P9-EMC-943

How many times have you been unable to think of the exact word to express your thought? More often than you'd care to admit? Besides being an embarrassment and annoyance, your inability to find the right word might cause others to misunderstand you.

The Merriam-Webster Pocket Dictionary of Synonyms

solves your problem by telling you precisely what words mean. With this authoritative reference, you need never worry about misusing a word. You will know the subtle distinctions between similar words and enrich the effectiveness of your vocabulary.

A Merriam-Webster®

The Merriam-Webster Pocket Dictionary of Synonyms

PUBLISHED BY POCKET BOOKS NEW YORK

POCKET BOOKS, a division of Simon & Schuster, Inc.
1230 Avenue of the Americas, New York, N.Y. 10020

Published by arrangement with G. & C. Merriam Co.

ISBN: 0-671-50445-2

First Pocket Books printing April, 1972

15 14 13 12 11

PREFACE

The Merriam-Webster Pocket Dictionary of Synonyms is a newly edited work based on *Webster's New Dictionary of Synonyms,* which rapidly has become a favorite book among readers and writers who wish to understand, appreciate, and make nice discriminations in the use of English words that are similar in meaning. The *Pocket Dictionary* is intended to fill a widespread need for a compact and readily available work devoted to synonymy. Its editors have rewritten and sharpened discriminations of groups of synonyms selected as particularly likely to be of general interest. Especial attention has been given to updating quotations and other illustrative material to assure accurate reflection of today's English.

The core of this book is the discriminating synonymy articles. It is not the book's purpose to assemble mere word-finding lists for consultants with a vague notion of the sort of word they seek. Rather, it provides them with the means of making clear comparisons between words of a common denotation and enables them to distinguish those differences in implications, connotations, and applications that determine the precisely suitable word for a particular situation of use. Additionally. the book includes alphabetically arranged cross-reference entries that indicate all articles in which the headword occurs and list its antonyms when these exist.

The nature of synonyms and antonyms

In the narrowest sense a synonym may be defined as a word that affirms exactly the meaning of a word with which it is synonymous. In this restricted sense there are few genuine synonyms and these mostly spelling variants of common origin (as such adjective pairs as *catachrestic, catachrestical*). For the purpose of this book words are considered to be synonyms if in one or more of their senses they are interchangeable without significant alteration of denotation but not necessarily without shifts in peripheral aspects of meaning (as connotations and implications).

Similarly, an antonym can be construed narrowly as a word that negates exactly the meaning of a word with which it is antonymous. Antonyms in this narrow sense are even less common than correspondingly defined synonyms. In this book a word is considered an antonym of another word if in one or more of its senses it negates the denotation of the latter but not necessarily without shifts in peripheral aspects of meaning.

The discriminating article

Each article begins with a list in boldface type of words to be discriminated (as **abolish, annihilate, extinguish**). The first word in the list is ordinarily the most general in application or the most central in meaning. Each list is followed by a brief statement of the area of meaning in which the group is to be compared, prefixed by the italicized words *shared meaning* (as **abolish** . . . *shared meaning* : to make nonexistent). Following this each word is discussed and appropriately illustrated in turn and in the order of its appearance in the list. Illustrations are set off between a pair of angle brackets and the illustrated words are italicized (as **Abolish** implies . . . <*abolish* a poll tax> <no plan will be acceptable unless it *abolishes* poverty – G. B. Shaw>). When the first word discriminated has an antonym, this appears as the final item of the article prefaced by the boldface italic abbreviation ***ant*** (as **abolish** . . . ***ant*** establish). Such an antonym or group of antonyms applies only to the first word of a discriminated group. Antonyms of other members of a group will be found at the appropriate cross-reference entry.

The cross-reference entry

Every word discriminated in a synonymy article has a boldface entry at its alphabetical place. Primarily this directs attention to each article in which it is discriminated (as **affinity** – see ATTRACTION, LIKENESS; which indicates that different meanings of the word *affinity* are discriminated in groups headed by **attraction** and **likeness**). Where antonyms exist they are listed immediately after the pertinent directional reference (as **aggravate 1** see INTENSIFY ***ant*** alleviate **2** see IRRITATE ***ant*** appease).

A DICTIONARY
OF
DISCRIMINATED SYNONYMS
WITH ANTONYMS

abandon *vb* **1 abandon, desert, forsake** *shared meaning* : to give up completely. **Abandon** can suggest complete disinterest in the future of what is given up <the picnickers *abandoned* their lunch to the ants> <no decent man *abandons* his family> **Desert** implies a relationship (as of occupancy or guardianship); it can suggest desolation <*deserted* farms growing up to brush> or culpability <soldiers who *desert* their posts> **Forsake** implies a breaking of a close association by repudiation or renunciation <all his knights and courtiers had *forsaken* him; not one came to his help – Matthew Arnold> <the young man *forsook* his parents to found a family of his own> ***ant*** reclaim
2 see RELINQUISH ***ant*** cherish (*as hopes*), restrain (*oneself*)
abandon *n* – see UNCONSTRAINT ***ant*** self-restraint
abase, demean, debase, degrade, humble, humiliate *shared meaning* : to lessen in dignity or status. **Abase** may suggest abjectness or servility or a feeling of personal inferiority <whose women are traditionally *abased* to the level of more or less beloved domestic animals – John Hersey> <the legislature met . . . to *abase* itself and undo its bad work – *Encyc. Americana*> **Demean** can suggest unsuitable behavior or association as the cause of loss of status <a *demeaning* subservience> <outrages against whatever *demeans* the black man in a predominantly white society – and thereby *demeans* the white – Roderick Nordell> **Debase** emphasizes loss of worth or quality <*debase* a currency> and especially deterioration of moral standards <a man *debased* by years of debauchery> **Degrade** suggests a downward step, sometimes in rank, more often in ethical stature, and typically implies a shameful or corrupt end <there is nothing *degrading* about honest labor> <those sins of the body which smear and sully, debase and *degrade* – J. T. Farrell> **Humble** frequently replaces *degrade* when the ignominy of a reduction in status is to be emphasized <they were delighted to see the bully *humbled* by a boy half his size> **Humiliate** stresses the shame and wounded pride of one who is abased or degraded <when we ask to be humbled, we must not recoil from being *humiliated* – Christina Rossetti> ***ant*** exalt, extol
abash – see EMBARRASS ***ant*** embolden, reassure
abate 1 see DECREASE
2 abate, subside, wane, ebb *shared meaning* : to die down in force or intensity. **Abate** stresses a progressive diminishing <companies should . . . take concrete steps to *abate* any air pollution they can – E. S. Muskie> while **subside** suggests a falling to a low level and an easing of turbulence <the wind *abated* and the waves were *subsiding*> **Wane** adds to *abate* an implication of fading or weakening <a *waning* moon> and is often used of something good or impressive or intense <after the first flush of excitement, the interest . . . began to *wane* – V. G. Heiser> **Ebb** suggests a gradual waning, especially

of something that commonly comes and goes <capacity to resist *ebbed* away – Oscar Handin> ***ant*** rise, revive
abbey – see CLOISTER
abbreviate – see SHORTEN ***ant*** elongate, lengthen
abdicate, renounce, resign *shared meaning* : to give up formally or definitely. **Abdicate** applies basically to the formal relinquishing of sovereign state or power <the king was forced to *abdicate*> but it is also appropriately used to indicate a giving up (as of duty or authority) by neglect or evasion <moderate and responsible leadership was ineffectual ... many simply *abdicated* their responsibility to act and to speak – J. K. Javits> **Renounce** may be chosen when the sacrifice, especially to some higher or moral end, involved in the relinquishment requires stress <the king *renounced* his throne to obtain peace> and in some cases the aspect of sacrifice becomes predominant <the sort of woman who has *renounced* all happiness for herself and who lives only for a principle – T. S. Eliot> **Resign** applies especially to the giving up of an unexpired office or trust and often implies an asking of permission to do so <when the secretary *resigned* the president asked him to stay on until a successor was found> ***ant*** assume, usurp
abet – see INCITE ***ant*** deter
abeyant – see LATENT ***ant*** operative, active
abhor – see HATE ***ant*** admire (*as persons or qualities*), enjoy (*something that is a matter of taste*)
abhorrent **1** see HATEFUL ***ant*** admirable, enjoyable
2 see REPUGNANT ***ant*** congenial
abide **1** see BEAR
2 see CONTINUE ***ant*** pass
3 see STAY ***ant*** depart
abject – see MEAN *adj* ***ant*** exalted (*as in rank*), imperious (*as in manner*)
able, capable, competent, qualified *shared meaning* : having power or fitness for work. Placed after the noun, *able* (followed by *to*) and *capable* (followed by *of*) give no indication of the degree of development of the power or fitness <an old man still *able* and willing to work> <not everyone is *capable* of living a spiritual life> Similarly used, *competent* suggests mere fitness <a servant *competent* to serve at table> while *qualified* suggests competence acquired through training <men who are more *qualified* in education and experience, but are making less money – T. M. Martinez> When preceding the noun, **able** is likely to suggest ability above the average demonstrated in performance <these courses can be a challenge to the most *able* student – Fern Witham> **Capable** stresses the having of qualities fitting one for work but does not imply outstanding ability <a *capable* boy can easily learn to drive a car> **Competent** and **qualified** imply possession of sufficient proficiency in an activity or occupation for effective performance, but the latter additionally suggests compliance with set standards (as of training and testing of one's competence) <a *competent* housekeeper> <a *qualified* electrician> ***ant*** inept, unable
abnegation – see RENUNCIATION ***ant*** indulgence, self-indulgence
abolish, annihilate, extinguish *shared meaning* : to make nonexistent. **Abolish** implies a putting to an end chiefly of things that are the outgrowth of law, customs, and conditions of existence <*abolish* a poll tax> <no plan will be acceptable unless it *abolishes* poverty – G. B. Shaw> **Annihilate** suggests a complete wiping out of existence of something material or immaterial <the homes and cities of the United States itself can be *annihilated* by enemy attack – Aidan Crawley> **Extinguish** is likely to suggest a complete but gradual ending (as by stifling, choking, or smothering) <a

religion of their own which was thoroughly and painfully *extinguished* by the Inquisition – T. S. Eliot> ***ant*** establish
abominable – see HATEFUL ***ant*** laudable, delightful
abominate – see HATE ***ant*** esteem, enjoy
aboriginal – see NATIVE
abortion, miscarriage *shared meaning* : expulsion of a fetus or embryo before it is capable of living independently. **Abortion** may suggest deliberate induction of the process either illicitly or for therapeutic reasons. In medical use *abortion* also denotes the expulsion of a human fetus or embryo during the first 12 weeks of pregnancy without regard to the cause. **Miscarriage** suggests a natural rather than an induced expulsion. In medicine it specifically applies to expulsion between the 12th and 28th weeks and before the fetus is able to live independently.
abound – see TEEM ***ant*** fail
aboveboard – see STRAIGHTFORWARD ***ant*** underhand, underhanded
abridge – see SHORTEN ***ant*** expand, extend
abridgment, abstract, epitome, synopsis, conspectus *shared meaning* : a shorter version of a larger work or treatment. **Abridgment** implies reduction in compass with retention of relative completeness <an *abridgment* of a dictionary> **Abstract** applies to a summary of points (as of a document or proposed treatment) and implies a skeletal form. **Epitome** suggests the briefest possible presentation of a complex whole that still has independent value <the *Paternoster* . . . is [an] *epitome* . . . of all the psalms and prayers written in the whole scripture – John Hooper> **Synopsis** and **conspectus** imply the giving of the crucial points by which something (as a treatise or subject) can be quickly comprehended. *Synopsis,* however, often suggests an outline or series of headings and *conspectus* a coherent account that gives a bird's-eye view. ***ant*** expansion
abrogate – see NULLIFY ***ant*** establish, fix
abrupt **1** see PRECIPITATE ***ant*** deliberate, leisurely
2 see STEEP ***ant*** sloping
absolute – see ULTIMATE ***ant*** conditioned
absolution – see PARDON ***ant*** condemnation
absorb **1 absorb, imbibe, assimilate** *shared meaning* : to take something in so as to become permeated by it. **Absorb** is likely to suggest a loss of identity in what is taken in or an enrichment of what takes in <had somehow *absorbed* . . . a weird mixture of the irresponsible, megalomaniacal ideas which erupted . . . during the nineteenth century – W. L. Shirer> <the liquid was *absorbed* by the dough> **Imbibe** often implies drinking, but like *absorb* it can suggest a soaking up <dry soil *imbibes* (or *absorbs*) the rainfall> In extended use it implies a taking in with noticeable or profound effect <where parents . . . send their young to *imbibe* education and healthy air in equal parts – Mollie Panter-Downes> **Assimilate** stresses an incorporation into the substance of the body or mind <one *assimilates* a foreign language and uses it in communication – W. E. Cole> ***ant*** dissipate (as *time, energies*)
2 see MONOPOLIZE
abstain – see REFRAIN ***ant*** indulge
abstemiousness – see TEMPERANCE ***ant*** gluttony
abstinence – see TEMPERANCE ***ant*** self-indulgence
abstract – see ABRIDGMENT ***ant*** amplification
abundant – see PLENTIFUL ***ant*** scarce
abuse, vituperation, invective, obloquy, scurrility, billingsgate *shared meaning* : vehemently expressed condemnation or disapproval. **Abuse** stresses harsh-

ness and unfairness of verbal attack <he would treat her to a virtuosity of *abuse,* acidly light and exaggerated – H. C. Hervey> **Vituperation** suggests an overwhelming flood of abuse <presidents were nagged beyond endurance, and senators, and congressmen: no one could escape the vials of her *vituperation* – F. L. Pattee> **Invective** implies fully as much vehemence but usually suggests logical presentation or cogent expression and public attack <the ominous muttering mounting to faint howls as with infuriated relish he prepared the roaring *invective* of the morning's tirade – Thomas Wolfe> **Obloquy** suggests defamation and consequent disgrace <those who . . . stood by me in the teeth of *obloquy,* taunt and open sneer – Oscar Wilde> **Scurrility** stresses viciousness of attack and coarseness or foulness of language <interrupted in his defense by ribaldry and *scurrility* from the judgment seat – T. B. Macaulay> **Billingsgate** implies practiced fluency and variety of obscene or profane abuse <*billingsgate* reduces language to a blunt instrument . . . [that] tends to demean the person using it, rather than the person it is used against – R. Baker> ***ant*** adulation

abutting – see ADJACENT

abysmal – see DEEP

academic – see PEDANTIC, THEORETICAL

accede – see ASSENT ***ant*** demur

accept – see RECEIVE ***ant*** reject

acceptation – see MEANING

accidental **1 accidental, casual, fortuitous, contingent** *shared meaning* : happening by chance. **Accidental** is very literal, rarely suggesting more than chance or unexpected occurrence <an *accidental* meeting> **Casual** may stress lack of real or apparent premeditation or intent even to the point of obscuring the implication of chance <propped with their elbows on the mantel in the *casual* earnestness of debate – Thomas Wolfe> **Fortuitous** so strongly stresses chance that it may connote entire absence of cause <the good frame of the universe was not the product of chance or *fortuitous* concourse of particles of matter – Sir Matthew Hale> **Contingent** implies both possibility and uncertainty and dependence on other or future events <she would divide her fortune between them, *contingent* upon their having male heirs – John Cheever> ***ant*** planned

2 accidental, incidental, adventitious *shared meaning* : not being part of the real or essential nature of something. **Accidental** retains its basic notion of chance occurrence but may also imply nonessential character <some of the colors were mineral in the rock itself: but others were *accidental,* due to water from the melting snow – T. E. Lawrence> **Incidental** suggests a real, sometimes a designed, relationship but one which is secondary and nonessential. An *incidental* advantage is one that might have been anticipated but is not regarded as of first importance <the poet's function of finding the universal in the *incidental* and the eternal in the transitory – *Current Biog.*> **Adventitious** implies a lack of essential relationships and may suggest casual addition or irrelevance <in works of imagination and sentiment . . . meter is but *adventitious* to composition – William Wordsworth> ***ant*** essential

accommodate 1 see ADAPT ***ant*** constrain

2 see OBLIGE ***ant*** discommode

accomplish – see PERFORM ***ant*** undo

accomplishment – see ACQUIREMENT

accord 1 see AGREE 3 ***ant*** conflict

2 see GRANT ***ant*** withhold

accordingly – see THEREFORE

accountable – see RESPONSIBLE ***ant*** unaccountable

accouter – see FURNISH
accredit – see APPROVE
accurate – see CORRECT *adj* ***ant*** inaccurate
accustomed – see USUAL
acerbity – see ACRIMONY ***ant*** mellowness
achieve **1** see PERFORM ***ant*** fail
2 see REACH ***ant*** miss (*getting or attaining*)
achievement – see FEAT ***ant*** failure
acid – see SOUR ***ant*** bland, sweet, alkaline
acidulous – see SOUR
acknowledge, admit, own, avow, confess *shared meaning* : to disclose against one's will or inclination. **Acknowledge** implies the disclosing of something that has been or might have been concealed <*acknowledge* a fault> <smarting at his too candid criticism, all the more because in my heart I *acknowledged* its truth – W. H. Hudson †1922> **Admit** often stresses reluctance to disclose or concede <at last the government at Washington *admitted* its mistake – which governments seldom do – Willa Cather> **Own** applies to acknowledgment of something in close relation to oneself <would not *own* his mistake> <let me *own* I'm an aesthetic sham – W. S. Gilbert> **Avow** implies open or bold declaration of what one might be expected to be silent about <many . . . who thought they had had the experience, could not bring themselves to relate it in public; others *avowed* they felt the conviction and elation – Lois B. Wills> <had an *avowed* hostility toward his parents> **Confess** usually applies to something felt to be wrong; thus, one *admits* an error but *confesses* a crime. Sometimes, however, it may imply no more than deference to the opinion of others <I *confess* I don't quite see how your plan will work> ***ant*** deny
acme – see SUMMIT
acquaint – see INFORM
acquiesce – see ASSENT ***ant*** object
acquire – see GET ***ant*** forfeit
acquirement, acquisition, attainment, accomplishment *shared meaning* : a power or skill won through exertion or effort. **Acquirement** implies achievement as the result of continued self-cultivation rather than of natural gifts <men of the greatest genius have not been most distinguished for their *acquirements* at school – William Hazlitt> **Acquisition** stresses eagerness of effort and the inherent value of what is gained <no philosopher would resign his mental *acquisitions* for the purchase of any terrestrial good – T. L. Peacock> **Attainment** applies especially to distinguished achievements (as in the arts or sciences) and suggests fully developed talents <a man of unusual character and remarkable *attainments* in his field> **Accomplishment** often adds to *acquirement* the notion of socially rather than basically useful skills <as for girls . . . they didn't really count, and if they succumbed to the lure of mere "*accomplishments*" such as French, music, or art – H. S. Commager>
acquisition – see ACQUIREMENT
acquisitive – see COVETOUS ***ant*** sacrificing, abnegating
acquit – see BEHAVE
acrimony, acerbity, asperity *shared meaning* : temper or language marked by irritation, anger, or resentment. **Acrimony** implies bitterness or ill will and the power to sting or blister with verbal attack <we all know how easy it is to . . . defend a pet theory with *acrimony* – A. T. Quiller-Couch> **Acerbity** implies sourness as well as bitterness and applies especially to mood <of an equable temper, with only such *acerbities* and touchinesses as are generally to be found in those who have had a love affair in their youth

and remained . . . unwed because of it – Virginia Woolf> **Asperity** suggests quickness of temper and sharpness of resentment, usually without bitterness <told him with some *asperity* to mind his own business> ***ant*** suavity

act – see ACTION 1

action **1 action, act, deed** *shared meaning* : something done or effected. **Action** refers primarily to the process of acting; **act** and **deed** to the result, the thing done. An *action* commonly involves a period of time, a process involving more than one step, or the possibility of repetition; an *act* is more frequently thought of as momentary or instantaneous and as individual <the rescue of a shipwrecked crew is a heroic *action,* the launching of a lifeboat, a brave *act*> *Deed* is used appropriately to describe an act that is illustrious or remarkable <the *deed* is worthy doing – Shak.>

2 see BATTLE

activate – see VITALIZE ***ant*** arrest

actual – see REAL ***ant*** ideal, imaginary

actuate – see MOVE

acumen – see DISCERNMENT ***ant*** obtuseness

acute **1** see SHARP ***ant*** obtuse

2 acute, critical, crucial *shared meaning* : full of uncertainty as to outcome. **Acute** stresses intensification, often rapid, of something (as a situation or need, symptoms, or emotional conflict) toward a resolving or breaking point <particularly *acute* is the possibility of war breaking out as a result of a sudden unanticipated flare-up – Stanley Kubrick> <the first society in human history to have mastered the problem of *acute* scarcity – A. S. Kaufman> **Critical** adds to *acute* implications of imminent change, of attendant suspense, and of decisiveness in the outcome <a *critical* shortage of food> <suffered such a *critical* illness . . . that the doctors attending him did not expect him to survive – *Current Biog.*> **Crucial** suggests a dividing of the ways and applies especially to something (as a test, a point, or a person) that will be decisive in the setting of a future course or direction <an awkward but *crucial* question – W. L. Shirer> <what is *crucial* is how injustices to women relate to the total human condition – Eulah C. Laucks>

adamant – see INFLEXIBLE ***ant*** yielding

adapt, adjust, accommodate, conform, reconcile *shared meaning* : to bring one into correspondence with another. To **adapt** is to fit or suit to something; it distinctively implies modification to meet new conditions <although he could somehow *adapt* himself to her tempers, it was this sudden change of mood that he felt he could never cope with – William Styron> <a tool *adapted* to several uses> To **adjust** is to bring into close correspondence or harmony, often by the use of tact or ingenuity <a delightful girl who could *adjust* to any confusion and who was at home in any society – J. A. Michener> <his sustained argument that . . . it was crippling for psychoanalysis to try to *adjust* a patient to the warpings of an unjust world – Norman Mailer> To **accommodate** is to reach a state of adaptation or adjustment by yielding or giving in to a necessary degree <he cannot change the system. He simply must learn to discipline and *accommodate* himself to it – W. E. Cole> To **conform** is to bring into harmony with a pattern, example, or principle <the attempt to *conform* nomadic Aboriginals to European customs and dress – *Australian Dict. of Biog.*> <legislators . . . grudgingly *conformed* to lower-court mandates – Trevor Armbrister> To **reconcile** is to demonstrate the fundamental congruity of things that seem incompatible <confidence in her own capacity to *reconcile* conflicting portraits of herself – Mary Austin> It sometimes suggests resignation <*reconciled* to his fate> ***ant*** unfit

adaptable — see PLASTIC ***ant*** inadaptable, unadaptable
address — see TACT ***ant*** maladroitness, gaucherie
adduce — see CITE
adept — see PROFICIENT ***ant*** inadept, bungling
adequate — see SUFFICIENT ***ant*** inadequate
adhere — see STICK
adherence, adhesion *shared meaning* : a sticking to or together. These words differ chiefly in their typical applications, **adherence** tending to be chosen when mental or moral attachment and **adhesion** when physical attachment is implied <called for *adherence* of the party platform to the laws defending freedom> <the *adhesion* of paint to a surface> ***ant*** nonadherence
adherent — see FOLLOWER ***ant*** renegade
adhesion — see ADHERENCE
adjacent, adjoining, contiguous, abutting, conterminous *shared meaning* : being in close proximity. **Adjacent** may or may not imply contact but always implies absence of anything of the same kind in between; thus, *adjacent* lots have a boundary in common while *adjacent* houses may be set well apart. **Adjoining** regularly implies a shared point or line of contact <they had *adjoining* rooms> **Contiguous** adds to *adjoining* the implication of meeting and touching along all or much of one side <a row of *contiguous* houses known as town houses> **Abutting** stresses the termination of one thing along a line of contact with another <land *abutting* on the road> <a laboratory *abuts* the main building> **Conterminous** may imply a considerable extent of common boundary <defending the side of Germany *conterminous* to France — W. E. H. Lecky> or it may apply to things enclosed by a continuous boundary whether close to or remote from one or another <the *conterminous* states of the United States> ***ant*** nonadjacent
adjoining — see ADJACENT ***ant*** detached, disjoined
adjourn, prorogue, dissolve *shared meaning* : to terminate the activities of (as a legislature). **Adjourn** implies suspension either until an appointed time of resumption or indefinitely <*adjourn* a meeting> <congress *adjourned* for the holiday season> **Prorogue** can be used similarly to *adjourn* but specifically it applies to action of the British crown or its representative whereby a parliament is adjourned and its uncompleted activities quashed so that they can only be taken up as new business by a succeeding parliament. **Dissolve** implies more permanency than *adjourn* or *prorogue* and in this relation specifically implies that the body ceases to exist as presently constituted so that an election must be held if it is to be reconstituted <the prime minister failed to win a vote of confidence and the parliament was *dissolved*>
adjure — see BEG
adjust — see ADAPT
administer — see EXECUTE
admire — see REGARD ***ant*** abhor
admission — see ADMITTANCE
admit **1** see ACKNOWLEDGE ***ant*** gainsay, disdain
2 see RECEIVE ***ant*** eject, expel
admittance, admission *shared meaning* : permitted entrance. **Admittance** usually refers to no more than a right to enter physically a particular place or building <an *admittance* fee> <*admittance* forbidden without special permission> **Admission** has acquired additional implications and is likely to be preferred when the notion of privilege is to be indicated or when the permitted entrance is more than purely physical <the *admission* of aliens into a country> <students seeking *admission* to the better colleges should apply early>

admonish – see REPROVE *ant* commend

ado – see STIR

adopt, embrace, espouse *shared meaning* : to take something (as an opinion, policy, or practice) as one's own. **Adopt** may stress the voluntary assumption that one did not originate <social and economic innovations on the Continent that . . . could be *adopted* with advantage in Britain – *Current Biog.*> <far from looking glum, she had *adopted* a winning manner – Edith Sitwell> **Embrace** is likely to stress willingness or eagerness to accept <the Italian people, at heart, had never . . . *embraced* fascism. They had merely suffered it, knowing that it was a passing phase – W. L. Shirer> **Espouse** adds to *embrace* the implication of close attachment (as to a cause) with a sharing of fortunes for better or worse <the spirit of uncompromising individualism that would eventually *espouse* the principle of democracy in church and state – V. L. Parrington> *ant* repudiate, discard

adore – see REVERE *ant* blaspheme

adorn, decorate, ornament, embellish, beautify, deck, bedeck, garnish *shared meaning* : to add something to with the intent of making more attractive. **Adorn** is likely to stress the addition, often of something beautiful in itself <a stately room *adorned* by delicate frescoes> <as a bride *adorns* herself with her jewels – *Isa* 61:10 (RSV)> **Decorate** implies the addition of color or interest to what is dull or monotonous <pathways, *decorated* with ornamental trees and shrubs – Tom Marvel> but it may suggest gaudiness or a concealing of defects <they are not beautiful: they are only *decorated* – G. B. Shaw> **Ornament** can imply a decorating by addition of something extraneous as an adjunct or accessory <whose bridle was *ornamented* with silver bells – Sir Walter Scott> **Embellish** tends to stress the act of an agent rather than the effect of a thing and may suggest the adding of superfluous or adventitious elements <the children, wearing their satin ribbons *embellished* with a picture of a fountain – Gerald Carson> **Beautify** may imply either an enhancing of real beauty <the eternal orbs that *beautify* the night – P. B. Shelley> or a counterbalancing of plainness or ugliness to produce an effect of beauty <a rough embankment *beautified* by shrubs and vines> **Deck** and **bedeck** imply the addition of something that contributes to gaiety, splendor, or showiness <a room *decked* with holiday greens> <as fine as any prince, ablaze with jewels, *bedecked* with yards of snowy lace and fine embroidery – Frank Yerby> <likes to *deck* out his little person in splendor and fine colors – W. M. Thackeray> **Garnish** implies a giving of final touches of order and ornament in preparation for use or service <the old-fashioned polemical sermon . . . *garnished* with quotations in Greek – Van Wyck Brooks> The word is used especially in cookery <*garnish* a broiled fish with lemon and parsley> *ant* disfigure

adroit **1** see CLEVER *ant* maladroit

2 see DEXTEROUS *ant* stolid

adumbrate – see SUGGEST 2

advance **1 advance, forward, further, promote** *shared meaning* : to help to move ahead. *Advance, forward,* and *further* are virtually interchangeable though **advance** more than the others may lay stress on the movement forward or the effectiveness of the assistance <the warm rain greatly *advanced* the early planting> <the award is made annually to the Negro who has done the most to *advance* race relations – *Current Biog.*> while **forward** is seldom applied to persons and may stress the activity or moral force intended to achieve the movement ahead <the high school as a means of *forwarding* the education of all youth – T. H. Briggs> **Further** may put less stress upon the movement forward and a great deal on the activity or aid or force that produces it <a man willing to go to any extremes to *further*

his ends> <her sole object . . . was to *further* him, not as an artist but as a popular success – Van Wyck Brooks> **Promote** may almost lose the notion of movement ahead in its strong stressing of the activity of assisting, encouraging, or fostering <that particular effort to *promote* myself ended in fiasco – Norman Mailer> <seeking to *promote* interfaith as well as interracial harmony – *Current Biog.*> ***ant*** retard, check
2 see CITE

advanced – see LIBERAL 2 ***ant*** conservative

advantageous – see BENEFICIAL ***ant*** disadvantageous

adventitious – see ACCIDENTAL 2 ***ant*** inherent

adventurous, venturesome, daring, daredevil, rash, reckless, foolhardy *shared meaning* : exposing oneself to danger beyond what is called for by duty or courage. **Adventurous** may apply to a disposition to encounter danger or to explore the new and unknown <an America that is completed . . . with no *adventurous* frontiers left for pioneering – *Current Biog.*> <China's current distress should not tempt us into anything *adventurous* . . . the U.S. cannot blunder into another war with China by miscalculation – *Commonweal*> **Venturesome** frequently implies an excessive tendency to take chances <the package of debenture plus warrant . . . offering an opportunity for considerable profit for the *venturesome* buyer – H. H. Biel> <in 1919 Alcock and Brown undertook the first and highly *venturesome* crossing of the Atlantic by air – *Manchester Guardian Weekly*> **Daring** heightens the implication of fearlessness and may suggest boldness in action or thought <a *daring* and crafty captain, as careless of his own life as of other folk's – Charles Kingsley> <they had been impetuous and *daring,* making up their minds in a couple of flashes, and without any fear . . . of what might happen – J. T. Farrell> **Daredevil** implies ostentation in daring and is especially applicable to public performers <a *daredevil* acrobat> or to showy feats <*daredevil* feats sometimes performed in the sperm-whale fishery – Herman Melville> **Rash** implies imprudent haste and lack of thought <any *rash* fool may marry – Clifton Fadiman> <like a *rash* exorcist, I was appalled by the spirit I had raised – L. P. Smith> **Reckless** stresses heedlessness or carelessness of consequences <a *reckless* driver who endangers everyone on the street> <he had frightfully dissipated his little capital. How wild and *reckless* he had been – W. M. Thackeray> **Foolhardy** implies a foolish daring or recklessness especially when not supported by the worth or likelihood of success < the perfectly *foolhardy* feat of swimming the flood – Sinclair Lewis> <brave and valiant and *foolhardy* though they were, the Poles were simply overwhelmed by the German onslaught – W. L. Shirer> ***ant*** unadventurous, cautious

adversary – see OPPONENT ***ant*** ally

adverse, inimical, antagonistic, counter, counteractive *shared meaning* : so opposed as to cause often harmful interference. **Adverse** describes what is harmful, unfavorable, difficult, or detrimental <what very small things in *adverse* circumstances suffice to make people happy – a little food, warmth, and something to look forward to – Hervey Allen> and may imply an often decisive or fateful opposition <an *adverse* decision of the court stripped him of his wealth> **Inimical** tends to suggest hostility or malevolence as a source of opposition <some had always been, and remained his constant opponents, some grew to be so . . . all were *inimical.* If ever there were a man who had to live spiritually alone it was he – Hilaire Belloc> <the courageous thinker must look the *inimical* aspects of his environment in the face, and accept the stern fact that the universe is hostile – D. C. Peattie> **Antagonistic** usually implies mutual opposition and may suggest incompatibility or even irreconcilability <*antagonistic* interracial reactions> <the *antagonistic* principles of aristocracy and democracy – V. L. Parrington> **Counter** need not imply hostility but it does imply inevitable opposing contact with resulting conflict or tension <whirlpools caused by *counter* currents in a stream> <a sally of the tongue may invite a *counter* sally of the fists – V. L. Parrington> **Counteractive** differs from *counter* chiefly in implying a termination or destruction of one of the things opposed <*counteractive* measures against an epidemic> ***ant*** propitious

adversity – see MISFORTUNE ***ant*** prosperity

advert – see REFER

advertise – see DECLARE

advice, counsel *shared meaning* : recommendation as to a decision or a course of conduct. These nouns and their corresponding verbs, **advise** and **counsel**, are often used interchangeably though they can carry quite distinctive implications. **Advice** and **advise** in themselves imply little about the quality of the recommendation or the qualifications of the advisor <*advise* a friend in the choice of a tie> <unsought *advice* is seldom helpful> but they may be specifically used with reference to persons qualified by training or employed to make technical recommendations <an extension specialist who *advises* apple growers on their spray schedule> **Counsel** is more likely to stress the fruit of wisdom and experience and suggests deliberation. It tends to presuppose more weighty occasions than *advice* or more authority in the one who counsels <he asked his father's *advice* and together they sought their pastor's *counsel*> <we must . . . find out why he did what he did, and *counsel* with him – R. F. Lewis>

advisable – see EXPEDIENT ***ant*** inadvisable

advise – see ADVICE

advocate – see LAWYER

affable – see GRACIOUS ***ant*** reserved

affect **1 affect, influence, touch, impress, strike, sway** *shared meaning* : to produce or have an effect upon (as a person). **Affect** implies the acting of a stimulus capable of producing a response or reaction <our eardrums are *affected* by ten octaves, at most, out of the endless range of sounds – James Jeans> When its object is a person *affect* usually implies an intellectual or emotional response <the sight *affected* her to tears> **Influence** implies a force that brings about a change or determines a course or stand <a secretion that *influences* growth rate in young animals> <Bauhaus methods still *influenced* education in art, architecture, and town planning – *Current Biog.*> **Touch** comes close to *affect* but it tends to carry a vivid suggestion of close contact and then may connote stirring, arousing, or harming <forms of social and domestic life . . . *touched* with a spice of uncertainty and menace – Thomas Wolfe> <for the first time powerfully *touched* by the presence of a woman – Sherwood Anderson> **Impress** is likely to stress the depth and lastingness of the effect <only one of the speeches *impressed* him> <her manner should be reserved and dignified; she would allow nothing to *impress* her – Victoria Sackville-West> **Strike** is similar to but weaker in suggestions than *impress* but may distinctively convey the notion of sudden sharp perception or appreciation <*struck* by the solemnity of the occasion> <you may buy whatever *strikes* your fancy> **Sway** implies the acting of influences that are not resisted or are irresistible, with resulting change in character or course of action <he is *swayed* by fashion, by suggestion, by transient moods – H. L. Mencken>

2 see ASSUME

affectation – see POSE ***ant*** artlessness

affecting – see MOVING

affection – see FEELING ***ant*** antipathy
affiliated – see RELATED ***ant*** unaffiliated
affinity – see ATTRACTION, LIKENESS
affirm – see ASSERT ***ant*** deny
affix – see FASTEN ***ant*** detach
afflict, try, torment, torture, rack *shared meaning* : to inflict on a person something (as suffering, disease, distress, or embarrassment) that he finds hard to bear. **Afflict** is a very general term applicable to almost any agent that causes distress <*afflicted* with a head cold> <shyness *afflicts* her like a disease> <the violence and the dark disorder that so *afflict* our lives – E. M. Kennedy> **Try** suggests an imposing of something that taxes the powers of endurance or self-control <a *trying* interview> <it *tried* her that he gave her no encouragement – Willa Cather> **Torment** suggests persecution or the repeated infliction of suffering or annoyance <horses *tormented* by flies> <he would like to love . . . his two daughters without the *tormenting* if nonetheless irremediable vexation that they closet his life in the dusty web of domestic responsibilities – Norman Mailer> **Torture** adds the implication of such mental or physical pain as causes one to writhe in distress <an idea of what a pulsating sciatica can do in the way of *torturing* its victim – Arnold Bennett> <the unseen grief that swells with silence in the *tortured* soul – Shak.> **Rack** suggests a pulling or tugging this way and that beyond endurance and in a manner suggestive of the strains inflicted by an instrument of torture <*racked* by doubts of his friend's loyalty> <Thucydides' world was a place *racked* and ruined and disintegrated by war – Edith Hamilton> ***ant*** comfort
affluent – see RICH ***ant*** impecunious, straitened
afford – see GIVE ***ant*** deny
affront – see OFFEND ***ant*** gratify
afraid – see FEARFUL ***ant*** unafraid, sanguine
age *n* – see PERIOD
age *vb* – see MATURE
agent – see MEAN *n*
aggravate **1** see INTENSIFY ***ant*** alleviate
2 see IRRITATE ***ant*** appease
aggregate – see SUM ***ant*** individual, particular
aggressive, militant, assertive, self-assertive, pushing, pushful, pushy *shared meaning* : conspicuously or obtrusively active or energetic. **Aggressive** implies a disposition to dominate often in disregard of others' rights or in determined and vigorous pursuit of one's ends <as intolerant and *aggressive* as any of the traditional satirists – C. D. Lewis> **Militant** similarly implies a fighting disposition but is less likely to suggest self-seeking than devotion to a cause, movement or principle <*militant* civil rights leaders> <*militant* in fighting to get for workers a larger share of the national income – *Time*> **Assertive** suggests bold self-confidence especially in the expression of opinion <the postwar political passivity of Bonn will increasingly be replaced by active and *assertive* policies – Herman Kahn> <an *assertive,* opinionated, likable fellow – V. L. Parrington> **Self-assertive** adds a connotation of unpleasant forwardness or brash self-confidence <*self-assertive* and ill-bred bourgeois – Edmund Wilson> **Pushing** and **pushful** may praise by implying ambition, energy, and enterprise <an energetic, *pushing* youth, already intent on getting on in the world – Sherwood Anderson> <the *pushful* energetic man of business – Aldous Huxley> but both as well as **pushy** may blame by implying snobbishness or crude intrusiveness <ignorant, *pushful,* impatient of restraint and precedent – H. L. Mencken> <Aunt Hattie, a *pushing* and impecunious member of the farflung Apley clan –

W. H. Chamberlin> <his motive power derives from ... the *pushiest* ambition since Alexander the Great – R. L. Taylor>

agile, nimble, brisk, spry *shared meaning* : acting or moving with easy alacrity. **Agile** implies dexterity and ease in mental or physical action <boys *agile* as monkeys scrambled up the slope> <the work of a ... sympathetic intelligence, *agile,* humane, and ... persuasive – A. D. Culler> **Nimble** stresses lightness and swiftness of action or thought and often implies a darting here and there <*nimble* as a squirrel> <a masterly comic, *nimble* performance of a lovable knave – *New Yorker*> **Brisk** suggests liveliness, animation, or vigor of movement or action, sometimes with a hint of hurry and flurry <a *brisk* and birdy little man with a chirping, cheerful voice – Thomas Wolfe> <trade was *brisk* as word got around that for every patron there was a free drink – Gerald Carson> **Spry** is likely to stress a capacity for quick action that is unexpected (as by reason of age or infirmity) <a *spry* old lady> <his *spry,* youthful vigor and unimpaired energy – Hervey Allen> ***ant*** torpid

agitate **1** see DISCOMPOSE ***ant*** calm, tranquilize

2 see SHAKE ***ant*** quiet, lull, still

agnostic – see ATHEIST

agony – see DISTRESS

agree **1** see ASSENT ***ant*** protest (*against*), differ (*with*)

2 agree, concur, coincide *shared meaning* : to come into or be in harmony regarding a matter of opinion. **Agree** implies unity or complete accord, often arrived at by discussion and adjustment of difference <on some points we all can *agree*> **Concur** tends to suggest cooperative or harmonious thinking or acting toward a given end or for a particular purpose <for the creation of a masterwork of literature two powers must *concur,* the power of the man and the power of the moment – Matthew Arnold> but sometimes implies no more than approval (as of a decision reached) <he *concurred* with the committee> **Coincide,** which is usually used of opinions, judgments, wishes, or interests rather than people, implies an agreement amounting to identity of opinion <their wishes exactly *coincide* with my desire> <private groups whose interests did not *coincide* with national defense – T. W. Arnold> ***ant*** differ, disagree

3 agree, tally, square, conform, accord, comport, harmonize, correspond, jibe *shared meaning* : to go or exist together without conflict or incongruity. **Agree** is a general term applicable to any precise going, existing, or fitting together <the conclusion *agrees* with the evidence> **Tally** implies an agreement like that between two correct sets of accounts, matching not only in overall conclusions but detail by detail <your story *tallies* closely with earlier accounts> <pain and pleasure no more *tally* in our sense than red and green – Robert Browning> **Square** suggests showing a precise or mathematically exact agreement <the corporation must, if it is to survive, *square* itself with the basic beliefs of the American people – E. C. Lindeman> **Conform** implies a fundamental likeness in form, in nature, or in essential quality <my views of conduct ... *conform* with what seem to me the implications of my beliefs – T. S. Eliot> **Accord** implies perfect fitness in a relation or association (as in character, spirit, quality, or tone) <the common doctrine of liberty *accorded* with the passions released by the Revolution – V. L. Parrington> **Comport,** like *accord,* is likely to stress the fitness or suitability of an agreement <the emphasis on the beautiful ... that *comports* with the conventional conception of culture as a life of traditionally molded refinement – Edward Sapir> *Harmonize* and *correspond* may apply to the relation of dissimilar things but **harmonize** stresses their blending to form a congruous or pleasing whole <from the waves, sound . . . broke forth *harmonizing* with solitude – P. B. Shelley> while **correspond** stresses their matching, complementing, or answering to each other <fulfillment seldom *corresponds* to anticipation> <the fin, wing, and arm *correspond* to one another> **Jibe**, rather broad in application, may sometimes be closely equivalent to *agree*, sometimes to *harmonize*, and sometimes to *accord* <his actions do not *jibe* with his words> <his looks *jibed* with the stage driver's description of him – Luke Short> ***ant*** differ (*from*)

agreeable – see PLEASANT ***ant*** disagreeable
aid – see HELP ***ant*** impediment
ail – see TROUBLE
aim – see INTENTION
air *n* – see MELODY, POSE
air *vb* – see EXPRESS
akin – see SIMILAR ***ant*** alien
alacrity – see CELERITY ***ant*** languor
alarm – see FEAR ***ant*** assurance, composure
albeit – see THOUGH
alert 1 see INTELLIGENT
2 see WATCHFUL ***ant*** supine
alibi – see APOLOGY
alien – see EXTRINSIC ***ant*** akin, assimilable
alienate 1 see ESTRANGE ***ant*** unite, reunite
2 see TRANSFER
align – see LINE
alike – see SIMILAR ***ant*** different
alive 1 see AWARE ***ant*** blind (*to*)
2 see LIVING ***ant*** dead, defunct
all – see WHOLE ***ant*** part (*of*)
all-around – see VERSATILE
allay – see RELIEVE ***ant*** intensify
allege – see CITE ***ant*** contravene, traverse
allegiance – see FIDELITY ***ant*** treachery, treason
alleviate – see RELIEVE ***ant*** aggravate
allied – see RELATED ***ant*** unallied
allocate – see ALLOT

allot, assign, apportion, allocate *shared meaning* : to give as a share, portion, role, or lot. **Allot** implies more or less arbitrary or haphazard selection and in itself conveys no suggestion of a fair or equal distribution <each child was *allotted* some household chore> <nature . . . propels us like children through the role she has *allotted* us – D. C. Peattie> **Assign** stresses authoritative and usually fixed allotment without implying equitable distribution <usually *assigned* me not to the main line of research in the laboratory, but to side issues – Maria G. Mayer> <chose *Macbeth* as the forthcoming play and *assigned* herself the role of Lady Macbeth – *Current Biog.*> **Apportion** implies a dividing according to some principle, sometimes of equivalence in sharing but more often of a proportionate distribution <his guardians had *apportioned* to him an allowance . . . adequate to his position – Benjamin Disraeli> <the duty of husbanding and *apportioning* the meager food stores of the party – W. J. Ghent> **Allocate** is used chiefly with respect to material resources or powers and implies usually a definite appropriation to a particular individual or group or for a particular use <these provisions . . . make it difficult for the state to

allocate money for pressing needs – Trevor Armbrister> <if the political community is to *allocate* functions and duties, it must have legal principles to guide and measure the allocation – R. M. Hutchins>

allow – see LET ***ant*** inhibit

allowance – see RATION

allude – see REFER

allure – see ATTRACT ***ant*** repel

almost – see NEARLY

alone, solitary, lonely, lonesome, lone, lorn, forlorn, desolate *shared meaning* : isolated from others. All these terms may refer not only to the fact of isolation but to the resultant emotional reaction. **Alone** stresses the objective fact of being by oneself with slighter notion of emotional involvement than most of the remaining terms <some people are happier when they are *alone*> <the upstart Americans, who, isolated and *alone,* would easily succumb – W. L. Shirer> **Solitary** may indicate aloneness as a chosen course <Netta loved these *solitary* interludes . . . . She could dream things there – J. C. Powys> but perhaps more often it suggests sadness at the loss or lack of usual connections or consciousness of isolation <left *solitary* by the death of his wife> **Lonely** adds to *solitary* the suggestion of longing for companionship <the comfort of that thought nestled into her, to wait to be taken out and looked at again in *lonely* times – Theodore Sturgeon> **Lonesome** heightens the implication of dreariness and longing <an only child often leads a *lonesome* life> <don't be *lonesome* while we are away> **Lone** may replace either *lonely* or *lonesome* but typically is as objective as *alone* <a *lone* robin pecking at the lawn> **Lorn** suggests recent separation or bereavement <when *lorn* lovers sit and droop – W. M. Praed> **Forlorn** stresses dejection, woe, and listlessness at separation from someone or something dear <as *forlorn* as King Lear at the end of his days – G. W. Johnson> **Desolate** most strongly suggests inconsolable grief and the barrenness of a life made isolated (as by death or desertion) <for her false mate has fled and left her *desolate* – P. B. Shelley> ***ant*** accompanied

aloof – see INDIFFERENT ***ant*** familiar, close

alter – see CHANGE *vb* ***ant*** fix

altercation – see QUARREL ***ant*** concurrence, accord

alternate *adj* – see INTERMITTENT ***ant*** consecutive

alternate *vb* – see ROTATE

alternative – see CHOICE *n*

although – see THOUGH

altitude – see HEIGHT

amalgamate – see MIX

amateur, dilettante, dabbler, tyro *shared meaning* : one who follows a pursuit without attaining proficiency or professional status. **Amateur** is likely to denote one with taste or liking for something rather than expert knowledge and in such use may be contrasted with *connoisseur* <affected the pose of the gentleman *amateur* of the arts – F. H. Ellis> but it may also stress personal rather than professional interest, especially in an activity requiring skill and in sports may specifically denote one not accepting direct remuneration <a leading *amateur* golfer> **Dilettante** often implies elegant trifling in the arts but may also distinguish the lover of an art from its skilled practitioner <not content to be a mere *dilettante* he studied under a leading musician and spent hours in practice> **Dabbler** implies a lack of serious purpose, but it suggests desultory habits of work and lack of persistence rather than a predetermined standing aside from active participation in a pursuit <a *dabbler* in magic and mysticism unwilling to delve deeply into esoteric lore> **Tyro** suggests inexperience and the resultant incompetence and crudity <the leaders of today were yesterday's *tyros*>and sometimes it implies a crass unawareness of one's limitations <"A noble theme!" the *tyro* cried, and straightway scribbled off a sonnet. "A noble theme," the poet sighed, "I am not fit to write upon it" – Carolyn Wells> ***ant*** professional, expert

amaze – see SURPRISE 2

ambiguous – see OBSCURE ***ant*** explicit

ambition, aspiration, pretension *shared meaning* : strong desire for advancement or success. **Ambition** applies to the desire for personal advancement and may suggest either a praiseworthy will to better oneself or an overweening self-assurance <it was her *ambition* for me which proved the deciding factor – David Fairchild> <you can only see him through a fog of *ambition* and jealousy . . . you're so unbalanced with your little success – Herman Wouk> **Aspiration** implies a striving after something higher than oneself or one's present status which typically is ennobling or uplifting <that spirit of his in *aspiration* lifts him from the earth – Shak.> but sometimes it may suggest presumption or folly on the part of the striver <assured that he need regard no woman as too high for his *aspirations* – Anthony Trollope> **Pretension** suggests ardent desire for recognition of accomplishment without actual possession of the qualifications that would justify it <decided to emigrate because his farm resources . . . were inadequate for his *pretensions* – T. H. Irving> <a man of large *pretensions* but small accomplishments>

amble – see SAUNTER

ambush – see SURPRISE

ameliorate – see IMPROVE ***ant*** worsen, deteriorate

amenable 1 see OBEDIENT ***ant*** recalcitrant, refractory
2 see RESPONSIBLE ***ant*** independent (*of*), autonomous

amend – see CORRECT *vb* ***ant*** debase, impair

amerce – see PENALIZE

amiable, good-natured, obliging, complaisant *shared meaning* : having or showing a will to please. **Amiable** implies qualities (as friendliness, affability, or kindliness) that tend to inspire liking <had a dignity and a self-assurance that many Americans lacked. They were *amiable,* calm, independent – Edmund Wilson> Sometimes it may suggest mildness of temper <married a gentle *amiable* girl> or even lack of proper firmness or strength <a man too *amiable* to be a success> **Good-natured** implies a cheerful willingness to please or to be helpful and sometimes to permit undue impositions <a loud brisk *good-natured* woman as ready to mother her neighbors as her children> **Obliging** stresses a readiness to be helpful or to accommodate to the wishes of others <was very *obliging,* and offered to do anything in his power – Bram Stoker> **Complaisant** implies a courteous or sometimes a weakly amiable desire to please or to be agreeable <boss-ridden conventions turned him down for more *complaisant* candidates – Allan Nevins & H. S. Commager> ***ant*** unamiable

amicable, neighborly, friendly *shared meaning* : exhibiting goodwill or an absence of antagonism. **Amicable** seldom implies more than that the parties concerned are not disposed to quarrel or are at peace with each other <after years of *amicable* intercourse a dispute arose> **Neighborly** may suggest goodwill and kindliness and a disposition to live on good terms with those with whom one must associate because of their proximity <a lover of men, the most *neighborly* soul in the world, mingling freely with all classes – V. L. Parrington> <cared for our place while we were gone in the most *neighborly* way> **Friendly** tends to be more positive in its implication of cordiality and often suggests a greater warmth of feeling <gave us a *friendly* encouraging nod> <a *friendly* outgoing personality> ***ant*** antagonistic

amnesty – see PARDON

amoral – see IMMORAL

amount – see SUM

ample 1 see PLENTIFUL *ant* scant, meager

2 see SPACIOUS *ant* meager, circumscribed

amplify – see EXPAND *ant* abridge, condense

amulet – see FETISH

amuse, divert, entertain *shared meaning* : to pass or cause to pass one's time pleasantly. **Amuse** is likely to suggest engaging the attention so as to keep one interested or engrossed usually lightly or frivolously <the errors he made in pitch and in language would be so *amusing* that the geishas would giggle with delight – Norman Mailer> <he has something to say that will either *amuse* or help his audience – W. J. Reilly> **Divert** implies the distracting of the attention (as from duty or worry) especially by something that causes laughter or gaiety <spent a *diverting* interlude at the shore> <he was *diverted,* though his face betrayed no sign of his amusement – C. B. Kelland> **Entertain** suggests the activity of supplying amusement or diversion often by planned or specially contrived methods <the problems involved in *entertaining* over a hundred people> <they were *entertained* by a program of chamber music> *ant* bore

analogous – see SIMILAR

analogue – see PARALLEL

analogy – see LIKENESS

analytic *or* **analytical** – see LOGICAL *ant* inventive, creative, constructive

analyze, resolve, dissect, break down *shared meaning* : to divide a complex whole into its component parts or constituent elements. **Analyze** suggests separating or distinguishing the component parts of something (as a substance, a process, or a situation) so as to discover its true nature or inner relationships <the effects of false and pernicious propaganda cannot be neutralized except by . . . *analyzing* its techniques and seeing through its sophistries – Aldous Huxley> <*analyze* a mixture of chemicals> **Resolve** does not commonly presuppose a personal agent and often stresses the fact of change of form, of metamorphosis, rather than necessarily indicating separation into components <the objective . . . of the microscope, for through its power to *resolve* minute structure, we see small objects crisp and clear – D. A. Burgh> <had to be a trick of the eye, a false evaluation . . . that in a moment would *resolve* itself into a sun-flash on an airplane – Theodore Sturgeon> **Dissect** suggests a searching analysis by or as if by laying bare parts for individual scrutiny <*dissect* a cat in the study of anatomy> < a complicated record must be *dissected,* the narratives of witnesses, more or less incoherent and unintelligible, must be analyzed – B. N. Cardozo> **Break down** suggests methods (as classifying, itemizing, or subgrouping) by which a complicated whole is divided into more manageable units <particularly interested in the way he *broke down* a major problem into a number of relatively minor decisions – R. J. Bryant> *ant* compose, compound, construct

anathematize – see EXCLUDE

anatomy – see STRUCTURE

ancient – see OLD *ant* modern

anecdote – see STORY

anger, ire, rage, fury, indignation, wrath *shared meaning* : emotional excitement induced by intense displeasure. **Anger,** the most general term, names the emotional reaction but in itself suggests no degree of intensity and implies nothing about justification or manifestation <could scarcely hide his *anger* at their answer> <he saw the calf, and the dancing: and

Moses' *anger* waxed hot – *Exod* 32:19 (AV)> **Ire** is likely to occur in more literary contexts and may suggest greater intensity than *anger,* often with an evident display of feeling <undismayed by the dark flush of *ire* he had kindled – George Meredith> **Rage** adds to *anger* the notion of loss of self-control with usually strong outward display of emotion that reflects inner turmoil and frustration <flew into the greatest *rage* of his life. This was the end, he shrieked.... There was nothing but treason, lies, corruption, and cowardice – W. L. Shirer> <had been on the verge of roaring again with *rage* – James Purdy> **Fury** is overmastering destructive rage verging on madness <head held high, her stiff back and neck eloquently expressive of outraged innocence and suppressed *fury* – Thomas Wolfe> <in his *fury* made sudden decisions which would prove utterly disastrous – W. L. Shirer> **Indignation** implies anger that is provoked by what one considers mean, shameful, outrageous, or unworthy <whose souls no honest *indignation* ever urged to elevated daring – P. B. Shelley> <the crime of aggression arouses their moral *indignation* – A. O. Wolfers> **Wrath** may imply either rage or indignation but is likely to suggest a desire or intent to avenge or punish <rose in his *wrath* and struck his tormentor to the floor> <let not the sun go down upon your *wrath* – *Eph* 4:26 (AV)> *ant* pleasure, gratification, forbearance

angle – see PHASE

anguish – see SORROW *ant* relief

animadversion, stricture, aspersion, reflection *shared meaning* : adverse criticism. **Animadversion** implies criticism prompted by prejudice or ill will <Maty's *animadversions* hurt me more. In part they appeared to me unjust, and in part ill-natured – William Cowper> **Stricture** implies censure that may be either ill-natured or judicious <very severe *strictures* must be passed on an author and on the publisher who produce a work now exceeding 1,000 pages without providing an index – *Times Lit. Supp.*> **Aspersion** imputes a slanderous character to the criticism <I defy the world to cast a just *aspersion* on my character – Henry Fielding> **Reflection** often implies indirect aspersion or criticism by oblique comment <the film disappeared ... apparently at the behest of Fascist authorities who considered it a *reflection* on their regime – *Current Biog.*> <the fact is ... that a good job done by an assistant is a *reflection* on the ability of the senior – L. L. Jones> *ant* commendation

animadvert – see REMARK

animal see CARNAL *ant* rational

animate *adj* – see LIVING *ant* inanimate

animate *vb* – see QUICKEN

animated 1 see LIVELY *ant* depressed, dejected
2 see LIVING *ant* inert

animosity – see ENMITY *ant* goodwill

animus – see ENMITY *ant* favor

annals – see HISTORY

annihilate – see ABOLISH

announce – see DECLARE

annoy 1 **annoy, vex, irk, bother** *shared meaning* : to disturb and nervously upset a person. **Annoy** may imply a wearing on the nerves by persistent, often petty unpleasantness <an *annoying* cough> but as often suggests a purely temporary disturbance or display of irritation <it's easy to become *annoyed* over trifles> **Vex** implies greater provocation and stronger disturbance and may suggest anger, perplexity, or anxiety in the reaction of the one affected <why *vex* your mind with an unsolvable problem?> <faulty translation that so *vexes* teachers – C. H. Grandgent>**Irk** stresses difficulty

in enduring and resulting weariness or impatience of spirit <discovered that his orderliness had *irked* her just as much as her disorder had *irked* him – Victoria Sackville-West> **Bother** may imply either a bewildering or an upsetting and regularly suggests interference with one's comfort or peace of mind <I do not want any more to be *bothered* with the kind of contemporary conflicts that I used to go out to explore – Edmund Wilson> <passed a restless night, *bothered* by dreams and mosquitoes> ***ant*** soothe
2 see WORRY
annul – see NULLIFY
anomalous – see IRREGULAR
anomaly – see PARADOX
answer **1 answer, respond, reply, rejoin, retort** *shared meaning* : to say or write or do something in return. **Answer** conveys the fact of a logical or practical satisfying of a question, demand, call, or need <the boy *answered* the teacher's question> <rough boards will *answer* our purpose> <he was most attracted to Shelley whose classical learning and visionary imagination *answered* to characteristics of his own – Ian Jack> **Respond** may suggest a ready, willing, or spontaneous answering to a stimulus <Luigi's wife *responding* to a nod, comes in with wine and glasses – C. L. Sulzberger> <the power to *respond* to reason and truth exists in all of us – Aldous Huxley> **Reply** implies making a return that covers the same ground as the stimulus (as a question, charge, or argument) and may focus attention on the quality of the return <three deep throaty blasts announce the approaching ship, to which the bridge *replies* with a like number of shrill signals – *Amer. Guide Series: Minn.*> <*replied* easily to her quizzing> **Rejoin** is basically applicable to any making of an answer but is likely to be chosen to imply one that is sharp or pointed and made in response to an ill-taken remark or an implied criticism <he *rejoined* to the boy's greeting with a sour "late again, I see."> **Retort** implies a retaliatory response to some criticism, rebuke, charge, or argument <I had . . . uttered a number of trenchant sayings upon female novelists. But the amusement changed to dismay when the ladies began to *retort* – A. T. Quiller-Couch>
2 see SATISFY 3
answerable – see RESPONSIBLE
antagonism – see ENMITY ***ant*** accord, comity
antagonist – see OPPONENT ***ant*** supporter
antagonistic – see ADVERSE ***ant*** favoring, favorable
antagonize – see OPPOSE ***ant*** conciliate
antecedent *n* – see CAUSE ***ant*** consequence
antecedent *adj* – see PRECEDING ***ant*** subsequent, consequent
anterior – see PRECEDING ***ant*** posterior
anticipate **1** see FORESEE
2 see PREVENT ***ant*** consummate
anticipation – see PROSPECT ***ant*** retrospect
antinomy – see PARADOX
antipathy – see ENMITY ***ant*** taste (*for*), affection (*for, toward*)
antiquated – see OLD ***ant*** modernistic, modish
antique – see OLD ***ant*** modern, current
antisocial – see UNSOCIAL ***ant*** social
antithetical – see OPPOSITE
anxiety – see CARE ***ant*** security
anxious – see EAGER ***ant*** loath
apathetic – see IMPASSIVE ***ant*** alert
ape – see COPY

aperture, interstice, orifice *shared meaning* : opening allowing passage through or in and out. **Aperture** applies to an opening, whether a flaw or an essential element, in something that otherwise presents a solid or closed surface or structure <light entered through an *aperture* in the cave roof> <the *aperture* of a camera> **Interstice** applies to an unfilled space or break in the continuity of a mass or fabric and especially to openings in something loose in texture, coarse-grained, layered, or piled up <moss growing in the *interstices* of an old stone fence> <problems which escape out of scientific hands like noxious insects into the *interstices* of the social fabric – L. C. Eiseley> **Orifice** applies to an opening that functions as or suggests a mouth or vent <the *orifice* of the bladder>

apex – see SUMMIT

aplomb – see CONFIDENCE ***ant*** shyness

apocryphal – see FICTITIOUS

apologia – see APOLOGY

apology, apologia, excuse, plea, pretext, alibi *shared meaning* : matter offered in explanation or defense (as of an act, a policy, or a view). **Apology** usually implies that one has been to a greater or less degree in the wrong and may suggest either a defense that brings forward palliating circumstances or a frank admission of error with an expression of regret by way of reparation <publicly offered *apology* to their customers for the inconvenience that had been caused> <said by way of *apology* that he would have met them if he had known when they were arriving> Sometimes *apology,* like **apologia,** implies no admission of guilt or error but rather a desire to clear the grounds for some course, belief, or position that appears wrong to others <*apologies* for various . . . doctrines of the faith – J. H. Newman> <memoirs are often in fact *apologias,* even if, with the wisdom of hindsight, their author recognizes and admits occasional errors of judgment – *Times Lit. Supp.*> **Excuse** implies an intent to avoid or remove blame or censure <a devilishly smooth impostor, awaiting their slightest blunder as an *excuse* to move in – J. D. Salinger> <there is no *excuse* for carelessness> **Plea** stresses argument or appeal to others for understanding or sympathy or mercy <dreaded the arguments, their tear-stained *pleas* and her own misery for . . . adding to the portion of their unhappiness – Bernard Malamud> <their *pleas* for mercy went unheard> **Pretext** suggests subterfuge and the offering of a reason or motive other than the true one in excuse or explanation <he made my health a *pretext* for taking all the heavy chores, long after I was as well as he was – Willa Cather> **Alibi** implies a desire to shift blame or to avoid punishment and commonly connotes plausibility rather than truth in the explanation offered <offered as an *alibi* his absence from town at the time of the crime> <federal taxes are already being used as an *alibi* for cuts in local school budgets – H. M. Groves>

appall – see DISMAY ***ant*** nerve, embolden

appalling – see FEARFUL 2 ***ant*** reassuring

apparent 1 apparent, illusory, illusionary, seeming, ostensible *shared meaning* : not actually being what it appears to be. **Apparent** suggests an appearance to the unaided senses that is not or may not be borne out by more rigorous examination or more perfect knowledge <appropriate actions are guided by perception of the underlying situation, which may very well be at variance with the *apparent* situation – F. C. Cameron> <absolutism leads to moral confusion through the doctrine that *apparent* evil is really good – J. E. Smith> **Illusory** and **illusionary** definitely imply a false impression based on deceptive resemblance or faulty observation, as influenced by emotions that prevent a clear view <an *illusory* ideal that has bemused man's under-

standing – M. J. Adler> <a lower-class woman in Rome who sees in the glamor of cinema an *illusionary* hope for her daughter's success – *Current Biog.*> **Seeming** implies a character in one thing that gives it the semblance of another; sometimes it suggests an intent to deceive or delude <these *seeming* simplicities are craftily charged . . . with secondary purposes, ulterior intimations – C. E. Montague> **Ostensible** applies chiefly to reasons or motives and suggests discrepancy between an openly declared or logically implicit aim or reason and the true one <his *ostensible* frankness concealed a devious scheme> <gave as their *ostensible* reason for leaving their fear of the storm> ***ant*** real

2 see EVIDENT ***ant*** inapparent, unintelligible

appear – see SEEM

apperception – see RECOGNITION

appetizing – see PALATABLE ***ant*** nauseating

appliance – see IMPLEMENT

applicable – see RELEVANT ***ant*** inapplicable

apply – see RESORT

appoint – see FURNISH

apportion – see ALLOT

apposite – see RELEVANT ***ant*** inapposite, inapt

appraise – see ESTIMATE

appreciable – see PERCEPTIBLE ***ant*** inappreciable

appreciate **1** see UNDERSTAND ***ant*** depreciate

2 appreciate, value, prize, treasure, cherish *shared meaning* : to hold in high estimation. **Appreciate** may suggest a level of understanding that allows one to admire critically or enjoy with discrimination <a . . . man with a most aggressive determination to see, to know and to *appreciate* all of his command – J. A. Michener> but often it stresses merely a response of warm approval, keen enjoyment, or gratitude <in his youth, he had starved often enough . . . to make him *appreciate* any free meal – Helen MacInnes> **Value** implies rating something highly for its essential or intrinsic worth <I *value* your opinion because I know it is sincere> <what she particularly *valued* was the freedom the theatricals gave her – Herman Wouk> **Prize** implies taking a deep pride in or setting great store by <the liberals, who *prized* an undogmatic, truth-seeking attitude toward religion – Lois B. Wills> <we seldom *prize* commonplace pleasures> **Treasure** emphasizes jealously guarding or keeping something as being precious or irreplaceable <*treasuring* family heirlooms> <other people . . . *treasure* memorable moments in their lives – Walker Percy> **Cherish** implies a special love and care of something that is an object of deep-seated, long-lasting, or even irrational attachment <the Southerners *cherished* still their old rage against the northern invaders – Edmund Wilson> <others are tortured between their *cherished* idea of university standards and their sense of guilt about black experience in America – Max Lerner> ***ant*** despise

apprehend – see FORESEE

apprehensive – see FEARFUL ***ant*** confident

apprentice – see NOVICE

apprise – see INFORM

approach – see MATCH

appropriate *vb* **appropriate, preempt, arrogate, confiscate** *shared meaning* : to seize high-handedly. **Appropriate** stresses making something one's own or converting it to one's own use without authority or with questionable right <to the natives it is sacrilegious . . . for the white men to *appropriate* the sacred watering places – Rex Ingamells> **Preempt** adds to *appropriate* the notion of beforehandedness and suggests a stronger action (as a seizure) in taking something wanted or needed by others <*preempted* the lion's share of the profits> <necessary but unlovely adjuncts of living having *preempted* much of the Hudson's shoreline – E. J. Kahn> **Arrogate** implies an unwarranted and usually an insolent or presumptuous claim to something (as a right, power, or function) usually to the exclusion of others with often juster claims <not even in medieval times . . . had any German *arrogated* such tyrannical power, nominal and legal as well as actual, to himself – W. L. Shirer> **Confiscate** stresses the exercise of authority in seizing and does not ordinarily imply impropriety or an intent to turn the property of another to one's own advantage <the teacher *confiscated* the slingshot> <the . . . government *confiscated* his property and condemned him to death – S. E. Ambrose>

appropriate *adj* – see FIT

approve, endorse, sanction, accredit, certify *shared meaning* : to have or express a favorable opinion. **Approve** implies commendation or agreement and may suggest a judicious attitude <fools admire, but men of wits *approve* – Joseph Furphy> <understood his purpose and *approved* of his aims – S. E. Ambrose> **Endorse** adds to *approve* the implication of publicly expressed support <agreed to accept nomination only if *endorsed* by all sixty-seven county chairmen – *Current Biog.*> <the basic dishonesty of public figures *endorsing* products they never use> **Sanction** implies both approval and authorization and may suggest the providing of a standard <some churches that permit divorce do not *sanction* remarriage> <these statements are *sanctioned* by common sense – Joseph Gilbert> **Accredit** and **certify** usually imply official endorsement and conformance with a set standard; choice is determined by idiom rather than basic difference in meaning. Thus, one speaks of an *accredited* dairy herd but *certified* milk, an *accredited* school but a *certified* teacher. *Accredited* occasionally implies general public acceptance or approval <if any . . . break away from *accredited* custom – W. R. Inge> ***ant*** disapprove

approximately – see NEARLY ***ant*** precisely, exactly

apropos – see RELEVANT ***ant*** unapropos

apt 1 see FIT ***ant*** inapt, inept

2 see QUICK

arcane – see MYSTERIOUS

arch – see SAUCY

ardent – see IMPASSIONED ***ant*** cool

ardor – see PASSION ***ant*** coolness, indifference

arduous – see HARD ***ant*** light, facile

argot – see DIALECT

argue – see DISCUSS

arid – see DRY ***ant*** moist, verdant

arise – see SPRING

aristocracy – see OLIGARCHY

arm – see FURNISH ***ant*** disarm

aroma – see SMELL ***ant*** stink, stench

arrange 1 see NEGOTIATE

2 see ORDER ***ant*** derange, disarrange

arrant – see OUTRIGHT

array – see LINE ***ant*** disarray

arrogant – see PROUD ***ant*** meek, unassuming

arrogate – see APPROPRIATE *vb* ***ant*** renounce, yield

art, skill, cunning, artifice, craft *shared meaning* : the faculty of carrying out expertly what is planned or devised. **Art** may be used interchangeably with the remaining terms, but in its most distinctive use it contrasts with them in implying a personal unanalyzable creative power <there's a great *art* in doing these things properly – G. B. Shaw> <praised be the *art* whose subtle power could stay yon cloud, and fix it in that glorious shape – William Wordsworth> <[management is] the *art* of getting things done through other people – L. A. Appley> **Skill** stresses technical knowledge and proficiency <one acquires *skill* through constant practice> <he lacked the *skill*, subtlety, and soundness of instinct to come up with any adroit new responses – J. T. Farrell> **Cunning** suggests ingenuity and subtlety in devising, inventing, or executing <high-ribbed vault . . . with perfect *cunning* framed – William Wordsworth> **Artifice**, though implying skill or intelligence in contriving or devising, is likely to suggest a certain lack of real creative power, a degree of artificiality <a travesty on nature. An *artifice* so masterfully contrived that . . . it holds a novel and fascinating beauty – Terry Southern> <not a show of *artifice* . . . but a genuine creative effort – H. C. Hervey> **Craft** can imply ingenuity and skill <about to display the sensational results of his *craft* to the audience – Roald Dahl> but more than the other words it tends to imply competence in workmanship and facility in the use of tools, techniques, or materials (as of a trade, profession, or art) <a sense of scholarship – and also a *craft* of translation – capable both of hearing what the classics say and also remaining loyal to ourselves – William Arrowsmith> <a gem wrought with all the *craft* of a Cellini>

artful – see SLY ***ant*** artless

article – see THING

articulate – see VOCAL ***ant*** inarticulate, dumb

articulation – see JOINT

artifice – see ART, TRICK

artificial, factitious, synthetic, ersatz *shared meaning* : brought into being not by nature but by human art or effort. **Artificial** may be applied to anything that is not produced by natural conditions but is in some sense a human creation <most of the inequalities in the existing world are *artificial* – Bertrand Russell> but it especially describes something that has a counterpart in nature or imitates something found in nature <*artificial* heat> <*artificial* flowers> It may, but need not, imply inferiority in what it describes. **Factitious** applies to intangibles (as emotions, reasons, or states of mind) that are not the product of real circumstances but are more or less artfully produced or induced to serve some end <created a *factitious* demand by spreading rumors of shortages> <stood for Parliament and played the game of politics upon *factitious* issues – H. G. Wells> **Synthetic** as applied to material things implies a product of the same class as a natural product but produced in another way by human effort; thus, an *artificial* rose however close its resemblance to a natural rose shares none of its fundamental qualities while a *synthetic* ruby not only looks like but is chemically the same as a natural ruby <*artifical* silk is not true silk since it is woven from *synthetic* fibers that are chemically unrelated to silk> **Ersatz**, a recent word in English, is often used as a synonym of *artificial* or *synthetic* when it is desired to stress the notion of substitution, typically of an inferior product for a better (as one that has become scarce or is being diverted from its normal use) <the search for *ersatz* . . . materials was unceasing. Sugar from sawdust; flour from potato meal; gasoline from wood and coal – John Gunther> <students respect learning in their professors and quickly detect *ersatz* provender forked out by glib verbalists – *Library Jour.*> ***ant*** natural

artless – see NATURAL ***ant*** artful, affected

ascend, mount, climb, scale *shared meaning* : to move upward to or toward a summit. **Ascend** implies little more than progressive upward movement

<the car *ascended* the steep grade> or sometimes movement toward a source <ships *ascending* the river> **Mount** is more likely to imply a getting up upon something raised <*mount* a horse> <the condemned man *mounted* the scaffold> **Climb** suggests the effort involved in upward movement and is appropriately used when difficulty of progress is implicit in the situation <*climb* a tree to rescue a stranded cat> <subsequently *climbed* slowly back to stardom on the stage – *Current Biog.*> **Scale** is likely to add to *climb* notions of skilled dexterity and adroitness <*scale* a high wall> <he *scaled* French cliffs under simulated battle conditions side by side with hardened American troops – *Current Biog.*> ***ant*** descend

ascendancy – see SUPREMACY

ascertain – see DISCOVER

ascetic – see SEVERE ***ant*** luxurious, voluptuous

ascribe, attribute, assign, impute, refer, credit *shared meaning* : to lay something to the account of a person or thing. **Ascribe** may suggest tentative, conjectural, inferential, or traditional indication of cause, character, or relationship <she *ascribed* human traits to the inanimate sun – R. K. Corbin> <they have *ascribed* their victories – in superstitious terms – to the operations of fortune – A. J. Toynbee> **Attribute** implies less tentativeness than *ascribe* and may suggest the plausibility and appropriateness of the indicated relation <this broad expansion of federal power cannot be *attributed* solely to the activities of greedy bureaucrats – Trevor Armbrister> <*attributing* her failure to her feeble health> **Assign** implies an ascribing with certainty often after study and deliberation <anthropologists *assign* the skull to the late Pleistocene> <the importance we *assign* to cleanliness> **Impute** implies an ascribing of something that brings discredit, often by way of accusation or blame <how dare you, sir, *impute* such monstrous intentions to me? – G. B. Shaw> **Refer** suggests an assigning of something to a class or to an origin or cause <at least one half of their bad manners may be *referred* to their education – A. T. Quiller-Couch> **Credit** implies an ascribing of something to some person or thing especially as its author, agent, source, or explanation <[his] admirers *credit* him with a new cinematic language – *Current Biog.*>

ashen – see PALE

ashy – see PALE

asinine – see SIMPLE ***ant*** sensible, judicious

ask 1 ask, question, interrogate, query, inquire *shared meaning* : to address a person in an attempt to elicit information. **Ask** is the most general term for putting a question <*ask* them where they live> <is America an empire? It is a question which no American cares to *ask* himself – Henry Fairlie> **Question** usually suggests putting one question after another (as in examining or teaching) <police *questioned* the suspect closely> <*question* a boy about his school> **Interrogate** implies formal or systematic questioning and stresses a search for facts <students . . . surround me on the lawn and *interrogate* me with . . . fervor and skill – M. S. Eisenhower> **Query** is likely to imply a desire for authoritative information or the resolution of a doubt <standard operating procedure would be to *query* the order – J. G. Cozzens> **Inquire** implies a searching for facts or for truth, often specifically by asking questions <his second nature . . . is to *inquire,* to balance, and to evaluate – M. D. Geismar> <*inquire* about his connections>

2 ask, request, solicit *shared meaning* : to seek to obtain by making one's wants known. **Ask** implies merely the statement of the desire <*ask* for a glass of water> **Request** implies greater formality and courtesy and may be preferred to *ask* when there is doubt that what is sought will be forthcoming <*request* a loan> <he . . . *requests* to be excused from the un-

grateful task – G. S. Faber> **Solicit** suggests a calling attention to one's wants in the hope of having them satisfied <*solicit* funds for charity> <our interest is *solicited* by the characters themselves rather than by anything that they do – A. J. Ayer>

asocial – see UNSOCIAL ***ant*** social

aspect – see PHASE

asperity – see ACRIMONY ***ant*** amenity

asperse – see MALIGN

aspersion – see ANIMADVERSION

asphyxiate – see SUFFOCATE

aspiration – see AMBITION

assail – see ATTACK

assassinate – see KILL

assault – see ATTACK

assemble – see GATHER ***ant*** disperse

assent, consent, accede, acquiesce, agree, subscribe *shared meaning* : to concur with what someone else has proposed. **Assent** implies an act involving understanding or judgment and applies especially to propositions or opinions <the council *assented* to the mayor's proposal only after careful study> **Consent** involves the will or feelings and indicates compliance with the wishes of another (as in concurring or assenting) <whatever you ask of me I will *consent* to – George Meredith> <he had really no choice but to agree . . . and gloomily he *consented* – Norman Mailer> **Accede** implies a yielding, often under pressure, of assent or concession <where it becomes desirable . . . to *accede* to such demands of the Negro community as are in the least way plausible – W. F. Buckley> <*acceding* to her pleas, he granted her another period of six months in which to make good – *Current Biog.*> **Acquiesce** implies tacit acceptance or forbearance of opposition <no organism *acquiesces* in its own destruction– H. L. Mencken> <if we *acquiesce* in this poorly disguised swindle – Sam Hunter> **Agree** often carries an implication of previous difference of opinion and may suggest the steps (as persuasion, negotiation, or discussion) that have brought about a change <reluctantly *agreed* to let his son choose his own college> <this inability to *agree* on what the disagreement amounts to – M. K. Drapkin> **Subscribe** implies not only consent or assent but hearty approval and a willingness to go on record <I don't *subscribe* to this American system of child raising – Ludwig Bemelmans> <your brother *subscribes* completely to our complaint> ***ant*** dissent

assert 1 assert, declare, affirm, protest, avow *shared meaning* : to state or put forward positively usually in anticipation of denial or objection or in the face of it. **Assert** applies to firm statement in the absence of proof; it may imply either assurance based on knowledge or unjustified, even brash, confidence in one's own position <he *asserted* that he could be of significant help to the Allies but his was an impotent military force – S. E. Ambrose> **Declare** adds to *assert* an implication of open or public statement <the Supreme Court *declared* that segregation in the schools was unconstitutional> **Affirm** implies conviction of truth and willingness to stand by one's statement because of evidence, experience, or faith <science has become too complex to *affirm* the existence of universal truths – Henry Adams> <*affirmed* his faith in his son's innocence> **Protest** stresses emphasis in affirmation, especially in the face of doubt <I here *protest,* in sight of heaven . . . I am clear – Shak.> <*protested* her ignorance of the cause of the quarrel> **Avow** stresses frank declaration and acknowledgment of personal responsibility for the statement being made <I am not . . . surprised that my church is facing boldly its *avowed* responsibility, which it has never

failed to fulfill – John Rock> <the modest procedure is not to *avow* loudly . . . our love of truth – G. W. Sherburn> ***ant*** deny, controvert

2 see MAINTAIN

assertive – see AGGRESSIVE ***ant*** retiring, acquiescent

assess – see ESTIMATE

assiduous – see BUSY ***ant*** desultory

assign – see ALLOT, ASCRIBE, PRESCRIBE

assignment – see TASK

assimilate – see ABSORB

assimilation – see RECOGNITION

assist – see HELP ***ant*** hamper, impede

associate – see JOIN

assuage – see RELIEVE ***ant*** exacerbate, intensify

assume, affect, pretend, simulate, feign, counterfeit, sham *shared meaning* : to put on a false or deceptive appearance. **Assume** often implies a justifiable motive rather than an intent to impose upon <*assumed* a cheerful air as he entered the sickroom> **Affect** implies making a show of possessing, preferring, or using something, usually for effect <[he] *affected* to ignore the press and public protests, but he steered clear of disaster and took some risks to protect the interests of property owners – *Australian Dict. of Biog.*> <a very kind and gentle man for all his *affected* toughness and gruffness – *Current Biog.*> **Pretend** implies overt profession of what is false, but in itself it suggests nothing about the motive <my book does not *pretend* to scholarship, only to a desire to help the average reader – Anthony Burgess> <[the boy] *pretended* that he was his father and was walking through the fields as he had seen his father walk – James Baldwin> **Simulate** suggests an intent to deceive and implies an assumption of the characteristics of something else by imitating its appearance or outward signs <listened to the protest with *simulated* concern> <they sang better than in church, without . . . the falsity of *simulated* joy – J. T. Farrell> **Feign** implies more invention than *pretend,* less specific imitation than *simulate* <*feign* an injury to escape an unwelcome task> **Counterfeit** may imply imitation that attains a high level of accuracy <*counterfeited* coins> <are you not mad indeed? or do you but *counterfeit?* – Shak.> **Sham** stresses an intent to deceive, but it often suggests such obvious deception as should fool only the gullible <when the curtain falls there are more actors *shamming* dead upon the stage than actors upright – H. A. L. Craig>

assurance 1 see CERTAINTY ***ant*** mistrust, dubiousness

2 see CONFIDENCE ***ant*** diffidence, alarm

assure – see ENSURE ***ant*** alarm

astonish – see SURPRISE 2

astound – see SURPRISE 2

astral – see STARRY

astute – see SHREWD ***ant*** gullible

atheist, agnostic, deist, freethinker, unbeliever, infidel *shared meaning* : one who does not take an orthodox religious position. An **atheist** is one who denies the existence of God and rejects all religious faith and experience; in some uses the term can convey ideas of reprehensible license of opinion and menacing godlessness. An **agnostic** withholds belief (without necessarily denying the possible existence of a supreme being) because he is unwilling to accept the evidence of revelation and spiritual experience; *agnostic* is often extended to nonreligious uses without loss of its basic notion of withholding belief <the younger men . . . were political *agnostics* . . . neither fully accepting nor disowning socialist doctrine – Claire Sterling> A **deist** rejects the concept of a supreme being as ruler and guide of man and the universe though he accepts a god as creator and final judge of man. A **freethinker** is likely to have lost his earlier faith and rejected the tenets of revealed or established religion in favor of what he finds rational or credible. An **unbeliever** is one who lacks or has lost religious faith; the word is more negative than *freethinker* and carries no implication of a substitute for faith <he had once been a believer, a believing Baptist, and is now an *unbeliever* – Joseph Mitchell> An **infidel** is a person belonging to another major religion than one's own and usually to one antagonistic to one's own <to the medieval Christian the Muhammadan was an *infidel*, as was the Christian to the Muhammadan> *ant* theist

athirst – see EAGER

atrocious – see OUTRAGEOUS *ant* humane, noble

attach – see FASTEN *ant* detach

attack, assail, assault, bombard, storm *shared meaning* : to make an onslaught upon. All have primary military application, but all have additional and distinctive extended use. **Attack** implies aggression or aggressiveness and usually a taking of the initiative in entering into an engagement or struggle <if she [France] wanted to *attack* the dollar, this would be a good time to demand reimbursement, for the dollar is shaky – Waverley Root> <*attack* a problem in engineering> **Assail** suggests the action of one who would conquer by repeated blows <the rain *assailed* him and thorns tore him – H. G. Wells> <continued to *assail* extravagances, especially in the foreign services – *Current Biog.*> **Assault** implies vigor of action and often an intent to overpower by suddenness and violence of onslaught <daily in our newspapers we are *assaulted* with a host of ... issues – M. S. Eisenhower> <a universal hubbub wild of stunning sounds ... *assaults* his ear – John Milton> **Bombard** is distinguishable from *assail* in its stronger implication of importunity or of multiplicity of continued pestering attacks <information *bombards* us via transistor radios, bulletin boards, newspapers, neon signs, TV, 3rd class mail, ad infinitum – Frank McLaughlin> <Negroes are ill at ease in the land of their birth. They are *bombarded* with the slogans of democracy, liberty, freedom, equality, but they are not allowed to participate freely in American life – St. Clair Drake & H. R. Cayton> **Storm** suggests the violence of the unleashed forces of nature <he *stormed* out of the house, his feelings in such a turmoil that he did not know where to go – John Cheever> and usually connotes an attempt to sweep away opposition (as by swiftness and violence of assault) <who think to *storm* the world by dint of merit – Robert Burns>

attain – see REACH

attainment – see ACQUIREMENT

attempt, try, endeavor, essay, strive, struggle *shared meaning* : to make an effort to do something. **Attempt** implies an actual beginning of or venturing upon something and often suggests failure or the likelihood of failure <do not *attempt* to take the car out in such weather> <here Shakespeare tackled a problem which proved too much for him. Why he *attempted* it at all is an insoluble puzzle – T. S. Eliot> **Try**, though often interchangeable with *attempt*, may distinctively suggest effort or experiment directed toward an end <you can do it if you really *try*> <they *try* to consult original sources wherever possible – *Current Biog.*> **Endeavor** heightens the implication of exertion and often connotes a striving to fulfill a duty or obey a sense of fitness <the best evidence a gentleman could give a lady of his respect and affection, was to *endeavor* in a friendly way, to rectify her foibles – Royall Tyler> <forces of disorder would take advantage of the situation to *endeavor* to break down governmental authority – S. E. Ambrose> **Essay** implies difficulty in the thing to be accomplished, but it also suggests tentative trying or experimenting <both *essay* virtually the same task: to describe the profound changes their countries have seen since the war – *Times Lit. Supp.*> *Strive* and *struggle* heighten the notion of difficulties to be overcome and stress the exertion involved. Distinctively, **strive** suggests persistent effort to overcome or surmount obstacles <the humanitarian values and goals which we are *striving* to maintain – *Science*> <*strive* to overcome a bad habit> **Struggle** is more likely to suggest a tussling or wrestling (as with adverse forces or in an effort to extricate oneself from what impedes or fetters) <the musicians *struggled* toward the raft in hip deep water – William Styron> <heroes fallen or *struggling* to advance – William Wordsworth> <the story of the human spirit *struggling* with sin – R. A. Hall> ***ant*** succeed

attend – see TEND

attentive – see THOUGHTFUL ***ant*** inattentive, neglectful

attitude – see POSITION

attorney – see LAWYER

attract, allure, charm, captivate, fascinate, bewitch, enchant *shared meaning* : to draw another by exerting a compelling influence. **Attract** is broad in application and stresses only the fact of having or exerting power to draw <bees *attracted* by flowers> <increased salaries necessary to *attract* the best teachers – Nancy Sandrof> **Allure** implies an enticing by what is fair, pleasing, or seductive <the beauty that *allured* men for pleasure had failed to hold them – Ellen Glasgow> **Charm** may suggest magic and commonly implies a power to evoke or attract admiration <this being who at one moment would goad one into such a paroxysm of indignation . . . and who next moment would *charm* one into such a state of subjection – Victoria Sackville-West> **Captivate** implies an often transitory capturing of the fancy or feelings <a place of natural beauty that *captivated* the visitor – W. L. Shirer> **Fascinate,** like *charm*, may suggest a magical influence, but it usually stresses the ineffectiveness of resistance or the helplessness to escape from the one that fascinates <the big white face that to me was something so strange and *fascinating* there were occasions when I could hardly bring myself to look away from it – Roald Dahl> <at once *fascinated* and repelled by the disclosures – Herman Wouk> *Bewitch* and *enchant* share an underlying hint of supernatural force or action, but **bewitch** in typical use implies exertion of an overwhelming power of attraction <*bewitched* by her grace and beauty> <heavens grant that Warwick's words *bewitch* him not – Shak.> while **enchant** is more likely to suggest a power to evoke joy and delight or ecstatic admiration in the one affected <*enchanted* by the play of light and shade> <what *enchants* him in this case was the nicety of . . . procedure, which began by deceiving and ended by murdering – Murray Kempton> ***ant*** repel

attraction, affinity, sympathy *shared meaning* : the relationship existing between things or persons that are naturally or involuntarily drawn together. **Attraction** implies the possession by one of qualities that tend to draw another to it <he came, radiating pride, love, and masculine *attraction*, the bridegroom in his hour of power – Herman Wouk> <the *attraction* of a magnet for iron> **Affinity** implies a susceptibility or predisposition on the part of the one that is attracted and by precise users is restricted to relationships involving people or occasionally their institutions or qualities <[he] became . . . aware of his *affinity* with the pioneers of modern art – *Current Biog.*> <the plan affirms a general *affinity* between the police and the military – both refer to outsiders as "civilians" – Allen Young> **Sympathy** implies a reciprocal relationship between individuals usually based on a shared susceptibility or common capacity for interaction <a large

statue by Epstein. A lovely thing, mind you, but surely not quite in *sympathy* with its surroundings – Roald Dahl> <contemplation of the older thought-patterns which require a vigorous imaginative *sympathy* provides far greater stimulus to the mind – C. L. Wrenn> <felt an inexplicable *sympathy* between them as if they had always been together>

attribute *n* – see QUALITY, SYMBOL

attribute *vb* – see ASCRIBE

audacity – see TEMERITY ***ant*** circumspection

augment – see INCREASE ***ant*** abate

auspicious – see FAVORABLE ***ant*** inauspicious, ill-omened

austere – see SEVERE ***ant*** warm, ardent

authentic, genuine, veritable, bona fide *shared meaning* : being actually and precisely what is claimed. **Authentic** stresses fidelity to actuality and fact and may suggest authority or trustworthiness in determining this relation <the existentialist . . . usually describes only in negative terms the social order that might encourage men to make the most *authentic* choices – D. H. Wrong> <confirmed both by legend and *authentic* record – J. A. Froude> **Genuine** implies accordance with an original or a type without counterfeiting, admixture, or adulteration <*genuine* maple syrup> but it may stress sincerity or the absence of factitiousness <*genuine* piety> **Veritable** implies a correspondence with truth and typically conveys a suggestion of affirmation <his books . . . were written in the grip of a terrible fever, a *veritable* trance, a state of self-induced intoxication – W. L. Shirer> Sometimes its use is hyperbolic and then merely asserts the justice of the designation <he is a *veritable* fool> **Bona fide,** though often used in place of *authentic* or *genuine,* can distinctively apply when good faith or sincerity is in question <*bona fide* residents who . . . maintained homes in no other places – *Harper's*> ***ant*** spurious

authenticate – see CONFIRM ***ant*** impugn

author – see MAKER

authoritarian – see TOTALITARIAN ***ant*** liberal, anarchic

authority – see POWER 3

automatic – see SPONTANEOUS

autonomous – see FREE *adj*

avaricious – see COVETOUS ***ant*** generous

avenge, revenge *shared meaning* : to punish one who has wronged oneself or another. Though the two terms are sometimes used interchangeably each can convey shades of meaning not inherently present in the other. **Avenge** is likely to be preferred when the agent is serving the ends of justice or vindicating another or when a just or merited punishment is administered <*avenge,* O Lord, thy slaughtered saints – John Milton> <he had an insult to *avenge,* a dishonor to be washed off his . . . escutcheon – J. T. Farrell> **Revenge,** though it may imply a desire for vindication or an aim to serve the ends of justice, is more likely to suggest a desire to retaliate, to get even, to pay back in degree or kind, and therefore tends to connote such states as malice, spite, or unwillingness to forgive <the idea . . . gave him promise – however remote – of *revenging* himself in a most devilish manner upon his greatest enemies – Roald Dahl>

average, mean, median, norm *shared meaning* : something (as a quantity) that represents a middle point between extremes. An **average** is exactly or approximately the quotient obtained by dividing the sum total of a set of figures by the number of figures <the *average* of 3, 9, and 12 is 8> Thus, *averages* provide a means of estimating something (as output or proficiency) that varies from case to case <he graduated from high school with an *average* of 82> **Mean** in general use is likely to refer to something (as a condition, quality, intensity, or rate) that lies midway between two extremes <observe a happy *mean* between abjectness and arrogance> <the annual temperature *means* vary with altitude> **Median** applies to the point at which as many instances are greater as are smaller; thus, the *average* of 3, 4, 5, 8, and 10 is 6 but the *median* of the same set of numbers is 5. **Norm** denotes the computed or estimated average of a large group, class, or grade and often implies a standard of reference <his health improved and he scored well above the *norm* in his fifth-grade subjects> ***ant*** maximum, minimum

averse – see DISINCLINED ***ant*** avid (*for*), athirst (*for*)

avert – see PREVENT 2

avid – see EAGER ***ant*** indifferent, averse

avoid – see ESCAPE ***ant*** face, meet

avow **1** see ACKNOWLEDGE ***ant*** disavow
2 see ASSERT

await – see EXPECT ***ant*** despair

awake – see AWARE

award – see GRANT

aware, cognizant, conscious, sensible, alive, awake *shared meaning* : having knowledge of something and especially of something not generally known or apparent. **Aware** suggests vigilance in observing and alertness in interpreting what is observed <an academic community, dedicated to rational and *aware* problem-solving – Richard Stith> <the *aware* person is alive because he knows how he feels, where he is and when it is – Eric Berne> **Cognizant** implies possession of special or certain knowledge, often from firsthand sources <through the servants, or from other means, he had made himself *cognizant* of the projected elopement – Anthony Trollope> **Conscious** may imply a calling into the forefront of awareness of something already perceptible to the mind or senses <became *conscious* of the beating of his heart as he waited there> <one must suppose that the counselor's perception, though accurate, remained below the level of *conscious* awareness – F. C. Cameron> or it may imply an extreme or dominating awareness, even a preoccupation <a race-*conscious* politician> <these two egoists, both acutely *conscious* of the historic roles they were playing, were constantly bickering – S. E. Ambrose> **Sensible** implies direct or intuitive perception especially of intangibles or of emotional states or qualities <even he was *sensible* of the decorous atmosphere – James Joyce> and it may be used appropriately to acknowledge awareness or appreciation (as of an injury, a slight, a courtesy, or a favor) <I am quite *sensible* of the wrong you did me> **Alive** may suggest vivid awareness or keen certain perception <his educational philosophy is . . . not sufficiently *alive* to the unprecedented problems of opening up high culture to every citizen – Michael Harrington> **Awake** is more likely to suggest an aroused state and alert watchfulness <they are not *awake* to the risks they run> <one of those *awake* institutions watching . . . both the building and the essential creativity with which to fill it – Louis Chapin> ***ant*** unaware

awe – see REVERENCE

awful – see FEARFUL 2

awkward, clumsy, maladroit, inept, gauche *shared meaning* : not marked by ease and smoothness (as in acting or functioning). **Awkward** is widely applicable (as to persons, things, or situations) and may convey a wide range of suggestions (as of unhandiness, inconvenience, lack of tact or control, or embarrassment) in various locutions; thus, an *awkward* tool is one that is unhandy to use, an *awkward* person lacks muscular control, an *awkward* situation may be either inconvenient or embarrassing <saying

the strained and *awkward* things that people always say when they talk of death – Thomas Wolfe> **Clumsy** stresses stiffness and heaviness and is often applied to what is lumbering or ponderous <a *clumsy* farm horse> <thick *clumsy* boots> As applied to persons and their acts it is likely to imply a lack of expertness and adroitness, often with a suggestion of bungling <made a *clumsy* apology> <two weeks on the job, he was almost beginning to feel less *clumsy* – Thomas Pynchon> **Maladroit** implies a deficiency of tact or a clumsiness in human relationships that often results in embarrassment or causes resentment <a *maladroit* reply to a civil question> <his last-minute attempts to influence the party platform, while philosophically proper, were politically *maladroit* – J. A. Michener> **Inept** stresses inappropriateness and often carries a suggestion of futility or absurdity <the fourth debate was about as *inept* a performance as one could witness, with neither man saying anything new or even repeating the old effectively – J. A. Michener> <saying things that were *inept,* maudlin, unhinged – William Styron> **Gauche** applies especially to a lack of ease arising from shyness, inexperience, or ill-breeding <there is almost always a lag between the time the *gauche* new arrival achieves success and the time those who got there first accept him as an equal – I. S. Rohter> ***ant*** handy, deft, graceful

baby – see INDULGE
back – see RECEDE
backbone – see FORTITUDE ***ant*** spinelessness
backslide – see LAPSE
bad, ill, evil, wicked, naughty *shared meaning* : not ethically acceptable. **Bad** is a very general term applicable to anyone or anything reprehensible, for whatever reason and to whatever degree <such a *bad* boy, he won't stay in the yard> <almost as *bad,* good mother, as kill a king, and marry with his brother – Shak.> **Ill** may suggest an active malevolence or vicious intent <it was *ill* counsel had misled the girl – Alfred Tennyson> <an *ill* deed> but sometimes it goes no further than to attribute objectionableness or inferiority to something or someone <the boy disobeyed his master's advice with the usual *ill* consequences – Elinor Cullen> <a man held in *ill* repute by his contemporaries> **Evil** may add to *bad* a strong suggestion of the sinister or the baleful <looked at Charles with an *evil* shine in his old eyes, and I knew he was going to say something wicked – Shirley Jackson> <he knew nothing bad about him, but he felt something *evil* – Willa Cather> **Wicked** usually implies serious moral reprehensibility <*wicked* sorcerers who have done people to death by their charms – J. G. Frazer> or it may suggest malevolence and malice <brooding in silence over his failure, the eyes veiled and *wicked* – Roald Dahl> **Naughty** which was once a close synonym of *wicked* <the congregations of *naughty* men have sought after my soul – *Bk. of Com. Prayer*> is in current use restricted to trivial misdeeds (as of children) <he had been very *naughty* that day, teased the cat, made his sister cry, and answered back when mother scolded him> or used to suggest reprehensibility in a light or playful way <the still popular, and still *naughty,* and perpetually profane *Decameron* – Gilbert Highet> ***ant*** good
badger – see BAIT
baffle – see FRUSTRATE
bag – see CATCH

bait, badger, heckle, hector, hound, chivy *shared meaning* : to harass persistently or annoyingly. **Bait** suggests wanton cruelty or malicious delight in persecution often of a weak or defenseless opponent and is more likely to be used of utterances than of physical harassment <*baiting* these hapless citizens who had the gall to have Japanese parents – G. S. Schuyler> **Badger** suggests persistent bedeviling with tactics designed to confuse, madden, or enervate <*badger* a witness on cross-examination> <the mill foreman so taunted the workers, so *badgered* them and told them that they dared not quit – Sinclair Lewis> **Heckle** implies persistent interruptive questioning of a speaker in order to confuse or discomfit him <infuriates some of his fellow Justices by *heckling* lawyers who appear before the Court – *Saturday Rev.*> **Hector** always carries a suggestion of bullying and implies a scolding or domineering attack <we are . . . not to be *hectored*, and bullied, and beat into compliance – Henry Fielding> *Hound* and *chivy* both suggest relentless pursuit, but **hound** implies persistent and long-continued persecution <the detective's prey . . . is degraded from the right to mercy, and is *hounded* without a qualm to his public humiliation – Gershon Legman> while **chivy** is more likely to imply merciless teasing or annoyance past the endurance of the victim <having seen two successive wives of the delicate poet *chivied* and worried into their graves – Joseph Conrad>

balance – see COMPENSATE

bald – see BARE

baleful – see SINISTER *ant* beneficent

balk – see FRUSTRATE *ant* forward

balky – see CONTRARY

ban – see FORBID

banal – see INSIPID *ant* original, recherché

bane – see POISON

baneful – see PERNICIOUS *ant* beneficial

banish, exile, deport, transport *shared meaning* : to remove by authority or force from a country, state, or sovereignty. To **banish** is to compel one to leave a place or country, although not necessarily his own, either permanently or for a fixed time, and with or without restriction to a particular place <*banish* an enemy of the king> <the spiritual leader of the Greek Cypriots . . . had been *banished* to the Seychelles Islands – *Current Biog.*> To **exile** is to banish or cause to depart under constraint from one's own country; the word may connote expulsion by degree or by compulsion of circumstances and suggests a prolonged absence <*exiled* for his part in the rebellion> <American writers who *exile* themselves in France> To **deport** is to send a person out of a country of which he is not a citizen, often to the country from which he came <*deport* a criminal> To **transport** is to banish a person convicted of a crime to a particular place (as a penal colony) <many of Australia's pioneers were *transported* men who had served out their time>

bankrupt – see DEPLETE

barbarian, barbaric, barbarous, savage *shared meaning* : characteristic of uncivilized man. **Barbarian** often implies a state midway between tribal savagery and full civilization <far from being savages . . . [they] were a *barbarian* people with a highly developed culture – Geoffrey Grigson & C. H. Gibbs-Smith> *Barbaric* and *barbarous* are more likely to apply to what is felt as characteristic of or fitting to a barbarian stage of development. **Barbaric** tends to imply a wild profusion and lack of restraint that is indicative of crudity of taste and lack of self-restraint <this audacious and *barbaric* profusion of words – chosen always for their color and their vividly expressive quality – Arthur Symons> **Barbarous** is more likely to imply uncivilized cruelty or ruthlessness or sometimes complete lack of cultivated taste and refinement <people of such great stupidity and such *barbarous* practices that the Administration has seen fit to quarantine them – W. S. Burroughs> <the *barbarous* conflicts between nations that call themselves Christian – Edmund Wilson> **Savage** in its basic use implies less advance toward civilization than *barbarian* <a *savage* tribe with a gathering economy> In its extended use it is ordinarily very close to *barbarous* <children . . . taught to fight, to menace, and to struggle in a world of *savage* violence and incessant din, they had the city's qualities stamped into their flesh – Thomas Wolfe> <a *savage* attack> ***ant*** civilized

barbaric – see BARBARIAN ***ant*** restrained, refined, subdued

barbarous 1 see BARBARIAN ***ant*** civilized, humane
2 see FIERCE ***ant*** clement

bare, naked, nude, bald, barren *shared meaning* : deprived of naturally or conventionally appropriate covering. In reference to bodily matters **bare** usually applies to body parts and implies, without connotation, absence of covering <*bare* feet> **Naked** implies complete lack of covering and is essentially a neutral word, acquiring its varied suggestions from its context <a fat *naked* baby> <a *naked* savage> <blowsy *naked* wenches leaning out of upper windows> **Nude,** a very close synonym of *naked,* is likely to be preferred when the reference is to art <had three *nude* statues in the exhibition> and **bald** applies specifically to the absence of hair on the head. But all of these words have more general applications. In such use **bare** typically stresses the absence of something usually expected <a *bare* room stripped of all nonessentials> <scorched and blackened by the long summer, the country was as *bare* as a conquered province – Ellen Glasgow> **Naked** tends to suggest exposure or revelation <the display of power was *naked* and arbitrary – Arthur Knight> <woods stand *naked,* ways and fields lie white – Inez & Kemp Malone> **Nude** is essentially neutral and literal <a broad *nude* valley – R. L. Stevenson> and **bald** may indicate the absence of an expected upper covering <the *bald* treeless summit of a mountain> or it may imply severe plainness and lack of adornment <a *bald* summary of a book that is both deep and complex – Julian Gloag> **Barren** implies absence of natural or appropriate covering but is likely to stress an underlying impoverishment, impotence, or aridity <intersperse with verdure and flowers the dusty deserts of *barren* philology – Samuel Johnson> <a wilder, *barrener,* more desolate land . . . could hardly be found – D. L. Sharp> ***ant*** covered

barefaced – see SHAMELESS ***ant*** furtive

barren 1 see BARE
2 see STERILE ***ant*** fecund

barrister – see LAWYER

base *n* **base, basis, foundation, ground** *shared meaning* : something on which another thing is built up and by which it is supported. **Base** implies, though often obscurely, an underlying element that supports something material or immaterial <a curiosity that set a ready *base* for learning – W. J. Pelton> <the *base* of a column> <a water-*base* paint> **Basis,** similar in meaning, is rarely used of material things and usually carries a more definite implication of support <the Government has begun to lay a sounder *basis* for a higher rate of growth in the future – R. M. Titmuss> **Foundation** tends to imply solidity in what underlies and supports and fixity or stability in what is supported <the exposure of unsuspected depravity in the highest circles shook the social fabric to its *foundations* – Lucius Beebe> <I detest that word . . . for no recognizable reason. I do seem to lack *foundation* for my beliefs and preju-

dices – *Saturday Rev.*> **Ground** suggests solidity and is likely to imply a substratum comparable to the earth in its capacity to support and sometimes to justify <the state of our whole life is estrangement . . . because we are estranged from the *Ground* of our being – Paul Tillich> <summarily discharged on the *ground* of his questionable associates> ***ant*** top

base *adj* **base, low, vile** *shared meaning* : contemptible because beneath what is expected of the average man. **Base** stresses the ignoble; it may suggest cruelty, treachery, greed, or grossness <*base* self-centered indulgence and selfish ambition – W. R. Inge> <there is nothing more *base* than betrayal of a benefactor> **Low** may connote crafty cunning, vulgarity, or immorality and regularly implies an outraging of one's sense of decency or propriety <a *low* comic> <sporting events of a *low* type, such as setting on men, women, or animals to fight – G. M. Trevelyan> **Vile,** the strongest of these words, tends to suggest disgusting depravity or filth <a *vile* remark> <[orders] commanding him to commit the *vilest* war crimes – W. L. Shirer> ***ant*** noble

bashful – see SHY ***ant*** forward, brazen

basis – see BASE

bathos – see PATHOS

batter – see MAIM

battle, engagement, action *shared meaning* : a meeting between opposing forces. All apply primarily to military encounters, and in this use **battle** appropriately describes general and prolonged combat while **engagement** stresses the actual contact between forces and may apply to either a major battle or a minor skirmish. **Action** may effectively replace either *battle* or *engagement* when it is desired to stress the active give-and-take of offensive and defensive efforts. These primary values and distinctions are likely to be retained in extended use of the words. **Battle** then can imply a major extended struggle or controversy <the advocates of the old classical education have been . . . fighting a losing *battle* for over half a century – W. R. Inge> **Engagement,** while stressing contact between forces, tends to replace the suggestion of hostility with one of interaction <there must be an *engagement* between the observer and the observed, an *engagement* wherein interest in the observed religion is not limited to a recognition of its importance as a social or cultural factor – P. H. Ashby> **Action** can suggest an active give-and-take in attaining an end or resisting a pressure <in the field of *action,* a nation exercises power in three general ways – through assistance, reward, or retaliation – S. K. Padover> <she kept up a fierce rearguard *action* . . . against any kind of clothes that looked grown-up – Herman Wouk>

bear **1** see CARRY

2 bear, suffer, endure, abide, tolerate, stand, brook *shared meaning* : to put up with something trying or painful. **Bear** is likely to imply a capacity to sustain what is distressing or hurtful without flinching or faltering <make the water as hot as you can *bear* it> <some people are better able to *bear* pain than others> <we had no choice but to *bear* the loss> **Suffer** suggests acceptance or passivity rather than courage in bearing <the indignities she was made to *suffer* – Victoria Sackville-West> <the Italian people, at heart, had never . . . embraced facism. They had merely *suffered* it, knowing that it was a passing phase – W. L. Shirer> **Endure** implies meeting difficulties or trials with firm resolution <he had not saved her, he had not taught her faith enough to *endure* disaster – William Styron> **Abide** may come close to *suffer* in suggesting acceptance without resistance or protest <what fates impose, that man must needs *abide* – Shak.> but is largely restricted to negative constructions <I cannot *abide* her constant chatter> **Tolerate**

suggests overcoming or successfully controlling an impulse to resist, avoid, or resent something injurious or distasteful <its views were supported or *tolerated* by most of the leaders – Lois B. Wills> <[he] swallowed an injustice which others would not have *tolerated* – R. G. Adams> **Stand** emphasizes strongly an ability to bear without discomposure or flinching <people who cannot *stand* the sight of blood> **Brook** can come close to *tolerate* <the General could ill *brook* the opposition of his son – Jane Austen> but in its usual negative construction it implies self-assertion or even defiance <restraint she will not *brook* – John Milton>

bearing, deportment, demeanor, mien, manner, carriage *shared meaning* : the way in which a person outwardly manifests his personality or attitude. **Bearing,** the most general of these words, now usually implies characteristic posture <a tall portly man with an impressive *bearing*> **Deportment** applies especially to one's actions in their relations to the external amenities of life and tends to stress the influence of breeding or training <all the thousand and one artificialities which go to make up feminine *deportment* – Max Peacock> **Demeanor** applies especially to one's attitude as shown in one's behavior in the presence of others <in later life her self-assertiveness and quick temper . . . gave her a formidable *demeanor* – Jean I. Martin & P. L. Brown> **Mien** referring to both bearing and demeanor, is likely to suggest mood and therefore may stress transience <usually presents a *mien* of solemnity – *Current Biog.*> **Manner** implies customary or characteristic way of interacting socially <stopped to speak, after the *manner* of the country – Ellen Glasgow> <her kindly *manner* soothed the frightened children> **Carriage** applies chiefly to habitual posture in standing or walking <has a lithe strong body and superb *carriage* – Elenore Lester>

beat – see CONQUER

beautiful, lovely, handsome, pretty, comely, fair *shared meaning* : aesthetically or sensuously pleasing. **Beautiful** is applied to what excites the keenest pleasure not only of the senses but also, through the medium of the senses, of mind and spirit. It may suggest an approach to or a realization of perfection <they are not *beautiful:* they are only decorated – G. B. Shaw> <the *beautiful* character of her husband, and his entire worthiness of her noble and deeply religious nature – Mabel F. Hale> **Lovely** is likely to imply a keen emotional delight rather than deep intellectual or spiritual pleasure and is especially applicable to what impinges primarily on the senses <a *lovely* rose> <why ever wast thou *lovely* in my eyes – Shak.> **Handsome** implies approval of something as conforming to a standard (as of regularity, symmetry, fitness of proportion, or quality of workmanship) <a *handsome* purse> In reference to persons it may suggest pleasing appearance and dignified charm rather than beauty <a tall *handsome* woman looking younger than her years> **Pretty** applies especially to something that pleases by its delicacy, grace, or charm rather than by its perfection or elegance <a group of *pretty* girls> It is likely to carry a derogatory note when applied to males or things felt as male. **Comely** is like *handsome* in suggesting cool approval rather than emotional response <the construction [was] . . . neat, *comely,* enigmatic, and rather dull – Christopher Rand> <a *comely* matron> **Fair** is likely to suggest a beauty based on purity, flawlessness, or freshness <it was a good house, and soon it would be cleaned and *fair* again – Shirley Jackson> <the girl was certainly *fair* to look upon. Many heavens were in her sunny eyes – Herman Melville> ***ant*** ugly

beautify – see ADORN ***ant*** uglify

bedeck – see ADORN

beg, entreat, beseech, implore, supplicate, adjure, importune *shared meaning* : to ask or request urgently. **Beg** suggests earnestness or insistence especially in asking a favor <the author has not been able to think of a better word and he *begs* the reader's indulgence – Joseph Church> <the boy *begged* for help> **Entreat** implies an attempt to persuade or to overcome resistance in another <he began to *entreat* the Colonial Office for a colonial appointment – *Australian Dict. of Biog.*> <*entreat* him to hold his revengeful hand – Lucy M. Montgomery> **Beseech** implies eager urgency and often anxiety or solicitude <she *besought* him, for his soul's sake, to speak the truth – Rudyard Kipling> **Implore,** often interchangeable with *beseech,* can suggest greater urgency in the plea and deeper or more intimate concern in the pleader <*implored* another chance to prove his innocence> **Supplicate** suggests a posture of humility or a prayerful attitude <invite, entreat, *supplicate* them to accompany you – Earl of Chesterfield> <fall on his knees and *supplicate* the God of his fathers – S. L. Terrien> **Adjure** implies enjoining as well as pleading and suggests the involvement of something sacred <I *adjure* thee by the living God, that thou tell us whether thou be the Christ – *Mt* 26:63 (AV)> **Importune** is likely to suggest repeated attempts to break down resistance and often connotes an annoying pertinacity <had *importuned* her day after day to try a canoe excursion – Herman Wouk> <her father's ways . . . the everlasting dumb *importuning* of her just to be good – Walker Percy>

beggarly – see CONTEMPTIBLE

begin, commence, start, initiate, inaugurate *shared meaning* : to take the first step (as in a course, process, or operation). **Begin** (implying opposition to *end*) and **commence** (implying opposition to *conclude*) are identical in meaning though the former is often preferred in less formal contexts and the latter when the situation involves real or fancied formality; thus, one *begins* to wash the dishes but one *commences* a lawsuit <*begin* a trip> <*commence* to keep a diary> <given the opportunity to follow up a research project so brilliantly *commenced*> **Start,** though sometimes used as though it were freely interchangeable with *begin* and *commence,* can carry quite distinctive implications based especially on its opposition to *stop. Start* is likely to suggest a setting out from a point, often after inaction or waiting <he was nearly seven before he *started* school> <they looked about hesitantly, no one wanting to *start* a conversation> <shouldn't you be *starting* for home soon?> **Initiate** stresses the taking of a first step but implies nothing about an end or ending <she *initiated* . . . a special project aimed at curing venereal diseases among prostitutes – *Current Biog.*> <the art of recording thought, invented ages ago, *initiated* history – A. C. Morrison> **Inaugurate** retains from its more frequent sense of to induct into office, a hint of a ceremonial beginning <*inaugurating* a terror which would become dreadfully familiar to hundreds of millions – W. L. Shirer> <a passionately modern mind who feels that science has *inaugurated* a new era – J. C. Powys> ***ant*** end

beguile – see DECEIVE, WHILE

behave, conduct, comport, deport, acquit *shared meaning* : to act or to cause or allow (oneself) to act in a particular way. **Behave** implies a standard <he *behaved* very badly toward his family> and when used without modifiers indicates conduct judged proper or seemly <most children will *behave* if they understand what is wanted> **Conduct** implies action or behavior that shows one's capacity for self-control and self-direction <her manner should be reserved and dignified; . . . she would *conduct* herself as though staying at Chevron were quite the ordinary thing for her to do

– Victoria Sackville-West> **Comport** is likely to appear in more formal context than *behave* and *conduct* and sometimes may convey the notion of conforming to what is expected (as of one's position or by one's peers) <a man is judged now by how well he *comports* himself in the face of danger – J. W. Aldridge> **Deport** is a close synonym of *comport* and may stress conformance to a code <*deported* himself like a gentleman of the old school> **Acquit** retains from other of its senses the notion of judgment and applies especially to conduct under stress <he *acquitted* himself well in the emergency> ***ant*** misbehave

behindhand – see TARDY ***ant*** beforehand

belie – see MISREPRESENT ***ant*** attest

belief **1 belief, faith, credence, credit** *shared meaning* : an assent or act of assenting to something offered for acceptance. **Belief** may suggest no more than mental acceptance without directly implying certitude or certainty on the part of the believer <just one single example of real unreason is enough to shake our *belief* in everything – Theodore Sturgeon> <buoyed up by the glorious *belief* . . . that he was at last in triumphant control of his destiny – Thomas Wolfe> **Faith** implies certitude and full trust and confidence in the source whether there be objective evidence or not <*faith* is the substance of things hoped for, the evidence of things not seen – *Heb* 11:1 (AV)> **Credence** implies intellectual acceptance but conveys nothing about the validity of the grounds for such acceptance <a rumor that gained wide *credence*> **Credit** implies acceptance on grounds other than proof, often specifically on the past reputation of the source <I'm inclined to give *credit* to his story for he has always been truthful> <what *credit* can be attached to an anonymous report?> ***ant*** unbelief, disbelief
2 see OPINION

believable – see PLAUSIBLE ***ant*** unbelievable

believe – see KNOW ***ant*** disbelieve

belittle – see DECRY ***ant*** aggrandize, magnify

bellicose – see BELLIGERENT ***ant*** pacific, amicable

belligerent, bellicose, pugnacious, combative, quarrelsome, contentious *shared meaning* : having or taking an aggressive or truculent attitude. **Belligerent** implies being actively at war or in an actively hostile mood <*belligerent* nations> <attacked the amendment in a hotly *belligerent* speech> **Bellicose** suggests a desire or readiness to fight or, sometimes, to stir up a fight <was there ever a people so *bellicose* in politics, so reckless and raucous in hostility – and then so unpugnacious in pitched combat – *Life*> **Pugnacious** and **combative** are more likely to apply to fixed qualities of disposition or character; they need not, however, convey the impression of pettiness or ill nature or of needlessly seeking cause for disagreement that is so strongly present in the otherwise similar **quarrelsome** <the Scotch are certainly a most *pugnacious* people; their whole history proves it – G. H. Barrow> <combat in the field of sports . . . [is] generally approved. The *combative* impulses in human nature may thus find an expression – M. R. Cohen> <on the days they worked they were good-natured and cheerful . . . on our idle days they were mutinous and *quarrelsome* – Benjamin Franklin> <a tense *quarrelsome* man, rarely at peace even with himself> **Contentious** is likely to suggest perversity of temper and wearisome persistence in dispute <the most *contentious*, quarrelsome, disagreeing crew – George Berkeley> ***ant*** friendly

bemoan – see DEPLORE ***ant*** exult

bend – see CURVE ***ant*** straighten

beneficial, advantageous, profitable *shared meaning* : bringing good or gain. **Beneficial** can describe whatever is conducive to well-being and especially to personal health and feeling or to social welfare <a climate *beneficial* to asthma> <the rain was *beneficial* to the sprouting seeds> **Advantageous** suggests alternatives and stresses a choice that brings superiority or greater success in attaining an end <the social graces so necessary to any young girl preparing for an *advantageous* marriage – H. C. Hervey> **Profitable** suggests the yielding of useful or lucrative returns <the teaching of new skills to those seeking *profitable* ways to fill their time and improve their talents – Nancy Sandrof> <a *profitable* investment> ***ant*** harmful, detrimental

benign – see KIND ***ant*** malign
benignant – see KIND ***ant*** malignant
berate – see SCOLD
beseech – see BEG
bestow – see GIVE
betray – see REVEAL
better – see IMPROVE ***ant*** worsen
bewail – see DEPLORE ***ant*** rejoice
bewilder – see PUZZLE
bewitch – see ATTRACT
bias *n* – see PREDILECTION
bias *vb* – see INCLINE
bid – see COMMAND ***ant*** forbid
biddable – see OBEDIENT ***ant*** willful
big – see LARGE ***ant*** little
billingsgate – see ABUSE
bind – see TIE ***ant*** loose, unbind
birthright – see HERITAGE
biting – see INCISIVE
bizarre – see FANTASTIC ***ant*** chaste, subdued
blamable – see BLAMEWORTHY
blame – see CRITICIZE

blameworthy, blamable, guilty, culpable *shared meaning* : deserving reproach or punishment for some act or course of action. **Blameworthy** and **blamable** acknowledge the fact of censurable quality in what is described but in themselves imply nothing about the degree of reprehensibility involved <anyone . . . who falls below the level of the high spirit of national unity which alone can give national salvation is *blameworthy* – Sir Winston Churchill> <the memories of infinitesimal neglects that began to show now preposterously *blamable* – Mary Austin> **Guilty** implies responsibility for or consciousness of crime, sin, or, at the least, grave error or misdoing <the defendant was found *guilty* of murder> <suspicion always haunts the *guilty* mind: the thief doth fear each bush an officer – Shak.> **Culpable** usually suggests less stringent blame than *guilty* and is likely to connote malfeasance or errors of ignorance, omission, or negligence <the avaricious victims were almost as *culpable* as the confidence man who tricked them> <*culpable* neglect> <is it not . . . *culpable* and unworthy, thus beforehand to slur her honor? – P. B. Shelley> ***ant*** blameless

blanch – see WHITEN
bland 1 see SOFT ***ant*** pungent, piquant, savory, tasty
2 see SUAVE ***ant*** brusque
blank – see EMPTY
blatant – see VOCIFEROUS ***ant*** decorous, reserved

blaze, flame, flare, glare, glow *shared meaning* : a brightly burning light or fire or something suggesting this. **Blaze** implies rapidity in kindling of material and the radiation of intense heat and light <the crackle and *blaze*

of dry oak logs> <burned with a *blaze* that lighted the whole town> <the angry *blaze* of her eyes> **Flame** suggests a darting tongue or tongues of fire <the *flames* rose above the burning building> <their exile fanned the smoldering spirit of Moroccan nationalism into *flame* – *Current Biog.*> **Flare** stresses a sudden rapid burst of fire or flame against a dark background (as of a dying fire) <the sudden *flare* of a match> In extended use it implies both suddenness and intensity <a *flare* of temper> **Glare** is likely to connote oppressive brilliance (as of a strong unshielded light) <the *glare* of a searchlight> <the *glare* of the sun on snow> <his days were passed in the *glare* of publicity – John Buchan> **Glow** is more likely to suggest a temperate burning that yields light without flame or glare or gentle warmth and radiance <the comforting *glow* of coals on the hearth> <an amiable *glow* put within him by a bottle of moselle wine – Robert McAlmon> <the healthy *glow* of his windburned cheeks>

bleach – see WHITEN

blemish, defect, flaw *shared meaning* : an imperfection. **Blemish** applies especially to something that affects only the surface or appearance <a *blemish* on an apple> or to something felt as similarly trivial <he studiously perfected nature by correcting all the little *blemishes* of manner and little weaknesses of character in order to produce an immaculate effect – V. L. Parrington> **Defect** applies to an imperfection that impairs worth or function <the basic *defect* in starvation is chemical: an inadequate supply of the raw materials needed for the maintenance of the normal structure and function of the organism – Josef Brožek> <there has been a *defect* in the mechanics of foreign policy formulation and execution – J. P. Roche> **Flaw** implies a defect in continuity or cohesion that is likely to cause failure under stress <a hidden *flaw* in a casting> <jealousy is the catalyst of Othello's inner *flaw*. . . . His *flaw* is nothing less than original sin, the sin of all mankind in its sense of inferiority: to play God – John Ciardi> ***ant*** immaculateness

blench – see RECOIL

blend – see MIX ***ant*** resolve

blink – see WINK

blithe – see MERRY ***ant*** morose, atrabilious

block – see HINDER

blot – see STIGMA

blot out – see ERASE

blowsy – see SLATTERNLY ***ant*** smart, spruce, dainty

bluff, blunt, brusque, curt, crusty, gruff *shared meaning* : abrupt and unceremonious in manner or speech. **Bluff** suggests good-natured outspokenness and unconventionality <this big, *bluff,* genial idol of the Viennese lower middle classes – W. L. Shirer> <answered with *bluff* good humor> **Blunt** implies such directness and plain speaking as to suggest carelessness of the feelings of others <the *blunt* fashion of people confident that right is on their side – Brendan Gill> <a *blunt* man. He is often brutal. He has never seemed to me to be devious – Sumner Welles> **Brusque** suggests abruptness in manner or speech, often with a strong hint of ungraciousness <these sharp comments and *brusque* retorts unnerved his challenger> <defended his old friend who, he said, had a *brusque* and rough manner but carried out his duties . . . efficiently and well – *Australian Dict. of Biog.*> **Curt** implies disconcerting shortness or rude conciseness <a *curt* reply to a harmless question> <his manner was *curt* and preoccupied> **Crusty** suggests a harsh or surly manner that may conceal an inner mellowness or kindliness <a *crusty* old bachelor> <far from being dull, the book is an extremely lively and *crusty* essay on politics – the Cabinet being the

thread on which he strings his very sensible and very individual notions – Janet Malcolm> **Gruff** implies a hoarse or husky speech that may suggest bad temper but is as likely to suggest shyness or embarrassment <*gruff*, disagreeable, sarcastic remarks – W. M. Thackeray> <a *gruff* surface that hid a heart of gold> ***ant*** smooth, suave

blunder – see ERROR

blunt 1 see BLUFF ***ant*** tactful, subtle
2 see DULL ***ant*** keen, sharp

boast, brag, vaunt, crow *shared meaning* : to express pride in oneself or one's accomplishments. **Boast,** the most general term, is likely to imply ostentatiousness and a degree of exaggeration <a man ready to *boast* of every trivial success> but it may also imply a claiming with proper and justifiable pride <the town *boasted* a general store, a bank, and an inn> **Brag** is a more forceful term that regularly conveys a strong notion of exaggeration and conceit and often implies a crude attempt at self-glorification <he *bragged* incessantly – no one, to hear him tell it, had such crops, such stock, such a loving wife, such clever children> <*brag* about a raise in pay> **Vaunt** usually connotes more pomp and bombast than *boast* and less crudity or naïveté than *brag* <charity *vaunteth* not itself, is not puffed up – *1 Cor* 13:4 (AV)> <too . . . sophisticated, hypercritical and ashamed of *vaunting* ourselves to claim credit where credit is due – Robert Moses> **Crow** usually implies exultant boasting or blatant bragging in a manner suggestive of the crowing of a cock over the defeat of a rival <the barrister *crowed* with triumph but the professor was in no way put out – Cyril Kersh> ***ant*** depreciate (*as oneself*)

bodily, physical, corporeal, corporal, somatic *shared meaning* : of or relating to the human body. **Bodily** suggests opposition to *mental* or *intellectual* <*bodily* pleasures> <*bodily* illness is more easy to bear than mental – Charles Dickens> **Physical** is vaguer in reference and puts less stress on organic structure; thus, specific *bodily* pains can result from generalized *physical* exertion; a sense of *physical* well-being tends to accompany *bodily* health. **Corporeal** implies an opposition to *immaterial* or *spiritual* <until, the breath of this *corporeal* frame . . . almost suspended, we are laid asleep in body, and become a living soul – William Wordsworth> <the spiritual life commences where the *corporeal* existence terminates – J. G. Frazer> **Corporal** is likely to apply to things that affect the body unpleasantly <*corporal* punishment> **Somatic** is preferred in technical use to *bodily* and *corporeal* because of its freedom from theological and literary connotations and in such use often carries an implied opposition to *psychical* <*somatic* structure> <*somatic* response to stimulation> <a *somatic* disorder>

boisterous – see VOCIFEROUS

bombard – see ATTACK

bombast, rhapsody, rant, fustian *shared meaning* : speech or writing characterized by high-flown pomposity or pretentiousness. **Bombast** implies verbose grandiosity or inflation of style disproportionate to the thought <nonsense gives place to sense, *bombast* to a hard-boiled and cynical lucidity – Aldous Huxley> **Rhapsody** applies to an ecstatic or effusive utterance governed more by the feelings than by logical thought <he writes as though he had uncovered a new religion and thought it deserved a *rhapsody* – *New Yorker*> and may specifically describe an excess of more or less incoherent praise <she went into *rhapsodies* over their new house> *Rant* and *fustian* are both distinctly derogatory, but **rant** stresses extravagance or violence in expressing and **fustian** the banality of what is expressed <the hoarse *rant* of the demagogue fills the air and distracts the people's minds – Max Ascoli> <its characters speak the *fustian* of pretentious books – C. E.

Montague> <he, whose *fustian's* so sublimely bad, it is not poetry but prose run mad – Alexander Pope>
bona fide – see AUTHENTIC ***ant*** counterfeit, bogus
bondage – see SERVITUDE
bon vivant – see EPICURE ***ant*** ascetic
bookish – see PEDANTIC
boorish, churlish, loutish, clownish *shared meaning* : uncouth in manner or appearance. **Boorish** stresses rudeness of manner or crudity which may reflect insensitiveness based on lack of culture and experience or mere unwillingness to be agreeable <early grammarians . . . felt that failure to distinguish such forms phonetically was barbarous and *boorish* – C. E. Reed> <I'm rude and I'm *boorish* and I discovered . . . I could be all these things and worse and that there would still be plenty of people to lick my boots – John Cheever> **Churlish** suggests surly unresponsiveness and ungraciousness <gave a *churlish* refusal to her request> **Loutish** implies bodily clumsiness usually accompanied by crude stupidity <a *loutish* drunk staggering toward us . . . muttering scurrilities to himself – James Morris> **Clownish** may come close to *loutish* but is somewhat more likely to connote an earthy ignorance and simplicity rather than stupidity <*clownish* peasant staring with vacant eyes at her great boots – W. B. Yeats> <fleshiness as a by-product of a wild farcical exuberance of the *clownish* and swinish side of man – W. L. Sullivan> ***ant*** gentlemanly
boost – see LIFT
booty – see SPOIL
border, margin, edge, rim, brim, verge, brink *shared meaning* : a line or outer part that marks the limit of something. **Border** can apply to a surface just within a boundary <the *border* of a rug> or to the boundary itself <I had at last reached the *border* of the forest – W. H. Hudson †1922> **Margin** applies to a border of definite width that is usually distinguishable from the remaining surface <the broad white *margin* of the page> <the weedy *margin* of a lake> In extended use it retains the notion of a distinguishable, often anomalous, zone <the Negro . . . has been living on the *margin* between totalitarianism and democracy for two centuries – Norman Mailer> **Edge** applies to the line made by two converging surfaces (as of a knife or a box) <the *edge* of a table> Often it implies sharpness <put an *edge* on this knife> or in extended use a cutting quality <the *edge* of Grandfather's voice slashed between them – Padma Perera> **Rim** applies usually to the border or edge of something circular <the *rim* of a wheel> <the *rim* of a glass> **Brim** applies to the upper rim of a vessel or of whatever retains a liquid <the pitcher was filled to the *brim*> <melting snows filled the streams to the *brim*> **Verge** applies to a line or very narrow margin that separates one thing from another <a row of white palings which marked the *verge* of the heath – Thomas Hardy> and in extended use tends to stress the closeness of one thing or condition to another or the likelihood of one state being transformed into another <on the *verge* of a nervous breakdown> <young talent on the *verge* of stardom – *Current Biog.*> **Brink** applies to the edge of something steep <the *brink* of a precipice> and in extended use regularly carries an ominous note that suggests the likelihood of abrupt transition (as from a better state to a worse) <the state stood on the *brink* of a fiscal crisis – Richard Steele> <moving ever closer to the *brink* of war>
boredom – see TEDIUM ***ant*** amusement
bother – see ANNOY ***ant*** comfort
bough – see SHOOT
bountiful – see LIBERAL

bouquet — see FRAGRANCE
brag — see BOAST ***ant*** apologize
branch — see SHOOT
brand — see STIGMA
brandish — see SWING
brash — see SHAMELESS ***ant*** wary
brazen — see SHAMELESS ***ant*** bashful
break down — see ANALYZE
bridle — see RESTRAIN, STRUT
bright, brilliant, radiant, luminous, lustrous *shared meaning* : shining or glowing with light. **Bright** implies emitting or reflecting a high degree of light <the moon was almost *bright* enough to read by> **Brilliant** implies intense often sparkling brightness <light seemed to be dissolved in the air all around her, *brilliant* yellow – Herman Wouk> <the pictures are *brilliant* but they glitter through a mist of reverie – Kenneth Rexroth> **Radiant** basically describes whatever gives off radiation (as rays of light) <the *radiant* sun warming the earth> but often it is used interchangeably with *bright* <in warlike armor drest, golden, all *radiant* – P. B. Shelley> <it was a *radiant* night . . . far away in the sky the moon shone in tumbled clouds – Elizabeth M. Thomas> **Luminous** implies emission of steady, suffused, glowing light by reflection or in surrounding darkness <a *luminous* watch dial> <the drapes . . . opened on icy stars, a *luminous* sky – David Madden> **Lustrous** stresses an even, rich light from a surface that reflects efficiently without sparkle or glitter <a *lustrous* heavy silk> <the *lustrous* salvers in the moonlight gleam – John Keats> ***ant*** dull, dim
brilliant — see BRIGHT ***ant*** subdued
brim — see BORDER
brink — see BORDER
brisk — see AGILE ***ant*** sluggish
bristle — see STRUT
brittle — see FRAGILE ***ant*** supple
broach — see EXPRESS
broad, wide, deep *shared meaning* : having horizontal extent. *Broad* and *wide* apply to a surface measured or viewed from side to side <a *broad* (or *wide*) path> but **broad** is likely to be preferred when full horizontal extent is considered <his shoulders are *broad*> and **wide** is more common when units of measurement are specified <a fireplace six feet *wide*> or implied by the presence of limiting features <a *wide* doorway> **Deep** applies specifically to extent from front to back <a *deep* but narrow closet> <the lot is *deep* enough to let us have a garden at the back> ***ant*** narrow
brook — see BEAR
brusque — see BLUFF ***ant*** unctuous, bland
bucolic — see RURAL ***ant*** urbane
build — see PHYSIQUE
bulge — see PROJECTION
bulk, mass, volume *shared meaning* : the aggregate that forms a body or unit. **Bulk** is applied mainly to what is or appears to be inordinately large or heavy <the *bulk* of ancient minster – William Wordsworth> and often more or less shapeless <on the living sea rolls an inanimate *bulk* – P. B. Shelley> **Mass** suggests an aggregate made by piling together items usually of the same kind <a *mass* of debris left by the flood> <the moral imbecility on which he relies . . . [is] characteristic not of men and women as individuals, but of men and women in *masses* – Aldous Huxley> <rich *masses* of clumped shrubbery – Thomas Wolfe> **Volume** applies to an aggregate without shape or outline and capable of flowing or fluctuating

<a tremendous *volume* of water flowed over the dam> These terms are also comparable as applied to quantity or amount: **bulk** and **mass** then apply to the greater part or a large proportion of something objective <the *bulk* of my time was spent in study> <the *mass* of our imports is raw material> **Volume,** however, can apply either to a total amount, especially when variable <expected an increased *volume* of business this year> or to a considerable quantity <the crops will be damaged unless we get rain in *volume* soon>

bunch — see GROUP

burdensome — see ONEROUS ***ant*** light

burglary — see THEFT

burlesque — see CARICATURE

bury — see HIDE

business **1** **business, commerce, trade, industry, traffic** *shared meaning* : activity concerned with the supplying and distributing of commodities. **Business** may be a broadly inclusive term but in its most precise use it specifically designates the activities of those engaged in the purchase or sale of commodities or in related financial transactions <the *business* of a ship chandler> *Commerce* and *trade* are often applied interchangeably to the activities of those engaged in the exchange of commodities especially on a large scale, but **commerce** is likely to be chosen when the activities involve nations or states and **trade** when they are between different business organizations in the same nation or when specific commodities are involved <the recent improvement in German *commerce*> <developed a large *trade* in raw furs> **Industry** applies chiefly to activities involving the production of commodities (as by processing or manufacturing) <the increasing automation of *industry*> **Traffic,** primarily applies to the operation and functioning of public carriers of goods and persons <nurtured by land and water *traffic,* it grew into a commercial center – *Amer. Guide Series: Ark.*> but it may also come close to *commerce* and *trade* in applying to the activities of those engaged in the exchange of commodities <perishable and livestock *traffic* . . . consigned to other than morning markets – *Farmer's Weekly* (*So. Africa*)> It may also specifically denote illicit or improper business activity <when there are no more addicts to buy junk there will be no junk *traffic* – W. S. Burroughs> <maintained a *traffic* in stolen goods>

2 see WORK 2

bustle — see STIR

busy, industrious, diligent, assiduous, sedulous *shared meaning* : actively engaged or occupied (as in work or in accomplishing some end). **Busy** stresses activity as opposed to idleness or leisure <had plenty of work to keep her *busy*> but does not in itself imply anything about the utility or effectiveness of the activity <"I'm so *busy* I can't get anything done," is no joke for many executives – Peter Drucker> **Industrious** implies characteristic or habitual attentiveness to one's business, work or avocation and continual earnest application <a vigorous and *industrious* girl, who, single-handed, kept the farm in a sort of order – Dorothy Sayers> **Diligent** suggests earnest application to a particular activity or pursuit <a *diligent* student> <a *diligent* search failed to find the lost package> **Assiduous** stresses careful and unremitting application <she also became increasingly *assiduous* in her slavish attentions, until . . . one would almost have thought that her duty toward him was her very life – Thomas Wolfe> **Sedulous** stresses painstaking and persevering application to a business or enterprise <would never fail in *sedulous* attention to his wants – Mary E. Freeman> <after weeks of *sedulous* and disheartening analysis, eventually ferreted out the source – W. H. Wright> ***ant*** idle, unoccupied

butchery – see MASSACRE

by, through, with *shared meaning* : used as a function word to qualify (a following word or phrase) as an agent, means, or instrument. **By** is followed commonly by the agent or causative agency <a wall built *by* the Romans> <destroyed *by* fire> <books *by* modern writers> **Through** implies intermediacy; it is followed by the name of someone or something that serves as the medium or means by which an end is gained or an effect is produced <remained close to his wife and daughters *through* many letters and frequent weekend visits – *Current Biog.*> <he spoke *through* an interpreter> <who can take pride in a position gained *through* influence?> **With** is more often followed by the name of the instrument through which a causative agent or agency works <eat *with* a fork> <the boy struck at the snake *with* a stick> but it may take for its object something not consciously used as an instrument but serving as the instrumentality by which an effect is produced <he amused the crowd *with* his antics> <up-to-date information presented *with* clarity and precision has made it the most widely accepted dictionary – *Circle & Monogram*>

cabal – see PLOT

cadence – see RHYTHM

calamity – see DISASTER *ant* boon

caliber – see QUALITY 2

call *vb* – see SUMMON

call *n* – see VISIT

calling – see WORK 2

callow – see RUDE *ant* full-fledged, grown-up

calm, tranquil, serene, placid, peaceful *shared meaning* : quiet and free from whatever disturbs or hurts. **Calm** draws from its primary application to the sea or weather a suggestion of freedom, real or apparent, from agitation, even in the face of provocation and danger <each day they faced the perils of the streets with hearts as *calm* as if they were alone upon a country road – Thomas Wolfe> **Tranquil** suggests a deeper or more settled composure with little if any implication of previous agitation <a *tranquil* trust in God amid tortures and death too horrible to be related – J. L. Motley> <on the balmy zephyrs *tranquil* rest the silver clouds – John Keats> **Serene** suggests a lofty and unclouded tranquillity <[he] seemed strangely *serene* that evening, as though having made up his mind to die . . . had brought a peace of mind and spirit – W. L. Shirer> <there remains the *serene* distillation of his art – the essence of a lifetime devoted to the creation of beauty – *Current Biog.*> **Placid** may stress lack of agitation rather than the peace and composure that can account for this <the *placid* common sense of Franklin – J. R. Lowell> Sometimes it may convey a hint of stupidity or unresponsiveness as the cause <a *placid* public, comfortable in its delusion that the regulatory agencies are holding profits to the mythical six percent – Miles McMillin> **Peaceful** implies repose or attainment of tranquillity often in contrast with or following strife or turmoil or bustle <I am grown *peaceful* as old age tonight – Robert Browning> *ant* stormy, agitated

calumniate – see MALIGN *ant* eulogize, vindicate

cancel – see ERASE

cancer – see TUMOR

candid – see FRANK ***ant*** evasive
canon – see LAW
cant – see DIALECT
canting – see HYPOCRITICAL
capable – see ABLE ***ant*** incapable
capacious – see SPACIOUS ***ant*** exiguous (*as of spaces or containers*)
capitulate – see YIELD
capitulation – see SURRENDER
caprice, freak, whim, vagary, crotchet *shared meaning* : an arbitrary and typically fanciful or impractical notion. **Caprice** emphasizes the lack of apparent motivation and is likely to suggest willfulness <my cousin's pet *caprice* is to affect a distaste for art, to which she is passionately devoted – G. B. Shaw> <the Villa was an altar of indulgence to every architectural *caprice* and whim – Ludwig Bemelmans> **Freak** suggests an impulsive causeless change of mind, like that of a child or a lunatic <follow this way or that, as the *freak* takes you – R. L. Stevenson> **Whim** is more likely to suggest a quaint, fantastic, or humorous turn of mind or inclination that may lead to freakish or capricious acts or behavior <a young lady . . . who had strange *whims* of fasting – George Eliot> <he dreaded some outrageous *whim* that might tickle the youth's sense of humor, and lead him to any wanton *freak* – John Collier> **Vagary** suggests strongly the erratic, irresponsible, or extravagant character of a notion <straight they changed their minds, flew off, and into strange *vagaries* fell – John Milton> <it does not lie within the responsibility of a public library to indulge every *vagary* of human taste – Kathleen Molz> **Crotchet** implies a perversely heretical or eccentric opinion or preference, especially on some trivial matter <a . . . habitation that had yielded at every point to the *crotchets* and meanderings of a growing family – John Cheever> <she was eccentric . . . full of *crotchets*. She never drank water without some vinegar in it – to cleanse it, she said – Robert Henderson>
capricious – see INCONSTANT ***ant*** steadfast
captious – see CRITICAL ***ant*** appreciative
captivate – see ATTRACT ***ant*** repulse
capture – see CATCH
cardinal – see ESSENTIAL ***ant*** negligible
care, concern, solicitude, anxiety, worry *shared meaning* : a troubled or engrossed state of mind or the thing that causes this. **Care** implies possession of a mind weighed down by responsibility or disquieted by apprehension <the king . . . most sovereign slave of *care* – H. D. Thoreau> <free . . . to go where she liked and do what she liked. She had no responsibilities, no *cares* – Arnold Bennett> **Concern** implies not only a troubled state of mind but also the interest, respect, affection, or responsibility that leads to this state <felt a deep *concern* about his father's health> <[his] *concern* . . . in the problems of human settlements stems from his own early experience as a refugee – *Current Biog.*> **Solicitude** implies great concern or sometimes apprehension and connotes either thoughtful or hovering attentiveness (as to one in pain, illness, or distress) <cared for the sick child with the greatest *solicitude*> <even the more peaceful hours . . . had beneath them a perpetual undercurrent of apprehensive *solicitude* – Havelock Ellis> **Anxiety** stresses anguished uncertainty and apprehension (as of misfortune or failure) <search parties had been organized and the two women speculated with deep *anxiety* on whether or not little Pamela had died of exposure – John Cheever> **Worry** suggests often prolonged or futile fretting over problems or situations that are a cause for solicitude or anxiety <there seemed no end to her *worries*> <in a state of *worry* because of fear for the loss of her commercial eminence – A. F. Harlow>

careful, meticulous, scrupulous, punctilious *shared meaning* : showing close attention to details (as of behavior or performance). **Careful** implies concern for whatever is in one's charge or for the way in which one's duties or tasks are met <a *careful* mother> <the doctor made a *careful* examination of his patient> **Meticulous** implies a carefulness marked by extreme attentiveness to detail or sometimes by a timorous fussiness about trifles <made as all good modern dictionaries are made: through a painstaking, *meticulous* process of recording, analyzing, defining – R. R. Lodwig & E. F. Barrett> <like most converts, *meticulous* over points of ritual – C. D. Lewis> **Scrupulous** implies painstaking attention to what is proper, fitting, or ethical <[he] was *scrupulous,* and certain accepted conventions had forced him to satisfy his conscience – Victoria Sackville-West> <the ethical responsibility . . . to be *scrupulous* in . . . reporting – *NEA Jour.*> **Punctilious** implies knowledge of fine points (as of law, etiquette, ceremony, or morality) and an often finicky or excessive attention to these <fussy about the *punctilious* observation of orders – Willa Cather> <uncivilized people often pay *punctilious* attention to rules of etiquette – W. G. Sumner> ***ant*** careless

caress, fondle, pet, cuddle *shared meaning* : to show affection by touching or handling. **Caress** implies expression of affection by gentle stroking or patting <his hand strayed over the desk. He might have been *caressing* the wood – Norman Mailer> **Fondle** implies doting fondness and sometimes lack of dignity; it may suggest more intimacy (as in hugging or kissing) and less gentleness than *caress* <all that he was good for, she said, was to *fondle* and fumble and kiss – Robert Graves> **Pet** basically applies to caressing or fondling children or animals <*pet* a cat> but may also apply to excessive indulgence <a spoiled *petted* child> or in recent use to amorous fondling in which it may suggest undue or improper familiarity <a girl is . . . more popular with boys if she *pets* – Valeria H. Parker> **Cuddle** applies to a close but gentle embracing designed to soothe and comfort <*cuddle* a frightened puppy> <little boys . . . who have kind mammas to *cuddle* them – Charles Kingsley>

caricature, burlesque, parody, travesty *shared meaning* : a comic or grotesque imitation. **Caricature** implies ludicrous exaggeration or distortion of characteristic or peculiar features (as of a person, a group, or a people) for the sake of satire or ridicule <*caricature* is a very special kind of portraiture, permitting extravagance and enunciating the awkward and uncomplimentary – *Christian Science Monitor*> **Burlesque** implies mockery through distortion of relationships (as by giving a trivial topic mock-heroic treatment or handling a serious subject frivolously) <exaggerated the elegant gestures of an old-world beau, crooking his arms and swinging his huge rear and huger paunch in an amazingly funny *burlesque* – Herman Wouk> **Parody** implies a more intellectual, less emotional critical approach and applies particularly to a substantial piece of work that, by applying a writer's stylistic peculiarities to an inappropriate subject, holds him up to ridicule <*parody* is an extremely limited form that appeals almost entirely to the intelligence . . . done supremely well . . . it gives us a pleasure similar to that which we get from an essay of Matthew Arnold's – Frank O'Connor> <a *parody* must imitate the original well, effectively exaggerating its peculiarities and weaknesses . . . to be good it must be sharp – Jacob Brackman> **Travesty** implies use of an extravagant or absurd style that at once demeans the user and his topic <it should never be the object of a satirist to make a *travesty* of a genuine work of art – Ira Kitchell> All these terms may be extended to situations and things that involve gross distortion, usually with a suggestion of distaste rather than amusement <his report is a *caricature* of the facts> <an organization that is a *burlesque* on traditional reli-

gion> <dizzy bright chatter . . . like a cruel *parody* of Manhattan small talk – Herman Wouk> <these *travesties* against the social conscience of the wealthiest nations on earth – L. H. Keyserling>

carnage – see MASSACRE

carnal, fleshly, sensual, animal *shared meaning* : having or showing a physical rather than an intellectual or spiritual orientation or origin. **Carnal,** though sometimes quite neutral, is likely to connote not merely man's bodily but his lower nature and appetites <*carnal* desires> <the superiority of the spiritual and eternal over the *carnal* and temporal had to be vindicated – H. O. Taylor> **Fleshly** is close to *carnal* in meaning but is likely to be less derogatory or even mildly apologetic in implication <punishments were set for the *fleshly* sins of monks and nuns and clergy – H. O. Taylor> **Sensual** may apply to any gratification of bodily desire but commonly implies sexual appetite or gross concentration on bodily satisfactions <a coarse heavy face, loose-featured, red, and *sensual* – Thomas Wolfe> **Animal** stresses a relation with man's physical as distinguished from his rational nature usually without definitely derogatory suggestion <the *animal* smell of sweating boys – Padma Perera> <in a ready-made dinner jacket which in no way destroyed his *animal* grace – Stella D. Gibbons> ***ant*** spiritual, intellectual

carping – see CRITICAL ***ant*** fulsome

carriage – see BEARING

carry, bear, convey, transport *shared meaning* : to move something from one place to another. **Carry** tends to emphasize the means by which something is moved or the fact of supporting it off the ground while moving <*carry* a load on one's back> <scientists have studied orbits to *carry* spacecraft close to the sun – I. M. Levitt> **Bear** stresses the effort of supporting or sometimes the importance of what is carried <a wagon designed to *bear* heavy loads> <the envoys *bore* rich gifts> **Convey** is likely to apply to things that move continuously or in mass <a belt that *conveys* finished parts to the shipping room> <the pipelines that *convey* gas to our cities> **Transport** puts the stress on the orderly movement of persons or goods often over considerable distances by a professional carrier <the speed with which troops are *transported* by air> <trucks *transporting* produce from farm to market>

cartel – see MONOPOLY

case – see INSTANCE

cast – see DISCARD, THROW

castigate – see PUNISH

casual **1** see ACCIDENTAL
2 see RANDOM ***ant*** deliberate

cataclysm – see DISASTER

catastrophe – see DISASTER

catch **1 catch, capture, trap, snare, entrap, ensnare, bag** *shared meaning* : to get into one's possession or under one's control by or as if by taking or seizing. **Catch,** the most general and ordinary term, is likely to imply that the thing laid hold of has been in flight, in concealment, or in motion and that appropriate action has led to its arrest <the boy *caught* the ball> <the police *caught* the thief> **Capture** suggests taking by overcoming resistance or difficulty <*capture* an enemy stronghold> <failed to *capture* the leadership of his party> *Trap, snare, entrap,* and *ensnare* all imply catching by or as if by a device that holds the one caught at the mercy of his captor, but **trap** can imply a literal trap <*trap* woodchucks> and **snare** a literal snare <*snare* a rabbit> while **entrap** and **ensnare** usually imply figurative seizure <the conscientious teacher *ensnared* in an atmo-

sphere of too much love for his class – R. G. Frost> <as if he would clear away some entanglement which had *entrapped* his thoughts – Louis Bromfield> **Bag** implies unquestionable success in seizing a difficult quarry by skill, stealth, or artifice, often with a suggestion of a hunter's craft <had the satisfaction of *bagging* the tricky rascal who had lighted still another fire – Frank Cameron> <the *bagging* of a fortune, the ruin of . . . trusting speculators – Sinclair Lewis> ***ant*** miss

2 see INCUR

categorical – see ULTIMATE

cause, determinant, antecedent, reason, occasion *shared meaning* : something that produces an effect or result. **Cause** applies to an event, circumstance, or condition or to any combination of these that brings about or helps to bring about an effect <one of the *causes* of her difficulty was an almost pathological shyness> <water and soil pollution are the root *causes* of mortality in the tropics – V. G. Heiser> **Determinant** applies to a cause that fixes the nature of what results as a product or outcome <the prime *determinant* of Rocky Mountain history has been the geology of that region, with its ore bodies containing gold, silver, copper, lead – K. F. Mather> **Antecedent** applies to what has preceded and therefore may be in some degree responsible for what follows or derives or descends from it <the *antecedents* of emperor-worship lay far back in history – John Buchan> **Reason** applies to a traceable or explainable cause of a known effect <there's always a *reason* for everything, and if we don't know it, we can find it out – Theodore Sturgeon> **Occasion** applies to a particular time or situation at which underlying causes become effective; thus, the *cause* of a war may be a long-time deep-rooted antipathy between peoples, its *occasion* some trivial incident.

caution – see WARN

cautious, circumspect, wary, chary *shared meaning* : marked by prudent attentiveness and discretion toward danger or hazard. **Cautious** can imply the promptings of fear (as of failure or of harm to oneself or others) and suggest forethought in planning or prudence in proceeding designed to minimize risk <a *cautious* investor> <physicians necessarily take a *cautious* attitude toward new compounds – Elizabeth Ogg> **Circumspect** stresses prudence, discretion, vigilance, and the weighing of consequences lest harm may inadvertently occur <was more *circumspect* than might have been expected. He did not want to lay himself open, he said, to the machinations of his "deadly enemy" – W. L. Shirer> **Wary** stresses suspiciousness and may imply a fear less well-grounded than *cautious* implies <somewhat superstitious . . . [he] is *wary* of innovations – *Current Biog.*> or alertness and cunning in escaping dangers <he was *wary,* and showed no disposition to marry – Victoria Sackville-West> **Chary** implies a cautious reluctance to give, act, or speak freely <I have had to be *chary* of concrete examples – M. J. Adler> <experience had taught him to be *chary* about putting anything in writing> ***ant*** adventurous, temerarious

cease – see STOP

celebrate – see KEEP

celebrated – see FAMOUS ***ant*** obscure

celerity, alacrity, legerity *shared meaning* : quickness in movement or action. **Celerity** stresses speed, especially in working <the human brain . . . acts at times with extraordinary *celerity* – B. N. Cardozo> <anxious to get home before dark, they finished their task with *celerity*> **Alacrity** emphasizes promptness in response more than swiftness in movement <respond to an invitation with *alacrity*> but it may also imply a cheerful readiness

<returned to his chore with *alacrity*> or alert activity <the *alacrity* with which he sprang from the vehicle – T. L. Peacock> **Legerity** implies lightness and ease as well as swiftness <when the mind is quickened ... the organs ... newly move, with ... fresh *legerity* – Shak.> <the *legerity* of the French mind made the ... visitor quick to comprehend his desire for solitude – Elinor Wylie> ***ant*** leisureliness

censorious – see CRITICAL ***ant*** eulogistic

censure – see CRITICIZE ***ant*** commend

ceremonial, ceremonious, formal, conventional *shared meaning* : marked by attention to or adhering strictly to prescribed forms, procedures, and details. *Ceremonial* and *ceremonious* both imply strict attention to what is prescribed (as by custom, a formal or informal code, or established ritual) but **ceremonial** is more likely to apply to things that are themselves ceremonies or an essential part of ceremonies <he read in a synthetic *ceremonial* tone of voice that sounded preposterous ... but he was conducting the marriage ceremony precisely as he had conducted countless previous ones – J. T. Farrell> while **ceremonious** more often applies to persons addicted to ceremony or to acts attended by ceremony <a *ceremonious* old gentleman> <the cold bath that he took each morning was *ceremonious* – it was sometimes nothing else since he almost never used soap – John Cheever> **Formal** applies both to things prescribed and to persons obedient to custom; it is more likely to suggest set forms than external ceremonies and often conveys the notion of stiff, restrained, or old-fashioned behavior <yielded a kiss at her door, after some *formal* reluctance, in a way that made it seem an old-fashioned courtesy – Herman Wouk> <make a *formal* report to the board of trustees> **Conventional** implies accord with general custom and usage <a *conventional* courtesy> and often suggests lack of originality or independence <the debate ... had a cautious, almost querulous, tone often detectable in Congress when the *conventional* wisdom is being challenged – John Walsh> <they are not moral; they are only *conventional* – G. B. Shaw>

ceremonious – see CEREMONIAL ***ant*** unceremonious, informal

certain – see SURE ***ant*** uncertain

certainty, certitude, assurance, conviction *shared meaning* : a state of being free from doubt. *Certainty* and *certitude* are very close, but **certainty** tends to stress the existence of objective unquestionable proofs and **certitude** to emphasize a faith strong enough to resist all attack <*certitude* is not the test of *certainty.* We have been cocksure of many things that were not so – O. W. Holmes †1935> <*certitude* is a mental state: *certainty* is a quality of propositions – J. H. Newman> **Assurance** stresses sureness and confidence rather than certainty and usually suggests implicit reliance on oneself or one's powers, intuitions, or methods or, alternatively, complete trust in another <faith is the *assurance* of things hoped for – *Heb* 11:1 (RSV)> <in these noble proportions was written quietly a message of luxurious well-being and *assurance* – Thomas Wolfe> **Conviction** usually implies previous doubt or uncertainty and is therefore appropriately applied to the state of mind of one who has become convinced <his brother ... was not fully seized of the *conviction* that "accuracy is a duty and not a virtue"– John Carter> <he could not evade the ... *conviction* that she was the Church speaking, rebuking him – H. C. Hervey> ***ant*** uncertainty

certify – see APPROVE

certitude – see CERTAINTY ***ant*** doubt

chance – see HAPPEN

change *vb* **change, alter, vary, modify** *shared meaning* : to make or become different. *Change* and *alter* are sometimes interchangeable; thus, conditions may *change* (or *alter*) for the better. **Change,** however, is more likely to imply an essential difference even amounting to a loss of identity or a substitution of one thing for another <can the Ethiopian *change* his skin, or the leopard his spots? – *Jer* 13:23 (AV)> <the principle by which the law was adapted to *changing* conditions by new ways of interpreting the scriptural text – Edmund Wilson> while **alter** tends to stress differences in some particular aspect without implying loss of identity <*alter* a skirt by shortening the hem> <the ordinary citizen, they said resignedly, can do nothing to *alter* the streams of history – M. S. Eisenhower> **Vary** stresses a breaking away from sameness, duplication, or exact repetition and frequently implies a difference or series of differences due to change <the temperature *varied* widely during the day> <Thomas's lifelong habit of *varying* himself in order to beguile whomever he was with, which enabled him to charm nearly everyone he was not trying to offend – Naomi Bliven> **Modify** suggests a difference that restricts, limits, or adapts to some new end <persuaded the senator to *modify* his opposition to the new tax> <the wing of a bird is an arm *modified* for flying>

change *n* **change, mutation, permutation, vicissitude** *shared meaning* : altered state. **Change,** the most general term, can apply not only to any alteration whether essential or superficial, transient or permanent, but also to any substitution of one thing for another <sensed a *change* in her attitude> <laid out a *change* of clothing> <poor faithful dogs, lovers of novelty and *change* of scene – Agnes Repplier> **Mutation** stresses lack of permanence and stability and presents change as inevitable <the vast *mutations* wrought by the Norman conquest – C. L. Wrenn> <O world! But that thy strange *mutations* make us hate thee, life would not yield to age – Shak.> **Permutation** implies transposition within a group or combination of things that, through a change in internal relations, presents a new form to what is essentially unchanged <a man all of words, his only tools, he tried them in every *permutation* his desperate imagination could invent – Joseph Whitehill> <featuring almost unlimited *permutations* and combinations of individual prefabricated components, to give the user a building for any need – Carl Heyel> **Vicissitude** implies a change so great as to seem a substitution for, or a reversal of, what has been and typically is applied to a change that has the character of a revolution or upheaval <poets have continued, uninterrupted by the *vicissitudes* of reform and revolutions, to express in uncomplicated language their simple pleasure in those natural phenomena – C. L. Wrenn>

character – see DISPOSITION, QUALITY, TYPE

characteristic, individual, peculiar, distinctive *shared meaning* : revealing a special quality or identity. **Characteristic** stresses the revelation of what distinguishes and serves to identify a person, thing, or class <the balance between old and new is *characteristic* . . . of his style and technique – *Current Biog.*> <a fertile oasis possesses a *characteristic* color scheme of its own – Aldous Huxley> **Individual** stresses qualities that distinguish one from other members of its class or group <one could hardly maintain the courage to be *individual,* to speak with one's own voice – Norman Mailer> <each of us had our *individual* foibles> **Peculiar** may come very close to *individual* but typically stresses the rarity or uniqueness of what pertains to an individual or class <life, considered in this manner . . . is a long stretch full of variety, in which every hour and circumstance have their *peculiar* merit – Victoria Sackville-West> <a drowsy fervor of manner and tone which was quite *peculiar* to her – Thomas Hardy> **Distinctive** implies qualities that are distinguishing and uncommon and are often worthy of special recognition or praise <although many Christians have always held this belief, no

[earlier] church developed it as a *distinctive* doctrine – *Current Biog.*> <the exquisite craftsmanship . . . that has given to free verse . . . its most *distinctive* qualities – J. L. Lowes>

charge *vb* – see COMMAND

charge *n* – see PRICE

charity – see MERCY ***ant*** malice, ill will

charm *n* – see FETISH

charm *vb* – see ATTRACT ***ant*** disgust

charter – see HIRE

chary – see CAUTIOUS

chase – see FOLLOW 2

chaste, pure, modest, decent *shared meaning* : free from all taint of what is lewd or salacious. **Chaste** primarily implies a refraining from acts, thoughts, or desires that are not virginal or sanctioned by marriage vows <strew me over with maiden flowers, that all the world may know I was a *chaste* wife to my grave – Shak.> In broader use it may imply freedom from or avoidance of whatever cheapens or debases <the *chaste* beauty of a work of art> <the *chaste* and abstracted intellect of the scholar – Elinor Wylie> **Pure** differs from *chaste* in implying innocence and absence of temptations rather than control of one's impulses and actions <a generation that had admired piquante women . . . was now confronted by simple beauty, *pure* and undeniable – Stella D. Gibbons> <come, pensive nun, devout and *pure* – John Milton> *Modest* and *decent* are often interchangeable, especially with reference to behavior and dress as outward manifestations of inner purity, but **modest** may stress absence of characteristics (as brazenness or boldness) unbefitting to one who is by nature pure and chaste while **decent** is more likely to stress due regard for what is conventionally seemly or proper <always dressed in a dainty *modest* way> <the pure bashful maiden was too *modest*, too tender, too trustful – W. M. Thackeray> <wore his best, a *decent* sober suit fit for a wedding or a funeral> <he no longer prayed . . . yet he felt that religion was *decent* and right, an essential in an honest man's life – Pearl Buck> ***ant*** lewd, wanton, immoral

chasten – see PUNISH ***ant*** pamper, mollycoddle

chastise – see PUNISH

cheap – see CONTEMPTIBLE ***ant*** noble

cheat, cozen, defraud, swindle, overreach *shared meaning* : to get something by dishonesty or deception. **Cheat** suggests deceit and tricks that are intended to escape observation <*cheat* at cards> <he could not escape his honesty, it was bedrock; to *cheat* would cause an explosion in him – Bernard Malamud> **Cozen** implies more artfulness and craft, especially by persuasion, in attaining some thing or end <a man who was *cozened* into leaving every shilling away from his own children – Anthony Trollope> **Defraud** stresses depriving one of what is rightfully his and implies the use of misleading statements and perversion of truth rather than artful persuasion <*defraud* a widow of her share of her husband's estate> <freedom of speech and press does not include . . . the right to deceive or *defraud* – T. P. Neill> **Swindle** implies large-scale cheating and abuse of confidence for gain and is primarily applicable to the obtaining of money by false pretenses <we must cease to regard ourselves . . . as men who have a right to exploit, oppress, and *swindle* the Chinese because they are an "inferior" race – Bertrand Russell> **Overreach** implies getting the better of another in dealing or bargaining, typically by unscrupulous methods or crafty cheating <the suspicion that most of the talk they [the deaf] cannot hear consists in plottings and schemings to *overreach* or get around them – J. G. Cozzens>

check – see RESTRAIN *ant* accelerate (*of speed*), advance (*of movements, plans, hopes*), release (*of feelings, energies*)
cheek – see TEMERITY *ant* diffidence
cheerful – see GLAD *ant* glum, gloomy
cherish – see APPRECIATE *ant* neglect
chide – see REPROVE *ant* commend
childish, childlike *shared meaning* : having qualities natural or suitable to a child. When used of adults, their behavior, or characteristics, the two words are quite dissimilar in implications. **Childish** tends to suggest such less admirable and less pleasing qualities of childhood as helplessness, peevishness, and mental immaturity <his parents . . . were both getting *childish* and needed care and yet they resented any loss of authority – Pearl Buck> <the deliberately *childish* antics of comedians: the affected high voices, the giggles, the silly faces – Herman Wouk> **Childlike,** by contrast, stresses the admirable qualities of the child (as trust, innocence, simplicity, and straightforwardness) <her brow and eyes and hair are beautiful and *childlike* – Mabel F. Hale> <retained into old age a *childlike* grace and dignity>
childlike – see CHILDISH
chimerical – see IMAGINARY *ant* feasible
chivalrous – see CIVIL *ant* churlish
chivy – see BAIT
choice *n* **choice, option, alternative, preference, selection, election** *shared meaning* : the act or opportunity of choosing or the thing chosen. **Choice** usually implies the right or privilege to choose freely from a number (as of persons, things, or courses) <*choice* . . . suggests scarcity . . . . It implies a set of things that are available, called opportunities. And it implies a criterion of selection called preferences. The act of rational *choice* is the act of selecting the best, the most preferred, opportunity – R. A. Mundell> **Option** stresses a specifically given right or power to choose among two or more mutually exclusive items <took an *option* to buy a farm> <the many *options* for careers open to present-day youth> **Alternative** implies a necessity to choose, usually between two mutually exclusive things <the only *alternative* to war was submission> but sometimes between more than two things when it is felt that those not chosen constitute a class opposed to the one that is, or is to be, selected <we must review all the *alternatives* before deciding on a course of action> **Preference** is likely to stress personal bias and predilection as a basis of choice. Typically it implies fixed or habitual choice <he works from *preference* rather than necessity> but often such choice overruled by other considerations <our *preference* is for the coast but business forces us to live inland> <sacrificed his *preference* for a quiet evening to take his wife dancing> **Selection** implies a wide range of choice and often the need of thought and discrimination in choosing <schools attempted . . . to cultivate discrimination and to furnish the material on which *selection* can be founded – C. H. Grandgent> **Election** is likely to imply a formal choosing after deliberation and typically a choosing for some explicit role, duty, or function <if . . . both an express warranty and deceit are present . . . the buyer will have an *election* of remedies – L. B. Howard>
choice *adj* **choice, exquisite, elegant, rare, dainty, delicate** *shared meaning* : having qualities that appeal to a cultivated taste. **Choice** stresses preeminence in quality or kind <a *choice* gem> <the *choice* and master spirits of this age – Shak.> **Exquisite** implies such perfection (as in workmanship or design) as is likely to be appreciated only by the most cultivated taste <a cameo cut with *exquisite* detail> <the line, "Bare ruin'd choirs where

late the sweet birds sang" – one of the most *exquisite* in English poetry – Leonard Wolf> **Elegant** applies to what is rich and luxurious but restrained by good taste <*elegant* in dress, always excellently correct, he wore fresh garments every day – Thomas Wolfe> In application to persons or their literary or scholarly work *elegant* is likely to imply dignified graciousness, restrained grace, or effective simplicity <however *elegant* and memorable, brevity can never, in the nature of things, do justice to all the facts of a complex situation – Aldous Huxley> <[his] thought and expression in economics have always been *elegant* and enviable. He excels in analyses – *Times Lit. Supp.*> **Rare** basically implies distinction in merit, outstanding excellence, or superlative quality but from other senses commonly retains a notion of uncommonness or scarcity <he was, in his good moods, *rare* company – Herman Wouk> <the *rarest* cordials old monks ever schemed to coax from pulpy grapes – Amy Lowell> **Dainty** may come close to *choice* when describing things which give delight to a fastidious taste <a *dainty* dish> but more often it stresses smallness coupled with exquisiteness <those *dainty* limbs, which Nature lent for gentle usage and soft delicacy – John Milton> **Delicate,** like *dainty,* implies an appeal to a fastidious taste but it stresses fineness, subtlety, or fragility rather than smallness in the thing described <the most wonderful and *delicate* design composed entirely of flowers – Roald Dahl> <the robust flavor of some wines will completely dominate *delicate* dishes and vice versa – J. D. Palmer> ***ant*** indifferent

choke – see SUFFOCATE

choleric – see IRASCIBLE ***ant*** placid, imperturbable

chore – see TASK

chroma – see COLOR

chronic – see INVETERATE ***ant*** acute (*of illness*)

chronicle – see HISTORY

chunky – see STOCKY

churlish – see BOORISH ***ant*** courtly

circadian – see DAILY

circle – see SET *n*

circuit – see CIRCUMFERENCE

circumference, perimeter, periphery, circuit, compass *shared meaning* : a continuous line enclosing an area. **Circumference** and **perimeter** apply to the line enclosing a circle or ellipse and therefore also to the closed curve marking the section of a sphere or cylinder. Additionally, *circumference* is applicable to what is felt as having a center <that mysterious intellectual magnetism that enlarges the *circumference* of his ego – J. C. Powys> and *perimeter* to the bounding line of any area or the bounding surface of a solid. **Periphery,** though sometimes interchangeable with *perimeter,* is likely to apply to outer parts or limits as contrasted with internal or central regions <the drift toward the *periphery* of the great metropolitan districts – Oscar Handlin> **Circuit** applies to a route, or often a journey, around a periphery or sometimes to any path that comes back to its point of beginning <the hands of the clock made a *circuit* of the face> <setting up a regular *circuit* of campfire meetings . . . for churchless southwestern areas – *Time*> **Compass** is likely to refer to the area or space enclosed within a perimeter <within thy crown, whose *compass* is no bigger than thy head – Shak.> or to the ground that figuratively might be passed over by the leg of a compass in describing a circle <another soldier . . . followed his trail, went on to make a wide *compass,* and get as far as Zuñi – Bernard De Voto>

circumscribe – see LIMIT ***ant*** expand, dilate

circumspect – see CAUTIOUS ***ant*** audacious
circumstance – see OCCURRENCE
circumstantial, minute, particular, detailed *shared meaning* : dealing with a matter point by point. **Circumstantial** suggests treatment (as in a narrative or report) that fixes in time and place with precise mention of concrete details and happenings <a *circumstantial* account of an accident> **Minute** stresses interest in or inclusion of every detail and implies exhaustiveness and meticulous exactness (as in investigating or reporting) <made a *minute* scientific examination of the bullets – W. H. Wright> **Particular** implies zealous attention to every feature or item <I think myself obliged to be very *particular* in this relation, lest my veracity should be suspected – Jonathan Swift> **Detailed** implies abundance rather than exhaustiveness in detail <his *detailed* recital of his troubles with the Internal Revenue Service – *Current Biog.*> ***ant*** abridged, summary
circumvent – see FRUSTRATE ***ant*** conform (*to laws, orders*), cooperate (*with persons*)
citation – see ENCOMIUM
cite **1** see SUMMON
2 see QUOTE
3 cite, advance, allege, adduce *shared meaning* : to bring forward (as in explanation, proof, or illustration). **Cite** implies a bringing forward of something as relevant, cogent, or specific to an inquiry or discussion <asked a senator if he could *cite* a single piece of legislation enacted solely for the benefit of the public – Trevor Armbrister> <*cited* the school dropout rate as evidence that we are squandering one of our most valuable national resources – *Johns Hopkins Mag.*> **Advance** stresses the notion of bringing forward for consideration or study without implications as to the validity of what is brought forward <the idea has been *advanced* as a theoretical possibility> **Allege** often carries a strong suggestion of doubt about the validity of what is brought forward <those whose senses are *alleged* to be subject to supernatural impressions – Sheridan Le Fanu> and sometimes amounts to a disclaimer of responsibility for the assertion <the presence, real or *alleged*, of some hostile group – John Dewey> **Adduce** is often very close to *cite* but more specifically it applies to a bringing forth (as of evidence, facts, instances, or arguments) in support of a position or contention <reasons *adduced* by those who doubt the interstellar origin of UFOs – Stanley Kubrick>
citizen, subject, national *shared meaning* : a person owing allegiance to and entitled to the protection of a sovereign state. **Citizen** is preferred for one owing allegiance to a state in which the sovereign power is retained by the people and sharing in the political rights and responsibilities of those people. **Subject** is applicable to a person who owes allegiance to a personal sovereign whether this sovereign rules directly or as a figurehead. **National** varies widely in both application and implication but in its most typical use applies to one who may claim the protection of a state whether or not he is an actual citizen or subject and especially to such a one living or traveling outside that state <the Filipinos were formerly *nationals* though never *citizens* of the United States> <the *subjects* of a limited monarchy have essentially the same rights and duties in respect to the state as the *citizens* of a republic>
civil, polite, courteous, gallant, chivalrous *shared meaning* : observant of the forms required by good breeding. **Civil** commonly suggests the bare fulfillment of the requirements of social intercourse, amounting frequently to no more than the avoidance of actual rudeness <it was an entirely *civil*

greeting, but that was all you could say of it – Christopher La Farge> **Polite** is more positive than *civil* and commonly implies polish of manners and address though not necessarily warmth or cordiality of manner <the cultured, precise tone, *polite* but faintly superior – William Styron> <they are . . . not considerate, only *polite* – G. B. Shaw> **Courteous** implies an actively considerate and sometimes rather stately politeness <he is gentle, *courteous* and considerate with his associates – *Current Biog.*> <this love was *courteous,* delicately ceremonial, precise – H. O. Taylor> *Gallant* and *chivalrous* imply courteous attentiveness, especially to women but **gallant** is likely to suggest spirited and dashing behavior and ornate or florid expression <talking . . . rapidly, paternally and lovingly . . . he was saying the most *gallant* things imaginable – William Styron> while **chivalrous** tends to suggest high-minded and disinterested attentions <she had fainted from weakness and he had felt strangely *chivalrous* and paternal – Ellen Glasgow> ***ant*** uncivil, rude

claim – see DEMAND ***ant*** disclaim, renounce

clamorous – see VOCIFEROUS ***ant*** taciturn

clandestine – see SECRET ***ant*** open

clear 1 **clear, transparent, translucent, pellucid, limpid** *shared meaning* : capable of being seen through. **Clear** implies absence of all such impediments to vision as clouds, haze, or turbidity <water *clear* as glass> <a *clear* bright sky> **Transparent** applies to whatever can be seen through clearly and sharply <fine *transparent* window glass> <a robe of *transparent* silk> **Translucent** applies to what permits the passage of light but not a clear vision of objects beyond it <under the glassy, cool, *translucent* wave – John Milton> <the *translucent* skin showing the radiant rose beneath – W. H. Hudson †1922> **Pellucid** suggests a shining clearness like that of crystal <more *pellucid* streams, an ampler ether, a diviner air – William Wordsworth> <her large, dark-grey, *pellucid* eyes – D. H. Lawrence> **Limpid** implies the soft clearness of pure water <a *limpid* stream, through which we see to the very bottom – Lindley Murray> ***ant*** turbid

2 **clear, perspicuous, lucid** *shared meaning* : quickly and easily understood. **Clear** implies freedom from obscurity, ambiguity, or undue complexity <it is *clear* that I was wrong> <make it *clear* that you will be late> <a *clear* statement of the events that took place> **Perspicuous** lays more stress than *clear* on the medium of expression and frequently connotes an effective simplicity and elegance of style <extreme conciseness of expression, yet pure, *perspicuous,* and musical, is one of the grand beauties of lyric poetry – Thomas Gray> **Lucid** suggests a clear logical coherence and evident order of arrangement <his descriptions of the most complicated organic structures are astonishingly *lucid* – Aldous Huxley> ***ant*** unintelligible, abstruse

3 see EVIDENT ***ant*** unclear

clear-cut – see INCISIVE

cleave 1 see STICK ***ant*** part

2 see TEAR

clemency – see MERCY ***ant*** harshness

clever 1 see INTELLIGENT ***ant*** dull

2 **clever, adroit, cunning, ingenious** *shared meaning* : having or showing practical intelligence or skill in contriving. **Clever** stresses quickness, deftness, or aptitude, usually mental but occasionally physical, and may suggest mere facileness rather than true competence <her unfailing run of bright talk, which always sounded *clever* even when there was nothing in it – Herman Wouk> **Adroit** suggests greater shrewdness and astuteness than *clever* and may imply the skillful, or even crafty, use of expedients to attain one's ends

<De Gaulle's *adroit* maneuvering soon brought ruin to Roosevelt's policy – S. E. Ambrose> <the cool prudence, the sensitive selfishness, the quick perception of what is possible, which distinguish the *adroit* politician – J. R. Green> **Cunning,** especially as applied to craftsmen and artists, implies skill in creating or constructing <he knew how . . . to construct a plot, he was *cunning* in his manipulation of stage effects – T. S. Eliot> <his hand has lost none of its old *cunning*> **Ingenious** stresses the power of inventing or discovering, sometimes it implies brilliancy of mind, sometimes mere cleverness <the *ingenious* Yankee, quick to adapt himself everywhere, easily extricating himself from situations – Matthew Josephson>
climax – see SUMMIT
climb – see ASCEND ***ant*** descend
cling – see STICK
clique – see SET *n*
cloak – see DISGUISE ***ant*** uncloak
clog – see HAMPER ***ant*** expedite, facilitate
cloister, convent, monastery, nunnery, abbey, priory *shared meaning* : a house of persons living under religious vows. *Cloister* and *convent* are both general terms denoting a place of retirement from the world for members of a religious community. In such use **cloister** stresses retirement from the world and **convent,** community living. Basically, **monastery** denotes a cloister for monks; in practice it is often applied to a convent for men, less often for women, who combine the cloistered life with useful service (as teaching, preaching, or scholarly activity). **Nunnery,** which specifically denotes a cloister for nuns, is increasingly displaced by *convent* with the same meaning. A monastery or nunnery governed, respectively, by an abbot or abbess is an **abbey;** by a prior or prioress, a **priory.** A *priory* is subordinate in rank to, but often, independent of, an *abbey.*
close *vb* **close, end, conclude, finish, complete, terminate** *shared meaning* : to bring or come to a stopping point or limit. **Close** usually carries over from another sense the idea of action on something that is in some way open as well as unfinished <*close* an account> <*close* a debate> <recall those nights that *closed* thy toilsome days – Alexander Pope> **End** conveys a stronger sense of finality <he has endeavored to *end* the sharp dichotomy between undergraduate education and graduate professional study – *Current Biog.*> and usually implies a progress or development which is felt as having been carried through <the harvest is past, the summer is *ended,* and we are not saved – *Jer* 8:20 (AV)> **Conclude** can imply a formal closing (as of a speech or a meeting) and may stress less the fact than the form of that closing <*concluded* his speech with a plea for unity> or it can be very close to *close* or *end* <*concluded* their game and went home> **Finish** implies that something proposed or undertaken has been done and it may, therefore, connote the completion of a final step in a process (as of elaboration or perfecting) <*finished* the dress by carefully pressing the seams> <I have *finished* the work which thou gavest me to do – *Jn* 17:4 (AV)> **Complete** implies a finishing that removes all deficiencies or accomplishes whatever has been undertaken <[his] education was ended, if not *completed* – J. T. Farrell> <this computer solved a problem . . . in two weeks that would have taken a hundred engineers a year to *complete* – Gilda L. Morse> **Terminate** implies the setting of a limit in time or space <he had never seen the instrument that was to *terminate* his life – Charles Dickens> <the path *terminated* in a sunny clearing>
close *adj* **1 close, dense, compact, thick** *shared meaning* : having constituent parts that are massed tightly together. **Close** may apply to weave or texture <a paper of fine *close* texture> <between the *close* moss violet-inwoven

– P. B. Shelley> but more often it applies to something made up of separate items that are or seem pressed together <troops in *close* formation> <a *close* ill-drained soil> **Dense** implies compression of parts or elements so close as to be almost impenetrable <a *dense* fog> <he had retreated inside himself, as into a *dense* thicket . . . seemed to peer out blindly from a complicated darkness – H. C. Hervey> **Compact** suggests a firm union or consolidation of parts within a small compass and may imply neatness and effectiveness of arrangement <he was all *compact* and under his swart, tattooed skin the muscles worked like steel rods – Herman Melville> **Thick** usually applies to something that is condensed or made up of abundant concentrated parts <a *thick* head of hair> <make the gruel *thick* and slab – Shak.> ***ant*** open

2 see STINGY ***ant*** liberal

clownish – see BOORISH ***ant*** urbane

cloy – see SATIATE ***ant*** whet

clumsy – see AWKWARD ***ant*** dexterous, adroit, facile

cluster – see GROUP

clutch *vb* – see TAKE

clutch *n* – see HOLD

coalesce – see MIX

coarse, vulgar, gross, obscene, ribald *shared meaning* : offensive to good taste or moral principles. **Coarse** suggests unrefined crudeness, indelicacy, or robust roughness <what passed for love in the plays of his time did usually deserve the *coarser* name – Bonamy Dobrée> <simple parables of the *coarse* businessman and the sensitive intellectual – Bernard De Voto> **Vulgar** describes what may offend good taste and decency and may suggest a boorish lack of breeding <Burns is often coarse, but never *vulgar* – Lord Byron> <her father is a . . . *vulgar* person, mean in his ideals and obtuse in his manners – John Erskine †1951> **Gross** stresses crude animal inclinations and lack of refinement <merely *gross,* a scatological rather than a pornographic impropriety – Aldous Huxley> <the *grossest* insinuation, the frankest accusation were common form – Bonamy Dobrée> **Obscene** is the strongest of these words in stressing impropriety, indecency, or nastiness <an *obscene* but unforgettable fantasy in which the contours of human decency have been permanently and irredeemably eroded – Hilton Kramer> <*obscene* language> <an *obscene* misuse of our power which has offended the sensibilities of the civilized world – *Between The Lines*> **Ribald** regularly applies to the witty or humorous that gains its effect by broad indecency or crude earthiness <a *ribald* folksong about fleas in straw – J. L. Lowes> ***ant*** fine, refined

cocksure – see SURE ***ant*** dubious, doubtful

coerce – see FORCE

coeval – see CONTEMPORARY

cogent – see VALID

cogitate – see THINK 2

cognate – see RELATED

cognizant – see AWARE ***ant*** ignorant

cohere – see STICK

coincide – see AGREE ***ant*** differ

coincident – see CONTEMPORARY

collate – see COMPARE

collect – see GATHER ***ant*** disperse, distribute

collected – see COOL ***ant*** distracted, distraught

color, chroma, hue, shade, tint, tinge *shared meaning* : a property of a visible thing that is recognizable in the light and is distinct from properties (as shape or size) that are apparent in dusk. **Color** is the ordinary and generic term for this property and specifically applies to the property of things seen as red, yellow, blue, and so on as distinguished from gray, black, or white. **Chroma** is a technical equivalent for this specific application of *color.* **Hue** may be a close synonym of *color* <as brown in *hue* as hazelnuts and sweeter than the kernels – Shak.> but typically it suggests gradation or modification of primary colors <the work of an inspired painter can reveal to us the *hues* and shades of twilight – Colin Clark> **Shade,** also interchangeable with *color,* more usually indicates a gradation of a color or hue according to lightness or brightness <use a paler *shade* of blue for the curtains> **Tint** usually applies to color that is pale or faint or diluted (as with white) <colors as pure and delicate as the *tints* of early morning – Willa Cather> **Tinge** distinctively applies to color that modifies other color (as by mingling with or overlaying) <embarrassment brought a *tinge* of red to her pale cheeks> <autumn bold, with universal *tinge* of sober gold – John Keats>

colorable – see PLAUSIBLE

colossal – see HUGE

comatose – see LETHARGIC ***ant*** awake

combat – see OPPOSE ***ant*** champion, defend

combative – see BELLIGERENT ***ant*** pacifistic

combine – see JOIN ***ant*** separate

comely – see BEAUTIFUL ***ant*** homely

comfort, console, solace *shared meaning* **:** to act to ease the grief or sufferings of another. **Comfort** implies imparting cheer, strength, or encouragement as well as lessening pain <he hath sent me . . . to *comfort* all that mourn – *Isa* 61:1-2 (AV)> **Console** emphasizes the alleviating of grief or the mitigating of a sense of loss rather than distinct or full relief <if you really want to *console* me, teach me rather to forget what has happened – Oscar Wilde> **Solace** suggests a lifting of spirits, as often from loneliness or boredom as from grief or pain <he *solaced* his cares by classical studies – Richard Garnett †1906> <see the Romantic poet as a solitary nightingale singing to *solace* his own private agony – C. R. Woodring> ***ant*** afflict, bother

comfortable, cozy, snug, easy, restful *shared meaning* **:** enjoying or providing circumstances that make for contentment and security. **Comfortable** implies the absence of whatever gives trouble, pain, or distress to body or mind <they drove home together . . . in *comfortable* silence – Stella D. Gibbons> Sometimes it additionally suggests a pleasant quality based on habitual use or association <a disreputable but *comfortable* and treasured old jacket> **Cozy** suggests comfortableness derived from warmth, shelter, ease, and friendliness <the *cozy* talk by the fireside – J. R. Green> <a *cozy* room with mellow light and close-drawn curtains> It regularly suggests intimacy and close association <desirous of living on the *cozy* footing of a father-in-law – Herman Melville> and can sometimes be derogatory in implying close association for devious purposes <meant the end of *cozy* arrangements in which they had seemingly grasped . . . the best of all worlds – R. J. Barber> **Snug** suggests possession of just so much (as of space, freedom, or money) as is needed for secure well-being <all the gypsies and showmen . . . lay *snug* within their carts and tents – Thomas Hardy> <I was completely isolated in my own luxurious shell, as *snug* as a hermit crab – Roald Dahl> **Easy** implies relief from or absence of anything likely to cause physical or mental discomfort or constraint <he was *easy* as an old shoe> <it was the desultory talk of the old days but it was *easy* and comfortable – Pearl Buck> **Restful** applies to whatever induces or contributes to relaxation or rest <a *restful,* friendly room, fitted to the uses of

gentle life – Mary Austin> or to the state of mind of one who is both comfortable and relaxed <that peace which the world can give – the *restful* sense of snuggling up close to a centre – C. E. Montague> ***ant*** uncomfortable, miserable

comic – see LAUGHABLE ***ant*** tragic

comical – see LAUGHABLE ***ant*** pathetic

command *vb* **command, order, bid, enjoin, direct, instruct, charge** *shared meaning* : to issue orders. *Command* and *order* imply authority and usually some degree of formality and impersonality, but **command** stresses official exercise of authority while **order** may suggest peremptory or arbitrary exercise; thus, a military officer or the captain of a ship *commands;* a landowner *orders* a trespasser off his premises <one is likely to resent being *ordered,* except by those who have a right to *command*> **Bid** suggests giving orders or directions (as to children or servants) directly and orally <she *bade* him be seated> It may carry more than a hint of firmness or curtness <seized him by the collar and sternly *bade* him cease making a fool of himself – G. B. Shaw> *Enjoin, direct,* and *instruct,* though less imperative than *command* and *order,* all imply an expectation of obedience. **Enjoin** adds to the idea of authority the implication of urging or warning <I *enjoin* upon all citizens to cooperate with the government – F. D. Roosevelt> **Direct** may suggest either a routine or a mandatory order often on specific points of procedure or activity <why otherwise does it [the Constitution] *direct* the judges to take an oath to support it? – John Marshall> **Instruct,** close to *direct,* may suggest greater formality or greater explicitness in directing <*instructed* her to go early to the market> **Charge** is likely to add to the idea of ordering that of imposing as an obligation <she must have faith, she *charged* herself. She must believe implicitly – H. C. Hervey> ***ant*** comply, obey

command *n* – see POWER 3

commemorate – see KEEP

commence – see BEGIN

commensurable – see PROPORTIONAL ***ant*** incommensurable

commensurate – see PROPORTIONAL ***ant*** incommensurate

comment – see REMARK

commentate – see REMARK

commerce – see BUSINESS

commingle – see MIX

commit, entrust, confide, consign, relegate *shared meaning* : to assign (as to a person or place) especially for care or safekeeping. **Commit** may express merely the idea of delivering into another's charge <*commit* the management of an estate to an agent> or it may have the special sense of a transfer to a higher power or to a place of custody <into thine hand I *commit* my spirit – *Ps* 31:5 (AV)> <*commit* a person to prison> **Entrust** implies committing with trust and confidence <*entrust* a friend with a secret> **Confide** implies entrusting with entire reliance or assurance <the defense of our island was still *confided* to the militia – T. B. Macaulay> **Consign** frequently suggests such transfer or delivery as removes what is transferred from one's immediate control <*consign* goods to an agent for sale> or as precludes altering one's decision <cleared his desk and *consigned* most of his papers to the flames> **Relegate** applies to consigning to a particular class, position, or sphere, often with an implication of setting aside or getting rid of <old furniture, *relegated* to the attic>

commodious – see SPACIOUS

common 1 see RECIPROCAL ***ant*** individual

2 common, ordinary, plain, familiar, popular, vulgar *shared meaning* : being what is generally met with and not in any way special, strange, or unusual. **Common** implies usual everyday quality or frequency of appearance <a *common* error> <he lacks *common* honesty> but it may additionally imply a degree of inferiority or coarseness <the *common* herd> <O hard is the bed . . . and *common* the blanket and cheap – A. E. Housman> **Ordinary** expresses more definitely accordance with the regular order of things <his face is just the *ordinary* face of an *ordinary* man, a mixture of small worries and pleasures, hopes and disappointments, a few simple longings, several deep frustrations – Helen MacInnes> **Plain** is likely to stress possession of the qualities of ordinary people and may suggest homely simplicity <the *plain* people everywhere . . . wish to live in peace with one another – F. D. Roosevelt> <as *plain* as an old shoe in dress, mannerisms, and the way he runs his business – *Time*> **Familiar** stresses the fact of being generally known and easily recognized <in spotting the ridiculous and the false in *familiar* situations, she does not spare herself – *Current Biog.*> <a *familiar* melody> *Popular* and *vulgar* imply commonness that arises from general acceptance especially by the common people of a country or period <*popular* fallacies> <the *vulgar* tongue> **Popular** is more likely to stress widespread currency or favor among the people <a *popular* tune to be sung in the car or the shower is still a nice thing – Renata Adler> <books . . . designed for the *popular* reader – Elizabeth Spencer> while **vulgar** usually carries derogatory connotations (as of inferiority or coarseness) <the meaningless and *vulgar* bustle of newspaper offices – Stella D. Gibbons> <blindness to the *vulgar* world was the essence of [Boston] Brahmanism – Alden Whitman> *ant* uncommon, exceptional

common sense – see SENSE

communicate, impart *shared meaning* : to convey or transmit something intangible (as information, feelings, or qualities). **Communicate** is more likely to stress the result and imply the making common to those concerned the knowledge or quality conveyed <his courage *communicated* itself to his followers> <great books are original communications. Their authors are *communicating* what they themselves have discovered – M. J. Adler> <it is the function of the fine arts to *communicate* values – Adelbert Ames, Jr.> **Impart** tends to stress the process of the transfer and to suggest sharing what is primarily one's own <the smoke *imparted* its odor to his clothes> <there is a core of indubitable knowledge in education, but most of the teacher's task consists in *imparting* methods for understanding what is still unknown – Zechariah Chafee, Jr.> <he *imparted* to you his vision of tomorrow's world – *Saturday Rev.*>

compact – see CLOSE *adj*

compare, contrast, collate *shared meaning* : to set side by side in order to show likenesses and differences. **Compare** implies as an aim the showing of relative values or excellences or a bringing out of characteristic qualities, whether they are similar or divergent; **contrast** implies as an aim the emphasizing of differences; thus, one may *compare* the movement of the *Odyssey* with that of the *Aeneid* to arrive at their distinctive qualities; one may thereupon *contrast* the buoyancy and rapidity of the one with the stateliness and dignity of the other. One thing is *compared with* another, as above: it is *compared to* another when it is formally represented on the basis of a real or imagined similarity as being like the other; thus, Pope *compares* Homer *with* (not *to*) Vergil but he *compares* Homer *to* (not *with*) the Nile, pouring out his riches with a boundless overflow <*compare* two cars to decide which will better suit our needs> <content to lounge . . . and listen to her prattle, *contrasting* her with other women and thinking how deliciously ingenuous she was – Victoria Sackville-West> **Collate** implies minute and critical comparison in order to detect points of agreement and divergence <he has visited all Europe . . . not to collect medals, or *collate* manuscripts: but . . . to compare and *collate* the distresses of all men in all countries – Edmund Burke>

compass *vb* – see REACH

compass *n* – see CIRCUMFERENCE

compassion – see SYMPATHY

compatible – see CONSONANT *ant* incompatible

compel – see FORCE

compendious – see CONCISE

compendium, syllabus, digest, survey, sketch, précis *shared meaning* : a brief treatment of a subject or topic. A **compendium** gathers together and presents in concise, often outline, form all the essential facts and details of a subject <dictionaries, linguistic atlases, *compendia* of usage, and scholarly grammars are important tools – A. H. Marckwardt> A **syllabus** gives the material necessary for a comprehensive view of a whole subject, often in the form of a series of heads or propositions <no party program, no official *syllabus* of opinions, which we all have to defend – W. R. Inge> A **digest** presents a body of information gathered from many sources and arranged for convenience in use <prepare a *digest* of current events for the use of a candidate> A **survey** is a brief but comprehensive treatment presented often as a preliminary to further study or discussion <an effort to determine, through a broad *survey* of its more salient features, the fundamental nature of the movement – G. C. Sellery> A **sketch** is a slight, tentative, usually preliminary presentation subject to later change, emendation, and amplification <we can give you the merest *sketch* of our plans just now> A **précis** is a precise clear-cut statement or restatement of fundamentals, often in the form of a report or summary that suggests the style or tone of an original <my *précis* . . . is scientifically inadequate, but it sums up the complicated subject in terms intelligible to such laymen as myself – Irving Kolodin> <the summary . . . will be much appreciated by those who want a *précis* of the scattered material on the Carib – Douglas Taylor>

compensate 1 compensate, countervail, balance, offset *shared meaning* : to make up for what is excessive or deficient, helpful or harmful in another. **Compensate** implies making up a lack or making amends for loss or injury <she worked without salary, but was *compensated* by a feeling of achievement that gave her confidence – *Current Biog.*> <crippled in early life so that he could not be a sailor, [he] more than *compensated* by painting ships, harbors, and coastal scenes – S. E. Morison> **Countervail** implies counteracting a usually bad or harmful influence or overcoming damage caused by it <when the technology of a time is powerfully thrusting in one direction, wisdom may well call for a *countervailing* thrust – Marshall McLuhan> <the absence of fuss . . . *countervailed* any tendency to self-importance – Sylvia T. Warner> **Balance** implies the equalizing or adjusting of things that are contrary or opposed so that no one outweighs another or can exert a harmful influence on the whole <the pressures of business, labor, and farmers . . . manage to check and *balance* each other – Max Ascoli> <caution warned her not to allow . . . anything to disturb her equilibrium; her present peace of mind was too precious – and too precariously *balanced* – H. C. Hervey> **Offset** implies neutralizing one thing's good or evil effects by the contrary effect of another <every advance in medicine will tend to be *offset* by corresponding advance in the survival rate of individuals cursed by some genetic insufficiency – Aldous Huxley> **2** see PAY

compete – see RIVAL

competent 1 see ABLE ***ant*** incompetent
2 see SUFFICIENT

complaisant – see AMIABLE ***ant*** contrary, perverse

complete *adj* – see FULL ***ant*** incomplete

complete *vb* – see CLOSE *vb*

complex, complicated, intricate, involved, knotty *shared meaning* : having confusingly interrelated parts. **Complex** suggests the unavoidable result of bringing together various elements (as parts, notions, or details) and does not imply a fault or failure <a *complex* mechanism> <the nature of oratory is such that there has always been a tendency among politicians and clergymen to oversimplify *complex* issues – Aldous Huxley> **Complicated** may heighten notions of difficulty in understanding, solving, or dealing with <a *complicated* mathematical problem> <*complicated* machinery has had to be matched by *complicated* social arrangements, designed to work as smoothly and efficiently as the new instruments of production – Aldous Huxley> **Intricate** suggests difficulty of understanding or appreciating quickly because of perplexing interconnecting, interweaving, or interacting of parts <science had not become so *intricate* as to discourage those who wished to know a little of everything – S. E. Morison> <complex in themselves, and *intricate* in their interaction – H. O. Taylor> **Involved** implies extreme complication in which parts are so interwoven or turned upon themselves as to almost defy resolution; often the word suggests needless complexity or even illogical disorder <a needlessly *involved* explanation> <public issues are so large and so *involved* that it is only a few who can hope to have any adequate comprehension of them – G. L. Dickinson> **Knotty** suggests such complication and entanglement as makes solution or understanding improbable <ethical problem-solving and decision-making are growing *knottier* all the time – Joseph Fletcher> ***ant*** simple

complicated – see COMPLEX ***ant*** simple

comply – see OBEY ***ant*** command, enjoin

component – see ELEMENT ***ant*** composite, complex

comport – see AGREE 3, BEHAVE

composed – see COOL ***ant*** discomposed, anxious

composure – see EQUANIMITY ***ant*** discomposure, perturbation

comprehend – see INCLUDE, UNDERSTAND

compress – see CONTRACT ***ant*** stretch, spread

compunction – see PENITENCE, QUALM

conceal – see HIDE ***ant*** reveal

concede – see GRANT ***ant*** dispute

conceive – see THINK

concern – see CARE ***ant*** unconcern

concert – see NEGOTIATE

concise, terse, succinct, laconic, summary, pithy, compendious *shared meaning* : very brief in statement or expression. **Concise** implies the elimination of whatever is superfluous or elaborative <it may not be "easy" reading, for it is highly *concise* and concentrated; but it is lucid, precise and often brilliantly epigrammatic – Stanley Hoffmann> **Terse** implies conciseness that is both pointed and elegant <in the *tersest,* clearest aphoristic form – Glenway Wescott> or sometimes such extreme conciseness as to be curt or brusque <can be so *terse* in his speech that he drops the definite or indefinite article – *Current Biog.*> <the *terse* style in which Mrs. Sayce is obliged to couch her notes sometimes forces her to be excessively dogmatic – *Times Lit. Supp.*> **Succinct** implies precise expression without waste of words <a *succinct* reply> <tells a good story in *succinct* sentences – D. P. Weeks> **Laconic,** as likely to apply to a person as his utterances, implies brevity to the point of seeming rude, indifferent, or mysterious <a *laconic,* hard-bitten, close-talking fellow. He is literally curt – Walker Gibson> <the *laconic* announcement was made . . . that the sentences of death had been carried out – *Manchester Guardian Weekly*> **Summary** suggests the statement of main points without elaboration or explanation <the swift and *summary* record of crowded and delightful days – Havelock Ellis> <a *summary* order> **Pithy** applies to what is not only succinct but rich in meaning and therefore especially forceful or telling <a *pithy* epigram> <the best and *pithiest* description of what really happened – Bernard Fall> **Compendious** applies to material that is at once full in scope and concise and brief in treatment; specifically, it suggests a compendium <the *compendious* scholarly words which save so much trouble – T. E. Brown> *ant* redundant

conclude 1 see CLOSE *vb ant* open
2 see INFER

conclusive, decisive, determinative, definitive *shared meaning* : bringing to an end. **Conclusive** applies especially to reasoning or logical proof that puts an end to debate or questioning <a very persuasive if not a *conclusive* argument – John Marshall> **Decisive** applies to something (as an act, event, influence, or argument) that puts an end to controversy or competition, to vacillation, to uncertainty, or to insecurity <a *decisive* battle> <[his] contributions . . . have been *decisive* in integrating the diverse views of the Darwinian and Mendelian schools of evolutionary thought – *Current Biog.*> **Determinative** applies chiefly to matters (as decisions, judgments, or influences) that put an end to uncertainty and give a fixed direction or goal to something (as a life, a course, or a movement) <[regulations] which redefined . . . the corporate characteristics which would be *determinative* of whether an unincorporated organization should be taxed as a corporation – *Arthur Young Jour.*> **Definitive,** often opposed to *tentative* or *provisional,* applies to whatever is put forth as final and as serving to make further study, questioning, or dispute pointless <a *definitive* history of New England glass> <it seems to be impossible to make any *definitive* judgment concerning the mechanical properties of the soil – Thomas Gold & B. W. Hapke> *ant* inconclusive

concourse – see JUNCTION

concur – see AGREE *ant* contend, altercate

condemn – see CRITICIZE

condense – see CONTRACT *ant* amplify (*a speech, article*)

condescend – see STOOP *ant* presume

condition *n* – see STATE

condition *vb* – see PREPARE

condone – see EXCUSE

conduce, contribute, redound *shared meaning* : to lead to an end. **Conduce** implies having a predictable tendency to further an end or to lead to as an end <characterizes the "essential nature" of religion in terms of its functions, particularly the social function of *conducing* to altruistic conduct – Irving Singer> <everything just now *conduces* to a serenity not very natural to my temperament – O. W. Holmes † 1935> **Contribute** distinctively applies to one factor of a group of influential factors that has an effective part in furthering an end or producing a result <the delayed rains *contributed* to the poor harvest> <their studies *contributed* much to our knowledge of the past> **Redound** implies leading to an unplanned end or state by or as if by a flow of consequences <if men are permitted to work for private gain their efforts in the competitive market will *redound* to the general good of society – Lucius Garvin> <seekers often make mistakes, and I wish

mine to *redound* to my own discredit only – Matthew Arnold> ***ant*** ward (*off*)

conduct **1 conduct, manage, control, direct** *shared meaning* : to use one's powers (as of skill or authority) to lead, guide, or dominate. **Conduct** may imply a leader's supervision or responsible guidance in a chosen course <*conduct* an orchestra> <this document . . . provides a particularly glaring instance of the tendency to *conduct* foreign and military policy not on their own merits, but as exercises in public relations – H. J. Morgenthau> but often the idea of leadership is lost or obscured and stress is placed on the fact of carrying something on or out <*conduct* a debate> <little research has been *conducted* on other forms of deafness – *Current Biog.*> **Manage** implies direct handling and manipulating or maneuvering toward an end or result <the key to *managing* yourself effectively is to *manage* your time effectively – R. J. Bryant> <only a person with a candid mind . . . can appreciate the full fun of an intrigue when they begin to *manage* one for the first time – Stella D. Gibbons> **Control** stresses the idea of authoritative guidance and may imply a regulating or restraining to keep within bounds or on course <*control* a fractious horse> <no attempt was made . . . to *control* by public authority the production and distribution of wealth – G. L. Dickinson> but sometimes implies domination or subjection to one's own will or interests <business has *controlled* the legislature through a coalition of rural lawmakers – Trevor Armbrister> **Direct** implies constant guiding and regulating so as to achieve smooth efficient operation <*direct* a research program>
2 see BEHAVE ***ant*** misconduct

confer – see GIVE

confess – see ACKNOWLEDGE ***ant*** renounce (*one's beliefs, principles*)

confide – see *commit*

confidence, assurance, self-possession, aplomb *shared meaning* : a state of mind or a manner marked by easy coolness and freedom from uncertainty, diffidence, or embarrassment. **Confidence** stresses faith in oneself and one's powers, usually on sound grounds and without conceit or arrogance <the *confidence* that springs from complete mastery of his subject – C. H. Grandgent> **Assurance** differs from *confidence* in its stronger implication of certainty <to face a good orchestra [as conductor] with inward and outward authority and *assurance* – J. N. Burk> and, when directed toward one's own powers, is likely to carry a note of arrogance or suggest a lack of objectivity in assessing their worth <their religion . . . hammered into them a self-righteous pride, a conceited *assurance* of moral superiority – J. T. Farrell> **Self-possession** implies an ease or coolness under stress that reflects perfect self-control and command of one's powers and facilities <that carefully cultivated air of quiet *self-possession,* suggesting inner repose and serenity – Harold Strauss> <answered the insolent question with complete *self-possession*> **Aplomb** applies to the bearing or behavior under difficult circumstances of a person with marked *assurance* or *self-possession* but it seldom carries the unpleasant connotation often felt in *assurance* <he demonstrated *aplomb* worthy of a veteran when, his silk breeches having split, he played an entire act sitting down – *Current Biog.*> ***ant*** diffidence

configuration – see FORM

confine – see LIMIT

confirm, corroborate, substantiate, verify, authenticate, validate *shared meaning* : to attest to the truth or validity of something. **Confirm** implies the removal of doubts by an authoritative statement or an indisputable fact <the president *confirmed* the report that he would not seek reelection> <repeated tests *confirmed* the water as the source of the epidemic> **Corroborate**

suggests the strengthening of one piece of evidence by another or, sometimes, additional evidence supporting something already more or less accepted <bystanders *corroborated* his story of the accident> <the material illustrates and *corroborates* what has already become known from other sources – G. F. Kennan> **Substantiate** presupposes something needing to be demonstrated or proved and implies the providing of evidence tending to this end <reference material to support, *substantiate*, or enlarge upon the text – Frank Mortimer> <a deed that *substantiated* their claim to the disputed land> **Verify** implies the establishment of correspondence, often point by point, of actual fact or details with those proposed or guessed at; thus, one *verifies* a suspicion, a fear, or a probability by awaiting the outcome of the relevant situation. In more general use the notion of comparison tends to be stressed; thus, one *verifies* the quotations in an essay by checking them against the original text; one *verifies* an account by checking the statement against all pertinent records of receipt and disbursal <ran a survey to *verify* the landmarks> **Authenticate** implies establishment of genuineness or validity by authoritative or expert dicta <the manuscript was *authenticated* by experts at the museum> <the court formally *authenticated* the grant of land> **Validate** is close to *authenticate* but is somewhat more likely to be chosen in reference to papers requiring an official signature or seal before they are considered valid <*validate* a passport> It is also used when the soundness of a judgment, policy, or belief is in question <the expansion of demand which alone can *validate* the policy – J. A. Hobson> ***ant*** deny, contradict

confirmation – see FORM
confirmed – see INVETERATE
confiscate – see APPROPRIATE *vb*
conflict – see DISCORD ***ant*** harmony
confluence – see JUNCTION
conform 1 see ADAPT
2 see AGREE 3 ***ant*** diverge
confound 1 see MISTAKE ***ant*** distinguish, discriminate
2 see PUZZLE
confuse – see MISTAKE ***ant*** differentiate
confute – see DISPROVE
congenial – see CONSONANT ***ant*** uncongenial, antipathetic (*of persons*), abhorrent (*of tasks, duties*)
congenital – see INNATE
congratulate – see FELICITATE
congregate – see GATHER ***ant*** disperse
congruous – see CONSONANT ***ant*** incongruous

conjecture, surmise, guess *shared meaning* : to draw an inference from slight evidence or (as nouns) an inference so drawn. **Conjecture** implies forming an opinion or judgment on evidence insufficient for definite knowledge <Kepler's series of *conjectures* as to the orbit of Mars – G. H. von Wright> <what the circumstances were that favored this tendency to segregation and change can be only *conjectured* – A. L. Kroeber> **Surmise** implies even slighter evidence and suggests the influence of imagination or suspicion <one can only *surmise* what powerful currents of apathy and hopelessness must be eroding the morale of the Ceylonese villager – Norman Cousins> <what he expressed as a mere *surmise* was transcribed by others as a positive statement – Richard Semon> **Guess** usually implies arrival at a conclusion on bases other than material and pertinent evidence and is likely to suggest the use of intuition or suspicion and a reliance upon chance for verification

<your *guess* as to his intent is as good as mine> <she didn't want to ride on the roller-coaster and he *guessed* that her ideas of pleasure were more sophisticated – John Cheever>

connect – see JOIN *ant* disconnect

connotation – see under DENOTE

connote – see DENOTE

conquer, defeat, vanquish, overcome, surmount, subdue, subjugate, reduce, overthrow, rout, beat, lick *shared meaning* : to get the better of by force or strategy. *Conquer* and *defeat* are the most general terms but typically **conquer** implies a major action, all-inclusive effort, and a more or less permanent result, while **defeat** implies merely the fact of getting the better of an adversary at a particular time often with no more than a temporary checking or frustrating; thus, one *conquers* a nation, a disease, or a bad habit when one so completely gets the better that the thing conquered is no longer a matter for serious consideration or concern. On the other hand one *defeats* an enemy in battle, a player in a tennis match, or an argument in a debate with full awareness that the situation may well be reversed at the next encounter. **Vanquish**, though like *conquer* in implying complete defeat, carries far less implication of finality. **Overcome** implies an opposing, often fixed, obstacle that can be dealt with only with difficulty or after a hard struggle <*overcome* a legal obstacle> <*overcome* a physical handicap> <only a large team working for years could have *overcome* the abundance of available material – *Times Lit. Supp.*> **Surmount** differs from *overcome* chiefly in implying a surpassing or exceeding rather than an overcoming in face-to-face confrontation <the technical problems to be *surmounted* – K. F. Mather> *Subdue, subjugate,* and *reduce* throw emphasis on the condition of subjection resulting from defeat. **Subdue** implies a bringing under control by or as if by overpowering <the police *subdued* the unruly drunk> <all violence or recklessness of feeling has been finally *subdued* – Willa Cather> **Subjugate** stresses a bringing into and keeping in subjection and often implies a humbled or servile state in what is subjugated <*subjugate* a wild horse> <never dreamed of liberating all men, but only of liberating a few by *subjugating* the rest – Raghavan Iyer> <*subjugate* one's prejudices> **Reduce** implies surrender and submission usually as the result of overwhelming by or as if by military action and often following destruction of the facilities without which resistance or defense is impossible <*reduce* a fortress by siege and shelling> <they found the settlement *reduced* to the last stage of wretchedness. The colonists were discouraged, diseased, and starving – S. E. Morison> **Overthrow** is much like *overcome* but stresses the bringing down or destruction of enemy power rather than the effort of attaining this end <there was no opposition leader in sight who had the slightest chance of *overthrowing* him, and if he were *overthrown* chaos would follow – S. E. Ambrose> **Rout** suggests such complete defeat as causes flight or complete dispersion and disorganization of the adversary <the guerrillas *routed* the attacking force> <a joke was a good way . . . to escape involvement, to twist an argument, to *rout* an opponent – Helen MacInnes> *Beat* and *lick*, characteristic of a less formal mode of expression, come close to *defeat* in meaning. **Beat**, in this use, is rather neutral though occasionally it may imply the finality but not the scope of *vanquish* <*beat* an opponent at cards> <*beat* the enemy in a pitched battle> while **lick** is likely to imply a complete humbling or reduction to ineffectiveness of the one defeated <*lick* a problem> <we've got the outfit to *lick* the wilderness – S. H. Adams>

conquest – see VICTORY

conscientious – see UPRIGHT ***ant*** unconscientious, unscrupulous

conscious – see AWARE ***ant*** unconscious

consecrate – see DEVOTE

consecutive, successive *shared meaning* : following one after the other. **Consecutive** stresses immediacy in following, regularity or fixedness of the order, and the close connection (as in time, space, or logic) of the units, while **successive** is applicable to things that follow regardless of differences (as in duration, extent, or size) or of the length of the interval between the units. Thus, one would speak of nine, ten, and eleven as *consecutive* numbers since they follow one another in immediate and regular order, but of flashing the *successive* numbers three, eleven, and seven on a screen since the order would be neither immediate nor regular; one would speak of *successive* (not *consecutive*) leap years since the order though regular is not immediate and of *successive* strokes of a piston since, though immediate, they need not be regular <strung together his rich miscellany to form a *consecutive* narrative – B. J. Hendrick> <war vies with magic in its efforts to get something for nothing . . . to enjoy the rewards of *consecutive* and tedious labor without having lifted a finger in work – Lewis Mumford> <recommended for replacement by a special Harvard report . . . as well as by *successive* reports of Boston superintendents – Efrem Sigel> <the product of the *successive* labors of innumerable men – Lewis Mumford> ***ant*** inconsecutive

consent – see ASSENT ***ant*** dissent

consequence **1** see EFFECT ***ant*** antecedent
2 see IMPORTANCE

consequently – see THEREFORE

conserve – see SAVE ***ant*** waste, squander

consider, study, contemplate, weigh *shared meaning* : to apply one's mind to something (as an idea, a problem, or a proposed course of action) in order to increase one's knowledge or understanding of it or to reach a decision about it. **Consider** can suggest a mere applying of one's mind <we will certainly *consider* your suggestion> but it may imply careful attention often from a definite point of view <marriage is an action too freely practiced and too seldom adequately *considered* – Rose Macaulay> or it may imply a casting about in order to reach an acceptable conclusion, opinion, or decision <when I came to *consider* his conduct, I realized that he was guilty of a confusion – T. S. Eliot> **Study** implies sustained purposeful concentration with such careful attention to details as is likely to reveal the possibilities, applications, variations, or relations of the thing studied <the engineers *studied* the proposed dam site> <*study* lecture notes in preparing for an examination> **Contemplate** implies the focusing of one's thoughts upon something, often with little indication of purpose or result <fine gentlemen and fine ladies are charming to *contemplate* in history – Bertrand Russell> but sometimes with a clear indication of considering as a possible choice among alternatives <this man who fifty years before had made us so miserable that I had once *contemplated* suicide – Roald Dahl> **Weigh** implies examination of conflicting claims or evidence in order to evaluate something or to reach a decision or choice <the jury must *weigh* the evidence carefully> <against the evils of monopoly and oligopoly must be *weighed* the possible . . . dynamic efficiencies that they may introduce – P. A. Samuelson>

considerate –see THOUGHTFUL ***ant*** inconsiderate

consign – see COMMIT

consistent – see CONSONANT ***ant*** inconsistent

console –see COMFORT

consonant, consistent, compatible, congruous, congenial, sympathetic *shared meaning* : being in agreement one with another or agreeable one to another. **Consonant** implies the absence of elements making for discord or difficulty <we are . . . embarking on new programs where they are *consonant* with the University's mission – M. S. Eisenhower> <rational propaganda in favor of action is *consonant* with the enlightened self-interest of those who make it and those to whom it is addressed – Aldous Huxley> **Consistent** is more likely to stress absence of contradiction between things or between details of the same thing <*consistent* with the . . . ethic of his day, he started his career at nineteen in menial labor – in his father's company – *Johns Hopkins Mag.*> <[presented] a strong, *consistent,* and all but exhaustive case for a natural science of human behavior – Harry Prosch> **Compatible** implies a capacity for existing together without disagreement, discord, or disharmony <the dominant party . . . advocates a moderate socialism *compatible* with free enterprise – *Current Biog.*> **Congruous** is more positive in suggesting a pleasing effect resulting from fitness or appropriateness of constituent elements < it is *congruous* . . . that poetry should work towards feeling by way of the intellect – Bonamy Dobrée> <thoughts *congruous* to the nature of their subject – William Cowper> **Congenial** implies a generally satisfying harmony between personalities or a fitness to one's personal taste <there is a strand in . . . our national character that is all too *congenial* to the spirit of crusading ideology – J. W. Fulbright> <deprived . . . of one another's *congenial* company – Edmund Wilson> **Sympathetic** is likely to suggest a more subtle or quieter kind of harmony than *congenial* <I am not very *sympathetic* to this frame of mind – Naomi Bliven> <he returned . . . as a scholar, *sympathetic* critic, and educator – *Current Biog.*> ***ant*** inconsonant

conspectus – see ABRIDGMENT

conspicuous – see NOTICEABLE ***ant*** inconspicuous

conspiracy – see PLOT

constant 1 see CONTINUAL ***ant*** fitful
2 see FAITHFUL ***ant*** inconstant, fickle

constituent – see ELEMENT ***ant*** whole, aggregate

constitution – see PHYSIQUE

constrain – see FORCE

constrict – see CONTRACT

consume – see MONOPOLIZE, WASTE

contaminate, taint, pollute, defile *shared meaning* : to make impure or unclean. **Contaminate** implies intrusion of or contact with an outside source as the cause <water *contaminated* by industrial wastes> <dispersing from the sky vast quantities of radioactive dust particles . . . *contaminating* entire cities – Norman Cousins> **Taint** stresses the effect rather than the cause, implying the loss of purity or cleanliness or the development of corruption or decay that naturally follows contamination <*tainted* meat> <his unkindness may defeat my life, but never *taint* my love – Shak.> **Pollute,** sometimes interchangeable with *contaminate,* may distinctively imply that the process which begins with contamination is complete and manifest and that what was pure or clean has become foul, poisoned, or filthy <the *polluted* waters of Lake Erie, in parts no better than an open cesspool> <saw a worldwide . . . plot to *pollute* science and thereby destroy civilization – W. L. Shirer> **Defile** strongly implies befouling of what ought to be kept clean and pure or held sacred and commonly suggests violation or desecration <*defile* a hero's memory with slanderous innuendo> <an evil bird that *defiles* his own nest – Hugh Latimer>

contemn – see DESPISE

contemplate – see CONSIDER
contemporaneous – see CONTEMPORARY
contemporary, contemporaneous, coeval, synchronous, simultaneous, coincident *shared meaning* : existing or occurring at the same time. **Contemporary** is likely to apply to people and what relates to them, **contemporaneous** to events; both depend on the context to identify the time regarding which agreement is implied. *Contemporary,* but not *contemporaneous,* may refer to the present but only as being the same time as that of the speaker or writer. Thus, a history of the 15th century based on *contemporary* accounts is one based on 15th century accounts; geological features are *contemporaneous* if they were laid down at the same time in geological history <love of school is not *contemporaneous* with residence therein; it is an after product – C. H. Grandgent> <Shakespeare was *contemporary* with Cervantes> <his books are filled with *contemporary* comment for he is always aware of the world about him> **Coeval** implies contemporaneousness at a remote time or for a long period <Engineering . . . is *coeval* with civilization – Harold Hartley> <as an investigative discipline, history is *coeval* with science – M. J. Adler> **Synchronous** implies exact correspondence between or during usually brief periods of time <the satellites will be placed in *synchronous* orbits – *Science News*> <the *synchronous* action of a bird's wings in flight> **Simultaneous** implies exact coincidence at a point or instant of time <the shots were *simultaneous*> <they held separate but *simultaneous* meetings> **Coincident** applies to events regarded as happening or falling at the same time and tends to minimize any notion of causal relationships <the growth of the mine union movement was *coincident* with the growth of business and manufacturing – T. R. Hay>
contemptible, despicable, pitiable, sorry, scurvy, cheap, beggarly *shared meaning* : arousing or deserving scorn or disdain. **Contemptible** may imply any quality provoking scorn or a low standing on a scale of values <a culture which in its primitive way is by no means *contemptible* – MacDonald Hastings> <the intellectual and emotional life of ordinary people is a very *contemptible* affair – Oscar Wilde> **Despicable** may imply utter worthlessness and usually suggests arousing an attitude of moral indignation <the downright *despicable* manner in which thousands of neophyte salesmen are recruited and discarded each year – J. B. Woy> <even excellent science could and did often make *despicable* morality – Christian Gauss> **Pitiable** applies to what inspires mixed contempt and pity and often attributes weakness (as of spirit or action) in the inspiring agent <his ignorance was *pitiable*> <the resorting to epithets . . . is a *pitiable* display of intellectual impotence – M. R. Cohen> **Sorry,** often interchangeable with *pitiable,* can distinctively imply contemptible or ridiculous inadequacy, wretchedness, or sordidness <a lean, *sorry,* jackass of a horse – Laurence Sterne> <the galvanized tub was a *sorry* excuse for a modern bath> **Scurvy** adds to *despicable* an implication of arousing disgust <a *scurvy* trick to play on a friend> **Cheap** may imply contemptibility resulting from undue familiarity or accessibility <had I so lavish of my presence been . . . so stale and *cheap* to vulgar company – Shak.> but more often it, together with **beggarly,** implies contemptible pettiness, meanness, or paltriness <every *cheap* critic . . . earned a few headlines by abusing the concept of government-sponsored art – J. A. Michener> <the poorest and most *beggarly* things . . . in the whole range of criticism – George Saintsbury> ***ant*** admirable, estimable, formidable
content *adj* – see under SATISFY 1
content *vb* – see SATISFY 1
contented – see under SATISFY 1

contention – see DISCORD
contentious – see BELLIGERENT ***ant*** peaceable
conterminous – see ADJACENT
contiguous – see ADJACENT
continence – see TEMPERANCE ***ant*** incontinence
continent – see SOBER ***ant*** incontinent
contingency –see JUNCTURE
contingent – see ACCIDENTAL

continual, continuous, constant, incessant, perpetual, perennial *shared meaning* : characterized by continued occurrence or recurrence. **Continual** can distinctively imply a close or unceasing succession or recurrence; **continuous,** an uninterrupted continuity or union (as of objects, events, or parts) <there were *continual* quarrels – W. B. Yeats> <their life together was one *continuous* quarrel> <there was a *continual* chorus of the creaking timbers and bulkheads – Jack London> <history . . . is *continuous* and each period must be related to its past as well as to its future – Stella Brook> Sometimes *continual* stresses the idea of going on indefinitely (though not without interruption) and *continuous* that of unbroken connection; thus, *continual* work is available day after day; one finishes a job by *continuous* work when one begins it and carries it to a conclusion without interruption. **Constant** implies uniform or persistent occurrence or recurrence <the relative goodness that accrues from *constant* and compatible association – H. C. Hervey> <such a career meant *constant* toil – John Buchan> **Incessant** implies ceaseless or uninterrupted activity and is likely to describe something felt as undesirable or distasteful <to struggle in a world of savage violence and *incessant* din – Thomas Wolfe> <the dread consequences of a regime's calculated and *incessant* propaganda – W. L. Shirer> **Perpetual** implies unfailing repetition or lasting duration <suffered from *perpetual* colds> <weary . . . of *perpetual* state business and *perpetual* honors; he wanted a rest – Robert Graves> **Perennial** implies enduring existence often through constant renewal <the *perennial* fight he led for tax reform – Charles Mandel> ***ant*** intermittent

continuance – see CONTINUATION

continuation, continuance, continuity *shared meaning* : a persisting in being or continuing or an instance revealing such persistence. **Continuation** suggests prolongation or resumption <the *continuation* of a street> <the *continuation* of the meeting was postponed> **Continuance** implies duration, perseverance, or persistent lingering <eleven years' *continuance* – Shak.> <patient *continuance* in well doing – *Rom* 2:7 (AV)> **Continuity** stresses uninterrupted or unbroken connection, sequence, or extent <a company benefits from *continuity* of management> <the life of ancient Rome, its unbroken *continuity* through the centuries – H. N. Fowler>

continue, last, endure, abide, persist *shared meaning* : to exist over a period of time or indefinitely. **Continue** applies to a process going on without ending <what a man is as an end perishes when he dies; what he produces as a means *continues* to the end of time – Bertrand Russell> **Last** may stress existing beyond what is expected or normal, especially when unqualified <a *lasting* odor> <a cleaner that *lasts* and *lasts*> but it readily loses this distinctive implication <the tire *lasted* only three months> **Endure** adds to *last* the implication of resistance to destructive forces or agents <it is conceivable that the only book to *endure* might be a well-thumbed copy of the Army's survival manual – M. J. Adler> **Abide** implies stable and constant existing, especially as opposed to mutability <though much is taken, much *abides* – Alfred Tennyson> <an artistic product of deep and *abiding* beauty – Alan Rich> **Persist** suggests outlasting the normal or appointed time <some fruits *persist* on the trees all winter> Often it connotes obstinacy or doggedness <the extinction that overtook all those forms that *persisted* too long in the direction of their old lines – G. G. Simpson>

continuity – see CONTINUATION

continuous – see CONTINUAL ***ant*** interrupted

contort – see DEFORM

contour – see OUTLINE

contract **1** see INCUR

2 contract, shrink, condense, compress, constrict, deflate *shared meaning* : to decrease in bulk or volume. **Contract** applies to any drawing together of bounding surfaces or component particles or to a reducing of area, compass, or length <his irises *contracted* to accommodate the light – H. C. Hervey> <molten metal *contracts* as it cools> **Shrink** implies a contracting or loss of material and stresses a falling short of original dimensions <wool *shrinks* badly when washed in too hot water> <problems don't *shrink* simply as a result of being set aside – R. J. Bryant> **Condense** indicates reduction of space occupied with resulting greater compactness and often implies some significant change in form or state <*condense* a gas to a liquid> <*condense* an essay into a single paragraph> **Compress** implies the application of pressure which closes vacuities, forces out unwanted matter, or causes amorphous loose material to become compact and often of definite form <*compress* cotton into a bale> <a formidable apparatus . . . to contain and *compress* the woman's bulging figure into a neat streamlined shape – Roald Dahl> **Constrict** implies a narrowing by contraction or squeezing <an artery *constricted* by disease> and, especially in extended use, may suggest a resulting stress or distress <the . . . taboos which ruled over and *constricted* our literary taste at the turn of the century – M. D. Geismar> **Deflate** implies a contracting that results from reduction of internal pressure; thus, one *deflates* a balloon by letting the contained air escape. Especially in extended use *deflate* tends to stress the limp or empty state that results <in his lecture on temperance he *deflated* those who felt too superior to associate with a reformed drunkard – Ruth P. Randall> ***ant*** expand

contradict – see DENY ***ant*** corroborate

contradictory – see OPPOSITE

contrary **1** see OPPOSITE

2 contrary, perverse, restive, balky, froward, wayward, delinquent *shared meaning* : unwilling or unable to conform to custom or submit to authority. **Contrary** implies a temperamental unwillingness to accept dictation or advice <the most *contrary* man in the world – he never wants to do what the rest of us do> **Perverse** implies a running counter to what is right, true, correct, or normal; it often suggests constitutional wrongheadedness or cranky or even unwholesome opposition to what is generally accepted <*perverse* disputings of men of corrupt minds, and destitute of the truth – *1 Tim* 6:5 (AV)> <the *perverse* wish to flee . . . not from the laws and customs of the world but from its force and vitality – John Cheever> **Restive** implies an obstinate refusal to submit to constraint and often carries more than a suggestion of restlessness under or impatience with control <the common man . . . is increasingly *restive* under the state of "things as they are" – Thorstein Veblen> <controlled his *restive* horse with a firm hand> **Balky** implies a refusal to proceed or acquiesce and may suggest the absence of an evident or logical reason for such behavior <a *balky* mule that often refused to budge from his stall> <will appeal directly to the voters for support if Congress gets *balky* – *Look*> **Froward**, typically in historical settings, implies contrariness as a characteristic and often suggests an arrogant resistance to control <thou art *froward* by nature, enemy to peace – Shak.> *Wayward* and *delinquent* both apply to one who is so perverse as to be beyond the control of those in authority over him. Distinctively, **wayward** stresses a going of one's own way, however wanton, capricious, or depraved it may be while **delinquent** stresses failure to do what is right, proper, or normal and is more likely to imply criminal failure to conform <a *wayward* girl knowing no law but her own whim> <those moral wildernesses of civilized life which . . . [he] automatically condemns as *deliquent* or evil or immature or morbid – Norman Mailer> ***ant*** complaisant

contrast – see COMPARE

contravene – see DENY ***ant*** uphold (*law, principle*), allege (*right, claim, privilege*)

contribute – see CONDUCE

contrition – see PENITENCE

control *vb* – see CONDUCT

control *n* – see POWER 3

controvert – see DISPROVE ***ant*** assert

conundrum – see MYSTERY

convene – see SUMMON ***ant*** adjourn

convent – see CLOISTER

conventional – see CEREMONIAL ***ant*** unconventional

converse – see SPEAK

convert *vb* – see TRANSFORM

convert *n* **convert, proselyte** *shared meaning* : a person who has embraced another faith than the one to which he formerly adhered. **Convert** implies a sincere and voluntary change (as in creed, opinion, or belief); it is, therefore, the designation likely to be preferred by the church, the party, or the school of thought of which the person changing has become a new member <the first American novelist to become a . . . *convert* to naturalism – Malcolm Cowley> **Proselyte** basically denotes a convert to another religion; in more general use the term may suggest less a reverent or convicted or voluntary embracing of something than a yielding to persuasions or special inducements <ye compass sea and land to make one *proselyte* – *Mt* 23:15 (AV)> *Proselyte,* therefore, is likely to be preferred by the members of a church, party, or school of thought to designate a former member who has been converted to another faith.

convey – see CARRY, TRANSFER

conviction – see CERTAINTY, OPINION

convincing – see VALID

convoke – see SUMMON ***ant*** prorogue, dissolve

convulse – see SHAKE

convulsive – see FITFUL

cool, composed, collected, unruffled, imperturbable, nonchalant *shared meaning* : actually or apparently free from agitation or excitement. **Cool** may imply calmness, deliberateness, or dispassionateness <minds that are to our minds as ours are to the beasts in the jungle – intellects vast, *cool* and unsympathetic – Orson Welles> <suave, polished, *cool,* detached – he was the very model of what a great captain of finance . . . should be – Thomas Wolfe> **Composed** implies freedom from signs of agitation or excitement, especially as a characteristic of a sedate decorous temperament or as the result of self-discipline <she was *composed* without bravado, contrite without sanctimoniousness – Agnes Repplier> <his manner was quietly *composed,* he spoke to the point but calmly and easily> **Collected** implies a concentration of the faculties that shuts out or overcomes distractions <be *collected:* no more amazement – Shak.> <such an intellect . . . cannot be at a loss, cannot but be patient, *collected,* majestically calm – J. H. Newman> **Unruffled** implies apparent serenity and poise in the face of setbacks or in the midst of excitement <his *unruffled* confidence in the self-sufficiency of his intuition . . . is always vindicated – *Current Biog.*> **Imperturbable** implies such fixed coolness and assurance that one cannot be ruffled or discomposed even under severe provocation; more than the other terms it implies a quality of temperament rather than a response to circumstances <a very good-looking, rosy little man with . . . a soft voice and a manner of *imperturbable* urbanity – H. G. Wells> **Nonchalant** stresses an easy coolness of manner or a casualness that may suggest indifference or unconcern <drove the car with *nonchalant* disregard of the law> or sometimes no more than jaunty self-confidence <while he tried to be *nonchalant* . . . he was cursing the men he saw go by laughing with girls – Sinclair Lewis > ***ant*** ardent, agitated

copious – see PLENTIFUL ***ant*** meager

copy *n* – see REPRODUCTION ***ant*** original

copy *vb* **copy, imitate, mimic, ape, mock** *shared meaning* : to make something so that it resembles an existing thing. **Copy** implies duplicating a model as closely as the materials, one's skill, or the circumstances allow <students *copying* the paintings of the masters> <tried to *copy* her sister's easy manner> **Imitate** stresses following something as a pattern or model without precluding intentional variation <the music *imitates* a storm> and it may imply inferiority in the end product <plaster was originally painted to *imitate* marble – *Amer. Guide Series: Minn.*> **Mimic** implies a close copying especially of voice or mannerisms for sport or for lifelike simulation or representation <he attends even to their air, dress, and notions, and imitates them liberally and not servilely; he copies but does not *mimic* – Earl of Chesterfield> **Ape** implies close copying, sometimes seriously, sometimes in the spirit of mimicry <in dress and habits, *ape* the Arabs around them – G. W. Murray> Often it suggests such clumsy mimicry of what one admires as subjects one to scorn and contempt <the lower classes *aped* the rigid decorum of their "betters" with laughable results – Harrison Smith> **Mock** commonly adds to *mimic* the implication of a derisive intent; it applies particularly to the imitation of sounds or movements of another <the babbling echo *mocks* the hounds – Shak.> <thoughtless children *mocking* a cripple's halting gait> ***ant*** originate

coquet – see TRIFLE

cordial – see GRACIOUS

corner – see MONOPOLY

corporal – see BODILY

corporeal – see BODILY

correct *vb* **1 correct, rectify, emend, remedy, redress, amend, reform, revise** *shared meaning* : to make right what is wrong. **Correct** implies taking action to eliminate errors, faults, deviations, or defects <*correct* a misstatement> <*correct* a naughty child> <take magnesia to *correct* an acid stomach> **Rectify** implies the existence of something that needs straightening out and effective action to this end <*rectify* a mistake in an account> <discovered many flaws in the jurisdictions of the courts . . . and stimulated the legislature to *rectify* them – J. M. Bennett> **Emend** implies alteration by way of correction (as of a text or manuscript). **Remedy** implies removing or making harmless a cause of trouble, harm, or evil <the crime can never be *remedied,* it can only be expiated – C. D. Lewis> **Redress** implies making compensation or reparation for unfairness, injustice, or imbalance <the necessity to try to help *redress* past injustices – Dorothy G. Singer> <the wrongs

that were to be righted, the grievances to be *redressed,* the abuses to be done away with – Malcolm Muggeridge> *Amend, reform,* and *revise* imply an improving by making corrective changes. **Amend** usually suggests relatively slight changes <laws that are not repealed are *amended* and *amended* – G. B. Shaw> **Reform** implies drastic changes intended to eliminate flaws, often to the point of imparting a new form or character <*reform* an inefficient school system> <the fact is that the world does not care to be *reformed* – S. M. Crothers> **Revise** implies a detailed search for imperfections and their correction in an attempt to attain excellence or perfection <*revise* a manuscript before submitting it for publication> <the government would undertake extensive measures . . . to *revise* the penal code and tighten fiscal regulations – *Current Biog.*>
2 see PUNISH

correct *adj* **correct, accurate, exact, precise, nice, right** *shared meaning* : conforming to fact, standard, or truth. **Correct** means hardly more than freedom from fault or error, often as judged by some conventional or acknowledged standard <his answers on the test were all *correct*> <two women . . . both middle-aged, carefully coiffured and dressed, listening with small, *correct* smiles – Helen MacInnes> **Accurate** implies fidelity to fact or truth attained by the exercise of care <an *accurate* analysis of a mixture> <a reasonably *accurate* and refined use of the mother tongue – C. W. Eliot> **Exact** emphasizes strictness or rigor of conformance without either exceeding or falling short of what is meet <what is the *exact* amount of the bill?> <a power of intuition greater than that of an *exact* investigator – Havelock Ellis> **Precise** adds to *exact* an emphasis on sharpness of definition or delimitation <no one definition of economics is *precise* – P. A. Samuelson> <*precise* statements of principles – A. C. Benson> **Nice** implies great, sometimes excessive, precision and delicacy (as in doing, discriminating, or stating) <she has a *nice* hand with pastry> <the *nice* and subtle ramifications of meaning were not easily avoided by a mind intent upon accuracy – Samuel Johnson> **Right,** though often interchangeable with *correct,* tends to have a stronger positive emphasis on conformity to fact or truth rather than mere absence of error or fault <you did very well, all your answers were *right*> <the police learned the *right* name of the missing man> ***ant*** incorrect

correlate – see PARALLEL

correspond – see AGREE 3

corroborate – see CONFIRM ***ant*** contradict

corrupt *vb* – see DEBASE

corrupt *adj* – see VICIOUS

coruscate – see FLASH

cost – see PRICE

costly, expensive, dear, valuable, precious, invaluable, priceless *shared meaning* : having a high value or valuation, especially in terms of money. *Costly, expensive, dear* refer to the expenditure or sacrifice involved in obtaining something. **Costly** implies high price and may suggest justifying qualities (as rarity or excellence of workmanship or material) <I took a *costly* jewel from my neck. A heart it was, bound in with diamonds – Shak.> **Expensive,** too, implies high price but is likely to suggest that the cost is beyond the thing's worth or the buyer's means <eggs are very *expensive* just now> **Dear,** opposed to *cheap,* commonly suggests a high, even exorbitant, price or excessive cost, usually due to factors other than the thing's inherent worth <high wages of building labor bring *dearer* housing – J. A. Hobson> **Valuable** may suggest the price that a thing will bring on sale or exchange <disposing of a *valuable* store of furs – I. B. Richman> but it is as likely to suggest worth measurable in other terms (as usefulness, serviceableness, or enjoyableness) <his year on Wall Street now seems to him the most *valuable* he ever spent – *Current Biog.*> **Precious** can apply to what is costly because scarce or irreplaceable <a *precious* gem> or it can emphasize the notions of *valuable* when applied to something whose value is not computable in money <*precious* friends hid in death's dateless night – Shak.> **Invaluable** and **priceless** imply worth that cannot be estimated, but in practice their use tends to be hyperbolical and often they substitute for *precious* <a *priceless* jewel> <he gave us *invaluable* assistance> ***ant*** cheap

coterie – see SET *n*

counsel – see ADVICE, LAWYER

counselor – see LAWYER

count – see RELY

countenance – see FAVOR

counter – see ADVERSE

counteractive – see ADVERSE

counterfeit *vb* – see ASSUME

counterfeit *n* – see IMPOSTURE

counterpart – see PARALLEL

countervail – see COMPENSATE

courage, mettle, spirit, resolution, tenacity *shared meaning* : mental or moral strength to resist opposition, danger, or hardship. **Courage** implies firmness of mind and will in the face of danger or extreme difficulty <but screw your *courage* to the sticking place, and we'll not fail – Shak.> <his friends had the *courage* to talk . . . but not to act – W. L. Shirer> **Mettle** suggests an ingrained capacity for meeting strain or stress with fortitude and resilience <a situation to try the *mettle* of the most resolute man among them> **Spirit** suggests a quality of temperament that enables one to hold one's own against opposition, interference, or temptation <successive crop failures had broken the *spirit* of the farmers – Willa Cather> **Resolution** stresses firm determination to achieve one's ends <approach an unpleasant task with *resolution*> <saw that England was saved a hundred years ago by the high spirit and proud *resolution* of a real aristocracy – W. R. Inge> **Tenacity** adds to *resolution* the implications of stubborn persistence and unwillingness to acknowledge defeat <the *tenacity* of the bulldog breed> <proved himself a negotiator of great ability and *tenacity* – *Current Biog.*> ***ant*** cowardice

court – see INVITE

courteous – see CIVIL ***ant*** discourteous

covert – see SECRET ***ant*** overt

covet – see DESIRE ***ant*** renounce (*something desirable*)

covetous, greedy, acquisitive, grasping, avaricious *shared meaning* : having or showing a strong desire for possessions, especially material possessions. **Covetous** implies intense desire, often for what is rightfully another's <settlers brought fine hunting dogs . . . of which the Indians were so *covetous* that a day was set each year when settlers traded dogs – *Amer. Guide Series: Va.*> In a more derogatory use *covetous* may stress envy or a wrongful intent to acquire what is another's <dark hints that the *covetous* British were always on the verge of stealing France's colonies – S. E. Ambrose> **Greedy** stresses lack of restraint and often of discrimination in desire <a man *greedy* for power> <he loved learning; he was *greedy* of all writings and sciences – G. G. Coulton> **Acquisitive** implies both eagerness to possess and ability to acquire and keep <the prospects of marriage deepened the *acquisitive* instincts in Edward Haslatt. These were already strong, for he

was of a nature that drew to himself what he wanted, and what he had he held – Pearl Buck> **Grasping** adds to *covetous* and *greedy* a strong implication of selfishness and often suggests the use of unfair or ruthless means in satisfying one's wants <people who are hard, *grasping* ... and always ready to take advantage of their neighbors, become very rich – G. B. Shaw> **Avaricious** implies obsessive acquisitiveness, especially of hoardable wealth and often emphasizes miserly stinginess <an unremitting, *avaricious* thrift – William Wordsworth> <[they] were furtively *avaricious;* they couldn't help being stingy, since parsimony ran in their blood – Victoria Sackville-West>

cower – see FAWN
coy – see SHY ***ant*** pert
cozen – see CHEAT
cozy – see COMFORTABLE
craft – see ART
crafty – see SLY
cranky – see IRASCIBLE
crass – see STUPID ***ant*** brilliant
crave – see DESIRE ***ant*** spurn
crawl – see CREEP
craze – see FASHION
create – see INVENT
creator – see MAKER
credence – see BELIEF
credible – see PLAUSIBLE ***ant*** incredible
credit *n* – see BELIEF
credit *vb* – see ASCRIBE

creep, crawl *shared meaning* : to move along a surface in a prone or crouching posture. **Creep** is more often used of quadrupeds or of human beings who move on all fours and proceed slowly, stealthily, or silently <the cat *crept* up on the mouse> <a baby *creeps* before he walks> and **crawl** of animals with no legs or many small legs that seem to move by drawing the body along a surface or of human beings who imitate such movement <the snake *crawled* back into his hole> <shuddered as a centipede *crawled* across his leg> <the injured man tried to *crawl* to the door> In extended use both words can imply intolerable slowness <tomorrow, and tomorrow, and tomorrow, *creeps* in this petty pace from day to day – Shak.> <men are going to work, their automobiles *crawling* eastward along the highway – William Styron> and both can imply a slow advancement (as of a person) into favor or a particular, often favorable, position. In this use *creep* is likely to suggest stealthy, insinuating, or insidious methods <a foreboding *crept* into him – Bernard Malamud> <*creep* and intrude into the fold – John Milton> and *crawl* abject obsequiousness <Cranmer ... hath *crawled* into the favor of the king – Shak.>

crime – see OFFENSE 2
cringe – see FAWN
cripple – see MAIM, WEAKEN
crisis – see JUNCTURE
crisp – see FRAGILE, INCISIVE
criterion – see STANDARD

critical 1 **critical, hypercritical, faultfinding, captious, carping, censorious** *shared meaning* : exhibiting the spirit of one who looks for and points out faults and defects. **Critical** may imply objectivity and an effort to see a thing clearly so that its good points may be distinguished from its bad and so that the thing as a whole may be fairly judged or valued <paperbacks

. . . present up-to-date information which should assist in "*critical* thinking" – Martha T. Boaz> <perhaps the *critical* mind was too analytical, too pragmatic, for the creative to be bold enough to assert itself – Helen MacInnes> Sometimes *critical* so stresses awareness of faults as to suggest loss of objectivity and fairness of judgment <she had been half mocked and half admired in the highly *critical* society of the Bronx gutters, where her nickname had been Lady Pieface – Herman Wouk> In the latter use, **hypercritical** may be preferred to *critical* as being more explicit and unambiguous <constant *hypercritical* belittling of the efforts of others – Harold Rosen & H. E. Kiene> **Faultfinding** suggests persistent, picayune, often ill-informed criticism and may imply an exacting querulous temperament not readily to be satisfied <a nagging *faultfinding* wife> **Captious** and **carping** usually imply perverse ill-natured faultfinding <after reading a work of such amplitude it seems *captious* to protest that the motivating forces . . . are inadequately analyzed – Geoffrey Bruun> <curiosity about words can . . . rarely survive *carping* criticism or harsh correction – Miriam B. Goldstein> **Censorious** implies a disposition to be both severely critical and highly condemnatory <such is the mode of these *censorious* days, the art is lost of knowing how to praise – John Sheffield> <one who thus berated pope and clergy might be *censorious* of princes – H. O. Taylor> ***ant*** uncritical

2 see ACUTE

criticize, reprehend, blame, censure, reprobate, condemn, denounce *shared meaning* : to find fault with openly. **Criticize** usually implies an unfavorable judgment or a pointing out of faults and defects <the book . . . was *criticized* on the grounds that sources were not indicated – *Times Lit. Supp.*> **Reprehend** implies both criticism and rebuke <*reprehend* not the imperfection of others – George Washington> **Blame,** basically opposed to *praise,* may imply a mere critical dispraising <some judge of authors' names, not works, and then nor praise nor *blame* the writings, but the men – Alexander Pope> Often, however, it conveys a strong imputation of wrongdoing or guilt <you have no one to *blame* for your plight but yourself> <dimly conscious that something was wrong, he *blamed* it on his father – E. L. Acken> or it may imply ultimate responsibility with or without guilt <he *blamed* himself for the failure on the agricultural front – T. P. Whitney> **Censure** carries a stronger suggestion of authority and implies a more or less formal reprimand <these austere tyrants seized with delight upon so estimable an excuse for *censuring* a member of the set they deprecated – Victoria Sackville-West> **Reprobate** implies strong disapproval or firm refusal to sanction <that wanton eye so *reprobated* by the founder of our faith – L. P. Smith> <*reprobated* what he termed the heresies of his nephew – Washington Irving> **Condemn** implies a final decision or definitive judgment and usually suggests one that is both unfavorable and merciless <by all the standards . . . [the building] would be *condemned* as expensive, pretentious, noisy and unsafe – John Cheever> **Denounce** adds to *condemn* the notion of public declaration <in all ages, priests and monks have *denounced* the growing vices of society – Henry Adams>

crooked, devious, oblique *shared meaning* : not straight or straightforward. **Crooked** may imply the presence of material curves, bends, or twists <a *crooked* road> <trees with *crooked* branches interlaced> or it may imply departure from a right and proper course and then usually suggests cheating or fraudulence <they are a perverse and *crooked* generation – *Deut* 32:5 (AV)> <set up a *crooked* deal to force his partner out of the business> **Devious** basically implies a departure from a direct or usual course <picked a *devious* path between the ridges> <returned home by a *devious* route

to avoid the waiting bully> In application to persons or their acts or practices *devious* is likely to imply unreliability, shiftiness or trickiness, or, sometimes, obscurity <resentments . . . which lurk beneath the surface and come out only indirectly in small *devious* acts and words of hostility – Anna W. M. Wolf & Lucille Stein> <his name was on the door as an attorney, but his living was earned by other and more *devious* means – Thomas Wolfe> **Oblique** implies departure from a horizontal or vertical direction <an *oblique* line dividing a rectangle into two equal triangles> and in extended use suggests indirection or lack of straightforwardness <the charges were *oblique* . . . and the confrontation forensic rather than substantial and direct – B. L. Felknor> <constituted a direct attack on current Republican policies and an *oblique* attack on Nixon – J. A. Michener> ***ant*** straight

cross – see IRASCIBLE

crotchet – see CAPRICE

crow – see BOAST

crowd, throng, crush, mob, horde *shared meaning* : an assembled multitude, usually of persons. **Crowd** implies a massing together and, often, a loss of individuality <a *crowd* is chaotic, has no purpose of its own and is capable of anything except intelligent action and realistic thinking – Aldous Huxley> **Throng** tends to stress physical factors and is likely to imply movement and pushing and shoving rather than density and loss of identity <there were *throngs* of people at the sale> **Crush** stresses compact concentration that makes for discomfort <the Governor . . . disappeared in a *crush* of handshaking and hugging well-wishers – *New Yorker*> **Mob** may be a casual intensive for *crowd* <you never saw such a *mob* as filled the streets this noon> but distinctively and specifically it can denote a disorderly crowd and especially one bent on riotous or destructive action <[it] was but a *mob* – good enough for street fighting but of little worth as a modern army – W. L. Shirer> **Horde** can apply to a crowd or throng or to a multitude linked together (as by common interests or problems); it is likely to be chosen when a depreciatory term is sought, for it tends to carry over from other of its senses a mood that imputes an inferior, rude, or savage character to the constituent individuals <*hordes* of teen-agers claimed him as their hero – *Current Biog.*> <unpolluted . . . by their brief contact with the touristic *horde* – Arnold Bennett>

crucial – see ACUTE

crude – see RUDE ***ant*** consummate, finished

cruel – see FIERCE ***ant*** pitiful

crush – see CROWD

crusty – see BLUFF

cryptic – see OBSCURE

cuddle – see CARESS

culmination – see SUMMIT

culpable – see BLAMEWORTHY

cumbersome – see HEAVY

cumbrous – see HEAVY

cunning *adj* **1** see CLEVER
2 see SLY ***ant*** ingenuous

cunning *n* – see ART

curb – see RESTRAIN ***ant*** spur

cure, heal, remedy *shared meaning* : to rectify an unhealthy or undesirable condition. *Cure* and *heal* may apply interchangeably to both wounds and disease <pierced to the soul with slander's venomed spear, the which no balm can *cure* – Shak.> <physician, *heal* thyself – *Lk* 4:23 (AV)> More often **cure** implies restoration to health after disease, **heal**, restoration to soundness of an affected part after a wound or lesion <his indigestion was *cured* by a change of diet> <the burn on his wrist *healed* slowly> The same distinction is likely to persist in extended use, with *cure* applicable when a condition (as a state of mind or a habit of behavior) is under discussion and *heal* when a specific incident or event is involved; thus, one might reason with two estranged friends hoping to *cure* their mutual distrust and thereby *heal* the breach between them <if you can compass it, do *cure* the younger girls of running after the officers – Jane Austen> <the troubles . . . had not been forgotten, but they had been *healed* – William Power> **Remedy** implies the use of remedies to improve, alleviate, or cure an abnormal or undesirable condition, be it of the body, the mind, or society <seeking means to *remedy* the common cold> <I had nothing to say, and went on to graduate study in psychology, hoping to *remedy* that shortcoming – B. F. Skinner>

curious, inquisitive, prying *shared meaning* : interested in what is not one's personal or proper concern. **Curious,** the most general and the only neutral one of these words, basically implies an eager desire to learn or to know <*curious* onlookers were held back by the police> <children are *curious* about everything> **Inquisitive** applies to habitual and impertinent curiosity and usually suggests quizzing and peering after information about what is none of one's concern <*inquisitive* old women watching from behind drawn curtains> <they grew *inquisitive* after my name and character – *Spectator*> **Prying** adds to *inquisitive* the implication of busy meddling and officiousness <I will not bare my soul to their shallow *prying* eyes – Oscar Wilde> ***ant*** incurious, uninterested

current *adj* – see PREVAILING ***ant*** antique, antiquated, obsolete

current *n* – see TENDENCY

curse – see EXECRATE ***ant*** bless

cursory – see SUPERFICIAL ***ant*** painstaking

curt – see BLUFF ***ant*** voluble

curtail – see SHORTEN ***ant*** protract, prolong

curve, bend, turn, twist *shared meaning* : to swerve or cause to swerve from a straight line or course. **Curve** can describe any deviation that suggests an arc of a circle or an ellipse <swifts . . . swoop out from their nests in the cliffs and *curve* over the town – Geoffrey Grigson & C. H. Gibbs-Smith> <*curved* her lips into a welcoming smile> **Bend** suggests a yielding to force and implies a point of departure from the anticipated, the regular, the normal, or the straight <the road *bent* sharply around the ledge> <somewhat prone to *bend* logic to meet the demands of argument – E. S. Bates> <pressure groups attempting to *bend* the government toward their special interests> **Turn** implies a change of direction essentially by rotation and not usually as a result of force or pressure <at the foot of the hill the path *turned* to the right> In broader use it typically implies giving or taking on a new direction or character <a good many novelists and critics have . . . been tempted into *turning* farmer – *Times Lit. Supp.*> <the fears . . . that teaching machines pose a threat to teachers, mechanize education, and *turn* students into robots – *Current Biog.*> **Twist** is likely to suggest a force having a spiraling effect throughout a length or course rather than at some one point <a rough track *twisted* up the mountain> or it may suggest a greater rotation than is usually implied by *turn* <I *twisted* my head to see what was going on at the back of the room> Often, especially in extended use, *twist* connotes a wrenching out of shape or an impressed distortion <hands gnarled and *twisted* by labor> <grotesque perversions of history, in which facts were fantastically *twisted* and even the simplest of words lost all meaning – W. L. Shirer>

custom — see HABIT
customary — see USUAL *ant* occasional
cutting — see INCISIVE
cynical, misanthropic, pessimistic, misogynic *shared meaning* : deeply distrustful. **Cynical** implies a setting of oneself apart from mankind often manifested in a sneering disbelief in human sincerity and integrity but sometimes in a vicious disregard of human rights or concerns <those *cynical* men who say that a democracy cannot be honest and efficient — F. D. Roosevelt> <the *cynical* practice of designing persons who exploit the idealism of youth and the gullibility of professors — B. G. Gallagher> **Misanthropic** implies a rooted dislike and distrust of one's fellowmen and an aversion to their society <I was in the early throes of a spell of *misanthropic* hermitism . . . I had, for various reasons, renounced the world of human endeavors and delights — John Barth> **Pessimistic** suggests a distrustful and gloomy view of things in general <a *pessimistic* philosophy> <a *pessimistic* old man, living alone in gloomy doubt of himself and all the rest of the world> **Misogynic** implies a specific deep-seated and fixed distrust in and aversion to women and all their works <a *misogynic* writer who portrays all women as scheming and selfish>

dabbler — see AMATEUR
daily, diurnal, quotidian, circadian *shared meaning* : of each or every day. **Daily** is used with reference to the ordinary concerns of the day or daytime <*daily* needs> <a *daily* newspaper> Distinctively, it may refer to weekdays as contrasted with holidays and Sundays and sometimes also Saturdays and it may imply an opposition to *nightly* <the *daily* anodyne, and nightly draught — Alexander Pope> **Diurnal** is used in contrast to *nocturnal* and occurs chiefly in poetic or technical context <rolled round in earth's *diurnal* course — William Wordsworth> <*diurnal* mammals that are active by day> **Quotidian** emphasizes the quality of daily recurrence <a *quotidian* fever> and may imply a commonplace, routine, or everyday quality to what it describes <an intellectual solemnity that only grudgingly permits its innermost concerns to be tested in the realm of *quotidian* experience — Hilton Kramer> **Circadian,** a chiefly technical term of recent coinage, differs from *daily* or *quotidian* in implying only approximate equation with the twenty-four hour day <*circadian* rhythms in insect behavior>
dainty **1** see CHOICE *adj ant* gross
2 see NICE
dally — see TRIFLE
damage — see INJURE
damn — see EXECRATE
damp — see WET
dangerous, hazardous, precarious, perilous, risky *shared meaning* : bringing or involving the chance of loss or injury. **Dangerous** applies to whatever has the power to cause harm or loss unless dealt with carefully and cautiously <a *dangerous* weapon> <*dangerous* drugs must be stored out of reach of children> <a very unrealistic, and therefore very *dangerous,* system of morality — Aldous Huxley> **Hazardous** differs from *dangerous* in its stress on the influence of chance in averting or precipitating harm; thus, a *hazardous* occupation is one in which a worker is exposed to dangers (as of injury or disease) that cannot be significantly lessened by his own care or efforts <we go on as though Presidents were immortal and immune

to illness for at least eight of their most *hazardous* years – R. G. Tugwell> **Precarious** stresses uncertainty or insecurity and its emphasis is likely to be on chance rather than risk; thus, *precarious* health is uncertain health, sometimes good, sometimes bad. Indirectly it can imply danger or hazard, especially as a factor in or source of uncertainty or insecurity; thus, *precarious* footing is so insecure (as from roughness or slipperiness) that it constitutes a hazard to safety <lyre-birds . . . lay only one egg, and its hatching seems rather *precarious* – Edmund Wilson> **Perilous** carries a stronger implication of the immediacy of threatened evil than *dangerous* <thousands of ships and planes guarding the long, *perilous* sea lanes – F. D. Roosevelt> **Risky** may come close to *perilous* in suggesting the imminence of harm or loss, but it is likely to stress foreknowledge and acceptance of this fact <so *risky* was travel that the . . . legislature specifically permitted travelers to carry concealed weapons – Carl Sandburg> <make a *risky* investment in hope of high returns> ***ant*** safe, secure

dank – see WET

daredevil – see ADVENTUROUS

daring – see ADVENTUROUS

dark 1 **dark, dim, dusky, murky, gloomy** *shared meaning* : more or less destitute of light. **Dark**, the ordinary and most general word, implies such lack of illumination, material, immaterial, or spiritual, as impairs one's ability to see or discriminate <a *dark* night> <it was *dark* under the trees> <the *dark* days that followed the declaration of war> <I am concerned . . . about the violence and the *dark* disorder that so afflict our lives – E. M. Kennedy> **Dim** suggests too feeble a light for things to be clearly visible <that *dim* world of deep winter and indoor candlelight – Robert Francis> or sometimes an enfeebling of sight or insight that interferes with seeing or perception <eyes *dim* with tears> <the sharing may be meagre and the comprehension *dim*, partial, or even subconscious, but people can hardly be united by something that they do not in some way feel – R. M. Hutchins> **Dusky** suggests deep twilight and the close approach of darkness <but comes at last the dull and *dusky* eve – William Cowper> **Murky** implies a heavy obscuring darkness like that caused by fog, smoke, or dust in air or mud in water <a *murky* golf course deserted, dusty with scudding wind and rain – William Styron> <tend to stretch their trickery . . . too far and to indulge in symbolism that seems a bit *murky* – John McCarten> **Gloomy** implies a serious interference with the normal radiation of light (as by clouds or heavy shade) and in both literal and extended use connotes pervading or oppressive cheerlessness <a *gloomy*, damp, heavily wooded area of East Prussia – W. L. Shirer> ***ant*** light

2 see OBSCURE ***ant*** lucid

daunt – see DISMAY

dawdle – see DELAY 2

dead, defunct, deceased, departed, late *shared meaning* : devoid of life. **Dead** is strictly applicable to whatever has lost life <a *dead* cat> <men *dead* in battle> <cutting *dead* branches from a tree> but is freely extended to whatever has lost an attribute (as energy, activity, or radiance) suggestive of life; thus, a *dead* fire is no longer burning, a *dead* telephone is no longer transmitting <every house contains *dead* books which will never be opened again – Margaret Lane> **Defunct** stresses cessation of active existence or operation <inherited a pittance under her *defunct* aunt's will> <a *defunct* baseball team> <a methodology derived third-hand from a *defunct* philosophy – Richard Lichtman> *Deceased, departed,* and *late* apply to persons who have died recently; **deceased** occurring especially in legal use, **departed**

in religious use, and **late** with reference to a person in a specific relation or status <his *late* wife> ***ant*** alive

deadly 1 deadly, mortal, fatal, lethal *shared meaning* : causing or capable of causing death. **Deadly** applies to whatever is certain or extremely likely to cause death <a *deadly* poison> <can release fumes that are *deadly*> <a *deadly* weapon> **Mortal** distinctively applies to what has caused or is about to cause death <a *mortal* wound> **Fatal** stresses the inevitability of eventual death; though often interchangeable with *mortal*, it is likely to be preferred when considerable time intervenes between the causative event and death <though he survived for some time, his injuries were ultimately *fatal*> and it is regularly used in predictions <I will not repeat your words . . . because the consequences to you would certainly be *fatal* – Henry Adams> **Lethal** applies to something which by its very nature is bound to cause death or which exists for the purpose of destroying life <took a *lethal* dose of morphine> <a *lethal* weapon> All these terms are capable of extension in which they are less weighty and typically imply a disconcerting, disturbing, or oppressing that may cause fear, dread, or distress rather than physical or spiritual death; thus, a *deadly* shaft of irony causes complete discomfiture; *mortal* terror is the most extreme terror; a *fatal* error is one that leads to the destruction of one's plans or hopes; a *lethal* verbal attack is utterly devastating <admired as much for its perceptive social criticism as for its urbane but *lethal* wit – *Current Biog.*> **2 deadly, deathly** *shared meaning* : leading toward death. In spite of their common meaning element, these often confused words are rarely if ever interchangeable. **Deadly** can apply to something so implacable, so virulent, or so ruthless that it can readily lead to death or destruction <a *deadly* hatred> <engaged in *deadly* conflict> or it can become little more than an intensive, implying an extreme of something <the *deadly* accuracy of his predictions> and especially of something unbearably unpleasant <the *deadly* monotony of her voice> **Deathly,** on the other hand, applies to what is felt as characteristic of or suggesting the approach of death <a *deathly* pallor> <I marked each *deathly* change in him – Robert Browning>

deal – see DISTRIBUTE, TREAT

dear – see COSTLY ***ant*** cheap

deathly – see DEADLY 2 ***ant*** lifelike

debar – see EXCLUDE

debase 1 debase, vitiate, deprave, corrupt, debauch, pervert *shared meaning* : to cause to become impaired and lowered in quality or character. **Debase** implies a loss of position, worth, value, or dignity <*debase* a coinage> <legislators represent people . . . not farms or cities or economic interests. . . . To the extent that a citizen's right to vote is *debased*, he is that much less a citizen. . . . The weight of a citizen's vote cannot be made to depend on where he lives – Earl Warren> **Vitiate** implies impairment through the introduction of something (as a fault or flaw) that destroys the purity, validity, or effectiveness of a thing <inappropriate and badly chosen words *vitiate* thought – Aldous Huxley> <party jealousies *vitiated* the whole military organization – *Times Lit. Supp.*> **Deprave** implies moral deterioration by evil thoughts or influences <he had to prove his own corruption by *depraving* someone he loved – Frank O'Connor> **Corrupt** implies a loss of soundness, purity, or integrity through the action of debasing or destroying influences <lay not up for yourselves treasures upon earth, where moth and rust doth *corrupt* – *Mt* 6:19 (AV)> <he was carried away by power, which, as it inevitably must, *corrupted* him, corroding his

mind and poisoning his judgment – W. L. Shirer> **Debauch** implies a demoralizing and depraving by corrupting influences (as self-indulgence, ease, or sensual pleasures); the word may suggest a weakening rather than a loss of good qualities (as purity and integrity) and often specifically connotes profligacy <an enchanted isle, where she *debauches* them with enervating delights and renders them oblivious to their duty – R. A. Hall> <factory methods . . . *debauched* Victorian design – *Country Life*> **Pervert** implies a twisting or distorting by which something is so altered as to be completely debased <*pervert* the facts to one's own advantage> <*perverting* justice for reactionary political ends – W. L. Shirer> ***ant*** elevate (*as taste*), amend (*as morals*)
2 see ABASE

debate – see DISCUSS

debauch – see DEBASE

debilitate – see WEAKEN ***ant*** invigorate

decadence – see DETERIORATION ***ant*** rise, flourishing

decay, decompose, rot, putrefy, spoil *shared meaning* : to undergo destructive dissolution. **Decay** suggests a gradual and not necessarily a complete deterioration from a prior state of soundness or perfection <infirmity, that *decays* the wise – Shak.> <as winter fruits grow mild ere they *decay* – Alexander Pope> **Decompose** stresses the idea of breaking down by chemical change <*decompose* water into hydrogen and oxygen> and often implies a corruption <the foul odor of *decomposing* food> **Rot** implies decay and decomposition, usually of or as if of animal or vegetable matter <fallen apples *rotting* on the grass> In extended use the term differs from *decay* in stressing stagnation rather than decline <the rest of the world is changing fast, and we've got to change with it or *rot* – Wilma Dykeman> <the Aztec regime and culture collapsed and the native crafts and arts *decayed* – R. W. Murray> **Putrefy** stresses the offensive quality of what decays or rots <corpses *putrefying* on the sun-drenched battlefield> **Spoil,** a more neutral word, is frequently chosen in place of *decay, rot,* or *putrefy* when the reference is to foodstuffs <put the meat in the refrigerator to keep it from *spoiling*>

deceased – see DEAD

deceitful **1** see DECEIVING
2 see DISHONEST ***ant*** trustworthy

deceive, mislead, delude, beguile *shared meaning* : to lead astray. **Deceive** implies imposing a false belief that causes bewilderment or helplessness or furthers the agent's purpose <it fell to [him] . . . to be contradicted by events, to be disappointed in his hopes, and to be *deceived* and cheated by a wicked man – Sir Winston Churchill> <because of the whisky, which had lulled and *deceived* their minds, their talk was repetitious and touched with a synthetic exaltation – William Styron> **Mislead** stresses a leading aside from the truth, usually by deliberately deceiving <a steady diet over the years of falsifications and distortions made a certain impression on one's mind and often *misled* it – W. L. Shirer> <the persons who have first deceived themselves are most effective in *misleading* others – John Dewey> **Delude** implies such deceiving or misleading as to make one a fool or a dupe or so befuddled as to be unable to distinguish the false from the true <we must not *delude* ourselves into thinking that there was anything like complete agreement – A. H. Marckwardt> **Beguile** implies the use of subtle or alluring devices, usually to mislead, deceive, or delude <marshlights to *beguile* mankind from tangible goods and immediate fruitions – Lewis Mumford> but sometimes to solace, amuse, or charm <the seven

poems were written to *beguile* the tedium of a sea voyage – V. L. Parrington> ***ant*** undeceive, enlighten

deceiving, deceitful *shared meaning* : tending to mislead. In spite of their common element of meaning these two frequently confused words are rarely if ever interchangeable. **Deceiving** stresses the perceived effect and is applicable to whatever tends to mislead either deliberately or by chance <the *deceiving* mildness of an early spring day> <her youth was masked by the *deceiving* sophistication of her conversation> **Deceitful** stresses the intent of the agent <a *deceitful* speech that concealed her motives well> When applied to persons *deceitful* is likely to imply a habitual propensity for deceit <presents the supple mediaeval devil in all his *deceitful* metamorphoses – H. O. Taylor> <she was a *deceitful*, scheming little thing – Israel Zangwill>

decency – see DECORUM

decent – see CHASTE ***ant*** indecent, obscene

deception, fraud, double-dealing, trickery, subterfuge *shared meaning* : deceitful practice or means designed or used to accomplish one's ends. **Deception** is a general term applicable to any sort of deceiving, for whatever purpose and by whatever means <a stage magician who was an adept at *deception*> <resorting to lies and *deception* to evade responsibilities> **Fraud** ordinarily implies culpable or even criminal deception and is especially applicable to misrepresentation or perversion of truth used to defraud another <a society, which encouraged savings and investment and solemnly promised a safe return from them and then defaulted? Was this not a *fraud* upon the people? – W. L. Shirer> **Double-dealing** implies duplicity and typically suggests an act or activities fundamentally at odds with one's professed attitude <they often say one thing and mean another, so that we may fairly accuse them of *double-dealing* – Muriel M. Jernigan> **Trickery** implies an attempt to dupe or befool or mislead; in its most typical uses it is likely to imply also sharp practice or dishonest intent <they held that the basest *trickery* or deceit was not dishonorable if directed against a foe – *Amer. Guide Series: R.I.*> but not infrequently it implies little more than skillful use of tricks to produce a desired effect <what seem to be chance artistic effects are usually the result of skilled *trickery* on the part of a conscious artist – J. A. Michener> **Subterfuge** implies deception by artifice and stratagem that is usually intended evasively (as in escaping responsibility or avoiding duty) <used her health as a *subterfuge* for neglecting the children> Often it implies substitution (as of a false explanation for the true one) <fired for editorial reasons that were a *subterfuge* for political ones – *Current Biog.*> <to wrap up the . . . unmentionable in a Latinized blanket has been an English *subterfuge* for a long time – Susie I. Tucker>

decide, determine, settle, rule, resolve *shared meaning* : to come or cause to come to a conclusion. **Decide** presupposes previous consideration and implies a cutting off of debate, doubt, or wavering <the time for deliberation has then passed. He has *decided* – John Marshall> <next, we have a conference to study this information and *decide* the best way to tackle the problem – Mary K. Dunlap> **Determine** adds the implication of setting limits or bounds and, therefore, of fixing something definitely or unalterably or inevitably; thus, one *decides* to give a party but *determines* the guests to be invited <she breaks away from the milieu of her youth where the size of the engagement ring *determines* the caliber of the bridegroom – M. D. Geismar> <unscheduled documentaries *determined* by news events and broadcast while the events are fresh – *Current Biog.*> **Settle** stresses finality and a bringing to an end of all doubt, wavering, or dispute <everything's *settled* now, you need not worry . . . ; there will be no fuss – Stella D. Gibbons> **Rule** implies a conclusion backed by authority (as of a court) <the judge *ruled* that the evidence was inadmissible> **Resolve** implies an expressed or clear decision to do or refrain from doing something <*resolved* to get to bed earlier>

decisive – see CONCLUSIVE ***ant*** indecisive

deck – see ADORN

declare 1 declare, announce, publish, advertise, proclaim, promulgate *shared meaning* : to make known publicly. To **declare** is to make known publicly, explicitly, and usually in a formal manner <*declared* his intention to refuse the nomination> <[they] take the position that there is no difference between right and wrong . . . except as the community *declares* itself upon them through law and custom – R. M. Hutchins> To **announce** is to declare, especially for the first time, something presumed to be of interest or intended to satisfy curiosity <*announce* the discovery of a new chemical element> <*announced* his intention to run for the senate seat> To **publish** is to make public especially through the medium of print <*publish* a report on an expedition> <the plan of action has not been *published* in detail – D. S. Campbell> To **advertise** is to call to public attention by repeated or widely circulated statements <deliberately *advertising* his willingness to make concessions – *Time*> Often the term connotes extravagance and lack of restraint <the Allies *advertised* these episodes to fill in a picture of German ruthlessness – F. L. Paxson> <his concept . . . does not make poetry sound as though it were on the defensive, . . . blatantly *advertising* itself as something other than poetry – Pier-Maria Pasinetti> To **proclaim** basically is to announce orally, loudly, and publicly <in his acceptance speech . . . [he] *proclaimed* a middle-of-the-road policy – *Current Biog.*> The term is often extended to any giving of wide publicity, especially when insistent, proud, bold, or defiant <the president *proclaimed* a day of mourning> To **promulgate** is to proclaim something with binding force (as a law or dogma) or something for which adherents are sought (as a theory or doctrine) <the edict was *promulgated* in all parts of the city> <men seeking to *promulgate* false prophesies>

2 see ASSERT

decline *vb* **decline, refuse, reject, repudiate, spurn** *shared meaning* : to turn away by not accepting, receiving, or considering. **Decline** implies courteous refusal, especially of invitations or offers <*decline* an invitation to dinner> <*decline* to answer personal questions> **Refuse** is more positive, implying decisiveness even to the point of ungraciousness <*refuse* to discuss a matter further> <he objected to the resolutions and *refused* his signature – *Australian Dict. of Biog.*> **Reject** implies a peremptory refusal by or as if by sending away or discarding <common sense, *rejecting* with scorn all that can be called mysticism – W. R. Inge> **Repudiate** implies a disowning or casting off as untrue, unauthorized, or unworthy of acceptance <nations that *repudiated* their debts> <permitting the husband to *repudiate* his wife at his own whim – Reuben Levy> **Spurn** carries an even stronger implication of disdain or contempt in rejecting than *repudiate* <universities in growing numbers are *spurning* government contracts that call for secret research – Elliot Carlson> <must *spurn* all ease, all hindering love, all which could hold or bind – Amy Lowell> ***ant*** accept

decline *n* – see DETERIORATION

decompose – see DECAY

decorate – see ADORN

decorum, decency, propriety, dignity, etiquette *shared meaning* : a code of rules respecting behavior or behavior that accords with such a code. Both *decorum* and *decency* imply existence of a code in accord with nature or reason; more specifically **decorum** suggests a code of rigid rules governing the behavior of civilized beings or behavior in accord with or as if in accord with such a code, while **decency** implies behavior according with normal self-respect or humane feeling for others or with what is fitting to a particular condition or station of life <a world where the *decorums* of trivial high society are infinitely more important than larger issues – Henry Hewes> <that opposition to the war which is strictly legal, which indeed has a very large measure of *decorum* – J. K. Galbraith> <conditions in which individual freedom and the social *decencies* of the democratic way of life will become impossible – Aldous Huxley> <some obscure sense of *decency* which prescribes that one doesn't reproach one's wife in this manner – William Styron> **Propriety** suggests an artificial standard of what is correct in conduct or speech <my whole life has been at variance with *propriety* – Lord Byron> and may be preferred to *decency* when merely seemly or fitting correctness is implied <*propriety* and necessity of preventing interference with the course of justice – O. W. Holmes †1935> **Dignity** implies a reserve or restraint in conduct prompted less by obedience to a code than by a sense of personal integrity or status <learning that art and music are not effete subjects beneath the intellectual *dignity* of a prospective engineer – *NEA Jour.*> <the Lewis County people . . . had a *dignity* and a self-assurance that many Americans lacked – Edmund Wilson> **Etiquette** is the usual term for the detailed rules governing manners and conduct in society and for the observance of these rules <always read the column on *etiquette* in her morning paper> ***ant*** indecorum, license

decoy – see LURE

decrease, lessen, diminish, reduce, abate, dwindle *shared meaning* : to grow or make less. **Decrease** suggests a progressive decline (as in size, amount, numbers, or intensity) <the water *decreases* in depth as you come toward shore> **Lessen** is close to *decrease* but is not ordinarily used with specific numbers; thus it is idiomatic to say that a fever has *lessened* or that it has *decreased* from 101° to 99°. **Diminish** emphasizes a perceptible loss and implies its subtraction from a total <an old port whose population *diminished* year by year – John Cheever> **Reduce** adds to *diminish* the implication of bringing down or lowering and typically suggests the operation of a personal agent <*reduce* production time by careful planning and scheduling> and is the most applicable of these words to lowering in rank, status, or condition <she was able to *reduce* male members of her audience to moonstruck lovers – Alton Cook> **Abate** presupposes something excessive (as in force, intensity, or amount) and it strongly implies a reducing that constitutes moderation of or relief from what oppresses <*abate* a tax> <no city is equipped with adequate authority to *abate* such noxious wastes from the atmosphere we breathe – T. O. Thackrey> **Dwindle** implies progressive lessening but unlike decrease is usually applied to things capable of growing evidently smaller or disappearing <interest in the program *dwindled* and meetings were rarely held and scarcely attended at all> <trade had *dwindled* to a mere trickle – W. L. Shirer> ***ant*** increase

decry, depreciate, disparage, belittle, minimize *shared meaning* : to give expression to one's low opinion of something. **Decry** implies open condemnation with intent to discredit <they respected each other, exchanged culinary memoirs, *decried* the eating habits of Americans – Ludwig Bemelmans> **Depreciate** implies a representation of something as of less value than that usually ascribed to it <true politeness in China demands that you should *depreciate* everything of your own and exalt everything belonging

to your correspondent – Frederic Hamilton> **Disparage** implies depreciation by indirect means such as slighting or invidious comparison <the critic . . . is generally *disparaged* as an artist who has failed – L P. Smith> *Belittle* and *minimize* both imply depreciation, but **belittle** suggests an effort to make a thing seem contemptibly small, and **minimize** to reduce it to a minimum or to make it seem either disparagingly or defensively as small as possible <*belittle* a suggestion> <*minimize* the risk in an investment> <the navy . . . was inclined to *minimize* its own losses – C. L. Jones> *ant* extol

dedicate – see DEVOTE

deduce – see INFER

deed *n* – see ACTION

deed *vb* – see TRANSFER

deep 1 **deep, profound, abysmal** *shared meaning* : having great extension downward or inward. In literal material applications *deep* and *profound* can imply extension downward from a surface or, less often, backward or inward from a front or outer part; in such use **deep** is the more general term, stressing the fact rather than the degree of such extension while **profound** connotes exceedingly great depth <a *deep* river> <*deep* wounds> <a gulf *profound* as that Serbonian bog . . . where armies whole have sunk – John Milton> In extended applications the terms diverge; *deep,* especially when used of persons or mental states or processes, tending to imply the presence or a need for the exercise of penetration or subtlety, sometimes of craft <felt *deep* concern for his brother's safety> <a *deep* and devious plot> <a little knowledge often estranges men from religion, a *deeper* knowledge brings them back to it – W. R. Inge> while *profound* may imply the need or presence of thoroughness; thus, a *deep* thinker probes into the ramifications and possibilities of a problem or situation; a *profound* thinker analyzes a problem in all its aspects until he has a comprehensive grasp of all the elements involved. **Abysmal** in both primary and extended use carries the idea of *abyss* and implies fathomless distance downward, backward, or inward <beyond the village the green of manioc fields lengthened into *abysmal* forests – H. C. Hervey> or often of measureless degree, especially with words denoting a lack of something <*abysmal* ignorance> <he had known the *abysmal* depletions that follow intellectual excess – Edmund Wilson>
2 see BROAD *ant* shallow

deep-rooted – see INVETERATE

deep-seated – see INVETERATE

deface, disfigure *shared meaning* : to mar the appearance of. **Deface,** usually applied to inanimate things, implies superficial injuries that impair the surface appearance <*deface* a building with scrawled indecencies> <it was a beautiful river, broad and blue and serene, with no cities *defacing* its shore – William Styron> **Disfigure,** as applied to a surface, implies deeper or more permanent injury than *deface* and is likely to be chosen when permanent impairment of the attractiveness or beauty of a person is in question; thus, one speaks of a face *disfigured* (not *defaced*) by smallpox; a *disfiguring* (not *defacing*) birthmark. In extended use, too, *disfigure* is likely to suggest a more serious, more enduring injury than *deface* <the baneful substitution of libido for love that has *disfigured* all the printed matter . . . and which has also largely *disfigured* life itself – *Saturday Rev.*> <Americans have a liking for the iconoclast, praise him, and with copious cash reward him. But when . . . he has passed by, they put back upon pedestals the images which he has *defaced* – W. L. Sullivan>

defame – see MALIGN

defeat — see CONQUER
defect — see BLEMISH
defend 1 defend, protect, shield, guard, safeguard *shared meaning* : to keep secure (as from danger or against attack). **Defend** implies warding off what immediately threatens or repelling what actually attacks <*defend* one's home against an intruder> <the independence of the Supreme Court of the United States should be *defended* at all costs – Walter Lippmann> **Protect** is likely to imply a securing by or as if by a covering <*protected* against cold by his heavy coat> <*protect* oneself against loss by insurance> <the ring of old forts which so far had *protected* the city successfully – P. W. Thompson> **Shield** suggests the intervention of a cover or barrier against imminent and specific danger <Heavens *shield* Lysander, if they mean a fray! – Shak.> <*shield* one's eyes against glaring light> **Guard** implies a standing watch over something to protect or secure it and usually connotes vigilance <*guard* a factory against saboteurs> <a room *guarded* by locked doors> <hazards that, if not *guarded* against over the years, can turn a teacher into a narrow-minded, humorless Milquetoast – Joseph Crescimbeni & R. J. Mammarella> **Safeguard** more strongly than any of the preceding words implies the use of protective measures where merely potential danger exists <the need to *safeguard* our cities from attack> <he was more than worldly-wise. He was *safeguarding* his own self-respect – Agnes Repplier>
ant combat, attack
2 see MAINTAIN
defer *vb* **1 defer, postpone, intermit, suspend, stay** *shared meaning* : to delay an action or proceeding. **Defer** suggests little more than a usually intentional putting off to a later date <*defer* payment on a note> <*defer* a decision until the facts are clear> Sometimes it implies a delay (as in fulfillment, attainment, or fruition) that is beyond one's control <hope *deferred* maketh the heart sick – *Prov* 13:12 (AV)> **Postpone** implies an intentional deferring, commonly to a definite time <the club meeting was *postponed* for a week because of the storm> **Intermit** implies a stopping for a time, often as a measure of relief and typically with the expectation of resumption after an interval <a fever that *intermitted* with great regularity> <pray to the gods to *intermit* the plague – Shak.> **Suspend** implies a stopping for a time usually for an evident reason and typically until some condition expressed or implied is met <bus service was *suspended* during the flood> <shall I *suspend* final decision until I have further evidence? – M. R. Cohen> **Stay** implies the interposition of an obstacle to something in progress; it may suggest a complete stopping but is as likely to suggest a delaying, slowing, or postponing <*stay* an execution> <when his mind fails to *stay* the pace set by its inventions, madness must ensue – C. D. Lewis>
2 see YIELD
deference — see HONOR ***ant*** disrespect
defile — see CONTAMINATE ***ant*** cleanse, purify
define — see PRESCRIBE
definite — see EXPLICIT ***ant*** indefinite, equivocal
definitive — see CONCLUSIVE ***ant*** tentative, provisional
deflate — see CONTRACT ***ant*** inflate
deform, distort, contort, warp *shared meaning* : to mar or spoil by or as if by twisting. **Deform** is the least specific of these terms, but it may suggest the loss of some particular excellence or essential <soul-killing witches that *deform* the body – Shak.> <[he] does not *deform* history to make a novelistic or moralistic point – *New Yorker*> **Distort** implies a twisting or wrenching out of the natural, regular, or true shape or form or direction and is

applicable not only to material things but to others (as minds, facts, or statements) that can be so twisted or wrenched <a face *distorted* with hate> <a simple and common way to *distort* the truth about any age is to discuss it primarily in terms of the age which succeeded it – *Times Lit. Supp.*> **Contort** differs from *distort* in suggesting such extreme distortion as to be grotesque or painful rather than a mere departure from the normal or natural <that most perverse of scowls *contorting* her brow – Nathaniel Hawthorne> <a generation of fearless children, not *contorted* into unnatural shapes, but straight and candid, generous, affectionate, and free – Bertrand Russell> **Warp** in physical application implies an uneven shrinking that draws and twists parts out of a flat plane <*warped* boards curling at the edges> and in extended use implies a force acting comparably so as to give something a bias, a wrong slant, or an abnormal direction or significance <all that had gone on in his *warped* but fertile brain – W. L. Shirer> <[feeling that] she was *warped* by a ludicrous out-of-date upbringing – Herman Wouk>

defraud – see CHEAT

deft – see DEXTEROUS ***ant*** awkward

defunct – see DEAD ***ant*** alive, live

degenerate – see VICIOUS

degeneration – see DETERIORATION

degrade – see ABASE ***ant*** uplift

deign – see STOOP

deist – see ATHEIST

delay 1 **delay, retard, slow, slacken, detain** *shared meaning* : to cause to be late or behind in movement or progress. **Delay** implies a holding back, usually by interference, from completion or arrival <heavy traffic *delayed* us on the return trip> <a plague upon that villain Somerset, that thus *delays* my promised supply – Shak.> **Retard** implies a slowing (as in moving or advancing) often by interference <the snow *retarded* our progress> <wives, who were trying at thirty-five to *retard* a faint dowdiness of flesh – William Styron> *Slow* (often followed by *up* or *down*) and *slacken* also imply a reduction in speed or rate of progress; thus, one may say that business is *slowing* down (or *slackening*); demand for new cars has *slackened* (or *slowed*) in recent months; but **slow** usually also implies deliberation or intention <he *slowed* his car as he approached the intersection> and **slacken**, an easing or letting up or relaxation (as of effort or determination) <he raised his foot from the pedal and the car *slackened* speed> <their rate of growth *slackens* as they age – L. P. Schultz> **Detain** implies a being held back past an appointed time, often with resulting delay (as in arrival or accomplishment) <*detain* a disobedient child after school> <he was *detained* by last minute details until he missed his plane> ***ant*** expedite, hasten

2 delay, procrastinate, lag, loiter, dawdle *shared meaning* : to move or act so slowly as to fall behind. **Delay** usually implies a putting off (as of a departure or beginning) <his mind was still *delaying* as to whether or no he would stop at the gate – Sylvia T. Warner> <genuine success seemed as usual to *delay* and postpone itself – Arnold Bennett> **Procrastinate** implies such a blameworthy delaying or indecision as results from indifference, laziness, or hesitation <to fumble, to vacillate, to *procrastinate* and so let war come creeping upon us almost unawares – W. A. White> **Lag** implies failure to maintain a speed or rate set by others <though several economic indicators were *lagging*, inflation continued unabated> <the rural children clearly *lagged* . . . when compared with the privileged urban children – N. S. Scrimshaw> *Loiter* and *dawdle* both imply delay in progress especially when walking, but **loiter** is more likely to suggest lingering or aimless sauntering or lagging behind <after breakfasting he walked down the hill and *loitered* about the little streets – Willa Cather> and it, alone, may imply a deliberate lingering with evil intent <suspicious persons who *loiter* in school buildings and on the surrounding grounds – J. E. Hoover> **Dawdle** carries a slighter implication of delay than *loiter* but a stronger connotation of idleness, aimlessness, or a wandering mind <children *dawdling* over their breakfast> <I did not hurry the rest of the way home; but neither did I *dawdle* – V. G. Heiser> ***ant*** hasten, hurry

delectation – see PLEASURE

delete – see ERASE

deleterious – see PERNICIOUS ***ant*** salutary

deliberate *adj* – see VOLUNTARY ***ant*** impulsive

deliberate *vb* – see THINK 2

delicate – see CHOICE *adj* ***ant*** gross

delight – see PLEASURE ***ant*** disappointment, discontent

delinquent – see CONTRARY

delirium – see MANIA

deliver – see RESCUE

delude – see DECEIVE ***ant*** enlighten

delusion, illusion, hallucination, mirage *shared meaning* : something accepted as true or real that is actually false or unreal. **Delusion** implies self-deception concerning facts or situations and typically suggests a disordered state of mind <*delusions* are false inferences usually based on reasonably accurate perception – J. L. Singer> <he misinterpreted all he heard and suffered from a *delusion* that his family hated him> **Illusion** implies an ascription of truth or reality to something that seems to normal perception to be true or real but in fact is not <the very men who had created this world in which every value was false ... saw themselves, not as creatures tranced by fatal *illusions,* but rather as the most knowing, practical, and hard-headed men alive – Thomas Wolfe> <*illusions* are rooted in individual human consciousness – R. J. Linnig> **Hallucination** basically implies the perception of usually visual impressions that have no reality but are the product of disordered function <[he] had a frightening *hallucination,* which persisted for some weeks after his last dose of peyote – *Trans-action*> but sometimes it differs little from *delusion* <that popular *hallucination,* from which not even great scientists are ... free – Lewis Mumford> **Mirage** is comparable with the foregoing words only in an extended sense in which it applies to a vision, dream, hope, or aim that one takes as a guide, not realizing that it is but illusory <this hope to find your people ... is a *mirage,* a delusion, which will lead to destruction if you will not abandon it – W. H. Hudson †1922>

demand, claim, require, exact *shared meaning* : to ask or call for something as or as if one's right or due. **Demand** implies peremptoriness and insistence and the claiming of a right to make requests that are to be regarded as commands <he no longer *demanded* such recognition. Instead he prayed for it – Sherwood Anderson> <students *demanding* a share in academic control> **Claim** implies a demand for the delivery or concession of something due as one's own or one's right; thus, one who *claims* a piece of property *demands* its delivery to him as his own; one who *claims* to have made a discovery *demands* recognition of the truth of his assertion <there is no right to freedom or life. But each man does *claim* such freedom – Samuel Alexander> **Require,** often interchangeable with *demand,* may distinctively imply an imperativeness arising from inner necessity and may seem less strident but more coolly insistent and exigent <his measure ... to *require*

all Congressmen to make public their spending on junkets overseas was buried in committee – *Current Biog.*> <to curtail the rising dropout rate will *require* creative and unorthodox ideas – *Johns Hopkins Mag.*> **Exact** implies not only demanding but getting what one demands <*exact* a promise from a friend> <*exact* payment of a note> <the mistake of *exacting* reparation in money and then lending Germany money with which to pay – Harry S Truman>

demean – see ABASE

demeanor – see BEARING

dementia – see INSANITY

demonstrate – see SHOW

demur – see QUALM

denotation – see under DENOTE

denote, connote *shared meaning* : to mean. In spite of their shared element of meaning these two terms are complementary rather than truly synonymous and cannot be interchanged without serious loss of precision. **Denote** (or its corresponding noun, **denotation**) applies to the definitive meaning content of a term: in a noun, the thing or the definable class of things or ideas which it names; in a verb, the act or state which is affirmed. **Connote** (or its corresponding noun, **connotation**) applies to the ideas or associations that are added to a term and cling to it, often as a result of personal experience but sometimes as a result of something extraneous (as a widely known context or connection with a widely known event). "Home", for example, *denotes* the place where one lives, but to one person it may *connote* comforts, intimacy, and privacy and to another hunger, cold, and abuse <*denotation* is fixed; *connotation* is flexible, varying widely with the background and experience of the individual> <the name . . . is said to signify the subjects *directly,* the attributes *indirectly;* it *denotes* the subjects . . . and *connotes* the attributes – J. S. Mill>

denounce – see CRITICIZE ***ant*** eulogize

dense **1** see CLOSE *adj* ***ant*** sparse (*of population, forests*), tenuous (*of clouds, air, masses*)
2 see STUPID ***ant*** subtle, bright

deny, gainsay, contradict, negative, negate, impugn, contravene *shared meaning* : to refuse to accept as true, valid, or worthy of consideration. To **deny** is to reject as untrue or invalid or to refuse to concede the existence or claims of <*deny* a request for higher wages> <it is hard to *deny* the justice of their morality – Francis Heisler> <the initiative . . . to *deny* the Polish people any independent existence of their own whatsoever, came from the Russians – W. L. Shirer> To **gainsay** is to oppose, usually by disputing the truth of what is put forward <his claim to a very important part in the movement cannot be *gainsaid* – Ian Jack> To **contradict** is to openly or flatly deny the truth of an assertion and usually to imply that the reverse is true <*contradict* a rumor> To **negative** is to refuse to assent to something (as a proposition, a suggestion, or a nomination) <the legislature *negatived* the proposed tax increase> Sometimes the term stresses a going counter to something and then implies disproof <the omission or infrequency of such recitals does not *negative* the existence of miracles – William Paley> To **negate** is to deny the existence, truth, or fact of something <*negated* and denied her own honest reactions – Sara H. Hay> To **impugn** is to attack not only the truth of a statement but the integrity of the person making it; the term may imply direct, often insulting questioning, disputing, or contradicting <his accuracy had often been *impugned,* his authority challenged – Osbert Sitwell> To **contravene** is to come into conflict less by intentional opposition than as a result of some inherent incompatibility

<ashamed to oppose the censor's morality, and afraid to *contravene* his authority, the writer's first reaction is to evade the censorship – Gershon Legman> <steps toward the mitigation of racial segregation and discrimination are often forestalled, since . . . these *contravene* the dicta of Southern customs and tradition – R. E. Jackson> *ant* confirm, concede

depart 1 see GO *ant* arrive, remain, abide
2 see SWERVE

departed – see DEAD

depend – see RELY

deplete, drain, exhaust, impoverish, bankrupt *shared meaning* : to deprive of something essential to existence or potency. **Deplete** implies a reduction in numbers, in quantity, or in mass or volume; in addition it regularly suggests the actual or potential harm done by such reduction; thus, crops *deplete* the soil when they draw excessive nutrients and leave its fertility impaired <California gold-seekers, their own fields *depleting,* headed for the new bonanza – Morton Cathro> **Drain** implies a depleting by or as if by the gradual withdrawal of fluid that can result in the deprivation of what is essential to existence and functioning <a burden of arms *draining* the wealth and labor of all peoples – D. D. Eisenhower> **Exhaust** differs from *drain* in implying a complete emptying or using up rather than a gradual depletion <*exhaust* all procedures for dealing with a problem> <the woodpile was nearly *exhausted* by winter's end> <the old ideas had been *exhausted* and the time was ripe for new ideologies – R. W. Murray> **Impoverish** implies a depletion or draining of something essential and stresses deprivation of what is essential to well-being or efficiency <children allowed to *impoverish* their minds with trashy reading> <a brilliant sun scorched the *impoverished* trees and sucked energy from the frail breezes – J. T. Farrell> **Bankrupt** suggests impoverishment to the point of imminent collapse <dainty bits make rich the ribs, but *bankrupt* quite the wits – Shak.>

deplore, lament, bewail, bemoan *shared meaning* : to manifest grief or sorrow for something. All carry a now usually figurative implication of weeping and sobbing. **Deplore** implies a judgment, often a moral judgment, with keen regretful objection to, sorrowful condemnation of, or grieving regret for what is in question <I sympathize with their problems but I deeply *deplore* the way they have tried to solve them> <they *deplore* the divorce between the language as spoken and the language as written – T. S. Eliot> **Lament** implies a strong and demonstrative expression of sorrow or mourning <yet I *lament* what long has ceased to be – P. B. Shelley> <jails where the members were given ample time to *lament* their errors – R. A. Billington> *Bewail* and *bemoan* imply sorrow or distress finding outlet in words or cries, **bewail** commonly suggesting the louder, **bemoan,** the more lugubrious expression of grief <and all wept, and *bewailed* her – *Lk* 8:52 (AV)> <the silver swans her hapless fate *bemoan,* in notes more sad than when they sing their own – Alexander Pope> but both words can lose much of their intensity and then suggest little more than querulous or mournful expressing of complaints and grievances <the Academy might have put the sculpture on view . . . instead of hiding it away upstairs like an invalid and then *bewailing* that nobody came to see it – Mollie Panter-Downes> <the governmental control which industrialists *bemoan* so consistently – Douglas McGregor>

deport – see BANISH, BEHAVE

deportment – see BEARING

deprave – see DEBASE

deprecate – see DISAPPROVE *ant* endorse

depreciate – see DECRY ***ant*** appreciate

depress, oppress *shared meaning* : to press or weigh down heavily. **Depress** implies a failure to withstand or bear up under a weight and stresses the resulting state (as of lowered activity or of dullness or dejection) <invariably, he is *depressed* in the morning, and it is no different today. He finds himself in the flat and familiar dispirit of nearly all days – Norman Mailer> <a market *depressed* by uncertainties> **Oppress** stresses the fact of a weight or burden bearing down but, unlike *depress,* does not directly imply either failure or success in withstanding <the strong glare from the glacier, which can *oppress* one even in the fog – Jeremy Bernstein> <the unhappiness of the household soon begins to *oppress* David – *New Yorker*> ***ant*** elate, cheer

deride – see RIDICULE

derive – see SPRING

description – see TYPE

desecration – see PROFANATION

desert – see ABANDON ***ant*** stick to, cleave to

design **1** see INTENTION ***ant*** accident
2 see PLAN

desire, wish, want, crave, covet *shared meaning* : to have a longing for something. *Desire, wish,* and *want* are often interchangeable especially in situations in which the degree of intensity of need or longing is not at issue <help *wanted*> <we can order any model you *wish;* simply tell us which one you *desire*> **Desire** is often felt as more formal and dignified, or even a little pompous <cleaning lady *desires* situation> It is, however, the strongest of the three words when one wishes to emphasize ardor of feeling and it may imply strong intention or fixed aim <more than any other thing on earth he *desired* to fight for his country – W. A. White> **Wish** is less strong and often connotes a vague or transient longing for the unattainable <*wishing* he could return to his childhood innocence> **Want,** interchangeable with *wish* in less formal contexts, may distinctively imply a longing for something which would fill a real need and which is actively hoped for <I have tried . . . to learn first what my partners *want* out of life – R. F. Lewis><a gentle , almost shy host who seems to *want* everyone to have a good time – Bert Burns> **Crave** suggests strongly the force of physical appetite or emotional need <*crave* peace and security after war> <what he *craved* was books of poetry and chivalry – E. A. Weeks> **Covet** implies an envious longing or strong eager desire, typically for what belongs to another <decadent civilizations that have elevated pain to an aesthetic and might *covet* humans as gladiators or torture objects – Stanley Kubrick> <we hate no people, and *covet* no people's land – Wendell Willkie>

desist – see STOP ***ant*** persist

desolate – see ALONE

despairing – see DESPONDENT ***ant*** hopeful

desperate – see DESPONDENT

despicable – see CONTEMPTIBLE ***ant*** praiseworthy, laudable

despise, contemn, scorn, disdain, scout *shared meaning* : to regard as beneath one's notice or unworthy of attention or interest. **Despise** implies an emotional reaction ranging from marked disfavor to utter loathing; distinctively it stresses a looking down upon a thing and evaluating it as mean, petty, weak, or worthless <the money he has was earned by his dead father whose memory he is inclined to *despise* – Roald Dahl> <bird and beast *despised* my snares, which took me so many waking hours at night to invent – W. H. Hudson †1922> **Contemn** implies a harsher but more intellectual or impersonal judgment <his own early drawings of moss roses and picturesque castles – things that he now mercilessly *contemned* – Arnold Bennett> **Scorn** implies quick, indignant, and profound contempt <*scorn* improper advances> <she envied, instead of *scorning*, their prodigious self-sufficiency – Victoria Sackville-West> <all his life he had *scorned* doctors and therapy, believing that medicine must be employed only in such mechanical matters as a broken limb – James Purdy> **Disdain** suggests a visible, often arrogant manifestation of aversion to what is felt as base or as beneath one <despised by those superior persons who *disdain* her as old-fashioned – M. R. Cohen> <the psychiatric patient is *disdained* and ridiculed by his fellow inmates – R. S. Banay> **Scout** stresses derision and also a refusal to consider the one in question seriously or as of any value, truth, or worth <Alice would have *scouted* . . . any suggestion that her parent was more selfish than saintly – G. B. Shaw> <we scorned presentiments and *scouted* occult influences – F. W. Crofts> *ant* appreciate

despoil – see RAVAGE

despondent, despairing, desperate, hopeless *shared meaning* : having lost all or nearly all hope. **Despondent** implies a deep dejection arising from a conviction of the uselessness of further effort <something dark and cold had settled over her thoughts. She could not shake it off though she told herself that it was unreasonable for her to feel so *despondent* – Ellen Glasgow> <he was often *despondent* about the future, could see no escape from world destruction> **Despairing** suggests the slipping away of all hope and often an accompanying despondency <the last *despairing* claim of a condemned culprit – H. T. Cockburn> <since he conceives of death as emptiness, he can, no matter how weary or *despairing*, wish for nothing but more life – Norman Mailer> **Desperate** implies such despair as prompts reckless action or convulsive struggle in the face of anticipated defeat or frustration <the bitter, *desperate* striving unto death of the oppressed race – Rose Macaulay> **Hopeless** suggests despair and the cessation of effort or resistance and often implies acceptance or resignation <while the new weapons systems grew more dreadful, the possibility of doing anything about them grew only more *hopeless* amid the insoluble dilemmas of the cold war – Walter Millis> *ant* lighthearted

destiny – see FATE

destitution – see POVERTY *ant* opulence

destruction – see RUIN *n*

desultory – see RANDOM *ant* assiduous (*study, search, or other activity*), methodical (*something designed, planned, constructed*)

detached – see INDIFFERENT *ant* interested, selfish

detail – see ITEM

detailed – see CIRCUMSTANTIAL

detain – see DELAY, KEEP 2

deterioration, degeneration, decadence, decline *shared meaning* : a falling from a higher to a lower level (as in quality, character, or vitality). **Deterioration**, the most general term, is applicable to any process or condition marked by impairment of some valuable quality (as freshness, soundness, or usefulness) <stored foods always undergo some *deterioration*> <a change in the man, a corrosion, a *deterioration* has set in – W. L. Shirer> **Degeneration** usually implies retrogression and a return to a simpler or more primitive state; as applied to persons it is likely to stress intellectual or moral retrogression <evolutionary *degeneration* is at least as likely in our future as is further progress – G. G. Simpson> <of all the dangers that confront a nation at war, this *degeneration* of national purpose . . . is the greatest – *New Republic*> **Decadence** presupposes previous attainment of maturity or excellence and implies a downturn leading toward senility or faultiness <at the turn of the century we all thought we knew what *decadence* meant – overripeness, overcivilization, a preoccupation with refined sensations . . . the essence of *decadence* is an excessive subjectivism – *Times Lit. Supp.*> <there was beauty . . . many fine things built for the contentment of hardy men – and there was *decadence* – more ships in bottles than on the water – John Cheever> **Decline,** sometimes interchangeable with *decadence,* is likely to differ from it in suggesting a more obviously downward course with greater evidence of deterioration and greater momentum and with less likelihood of arrest or recovery <the blind, mighty risings and *declines* of tides and winds and seasons – Peter Matthiessen> <along with a *decline* of average healthiness there may well go a *decline* in average intelligence – Aldous Huxley> ***ant*** improvement, amelioration

determinant – see CAUSE

determinative – see CONCLUSIVE

determine – see DECIDE, DISCOVER

detest – see HATE

detestable – see HATEFUL

detrimental – see PERNICIOUS ***ant*** beneficial

devastate – see RAVAGE

devastation – see RUIN *n*

develop – see MATURE

deviate – see SWERVE

devious – see CROOKED ***ant*** straightforward

devote, dedicate, consecrate, hallow *shared meaning* : to set apart for a particular use or end. **Devote** is likely to imply a giving up or setting apart because of compelling motives <*devoted* his evenings to study> <*devote* one's money to charity> <the student must feel he is a valuable member in an enterprise *devoted* to education and to discovery – M. S. Eisenhower> **Dedicate** implies solemn and exclusive devotion to a sacred or serious use or purpose <we Americans are *dedicated* to improvement – Louis Kronenberger> <she has *dedicated* her life to her family's comfort> **Consecrate** even more strongly than *dedicate* implies investing with a solemn or sacred character <when a church has been built and all the debt paid, it is solemnly *consecrated* to God's service by the bishop. But if any debt remains, it is *dedicated* but not *consecrated,* because we cannot give to God what does not belong to us – Pierce Middleton> In more general use, too, *consecrate* carries a strong connotation of almost religious devotion <a night of memories and of sighs I *consecrate* to thee – W. S. Landor> <rules or principles *consecrated* by time – Edmund Burke> **Hallow,** not normally used of oneself, may differ little from *dedicate* or *consecrate* <propaganda *hallowed* by the local traditions – Aldous Huxley> but, distinctively, can imply an ascription of intrinsic sanctity <in a larger sense we cannot dedicate, we cannot consecrate, we cannot *hallow* this ground. The brave men, living and dead, who struggled here, have consecrated it far above our poor power to add or detract – Abraham Lincoln> <let us hold fast the inheritance of our civil and religious liberties, which we have received from our fathers sealed and *hallowed* by their blood – W. E. Channing> <wherefore the Lord blessed the sabbath day, and *hallowed* it – *Exod* 20:11 (JPS)>

devotion – see FIDELITY

devout, pious, religious, pietistic, sanctimonious *shared meaning* : showing fervor in the practice of religion. **Devout** stresses genuine feeling and a mental or emotional attitude about religion leading to solemn reverence and fitting observance of rites and practices <a *devout* man, and one that feared God – *Acts* 10:2 (AV)> <I was often *devout*, my eyes filling with tears at the thought of God and for my sins – W. B. Yeats> **Pious** emphasizes faithful and dutiful performance of religious obligations; in comparison with *devout* it may stress outward evidence of religious faithfulness rather than inner marks of religious devotion <a *pious* man who never missed a sermon or omitted family prayers> <happy, as a *pious* man is happy when, after a long illness, he goes once more to church – Robert Hichens> Sometimes *pious* carries more than a hint of depreciation or suggestion of hypocrisy <a hypocrite – a thing all *pious* words and uncharitable deeds – Charles Reade> <a *pious* old fraud> **Religious** usually implies both devoutness and piety but its strongest suggestion is of assured faith in a God or gods and adherence to a way of life in consonance with that faith <a man may be moral without being *religious*, but he cannot be *religious* without being moral – F. W. H. Myers> <a truly *religious* man deplores his own moral failings and tries ... to bring his character and conduct more into accord with the precepts and practices of his religion – M. J. Adler> **Pietistic** basically stresses the emotional rather than the intellectual aspects of religion <the overly sentimental, almost exclusively *pietistic* and devotional temperament of some pastoral methods has caused a grave drop in the practice of religion – *Springfield* (*Mass.*) *Republican*> but, especially in popular use, *pietistic* may convey little more than the suggestion of overly emotional or sentimental piety <a hothouse *pietistic* atmosphere keeps seeping in which makes one gasp for spiritual fresh air – *Times Lit. Supp.*> **Sanctimonious** implies a mere pretension to or appearance of devoutness or piety and often suggests smugness <these *sanctimonious* hypocrites who laud righteousness and live most evilly>

dexterity – see READINESS *ant* clumsiness

dexterous, adroit, deft *shared meaning* : ready and skilled in physical movement or, sometimes, mental activity. **Dexterous** implies expertness with consequent facility and agility in manipulation or movement <seized one corner of the blanket, and with a *dexterous* twist and throw unrolled it – C. G. D. Roberts> <by force or by *dexterous* diplomacy – Walter Moberly> **Adroit,** less used with reference to purely physical skill, adds to *dexterous* an implication of ability to cope effectively, artfully, or cleverly with situations as they arise; thus, an *adroit* fencer is not only *dexterous* in body but able to anticipate his opponent and meet his every move without delay or bungling <she is *adroit* in the choice of words, has a fine appreciation of sentence rhythms and the color of speech – Haskel Frankel> **Deft** stresses lightness, neatness, and sureness of touch, either literal or figurative <with ... *deft* manipulations he reversed the car in the narrow road – W. H. Wright> <he had a *deft* (though not at all malicious) wit – Nat Hentoff> <a *defter* technique in marketing and advertising – Alfred Lief> *ant* clumsy

dialect, vernacular, lingo, jargon, cant, argot, slang *shared meaning* : a form of language that is not recognized as standard. **Dialect** applies commonly to a form of language persisting regionally or among the uneducated <*dialects* may in the course of time become separate languages, as happened to the *dialects* of Latin that became French, Spanish, ... and the other Romance languages – J. H. Friend> <*dialect* [is] a variant version of a language distinguished by its peculiar idiom, vocabulary, phonology .... A *dialect* usually impedes speech communication – John Nist> **Vernacular** applies basically to the everyday speech of the people in contrast to that of learned men <*vernacular* changes with the company. The informal vocabulary used by the educated man in his profession is blended with new words when he goes to a hardware store or a cocktail party. One does not descend to the *vernacular* so much as one moves laterally across different phases of it – Richard Bridgman> **Lingo** is a term of contempt for language not readily understood; it is equally likely to be applied to a strange foreign language, a dialect, or cultivated scholarly usage, according to the experience and background of the user <he soon settled into his new life, even adopting the flat . . . [local] *lingo* with its celebrated whine – L. M. Herrickson> <a *lingo* that few people understand or care about – C. C. Furnas> **Jargon** applies chiefly to the technical or esoteric language of a profession, trade, or cult <every profession has its own *jargon,* and we psychiatrists have ours – K. A. Menninger> but it stresses unintelligibility and may replace *lingo* when it is desired to emphasize the outlandish quality of language or usage <to the uninitiated *jargon* is meaningless or confusing – John Nist><without recourse to either hip *jargon* or learned explanations, he opens for the uninitiated the significance of the world of jazz – *Times Lit. Supp.*> **Cant** is applied derogatorily to language that is both peculiar to a group or class and intrinsically lacking in clarity or precision of expression <*cant* was especially applied in England to the whining tone affected by beggars, and was then transferred to the way of talking affected by religious hypocrites – Otto Jespersen> **Argot** applies specifically to the peculiar, often more or less secret language of a closely knit group <the American Negro has . . . developed his own *argot,* partly to put the white man off, partly to put him down – Daniel Stern> **Slang** designates a class of mostly recently coined and frequently short-lived terms and usages informally preferred to standard language as being forceful, novel, or voguish <*slang* cuts across social levels – A. H. Marckwardt> <*slang* [is] language, words, or phrases of a vigorous, colorful, metaphoric, or taboo nature, invented to transfuse fresh life into a vocabulary gone stale from too much standard and conventional usage – John Nist>

dictatorial, magisterial, dogmatic, doctrinaire, oracular *shared meaning* : imposing one's will or opinions on others. **Dictatorial** stresses autocratic high-handed methods and a domineering manner <had always told people what to do in a *dictatorial* tone and with a certain restrained impatience – Edmund Wilson> <the essentially *dictatorial* nature of questionnaires, even of relatively polite or inoffensive ones – R. F. Goldman> **Magisterial** stresses assumption or use of prerogatives appropriate to a magistrate or schoolmaster in forcing acceptance of one's opinions but is more likely to bespeak assurance of one's own correctness than mere domineering <the first section . . . a *magisterial* survey of the period's religious history, draws on much first-rate recent scholarship – H. F. May> **Dogmatic** basically implies authoritative laying down of principles or dogma as true and beyond dispute <now physics is, or should be, undogmatic; mathematics is, and must be, *dogmatic.* No mathematician is infallible; he may make mistakes; but he must not hedge – A. S. Eddington> In depreciative use *dogmatic* may imply an assertive or even arrogant assurance that discourages debate <the requirements of our modern society demand that people be trained to assume their share in solving wondrously complex problems and to avoid *dogmatic* decisions – G. M. Phillips> **Doctrinaire** is likely to imply a dogmatic disposition and often suggests an opposition to *practical* for it emphasizes a disposition to be guided by abstract or personal theories and doctrines in teaching, planning, or deciding, especially in matters affecting others or the general populace <it troubles even his admirers that he has become so sure of himself, that he is increasingly *doctrinaire,* that his sereneness has become indistinguishable from complacency – Milton Viorst> **Oracular** suggests the real or implied possession of hidden knowledge and a manner both cryptic and dogmatic or even pompously assured <his habit of *oracular* utterance when and possibly whenever he had a conviction – Ezra Pound> <he was fired as a security risk. . . . The anonymity of his discharge gave it *oracular* proportions, as if some tree or stone or voice from a cave had put the finger on him – John Cheever>

difference – see DISCORD

different, diverse, divergent, disparate, various *shared meaning* : unlike in kind or character. **Different** may imply little more than distinctness or separateness <several *different* people called> but sometimes it implies contrast or contrariness <the ways in which their English is *different* from the English used elsewhere – Randolph Quirk> **Diverse** implies marked difference and decided contrast <teaching must be restored to its rightful priority among the many *diverse* aims which universities have come to serve – M. S. Eisenhower> **Divergent** implies movement apart or along different courses and the unlikelihood of ultimate meeting or reconciliation <recognized that labor and capital have *divergent* interests – M. R. Cohen> **Disparate** implies such absolute or essential differences as make for a fundamental incongruity or incompatibility <maintains that specialized information from *disparate* fields must be coordinated to deal with specific social problems – *Current Biog.*> <the *disparate* elements of the medieval personality were as yet unblended – H. O. Taylor> **Various** commonly lays stress on the number of sorts or kinds <in *various* shapes of parsons, critics, beaus – Alexander Pope> <South America's strange fauna, with its animals as *various* as the jaguar, the cavy, and the sloth> ***ant*** identical, alike, same

difficult – see HARD ***ant*** simple

difficulty, hardship, rigor, vicissitude *shared meaning* : something obstructing one's course and demanding effort and endurance if one's end is to be attained. **Difficulty** can apply to any condition, situation, experience, or task which presents a problem hard to solve or seemingly beyond one's ability to suffer or surmount <the wise gods have put *difficulty* between man and everything that is worth having – J. R. Lowell> <they were determined to succeed; they met and solved each *difficulty* as it arose> **Hardship** stresses extreme suffering, toil, or privation but does not in itself imply either effort to overcome or patience in enduring <men to much misery and *hardship* born – John Milton> <they face the *hardships* of their comfortless lives with stolid indifference – P. E. James> **Rigor** suggests a hardship necessarily imposed upon one (as by an austere religion, a trying climate, or an exacting undertaking) <anything which might soften the *rigor* of his prison – J. H. Wheelwright> <did not intend to let the *rigors* of a strange land frighten her away – Green Peyton> **Vicissitude** applies to a difficulty or hardship incident to life or to a way of life, a career, or a course of action and commonly implies inevitability <the dwarfing *vicissitudes* of poverty – Francis Hackett> <the *vicissitudes* of time and chance have left only 9 of the 30 trees – *Amer. Guide Series: Mich.*>

diffident – see SHY ***ant*** confident

diffuse – see WORDY ***ant*** succinct

digest – see COMPENDIUM

dignity – see DECORUM

digress – see SWERVE

dilapidate – see RUIN *vb*

dilate – see EXPAND ***ant*** constrict, circumscribe, attenuate

dilemma – see PREDICAMENT

dilettante – see AMATEUR

diligent – see BUSY ***ant*** dilatory

dim – see DARK ***ant*** bright, distinct
diminish – see DECREASE
diminutive – see SMALL
diplomatic – see SUAVE
direct *vb* – see COMMAND, CONDUCT
direct *adj* **direct, immediate** *shared meaning* : uninterrupted. These words are frequently used with little distinction, although they are capable of conveying quite dissimilar connotations. **Direct** suggests unbroken connection between one thing and another (as between cause and effect, source and issue, or beginning and end) or a straight bearing of one upon the other, while **immediate** stresses the absence of any intervening medium or influence; thus, a *direct* cause leads straight to its effect, but an *immediate* cause (which may or may not be the *direct* cause) is the one which is the last link in a chain of causes and which actually precipitates an action; *direct* descent is descent in a straight line from a particular ancestor; one's *immediiate* family can include only one's parents, brothers and sisters, and children, the persons related to one without any intervening step <a hundred different complications in which we shall have a *direct* interest – F. D. Roosevelt> <the dangers of teaching are of a peculiar nature – psychological rather than physical, cumulative rather than *immediate* – Joseph Crescimbeni & R. J. Mammarella>
directly – see PRESENTLY
dirty, filthy, foul, nasty, squalid *shared meaning* : conspicuously unclean or impure. **Dirty** emphasizes the fact of the presence of dirt rather than an emotional reaction <children *dirty* from play> <a *dirty* littered street> **Filthy** carries a strong suggestion of offensiveness and typically suggests gradually accumulated dirt which besmears or begrimes rather than merely soils <a stained greasy floor, utterly *filthy*> <he was constantly drunk, *filthy* beyond all powers of decent expression – Leslie Stephen> **Foul** implies extreme offensiveness and an accumulation of what is rotten or stinking <the *foul* oil-and-garbage whiffs from the river – Herman Wouk> <the woman's breath, *foul* with a stale whiskey stench, was blown upon her, and she got suddenly a rank body smell, strong, hairy, female, and unwashed – Thomas Wolfe> **Nasty** applies to what is actually foul or is repugnant to one accustomed to or expecting freshness, cleanliness, or sweetness <we must check the plumbing, there's a *nasty* smell around the sink> <it's a *nasty* job to clean up after a sick cat> In practice *nasty* is often weakened to the point of being no more than a synonym of *objectionable* or *disagreeable* <had a *nasty* fall> <realized what a *nasty* time she had had for twenty years – Stella D. Gibbons> **Squalid** adds to the idea of dirtiness or filth that of utter slovenly neglect <living in *squalid* poverty> <*squalid* slums>
All these terms are applicable to moral uncleanness or baseness or obscenity. **Dirty** then stresses meanness or despicability <the creature's at his *dirty* work again – Alexander Pope> while **filthy** and **foul** describe disgusting obscenity or loathsome behavior <*filthy* language> <a *foul* story> and **nasty** implies a peculiarly offensive unpleasantness <a cheap and *nasty* imitation of the real thing – Robert Wilkes> Distinctively, **squalid** implies sordidness as well as baseness and dirtiness <a series of rather *squalid* little affairs that everybody knew about and nobody mentioned – Ngaio Marsh> The first four terms are also used of unpleasant weather especially when the user desires to convey a personal reaction to it <a *dirty* night outside> <the weather has been *foul* all week> ***ant*** clean
disability – see INABILITY
disable – see WEAKEN ***ant*** rehabilitate (*a disabled person*)
disaffect – see ESTRANGE ***ant*** win (*men to a cause, allegiance*)

disapprove, deprecate *shared meaning* : to feel or express an objection. **Disapprove** implies an attitude of dislike based on reasonable grounds (as social, ethical, or intellectual) and an unwillingness to accept or praise; it may, but need not, connote active rejection or condemnation <*disapprove* of a style of dress> <Lawrence *disapproved* of too much knowledge, on the score that it diminished men's sense of wonder – Aldous Huxley> <I *disapprove* of your choice though I concede your right to make it> **Deprecate** stresses the implication of regret, sometimes profound, sometimes diffident or apologetic <he seemed to *deprecate* his enormous bulk, half out of a little armchair, as he talked – George Plimpton> <this incisive analysis of the shortcomings of labor arbitration *deprecates* court enforcement of arbitration decrees – William Gibelman> ***ant*** approve

disaster, catastrophe, calamity, cataclysm *shared meaning* : an event or situation that is or is regarded as a terrible misfortune. **Disaster** implies an unforeseen mischance or misadventure that brings destruction (as of life or property) or ruin (as of projects, careers, or hopes) <the flood was a major *disaster* to the economy of the region> <such a war would be the final and supreme *disaster* to the world – Archibald MacLeish> **Catastrophe** is used of a disastrous conclusion and often emphasizes the idea of finality <prolongation of the ... war, with its increasing danger of universal *catastrophe,* threatens not only the lives of millions, but the humanitarian values and goals which we are striving to maintain – *Science*> **Calamity** applies to a grievous misfortune usually involving widespread or far-reaching loss or profound personal or public distress <*calamities* of nature such as flood and drought – *Notes & Queries on Anthropology*> <in time of great public *calamity* ... recourse was had to the sacrifice of a human scapegoat, who was to bear away all the sins and misfortunes of the people – J. G. Frazer> **Cataclysm,** which suggests an upheaval that overwhelms or shatters an existing order, is usually applied to the general or universal rather than the personal or particular <Hiroshima demonstrated how clean and easy and impersonal *cataclysm* could be – Jeanne L. Noble> <if all future world organization were rent asunder and if new *cataclysms* ... destroyed all that is left – Sir Winston Churchill> All these words and their derivatives are used less precisely in milder situations often to suggest the user's strong reaction to something <the dinner was a *disaster,* the guests late, the meat scorched> <fell into hysterics at every little household *catastrophe*> <you feel it a *calamity* today, by tomorrow you will have forgotten it> <he was subject to sudden *cataclysms* of violent whim and fancy, which he took for the demands of reason and efficiency – William Irvine>

disbelief – see UNBELIEF ***ant*** belief

disburse – see SPEND

discard, cast, shed, scrap, junk *shared meaning* : to get rid of as of no further use, value, or service. **Discard** implies the letting go or throwing away of something that has become presently useless or superfluous though often not intrinsically valueless <sorted and re-sorted his cargo, always finding a more necessary article for which a less necessary had to be *discarded* – Willa Cather> <we *discarded* so many things when we moved> **Cast,** especially when followed by *off, away,* or *out,* is likely to imply a forceful rejection or repudiation <*cast* scraps of food out for the chickens> <his wife was *casting* him off, half regretfully, but relentlessly – D. M. Lawrence> **Shed** is the usual term for seasonal or periodic casting of natural parts (as antlers, hair, or leaves) <a snake *shedding* its skin> and it also is appropriately used to imply a discarding of what has become burdensome, hampering, or uncomfortable <glad of a chance to *shed* her tight shoes>

<it is not easy to *shed* bad habits> **Scrap** can suggest permanent disposal <*scrap* an idea as impractical> but is likely to imply the possibility of salvage and of some further utility to another <*scrap* out-of-date machinery> **Junk** is close to *scrap* but carries less implication of residual value and tends to stress finality in disposal <the first big maker of electric appliances to *junk* fair-trade pricing – *Newsweek*> <*junk* something every day . . . *junk* your little jealousies, envies, and hatreds – *Read Mag.*>

discernment, discrimination, perception, penetration, insight, acumen *shared meaning* : keen intellectual vision. **Discernment** stresses accuracy (as in reading character or motives or appreciating art) <the whole book is conceived with enthusiasm and carried out in a similar manner backed by *discernment.* It gives an absorbing account of the art world – *Brit. Bk. News*> **Discrimination** emphasizes the power to distinguish and to select the excellent, the appropriate, and the true <nobody should reproach them for reading indiscriminately . . . only by so doing can they learn *discrimination* – *Times Lit. Supp.*> **Perception** implies quick acute discernment and delicacy of feeling <what we call understanding is merely the ability to identify our faults in others – with some tolerance and *perception* – H. C. Hervey> **Penetration** implies a searching mind that goes beyond what is obvious or superficial <good little novels, full of Gallic irony and *penetration* – *Time*> **Insight** emphasizes depth of discernment or of sympathetic understanding <throughout the years he has used . . . techniques or *insights* provided by abstract art, to express better his statements about men and the world – *Current Biog.*> <the ecstasy of imaginative vision, the sudden *insight* into the nature of things – Edmund Wilson> **Acumen** suggests consistent penetration coupled with soundness and shrewdness of judgment <business *acumen* and judicious handling of capital – William McFee> <it is clear and bold, reflecting astute scholarship and logical *acumen* – L. L. Gerson>

discharge – see FREE *vb,* PERFORM

disciple – see FOLLOWER

discipline – see PUNISH, TEACH

disclose – see REVEAL

discomfit – see EMBARRASS

discompose, disquiet, disturb, perturb, agitate, upset, fluster, flurry *shared meaning* : to destroy one's capacity for collected thought or decisive action. **Discompose** implies a usually minor degree of loss of self-control or self-confidence especially through emotional stress <his face was *discomposed.* His eyes gleamed angrily – Herman Wouk> **Disquiet** suggests the loss of one's sense of security or peace of mind and often the resulting uncertainty, distress, or fear <why art thou cast down, O my soul? and why art thou *disquieted* within me? – *Ps* 42:11 (AV)> <received *disquieting* news about her mother's health> **Disturb** emphasizes interference with one's mental or emotional peace or balance (as by worry, perplexity, disappointment, or fear) <what is *disturbing* me most . . . is the knowledge that I have made a monstrous fool of myself – Roald Dahl> <his passion for his cause *disturbed* me – W. A. White> **Perturb** implies deep disturbance and unsettlement of mind and emotions <[his] reaction to this must have *perturbed* even the imperturbable Russian – W. L. Shirer> <the unexpected threat *perturbed* the villagers> **Agitate** stresses loss of calmness and assurance and implies obvious signs of emotional excitement but need not suggest distress of mind as a cause <it was a happiness that *agitated* rather than soothed her – S. M. Crothers> <*agitated* at the prospect of so long a trip> **Upset,** like *agitate,* implies an emotional reaction, but it regularly presupposes an unpleasant cause (as disappointment, worry, or sorrow) <

felt *upset* and quelled and sat upon and I wasn't fond of the feeling – Theodore Sturgeon> <he was not at all *upset* by the challenge> **Fluster** suggests a bewildered agitation caused by unexpected or sudden demands <the type of man upon whose conversation his wife waits in a sort of meek attendance, like a *flustered* maid – William Styron> **Flurry** suggests the excited commotion induced by emergency demands <*flurried* by the need for haste, she quite forgot to pack her nightclothes> ***ant*** compose

disconcert – see EMBARRASS

discontinue – see STOP ***ant*** continue

discord, strife, conflict, contention, dissension, difference, variance *shared meaning* : the state of those who disagree and lack harmony or the acts and circumstances marking such a state. **Discord** implies such an intrinsic lack of harmony and concord as is likely to be marked by open quarreling or antagonism between persons and incongruity between things (as sounds or colors) <that voice . . . had a quality of stridence, dissonance, like two single high notes struck together hard in *discord* – Roald Dahl> <the controversies arising from this situation are bitter, and the *discord* is ominously apparent – H. A. Wagner> **Strife** throws emphasis on the struggle for dominance or superiority rather than on a fundamental disharmony <domestic fury and fierce civil *strife* – Shak.> <yet live in hatred, enmity, and *strife* among themselves – John Milton> **Conflict** usually stresses the action of forces in opposition <the French have been engaged in a . . . bloody *conflict* with Communist forces – *Young America*> but in static applications implies an irreconcilability <the age-old *conflict* between city and village – A. R. Williams> <the *conflict* of passion, temper, or appetite with the external duties – T. S. Eliot> **Contention** applies to strife or competition manifested in quarreling, disputing, or controversy <in spite of the violent *contentions* of the great . . . many of the cities of Italy were advancing in prosperity – C. E. Norton> **Dissension** implies strife and discord between persons or parties and typically stresses a breach between factions <*dissension* between right and left wings of a political party> <would he enjoy seeing hate and *dissension* spread over Western Europe; would he gloat over anarchy? – Helen MacInnes> **Difference** (often in the plural) and **variance** usually imply a clash arising in inherent dissimilarity (as in character, opinion, or nature) that makes for discord or strife <nationalists have always used force to settle their *differences* – H. S. Fowler> <even among the zealous patrons of a council of state the most irreconcilable *variance* is discovered concerning the mode in which it ought to be constituted – James Madison>

discover **1** see REVEAL

2 discover, ascertain, determine, unearth, learn *shared meaning* : to find out something previously not known to one. **Discover** may presuppose exploration, investigation, or chance encounter and always implies the prior actual or potential existence of what becomes known <make sure that the individual student has the maximum chance both to *discover* and to develop his talents – J. A. Perkins> <*discover* the solution to a problem> **Ascertain** presupposes awareness of ignorance or uncertainty and implies conscious effort (as by studying, questioning, or experimenting) to arrive at the truth or discover the relevant facts <had *ascertained* . . . that his son-in-law was among the living prisoners – Charles Dickens> **Determine,** otherwise close to *ascertain,* stresses the intent to establish facts or truth or to settle a controversy <science deals only with *determined,* repeatable aspects of nature – Adelbert Ames Jr.> <intensive psychological testing . . . went into *determining* which officers would make good unconventional fighting men – Robin Moore> **Unearth** implies a bringing to light of what

is forgotten or hidden <*unearth* an Elizabethan manuscript from among family records> <confess myself unable to *unearth* any sizzling inside story . . . any juicy revelations – James Morris> **Learn** implies the acquirement of knowledge; sometimes it suggests a planned and orderly acquisition based on study and practice <*learn* a trade> <*learn* to speak idiomatic English> but as often it may suggest a casual coming by knowledge, even without conscious intent <the world has *learnt* to accept as an everyday fact the uses of . . . communication satellites – *Times Lit. Supp.*> <we only now *learned* that you had come home>
3 see INVENT
discrete – see DISTINCT
discrimination – see DISCERNMENT
discuss, argue, debate, dispute *shared meaning* : to discourse about something in order to arrive at the truth or to convince others of the validity of one's position. **Discuss** implies an easy exchange of ideas, often exploratory in character or for the sake of clarifying issues <they themselves do the classroom cooking, and at the end of class they eat and *discuss* the results – *Current Biog.*> **Argue** implies conviction and the often heated adducing of reasons and evidence in support of one's position <I think I would have reasoned with her, tried to persuade her, *argued* and explained – Helen MacInnes> <deep-seated preferences cannot be *argued* about – you cannot *argue* a man into liking a glass of beer – O. W. Holmes †1935> **Debate** usually stresses formal or public argument between opposing parties <they had gathered a wise council to them of every realm, that did *debate* this business – Shak.> but it can also apply to inner discussion or deliberation in which one weighs one plan, or view, or objective against another <he *debated* whether to go to the theater or stay home and read> **Dispute** can be very close to *discuss* or *debate* <[Paul] spoke boldly for the space of three months, *disputing* and persuading the things concerning the kingdom of God – *Acts* 19:8 (AV)> but much more often it implies contentions or heated argument <she *disputed* with him over the bills for champagne and over the size of the tips he handed out when they traveled – Ludwig Bemelmans>
disdain – see DESPISE ***ant*** favor, admit
disdainful – see PROUD
disembarrass – see EXTRICATE
disencumber – see EXTRICATE
disentangle – see EXTRICATE ***ant*** entangle
disfigure – see DEFACE ***ant*** adorn
disgrace, dishonor, disrepute, shame, infamy, ignominy, opprobrium *shared meaning* : loss of esteem and good repute and the resulting denigration and contempt. **Disgrace** implies loss of favor or esteem or severe humiliation without in itself indicating whether or not this is merited <the boy was in *disgrace* because of his truancy> <summoned to serve on a jury and make decisions involving the *disgrace* or vindication . . . of your fellow creatures – G. B. Shaw> **Dishonor,** often used interchangeably with *disgrace,* can distinctively imply a falling from a previous condition of honor and often a loss of self-respect or self-esteem <he had an insult to avenge, a *dishonor* to be washed off his imaginary escutcheon – J. T. Farrell> <but now mischance hath trod my title down, and with *dishonor* laid me on the ground – Shak.> **Disrepute** implies a usually progressive passing out of favor often because of unproven or merely suspected irregularity of conduct <the hotel fell into *disrepute* among conservative people after the bar was added> <a deficiency on the part of one member [of a professional group] places burdens, if it does not bring *disrepute,* upon the

others – *AAUP Bull.*> **Shame** implies particularly humiliating disgrace or disrepute; though it need not imply personal guilt, it is likely to stress the strong emotional reaction of the one affected <*shame* [is] the sense of having failed to live up to one's desired image – Murray Blimes> <his mother had read it slowly several times; he feeling *shame* for her at the unease with which she read – Norman Mailer> **Infamy** stresses notoriety and usually implies such long-lasting well-deserved ill fame as arouses hatred and contempt <to be disgraced in the eye of the world, to wear the appearance of *infamy* while her heart is all purity, her actions all innocence, and the misconduct of another the true source of her debasement – Jane Austen> <a fortress of *infamy* and viciousness unmatched in the Western World – H. E. Rieseberg> **Ignominy**, though close to *infamy*, stresses the state of the one affected and the contemptibility or despicability of the disgrace or its cause <was she now to endure the *ignominy* of his abandoning her? – D. H. Lawrence> **Opprobrium** adds to *disgrace* the notion of being severely reproached or condemned <bring *opprobrium* on oneself by a dissipated life> <there has always been *opprobrium* attached to ignorance of grammar – Charlton Laird> ***ant*** respect, esteem

disguise, cloak, mask, dissemble *shared meaning* : to alter so as to hide the true appearance, identity, intention, meaning, or feelings. **Disguise** typically implies a deceptive change in physical appearance but may extend to a change in behavior or manner that serves to conceal a motive or attitude <I did my best to *disguise* a chronic shyness with an appearance of world-weariness – Cornelia O. Skinner> **Cloak** implies the assumption of something that covers and conceals identity or nature <intolerance and public irresponsibility cannot be *cloaked* in the shining armor of rectitude and righteousness – A. E. Stevenson †1965> **Mask** suggests the prevention of recognition of a thing's true character, nature, or presence usually by some obvious means; it need not imply pretense or deceitfulness <*mask* an ugly view with a vine-covered fence> <a burly man who tries to *mask* his sensitivity with gruffness – Neil Morgan> **Dissemble** stresses simulation for the purpose of deceiving as well as disguising and is used especially of feelings and opinions <said that the Negro had been trained to *dissemble* and conceal his real thoughts, as a matter of survival – M. S. Handler>

dishonest, deceitful, lying, mendacious, untruthful *shared meaning* : unworthy of trust or belief. **Dishonest** is broadly applicable to a breach of honesty or trust (as by lying, deceiving, stealing, or defrauding) <a *dishonest* statement> <*dishonest* employees> <her grief had a faintly *dishonest* ring – William Styron> **Deceitful** usually implies an intent to mislead and commonly suggests a false appearance or double-dealing in behavior <*deceitful* propaganda> As applied to persons it is likely to imply a proclivity for deceit <she was a *deceitful*, scheming little thing – Israel Zangwill> **Lying** is more likely to apply to a specific act or instance than a habit or tendency of telling untruths <a *lying* account of the incident> <silly newspapers and magazines for the circulation of *lying* advertisements – G. B. Shaw> **Mendacious**, less forthright than *lying*, may suggest bland or even harmlessly mischievous deceit <ships . . . where the masters, hearing his quality, set out wine and told him *mendacious* tales of their trade – J. H. Wheelwright> **Untruthful**, like *lying*, is an unequivocal term though somewhat less harsh in suggestion; it is applicable equally to acts and instances of lying and to people who lie <an *untruthful* child, always telling little fibs> <an *untruthful* report of a conversation> ***ant*** honest

dishonor – see DISGRACE ***ant*** honor

disinclined, hesitant, reluctant, loath, averse *shared meaning* : lacking the will or desire to do something indicated. **Disinclined** implies unwillingness based on mild distaste or disapproval <*disinclined* to go out in bad weather> <writers . . . *disinclined* to come to real grips with the vexed question of public control in industry – M. R. Cohen> **Hesitant** implies a holding back through fear, uncertainty, or disinclination <after a *hesitant* start she sailed through the evening bravely, and at the last curtain she received an ovation – Herman Wouk> **Reluctant** adds to *hesitant* a definite note of resistance or unwillingness <a *reluctant* witness> <the plight of *reluctant* students is even more hopeless, because they lack the will to learn even when study conditions are ideal – R. K. Corbin> **Loath** stresses the lack of harmony between what one anticipates doing and one's natural preferences; thus, one may be *loath* to believe a report that discredits a friend and equally *loath* to disbelieve a flimsy rumor that discredits an enemy <seemed *loath* to enter, yet drawn by some desire stronger than his reluctance – Willa Cather> **Averse** suggests a turning away from what is distasteful or unwelcome <the age . . . while demanding documented facts, was not at all *averse* from a spice of gossip – Bonamy Dobrée> <his impulses were generous, trustful, *averse* from cruelty – J. R. Green>

disinfect – see STERILIZE ***ant*** infect

disinterested – see INDIFFERENT ***ant*** interested, prejudiced, biased

disloyal – see FAITHLESS ***ant*** loyal

dismay, appall, horrify, daunt *shared meaning* : to unnerve and check by arousing fear, apprehension, or aversion. **Dismay** implies a loss of power or will to proceed because of sudden fear or anxiety or great perplexity <be not afraid nor *dismayed* by reason of this great multitude: for the battle is not yours, but God's. Tomorrow go ye down against them – *2 Chron* 20:15–16 (AV)> **Appall** can imply an overwhelming and paralyzing dread or terror <"Are you a man?" "Aye, and a bold one, that dare look on that which might *appall* the devil" – Shak.> but more often it implies such a sense of impotence as is aroused when one is confronted by something that perturbs, confounds, or shocks, yet is beyond one's power to alter <*appalled* by the magnitude of the tragedy – C. G. Bowers> <he clearly revealed himself to a fascinated and then *appalled* national audience as a bombastic bully, contemptuous of legal procedures – Nat Hentoff> **Horrify** may imply a shuddering revulsion from the gruesome or ghastly or hideous <*horrified,* he realized that he was witness to an exhibition incredibly medieval – an act of necromancy and self-torture – H. C. Hervey>Often, however, *horrify* comes close to *shock* and then implies little more than momentary agitation occasioned by something unexpected and distasteful (as a breach of decorum) <smoking right through soup, fish, meat, salad, and dessert in a way to *horrify* the epicure – Frances Perkins> **Daunt** suggests a cowing, subduing, disheartening, or frightening in a venture requiring courage <obstacles that would have *daunted* a man of less intrepid mind – Adeline Adams> ***ant*** cheer

dismiss – see EJECT

disparage – see DECRY ***ant*** applaud

disparate – see DIFFERENT ***ant*** comparable, analogous

dispassionate – see FAIR ***ant*** passionate, intemperate

dispatch *vb* – see KILL

dispatch *n* – see HASTE ***ant*** delay

dispel – see SCATTER

dispense – see DISTRIBUTE

disperse – see SCATTER ***ant*** assemble, congregate (*persons*), collect (*things*)

displace – see REPLACE

display – see SHOW 2

dispose – see INCLINE

disposition, temperament, temper, character, personality *shared meaning* : the dominant quality or qualities distinguishing a person or group. **Disposition** implies customary moods and attitude toward the life around one <a man of genial social *disposition*> <a pleasant white-haired widow surrounded by many potted plants that seemed to bloom and flourish in the fertile climate of her *disposition* – John Cheever> **Temperament** implies a pattern of innate characteristics that result from one's physical, emotional, and mental makeup <a phlegmatic *temperament*> <the electric amenities that pass between artistic *temperaments* at different tensions still find free play – J. L. Lowes> **Temper** implies the qualities acquired through experience that determine how a person or group meets difficulties or handles situations <there was a general confidence in her instinctive knowledge of the national *temper* – J. R. Green> <a less dogmatic *temper* is becoming apparent among the scientists themselves – Irving Babbitt> **Character** applies to the aggregate of moral qualities by which a person is judged apart from his intelligence, competence, or special talents <a man of mild and simple *character* – Roald Dahl> **Personality** applies to the aggregate of characteristics that gives individuality <the horses, whose *personalities* played an important part in these events, were, with few exceptions, beguiling – *New Yorker*> <that the Arab world accept the national *personality* of Israel as a sovereign, independent state – *Progressive*> <each man has his own *personality* and a unique combination of abilities, potentials, needs, desires, fears, and values – R. F. Lewis>

disprove, refute, confute, rebut, controvert *shared meaning* : to show or try to show by presenting evidence that something (as a claim, statement, or charge) is not true. **Disprove** stresses the success of the effort and the effective demonstration of the falsity, erroneousness, or invalidity of what is attacked <one hypothesis about the cause of a specific ailment is as good as another until *disproven* – H. M. Sapolsky> **Refute** stresses a logical method of disproving and is likely to suggest adducing of evidence, bringing forward of witnesses or authorities, and close reasoning <there is great force in this argument, and the Court is not satisfied that it has been *refuted* – John Marshall> **Confute** implies reducing an opponent to silence by or as if by an overwhelming argument; it commonly implies refutation, but it may also suggest such methods as raillery, denunciation, or sarcasm <Elijah ... *confuted* the prophets of Baal ... with ... bitter mockery of their god when he failed to send down fire from heaven – G. B. Shaw> <Satan stood ... *confuted* and convinced of his weak arguing and fallacious drift – John Milton> **Rebut**, though close to *refute,* differs in suggesting more formality of method and in not implying assured success in answering an opponent's arguments, evidence, or testimony <the author carefully examined and *rebutted,* point by point, many of the arguments – M. F. A. Montagu> <this presumption could be *rebutted* only by clear and convincing evidence to the contrary – *U. S. Code*> **Controvert** usually carries a dual implication of denying and of attempting to disprove what is put forward; it stresses the effort to refute without necessarily implying success in refutation <the thesis which is maintained by one school and *controverted* by another – A. J. Ayer> <however complicated the rules may be ... it is nearly always possible to *controvert* them by finding an example that does not fit – Charles Barber> ***ant*** prove, demonstrate

dispute – see DISCUSS ***ant*** concede

disquiet – see DISCOMPOSE ***ant*** tranquilize, soothe

disregard – see NEGLECT

disrepute – see DISGRACE ***ant*** repute

dissect – see ANALYZE

dissemble — see DISGUISE *ant* betray
dissension — see DISCORD *ant* accord, comity
dissipate 1 see SCATTER *ant* accumulate (*as possessions*), absorb (*as one's energies*), concentrate (*as one's thoughts*)
2 see WASTE
dissolve — see ADJOURN
distant, far, far-off, faraway, remote, removed *shared meaning* : not close in space, time, or relationship. **Distant** stresses separation and implies an obvious interval whether long or short <the pond was nearly a mile *distant* from their home> <held her sewing a bare six inches *distant* from her eyes> <went to live in a *distant* city> **Far** in most of its uses applies to what is a long way off <[he] took his journey into a *far* country — *Lk* 15:13 (AV)> <new studies ... uncover more and more of the *far* past — Allan Nevins> <he preferred to talk outdoors, and his voice was faint and *far,* like wind caught in a bottle — John Updike> **Far-off** stresses distance and is often preferred when distance in time is specifically implied <some misty *far-off* tomorrow when neither we nor our children can be inconvenienced — W. H. Ferry> **Faraway** differs little from *far-off* but may sometimes connote a hazy remoteness or even obscurity <a dreamy, *faraway* look came into Mr. Bohlen's eyes — Roald Dahl> <how long ago and *faraway* it was — that dim world of deep winter and indoor candlelight — Robert Francis> <a *faraway* concept of theoretical science — H. A. Klein> **Remote** suggests a far removal from one's point of view, time, or location and is likely to connote a consequent lessening of importance to oneself <the sands of a *remote* and lonely shore — P. B. Shelley> <finds the likelihood of a scholarly career *remote* — M. S. Eisenhower> <the danger [of nuclear war] increases . . . because the thing becomes more and more *remote* in people's minds — Jeremy Bernstein> **Removed** carries a stronger implication of separateness and may suggest a contrast not only in time and space but in character or quality <with peace as far *removed* as it had been at the time of his election — F. L. Paxson> <sought a quiet retreat, *removed* from the everyday world and its tensions>
distasteful — see REPUGNANT *ant* agreeable, palatable
distend — see EXPAND *ant* constrict
distinct 1 **distinct, several, separate, discrete** *shared meaning* : not being each and every one the same. **Distinct** implies that one thing is distinguishable by the eye or mind from another or others <in a few seconds she had her plan clearly in her head, with every detail as *distinct* as though the scheme had already been carried through — Stella D. Gibbons> <things similar in effect but wholly *distinct* in motive — Hilaire Belloc> **Several** indicates distinctness, difference, or separation from similar items <conduct these knights unto their *several* lodgings — Shak.> <her knowledge of three *several* tongues — Elinor Wylie> **Separate,** more common in modern usage, differs little in meaning from *several* <they went their *separate* ways> <these two modern masters created *separate* but related parts of a single work based on the music of Anton Webern — *Current Biog.*> **Discrete** strongly emphasizes individuality and lack of material connection despite apparent similarity or continuity <combining *discrete* tasks into processes that a single individual can control — M. A. Fried> <the dumb creation lives a life made up of *discrete* and mutually irrelevant episodes — Aldous Huxley>
2 see EVIDENT *ant* indistinct, nebulous
distinctive — see CHARACTERISTIC *ant* typical
distinguished — see FAMOUS
distort — see DEFORM

distract – see PUZZLE *ant* collect (*one's thoughts, one's powers*)
distress *n* **distress, suffering, misery, agony** *shared meaning* : the state of being in great trouble or in pain of body or mind. **Distress**, applicable to things as well as persons, implies circumstances that impose grave stress or strain and is likely to connote the possibility of or the need for relief <a ship in *distress*> <to pity *distress* is human; to relieve it is Godlike – Horace Mann> **Suffering** implies conscious endurance of pain or distress and often a stoical acceptance of it <it was not the magnitude or multiplicity of burdens that created martyrs and saints; it was the individual capacity to bear *suffering* – H. C. Hervey> **Misery** stresses the unhappy or wretched conditions attending distress or suffering; often it connotes sordidness, abjectness, or dull passivity <men will not long endure the *misery* of anarchy . . . they will prefer even the tyrant's order to no order at all – H. A. Deane> **Agony** suggests suffering so intense that both body and mind are involved in a struggle to endure the unbearable <and being in an *agony* he prayed more earnestly – *Lk* 22:44 (AV)> <she went through *agonies* of jealousy and remorse, and fantasies of revenge, which amazed her with their violence – Herman Wouk>
distress *vb* – see TROUBLE
distribute, dispense, divide, deal, dole *shared meaning* : to give out, usually in shares, to each member of a group. **Distribute** may apply to any manner of separating into parts and spreading out, equally or systematically or merely at random <*distribute* alms to the needy> <*distributed* the fertilizer over the field> <some companies *distribute* most of their income in the form of dividends> **Dispense** suggests the giving of a carefully weighed or measured part to each of a group, often as a right, as due, or according to need <he spends half his time in London; the other half he spends agreeably patronizing his dependents, riding round his estate on a nice day *dispensing* bounty – Victoria Sackville-West> <knew that passion was powerful, heady stuff, and must be prudently *dispensed* – the right proportions at the right moments – Roald Dahl> **Divide** stresses the separation of a whole into parts before giving out or delivering and, when unqualified, usually implies equality of the several parts <*divide* an orange between two children> <the grocer got along well with his assistant. They *divided* tasks and waited on alternate customers – Bernard Malamud> **Deal** (usually followed by *out*) implies the delivery piece by piece in turn to each of the members of a group <*dealt* out the cookies to the boys> **Dole** (also often followed by *out*) may imply a dispensing of alms to the needy <a prince *doling* out favors to a servile group of petitioners – Theodore Dreiser> but often it suggests scantiness or niggardliness in the amount dispensed and need not suggest a charitable intent <[the state] pays its capitol doorkeepers . . . twice as much as it *doles* out to its lawmakers – Trevor Armbrister> *ant* collect (*supplies*), amass (*as wealth*)
disturb – see DISCOMPOSE
diurnal – see DAILY
dive – see PLUNGE
diverge – see SWERVE *ant* converge (*as paths, roads, times*), conform (*as customs, habits, practices*)
divergent – see DIFFERENT *ant* convergent
diverse – see DIFFERENT *ant* identical, selfsame
divert – see AMUSE
divide **1** see DISTRIBUTE
2 see SEPARATE *ant* unite
divine – see FORESEE
division – see PART

divorce — see SEPARATE
divulge — see REVEAL
docile — see OBEDIENT ***ant*** indocile, unruly, ungovernable
doctrinaire — see DICTATORIAL
doctrine, dogma, tenet *shared meaning* : a principle accepted as valid and authoritative. **Doctrine** may imply authoritative teaching backed by acceptance by a body of believers or adherents <a catechism of Christian *doctrines*> <Islamic constitutional *doctrine* developed, during the first two centuries of Islam, as a rationalization of the existing practice — Guenter Lewy> but *doctrine* can be used more broadly to denote a formulated theory that is supported by evidence, backed by authority, and proposed for acceptance <the *doctrine* of organic evolution> **Dogma** implies a doctrine that is laid down as true and beyond dispute <in 1870 Pope Pius IX defined the *dogma* of papal infallibility> The term may connote arbitrary or even arrogant insistence on authority or imposition of authority <the *dogma* that the king can do no wrong> <a landowning and trading aristocracy soon emerged which . . . watched and controlled morals . . . and even dictated *dogmas* — Lois B. Wills> **Tenet** stresses acceptance and belief rather than teaching and applies to a principle held or adhered to <the *tenets* of Calvinism> <the whole *tenet* of my Church's belief is against . . . the freedom of the individual — J. A. Michener>
dogged — see OBSTINATE ***ant*** faltering
dogma — see DOCTRINE
dogmatic — see DICTATORIAL
doldrums — see TEDIUM ***ant*** spirits, high spirits
dole *n* — see RATION
dole *vb* — see DISTRIBUTE
dominant, predominant, paramount, preponderant, sovereign *shared meaning* : superior to all others in power, influence, or importance. **Dominant** applies to something that is uppermost because it rules or controls <a *dominant* race> <the idea of beauty and of a human nature perfect on all its sides, which is the *dominant* idea of poetry — Matthew Arnold> **Predominant** implies a sometimes transitory ascendancy and applies to what, at a particular time, exerts the most marked influence (as on a person or a situation) <purfication of the political process . . . must accompany any proposals to make this face of federalism *predominant* — R. M. Hutchins> <grammar was *predominant* in the curriculum — A. H. Marckwardt> **Paramount** implies supremacy in importance, rank, or jurisdiction <the United States should . . . begin to behave with the sense of confidence and restraint becoming to the *paramount* power of the day — Selig Harrison> <the welfare of the children must be the schools' *paramount* consideration> **Preponderant** implies an outweighing by the thing described of all other things with which it may reasonably come into comparison (as in importance, power, influence, force, or number) <always *preponderant* in numbers, and often in influence and power — H. O. Taylor> **Sovereign** implies quality or rank to which everything else is clearly inferior or subordinate <a *sovereign* remedy> <wearing . . . an amulet *sovereign* against all passion — Robert Browning> <the *sovereign* power of the pope over all forms of secular authority — G. H. Sabine> ***ant*** subordinate
domineering — see MASTERFUL ***ant*** subservient
dominion — see POWER 3
donate — see GIVE
doom — see FATE
dormant — see LATENT ***ant*** active, live
double-dealing — see DECEPTION

doubt – see UNCERTAINTY ***ant*** certitude, confidence

doubtful, dubious, problematic, questionable *shared meaning* : not affording assurance of the worth, soundness, success, or certainty of something or someone. *Doubtful* and *dubious* are sometimes used with little distinction <a *doubtful* (or *dubious*) reputation> <we are *dubious* (or *doubtful*) about their chances of success>, but **doubtful** is likely to postively impute worthlessness, unsoundness, failure, or uncertainty <their future prospects are very *doubtful*> <his title to the property is *doubtful*> while **dubious** can stress hesitation, mistrust, or suspicion (as in accepting, believing, or following); thus, a *doubtful* adherent to a party is one who cannot be counted on to be an actual adherent, a *dubious* adherent one whose adherence is less than wholehearted because of uncertainties in his own mind; *doubtful* friends are probably not real friends, *dubious* friends give rise to suspicion as to their worth or probity. **Problematic,** unlike the other terms, carries no suggestion of moral judgment and is applicable to any situation of which the outcome is quite unpredictable <the question . . . of hidden variables underlying the quantum theory is still *problematic* – D. Bohm & J. Bub> <success in the control of inflation remains *problematic*> **Questionable** may imply little more than the existence of doubt <the legality of his action is *questionable*> but often it suggests doubt about propriety and may imply strong or well-grounded suspicion (as about honesty or uprightness) <*questionable* conduct> <it seems inconceivable that such a man could be involved in *questionable* deals – Trevor Armbrister> ***ant*** positive

dowdy – see SLATTERNLY ***ant*** smart (*in dress, appearance*)

drag – see PULL

drain – see DEPLETE

dramatic, theatrical, dramaturgic, melodramatic, histrionic *shared meaning* : relating to plays and acting or having effects typical of acted plays. These words are chiefly comparable in extended application to behavior and expression that in its flamboyance or emotional quality suggests the theater more than life. **Dramatic** applies to something (as speech or action) having the power of deeply stirring the imagination or the emotions <he is a *dramatic,* almost hypnotic talker, and members of the teaching profession regard him as a born teacher, with a great sense of mission – Christopher Rand> <it was natural that the academic bickerings over doctrine . . . should be replaced by a *dramatic* emotionalism – Lois B. Wills> **Theatrical** is likely to suggest the artificiality of the theater and imply an often blatant appeal to the emotions especially through artificiality of voice, gesture, or action <he had already learned that with this people religion was necessarily *theatrical* – Willa Cather> <he knew . . . the swarthy man with a beard and turban might be an Indian prince . . . might be a rooming-house eccentric. This *theatrical* atmosphere of impermanence – this latitude for imposture – impressed him – John Cheever> **Dramaturgic** stresses technical fitness for stage production and may suggest the use of formal devices characteristic of stage production <every *dramaturgic* practice that subordinates the words to any other medium has trivialized the drama – E. R. Bentley> **Melodramatic** suggests an exaggerated emotionalism or an inappropriate theatricalism <since she was as emotionally unstable as her distinguished host, the account she has left . . . is lurid and *melodramatic,* and yet it is probably largely true – W. L. Shirer> **Histrionic** suggests speech, behavior, or appearance more suited to the theater than to everyday life <introduction into the liturgy of *histrionic* gestures, more suitable for a theatre than an oratory – E. K. Chambers> <demanded of himself and his musicians honest perfection, uncluttered by *histrionic* poses – *Current Biog.*>

dramaturgic – see DRAMATIC
draw – see PULL
dread – see FEAR
dreadful – see FEARFUL 2
drench – see SOAK
drift – see TENDENCY
drill – see PRACTICE
drive – see MOVE
droll – see LAUGHABLE
drowsy – see SLEEPY
drudgery – see WORK
drunk, drunken, intoxicated, inebriated, high, tipsy, tight, plastered *shared meaning* : conspicuously under the influence of intoxicating liquor. **Drunk** and **drunken** are the plainspoken, direct, and inclusive terms <he was dead *drunk* every payday> <a *drunken* man staggering down the street> *Drunken* may imply habitual excess in drinking <Stephano, my *drunken* butler – Shak.> and is also applicable to whatever proceeds from intoxication <a *drunken* brawl> **Intoxicated,** though sometimes interchangeable with *drunk,* is likely to be chosen as less derogatory when the degree of drunkenness is relatively slight <several of the students got *intoxicated* after the game> **Inebriated** implies such a state of intoxication that exhilaration or undue excitement results <half the members became *inebriated* and passed a tax on soft drinks sold at dog tracks – Trevor Armbrister> All four of these words are subject to extended use in which they usually imply an excess of or extreme display of emotion <*drunk* with divine enthusiasm – P. B. Shelley> <*drunken* with blood and gold – P. B. Shelley> <I dream that at Naples, at Rome, I can be *intoxicated* with beauty – R. W. Emerson> <*inebriated* with the exuberance of his own verbosity – Benjamin Disraeli> The remaining words are likely to occur in less formal context and ordinarily suggest increasing degrees of drunkenness: one is **high** whose grasp on reality is loosened by drinking; one is **tipsy** whose muscular and usually mental control is lessened by drinking; one is **tight** whose state of intoxication is obvious to the beholder; and one is **plastered** who has become wholly incompetent through intoxication. *ant* SOBER
drunken – see DRUNK *ant* sober
dry, arid *shared meaning* : lacking or deficient in moisture. **Dry** may suggest freedom from noticeable moisture either as a characteristic or a desirable state <a *dry* climate> <*dry* land> <a warm *dry* cellar> or it may suggest deficiency of moisture or the lack or loss of normal or needed moisture <August is often a *dry* month> <the roast was overcooked and *dry*> <the spring has gone *dry*> **Arid** implies destitution or deprivation of moisture and extreme dryness; in its typical applications to regions or territory it suggests waste or desert lands <the *arid* parts of the southwestern United States> <a bare *arid* stretch of country> In extended use in application to intellectual matters (as topics, writings, or sermons) *dry* is likely to imply lack of those qualities that compel interest or attention <read a *dry* report in a droning voice> and *arid* the absence of those qualities that mark a thing as worthwhile, fruitful, or significant <art history is becoming increasingly *arid* and pedagogical – *Times Lit. Supp.*> <the usual *arid* high-school text – J. W. Weigel> As applied to persons, their manner, or their words and expressions *dry* implies a loss of vital qualities (as youthful enthusiasm or human warmth and responsiveness) <he had grown thin and *dry* in the years that had passed and something dour in his nature had become plain – Pearl Buck> while *arid* implies an absence

of or an incapacity for these qualities <some *arid* matron made her rounds at dawn, sniffing, peering, causing blue-nosed maids to scour – Virginia Woolf> <this structural defect might have been overcome ... if the intellectual leadership were less *arid* – Barbara Ward> In a related use *dry,* but not *arid,* may suggest the assumption of repression of feeling and enthusiasm as a mannerism or for effect <a *dry* sense of humor> <a certain *dry* spirit of detachment and analysis – Aldous Huxley> ***ant*** wet

dubiety – see UNCERTAINTY ***ant*** decision

dubious – see DOUBTFUL ***ant*** cocksure (*state of mind, opinion*), reliable (*of things in general*), trustworthy (*of persons*)

ductile – see PLASTIC

dudgeon – see OFFENSE

dull 1 see STUPID ***ant*** clever, bright

2 dull, blunt, obtuse *shared meaning* : not sharp, keen, or acute. **Dull** applies physically to an edge or point that has lost its original sharpness through use <a *dull* knife> and in extended use suggests loss of original or usual quickness, zest, or pungency <he woke late feeling *dull* and tired> <there were cows and they looked at him dully with their great *dull* eyes – James Baldwin> <a kind of *dull* disappointment in the ordinariness and familiarity of it all – Henry Hewes> **Blunt** applies to an edge or end not designed to be sharp or keen <children should only be given scissors with *blunt* tips> and it can suggest innate or inherent lack of sharpness or quickness of feeling or perception <a *blunt* speech that offended some of his hearers> <*blunt* in perception and feeling, and quite destitute of imagination – A. C. Bradley> **Obtuse,** basically applicable to an angle or convergence of more than 90 degrees, can suggest more-or-less stupid lack of perception or sensitivity or inordinate bluntness (as of manner or speech) <most Americans, including those whose task it is to make foreign policy ... are disturbingly *obtuse* about the sensitivities of other nations – Vera M. Dean> ***ant*** sharp (*edge, point*), poignant (*sensation, feeling*), lively (*action, activity*)

dumb – see STUPID ***ant*** articulate

dumbfound – see PUZZLE

dumpy – see STOCKY

dupe, gull, trick, hoax *shared meaning* : to delude by underhand methods or for one's own ends. **Dupe** suggests unwariness in the person deluded <ineffectual innocents repeatedly *duped* by a tough enemy – R. J. Lifton> **Gull** stresses credulousness or readiness to be imposed on and made a fool of <*gull* who may, they will be *gulled!* They will not look nor think – Robert Browning> <the cheap, easy effects of fake elegance with which the public *gulls* itself – Ada L. Huxtable> **Trick,** though implying an intent to delude by means of a ruse or fraud, need not imply a vicious intent <a magician's success depends on his ability to *trick* his audience> Often it suggests the use of cunning and guile in attaining an end <enables some lawyers to *trick* us into bringing in the wrong verdict – W. J. Reilly> **Hoax** often applies to a tricking merely for fun or with the aim of demonstrating the extent of human gullibility and may imply an elaborate or painstaking deception <these eulogists sin in two respects. They *hoax* the reader and their book is as dreary as it is inaccurate – Richard Maney> <the ... Association ... now realizes that it has been scientifically *hoaxed* into advancing Kremlin propaganda – Eugene Lyons>

duplicate – see REPRODUCTION

dusky 1 see DARK

2 dusky, swarthy, tawny *shared meaning* : tending toward darkness and dullness. Though by no means so restricted, all three words find one of their commonest uses in the description of human appearance. **Dusky** applies to what is somewhat dark, whether with respect to light or color <*dusky* vapors of the night – Shak.> <a *dusky* blush rose to her cheek – Edith Wharton> <refuse to share the same sections of churches with their more *dusky* brethren and will send their children only to teachers with very light complexions – *Amer. Guide Series: La.*> *Swarthy* and *tawny* apply to hue or color only; **swarthy,** to a shade verging on or suggesting blackness, and **tawny,** to a yellowish-brown to sandy hue <a *swarthy* Ethiope – Shak.> <*tawny* Tartar – Shak.> <the fair complexions of the blue-eyed warriors of Germany formed a very singular contrast with the *swarthy* or olive hue [of the Moors] which is derived from . . . the torrid zone – Edward Gibbon> <the *tawny* oak doors were shut – John Gunther> <the hills . . . were no longer peaceful. In the dawnlight they were *swarthy* and dismal – Kenneth Roberts> ***ant*** light, bright

duty – see FUNCTION, OBLIGATION, TASK

dwell – see RESIDE

dwindle – see DECREASE

eager, avid, keen, anxious, athirst *shared meaning* : moved by a strong and urgent desire or interest. **Eager** implies ardor and enthusiasm and sometimes impatience at delay or restraint <students qualified for this experience, and *eager* to undertake the considerable labor it entails – R. M. Vogel> <a bevy of *eager* people spreading the gospel – J. A. Michener> **Avid** adds to *eager* the implication of insatiability or greed <an *avid* reader> <overly *avid* pursuit of a single theme has brought implications which are not true – R. B. Davis> **Keen** suggests intensity of interest and quick responsiveness in action <Washington was *keen* to follow up his Yorktown victory by a combined attack on Wilmington – S. E. Morison> **Anxious** suggests earnest desire but emphasizes fear of frustration, disappointment, or failure <the "have-not" nations are *anxious* to better their lot – Marston Bates> <What is the significance of this *anxious* hunt of the young thinker for the primal economic fact . . . ? – Cecil Sprigge> **Athirst** stresses yearning or longing and is unlikely to connote readiness for action <I that forever feel *athirst* for glory – John Keats> <older boys and girls . . . *athirst* for experience – *Saturday Rev.*> ***ant*** listless

earn – see GET

earnest – see SERIOUS ***ant*** frivolous

earth, world, universe *shared meaning* : the entire area in which man thinks of himself as living and acting. **Earth** is the usual designation of the material global body, the planet of the sun; it may suggest a distinction between this and bodies visible in the heavens <this goodly frame, the *earth* – Shak.> <the difference between the *Earth* as *a planet* and the *Earth* as *the planet.* The second is our familiar way of saying . . . "the one planet that matters, ours." – Wilson Follett> or, often, a distinction from heaven and hell <Thy will be done in *earth,* as it is in heaven – *Mt* 6:10 (AV)> **World** is more variable in reference than *earth,* with which it is often interchangeable; distinctively it may refer to the material earth and all the illimitable area perceptible to the senses <wherever we point the telescope . . . wherever we look with the microscope there we find beauty. It beats in through every nook and cranny of the mighty *world* – Rufus Jones> but more often it reflects from other senses a stress on human existence and may imply the sum total of human beings together with their interests and concerns <all the *world* loves a lover> or a particular part of this inclusive world bound by some common tie <the fascinating *world* of the theater> <the turbulence that can be observed today throughout the Islamic *world,* from North Africa to Pakistan and Indonesia – Guenter Lewy> or, specifically, to the part of the world devoted to secular as contrasted to religious or spiritual concerns <the *world,* the flesh, and the devil> <I too love the earth and hate the *world.* God made the first, and man . . . has made the second – George Santayana> **Universe** in its most basic use denotes the entire system of created things and physical phenomena regarded as a unit in its arrangement and operation <early students held that earth was the center of the *universe*> In more restricted use it may refer to any entire system of phenomenal items as perceived by limited human vision <he inhabited a different *universe* from that of common men – Aldous Huxley> <the problem is to devise sensors which . . . will respond to the significant features of the *universe* to be examined – E. B. Carne>

earthly, terrestrial, mundane, worldly *shared meaning* : belonging to or characteristic of the earth. **Earthly** can imply opposition to *heavenly* <*earthly* love> <if I have told you *earthly* things, and ye believe not, how shall ye believe, if I tell you of heavenly things? – *Jn* 3:12 (AV)> or, less often, to *celestial* <there must be a great triangle of *earthly* observation points for any continuous watch on interplanetary space – John Lear> **Terrestrial** in one common use implies usually opposition to *celestial* <a *terrestrial* globe> or it may imply a distinction between earth and the other solar planets <*terrestrial* magnetism> <*terrestrial* life> or, in technical astronomical use, between earth and those solar planets assumed to be earthlike and those others that are assumed to be unlike earth <the small, heavy, slowly rotating *terrestrial* planets (Mercury, Venus, Mars, and the Earth) – D. ter Haar> Often *terrestrial* stresses surface land, especially as a habitat and as distinguished from water, air, or trees <*terrestrial* birds> <electric light abolished the divisions of night and day, of inner and outer, and of the subterranean and the *terrestrial* – Marshall McLuhan> *Mundane* and *worldly* both imply a relation to the immediate concerns and activities of men; distinctively **mundane** is likely to suggest an opposition to what is eternal and stress transitoriness or impermanence <quaff the elixir and sweet essence of *mundane* triumph – L. P. Smith> or it may center attention on the practical, ordinary, or even humdrum <we suspect they [looks and fashion] sometimes affect buying decisions a great deal more than such *mundane* considerations as durability and comfort – *Consumer Reports*> <such *mundane* activities as washing dishes or driving an automobile – Ralph Linton> while **worldly** is likely to imply indifference to things of the spirit and preoccupation with mundane matters and the satisfaction of the appetites <they were young and pretty, trying to be chic and *worldly* – Helen MacInnes>

ease – see READINESS ***ant*** effort

easy – see COMFORTABLE ***ant*** disquieting, disquieted

ebb – see ABATE ***ant*** flow (*as the tide*)

eccentricity, idiosyncrasy *shared meaning* : singularity in behavior or an instance of this. **Eccentricity** retains its basic notion of being off center and in this use stresses divergence from the usual or customary; it may impute mild mental aberration as a cause <a quaint house in Wales, which they made quainter during their fifty-odd years of living together in joyous *eccentricity* – C. R. Woodring> <speaking French with an *eccentricity* that could not be ignored – F. M. Ford> <pamphlets attributed to the frontier hero and capitalizing on the picturesque *eccentricities* of backwoods life – J. D. Hart> **Idiosyncrasy** puts its primary stress on a strongly individual quality and correspondingly less on deviation from the usual or typical; it is likely to imply a following of one's peculiar bent or temperament (as in trait, trick, or habit) <a countenance which at once arrested and absorbed my whole attention on account of the absolute *idiosyncrasy* of its expression – E. A. Poe> <certain parts became so identified with favorites who played them often that the actor's *idiosyncrasies* were accepted as essential qualities of the original character – Margery Bailey>

economical – see SPARING *ant* extravagant

ecstasy, rapture, transport *shared meaning* : intense exaltation of mind and feelings. **Ecstasy** can imply a trancelike state in which consciousness of one's surroundings is lost and the mind is intent on what it contemplates (as with the mystic) or on what it conceives and creates (as with the inspired poet or artist) <like a mad prophet in an *ecstasy* – John Dryden> In more general use the term implies such overmastering and entrancing emotion as exalts the mind and overcomes the senses <she loved him with an acute, painful *ecstasy* that made her dizzy and blinded her to all the world besides – Rose Macaulay> **Rapture** can imply a lifting of the mind or soul out of itself by or as if by divine power so that it perceives things beyond the normal range of human vision, but usually its implication is one of intense bliss or utter delight <as a child I first read Pope's Homer with a *rapture* which no subsequent work could ever afford – Lord Byron> <totally dedicated to the world of natural history . . . his *rapture* in collecting plants went beyond considerations of personal safety and finance – D. S. Kalk> **Transport** applies to any violent or powerful emotion that lifts one out of one's self and usually provokes vehement expression or frenzied action <what a *transport* of enthusiasm! – W. S. Landor> <in art, as in poetry, there are the *transports* which lift the artist out of . . . himself – Walter Pater>

edge – see BORDER

educate – see TEACH

educe, evoke, elicit, extract, extort *shared meaning* : to draw out something hidden, latent, or reserved. **Educe** is likely to imply the development and outward manifestation of something potential or latent <techniques . . . which sooner or later could bring even the most sophisticated crowd to its feet, to make it scream in *educed* outrage – Stanley Elkin> **Evoke** implies a strong stimulus that arouses an emotion or interest or recalls an image or memory from the past <in any link between past and present there was potent magic, some power to *evoke* allegiance – H. C. Hervey> **Elicit** usually implies effort and skill in drawing something forth and often implies resistance in the person or thing that is the object of effort <the teacher who is enthusiastic about his material is more likely to *elicit* interest than is the bored teacher – R. K. Corbin> <*elicit* information from a reluctant witness by cross-examination> **Extract** basically implies the action of a force (as pressure or suction) <*extract* juice from an orange> and in more general use implies a comparable urging and pressing <he had not that faculty of *extracting* the essence from a heap of statements – Charles Dickens> <the court refused to accept the confession the police had *extracted* from the suspect> **Extort,** sometimes interchangeable with *extract,* is likely to intensify the notion of urgent action and even to evoke an image of wringing or wresting something from one who is reluctant to part with it <a . . . masterly demonstration of the icily admiring, the exactly just but obviously *extorted* tribute – G. W. Johnson> <*extort* a promise> <*extort* money from relatives>

eerie – see WEIRD

efface – see ERASE

effect *n* **effect, result, consequence, event, issue, outcome** *shared meaning* : a condition or occurrence traceable to a cause. **Effect** is the correlative of the word *cause* and applies to something that necessarily and directly follows upon or occurs by reason of a cause <low mortality, the *effect* of excellent social services in every village – William Petersen> <reports in psychiatric journals tend to establish a cause-and-*effect* link between certain drugs and psychosis – *Trans-action*> **Result** usually suggests an effect that terminates the action of a cause, and it applies more often than *effect* to material objects <relations . . . were much improved as a *result* of these meetings – *Current Biog.*> <his limp is the *result* of a childhood accident> **Consequence** is likely to suggest a direct but looser or more remote connection with a cause than either *effect* or *result;* specifically it can imply an adverse or calamitous effect, a chain of intermediate causes, or a complexity of effects <conceive how difficult it is to escape the dread *consequences* of a regime's calculated and incessant propaganda – W. L. Shirer> <the overall tax *consequences* should be the same whether a corporation sells its assets and then liquidates or makes a liquidating distribution of its assets to the stockholders – *Arthur Young Jour.*> **Event,** increasingly uncommon in this relation, carries the notion of an unpredictable or unforeseeable outcome <then very doubtful was the war's *event* – Edmund Spenser> <the happiness of Rome appeared to hang on the *event* of a race – Edward Gibbon> **Issue** usually denotes a result that is a solution (as of a problem) or a resolution (as of difficulty or a conflict) <the war was by then obviously proceeding toward a successful *issue* – F. M. Ford> **Outcome,** often interchangeable with *result* or *issue,* can suggest the interaction of complex, often conflicting forces and apply to the result of their joint causal action <the peoples of the coast, as an *outcome* of living in a corridor for armies, are an ethnic jumble – *Times Lit. Supp.*> ***ant*** cause

effect *vb* – see PERFORM

effective, effectual, efficient, efficacious *shared meaning* : producing or capable of producing a result or results. **Effective** emphasizes the actual production of or the power to produce an effect <*effective* thinking> <an *effective* rebuke> <Confucius . . . was more *effective* as a teacher than as a politician – Albert Newgarden> **Effectual** suggests the accomplishment of a desired result or the fulfillment of a purpose or intent and is most applicable when looking backward after the event <the remedy proved *effectual* and relieved her distress> <his recommendation was *effectual,* and I was . . . chosen – Edward Gibbon> **Efficient** may apply to what is actually operative and producing a result <it should be obvious that it is the conditions producing the end effects which must be regarded as the *efficient* causes of them – M. F. A. Montagu> or it may suggest an acting or a potential for action or use in such a way as to minimize loss or waste of energy in effecting, producing, or functioning <a strong tendency to break up cumbersome estates into small, *efficient* farms – Allan Nevins & H. S. Commager> As applied to human beings with this denotation, *efficient* suggests the exercise of qualities (as skill, care, and patience) that imply capability and competence <an *efficient* housewife plans her day carefully> **Efficacious** implies possession of a special power or virtue that gives effective power <quinine is still one of the most *efficacious* drugs in the control of malaria> <certain formulae of blessing especially *efficacious* against devils – Elinor Wylie> ***ant*** ineffective, futile

effectual – see EFFECTIVE ***ant*** ineffectual, fruitless

effeminate – see FEMININE ***ant*** virile

efficacious – see EFFECTIVE ***ant*** inefficacious, powerless

efficient – see EFFECTIVE ***ant*** inefficient

effort, exertion, pains, trouble *shared meaning* : the active use of energy in producing a result. **Effort** may suggest either a single action or persistent activity and usually implies the calling up or directing of energy by the conscious will <a community . . . is strong only to the extent that its members make the *effort* required to sustain and nourish it – J. A. Perkins> <with a final mighty *effort* he thrust the obstacle aside> **Exertion** may suggest the active exercise of a power or faculty <a . . . man, capable of close application of mind, and great *exertion* of body – Charles Dickens> but often it suggests laborious and exhausting effort <the Democratic Party in 1952 exhibited evidence of fatigue from an accumulation of strains and tensions following its *exertions* during a period of 20 years of great activity – *Americana Annual*> <I should have considered it as part of my duty, and the *exertion* would soon have been nothing – Jane Austen> **Pains** implies toilsome or solicitous care and is likely to connote conscientiousness in the agent <the courts have taken some *pains* to recognize the distinctive features of the academic community – J. A. Perkins> **Trouble** implies exertion that inconveniences or wastes time and patience <we owe a debt of gratitude . . . for the immense *trouble* he has been at to give us so complete an account of the vicissitudes of a typical . . . Victorian – *Times Lit. Supp.*> but often *trouble* loses its implication of inconvenience and time-wasting and is then a very close synonym of *pains* <always took the *trouble* to keep her house neat and shining> ***ant*** ease

effrontery – see TEMERITY

eject, expel, oust, evict, dismiss *shared meaning* : to drive or force out. **Eject** carries an especially strong implication of throwing or thrusting out from within and is applicable in almost any situation where this notion is prominent <the volcano *ejected* lava> <*eject* an intruder from one's house> <the sick puppy *ejected* a mass of worms> <the solar system had been formed out of matter *ejected* from the sun – S. F. Mason> **Expel** stresses a thrusting out or driving away and is more likely than *eject* to imply voluntary action <he was fired as a security risk . . . and the pain of being condemned or *expelled* by a veiled force may have accounted for his rage – John Cheever> <a century of emphasis upon facts . . . and a corresponding distrust of statements that cannot be verified, have *expelled* the excitement and greatness – William Arrowsmith> **Oust** implies removal or dispossession by power of the law, by force, or by the compulsion of necessity <agreements between the parties cannot *oust* the [Labor Relations] Board's jurisdiction – B. F. Tucker> <we moved into one of our smaller houses, *ousting* the tenant – W. A. White> <foretold . . . that continued advances in pharmaceutical remedies would ultimately *oust* surgery altogether – *Punch*> **Evict** means to turn out (as from one's home or place of business) by a legal or comparable process <tenants *evicted* for nonpayment of rent> <thousands of crofters were *evicted* to make way for large sheep farms – *London Calling*> **Dismiss** stresses a getting rid of something (as a case at law) by rejecting a claim or prayer and refusing it further consideration <this court reversed the judgment . . . and remanded the case with directions to *dismiss* it – R. B. Taney> or a disposing of something (as a fear, a grudge, or a problem) by ejecting it from the mind or thoughts <nonviolence as a political weapon . . . should not be *dismissed* lightly – *African Abstracts*> <we may *dismiss* these harmonizers as plainly ignorant of the history of religion – M. R. Cohen> ***ant*** admit

elastic, resilient, springy, flexible, supple *shared meaning* : able to endure strain (as from bending, twisting, or stretching) without being permanently altered or injured. **Elastic** implies the property of resisting deformation by stretching <rubber bands are *elastic*> **Resilient** implies an ability to recover shape quickly when the deforming force is removed <steel for springs must be very *resilient*> **Springy** combines the implications of *elastic* and *resilient* and stresses equally capacity to yield to and recover from strain <walking on a *springy* turf> **Flexible** applies to what can be bent without breaking; the term may, but need not, imply resilience <modern plumbing can be simplified by the use of *flexible* tubing> **Supple** applies to something that can be readily bent, twisted, or folded without any sign of injury <a *supple* fabric that drapes well> <*supple* joints and muscles>

In extended use these words retain their basic implications. **Elastic** stresses ease in stretching beyond normal or appointed limits <a very *elastic* conscience> <some principles there must be, however *elastic* – John Buchan> **Resilient** emphasizes a capacity for quick recovery (as of health or spirits) <the *resilient* health that permits him to take the tropics in stride – Bernard Taper> **Springy** may suggest youthful freshness and buoyancy <a *springy* step> <a *springy* fellow, well set up – Amy Lowell> **Flexible** implies an adaptable or accommodating quality <the company has a *flexible* policy about wage increases> <a *flexible* tax plan> <the teacher who is *flexible* and takes quick advantage of the individual student's current focus of interest is more likely to induce in the child a desire to write well than is the rigid teacher bound to a textbook – R. K. Corbin> **Supple,** in extended use applied chiefly to persons or their utterances, may imply little more than flexibility or ease in practice and action <sang with a lively, *supple* voice – Douglas Watt> or it may suggest flexibility tending on the one hand toward obsequious compliance, on the other to ready, even artful adaptability <he might have been naïve, opportunistic, shrewd, and devoted all at the same time. He was a highly complex and *supple* individual living in a highly complex and rigid society – Marvin Kalb> ***ant*** rigid

elect – see SELECT ***ant*** reprobate (*in theology*)

election – see CHOICE *n*

electrify – see THRILL

elegant – see CHOICE *adj*

element, component, constituent, ingredient, factor *shared meaning* : one of the parts, substances, or principles that make up a compound or complex thing. **Element** applies to anything that is a part of a compound or complex whole and often connotes irreducible simplicity <resolve a problem into its *elements* in order to solve it><the air had a close, dead smell compounded of many *elements* – Thomas Wolfe> *Component* and *constituent* may designate any of the substances or qualities that enter into the makeup of a complex product. **Component,** however, stresses the separate identity or distinguishable character of the elements; **constituent,** their essential and formative relation to the whole <the springs, gears, levers, cogs, and pivots that are *components* of a mechanism> <hydrogen and oxygen are *constituents* of water> **Ingredient** applies to any of the substances or materials that suitably combined form a mixture with qualities of its own that may be quite distinct from those of the unmixed constituents <iron and carbon are the *ingredients* of steel> <assemble the *ingredients* for a cake> <the most important *ingredient* of a good education is a good teacher – E. M. Kennedy> **Factor** applies to a constituent or element whose presence helps actively to perform a particular kind of work or to bring about a particular result <his wartime experience . . . was a *factor* in his choice of career – *Current Biog.*> <God . . . is not one of the *factors* for which science has to account – W. R. Inge> ***ant*** compound, composite

elevate – see LIFT ***ant*** lower

elevation – see HEIGHT

elicit — see EDUCE
eliminate — see EXCLUDE
elongate — see EXTEND ***ant*** abbreviate, shorten
elucidate — see EXPLAIN
elude — see ESCAPE
emanate — see SPRING
emancipate — see FREE *vb*
emasculate — see UNNERVE
embarrass, discomfit, abash, disconcert, rattle, faze *shared meaning* : to distress by confusing or confounding. **Embarrass** implies some influence that impedes thought, speech, or action and may be used of persons or of the things they plan or desire to do <a settlement would expose South Africa to an extremely *embarrassing* military, economic, and political confrontation with a nearby state — C. E. Crowther> <the somewhat too elaborate deference paid them by their neighbors *embarrassed* them and caused them to clothe their wealth in muted, simple gray — William Styron> **Discomfit** implies a hampering or frustrating and often suggests the skill and ease with which another is routed and thrown into confusion <an answer that *discomfited* the brash young salesman> **Abash** presupposes initial self-confidence or self-assurance and implies a sudden check to that mood by something that produces shame, shyness, or a conviction of inferiority <before her cool, experienced manner we were clumsy and *abashed* — John Barth> <a man whom no denial, no scorn could *abash* — Henry Fielding> **Disconcert,** whether referring to actions or plans or to persons, is likely to imply an upsetting or derangement that, in the case of persons, amounts to temporary loss of equanimity or assurance <it was enormously *disconcerting* to see these women of the Church out there in the shameless sunlight — H. C. Hervey> <her solemn unwinking stare that *disconcerted* self-conscious people — Rose Macaulay> **Rattle** more than *disconcert* stresses the disorganizing effect of the upsetting force and is likely to suggest a complete loss of accustomed poise and composure <hecklers trying to *rattle* a speaker> <*rattled* by hypothetical eyes spying upon her — Jean Stafford> **Faze,** found chiefly in negative constructions, may come close to *disconcert* or may carry added implications of *abash* and *rattle* <he had ice water in his veins. Nothing *fazed* him, not insult or anger or violence or getting his face beat into a hamburger — R. P. Warren>
embellish — see ADORN
emblem — see SYMBOL
embrace 1 see ADOPT ***ant*** spurn
2 see INCLUDE
emend — see CORRECT *vb* ***ant*** corrupt (*a text, passage*)
emergency — see JUNCTURE
emigrant, immigrant *shared meaning* : one that leaves one place to settle in another. Although both words are applicable to the same individual, they are not interchangeable because they represent opposing points of view: **emigrant** that of the place left and **immigrant** that of the new home. Thus, primitive horses developed in North America, but as conditions became unfavorable they left as *emigrants* and entered the Old World where they were domesticated and ultimately brought back to America with the settlers as *immigrants;* Britain has suffered the loss of many scientists as *emigrants* and the United States has gained much from these valuable *immigrants* <all Americans are *immigrants* for even the Indians came originally as *emigrants* from Asia>
eminent — see FAMOUS

emolument – see WAGE
emotion – see FEELING
empathy – see SYMPATHY
employ – see USE *vb*
employment – see WORK 2
empower – see ENABLE
empty 1 **empty, vacant, blank, void, vacuous** *shared meaning* : lacking contents which could or should be present. **Empty** implies a complete absence of contents, especially of usual or normal contents; **vacant**, an absence of appropriate contents or occupants <an *empty* bucket> <his purse was *empty*> <a *vacant* apartment> <*vacant* professorships> When qualifying the same noun, the words are likely to suggest distinctly different ideas; thus, an *empty* house contains neither furniture nor occupants while a *vacant* house is devoid of inmates and presumably for rent or for sale; an *empty* chair has no one sitting in it while a *vacant* chair has lost its usual occupant (as by death); an *empty* space contains nothing while a *vacant* space awaits appropriate filling. **Blank** stresses the absence of any significant, relieving, or intelligible features on a surface <the window faced a *blank* wall> Sometimes the void implies a vacancy intended to be filled; thus, a *blank* sheet of paper is one available for writing; a *blank* check is one with space left for insertion of a sum. **Void** implies absolute emptiness to the senses <sandy wilderness, all black and *void* – William Wordsworth> <the *void*, hollow, universal air – P. B. Shelley> **Vacuous** suggests the emptiness of a vacuum and is often applied hyperbolically to what lacks intelligence or significance <there was nothing to be read in the *vacuous* face, blank as a school notice-board out of term – Graham Greene> ***ant*** fill
2 see VAIN
emulate – see RIVAL
enable, empower *shared meaning* : to make one able to do something. Distinctively, **enable** implies provision of the means or opportunity, **empower**, provision of the power or delegation of the authority, to do something. Thus, a private income *enables* (not *empowers*) one to live without employment; courts are *empowered* (not *enabled*) by the legislature to try certain classes of cases <opportune variations . . . which at various times *enabled* the animals to cope with unpredictable changed conditions and so to escape . . . extinction – G. G. Simpson> <his wealth came earlier, *enabling* him to retire at fifty – *Johns Hopkins Mag.*> <one of the bills would *empower* federal courts to hear suits brought by citizens against governmental agencies for unwanted withholding of information – *Current Biog.*> <the emotion which *empowers* artists to create significant form – Clive Bell>
enchant – see ATTRACT ***ant*** disenchant
encomium, eulogy, panegyric, tribute, citation *shared meaning* : a formal expression of praise. **Encomium** implies warm enthusiasm in praise, especially of a person <the *encomiums* by my friend pronounced on humble life – William Wordsworth> **Eulogy** applies to a prepared utterance and especially a funeral oration or a sermon extolling the virtues and services of a person <I would rather have a plain coffin without a flower, a funeral without a *eulogy*, than a life without . . . love and sympathy – G. W. Childs> **Panegyric** carries a strong implication of elaborate, high-flown, rhetorical or poetic compliment <all *panegyrics* are mingled with an infusion of poppy – Jonathan Swift> **Tribute** applies alike to written or spoken praise or to an act that takes its place <I am appointed sole executor, a confidence I appreciate as a *tribute* to my lifelong friendship – H. G. Wells> <no *tribute* can be paid to them which exceeds their merit – John Marshall>

Citation may designate either the formal eulogy that accompanies the awarding of an honor or the specific mention of a person in military service in an order or dispatch.

encroach – see TRESPASS

end *n* **1 end, termination, ending, terminus** *shared meaning* : the point or line beyond which something does not or cannot go. **End** is the inclusive term, implying the final limit in time or space, in extent of influence, or in range of possibility <the *end* of a road> <the *end* of one's life> <we are at the *end* of our resources> <his answer put an *end* to speculation> **Termination** and **ending** apply to the end of something having predetermined limits or being completely finished <the *termination* of a base> <waiting for the *ending* of the meeting> The latter, but not the former, often includes a portion leading to the final point <a novel with an unusual *ending*> **Terminus** applies commonly to a point toward which one moves or progresses <New York is the *terminus* of many transportation systems> <the object is the starting point, not the *terminus,* of an act of perception – James Jeans> *ant* beginning

2 see INTENTION

end *vb* – see CLOSE *vb* *ant* begin

endeavor – see ATTEMPT

endemic – see NATIVE *ant* exotic, pandemic

ending – see END *ant* beginning

endorse – see APPROVE

endure 1 see BEAR

2 see CONTINUE *ant* perish

enemy, foe *shared meaning* : one who shows hostility or ill will. **Enemy** stresses antagonism that may, however, range from a deeply cherished hatred or a will to harm and destroy to no more than active or evident dislike or a habit of preying upon <since [in France] opposition is never considered to be legitimate, the Government has no opponents – only *enemies* – J.-F. Revel> <luck and he were, if not natural *enemies,* not good friends – Bernard Malamud> <pointed out a century ago that greed and short-sightedness were the natural *enemies* of a prudent resources policy – J. F. Kennedy> **Foe,** on the other hand, stresses active fighting or struggle rather than emotional reaction <give me the avowed, the erect, the manly *foe,* bold I can meet, – perhaps may turn his blow! – George Canning> In reference to antagonists of a nation at war *enemy* is the general term, *foe* being preferred chiefly in rhetorical or poetic use <we have met the *enemy,* and they are ours – O. H. Perry> <whispering with white lips – "The *foe!* They come!" – Lord Byron>

energetic – see VIGOROUS *ant* lethargic

energize – see VITALIZE

energy – see POWER *ant* inertia

enervate – see UNNERVE *ant* harden, inure

enfeeble – see WEAKEN *ant* fortify

engagement – see BATTLE

engaging – see SWEET *ant* loathsome

engineer – see GUIDE

engross – see MONOPOLIZE

enhance – see INTENSIFY

enigma – see MYSTERY

enigmatic – see OBSCURE *ant* explicit

enjoin – see COMMAND

enjoy – see HAVE

enjoyment — see PLEASURE *ant* abhorrence
enlarge — see INCREASE
enliven — see QUICKEN *ant* deaden, subdue
enmity, hostility, antipathy, antagonism, animosity, rancor, animus *shared meaning* : deep-seated dislike or ill will or a manifestation of such feeling. **Enmity** suggests positive hatred whether open or concealed <I will put *enmity* between thee and the woman — *Gen* 3:15 (AV)> **Hostility** suggests strong and usually open enmity showing itself in attacks or aggressive action <the *hostility* to institutions and standards which alarms me is demonstrated by only a small minority of students — H. A. Deane> *Antipathy* and *antagonism* are likely to imply a temperamental or constitutional basis for one's hatred or dislike. Distinctively **antipathy** suggests repugnance and a desire to avoid or reject while **antagonism** stresses the clash of temperaments and the quickness with which hostilities are provoked <the racial *antipathy* felt by Africans for Asians — *Times Lit. Supp.*> <inveterate *antipathies* against particular nations and passionate attachments for others should be excluded — George Washington> <the students at the prejudice workshop came in confident of their own freedom from serious prejudices, but they went out scared by the discovery of deep *antagonisms* that they had never sensed until then — R. L. Shayon> **Animosity** is likely to suggest angry vindictiveness and a desire to hurt or destroy its object <there was a natural *animosity* between the poor honest residents of the county and the rich debauched strangers who swept in — J. A. Michener> **Rancor** stresses bitterness and ill will and often implies the nursing of a grudge or grievance <small wonder at her feeling an unchristian *rancor* against the nation which had caused his death — C. S. Forester> **Animus** implies a usually prejudiced dislike and often malevolent or spiteful ill will <a large school of thought cherishes a curious *animus* against what it calls intellectualism — W. R. Inge> <students meet together . . . , think together, laugh together, and share a common *animus* against the authorities — L. S. Feuer> *ant* amity
ennui — see TEDIUM
enormous — see HUGE
enough — see SUFFICIENT
enrapture — see TRANSPORT
ensnare — see CATCH
ensue — see FOLLOW
ensure, insure, assure, secure *shared meaning* : to make an outcome sure. **Ensure** implies a making certain and inevitable <his passion for political autocracy *ensured* a mindless and provincial political absolutism — W. L. Shirer> <control of hiring was all that was necessary to *ensure* an honest, efficient civil service — D. R. Lindsay> **Insure** stresses the taking of necessary measures beforehand to make a result certain or to provide for any probable contingency <we worry about becoming a nation of spectators — yet we teachers help to *insure* it by demanding that kids sit passively while we talk — Frank McLaughlin> <to control intelligence in the attempt to *insure* only benevolent consequences would be a Pyrrhic victory sentencing the human race to ignorance, stagnation, and decadence — K. B. Clark> **Assure,** often interchangeable with *ensure* and *insure,* may distinctively express the notion of the removal of all doubt, uncertainty, or worry from the mind <he was *assured* of survival — H. C. Hervey> <a pure man forgives or pleads for mercy or *assures* the penitent — F. W. Robertson> **Secure** implies positive action to ensure safety, protection, or certainty against adverse contingencies <lock the door to *secure* us from interruption — Charles Dickens> <the proper way, they felt, to *secure* liberty to posterity was

to set up a representative government, limited in scope by a statement of natural rights with which no government may meddle – S. E. Morison>

enter, penetrate, pierce, probe *shared meaning* : to make way into something. **Enter**, the most general of these terms, may imply either a going in or a forcing a way in <he *entered* the house by the front door> <the bullet *entered* the fleshy part of his arm> **Penetrate** carries a strong implication of an impelling force or compelling power that effects entrance <the salt rain . . . *penetrates* the thickest coat – Richard Jefferies> Often, especially in extended use, *penetrate* can suggest qualities (as sharpness, keenness, or acuteness) that give something a power to effect entry into or passage through in either a tangible or an intangible manner <a cold that *penetrates* the very bones> <her *penetrating* voice> <we cannot *penetrate* the mind of the Absolute – W. R. Inge> <with her extraordinary intelligence she had *penetrated* his weakness, the ease with which he could be wounded – Pearl Buck> **Pierce** adds to *penetrate* a clear implication or suggestion of an entering point or wedge <they *pierced* both plate and mail – Edmund Spenser> <a passion like a sword blade that *pierced* me through and through – Vachel Lindsay> Often it imputes great poignancy or aesthetic effectiveness to the thing that pierces <the remembrance of all that made life dear *pierced* me to the core – W. H. Hudson †1922> **Probe** implies penetrating in order to investigate or explore something hidden from easy observation or knowledge <it is possible that unmanned spaceships will *probe* beyond the limits of the Solar System – M. G. H. Ligda> <he has *probed* into the relationship between dietary factors and renal hypertension and has explored the nutritional aspects of liver and kidney disease – *Current Biog.*> ***ant*** issue (*from* or *out*)

entertain – see AMUSE

enthuse – see THRILL

enthusiasm – see PASSION ***ant*** apathy

entice – see LURE ***ant*** scare

entire **1** see PERFECT ***ant*** impaired

2 see WHOLE ***ant*** partial

entrance – see TRANSPORT

entrap – see CATCH

entreat – see BEG

entrench – see TRESPASS

entrust – see COMMIT

envious, jealous *shared meaning* : begrudging another possession of something. In spite of their shared element of meaning, these words are not close synonyms and can rarely be interchanged without loss of precision or alteration of emphasis. **Envious** stresses a coveting of something (as riches or attainments) which belongs to another or of something (as success or good luck) which has come to another; it may imply an urgent, even malicious desire to see him dispossessed of what gives him gratification <some *envious* hand has sprinkled ashes just to spoil our slide – Eugene Field> <his successes were so repeated that no wonder the *envious* and the vanquished spoke sometimes with bitterness regarding them – W. M. Thackeray> or it may imply no more than a mild coveting without desire to injure <we are all *envious* of your new dress> <her *envious* interest in the great, the notorious, or the socially eminent – Victoria Sackville-West> **Jealous** is likely to stress intolerance of a rival for the possession of what one regards as peculiarly one's own possession or due, but sometimes it implies no more than intensely zealous efforts to keep or maintain what one possesses. The term can be used without derogation <proud of their calling, conscious of their duty, and *jealous* of their honor – John Gals-

worthy> <thou shalt have no other gods before me ... for I the Lord thy God am a *jealous* God – *Exod* 20:3–5 (AV)> but more often it carries a strong implication of distrust, suspicion, enviousness, or sometimes anger <stabbed by a *jealous* lover> <[they] were extremely *jealous* of one another, and in consequence suffered horrid torments – Stella D. Gibbons>

envisage – see THINK

envision – see THINK

ephemeral – see TRANSIENT

epicure, gourmet, gourmand, glutton, bon vivant *shared meaning* : one who takes pleasure in eating and drinking. **Epicure** implies fastidiousness and voluptuousness of taste and is applicable to a connoisseur not only of food but in any art involving both feasting and delicacy of taste <I am become a perfect *epicure* in reading; plain beef or solid mutton will never do – Oliver Goldsmith> **Gourmet** applies to a connoisseur in food and drink and suggests discriminating enjoyment <a studious *gourmet* and collector of recipes – Thomas Mario> **Gourmand** implies less fastidiousness and discernment than *gourmet,* but it suggests a hearty interest in and enjoyment of good food and drink rather than, as **glutton** does, greedy and voracious eating and drinking <eating habits ... of a determined gourmet, verging at times on those of a *gourmand* – E. J. Kahn> <the French love good eating – they are all *gourmands* – Laurence Sterne> <skillfully made delicacies from many countries ... in such vast array this season that they threaten to turn the gourmet into a *glutton* – Jane Nickerson> **Bon vivant** stresses liveliness and spirit in enjoying the pleasures of the table, especially in the company of others <he was also a *bon vivant,* a diner-out, and a storyteller – *Fraser's Mag.*> <somewhat of a *bon vivant,* and his wine was excellent – Sir Walter Scott>

epicurean – see SENSUOUS ***ant*** gross

episode – see OCCURRENCE

epitome – see ABRIDGMENT

epoch – see PERIOD

equable – see STEADY ***ant*** variable, changeable

equal *adj* – see SAME ***ant*** unequal

equal *vb* – see MATCH

equanimity, composure, sangfroid, phlegm *shared meaning* : the characteristic quality of one who is self-possessed and not easily disturbed or perturbed. **Equanimity** suggests a habit of mind that is disturbed rarely or only under great strain <his placidity of demeanor ... arose from ... the *equanimity* of a cold disposition – Anthony Trollope> <stoicism teaches men ... to accept with proud *equanimity* the misfortunes of life – W. R. Inge> **Composure** implies a controlling of mental or emotional agitation by an effort of will or as a matter of habit <his passions tamed and all at his control, how perfect the *composure* of his soul – William Cowper> **Sangfroid** implies great coolness and steadiness under strain and may suggest a constitutional coldness <with gigantic *sangfroid* I performed one of her own dances for her – Agnes de Mille> <bridge ... roulette and Monte Carlo – at all these she won and lost, with the same equable *sangfroid* – Rose Macaulay> **Phlegm** implies insensitiveness and suggests apathy of mind or sluggishness of temperament rather than self-control <there was a busy, bustling, disputatious tone about it, instead of the accustomed *phlegm* and drowsy tranquillity – Washington Irving> <a slow stolid man whose calm was no more than *phlegm*>

equip – see FURNISH

equitable – see FAIR ***ant*** inequitable, unfair

equity – see JUSTICE

equivalent – see SAME ***ant*** different
equivocal – see OBSCURE ***ant*** unequivocal
equivocate – see LIE
era – see PERIOD
eradicate – see EXTERMINATE

erase, expunge, cancel, efface, obliterate, blot out, delete *shared meaning* : to strike out something so that it no longer has effect or existence. **Erase** implies a wiping or rubbing out (as of letters or impressions) often in preparation for correction or replacement by new matter <*erase* a badly written line> In extended use it suggests a comparable eradication (as from the memory or mind) <have a few years totally *erased* me from your memory? – Thomas Gray> <altering the submarine's log and his own diary so as to *erase* any telltale evidence of the truth – W. L. Shirer> **Expunge** stresses a removal or destruction that leaves no trace <irrelevant testimony *expunged* from a court record> <the most primitive ways of thinking may not yet be wholly *expunged* – William James> **Cancel** basically implies a striking out of written material <*cancel* a line in a manuscript> but is widely applied to invalidating or nullifying by a variety of means; thus, a postage stamp is *canceled* with an indelible impression to prevent reuse; a ticket is *canceled* with a punch or by tearing; a will is *canceled* by physical destruction or replacement <sabbatical leaves are being postponed or *canceled* – D. A. Shepard> **Efface** stresses the complete removal of something by or as if by eliminating the surface of which it is a part <coins with dates *effaced* by wear> <while nations have *effaced* nations, and death has gathered to his fold long lines of mighty kings – William Wordsworth> **Obliterate and blot out** both imply a covering up or smearing over that hides all traces of a thing's existence <*obliterate* lines in a diagram with white ink> <the sun was nearly *blotted out* by the bitter brown haze – *Time*> but in extended use both terms tend to imply not hiding, but utter destruction <about half the island was *obliterated* in the Krakatau blast – R. C. Cowen> <then rose the seed of chaos, and of night, to *blot out* order, and extinguish light – Alexander Pope> **Delete** basically implies a deliberate exclusion, or a marking to direct exclusion, of written matter; in extended applications it often suggests arbitrariness in eradication <the censor *deleted* most of the letter> <*delete* a needed appropriation from the budget on grounds of economy>

error, mistake, blunder, slip, lapse *shared meaning* : a departure from what is true, right, or proper. **Error** suggests the existence of a guide and a straying from a right course through failure to make effective use of this; thus, a typographical *error* results when a compositor fails to read a manuscript correctly; an *error* in addition involves some failure in following the rules of addition; an *error* in conduct is an infraction of an accepted code of manners or morals <those who, with sincerity and generosity, fight and fall in an evil cause, posterity can only compassionate as victims of a generous but fatal *error* – Sir Walter Scott> **Mistake** implies misconception or inadvertence and usually expresses less severe criticism than *error* <*mistake* is defined as an erroneous mental conception which influences a person to act or to omit to act – L. B. Howard> <a *mistake* in spelling> **Blunder** commonly implies stupidity or ignorance as a cause and regularly attributes some degree of culpability <the reputation of Stalin has been dethroned and his *blunders* as a statesman have been denounced – Edmund Wilson> <we usually call our *blunders* mistakes, and our friends style our mistakes *blunders* – H. B. Wheatley> **Slip** stresses inadvertence or accident and applies especially to trivial but embarrassing mistakes <a social *slip* which makes us feel hot all over – L. P. Smith> **Lapse**, though sometimes in terchangeable with *slip,* is likely to stress forgetfulness, weakness, or inattention rather than accident <forever chiding him for his grammatical *lapses* – William Styron> In reference to moral transgression it tends to stress a falling from grace or below accepted or personal standards <for all his ... *lapses,* there was in him a real nobility, an even ascetic firmness and purity of character – Havelock Ellis>

ersatz – see ARTIFICIAL

erudite – see LEARNED

erudition – see KNOWLEDGE

escape, avoid, evade, elude, shun, eschew *shared meaning* : to get away or keep away from something one does not want to incur, endure, or encounter. **Escape** stresses the fact of getting away or being passed by, not necessarily through effort or by conscious intent <opportune variations ... enabled the animals to cope with unpredictable changed conditions and so to *escape* ... extinction – G. G. Simpson> <*escape* a storm by sheltering in an old barn> **Avoid** stresses forethought and caution in keeping clear of danger or difficulty <he usually limits his sports to boating, swimming, and bear hunting to *avoid* any muscular strain or injury that might impair his dancing – *Current Biog.*> **Evade** implies adroitness, ingenuity, or sometimes lack of scruple in escaping or avoiding <*evade* suspicion by spreading confusing rumors> <another, slightly more conservative, means of *evading* the speed of light's restrictions – Stanley Kubrick> <the king was so far away that his rules might be in large degree *evaded* if not defied – C. L. Jones> **Elude** usually stresses a slippery or baffling quality in the one that gets away <for are we not all fated to pursue ideals which seem eternally to *elude* us – L P. Smith> but it may come close to *evade* and then carry a strong suggestion of shifty unreliability and the use of stratagems in evasion <she is adept in *eluding* her obligations> <he *eludes* law by piteous looks aloft – Robert Browning> **Shun** often implies avoidance as a matter of habitual practice or policy <a man who always *shunned* unnecessary labor> and may imply abhorrence or repugnance as a reason <thus have I *shunned* the fire for fear of burning – Shak.> <a desolate wilderness ..., infested with malaria, and *shunned* by people – George Kish> **Eschew,** close to *shun* in basic meaning, is likely to stress practical, moral, or prudential grounds for avoidance <the Anglo-American public, still *eschewing* sex, turned to fiercer pleasures in the murder-mystery – Gershon Legman> <trained to *eschew* private passions and pursuits – E. A. Mowrer>

eschew – see ESCAPE ***ant*** choose

especial – see SPECIAL

espouse – see ADOPT

essay – see ATTEMPT

essential, fundamental, vital, cardinal *shared meaning* : so important as to be indispensible. **Essential** implies belonging to the very nature of a thing and therefore incapable of removal without destroying the thing or fundamentally altering its distinctive character <the most *essential* characteristic of mind is memory – Bertrand Russell> <the stamen and pistil are called *essential* organs because they are necessary if there is to be seed – J. W. McKay> **Fundamental** applies to something that forms a foundation without which an entire system or complex whole would collapse <the American Declaration of Independence and the United States Constitution put these freedoms into writing, and they have since been *fundamental* to the American system – R. L. Tobin> <consider a dragonfly, a rocket and a breaking wave. All three of them illustrate the same *fundamental* laws of motion – Aldous Huxley> **Vital** suggests something that is as necessary to a thing's continued existence or operation as air, food, and water are to living things

<it is *vital* that we produce graduates who have a more sensitive awareness of their ... surroundings – A. D. Trottenberg> <the Germans ... did not realize how *vital* to Britain's defenses radar was – W. L. Shirer> **Cardinal** aptly describes a factor on which an outcome turns or depends <I had become a *cardinal* piece on the chaotic chessboard of Monroe Street's sociology – Norman Mailer> <the *cardinal* virtue in the Shavian scale ... is responsibility; every creed he has attacked Shaw has attacked on the grounds of irresponsibility – E. R. Bentley>

establish – see SET *vb* ***ant*** uproot (*a tree, a habit, a practice*), abrogate (*a right, a privilege, a quality*)

esteem – see REGARD ***ant*** abomination, contempt

estimate, appraise, evaluate, value, rate, assess *shared meaning* : to judge a thing with respect to its worth. **Estimate** implies a judgment, considered or casual, that precedes or takes the place of actual measuring or counting or testing out <*estimate* the cost of replacing a furnace> <she had *estimated* him shrewdly when she compared him to the princess who felt the pea through four-and-twenty mattresses – Victoria Sackville-West> **Appraise** basically implies an intent to fix definitely and in the capacity of an expert the monetary worth of something <*appraise* an estate for purposes of taxation> and in extended use implies critical judging and an intent to give a final, precise, and accurate judgment <the scholarly eye of this trained historian resting on and *appraising* the turmoil and hysteria that marked the downfall of Adolf Hitler – Rosemary Benét> **Evaluate** suggests an intent to determine either the relative or intrinsic worth of something in terms other than monetary <*evaluate* the effectiveness of a new antibiotic> <Negroes want ... respect, dignity, the opportunity to grow and to be *evaluated* in terms of their worth as individuals – K. B. Clark> **Value** comes very close to *appraise* but does not imply authoritative or expert judgment <he *valued* his collection at several thousand dollars> and in extended use is likely to stress personal rather than critical judgment <he *values* her friendship very dearly> <disappointment at being *valued* under her expectations – Bernard Malamud> **Rate** adds to *estimate* the implication of placing in a scale of values <the law was long *rated* above the other professions> <as copper is *rated* very much above its real value, so silver is *rated* somewhat below it – Adam Smith> **Assess** basically applies to an appraising in order to assign a taxable value; in its extended use it implies precise evaluation usually as a prelude to further consideration or interpretation or as a guide to action <*assess* the damage done by a flood> <what is equal treatment in education? ... who is to be permitted to judge individual abilities, and who should *assess* academic performance and progress? – J. A. Perkins>

estrange, alienate, disaffect, wean *shared meaning* : to cause one to break a bond of affection or loyalty. Both *estrange* and *alienate* suggest a making foreign or strange (as by bodily or mental separation) and a consequent loss of sympathy amounting to indifference or hostility <a little knowledge often *estranges* men from religion, a deeper knowledge brings them back to it – W. R. Inge> <the veils of prejudice, ignorance and indifference that *alienate* man from man – Warren Hinckle> Distinctively, **estrange** can suggest a mutual indifference or hostility <welded the scattered *estranged* group ... into something like the close-knit tribal Family of the old country – Herman Wouk> while **alienate** is likely to be preferred when the blame can be fixed on one of the persons involved or on a person or thing not directly involved <born ... into a schismatic body called the Free Church of Scotland, membership of which was about as socially *alienating* in Britain

as Proust's Jewish mother was in France – John D. Scott> <a creative minority . . . who would like to contribute but are *alienated* by red tape – R. C. Angell> <her caprices and extravagance *alienated* her husband> **Disaffect** is likely to be used with reference to those from whom loyalty might naturally or reasonably be expected or demanded and stresses the effects (as unrest, discontent, or rebellion) of alienation without actual separation <the disloyalists tried to *disaffect* the militia, preaching treason – C. G. Bowers> <all hands were *disaffected* by the example of the ringleaders – R. L. Stevenson> **Wean** implies a commendable separating of one from someone or something on which he is weakly dependent or with which he is immaturely preoccupied <to *wean* your minds from hankering after fake Germanic standards – A. T. Quiller-Couch> <*weaned* my young soul from yearning after thine – Emily Brontë> ***ant*** reconcile

ethical – see MORAL ***ant*** unethical
etiquette – see DECORUM
eulogy – see ENCOMIUM ***ant*** calumny, tirade
evade – see ESCAPE
evaluate – see ESTIMATE
evanescent – see TRANSIENT
even 1 see LEVEL ***ant*** uneven
2 see STEADY
event – see EFFECT, OCCURRENCE
eventual – see LAST
evict – see EJECT
evidence – see SHOW

evident, manifest, patent, distinct, obvious, apparent, plain, clear *shared meaning* : readily perceived or apprehended. **Evident** implies the existence of unmistakable signs, all of which point to one conclusion <her enjoyment of the music was *evident*> <he stopped and looked about him as if not knowing what to do, and then, in *evident* confusion, forced himself to go on – Thomas Wolfe> **Manifest** implies an external display so evident that little or no inference is needed <the court's finding that the verdict is against the *manifest* weight of the evidence – L. B. Howard> **Patent** applies to a cause, effect, or significant feature that is clear and unmistakable once attention is drawn to it <three very *patent* reasons for the comparatively slow advance of our children – C. H. Grandgent> <*patent* defects, that is, those visible and apparent on inspection – L. B. Howard> **Distinct** implies such sharpness of outline or of definition that the thing requires no effort to see or discern <a neat *distinct* handwriting> <an amalgam of separate parts, no longer *distinct* – Terry Southern> **Obvious** implies such ease in discovering or accounting for that it may suggest conspicuity in the thing or little need of perspicacity in the discoverer <there was humiliation in being peddled here and there, a very *obvious* unmarried daughter – Herman Wouk> <acknowledged his *obvious* insincerity with brittle silence – H. C. Hervey> **Apparent** may be very close to *evident* but is likely to imply not merely inference from evidence but this plus more or less elaborate reasoning <it is *apparent* from comparison of their stories that one of the girls is lying> <by his subtle, repeated interpretations of the suites, he gradually made their beauty *apparent* – Current Biog.> *Plain* and *clear* both apply to something that is immediately apprehended or unmistakably understood, but **plain** implies lack of complexity, intricacy, or elaboration and **clear,** an absence of anything that confuses the mind or obscures the issues <his sermons were *plain* and sometimes they made a man angry, but at least one knew what they were about – Pearl Buck>

<all agreed that . . . it was Goering's *clear* duty under the decree to take over – W. L. Shirer> *ant* inevident
evil – see BAD *ant* exemplary, salutary
evince – see SHOW
evoke – see EDUCE
exact *vb* – see DEMAND
exact *adj* – see CORRECT *adj*
exacting – see ONEROUS *ant* easy, lenient
examine – see SCRUTINIZE
example – see INSTANCE, MODEL
exasperate – see IRRITATE *ant* mollify
exceed, surpass, transcend, excel, outdo, outstrip *shared meaning* : to go or be beyond a stated or implied limit, measure, or degree. **Exceed** implies going beyond a limit set by authority or established by custom or prior achievement <*exceed* a speed limit> <my wrath shall far *exceed* the love I ever bore – Shak.> **Surpass** may replace *exceed,* especially when superiority (as to a standard or in quality) is to be implied <he easily *surpassed* the previous record> <it is safe to say that in this play Middleton is *surpassed* by one Elizabethan alone, and that is Shakespeare – T. S. Eliot> **Transcend** implies a rising or extending notably above or beyond ordinary limits <nothing – simply nothing at all – *transcends* a cat's incomparable insincerity – Theodore Sturgeon> <a point of view *transcending* the purely human outlook on the universe – Laurence Binyon> **Excel** implies an attaining of superiority or even preeminence in accomplishment or achievement <a charming child who instinctively *excels* other children in all the social graces> <love divine, all love *excelling* – John Wesley> **Outdo,** less common than *surpass* or *excel* in highly formal context, is often preferred when there is an intent to connote the breaking of a previously established record <he hath in this action *outdone* his former deeds doubly – Shak.> <a competition in deceit in which, I admit, he *outdid* them – Owen Wister> **Outstrip,** also closely comparable to *surpass* and *excel,* is likely to suggest succeeding in or as if in a race <has civilization *outstripped* the ability of its users to use it? – Margaret Mead> <bituminous coal had far *outstripped* anthracite in the industrial markets – S. A. Hale>
excel – see EXCEED
excessive, immoderate, inordinate, extravagant, exorbitant, extreme *shared meaning* : going beyond a normal or acceptable limit. **Excessive** implies an amount or degree too great to be reasonable or endurable <driving at an *excessive* speed> <*excessive* lenity and indulgence are ultimately *excessive* rigor – John Knox> <*excessive* bail shall not be required, nor *excessive* fines imposed, nor cruel and unusual punishments inflicted – *U.S. Constitution*> **Immoderate** implies absence of desirable or needed restraint (as of the feelings or their expression) <*immoderate* laughter> <he was . . . too consistently moderate to be *immoderate* even in the virtue of moderation – J. C. H. Wu> **Inordinate** implies an exceeding of limits dictated by reason or good judgment <the great difficulty of living content is the cherishing of *inordinate* and unreasonable expectations – T. E. Brown> <an *inordinate* appetite> **Extravagant** often adds to *excessive* or *immoderate* the implications of a wild, lawless, prodigal, or foolish wandering from proper and accustomed limits <make *extravagant* claims for a new process> <lavish *extravagant* praise on a trivial accomplishment> The term often specifically implies prodigality in expenditure <she was rapacious of money, *extravagant* to excess – Henry Fielding> **Exorbitant** implies departure from accepted standards regarding amount or degree <a resolution to contract none of the *exorbitant* desires by which others are

enslaved – *Spectator*> In its frequent application to prices, demands, or exactions *exorbitant* is likely to connote extortion on the part of the agent and the infliction of hardships on the person affected <*exorbitant* profits> <blinded by so *exorbitant* a lust of gold, the youngster straightway tasked his wits, casting about to kill the lady – Robert Browning> **Extreme** may imply approach to the farthest limit possible <the *extreme* point to which man has yet penetrated in outer space> but more often it is used hyperbolically and means no more than of a notably high degree or exceeding what is usual or customarily accepted <the *extremer* manifestations of the avant-garde – *Times Lit. Supp.*> <he talks about family secrets in a candid way that would cause his parents *extreme* anguish if they knew – R. K. Corbin> ***ant*** deficient

excite – see PROVOKE ***ant*** soothe, quiet (*persons*), allay (*fears, anxiety*)

exclude, debar, eliminate, suspend *shared meaning* : to shut or put out. **Exclude** implies a keeping out of what is already outside by or as if by closing some barrier <*exclude* light from a room by closing the shutters> <minority groups who are *excluded* from some activities simply because their ancestors belonged to the less privileged classes – J. R. Everett> **Debar** stresses the effectiveness of an existent barrier in excluding one person or class from what is open or accessible to others <*debarred* by illness from participation in active sports> <*debarring* persons of foreign birth from exercising political rights – Edmund Wilson> **Eliminate** implies the getting rid of what is already within, typically as a constituent part of a system <*eliminate* waste from federal spending> <the President's request for legislation to *eliminate* air pollution – *Forbes*> <it is always wise to *eliminate* the personal equation from our judgments of literature – J. R. Lowell> **Suspend** implies temporary and commonly disciplinary removal (as from membership in an organization) or restraining (as from functioning or expression) <students *suspended* for cheating> <his mind had been *suspended* for nearly five hours in a state of palmy beatitude – William Styron> <De Gaulle *suspended* the Lebanon constitution after the Lebanese voted for independence – S. E. Ambrose> ***ant*** admit (*persons*), include (*things*)

exclusive – see SELECT ***ant*** inclusive

excuse *vb* **excuse, condone, pardon, forgive** *shared meaning* : to exact neither punishment nor redress for (an offense) or from (an offender). Both *excuse* and *condone* imply a passing over either without censure or without meet punishment. Distinctively, one may **excuse** specific acts (as faults, omissions, or neglects) especially in social or conventional obligations or the person responsible for these <*excuse* an interruption> <*excuse* a boy for his tardiness> Often the word implies extenuating circumstances <the injustice with which he had been treated would have *excused* him if he had resorted to violent methods of redress – T. B. Macaulay> or in some contexts self-justification <enabled . . . officers to *excuse* themselves from any personal responsibility for the unspeakable crimes which they carried out on . . . orders – W. L. Shirer> One more often **condones** either a kind of behavior (as dishonesty, folly, or violence) that constitutes a grave breach of the moral or legal code or a person or institution responsible for such behavior <the reasons for heavy drinking can be understood from a humanistic point of view, if not *condoned* – Gerald Carson> <we *condone* everything in this country – private treason, falsehood, flattery, cruelty at home, roguery, and double-dealing – W. M. Thackeray> *Pardon* (opposed to *punish*) and *forgive* (opposed to *condemn*) are often used interchangeably, but their implications can be distinct. One **pardons** when one remits the penalty rightfully due for admitted or proved offense whether slight or serious <the President has the power to *pardon* . . . persons found guilty of violating federal laws – J. N. Moody & J. F. X. McCarthy> <exaggeration may be *pardoned* to Mr. Briffault's enthusiasm for his cause, but this tolerance can scarcely be extended to misstatements of facts – *New Republic*> One **forgives** when one gives up all claim both to requital and to resentment or vengeful feelings <to err is human, to *forgive,* divine – Alexander Pope> <he *forgave* injuries so readily that he might be said to invite them – T. B. Macaulay> ***ant*** punish

excuse *n* – see APOLOGY

execrate, curse, damn, anathematize *shared meaning* : to denounce violently. **Execrate** implies intense loathing and usually furious passion <for a little while he was *execrated* in Rome; his statues were overthrown, and his name was blotted from the records – John Buchan> **Curse** and **damn** both suggest an invoking of divine vengeance and imply fervent angry denunciation by oaths or blasphemy; the former may seem somewhat more literary than the latter <in literature, with his usual charming violence, he *cursed* Conrad's style – F. A. Swinnerton> <he told me great tales of their cruelty, and he *cursed* them most bitterly – Hugh Walpole> <mentally *damned* the cook as the real cause of his distress – F. W. Crofts> <he *damned* the railroad for the delay> **Anathematize** implies solemn denunciation (as of an evil, a heresy, or an injustice); it is peculiarly applicable to formal yet impassioned denunciations (as by clergymen or moralists) <*anathematized* the leader of the Kentist insurgents – F. M. Stenton> <the "logical mind" spoke of original sin and *anathematized* the doctor. The rational mind spoke of the effect and *anathematized* the cause – Van Wyck Brooks>

execute 1 see PERFORM

2 execute, administer *shared meaning* : to carry out the declared intent of another. **Execute** implies the enforcing of specific provisions (as of a law, a will, a commission, or a command) <*execute* an order precisely as given> <where the heads of departments are the political or confidential agents of the executive, merely to *execute* the will of the president – John Marshall> <the law or a sentence is as much *executed* when a condemned felon is imprisoned as when he is put to death – R. G. White> **Administer** implies the continuing exercise of deputed authority in pursuance of only generally indicated goals <*administer* a trust fund for the benefit of the needy> <*administer* justice from the bench> <the territory was *administered* by France under a mandate>

3 see KILL

exemplar – see MODEL

exercise – see PRACTICE

exertion – see EFFORT

exhaust – see DEPLETE, TIRE

exhibit – see SHOW 2

exigency – see JUNCTURE, NEED *n*

exiguous – see MEAGER ***ant*** capacious, ample

exile – see BANISH

exorbitant – see EXCESSIVE ***ant*** just (*price, charge*)

expand, amplify, swell, distend, inflate, dilate *shared meaning* : to increase in size or volume. **Expand,** the most general term, may apply whether the increase comes from within or without or is induced by addition, by growth, or by unfolding of preexistent parts <the mercury *expanded* in the thermometer> <*expand* a business to meet demand> <we must *expand* the concept of conservation to meet the imperious problems of the new age – J. F. Kennedy> Distinctively, *expand* can imply enlargement by opening out <*expand* the chest with deep breaths> <flowers *expanding* in the

warm spring sun> **Amplify** implies the extension or enlargement of something that is inadequate <language extends and *amplifies* man but it also divides his faculties – Marshall McLuhan> <displaying her talent for *amplifying* the latent design and implication of ordinary subjects – *Current Biog.*> **Swell** implies gradual expansion beyond a thing's normal or original limits (as of size, volume, or quantity) <veterans *swelled* college enrollments in unprecedented numbers – E. M. Gerritz> <every misuse of power and trust will *swell* the resentment of the just – Jennie Flaherty> **Distend** implies expansion caused by pressure from within <sails *distended* by the wind> Often it implies an exceeding of normal or wholesome bounds <if in addition to the year's four seasons the fifth of famine tramples . . . the land and howls with the *distended* bellies of unfed babies – Frederic Morton> **Inflate** implies distension by or as if by the introduction of gas and often suggests a resulting instability or liability to collapse <*inflate* a balloon with helium> <poems . . . so *inflated* with metaphor, that they may be compared to the gaudy bubbles blown up from a solution of soap – Oliver Goldsmith> **Dilate** implies expansion in diameter and suggests a widening out of something circular <as round a pebble into water thrown *dilates* a ring of light – H. W. Longfellow> <some stirring experience . . . may swiftly *dilate* your field of consciousness – C. E. Montague> *ant* contract, abridge

expect, hope, look, await *shared meaning* : to anticipate in the mind some occurrence or outcome. **Expect** usually implies both a high degree of certainty and a marked sense of anticipation <they *expect* to be married in June> <instead of worrying about what to *expect* from his boss, the effective manager worries about what the boss should *expect* from him – R. J. Bryant> <he seems to require and *expect* goodness in his species as we do a sweet taste in grapes – Bernard Mandeville> **Hope** (often with *for*) implies little certainty but suggests confidence or assurance in the possibility that what one desires or longs for will happen <*hope* they will have a pleasant day for the wedding> <encouraged to *hope* for a college education – H. E. Scudder> **Look** followed by *to* is likely to suggest more strongly than *expect* a counting on or a freedom from doubt <they *looked* to their children to care for them in old age> <I never *look* to have a mistress that I shall love half as well – Henry Brooke> With *for, look* does not focus on assurance; it suggests rather an attitude of expectancy and watchfulness <we can scarcely *look* for their arrival before Monday> <I think we may *look* for a better result next year – F. T. Wood> **Await** often adds to *look for* the implication of being ready, mentally or physically, for the event; unlike the preceding words it can take for its subject the thing anticipated and for its object the one that anticipates <the punishment which *awaits* unrepented sin – R. A. Hall> <death *awaits* every man> <we *await* your decision as patiently as we can> *ant* despair (*of*)

expedient *adj* **expedient, politic, advisable** *shared meaning* : dictated by practical or prudential motives. In this use all three words imply a choice and indicate the basis on which it has been or is to be made. **Expedient** applies to what is definitely and usually immediately advantageous <there shall be appointed . . . such number of . . . justices of the peace as the president of the United States shall, from time to time, think *expedient* – John Marshall> Often the word implies opportuneness as well as advantageousness <they did not feel it *expedient* to interfere at this time> and may connote subordination of ethical principles to convenience or self-interest <a kind of mumbo jumbo to justify whatever current policy the government happens to find *expedient* – Edmund Wilson> or even be used in opposition to *right* <too fond of the right to pursue the *expedient*

– Oliver Goldsmith> **Politic** stresses the practical point of view and applies to whatever constitutes a judiciously or tactically sound course, action, or method; like *expedient* it tends to suggest material or even self-centered motives <whether it is not your interest to make them happy . . . . Is a *politic* act the worse for being a generous one? – Edmund Burke> <so long as it was *politic* to profess loyalty – V. L. Parrington> **Advisable** applies to what is practical, prudent, or advantageous but lacks the derogatory suggestions of *expedient* and *politic;* therefore it is the word of choice when a neutral objective statement of fact is to be made <it was not *advisable* to drive on through the mountains because of the night fogs – Harry Sylvester> <others find it *advisable* to read very slowly . . . saturating themselves with a book's very atmosphere – J. C. Powys> ***ant*** inexpedient

expedient ***n*** – see RESOURCE

expedition – see HASTE ***ant*** procrastination

expeditious – see FAST ***ant*** sluggish

expel – see EJECT ***ant*** admit

expend – see SPEND

expense – see PRICE

expensive – see COSTLY ***ant*** inexpensive

expert – see PROFICIENT ***ant*** amateurish

explain, expound, explicate, elucidate, interpret *shared meaning* : to make something clear or understandable. **Explain** implies a making of something plain or intelligible to one to whom it was previously obscure <*explain* the difference between two words> <puzzling things were *explained.* Contradictions melted away – Herman Wouk> **Expound** implies careful, elaborate, often learned setting forth of a subject in order to explain it (as in a sermon or treatise) <*expound* the gospel of salvation> <[it] *expounds* in clear, readable English the tremendous importance of the Roman legacy to our world – John Day> **Explicate** adds to *expound* the idea of detailed development or analysis of a topic <before I attempt to explain the moderate sense of the word "knowledge" . . ., let me *explicate* the too high or too strong sense of the term which I wish to exclude – M. J. Adler> <the kind of criticism that tries to "*explicate*" a poem through close textual analysis, rather than to assess it in relation to its author's other work – *Current Biog.*> **Elucidate** implies a throwing light on something obscure (as by explanation, exposition, or illustration) <plain exposition, in which the comparisons are not plaintive but *elucidating* – *New Yorker*> <the governor's speech *elucidated* his tax proposals> **Interpret** adds to *explain* the implication of using imagination or sympathy or special knowledge to make clear the meaning of something (as a dream, an abstraction, or a passage in a foreign language) that presents more than purely logical difficulty <the principle by which the Law was adapted to changing conditions by new ways of *interpreting* the scriptural text – Edmund Wilson> <a collection of 81 sayings . . . which . . . has been variously *interpreted* by various translators – Albert Newgarden>

explicate – see EXPLAIN

explicit, express, specific, definite *shared meaning* : perfectly clear and unambiguous. **Explicit** implies such plainness and distinctness that there is no room for ambiguity or reason for difficulty in interpretation <that there might be no mistake as to the meaning of his satire Brackenridge set down . . . an *explicit* statement of his purpose – V. L. Parrington> <his father gave him an *explicit* order to be home in time for supper> <the fourth condition makes *explicit* what was implied by the earlier statement – M. J. Adler> **Express** implies explicitness together with direct ness and forcefulness in utterance <give *express* credit in a report to the technician who actually performed the tests> <you disobeyed my *express* order> <an *express* provision of the act required that the codes should not promote monopolies – F. D. Roosevelt> **Specific** implies precision in reference or particularization in statement of the details covered or included <the teacher programs the machine with the *specific* needs of individual students in mind – *Johns Hopkins Mag.*> <he made several *specific* criticisms of our plan of procedure> **Definite** stresses precise and determinate limitations and the absence of uncertainty, indecision, or ambiguity <came to the *definite* conclusion that they would have to leave the farm> <it was a simple, clear, *definite* question – Sinclair Lewis> ***ant*** ambiguous

exploit – see FEAT

exposed – see LIABLE

expostulate – see OBJECT

expound – see EXPLAIN

express *adj* – see EXPLICIT

express *vb* **express, vent, utter, voice, broach, air** *shared meaning* : to let out what one thinks or feels. **Express** implies an impulse to reveal that may be variously manifested (as in words and action, in dress and habits, or in what one makes or produces) <believes that printing types and books should *express* contemporary conditions and fulfill contemporary needs – *Current Biog.*> <fashion should *express* the needs of women – Norman Norell> <there were so many different moods and impressions that he wished to *express* in verse – James Joyce> **Vent** stresses a strong inner compulsion to express something (as a pent-up emotion that demands an outlet) often in a highly emotional manner <went on in this vein for some time, getting into a tantrum; but . . . she finally took herself off to *vent* her irritation on the faithful Wacey – Victoria Sackville-West> <his heart's his mouth: what his breast forges, that his tongue must *vent* – Shak.> **Utter** implies the use of the voice, not necessarily in articulated speech <the dog *uttered* a whimper of pain> <such a grammar can be internally consistent, useful as an instrument of analysis, but inadequate as an explanation of how people actually *utter* – *Times Lit. Supp.*> <is any given truth any the less true for having been *uttered* more than once? – Theodore Sturgeon> **Voice** implies expression in words but not necessarily by vocal utterance <*voice* a complaint> <demonstrated an ability to find and *voice* national issues before other men were aware of them – Charles Mangel> **Broach** stresses mention for the first time, usually of something long thought over while awaiting an opportune moment for disclosure <know . . . with what brilliance of wit and vividness he adorns the philosophical themes he *broaches* – Harrison Smith> <he was sold on the idea as soon as they *broached* it – W. B. Ready> or one introduced for purposes of study and consideration <I *broached*, as a practical measure . . . the system which I had discussed tentatively . . . several years before – A. D. White> <the idea of a Trans-Saharan railway has been *broached*. Many arguments have been advanced – Emile Lengyel> **Air** implies an exposing or parading of one's view often in order to gain aid or relief or sympathy <[took] long walks together . . . *airing* their most intimate and improbable plans – John Cheever> ***ant*** imply

expression – see PHRASE

expunge – see ERASE

exquisite – see CHOICE *adj*

extend, lengthen, elongate, prolong, protract *shared meaning* : to draw out or add to so as to increase in length. Both **extend** and **lengthen** connote an increase of length either in space or time, but only the former can also connote increase in range (as of kinds, influence, or applicability); thus, a road can be *extended* or *lengthened;* one may *extend* or *lengthen* his stay; the power of a monarch, however, may be *extended* but not *lengthened* <the curriculum . . . was planned . . . to *extend* the children's interests, to open new doors to them – Eleanor McGrath> <time and again he has shocked, altered, and *extended* my view of the world – P. R. Bannes> <the *lengthening* of the average life span by more than twenty years since the last century – *Collier's Yr. Bk.*> **Elongate** usually implies increase in spatial length and frequently suggests stretching <as you travel along the rough road, the lake *elongates* towards you – George Farwell> <fractures in the lateral margins enabled the outer shell to *elongate* vertically – C. M. Nevin> <the British *elongating* their defense program – *Economist*> **Prolong** is likely to imply duration especially beyond usual or normal or pleasing limits <*prolong* an argument interminably> <that audience is accustomed to being distracted and does not like to be asked to concentrate or make a *prolonged* intellectual effort – Aldous Huxley> **Protract** adds to *prolong* the connotations of indefiniteness, needlessness, or boredom <many of the young talked despondently of the *protracted* Cold War and the seemingly inevitable nuclear holocaust – M. S. Eisenhower> <his temptation will be to *protract* negotiations on the minor points still outstanding – *New Statesman & Nation*> ***ant*** abridge, shorten

exterior – see OUTER ***ant*** interior

exterminate, extirpate, eradicate, uproot, wipe out *shared meaning* : to effect the destruction or abolition of something. **Exterminate** implies utter extinction and usually a killing off <the tribe had been *exterminated* . . . in their summer camp – Willa Cather> <the little businessmen . . . soon found themselves . . . being *exterminated* and forced back into the ranks of wage earners – W. L. Shirer> **Extirpate** implies the extinction of a class or kind (as a species or race) or sometimes of an idea or doctrine by or as if by destruction or removal of its means of propagation <the ancient Athenians had been *extirpated* by repeated wars and massacres – Robert Graves> <serpent worship which the Mosaic curse and Christianity alike have not succeeded in *extirpating* – Norman Douglas> **Eradicate** stresses the driving out or eliminating of something that has taken root or established itself firmly <the program to *eradicate* tuberculosis> <if you *eradicate* a fault you leave room for a worse one to take root and flourish – L P. Smith> **Uproot** differs from *eradicate* chiefly in implying a forceful or violent method suggestive of a tempest that tears trees out by their roots <political authority must confront the problems created by the *uprooting* of the old structure of society – Guenter Lewy> <hands . . . red with guiltless blood . . . *uprooting* every germ of truth – P. B. Shelley> **Wipe out** can imply extermination <a nerve gas that could *wipe out* the populations of enemy cities – *N.Y. Times*> but as often suggests a canceling or obliterating <*wipe out* a debt> <integration is the most vital factor . . . in *wiping out* stereotypes and allowing for greater acceptance and appreciation for individuality – Dorothy G. Singer>

external – see OUTER ***ant*** internal

extinguish – see ABOLISH

extirpate – see EXTERMINATE

extort – see EDUCE

extract – see EDUCE

extraneous – see EXTRINSIC ***ant*** relevant

extravagant – see EXCESSIVE ***ant*** restrained

extreme – see EXCESSIVE

extricate, disentangle, untangle, disencumber, disembarrass *shared meaning* : to free from what binds or holds back. **Extricate** implies the use of force or ingenuity in freeing from a difficult position or situation <resolve to bring an end to this war ... as quickly as it is physically possible to reach the essential agreement and *extricate* our men and our future from this bottomless pit – E. M. Kennedy> <the wily Austrian had once more *extricated* himself from a tight fix that might easily have proved disastrous – W. L. Shirer> **Disentangle** and **untangle** suggest painstaking separation of a thing from other things <he had become conscious of many undercurrents whose significance he was unable to *disentangle* – Victoria Sackville-West> <so picturesque a figure that biography is unable to *disentangle* him from legend – *Amer. Guide Series: N.C.*> <drank, set down his glass, and *untangled* his legs – Hamilton Basso> <aided in the reorganization of municipal administration, *untangled* financial difficulties – T. H. Jack> **Disencumber** implies a freeing from what weighs down, clogs, or imposes a heavy burden <he can call a spade a spade, and knows how to *disencumber* ideas of their wordy frippery – George Eliot> <*disencumber* oneself from heavy winter clothes> **Disembarrass** implies a release from what embarrasses by or as if by hampering, hindering, or impeding <*disembarrass* ourselves of the curse of ignorance and learn to work together – Alvin Johnson> <loved to *disembarrass* himself of all the apparatus of life – A. C. Benson> <decide to *disembarrass* themselves of him by killing or banishing him – Merran McCulloch>

extrinsic, extraneous, foreign, alien *shared meaning* : external to a thing, its essential nature, or original character. **Extrinsic** applies to what is distinctly outside the thing in question or is not contained in or derived from its essential nature <people whose religious practice is motivated by *extrinsic* factors like sociability and conformity – *Trans-action*> <the special quality of such presuppositions is that they are inherent and not *extrinsic* – Walter Moberly> **Extraneous** applies to what is on or comes from the outside and may or may not be capable of becoming an essential part <water is rarely free from *extraneous* matter> <style . . . is not – can never be – *extraneous* ornament – A. T. Quiller-Couch> **Foreign** applies to what is so different as to be rejected or repelled or, if admitted, to be incapable of becoming identified with or assimilated by the thing in question <*foreign* matter in a wound> <look round our world. . . . Nothing is *foreign:* parts relate to whole . . . ; all served, all serving: nothing stands alone – Alexander Pope> <the mysticism so *foreign* to the French mind and temper – W. C. Brownell> **Alien** is likely to add to *foreign* a suggestion of such strangeness as leads to incompatibility or even repugnance <he realized that he was in a far, *alien* land, without familiar signs and sights to succor his essentially timid heart – H. C. Hervey> <our apprehension of something more *alien,* something deeply antipathetic to ourselves – Edmund Wilson> ***ant*** intrinsic

exuberant – see PROFUSE ***ant*** austere, sterile

fabricate – see MAKE

fabulous – see FICTITIOUS

facet – see PHASE

facetious – see WITTY ***ant*** lugubrious

facility – see READINESS

facsimile – see REPRODUCTION

factitious – see ARTIFICIAL ***ant*** bona fide, veritable

factor – see ELEMENT
faculty – see POWER 2
fad – see FASHION
fag – see TIRE
failing – see FAULT ***ant*** perfection
fair 1 see BEAUTIFUL ***ant*** foul, ill-favored
2 **fair, just, equitable, impartial, unbiased, dispassionate, objective** *shared meaning* : free from favor toward either or any side. **Fair** implies an elimination of one's own interests, feelings, or prejudices so as to achieve a proper balance of conflicting interests <a *fair* distribution of a treat> <the judge's decision was absolutely *fair*> **Just** implies an exact following of a standard of what is right and proper <how much easier it is to be generous than *just* – *Junius*> **Equitable** implies a freer and less rigid standard than *just* and usually a fair and equal treatment of all concerned <a form of society which will provide for an *equitable* distribution of . . . riches – J. W. Krutch> **Impartial** stresses an absence of favor and prejudice in making a judgment <an *impartial* tribunal> <law shall be uniform and *impartial* – B. N. Cardozo> **Unbiased** stresses even more strongly the absence of prejudice and prepossession and the firm intent to be fair to all <*unbiased* by self-profit – Alfred Tennyson> <to furnish the cabinet with *unbiased* and helpful advice on matters of state – R. M. Dawson> **Dispassionate** suggests freedom from emotional involvement or the influence of strong feeling and may imply coolness or even coldness in judgment <a *dispassionate* and objective description of the region – G. M. Foster> <a *dispassionate* appraisal of an artist's work> **Objective** stresses a tendency to view events or phenomena as apart from oneself and therefore to be judged on purely factual bases and without reference to one's personal feelings or interests <we shall be like ice when relating passions and adventures . . . we shall be . . . *objective* and impersonal – William Troy> ***ant*** unfair
faith – see BELIEF ***ant*** doubt
faithful, loyal, constant, staunch, steadfast, resolute *shared meaning* : firm in adherence to whatever one owes allegiance. **Faithful** implies firm and unswerving adherence to an individual to whom one is united by some tie (as marriage, allegiance, or gratitude) or to a promise, oath, or pledge <a *faithful* husband is *faithful* to his marriage vows> **Loyal** implies firm resistance to any temptation to desert or betray <your wife, my lord; your true and *loyal* wife – Shak.> <they are not *loyal,* they are only servile – G. B. Shaw> **Constant** stresses continuing firmness of emotional attachment without necessarily implying strict obedience to promises or vows <I never knew a pair of lovers more *constant* than those two – Edna S. V. Millay> <a few came, straggling and reluctant and not at all *constant:* most quit after the first day – Thomas Pynchon> **Staunch** suggests fortitude and resolution in adherence and imperviousness to influences that would weaken it <ever a *staunch* Federalist, he viewed the policies of Jefferson and his followers with repugnance – E. E. Curtis> <Russia and China today are among the world's *staunchest* supporters of monogamous . . families – Gary Snyder> **Steadfast** implies a steady and unwavering course in love, allegiance, or conviction <which hope we have as an anchor of the soul, both sure and *steadfast* – *Heb* 6:19 (AV)> <narrow of vision but *steadfast* to principles – Agnes Repplier> **Resolute** can imply steadfastness or staunchness but is likely to emphasize firm determination as a quality of character <not . . . *resolute* and firm, but perverse and obstinate – Edmund Burke> <her first few years . . . would have defeated a less *resolute* actress – *Current Biog.*> ***ant*** faithless

faithless, false, disloyal, traitorous, treacherous, perfidious *shared meaning* : untrue to what has a right to one's fidelity or allegiance. **Faithless,** applicable to a person, an utterance, or an act, implies a breach of an obligation (as a vow or pledge) whether by specific betrayal or general untrustworthiness or mere neglect of actively proving devotion or faith <the remnant . . . have been abandoned by their *faithless* allies – P. B. Shelley> <he abandoned one wife and was *faithless* to another – J. R. Green> **False** stresses the fact of failure to be true to however great or small a degree <a *false* friend who helped to spread a malicious rumor> <to all who dealt with him he was equally *false* and tricky – J. R. Green> **Disloyal** implies lack of faithfulness to one to whom loyalty is owed <good party people think such open-mindedness *disloyal;* but in politics there should be no loyalty except to the public good – G. B. Shaw> **Traitorous** implies either actual treason or a serious betrayal of trust <a *traitorous* breach of confidence> <sedition, in our law, is *traitorous* behavior that falls short of treason because it does not actively levy war against the United States – M. T. Smelser & H. W. Kirwin> **Treacherous** implies readiness to betray trust or confidence or, as applied to things, to lead into peril or toward disaster by false or delusive appearances <*treacherous* allies who require constant watching> <a slippery *treacherous* slope> <up steep crags, and over *treacherous* morasses, he moved . . . easily – T. B. Macaulay> **Perfidious** adds to *treacherous* a strong implication of baseness or vileness <a *perfidious* attack on an ally> ***ant*** faithful

fake – see IMPOSTURE

false **1 false, wrong** *shared meaning* : neither true nor right. **False** rarely wholly loses its early implication of deceit. This is markedly so when the primary implication is one of contrariety between something said, thought, or concluded and reality or the facts <a *false* statement> <thou shalt not bear *false* witness against thy neighbor – *Exod* 20:16 (ASV)> It is present but less marked when the term applies to something viewed as opposed to a corresponding something real, genuine, or authentic; thus, *false* pearls simulate the appearance of but lack the quality and worth of real pearls; a *false* arch has the appearance of an architectural arch but does not have the structure or serve the purpose of a genuine arch; the pinxter flower is sometimes called *false* honeysuckle because of its resemblance to the true honeysuckle. Only in the sense of incorrect or erroneous does *false* largely lose the implication of deceit and even here there is often a suggestion of being beguiled or misled into believing the thing so described is true or right <so different from anything she had ever seen before that it had to be a trick of the eye, a *false* evaluation of size and speed and distance – Theodore Sturgeon> **Wrong** in its several senses is colored by its original implication of wryness or crookedness and implies basically a turning from a standard (as of truth, rectitude, or correctness) to its opposite. The word is both more forthright in denotation and less subtle in implication than *false;* thus, a *wrong* conception is one that is the reverse of the truth, while a *false* conception is not only *wrong* but the result of one's being deceived or intending to deceive; a *wrong* answer is merely erroneous, a *false* answer is both erroneous and lying <we took a *wrong* turning and lost our way> ***ant*** true

2 see FAITHLESS ***ant*** true

falsify – see MISREPRESENT

falter – see HESITATE

familiar **1 familiar, intimate** *shared meaning* : close to one another in spirit or indicative of such closeness. **Familiar** suggests the ease, informality, and

absence of reserve or constraint natural among members of a family or friends of long standing; it may apply to the relations, words, and actions of persons actually in such a situation <time and intercourse have made us *familiar* – Samuel Johnson> or to the attitude or the style of speaking or writing of persons who assume a comparable freedom and ease of address <the *familiar,* if not rude, tone in which people addressed her – Nathaniel Hawthorne> **Intimate** stresses the closeness and intensity rather than the mere frequency or continuity of personal association; it can suggest deep mutual understanding or the sharing of deeply personal thoughts and feelings <their hand grasp was very *intimate* and mutually comprehending – Arnold Bennett> <this girl's worldly wisdom . . . and *intimate* gossip about well-known people – Herman Wouk> As applied directly or indirectly to knowledge *intimate* differs from *familiar* not only in idiom but in implying close or deep study rather than mere acquaintance; thus, one is *familiar* with a situation when he has informed himself of important facts about it, one has an *intimate* knowledge of a situation who has added to familiarity a careful study of its fine points, ramifications, and interrelations; one is *familiar* with a poem who has read it and retained some notion of its content, one has *intimate* knowledge of a poem who has not only read it but studied it carefully and analyzed its content and relation to the poet's other work <has greatly contributed to the understanding of Africa . . . through his authoritative and *intimate* knowledge of that revolutionary continent – *Current Biog.*> ***ant*** aloof
2 see COMMON ***ant*** unfamiliar, strange
famous, renowned, celebrated, noted, notorious, distinguished, eminent, illustrious *shared meaning* : known far and wide. **Famous** implies little more than the fact of being, sometimes briefly, widely and popularly known <a *famous* athlete> <a locally *famous* recipe for plum cake> **Renowned** regularly and definitely implies not merely knowledge but acclaim and approbation <a *renowned* scientist> <royal kings . . . *renowned* for their deeds . . . for Christian service and true chivalry – Shak.> **Celebrated** stresses reception of popular or public notice and attention, especially in print <a *celebrated* kidnapping case> Often it implies public admiration or flattering attention <[she] had become as much *celebrated* for her writing as for her acting – *Current Biog.*> **Noted** suggests well-deserved public attention <a *noted* liberal editor> <one of the most *noted* racers and most noteworthy sires in American turf history> **Notorious** usually adds to *famous* a distinctly pejorative implication of questionableness, undesirableness, or evil <a *notorious* prostitute> <some weeds have become *notorious* in tropical forestry – C. J. Taylor> <it was the hangers-on that made Bucks County . . . *notorious.* The area was flooded with artists and writers and revolutionaries and people who never took baths – J. A. Michener> **Distinguished** implies acknowledged excellence or superiority <a *distinguished* statesman> <*distinguished* people are *distinguished* because of major strengths – not because of a lack of weaknesses – R. F. Lewis> **Eminent** implies conspicuousness for outstanding qualities and is applicable to one rising above others of the same class <among our famous present-day writers no one is really *eminent*> <John Bartram, America's most *eminent* naturalist – Harriet Zuckerman> **Illustrious** stresses enduring and merited honor and glory attached to a person or his deeds or qualities <boast the pure blood of an *illustrious* race – Alexander Pope> <his right noble mind, *illustrious* virtue – Shak.> ***ant*** obscure
fanciful – see IMAGINARY ***ant*** realistic
fancy *n* – see IMAGINATION ***ant*** experience
fancy *vb* – see THINK

fantastic **1** see IMAGINARY
2 fantastic, bizarre, grotesque *shared meaning* : conceived or made or carried out without evident reference to reality, truth, or common sense. **Fantastic** suggests fantasy and stresses the exercise of unrestrained imagination or unlicensed fancy. Its connotations range from absurd extravagance through remoteness from reality to mere ingenuity in devising <these methods of interpretation ... will otherwise seem gratuitously farfetched, *fantastic* – Edmund Wilson> <she was completely dazzled by him. His irruption into her life seemed not only *fantastic,* but unbelievable – Victoria Sackville-West> <a writer of *fantastic* ... fiction – *Times Lit. Supp.*> **Bizarre** applies to the sensationally queer or strange and implies violence of contrast or incongruity of combination <temple sculpture became *bizarre* – rearing monsters, fiery horses, great pillared halls teeming with sculptures – *Atlantic*> <confidence in the ignorance and the gullibility of the electorate has been demonstrated in some *bizarre* episodes in American politics – B. L. Felknor> **Grotesque** may apply to what is conventionally ugly but artistically effective <attained almost instant literary fame with his powerful and *grotesque* novel – *Current Biog.*> or it may suggest ludicrous ugliness or incongruity or awkwardness, often with sinister or tragic overtones <they are eyesores, *grotesque* of face, misshapen in figure, outlandish in dress, vulgar in manner – *Newsweek*> <there is ... something unreal, almost unbelievable, quite *grotesque,* in the diplomatic exchanges between Moscow and Berlin in these spring weeks – W. L. Shirer>
fantasy – see IMAGINATION
far – see DISTANT ***ant*** near, nigh, nearly
faraway – see DISTANT ***ant*** near, nigh, nearly
far-off – see DISTANT ***ant*** near, nigh, nearly
farther, further *shared meaning* : to a greater extent or degree : going or extending beyond. Although these words are often used interchangeably they were originally different words and can still be used distinctively to convey quite separate impressions. In such use **farther** basically implies a greater distance from a point in space or sometimes in time; **further** implies onwardness or an advance or an addition (as in movement or progression) not only in space but in time, quantity, or degree <the *farther* floe was pulling away in the grip of the tide – Berton Roueché> <the philosopher's hatred of and contempt for science ... goes back no *farther* than the beginning of the nineteenth century – Raymond Queneau> <De Gaulle's violent remarks ... *further* strained relations – S. E. Ambrose> <it is easy to feel that we are even *further* from equality and justice than we were in 1951 – Robert Blauner> In spite of this fundamental distinction in meaning there are many cases in which a meaningful choice is difficult indeed, since the ideas of distance from a point and of advance in movement may both be implied <I ... could get no *farther* than the first two or three chapters, so stupid did I find it – *Times Lit. Supp.*> <as we climb higher, we can see *further* – W. R. Inge>
fascinate – see ATTRACT
fashion *n* **1** see METHOD
2 fashion, style, mode, vogue, fad, rage, craze *shared meaning* : the choice or usage (as in dressing, decorating, or living) generally accepted by those who regard themselves as up-to-date and sophisticated. **Fashion** is thought of in general as the current conventional usage or custom of polite society or that determined by those who are regarded as leaders in the social, intellectual, literary, or artistic world <discriminating travelers who ... do not follow *fashion* ... but create it – *N.Y. Times Mag.*> <nowhere ... is *fashion* so exacting, not only in dress and demeanor, but in plastic art

itself – W. C. Brownell> **Style** often implies a distinctive fashion and may suggest the elegant or distinguished fashion chosen by persons of wealth and taste <*style* is the form imposed by art on life. . . . There is obviously no *style* without leisure, without exposure to good models, without a passion for improvement – Alan Simpson> **Mode** suggests the fashion of the moment among those anxious to appear elegant or sophisticated <the easy, apathetic graces of the man of the *mode* – T. B. Macaulay> **Vogue** stresses the prevalence or wide acceptance of a fashion <the virtue of being a good literary politician is that one can promote one's own fashion, be put in *vogue,* and so relax the bite of the snob – Norman Mailer> <the slender, undeveloped figure then very much in *vogue* – Willa Cather> **Fad** suggests caprice in taking up or in dropping a fashion <areas where the *fad* for sourdough bread is prevalent – Miriam S. Minnick> <trends, mingling neoanarchist patterns of political action with current Left Bank politico-intellectual *fads* – Edmond Taylor> **Rage** and **craze** stress intense or senseless enthusiasm in taking up or pursuing a fad <derivations from the Sanskrit, once all the *rage,* are now out of favor – Alan Pryce-Jones> <the current *rage* for . . . how-to-do-it material – W. I. Nichols> <the British *craze* for the monocle gave to the wearer the power of the camera to fix people in a superior stare – Marshall McLuhan>

fashion *vb* – see MAKE

fast, rapid, swift, fleet, quick, speedy, hasty, expeditious *shared meaning* : moving, proceeding, or acting with celerity. *Fast* and *rapid* are sometimes used without distinction, but **fast** is more likely to apply to a moving object and **rapid** to characterize the movement itself; thus, a *fast* horse is one capable of going at a *rapid* gait; a *fast* worker does *rapid* work. **Swift** suggests great rapidity, frequently coupled with ease or facility of movement <more *swift* than swallow shears the liquid sky – Edmund Spenser> **Fleet** adds the implication of lightness and nimbleness <*fleeter* than arrows, bullets, wind, thought, swifter things – Shak.> <like sails or clouds on a windy day, the dancers appeared, came together, and separated with a *fleet,* almost preoccupied urgency – Doris Hering> The remaining words, though applicable to persons and sometimes to things, are particularly likely to be used of actions. **Quick** suggests promptness and the taking of little time <slow to resolve, but in performance *quick* – John Dryden> <the teacher who is flexible . . . takes *quick* advantage of the individual student's current focus of interest – R. K. Corbin> <the boy is very *quick* on his feet> **Speedy** implies quickness of successful accomplishment and may also suggest unusual velocity <the *speedy* exhaustion of the soils that were being recklessly cropped – Lewis Mumford> <a *speedy* recovery> <forced in time of war to use the heavier-type *speedy* vehicles – John Kemp> **Hasty** suggests hurry and precipitousness rather than speed and often connotes a resulting confusion, disorder, or inefficiency <my wife . . . is often *hasty* in her judgment of strangers – Roald Dahl> <made a *hasty* departure from the overturned beehive> <clearheaded now, firmly master of a somewhat *hasty* heart . . . [he] persevered and won as patron a wealthy cement contractor – Kenneth Rudeen> **Expeditious** adds to *quick* the implication of efficiency <an *expeditious* worker> <stamped out the rebellion by the most *expeditious* means – Virginia Valentine> ***ant*** slow

fasten, fix, attach, affix *shared meaning* : to make something stay firmly in place. **Fasten** implies an action of securing (as by tying, buttoning, nailing, or locking) <*fasten* a calendar to the wall> <*fasten* a skirt with large buttons> <be sure you *fasten* the door when you leave> **Fix** implies an intent to keep something from falling down or from losing hold and is likely to suggest such methods as driving in or implanting deeply <*fix* a post in the earth> The word is more common in extended than in literal use in this sense <*fix* a face in one's memory> In some phrases where *fasten* and *fix* are both used freely, there may be a distinction in meaning that is subtle but significant; thus, to *fix* one's affection on someone connotes concentration and fidelity while to *fasten* one's affection on someone is likely to suggest covetousness or an effort to control or dominate; to *fix* blame suggests solid grounds for the accusation, but to *fasten* blame is likely to suggest factitious grounds or selfish motives <his heart is *fixed*, trusting in the Lord – *Ps* 112:7 (AV)> <all disliked the laws which Church and State were trying to *fasten* on them – Henry Adams> **Attach** suggests a connecting or uniting by or as if by a bond, link, or tie in order to keep things together <*attach* a sheet to the line with clothespins> <he is strongly *attached* to the cause of peace> <to this treasure a curse is *attached* – Bayard Taylor> **Affix** implies an imposing of one thing or another typically by such means as gluing, impressing, or nailing <a small hand mirror *affixed* to the wall by a nail – James Purdy> <a penalty *affixed* to hasty, superficial thinking – A. N. Whitehead> ***ant*** unfasten, loosen, loose

fastidious – see NICE

fatal – see DEADLY

fate, destiny, lot, portion, doom *shared meaning* : a predetermined state or end. **Fate** implies an inevitable and often an adverse outcome, condition, or end <let us, then, be up and doing, with a heart for any *fate* – H. W. Longfellow> <the *fate* of all language is change – David Mellinkoff> **Destiny** implies something foreordained and inescapable and is more likely to suggest a great or noble course or end than one to be feared or resisted <the symbol of the *destiny* of the Jewish people, whom no earthly power has ever been able to defeat – Bruno Bettelheim> *Lot* and *portion* imply a distribution by fate or destiny, **lot** distinctively imputing the action of blind chance and **portion** the apportionment of good and evil elements <whenever one of the people curses you . . . or otherwise mistreats you, as is the usual *lot* of a clown – Jack Altman> <her own misery for taking from the small sum of peace they had in the world, adding to the *portion* of their unhappiness – Bernard Malamud> <poverty was his *portion* all his days – Kemp Malone> **Doom** stresses finality and usually implies an unhappy or calamitous fate <involution is as much a law of nature as evolution. There is no escape from this *doom* – W. R. Inge> <lured unsuspecting ships to their *doom* on the rocks on dark and stormy nights – Richard Joseph>

fateful – see OMINOUS

fatigue – see TIRE ***ant*** rest

fatuous – see SIMPLE ***ant*** sensible

fault, failing, frailty, foible, vice *shared meaning* : an imperfection or weakness of character. **Fault** implies a not necessarily culpable failure to reach some standard of perfection (as in disposition, action, or habit) <he is all *fault* who hath no *fault* at all – Alfred Tennyson> <his lack of interest in theology is a weakness but not a major *fault* – C. H. Hopkins> **Failing** implies a usually minor shortcoming in character of which one may be quite unaware <pride . . . is a very common *failing*, I believe – Jane Austen> <has all the *failings* of our common lot – Ronald Rubinstein> **Frailty** implies a general or chronic proneness to yield to temptation <you don't stop being concerned with man because you recognize his essential absurdities and *frailties* and pretensions – Stanley Kubrick> **Foible** applies to a harmless weakness or idiosyncrasy more likely to be amusing or endearing than disfiguring <Miller did indeed sound at times the Hemingwayish note of a he-man historian among the literary sissies – his most damaging *foible*

– H. F. May> **Vice** suggests violation of moral law but does not in itself imply corruptness or defiance; often it is a general term for an imperfection or weakness and especially for one arising from a normal quality or appetite carried to excess <she was criminally proud. That was her *vice* – Arnold Bennett> <dogmatism is a form of arrogance and pride, a *vice,* concerning knowledge claims – J. W. Davis> ***ant*** merit

faultfinding – see CRITICAL

favor *n* **favor, goodwill, countenance** *shared meaning* : approving interest. **Favor** suggests an active interest and usually implies partiality or preference <claimed that the judge had shown *favor* to the defense> <one old maid who stood highest in her *favor* – Jack Altman> **Goodwill** implies positive friendliness and a willingness to contribute to the success or welfare of a person, a group, or a cause <an augury of the oncoming generation who can and will bring *goodwill* and a more generous humanity in the place of intolerance – B. H. Kizer> <a happy man . . . is a radiating focus of *goodwill* – R. L. Stevenson> **Countenance** stresses approval or sanction but does not necessarily imply helpfulness or friendliness <writers whose entirely orthodox views . . . have been refused official *countenance* – H. R. Trevor-Roper> <[they] were left without munitions of war, without arms, clothing, pay, or even *countenance* and encouragement – C. P. Curtis & Ferris Greenslet> ***ant*** disfavor, animus

favor *vb* – see OBLIGE

favorable, auspicious, propitious *shared meaning* : pointing toward a happy outcome. **Favorable** implies definitely that the persons involved are approving or helpful or that the circumstances are advantageous <both families were *favorable* to the match> <a hot dry summer, *favorable* to contemplative life out of doors – Joseph Conrad> <they tacked about seeking a *favorable* breeze to carry them down the bay> **Auspicious** suggests the presence of signs and omens and is applicable to something that is marked by favorable signs or is in itself regarded as a good omen <pay the boy . . . he brought *auspicious* news – Rudyard Kipling> <his generous contribution gave the campaign an *auspicious* start> **Propitious** describes, perhaps more mildly than *auspicious,* events or conditions that constitute favorable indications and is especially applicable in situations quite free from any discouraging note but not requiring the positive note of optimism that is so regularly a part of *auspicious* <[they arrived] at that *propitious* moment of recess between the departure of the sweepers and the arrival of the minor officials – Terry Southern> <after so *propitious* an opening it seemed that acerbities might be quelled, rivalries mitigated – S. H. Adams> ***ant*** unfavorable, antagonistic

fawn, toady, truckle, cringe, cower *shared meaning* : to act or behave with abjectness. **Fawn** implies seeking favor by servile flattery or exaggerated attention and submissiveness <they *fawn* on the proud feet that spurn them lying low – P. B. Shelley> <died, still *fawning* like the coward that he had always been – Bernard Pares> **Toady** suggests the attempt to ingratiate oneself by an abjectly menial or subservient attitude; it consistently implies a mean self-interest <in proportion as he submits and *toadies,* he also will dominate and bully – Margaret Mead> **Truckle** implies an obsequious subordination of oneself or submission of one's wishes, judgments, or opinions to those of a superior <he would *truckle* to no man – V. L. Parrington> <there are people who will always *truckle* to those who have money – Archibald Marshall> **Cringe** suggests a bowing and shrinking in physical or mental distress or fear or in servility <a dog *cringing* from a blow> <we *cringe* under the blasting wind on the highest slopes – C. S. Houston> <blatant he bids the world bow down, or *cringing*

begs a crust of praise – Rudyard Kipling> **Cower** implies intense, often cowardly fear and a shrinking away from its cause, usually someone who tyrannizes or dominates <*cowering* in their huts like so many rabbits in their burrows, listening in fear – Charles Kingsley> <the whole family *cowered* under Lady Kew's eyes and nose, and she ruled by force of them – W. M. Thackeray> ***ant*** domineer

faze – see EMBARRASS

fealty – see FIDELITY ***ant*** perfidy

fear 1 fear, dread, fright, alarm, panic, trepidation *shared meaning* : painful agitation in the presence or anticipation of danger. **Fear,** the most general term, implies apprehensive anxiety and often loss of courage <*fear* came upon me, and trembling – *Job* 4:14 (AV)> **Dread** is likely to add to *fear* the idea of intense reluctance to face or meet a person or situation and suggests aversion as well as anxiety <conscious that, for all the horror and the *dread*, the death was a marvelously exciting and dramatic experience – Herman Wouk> <we face the threat – not with *dread* and confusion – but with confidence and conviction – D. D. Eisenhower> **Fright** implies the shock of sudden, startling fear <the deer took *fright* and dashed off> <the sound produces a kind of horror that is something more than mere *fright* – Ernie Pyle> **Alarm** suggests such sudden and intense apprehension as is produced by newly perceived awareness of imminent danger <thou wast born amid the din of arms, and sucked a breast that panted with *alarms* – William Cowper> **Panic** implies unreasoning and overmastering fear and is likely to connote disordered and useless activity <fled in sudden *panic* from the safety of her home> <she began to wail in *panic.* Within a minute she was hysterical – Norman Mailer> **Trepidation** adds to *dread* the implication of timidity especially as manifested by trembling or by marked hesitation <I should very shortly perish of *trepidation* and suspense in so sinister an environment – Elinor Wylie> ***ant*** fearlessness

2 see REVERENCE ***ant*** contempt

fearful 1 fearful, apprehensive, afraid *shared meaning* : disturbed by fear. **Fearful** implies a timorous, worrying, or imaginative temperament more often than a real cause for fear <*fearful* that a storm would spoil their picnic> <the average individual is somewhat *fearful* of high speeds – H. G. Armstrong> **Apprehensive** suggests an immediate state of mind produced by having good grounds for fear and regularly implies a presentiment or anticipation of danger or evil <whole troops of . . . provincials, less *apprehensive* of servitude than of famine – Edward Gibbon> <leaving me miserable and *apprehensive* of some great trouble in store for all of us – Hugh Walpole> **Afraid** implies nothing about the validity of the motivation, but it does regularly imply a deep-seated reaction of fear and may connote weakness or cowardice often manifest in unwillingness to act or declare oneself <the trained reason is disinterested and fearless. It is not *afraid* of public opinion – W. R. Inge> <we have been much too much *afraid* of the Russians, and have allowed ourselves frequently to be bluffed by them – Edmund Wilson> ***ant*** fearless, intrepid

2 fearful, awful, dreadful, frightful, terrible, terrific, appalling *shared meaning* : of a kind to cause grave distress of mind. Additionally, all these words and their corresponding adverbs have a lighter, chiefly conversational value in which they are used as intensives and mean little more than *extreme* (or *extremely*). In their basic use, however, all convey an impression of which horror or fear is an integral part. **Fearful** applies to what produces fear, agitation, or loss of courage <our *fearful* trip is done, the ship has weathered every rack – Walt Whitman> **Awful** implies striking with an awareness of transcendent overpowering force, might, or significance <a

grave voice which, falling word by word upon his consciousness, made him stir inside with a grotesque and *awful* fear – William Styron> <the *awful* arithmetic of the atomic bomb – D. D. Eisenhower> **Dreadful** applies to what fills one with dread and suggests a power to make one shudder with mingled fear and aversion <cancer is a *dreadful* disease> <it is out of the self-knowledge gained by putting *dreadful* questions that man achieves his final dignity – L. C. Eiseley> **Frightful** implies such a startling or outrageous quality as produces utter consternation or a paralysis of fear <her husband's defection was a *frightful* shock> <a *frightful* spectacle of poverty, barbarity, and ignorance – T. B. Macaulay> **Terrible** suggests painfulness too great to be endured or a capacity to produce and prolong extreme and agitating fear <those five *terrible* days of war – *New Yorker*> <the Jewish God may be retributory and *terrible* but he is not preoccupied with torment – Edmund Wilson> <a human being devoid of hope is the most *terrible* object in the world – V. G. Heiser> **Terrific** applies to something intended or fitted to inspire terror (as by its size, appearance, or potency) <a lien on future growth and prosperity, like our *terrific* national debt of today – S. E. Morison> <a *terrific* outburst of fury> <the storm was *terrific* beyond imagining> **Appalling** describes what strikes one with dismay as well as with terror or horror <tumors destroy man in a unique and *appalling* way, as flesh of his own flesh, which has somehow been rendered proliferative, rampant, predatory, and ungovernable – F. P. Rous> <to ensure that he would perform under the *appalling* stress of eighteenth-century battle conditions – Walter Millis>

feasible – see POSSIBLE ***ant*** unfeasible, infeasible, chimerical (*schemes, projects, suggestions*)

feat, exploit, achievement *shared meaning* : a remarkable deed. **Feat** applies usually to an act involving physical strength, dexterity, or daring <sleights of art and *feats* of strength went round – Oliver Goldsmith> but it may also imply mental dexterity or technical skill in performing or doing <the conquest of the peoples of the Peruvian coast was not a very difficult military *feat* – P. E. James> <it is a rather remarkable intellectual *feat* and a considerable artistic one – Irving Kolodin> **Exploit** applies particularly to an adventurous, heroic, or brilliant deed <the Romans talked with admiration for a century of the far land to which Caesar had borne the eagles; and no *exploit* gave him more fame with his contemporaries – J. A. Froude> or sometimes to one merely sensational <his *exploits* included dressing up as the Sultan of Zanzibar to receive a civic welcome at Cambridge – *Irish Digest*> **Achievement** implies success hard won in the face of difficulty or opposition <great is the rumor of this dreadful knight, and his *achievements* of no less account – Shak.> <for one of the *achievements* of his group . . . he was later awarded a British decoration – *Current Biog.*>

fecund – see FERTILE ***ant*** barren

fee – see WAGE

feel – see TOUCH

feeling 1 see SENSATION

2 feeling, affection, emotion, sentiment, passion *shared meaning* : subjective reaction or response (as to a person or a situation) or an expression of this. **Feeling,** the general term, indicates the fact of a response (as of pleasure, pain, attraction, or repulsion) but in itself offers nothing about the nature, the quality, or the intensity of that response <it's the *feeling* you had when you were twelve, and summer-drenched, and you kissed a girl for the very first time and knew a breathlessness you were sure could never happen again – Theodore Sturgeon> Sometimes *feeling* implies a contrast with *judgment* and connotes lack of thought <her humanity was a *feeling,* not a principle – Henry Mackenzie> **Affection** applies mainly to feelings that are also inclinations or likings <that serene and blessed mood, in which the *affections* gently lead us on – William Wordsworth> <radiates a warmth and tender *affection* that few can resist – Jacques Nevard> **Emotion** applies particularly to feelings marked or accompanied by excitement or agitation <a sensation of strength, inspired by mighty *emotion* – George Eliot> <I could feel at once that the house still held anger, and I wondered that anyone could keep one *emotion* so long – Shirley Jackson> **Sentiment** suggests refined, sometimes romantic, and occasionally artificial or affected feeling and is likely to connote a larger intellectual element in the feeling than any of the other terms <that moral *sentiment* which exists in every human breast – George Bancroft> <a man of liberal *sentiments* and cultivated understandings – T. B. Macaulay> **Passion** suggests powerful or controlling emotion; far more than *affection,* it implies urgency of desire (as for possession or revenge) <[he] knew that *passion* was powerful, heady stuff, and must be prudently dispensed – Roald Dahl> <the ruling *passion,* be it what it will, the ruling *passion* conquers reason still – Alexander Pope>

feign – see ASSUME

feint – see TRICK

felicitate, congratulate *shared meaning* : to express pleasure in the success or good fortune of another. **Felicitate** is commonly felt as more formal in tone and carries a strong implication of recognizing the fortune or happiness of another and wishing him continuing success and satisfaction <*felicitate* parents on the birth of a child> **Congratulate** is the more common term and the wider in its range of applications; it usually implies that the congratulator regards the other as a person to whom good fortune has come or whose accomplishment merits praise, but in itself it says nothing about the degree of satisfaction the congratulator feels or the extent to which he wishes the other success <the losing candidate *congratulated* his successful opponent> <*congratulated* herself on so quickly finding a job> <the author is to be *congratulated* on his book – *Language*>

felicitous – see FIT ***ant*** infelicitous, inept, maladroit

female *n* **female, woman, lady** *shared meaning* : a person and especially an adult who belongs to the sex that is the counterpart of the male sex. **Female** emphasizes the idea of sex and is applicable not merely to humans but to all beings that can be distinguished by sex. Its ordinary use as a synonym for *woman* was once common <three smart-looking *females* – Jane Austen> but is now felt as derogatory or contemptuous <the backbiting of catty *females*> except in strictly scientific or statistical application <the population included 12,270 males and 14,731 *females*> **Woman** is the general neutral term, applicable to all adult female persons regardless of rank or character <an abandoned *woman* sodden with drink and riddled by disease> <she was one of the greatest *women* of our times> **Lady** specifically denotes a woman of rank and connotes the qualities (as of dress, fashion, and manner) associated with women of the privileged classes <inclined to remind you that she was a *lady* by birth – W. S. Maugham> but often it denotes a female person of admirable character without regard to rank <a *lady* . . . quiet, reserved, gracious, continent – W. D. Steele> or even becomes a merely courteous equivalent to *woman* <is the *lady* of the house in?> <we met several *ladies* we hadn't seen for years> though its indiscriminate substitution for *woman* (as in wash *lady,* char*lady*) carries courtesy into travesty.

female *adj* – see FEMININE ***ant*** male

feminine, female, womanly, womanlike, womanish, effeminate, ladylike *shared* *meaning* : of, characteristic of, or like a female, especially of the human species. **Feminine** applies to qualities or attributes or attitudes characteristic of women and not shared by men <a *feminine* approach to a problem> <disguised their feelings . . . beneath masks of smooth *feminine* guilelessness – William Styron> **Female** (opposed to *male*) applies to plants and animals as well as persons and stresses the fact of sex <the excess of *female* births over male> <use of *female* labor in cotton mills> **Womanly** suggests the qualities of the mature woman, especially those qualities that make her effective as wife and mother <her instincts were all *womanly* and housewifely. She liked to cook and sew, and she liked men – Robert McAlmon> **Womanlike** is more likely to suggest characteristically feminine faults and foibles <*womanlike,* taking revenge too deep for a transient wrong – Alfred Tennyson> **Womanish** is often used derogatorily in situations in which manliness might naturally be wanted or expected <*womanish* entreaties and lamentations – T. B. Macaulay> **Effeminate** emphasizes the softer and more delicate aspects of womanly nature and in its usual application to men implies lack of virility or masculinity <[France] was weak and *effeminate,* frivolous and inefficient, but to it nevertheless the world owed a huge . . . debt – S. E. Ambrose> <an *effeminate* and unmanly foppery – Richard Hurd> **Ladylike** suggests decorous propriety <all three were *ladylike* and well brought-up girls> or, in reference to males, may impute primness, daintiness, or lack of expected masculine force and strength <a bustling *ladylike* little man> ***ant*** masculine

ferocious – see FIERCE

fertile, fecund, fruitful, prolific *shared meaning* : producing or having the power to produce offspring or fruit. **Fertile** implies the power to reproduce in kind or to assist in reproduction and growth <*fertile* seeds> <a *fertile* soil> In extended application (as to the mind or to ideas) the term suggests readiness of invention or development <[his] first studies of art brought him under one of the most *fertile* teachers of his generation – Lewis Mumford> <in him were united a most logical head with a most *fertile* imagination – James Boswell> **Fecund** emphasizes abundance or rapidity in bearing fruits or offspring or, by extension, projects, inventions, or works of art <any social movement – particularly one that . . . is so *fecund* of new art forms, new styles of dress and demeanor, and . . . new ethical bases for human relationships – Fred Davis> **Fruitful** adds to *fertile* and *fecund* the implication of desirable or useful results <the "annihilation of distance" opens the way for either *fruitful* cooperation or disastrous collision – A. J. Toynbee> <Darwinism . . . is a *fruitful* theory of the means by which nature works – W. R. Inge> **Prolific** stresses rapidity of spreading or multiplying by or as if by natural reproduction <a *prolific* writer> <the defectives are appallingly *prolific;* the others have fewer children – G. B. Shaw> ***ant*** infertile, sterile

fervent – see IMPASSIONED

fervid – see IMPASSIONED

fervor – see PASSION

fetid – see MALODOROUS ***ant*** fragrant

fetish, talisman, charm, amulet *shared meaning* : an object believed useful in averting evil or attracting good. **Fetish** is literally applied to such an object regarded as sacred or magical among a primitive people; in extended use it applies to something, often intangible, that is cherished unreasonably or obsessively <the calorie-conscious America of the moment, where the renunciation of the good life in the midst of its overwhelming abundance is a national *fetish* – Lucius Beebe> **Talisman,** primarily applicable to a cut or engraved astrological figure held to have magical power (as to heal or protect), can denote something that seems to exert a magical, extraordinary, and usually happy influence <every cloud-lost spire of masonry was a *talisman* of power, a monument to the everlasting empire of American business – Thomas Wolfe> **Charm** applies basically to an object or a formula of words believed efficacious in repelling evil spirits or malign influences or attracting their opposites <a *charm* against the evil eye> Often it is used of something that exerts a compelling appeal or an irresistible attraction <allowed himself to fall under the spell of the boy's *charm* – Victoria Sackville-West> <a new and even greater *charm* – the fascination of the unknown and mysterious – W. H. Hudson †1922> **Amulet** applies especially to an inscribed ornament worn or carried on the person as a protection against evil <he too made gifts of small images which the Eskimo took to be *amulets* of great power and tied to the sorcerer's belt at his shoulder – Farley Mowat>

fetter – see HAMPER

fewer – see LESS

fib – see LIE

fickle – see INCONSTANT *ant* constant, true

fictitious, fabulous, legendary, mythical, apocryphal *shared meaning* : being the product of imagination or mental invention. **Fictitious** implies fabrication and suggests artificiality or contrivance more than deliberate falsification or deception <a *fictitious* reconstruction of primitive life before the coming of the white man – *Amer. Guide Series: Oregon*> Often the word suggests false evaluation <in booms as in panics the market value of a security is often *fictitious*> **Fabulous** stresses the marvelous or incredible character of something without distinctly implying impossibility or actual nonexistence <the *fabulous* mill which ground old people young – Charles Dickens> <seen, in some unknown coral island, the *fabulous* buried cache of forgotten pirates' plundering – Thomas Wolfe> <he [Lincoln] grows vaguer and more *fabulous* as year follows year – H. L. Mencken> **Legendary** suggests the elaboration of invented details and distortion of historical facts produced by popular tradition <the *legendary* kings of Ireland> <*legendary* history reported in the next generation that the elements had been pregnant with auguries: images had sweated; the sky had blazed with meteors – J. A. Froude> **Mythical** usually presupposes the working of the popular imagination and implies a fanciful often symbolic quality that partakes of the nature of myth <the most successful heroes and heroines in opera are *mythical* figures . . . they embody some element of human nature or some aspect of the human condition which is a permanent concern of human beings irrespective of their time and place – W. H. Auden> <the historical approach to experience (attempting to be true to the thing as it was), and the *mythical* approach (attempting to capture the constant element in the flux) – Alan Holder> **Apocryphal** implies an unknown or dubious source or origin for an account circulated as true or genuine <the story is told about *both* of them, which suggests it may be *apocryphal* – George Plimpton> <tales, possibly *apocryphal* and certainly embroidered, of his feats of intelligence work in the eastern Mediterranean – R. W. Firth> *ant* historical

fidelity, allegiance, fealty, loyalty, devotion, piety *shared meaning* : faithfulness to something to which one is bound by a pledge, by duty, or by a sense of what is right or appropriate. **Fidelity** implies strict and continuing faithfulness (as to an obligation, a promise, or a responsibility) <with close *fidelity* and love unfeigned to keep the matrimonial bond unstained – William Cowper> **Allegiance** suggests an adherence like that of a medieval vassal to his lord and implies an unswerving fidelity maintained even when conflicting obligations dispute its claim <Hitler held the *allegiance* and trust of this remarkable people to the last . . . they would follow him blindly . . . with a touching faith and even an enthusiasm . . . over the precipice to the destruction of the nation – W. L. Shirer> **Fealty** implies a fidelity acknowledged by the individual and as compelling as a sworn vow <when I do forget the least of these unspeakable deserts, Romans, forget your *fealty* to me – Shak.> **Loyalty** is likely to imply a more personal attachment and a more emotional relationship than *fidelity* or *fealty* and regularly denotes a faithfulness that is steadfast in the face of any temptation to defect, renounce, or betray <knew that he could count on his brother's *loyalty*> <he was no longer entirely at liberty; already part of his freedom was forfeit to a responsibility and a *loyalty* – H. C. Hervey> **Devotion** stresses zeal in service amounting to self-dedication <they gave the last full measure of *devotion* – Abraham Lincoln> <she applied her energies constructively, with *devotion* – Hudson Strode> **Piety** stresses fidelity to obligations regarded as natural and fundamental and the observance of duties required by such fidelity <filial *piety* involves loving and dutiful respect for one's parents> <scientific rationale . . . alone cannot satisfy, the deep nonlogical purposes and *pieties* that are the necessary cornerstone of any social edifice – H. J. Muller> ***ant*** faithlessness, perfidy

fierce, ferocious, barbarous, savage, cruel *shared meaning* : showing fury or malignity in looks or actions. **Fierce** describes men or animals that inspire terror because of their menacing aspect or their unrestrained fury in attack <the other Shape . . . black it stood as night, *fierce* as ten Furies, terrible as Hell – John Milton> or qualities, expression, or events characteristic of these <that *fierce,* unbending will which later would carry him so far despite seemingly insuperable obstacles – W. L. Shirer> **Ferocious** implies extreme fierceness and unrestrained violence and brutality <a pint of iron man, so tough, so *ferocious,* so sharp in the teeth that the wildest alley cat would have surrendered a freshly caught rat rather than contest the meal – Norman Mailer> <the *ferocious* slaughters instituted . . . by barbarian conquerors – Lewis Mumford> **Barbarous** implies a ferocity or mercilessness unworthy of civilized man <you have been wantonly attacked by a ruthless and *barbarous* aggressor. Your capital has been bombed, your women and children brutally murdered – Sir Winston Churchill> **Savage** implies the absence of inhibitions normally restraining civilized man when dealing with those he hates or fears or when filled with violent passion <the *savage* wars of religion – W. R. Inge> <the son . . . had been trained in *savage* Sicilian loyalty and lived only to avenge his father – G. K. Chesterton> **Cruel** implies indifference to suffering or even a positive pleasure in witnessing or inflicting it <as *cruel* as a schoolboy ere he grows to pity – Alfred Tennyson> <*cruel,* and full of hate and malice and a petty rage – G. D. Brown> ***ant*** tame, mild

figure – see FORM

filch – see STEAL

filthy – see DIRTY ***ant*** neat, spick-and-span

final – see LAST

financial, monetary, pecuniary, fiscal *shared meaning* : of or relating to money. **Financial** implies money matters conducted on a relatively large scale or involving some degree of complexity <the state is in serious *financial* difficulties> <the *financial* value of a college education> **Monetary** refers more directly to money, especially as coined, distributed, or circulating <*monetary* gold> <changing *monetary* standards> <economists find it helpful to organize their data both in real terms and in *monetary* terms – R. H. Wolf> **Pecuniary** implies reference to the practical uses of money especially as affecting the individual <he is always in *pecuniary* difficulties> <the *pecuniary* aims and class animosities of capitalist production – Lewis Mumford> **Fiscal** refers to money as providing public revenue or to the financial affairs of an institution or corporation <the *fiscal* year in the United States ends on June 30> <the nation's metropolises, stricken with *fiscal* anemia . . . have necessarily become organized on a dog-eat-dog . . . basis – N. E. Long>

fine – see PENALIZE

finical – see NICE

finicky – see NICE

finish – see CLOSE *vb*

fire – see LIGHT

firm, hard, solid *shared meaning* : having a texture or consistency that resists deformation. **Firm** implies such compactness and coherence and often elasticity of substance as provides resistance to pulling, distorting, cutting, or displacing <a *firm* close-woven cloth> <*firm* healthy flesh> <the ground was *firm* enough to walk on> **Hard** implies impenetrability or strong resistance to pressure or tension but not elasticity <*hard* steel> <diamond is one of the *hardest* substances> **Solid** implies such density and coherence as enable a thing to maintain a fixed form in spite of external deforming forces <ice is the *solid* form of water> or such firmness of construction or structure as makes a thing strong, stable, or sound <a substantial *solid* cottage> or the absence of empty spaces which might constitute a weakness <a *solid* wall firmly mortared together>

In extended use **firm** stresses stability, fixedness, or resolution <a *firm* purpose> <receptive to suggestions, he is, however, *firm* once a decision is made – *Current Biog.*> **Hard** implies obduracy or lack of normal responsiveness <a *hard* man to do business with> <the fellow's eyes were now sly and cunning as a cat's, now *hard* and black as basalt – Thomas Wolfe> <she was firm, but she was not *hard* – Archibald Marshall> **Solid** typically implies substantiality or genuineness <demand *solid* facts> <a *solid* meal> <rested in *solid* comfort> or it may imply complete reliability or sobriety <one of the most *solid* citizens of our community> <his scholarship was *solid* and sound – A. C. McGiffert> or sometimes unbroken continuity (as in time, feeling, or opinion) <there had been a *solid* week of rain> <the committee determined to present a *solid* front in support of the amendment> ***ant*** loose, flabby

fiscal – see FINANCIAL

fit *adj* **fit, suitable, meet, proper, appropriate, fitting, apt, happy, felicitous** *shared meaning* : right with respect to some end, need, use, or circumstance. **Fit** stresses adaptability or special readiness for use or action <food *fit* for a king> <but when to mischief mortals bend their will, how soon they find *fit* instruments of ill! – Alexander Pope> and it may connote competence or possession of needed qualification <he is no *fit* father for a decent family> <men *fit* to command> **Suitable** implies an answering to requirements or demands <university graduates who had been unable to find *suitable* jobs or any secure place in normal society – W. L. Shirer> **Meet** implies both suitability and a precise adaptation to a particular situation, need, or circumstance; regularly it suggests rightness or justness rather than mere absence of incongruity <it is very *meet,* right, and our bounden duty, that we should at all times and in all places, give thanks unto thee, O Lord – *Bk. of Com. Prayer*> <is it *meet* that an utter stranger should thus express himself? – W. S. Gilbert> **Proper** suggests a suitability through essential nature or accordance with custom <an amateur trespassing in a field *proper* to the legal authorities and the medical profession – *Times*

Lit. Supp.> <the *proper* study of mankind is man – Alexander Pope> **Appropriate** implies eminent or distinctive fitness and stresses the pleasing effect of congruity <often . . . *appropriate* actions are guided by perception of the underlying situation, which may very well be at variance with the apparent situation – F. C. Cameron> <dinners . . . with seven or eight courses and their *appropriate* wines – Lucius Beebe> **Fitting** implies harmony (as of mood, tone, or purpose) <news *fitting* to the night, black, fearful, comfortless and horrible – Shak.> **Apt** implies a fitness marked by nicety and discrimination <an *apt* reply to an impertinent question> <what time so *apt* for inculcating obedience . . . as this solemn hour – H. O. Taylor> **Happy** describes what is effectively or successfully appropriate <a *happy* choice of words that precisely conveyed his intent> <when academically talented students come together with dedicated scholars, a *happy,* mutually beneficial relationship is established – M. S. Eisenhower> **Felicitous** implies an aptness that is appropriate, telling, or graceful <I do not like mottoes but where they are singularly *felicitous* – Charles Lamb> <had a way of illuminating . . . factual data with *felicitous* theoretical insights – D. G. Mandelbaum> ***ant*** unfit

fit *vb* – see PREPARE

fitful, spasmodic, convulsive *shared meaning* : lacking steadiness or regularity (as in course, movement, or activity). **Fitful** stresses intermittence and implies an irregular succession or progress marked by fits and starts <after life's *fitful* fever he sleeps well – Shak.> <a *fitful* wind swept the cheerless waste – Joseph Conrad> **Spasmodic** adds to *fitful* the implication of great and repeated alterations of intensity (as of activity or effort or zeal) and is likely to stress opposition to whatever is sustained at a consistent and especially a high pitch <growth of the towns was *spasmodic* – *Amer. Guide Series; Mass.*> <a continuous discussion of international affairs, not *spasmodic* action at times of crisis – Clement Attlee> **Convulsive** suggests the breaking of regularity or quiet by uncontrolled movement or action; typically it connotes distress of body, mind, or spirit <the nation . . . made a *convulsive* effort to free itself from military domination – T. B. Macaulay> <there was a *convulsive* stir among the horses; a swinging of heads, a dipping of hindquarters; in a moment sand flew up from thudding hoofs, and they were off – L. P. Hartley> ***ant*** constant

fitting – see FIT ***ant*** unfitting

fix *vb* **1** see FASTEN

2 see SET *vb* ***ant*** alter, abrogate (*a custom, rule, law*)

fix *n* – see PREDICAMENT

flabbergast – see SURPRISE 2

flabby – see LIMP ***ant*** firm

flaccid – see LIMP ***ant*** resilient

flagitious – see VICIOUS

flagrant, glaring, gross, rank *shared meaning* : conspicuously bad or objectionable. **Flagrant** applies usually to offenses or errors so bad that they can neither escape notice nor be condoned <[war prisoners] were made to work in the armaments and munitions industries in *flagrant* violation of the Hague and Geneva conventions – W. L. Shirer> <ended their sinful career by open and *flagrant* mutiny and were shot for it – Rudyard Kipling> **Glaring** implies painful or damaging obtrusiveness to something that is conspicuously wrong, faulty, or improper <this evil is so *glaring,* so inexcusable – G. B. Shaw> <a *glaring* inconsistency in his argument> **Gross,** more likely to apply to human attitudes, qualities, or faults than to specific evil acts or serious offenses, implies an unbounded and wholly inexcusable badness in what it describes <at best he was guilty of *gross*

neglect> <a mannered, nervous laugh, he found *gross* and somehow unwholesome – William Styron> <Elizabethan and Jacobean poetry ... had serious defects, even *gross* faults – T. S. Eliot> **Rank** applies to what is openly and extremely objectionable and utterly condemned <O, my offense is *rank*, it smells to heaven – Shak.> <must lecture him on his *rank* disloyalty – David Walden>

flair – see LEANING

flame – see BLAZE

flare – see BLAZE

flash, gleam, glance, glint, sparkle, glitter, glisten, glimmer, coruscate, shimmer *shared meaning*: to send forth light. **Flash** implies a sudden and transient burst of light <the fireflies *flashed* their little lamps> **Gleam** suggests a steady light seen through an obscuring medium or against a dark background <I see the lights of the village *gleam* through the rain and mist – H. W. Longfellow> **Glance** suggests a bright darting light reflected from a moving surface <light from the moon *glanced* off the ruffled water> **Glint** implies quickly glancing or gleaming light <when the first sunshine through their dewdrops *glint* – J. R. Lowell> **Sparkle** suggests innumerable moving points of bright light <the sun was glinting through the leaves, *sparkling* the silver stream as it cascaded down – Edna Burress> **Glitter** implies a brilliant sparkling or gleaming <a landscape, *glittering* with sun and rain – Ambrose Bierce> but may carry a sinister connotation <eyes *glittering* greedily> **Glisten** applies to a soft persistent sparkling gleam from or as if from a wet or oily surface <snowy mountains *glistening* through a summer atmosphere – Washington Irving> **Glimmer** suggests a faint, obscured, or wavering gleam <the sadness of these *glimmering* dawns – Walker Percy> <flickering candles *glimmered* from each window> **Coruscate** implies the giving off or reflecting of light in repeated bright beams or flashes <polished brass, *coruscating* helmets and horses shining like table silver – Edith Wharton> **Shimmer** implies a soft tremulous gleaming or a blurred reflection <lovely, tuft-topped, skinny-trunked trees *shimmering* against the clear blue sky – John Weld> <the brick street, which *shimmered* now in the very hot sun – John Barth>

flashy – see GAUDY

flat – see INSIPID, LEVEL

flatulent – see INFLATED

flaunt – see SHOW 2

flavor – see TASTE

flaw – see BLEMISH

fleer – see SCOFF

fleet *vb* – see WHILE

fleet *adj* – see FAST

fleeting – see TRANSIENT ***ant*** lasting

fleshly – see CARNAL

flexible – see ELASTIC ***ant*** inflexible

flightiness – see LIGHTNESS ***ant*** steadiness, steadfastness

flimsy – see LIMP

flinch – see RECOIL

fling – see THROW

flippancy – see LIGHTNESS ***ant*** seriousness

flirt – see TRIFLE

floppy – see LIMP

flourish 1 see SUCCEED ***ant*** languish
2 see SWING

flout – see SCOFF ***ant*** revere

flow – see SPRING
fluctuate – see SWING 2
fluid – see LIQUID
flurry *n* – see STIR
flurry *vb* – see DISCOMPOSE
fluster – see DISCOMPOSE
foe – see ENEMY ***ant*** friend
fog – see HAZE
foible – see FAULT
foil – see FRUSTRATE

follow **1 follow, succeed, ensue, supervene** *shared meaning* : to come after something or someone. **Follow** may apply to a coming after in time, position, understanding, or logical sequence <a prayer *followed* the singing> <the bravest man I ever knew *followed* me up San Juan Hill – Theodore Roosevelt> **Succeed** implies a coming after immediately in a sequence determined by some rational cause or rule (as natural order, inheritance, election, or laws of rank) <prevent officeholders from *succeeding* themselves – Trevor Armbrister> <the University will receive . . . additional fellowships in each of the two *succeeding* years – M. S. Eisenhower> <a son waiting to *succeed* his father in the family business> **Ensue** commonly suggests a logical consequence or naturally expected development <that such a consequence . . . should *ensue* . . . was far enough from my thoughts – Jane Austen> <when his mind fails to stay the pace set by its inventions, madness must *ensue* – C. D. Lewis> **Supervene** suggests a following by something added or conjoined and often unforeseen or unpredictable <an event *supervened* that brought disaster to my uncle's family – George Santayana> <what generally spoils long novels is the untimely *supervening* creative fatigue – Arnold Bennett> ***ant*** precede (*in order*), forsake (*as a teacher*)

2 follow, chase, pursue, trail *shared meaning* : to go after or on the track of someone or something. **Follow** is the comprehensive term; it usually implies the lead or guidance of one going before and, in itself, gives no clue as to the purpose of the one that follows <*follow* a path to town> <the boys *followed* the cows to the barn> <police *following* up a clue> **Chase** implies speed in following, sometimes in order to catch what flees and sometimes to turn or drive away what advances <youngsters snatching at fun while they *chased* the dream of a happy marriage – Herman Wouk> <*chasing* the boys out of the orchard> **Pursue** usually suggests an attempt to overtake, reach, or attain often with eagerness or persistence, sometimes with hostile intent <over and over again . . . human societies have *pursued* a course that was suicidal, while defending values that they regarded as more important than survival – Margaret Mead> <*pursue* a course of study> <insists that the Church's duty is to redeem the drug-takers with love and care, rather than to *pursue* them with hatred and punishment – *Times Lit. Supp.*> **Trail** implies a following in the tracks of one gone before <*trail* a fugitive to his hiding place> <her mother . . . took it for granted that Margaret should *trail* as a small tug in her wake – Victoria Sackville-West> ***ant*** precede

follower, adherent, disciple, partisan, satellite *shared meaning* : one who attaches himself to another. **Follower**, the inclusive term, denotes one who attaches himself to the person or opinions of another <led his *followers* by a roundabout course to the town> <considered witches to be *followers* of the devil> **Adherent** stresses closeness and persistence of attachment <he has facts to present, plus some interesting speculations, which even *adherents* to other camps will find worth pondering – R. B. MacLeod> **Disciple** implies a devoted allegiance to one chosen or accepted as master and teacher <a *disciple* of . . . Gandhi, Shastri spent a number of years in prison for taking part in Gandhi's noncooperation movement – *Current Biog.*> <he had become the fanatical and fiercely absorbed *disciple* of a cult – H. C. Hervey> **Partisan** suggests a zealous and often prejudiced attachment <wrote frankly as a *partisan* of the liberals – W. A. White> <*partisans* of finnan haddie . . . might like to plan a pilgrimage to the tiny fishing village of Findon – Horace Sutton> **Satellite** suggests constant attendance on the person of a leader and is likely to imply subservient subordination to one stronger or dominating <Boswell was . . . made happy by an introduction to Johnson of whom he became the obsequious *satellite* – Washington Irving> <the central sun he became for a host of surrounding *satellites* – Irving Kolodin> ***ant*** leader

foment – see INCITE ***ant*** quell

fondle – see CARESS

fool, idiot, imbecile, moron, simpleton, natural *shared meaning* : one who is mentally defective. **Fool,** the general term, implies lack or loss of reason or intelligence and is applicable to the mentally deranged as well as the mentally deficient <he was a *fool* and liable . . . under the stress of bodily or mental disturbance, to spasmodic fits of abject fright which he mistook for religion – Norman Douglas> Often the word implies not mental deficiency but lack of judgment or prudence and is then usually a term of contempt varying from the mildly patronizing to the intensely offensive <a blue-eyed, black-haired *fool* of a fellow, whose tongue was loose at both ends and laced with wit – Pearl Buck> <a *fool* and his money is soon parted – James Howell> *Idiot, imbecile,* and *moron* are technical designations for mentally deficient persons. An **idiot** is incapable of connected speech and avoiding ordinary hazards and so needs constant attendance. An **imbecile** is incapable of earning a living but can be educated to attend to simple wants and to avoid most common dangers. A **moron** can learn a simple trade but requires close supervision in his work and life. In more general use *idiot* implies utter feeblemindedness, *imbecile* half-wittedness, and *moron* general stupidity. All three may also imply no more than mild derogation of a person or his conduct, especially as exemplified by a transitory lapse in judgment or good sense <you were a perfect *idiot* at the party> <what *imbecile* left the sewing basket in my chair?> <only a *moron* would believe him> **Simpleton,** usually a term of indulgent contempt, implies silliness or lack of expected sophistication <the squealing *simpletons* who gathered in fan clubs to worship an actor – Herman Wouk> **Natural,** which persists chiefly in historical context, applies to any congenitally feebleminded person <the man is not a *natural;* he has a very quick sense, though very slow understanding – Richard Steele>

foolhardy – see ADVENTUROUS ***ant*** wary

foolish – see SIMPLE

forbear – see REFRAIN

forbid, prohibit, interdict, inhibit, ban *shared meaning* : to debar one from using, doing, or entering or to order something not be used, done, or entered. **Forbid** implies absolute proscription and expected obedience and is appropriately used when the order is that of one in authority (as a parent, a teacher, or an employer) <*forbid* a child to leave the house> <smoking is *forbidden* on these premises> <suffer the little children to come unto me, and *forbid* them not – *Mk* 10:14 (AV)> **Prohibit** implies more generality and impersonality and suggests statutes and ordinances and restraints imposed for the good of all <the act was wrong in the sense that it was *prohibited* by law – B. N. Cardozo> <the colonists were *prohibited* from importing goods directly> **Interdict** implies prohibition by authority, usually civil or ecclesiastical authority, for a given time or a declared purpose <*interdict* trade with belligerent nations> <alcohol and tobacco are usually *interdicted* to the cardiac patient> **Inhibit** implies the imposition of restraint or restriction by authority, by the exigencies of time or situation, or by the operation of often involuntary self-restraint <a clause was . . . inserted which *inhibited* the Bank from advancing money to the Crown without authority from Parliament – T. B. Macaulay> <the fifty states of the United States are, each and all, officially sovereign, but the supremacy of the Federal government over them is not *inhibited* by that – A. J. Toynbee> **Ban** carries an implication of legal or social pressure as the source of prohibition and with it a strong connotation of condemnation or disapproval <more and more landlords were *banning* tenants with children – Dixon Wecter> <attempts have been made . . . to have Grass's writings *banned* as blasphemous and pornographic – *Current Biog.*> <these laws . . . were specific in naming the one weapon to be *banned* – R. W. Thorp> ***ant*** permit, bid

force *n* – see POWER

force *vb* **force, compel, coerce, constrain, oblige** *shared meaning* : to make someone or something yield. **Force** is the general term and implies the overcoming of resistance by the exertion of strength, power, weight, stress, or duress <the nature of power is such that even those who . . . have had it *forced* upon them, tend to acquire a taste for more – Aldous Huxley> <*force* one's way through a crowd> **Compel** differs from *force* in typically requiring a personal or personalized object; it can imply the exertion of authority or the working of an irresistible force <no ghetto will be *compelled* to accept colonial status – W. H. Ferry> <he knew that sooner or later hunger and thirst would *compel* him to come out> **Coerce** suggests the overcoming of resistance by severe methods (as violence or duress) or by threat and intimidation <there are more ways of *coercing* a man than by pointing a gun at his head – W. R. Inge> <no one can claim that he was *coerced* by bribery. This is reserved for threats and direct pleas – W. D. Falk> **Constrain** suggests a forcing by what does or seems to constrict, press, confine, or bind <*constrained* through poverty to live in the houses of others – Edith Sitwell> <the walls are high, the gates are strong . . . but true love never yet was thus *constrained* – P. B. Shelley> **Oblige** implies the constraint of necessity, sometimes physical, but often moral or intellectual <the prophetic mission of the family *obliges* it to fidelity to conjugal love in the face of the compromises and infidelities condoned in our culture – *Pilot*> <his health *obliged* him to retire at fifty>

forecast – see FORETELL

foregoing – see PRECEDING ***ant*** following

foreign – see EXTRINSIC ***ant*** germane

foreknow – see FORESEE

forerunner, precursor, harbinger, herald *shared meaning* : one who goes before or announces the coming of another. **Forerunner** may denote a personal messenger <there is a *forerunner* come from . . . the Prince of Morocco, who brings word the prince his master will be here tonight – Shak.> but it is freely applicable to whatever serves as a sign, presage, or warning of something to come <the Committee that became the government of liberated France and *forerunner* of the Fourth Republic – S. E. Ambrose><blustery March days that are *forerunners* of spring> **Precursor** applies to a person or thing that in some sense paves the way for the success or accomplishment of one that follows <a fascinating account of chemistry's *precursor,* alchemy – *Key Reporter*> <headaches . . . were the *precursors* of breakdown and helpless invalidism – V. S. Pritchett> **Harbinger** and

herald both apply, chiefly figuratively, to one that proclaims or announces the coming of a notable event <the sinister white owl . . . the *harbinger* of destruction – Alan Moorehead> <neither the changes they grudgingly assent to nor the occasional aggressive eruptions from the second city are viewed as the *harbingers* of a revolutionary order – Harvey Wheeler> <it was the lark, the *herald* of the morn – Shak.> <revolutions . . . were the *heralds* of social change – R. W. Livingstone>

foresee, foreknow, divine, apprehend, anticipate *shared meaning* : to know or prophesy beforehand. **Foresee** implies nothing about how the knowledge is derived and may apply to ordinary reasoning and experience <our failure to *foresee* all future problems – Vera M. Dean> <as far as can now be *foreseen* evolutionary degeneration is at least as likely in our future as is further progress – G. G. Simpson> **Foreknow,** stressing prior knowledge, usually implies supranormal powers or divine revelation as its source <they were willing to say that God *foreknows* the sin of those who are not elected to salvation – K. S. Latourette> <who would the miseries of man *foreknow* – John Dryden> **Divine** suggests a special gift, the assistance of a strange power, or exceptional discernment as the source of knowledge <I . . . *divined* that the best way of breaking down their reserve was to let them try to penetrate mine – Edith Wharton> <there was an important connection between the two families and . . . I have not *divined* what it really was – M. A. McCorison> **Apprehend** implies a degree of foresight often mingled with uncertainty, anxiety, or dread <they feel a deep and momentary uneasiness as if they *apprehended* how darkness can fall over the continents of the mind – John Cheever> <she *apprehended,* not without good cause, that his kingdom might soon be extended to her frontiers – T. B. Macaulay> **Anticipate** implies such foreknowledge as leads or allows one to take action about or respond emotionally to something before it happens <as the speech organs move into position to produce the /p/, they already *anticipate* part of the position for the following /i/ – W. G. Moulton> <sorrowfully *anticipating* the loss of their home when the new dam was built>

forestall – see PREVENT

foretaste – see PROSPECT

foretell, predict, forecast, prophesy, prognosticate *shared meaning* : to tell beforehand. **Foretell** applies to the telling of a future event by any procedure or from any source of information <some sorcerer . . . had *foretold,* dying, that none of all our blood should know the shadow from the substance – Alfred Tennyson> <Lombroso's marks of degeneration . . . supposedly *foretold* of a biological predisposition to commit crimes – M. F. A. Montagu> **Predict** commonly implies inference from facts or from accepted laws of nature <when the teen-ager female behaves in a certain coquettish manner, she is *predicting* that a male or males will respond in a particular manner – E. O. Milton> <an astronomer *predicts* the return of a comet from his knowledge of its path and of the behavior of heavenly bodies> **Forecast** adds the implication of anticipating eventualities and differs from *predict* in being usually concerned with probabilities rather than certainties; thus, one *forecasts* tomorrow's weather but one *predicts* the date and degree of the next solar eclipse <it is difficult to *forecast* just what the future utility of the machine in education will be – *Johns Hopkins Mag.*> <it seems fairly safe to *forecast* that, if the human race survives, it will have abandoned the ideal and the practice of national sovereignty – A. J. Toynbee> **Prophesy** either connotes inspired or mystic knowledge or implies great assurance in prediction <ancestral voices *prophesying* war – S. T. Coleridge> <wrinkled benchers often talked of him approvingly, and *prophesied* his rise – Alfred Tennyson> **Prognosticate** implies prediction based on signs and symptoms and often connotes skill in interpretation <the doctor was unable to *prognosticate* the outcome of the disease> <I neither will nor can *prognosticate* to the young gaping heir his father's fate – John Dryden>

forewarn – see WARN

forge – see MAKE

forget – see NEGLECT ***ant*** remember

forgetful, oblivious, unmindful *shared meaning* : losing from one's mind something once known or learned. **Forgetful** is likely to imply a propensity not to remember or a defective memory <bear with me, good boy, I am much *forgetful* – Shak.> but it may suggest careless negligence (as of duty) rather than weakness of memory <be not *forgetful* to entertain strangers – *Heb* 13:2 (AV)> **Oblivious** suggests failure to notice or remember as a result of external causes or conditions or of a determination to ignore <he is *oblivious* of all distractions when he is wrapped up in his work – E. J. Kahn> <she lay in deep, *oblivious* slumber – H. W. Longfellow> **Unmindful** is likely to imply inattention or heedlessness <*unmindful* of the passage of time> or a deliberate disregard <every person was willing to save himself, *unmindful* of others – Oliver Goldsmith>

forgive – see EXCUSE

forlorn – see ALONE

form *n* **form, figure, shape, conformation, configuration** *shared meaning* : outward appearance. **Form** usually suggests reference to both internal structure and external outline and often the principle that gives unity to the whole <the earth was without *form,* and void – *Gen* 1:2 (AV)> <the landscape varied from moment to moment because of changes in lighting rather than because of variations in *form* or mass or substance – Elizabeth P. Schafer> **Figure** applies chiefly to the form as determined by bounding or enclosing outlines <flowers have all exquisite *figures* – Francis Bacon> and it may apply to the lines or the visible form of a kind or type <it was hard to tell in the dim light whether the *figure* was that of a man or a woman> <her husband was a *figure* whose prototype one often encounters in stories of Jewish slums . . . – a man who, despite the squalor around him, managed to convey an impression of dignity, grave humor, and even wisdom – Bernard Taper> **Shape,** like *figure,* suggests an outline but carries a stronger implication of the enclosed body or mass <the color of his beard, the *shape* of his leg – Shak.> <believes that there are certain permanent qualities or values within human experience, but that these assume different *shapes* at different moments in history – Alan Holder> **Conformation** suggests the whole complicated structure of harmoniously arranged parts that underlies outward appearance <beef cattle of excellent *conformation*> <failed to find any relation between altitude tolerance and body stature or *conformation* – H. G. Armstrong> **Configuration,** too, emphasizes the disposition or arrangement of parts; it is the term of choice when the intent is to call attention to the pattern they form, especially over an extent of space or territory <the remarkable *configuration* of the Atlantic seabed – T. H. Huxley> <a network of roads following the *configuration* of the country – John Buchan> <when the shadows lengthen and the fire flickers low, all sorts of strange *configurations* creep out of the closets of our minds – Harvey Mindess>

form *vb* – see MAKE

formal – see CEREMONIAL ***ant*** informal

former – see PRECEDING ***ant*** latter

forsake – see ABANDON ***ant*** return to, revert to

forswear – see PERJURE
forth – see ONWARD
forthright – see STRAIGHTFORWARD ***ant*** furtive
fortitude, grit, backbone, pluck, guts, sand *shared meaning* : courage and staying power. **Fortitude** stresses firmness in enduring physical or mental hardships and suffering <it was the *fortitude* of the German soldier that saved the armies . . . from a complete debacle – W. L. Shirer> <a life of unremitting physical toil and mental anxiety combined with miserable health – no small test of *fortitude* – John Buchan> **Grit** stresses unyielding resolution and indomitableness in the face of hardship or danger <the foot soldier will still have to advance against strongly entrenched and fanatical troops, through sheer *grit* and fighting skill – Harry S Truman> **Backbone** emphasizes resoluteness of character and implies either ability to stand firm in the face of opposition or such determination and independence as requires no support from without <like conscience-stricken dogs they lost *backbone,* and visibly were in a condition to submit to anything – Kenneth Roberts> **Pluck** implies a willingness to fight or continue against odds <the energy, fortitude, and dogged perseverance that we technically style *pluck* – E. G. Bulwer-Lytton> **Guts,** often considered expressive but not entirely polite, stresses fortitude and stamina and implies effectiveness and determination in facing and coping with what alarms or repels or discourages <I indict the Government for lack of *guts,* for lack of determination, and [for] a lack of honesty – Richard Crawshaw> <if our representatives had the deep-down *guts* to enact two basic reforms – Charles Mangel> **Sand** is close to *grit* in basic meaning but may come close to *pluck* in suggesting an ability and will to withstand odds <no more pride than a tramp, no more *sand* than a rabbit – Mark Twain> ***ant*** pusillanimity
fortuitous – see ACCIDENTAL
fortunate – see LUCKY ***ant*** unfortunate, disastrous
forward *adv* – see ONWARD ***ant*** backward
forward *vb* – see ADVANCE ***ant*** hinder, balk
foul – see DIRTY ***ant*** fair, undefiled
foundation – see BASE ***ant*** superstructure
foxy – see SLY
fragile, frangible, brittle, crisp, friable *shared meaning* : easily broken. In spite of the common element of meaning these words are not freely interchangeable. **Fragile** implies extreme delicacy of material or construction and the need for careful handling <*fragile* porcelain figures> <this nation, molded in the heat of battle against tyranny . . . is not a *fragile* thing – W. O. Douglas> **Frangible** stresses an inherent susceptibility to be broken rather than a delicacy that leads easily to being broken; thus, a *frangible* bullet is one designed to shatter on impact with a target without penetrating <fabricating *frangible* nose and tail cones for airborne rockets – *Technical Survey*> **Brittle** implies hardness combined with inflexibility so that the thing has no give and is susceptible to quick snapping or fracture under pressure or strain <an old person's bones are likely to be *brittle*> The term is often extended to things or situations that are dangerously lacking in flexibility or elasticity <the campus mood is *brittle* enough to escalate the protests rapidly if the talks fall through – *Newsweek*> **Crisp** implies a firmness and brittleness that is desirable, especially in some foods <*crisp* hot toast> <a salad with *crisp* chilled cucumbers> In extended use it is likely to imply a fresh, clean-cut or incisive quality <*crisp,* cool, mountain air> <a languorous work, in the manner of Walter Scott, with occasional interludes of *crisp* brilliance – Anthony West> **Friable** describes something

that is easily crumbled or pulverized <a rich *friable* loam soil> <a *friable* sandstone, quite worthless for building> *ant* durable

fragment — see PART

fragrance, perfume, scent, incense, bouquet *shared meaning* : a sweet or pleasing odor. **Fragrance** usually suggests the odors of flowers or other pleasant plant material <flowers laugh before thee on their beds and *fragrance* in thy footing treads — William Wordsworth> <the *fragrance* of intoxicating odors — the resinous smell of pine, and the smells of grass and warm sweet clover — Thomas Wolfe> **Perfume** may suggest a stronger or heavier odor and applies especially to a prepared or synthetic liquid <the *perfume* of lilies had overcome the scent of books — John Galsworthy> <rose like a steam of rich distilled *perfumes* — John Milton> **Scent** is very close to *perfume* but of wider application because more neutral in connotation <the *scent* of the apples — Robert Frost> <a faint *scent* of lilacs was borne in by the evening breeze> **Incense** applies to smoke from burning material (as spices and gums) that disseminates a pleasing odor <the *incense* of burning apple logs> or to a comparable penetrating but pleasing odor <the breezy call of *incense*-breathing Morn — Thomas Gray> <grateful the *incense* from the lime-tree flower — John Keats> **Bouquet**, used especially of wine, applies to a delicate and distinctive complex odor that suggests the distinctive and savory quality of its source <the grateful smell of cooking pork grew every moment more perfect in *bouquet* — Ethel Anderson> <laboratory experiments show that salmon . . . can distinguish one stream's *bouquet* from that of another — Richard Mathews> *ant* stench, stink

frailty — see FAULT

framework — see STRUCTURE

frangible — see FRAGILE

frank, candid, open, plain *shared meaning* : showing willingness to say what one thinks or feels. **Frank** stresses lack of reserve or of reticence in expressing oneself and usually connotes freedom from such restraints as fear, shyness, secretiveness, or tact <[she] was rough and *frank* . . . ; she had brought herself up in a hard school, reinforcing her native candour — Victoria Sackville-West> <the grossest insinuation, the *frankest* accusation, were common form — Bonamy Dobrée> **Candid** suggests expression free from all evasion or insincerity and implies a character unwilling to dodge an issue or to yield in any degree to bias or fear <I am sure that he was *candid* with me. I am certain that he had no guile — W. A. White> **Open** implies both frankness and candor, but it often suggests more artlessness and naturalness than *frank* and less pressure of conscientiousness than *candid* <Truman was *open* and sincere [with reporters] and tried to satisfy everyone — *Current Biog.*> **Plain** suggests outspokenness, downrightness, and freedom from affectation or subtlety of expression <I am no orator, as Brutus is; but, as you know me all, a *plain* blunt man — Shak.> *ant* reticent

fraud — see DECEPTION, IMPOSTURE

freak — see CAPRICE

free *adj* **free, independent, autonomous, sovereign** *shared meaning* : not subject to the rule or control of another. **Free** stresses the complete absence of external control and the full right to make all one's own decisions <freedom makes a man to choose what he likes; that is, makes him *free* — A. T. Quiller-Couch> **Independent** implies a standing alone <an *independent*, stubborn man who knew what he wanted, a man who was firmly rooted, established, secure against calamity and want — Thomas Wolfe> Applied to a state, it implies lack of connection with any other having power to interfere with its citizens, laws, or policies <the initiative to partition Poland completely, to deny the Polish people any *independent* existence of their own whatsoever, came from the Russians – W. L. Shirer> In its most preçise use **autonomous** implies independence combined with freedom <a discipline which is . . . only a part of the whole picture cannot be completely *autonomous* – that is, in every way independent of all the rest – M. J. Adler> but in more general, and especially political, applications it implies independence from a central power only in matters of self-government <an *autonomous* dominion of an empire> <proposals for the establishment of *autonomous* school districts> **Sovereign** stresses the absence of a superior or central dominant power and implies supremacy within its field to what is so described or so designated <noble and most *sovereign* reason – Shak.> As applied to a ruling power, *sovereign* usually involves the ideas of complete political independence and of the possession of original and underived power <the king could not be *sovereign* if there were any immunities . . . outside his jurisdiction – Christopher Morris> *ant* bond

free *vb* **free, release, liberate, emancipate, manumit, discharge** *shared meaning* : to loose from constraint or restraint. **Free** implies a usually permanent removal from whatever binds, confines, entangles, or oppresses <*free* one's hair from a bramble> <*free* a man from prison> <*free* one's mind from a problem by discussing it with a friend> **Release** stresses a setting loose (as from restraint, confinement, or obligation) <death had *released* him from his suffering> <*release* me from my bands with the help of your good hands – Shak.> **Liberate,** a close synonym of the preceding words, tends to stress the resulting state of freedom <*liberate* birds from a cage> <a *liberating* mood of free intellectual inquiry that became part of his life – *Current Biog.*> **Emancipate** implies the liberation of a person from subjection (as to another person) or domination (as by custom or duties) and may suggest attaining a freedom to follow one's own judgment, conscience, or intelligence <pointed out war's *emancipating* effects on women – Jessie Bernard> **Manumit** implies emancipation from slavery <Darnall . . . was the son of a white man by one of his slaves, and his father executed certain instruments to *manumit* him – R. B. Taney> **Discharge** may imply liberation or merely ejection or emission from a confining that may or may not constitute restraint <*discharge* a prisoner> <*discharge* a hospital patient> <*discharge* a shot from a rifle> <the train *discharged* a horde of passengers>

freedom, liberty, license *shared meaning* : the power or condition of acting without compulsion. **Freedom** has a broad range and may imply total absence of restraint even as imposed by necessity, or moderate absence of restraint, or merely an unawareness of being unduly hampered or frustrated <*Freedom* . . . is to be understood in the medieval sense, when there was no abstract *freedom* but only countable *Freedoms,* each bestowed, none inherent, all subject to forfeiture – Martin Joos> **Liberty,** often interchangeable with *freedom,* is likely to carry more clearly either an implication of the power to choose (as one's course, beliefs, or utterances) <in totalitarian states there is no *liberty* of expression for writers and no *liberty* of choice for their readers – Aldous Huxley> or one of deliverance or relief from constraint or compulsion <from bondage freed, at *liberty* to serve as you loved best – Maurice Baring> **License** can imply unusual freedom (as from rules or restraints) permitted or tolerated because of special circumstances <poetic *license*> <reason and common sense were given full *license* to take no notice of pedants – Stuart Hampshire> but more often it implies an abuse of liberty by willfully following one's own course without regard to propriety or the rights of others <*license* they mean when they cry Liberty – John Milton> <Caesar's legions . . . were enjoying their victory in the *license* which is miscalled liberty – J. A. Froude> ***ant*** necessity

freethinker – see ATHEIST

frenzy – see MANIA

frequently – see OFTEN ***ant*** rarely, seldom

fresh – see NEW ***ant*** stale

friable – see FRAGILE

friar – see RELIGIOUS

friendly – see AMICABLE ***ant*** unfriendly, belligerent

fright – see FEAR

frightful – see FEARFUL **2**

fritter – see WASTE

frivolity – see LIGHTNESS ***ant*** seriousness, staidness

froward – see CONTRARY ***ant*** compliant

frown, scowl, glower, lower *shared meaning* : to put on a dark or malignant countenance or aspect. **Frown** implies a stern face and contracted brows that express concentration, bewilderment, or especially anger, displeasure, or contempt <the sedan's driver . . . turning his head to *frown* grotesquely at the man in the back . . ., and then to glare down the road ahead – Terry Southern> **Scowl** implies wrinkled down-drawn brows and a mood of sullenness or discontent <a spinner that would not rebel, nor mutter, nor *scowl,* nor strike for wages – R. W. Emerson> **Glower** implies a direct defiant or brooding stare and carries a strong connotation of intense resistant anger or contempt <he . . . stood *glowering* from a distance at her, as she sat bowed over the child – D. H. Lawrence> **Lower** implies a menacing darkness and sullenness of face or of aspect; the term is used with reference either to persons or to skies that give promise of foul weather <dark *lowers* the tempest overhead – H. W. Longfellow> ***ant*** smile

frowzy – see SLATTERNLY ***ant*** trim, smart

frugal – see SPARING ***ant*** wasteful

fruitful – see FERTILE ***ant*** unfruitful, fruitless

fruition – see PLEASURE

fruitless – see FUTILE ***ant*** fruitful

frustrate, thwart, foil, baffle, balk, circumvent, outwit *shared meaning* : to come between a person and his aim or desire or to defeat another's desire. **Frustrate** implies making vain or ineffectual all efforts, however vigorous or persistent <legislators backed by the sanction of powerful business lobbies *frustrating* the few good and intelligent men who are willing to labor in the maw of small-time politics – Willie Morris> **Thwart** suggests frustrating by running counter to or crossing one making headway <others had thrust themselves into his life and *thwarted* his purposes – George Eliot> **Foil** implies so checking or defeating as to discourage further effort <intelligence as a means to *foil* brute force – Lafcadio Hearn> **Baffle** implies frustrating by puzzling or confusing <the swiftness of his marches *baffled* alike flight and resistance – J. A. Froude> <with postwar verse, the . . . untutored reader is apt to admit himself quite *baffled* – C. D. Lewis> **Balk** suggests the interposing of obstacles and hindrances <snarled in a knot of words which *balks* the understanding – Edmund Wilson> **Circumvent** implies frustration by stratagem <*circumventing* his enemies by craft and driving them out . . . by force – P. N. Ure> **Outwit** implies craft and cunning in frustrating or circumventing <the skill with which she [Elizabeth I] had hoodwinked and *outwitted* every statesman in Europe – J. R. Green> ***ant*** fulfill

fugitive – see TRANSIENT

fulfill 1 see PERFORM *ant* frustrate, fail (in)
2 see SATISFY 3 *ant* fall short (of)

full, complete, plenary, replete *shared meaning* : containing all that is wanted or needed or possible. In spite of the common meaning element only *full* is freely interchangeable with the remaining words. **Full** may imply the inclusion of all that is needed or desirable <made a *full* confession> <sat down to a *full* meal at noon> or the presence of all that can be held or contained <a chest *full* of embroidered linens> <a *full* basket of fruit> **Complete** means full in the sense of having everything needed or wanted <a *complete* analysis of a problem> <their work was *complete* and perfectly done> **Plenary** adds to *complete* the implication of fullness without qualification and carries a strong suggestion of absoluteness; thus, *plenary* power is full power without any limitation or qualification; a *plenary* indulgence implies the remission of the entire temporal punishment due for one's sins <the *plenary* inspiration of the Bible – M. R. Cohen> <a *plenary* state of cleanliness – Arnold Bennett> **Replete,** usually followed by *with,* stresses abundance of supply and implies a being filled to the brim or to satiety <many schools had suddenly become great and *replete* with erudite scholars – Paul Goodman> <a warmly affectionate book, *replete* with both human and religious value – Frances Witherspoon> *ant* empty

fumigate – see STERILIZE

fun, jest, sport, game, play *shared meaning* : action or speech that provides amusement or arouses laughter. **Fun** usually implies laughter or gaiety but may imply merely a lack of serious or ulterior purpose <the object of kidding . . . is . . . to pass off untruth as truth just for the *fun* of it – Jacob Brackman> <they meant no harm; they just said it in *fun*> **Jest** implies lack of earnestness in what is said or done and may suggest hoaxing or teasing <a prank begun as a *jest* that ended in tragedy> <won fame by *jests* at the foibles of his time, but . . . his pen was more playful than caustic – S. T. Williams & J. A. Pollard> <mock not nor jest at anything of importance; break no *jests* that are sharp or biting – George Washington> **Sport** is likely to imply the arousing of laughter against someone typically by raillery and ridicule <make *sport* of a new boy at recess> **Game** may come very close to *sport* in its implications <made *game* of his unfortunate rival> but it may also apply to any activity carried on in a spirit of fun <there have been few poets more successful . . . in having fun with poetry. To Mr. Frost it is a pleasant *game* – Lewis G. Leary> **Play** which stresses an opposition to *earnest* can replace any of the other words when a thoroughly innocuous implication of lack of earnestness or seriousness is desired <sometimes words said in *play* wound as much as if they were said in earnest> <handling the problem that had baffled us was mere *play* for a man of his experience>

function 1 **function, office, duty, province** *shared meaning* : the acts or operations expected of a person or thing. **Function,** applicable to anything living, natural, or constructed, implies a definite end or purpose that the thing in question serves or is designed to serve or a particular kind of work it is intended to perform <the work of art and its maker had a *function* to fulfill which was essential for the existence of society – E. F. Sekler> <the *function* of language is twofold: to communicate emotion and to give information – Aldous Husley> **Office,** close to *function* in application to things, is more often applied to the function or work expected of a person by reason of his trade or profession or of his special relationship to others <it is the proper *office* of a parent to guide and correct his children> <O, pardon me for bringing these ill news, since you did leave it for my *office,* sir – Shak.> **Duty** applies to a task or responsibility imposed by

one's occupation, rank, status, or calling <the cook performed her *duties* well> <it is not only the right, but it is the judicial *duty* of the court, to examine the whole case – R. B. Taney> **Province** denotes a function, office, or duty that naturally or logically falls within one's range of jurisdiction or competence, sometimes as defined by customary practice <nursing does not belong to a man; it is not his *province* – Jane Austen> <the teaching of foreign language . . . is rapidly becoming the *province* of the schools rather than of higher education – Elton Hocking>
2 see POWER 2
fundamental – see ESSENTIAL
funny – see LAUGHABLE
furnish 1 see PROVIDE ***ant*** strip
2 furnish, equip, outfit, appoint, accouter, arm *shared meaning* : to supply one with what is needed (as for daily living or a particular activity). **Furnish** implies the provision of any or all essentials for performing a function or serving an end <such education as the local schools could *furnish* – G. F. Smythe> <*furnish* a bedroom in Danish modern style> **Equip** stresses the provision of what makes for efficiency in use or action; thus, a poorly *furnished* kitchen may be merely shabby or short in tables or chairs, but a poorly *equipped* kitchen is not adequately supplied with the utensils needed for cooking and other kitchen tasks <troops that were . . . *equipped* and trained to fight in the bitter cold and the deep snow – W. L. Shirer> **Outfit** stresses provision for a particular purpose (as a journey or a special activity) <*outfit* a boy for school> **Appoint** suggests complete and often elegant furnishings or equipment <a well-*appointed* office> <the interior has been *appointed* with pieces associated with the Colonial period – *Amer. Guide Series: N.Y.C.*> **Accouter** applies especially to the supplying of personal dress or equipment, usually for a particular activity <the fully *accoutered* members of a Wild West show – *Saturday Rev.*> **Arm** implies provision for effective action or operation, especially in war <*arm* a merchant ship for use as a privateer> <*armed* with wide powers and unlimited resources – T. D. McCormick>
further *adv* – see FARTHER
further *vb* – see ADVANCE ***ant*** hinder, retard
furtive – see SECRET ***ant*** forthright, brazen
fury – see ANGER
fuse – see MIX
fuss – see STIR
fussy – see NICE
fustian – see BOMBAST
fusty – see MALODOROUS
futile, vain, fruitless *shared meaning* : barren of result. *Futile* and *vain* parallel each other when they imply failure to realize an immediate aim <it was equally in *vain*, and he soon wearied of his *futile* vigilance – R. L. Stevenson> but **futile** is likely to connote the completeness of the failure or the unwisdom of the undertaking while **vain** in itself is unlikely to imply more than the simple fact of failure <all literature, art, and science are *vain* . . . if they do not enable you to be glad – John Ruskin> <opposition . . . had been so *futile* that surrender seemed the only course open – C. L. Jones> **Fruitless** can come close to *vain* but often suggests long and arduous effort or severe disappointment <he nursed a grievance and, with Scotch persistence, kept up for years his *fruitless* efforts at reinstatement – F. W. Ashley>

gag – see JEST

gain 1 see GET ***ant*** forfeit, lose

2 see REACH ***ant*** forfeit, lose

gainsay – see DENY ***ant*** admit

gall – see TEMERITY

gallant – see CIVIL

gallantry – see HEROISM ***ant*** dastardliness

game – see FUN

gape – see GAZE

garble – see MISREPRESENT

garish – see GAUDY ***ant*** somber

garner – see REAP

garnish – see ADORN

garrulous – see TALKATIVE ***ant*** taciturn

gather 1 gather, collect, assemble, congregate *shared meaning* : to come or bring together into a group, mass, or unit. **Gather,** the most widely applicable term, is usually neutral in connotation or may suggest literal or figurative plucking and culling or harvesting <the balloon start had *gathered* a little crowd of people – H. G. Wells> <*gather* a supply of firewood> **Collect** is sometimes interchangeable with *gather* <leaves *collected* along the fence> <*collect* information> but often it implies careful selection or orderly arrangement or a definitely understood end in view <boys who *collect* stamps can learn a great deal about the world they live in> <the mass of movable wealth *collected* in the shops and warehouses of London – T. B. Macaulay> **Assemble** stresses a close union of individuals and a conscious or a definite end in their coming or being brought together <individual ships were *assembled* from prefabricated parts in as little as four and one-half days – *Current Biog.*> <the right of the people peaceably to *assemble* – *U.S. Constitution*> <he was . . . a very memorable person. I won't attempt to *assemble* his many achievements and virtues here – J. D. Salinger> **Congregate** implies a spontaneous flocking together into a crowd or huddle, usually of similar types <pigeons *congregating* on a sunny roof> <the older people sat rather stiffly in the corners, the young men *congregated* uneasily in impermanent groups – Irwin Shaw>

2 see REAP

3 see INFER

gauche – see AWKWARD

gaudy, tawdry, garish, flashy, meretricious *shared meaning* : vulgarly or cheaply showy. **Gaudy** implies a tasteless use of overly bright, often clashing colors or excessive ornamentation <false eloquence, like the prismatic glass, its *gaudy* colors spreads on ev'ry place – Alexander Pope> **Tawdry** applies to what is not only gaudy but cheap and sleazy <she saw a *tawdry* mockery of sacred things, a bourgeois riot of expense, with a special touch of vulgar . . . sentimentality – Herman Wouk> <the woman . . . big, bovine, in a motley of cheap and *tawdry* clothes – William Styron> **Garish** describes what is distressingly or offensively bright <hide me from day's *garish* eye – John Milton> <this front room is furnished with *garish* theatrical magnificence – Arnold Bennett> **Flashy** implies momentarily brilliant performance or display that soon reveals itself as shallow or vulgar <two painted *flashy* women with fine legs – Graham Greene> <"what the public wants" is being translated into the *flashy,* the gadgety, the spectacular – R. F. Loewy> **Meretricious** stresses falsity and may be chosen when the notion to be conveyed is one of a tawdry show that beckons with a false allure or promise <girls who deck themselves with gems, false hair, and *meretricious* ornament, to chain the fleeting fancy of a man – W. S. Gilbert> <nor . . . is it rare for scholarly names to provide fig leaves of respectability for *meretricious* but stylish books – *Times Lit. Supp.*> <soldiers . . . circled displays of colored post cards and picked up *meretricious* mementos – James Baldwin> ***ant*** quiet (*in taste or color*)

gauge – see STANDARD

gaunt – see LEAN

gay – see LIVELY ***ant*** grave, sober

gaze, gape, stare, glare, peer, gloat *shared meaning* : to look at long and attentively. These words are seldom freely interchangeable because of the wide disparity in their implications about attitudes and motives. **Gaze**, the most neutral word, implies fixed and prolonged attention <and still they *gazed*, and still the wonder grew that one small head could carry all he knew – Oliver Goldsmith> <she *gazed* into his faded blue eyes as if yearning to be understood – Joseph Conrad> **Gape** adds to *gaze* the implication of stupid and openmouthed wonder <depicts man lost and blindly *gaping* amidst the chaos – Rhys Gwyn> <*gapes* round-eyed at the astonishing world – Rose Macaulay> **Stare** implies a fixed and direct, unwavering gaze (as of wonder, admiration, defiance, or abstractedness) <his eyes . . . *stared* down at me with a look of absolute vacuity – Roald Dahl> <[he] became a vegetarian after being *stared* down by a cow – Martin Cohen> **Glare** implies a fierce or angry staring <all . . . with countenance grim *glared* on him passing – John Milton> <where two armies *glare* at each other across a geographical line – Lindesay Parrott> **Peer** suggests a straining to see more closely or fully, often with narrowed eyes or from concealment <he *peered* sharply out of the corner of his eye like a spy who had to find out what was going on . . . without letting the passersby observe his interest – Thomas Wolfe> **Gloat** implies prolonged or frequent gazing on something, often in secret and usually with deep, even malignant or unholy satisfaction <to gaze and *gloat* with his hungry eye on jewels that gleamed like a glowworm's spark – H. W. Longfellow>

general – see UNIVERSAL

generic – see UNIVERSAL

generous – see LIBERAL ***ant*** stingy

genial – see GRACIOUS ***ant*** saturnine (*manner, disposition, aspect*), caustic (*remarks, comments*)

gentle – see SOFT ***ant*** rough, harsh

genuine – see AUTHENTIC ***ant*** counterfeit, fraudulent

germane – see RELEVANT ***ant*** foreign

get **1 get, obtain, procure, secure, acquire, gain, win, earn** *shared meaning* : to come into possession of. **Get** is very general in its meaning and simple and familiar in its use. Thus, one may *get* something by fetching <*get* a book from the shelf>, by extracting <*get* gold from ore>, by receiving <*get* a present>, or by earning <*get* good wages> **Obtain**, too, is rather general but tends to suggest attainment of something sought for, often after expenditure of time and effort <*obtain* a graduate degree> <the identity and a description of all suspicious and dangerous persons should be *obtained* – J. E. Hoover> **Procure** implies effort in obtaining something for oneself or another <pursued with unflagging energy his program of building up the armed services and *procuring* arms for them – W. L. Shirer> **Secure** may suggest safe lasting possession or control <safety against infection could be *secured* by the simple precaution of using safe, potable water – V. G. Heiser> or the gaining of what is hard to come by <*secure* bookings

for a new singer> <*secure* a site for a new library> **Acquire** is likely to suggest an adding to what is already possessed <*acquire* a taste for olives> <develop realistic policies to preserve those legal rights already ours and to *acquire* those legal rights we need – W. D. North> **Gain** adds to *obtain* the implication of struggle or competition and often imputes material value to the thing obtained <worked hard to *gain* an education> <he stood to *gain* a fortune if his scheme succeeded> **Win** may differ from *gain* in suggesting that favoring qualities or circumstances play a part in the gaining <contrasts the dedicated efforts of Communist nations to *win* over the African continent with the halfhearted assistance rendered by the Western powers – *Current Biog.*> <her excellent performance *won* her an award> **Earn** implies a correspondence between one's effort and what one gains thereby <no one without education can hope to *earn* an adequate income> <she had once *earned* a scolding from her nurse by filling her stockings with mud – G. B. Shaw>
2 see INDUCE

gibe – see SCOFF

gift, faculty, aptitude, bent, talent, genius, knack *shared meaning* : a special ability or an unusual capacity for doing or achieving something. **Gift** is likely to imply the favor of nature, of God, or of fortune <a *gift* of humor> <she has a real *gift* for arranging flowers – Edith Wharton> **Faculty** applies to either an innate or an acquired ability for a particular accomplishment or function <once a thing did become pertinent, he had an amazing *faculty* for absorbing it wholly – Terry Southern> **Aptitude** implies both a native capacity and a natural liking for a particular pursuit <people . . . who write from all sorts of motives other than a genuine *aptitude* for writing – Havelock Ellis> <the *aptitude* for calculated emotional imbalance that is so much a part of the professional actress – H. C. Hervey> **Bent** is very close to *aptitude* but is likely to stress inclination more strongly than ability <the free environment that helped them develop into more complete personalities through following their natural *bent* – Emmanuel Bernstein> <a novelist by trade, a symbolist by *bent* – C. W. Mann> **Talent** suggests a marked special ability without implying a mind of extraordinary power <some men have a *talent* for making money> <he had no *talent* for gardening – Elizabeth M. Thomas> **Genius**, a much stronger term than *talent*, usually suggests impressive inborn creative ability and often an inner driving energy that forces its possessor to achieve <in the contemporary novel *genius* is hard to find, *talent* is abundant – *Brit. Bk. News*> **Knack** stresses ease and dexterity in performance and usually implies aptitude in a minor matter <an uncommon *knack* in Latin verse – C. W. Eliot> <a *knack* for organizing and sustaining a nicely knit plot – W. F. Kerr>

gigantic – see HUGE

give, present, donate, bestow, confer, afford *shared meaning* : to convey to another as his possession. **Give** is the general term applicable to passing over anything by any means <*give* a boy a lift in one's car> <*give* my love to your mother and sisters – John Keats> <*give* alms> <*give* a silver urn as a wedding gift> **Present** carries a note of formality or ceremony <pray, *present* my respects to Lady Scott – Lord Byron> <the new ambassador *presented* his credentials> <*present* an award> **Donate** usually implies a publicized giving (as to a charity) <*donate* a piano to an orphanage> <*donate* a site for a new park> **Bestow** implies the settling of something on one as a gift and may imply condescension on the part of the giver <large gifts have I *bestowed* on learned clerks – Shak.> **Confer** implies a gracious giving (as of a favor or honor) <the Queen *confers* her titles and degrees – Alexander Pope> **Afford** implies a giving or bestowing especially as a natural or legitimate consequence of the character of the one that gives <do the laws of his country *afford* him a remedy? – John Marshall> <we have been misleading ourselves into believing that we are *affording* equal opportunities in education to all – A. H. Quie>

glad, happy, cheerful, lighthearted, joyful, joyous *shared meaning* : characterized by or expressing the mood of one who is pleased or delighted. **Glad** may be used in opposition to *sorry* to convey polite conventional expressions of pleasure <we are so *glad* you could come> or it may be used in opposition to *sad* to convey the idea of an actual lifting of spirits, delight, or even elation <wine that maketh *glad* the heart of man – *Ps* 104:15 (AV)> <his entire saintly life was *glad* with an invincible gaiety of spirit – H. O. Taylor> **Happy**, indistinguishable from *glad* in conventional expressions, can in other contexts distinctively imply a sense of well-being and complete content <nothing made him so *happy* as to be at home with his family> <anyone is *happy* who confidently awaits the fulfillment of his highest dreams – Thomas Wolfe> **Cheerful** suggests a strong spontaneous flow of good spirits <broke into a *cheerful* song as he strode along> <he kept throughout his life his youthful optimism and his *cheerful* trust in men – *Dict. of Amer. Biog.*> **Lighthearted** stresses freedom from worry, care, and discontent <he whistles as he goes, *lighthearted* wretch, cold and yet cheerful – William Cowper> <the *lighthearted*, pleasure-loving, cultivated spirit of its [Vienna's] people – W. L. Shirer> *Joyful* and *joyous* imply keen gladness or happiness with resulting elation, but **joyful** usually suggests an emotional reaction to a situation that calls forth rejoicing <in the day of prosperity be *joyful* – *Eccles* 7:14 (AV)> <and *joyful* nations join in leagues of peace – Alexander Pope> while **joyous** is more likely to apply to something that is by its nature filled with joy or a source of joy <all that ever was *joyous*, and clear, and fresh, thy music doth surpass – P. B. Shelley> <that *joyous* serenity we think belongs to a better world than this – Sir Winston Churchill> *ant* sad

glance – see FLASH
glare – see BLAZE, GAZE
glaring – see FLAGRANT
gleam – see FLASH
glean – see REAP
glee – see MIRTH *ant* gloom
glimmer – see FLASH
glint – see FLASH
glisten – see FLASH
glitter – see FLASH
gloat – see GAZE
gloomy – see DARK *ant* brilliant (*with reference to illumination*)
glorious – see SPLENDID *ant* inglorious
glow – see BLAZE
glower – see FROWN
glum – see SULLEN *ant* cheerful
glut – see SATIATE
glutton – see EPICURE
gluttonous – see VORACIOUS *ant* abstemious

go 1 **go, leave, depart, quit, withdraw, retire** *shared meaning* : to move out of or away from the place where one is. **Go** is the general term and is commonly used as the simple opposite of *come* <*go* to school> <*go* away for the day> **Leave** stresses the fact of separation from someone or something <*leave* one's hometown to take a new job> <we shall be sorry to see him *leave*> <he is *leaving* on the early plane> **Depart** carries a

stronger implication of separation than *leave* and is likely to suggest formality, especially when used as an opposite of *arrive* <a goddess of gone days, *departed* long ago – Edna S. V. Millay> <ships arrive and *depart* the landlocked harbor at the rate of one an hour – Franc Shor> <when her gentle spirit *departs* this life the world will be much poorer and less interesting – John Lane> **Quit** may add to *leave* the notion of freeing, ridding, or disentangling from something that burdens or tries <he *quitted* London to take refuge among the mountains – George Meredith> <*quit* a dull job> **Withdraw** suggests a deliberate removal for good reason <constrained by the strength of his convictions to *withdraw* from the Catholic Church – W. L. Sullivan> <the visitors *withdrew* when the doctor came into the room> **Retire** may be used interchangeably with *withdraw* but it is especially appropriate when it is desired to imply renunciation, retreat, or recession <*retire* from the world to a monastery> <when he dies or *retires,* a new manager must be found – G. B. Shaw> <plants and animals ... closely followed the *retiring* ice – John Muir † 1914> ***ant*** come
2 see RESORT
goad – see MOTIVE ***ant*** curb
goal – see INTENTION
good-natured – see AMIABLE ***ant*** contrary
goodwill – see FAVOR
gorge – see SATIATE
gorgeous – see SPLENDID
gossip – see REPORT
gourmand – see EPICURE
gourmet – see EPICURE
govern, rule *shared meaning* : to exercise power and authority in controlling others. **Govern** implies a keeping in a straight course or under proper control or in smooth operation for the good of the individual or the whole <to *govern* is to organize the common activities of a society. It may be much more than that, but so much is essential; power rests on organization; where there is no organization there is no government – *Times Lit. Supp.*> <I appeal to you to *govern* your temper – Charles Dickens> <formulating the principles which should *govern* the creation of proletarian literature – C. I. Glicksberg> **Rule** is likely to imply power to lay down laws which shall determine the action of others or to issue commands which must be obeyed, and it often suggests arbitrary or capricious exercise of power <resolved to ruin or to *rule* the state – John Dryden> <we can't let our parents *rule* our lives – Rose Macaulay> <[testified] that ... police stood idly by while white toughs *ruled* with bricks and clubs – *Springfield (Mass.) Union*>
grab – see TAKE
grace – see MERCY
gracious, cordial, affable, genial, sociable *shared meaning* : markedly pleasant and easy in social intercourse. **Gracious** implies kindliness and courtesy, especially to inferiors <heartened by her *gracious* reception of a nervous bow – G. B. Shaw> <*gracious* to everyone, but known to a very few – Willa Cather> **Cordial** stresses warmth and heartiness <a *cordial* greeting> <they gave us a *cordial* reception, and a hearty supper – Herman Melville> **Affable** implies easy approachability and readiness to respond pleasantly to conversation or requests or proposals <easy of approach and *affable* in conversation. They seldom put on airs – W. S. Maugham> **Genial** implies qualities such as warm sympathy or a sense of humor that make for good cheer <he was no fanatic and no ascetic. He was *genial,* social, even convivial – Goldwin Smith> <this sudden calm and the sense of

comfort that it brought created a more *genial* atmosphere over the whole ship – Roald Dahl> **Sociable** implies a genuine liking and need for the company of others and a usually genial readiness to engage in social intercourse even with strangers or inferiors <was genial and *sociable,* approachable at all times and fond of social intercourse – J. S. Reeves> <a very *sociable* fellow, prone to talk as long as he can find a listener – Jack London> *ant* ungracious

grand, magnificent, imposing, stately, majestic, grandiose *shared meaning* : large and impressive. **Grand** implies largeness of size or conception combined with handsomeness and dignity <the *grand* view from the summit> <we need the energies of our people – enlisted not only in *grand* enterprises, but . . . in those small splendid efforts that make headlines in the neighborhood newspaper instead of the national journal – R. M. Nixon> **Magnificent** implies an impressive largeness (as of substance or spirit), proportionate to scale without sacrifice of dignity or good taste <a cart drawn by a ponderous and *magnificent* black carthorse – Roald Dahl> <the *magnificent* marble town house celebrated as a world's wonder – J. L. Motley> but often the idea of largeness becomes submerged and *magnificent* stresses superiority, especially as contrasted with *plainness* or *insignificance* <wore a *magnificent* rose taffeta gown> <perhaps the most *magnificent* manifestation of poetic mysticism is the last canto – G. G. Coulton> **Imposing** implies impressive size and dignity <an *imposing* mansion dominated the village> <a tall *imposing* old man> **Stately** emphasizes dignity together with handsomeness and impressiveness and may carry a suggestion of larger than usual size <there was a majestic quality about this woman, something splendid, almost *stately* – Roald Dahl> <might hope for a period of yearly relaxation in London, ordered and increasingly *stately* as the natural frivolity of youth matured – Victoria Sackville-West> **Majestic** combines the implications of *imposing* and *stately* and adds a strong connotation of solemn grandeur <the voice . . . possessed a quality of roundness that was the roundness of the infinite – terrible, *majestic* and beautiful – William Styron> **Grandiose** implies a scope or size exceeding ordinary experience but is ordinarily applied derogatorily to inflated pretension or absurd exaggeration <Hegel's *grandiose* but utopian attempt to encompass the material world within the logical straitjacket of his own system – *Times Lit. Supp.*> <Hitler's *grandiose* plans for world conquest – W. L. Shirer>

grandiose – see GRAND

grant, concede, vouchsafe, accord, award *shared meaning* : to give as a favor or a right. One **grants,** usually to a claimant or a petitioner and often a subordinate, something requested or demanded that could be withheld <acceding to her pleas, he *granted* her another period of six months in which to make good in the theater – *Current Biog.*> <*grant* an interview to a reporter> One **concedes** something claimed or expected as a right, prerogative, or possession when one yields it reluctantly in response to a rightful or compelling claim <even his harshest critics *concede* him a rocklike integrity – *Time*> <the senator *conceded* the election soon after midnight> One **vouchsafes** when one grants something as a courtesy or as an act of gracious condescension <occasionally a true poet is *vouchsafed* to the world – Rumer Godden> As often used in supplications, the word implies humility in the suppliant <*vouchsafe,* O Lord: to keep us this day without sin – *Bk. of Com. Prayer*> One **accords** to another what is his due or in keeping with his character or status <children easily appreciate justice, and will readily *accord* to others what others *accord* to them – Bertrand Russell> One **awards** something that is deserved or merited; typically the word implies careful weighing of pertinent factors (as by a court of law or a judge in a contest or competition) <*award* a contract to build a new school> <*award* damages to an accident victim> <his victory was duly acclaimed . . . ; he was given the title of Imperator and *awarded* a triumph – John Buchan>

graphic, vivid, picturesque, pictorial *shared meaning* : giving a clear visual impression especially in words. All these words are applied primarily to works of art and typically to literature. **Graphic** stresses the evoking of a clear lifelike image <a *graphic* description of the face of a young Hindu at the sight of castor oil – C. R. Darwin> **Vivid** stresses the intense vital quality of either the stimulus or the response <figures so *vivid* that they seem to breathe and speak before us – L. P. Smith> <such materials provide more than mere knowledge . . . they afford a vicarious but *vivid* experience for the students – Elton Hocking> **Picturesque** suggests the presence of those qualities (as unfamiliarity, sharp contrasts, or mysterious charm) that make for a striking or effective picture <the *picturesque* force of his style – Nathaniel Hawthorne> <a venerable family mansion, in a highly *picturesque* state of semidilapidation – T. L. Peacock> **Pictorial** implies the aim of presenting a vivid picture with emphasis on colors, shapes, and spatial relations <you'll see other unfamiliar signs along the highway . . . but you'll find these *pictorial* devices are readily understandable – Russ Leadabrand> <he made *pictorial* drama out of the most commonplace intimacies of French bourgeois home life – J. T. Soby>

grasp *vb* – see TAKE

grasp *n* – see HOLD

grasping – see COVETOUS

grateful **1 grateful, thankful** *shared meaning* : feeling or expressing gratitude. **Grateful** is more commonly employed to express a proper sense of favors received from another person or persons <she . . . was happy to have the girl in her house, as if she was, at bottom, a lonely woman, *grateful* for any company – John Cheever> <the Queen herself, *grateful* to Prince Geraint for service done – Alfred Tennyson> **Thankful** is often preferred to express one's acknowledgment of divine favor or of what is vaguely felt to be providential <for what we are about to receive make us truly *thankful*> <Churchill was mildly amused and in any case *thankful* that "this most difficult man" was finally out of London – S. E. Ambrose> <you were very careless, you can be *thankful* that you were not badly hurt> ***ant*** ungrateful

2 see PLEASANT ***ant*** obnoxious

gratifying – see PLEASANT

grave – see SERIOUS ***ant*** gay

great – see LARGE ***ant*** little

greedy – see COVETOUS

green – see RUDE ***ant*** experienced, seasoned

grief – see SORROW

grievance – see INJUSTICE

grieve, mourn, sorrow *shared meaning* : to feel or express sorrow or grief. **Grieve** implies actual mental suffering, whether it is shown outwardly or not; often it connotes the concentration of one's mind on one's loss, trouble, or cause of distress <he *grieved*, like an honest lad, to see his comrade left to face calamity alone – George Meredith> <she might *grieve* . . . but she was gallant, she was proud; she would not whine – Victoria Sackville-West> **Mourn** stresses the outward expressions of grief, sincere or conventional, and usually suggests a specific cause (as the death of one near akin) <grieve for an hour, perhaps, then *mourn* a year and bear about

the mockery of woe to midnight dances, and the public show – Alexander Pope> **Sorrow,** sometimes interchangeable with either *grieve* or *mourn* when sincere mental distress is implied, may be preferred when the sense of regret or loss and of resultant sadness is to be stressed; it usually suggests an inner distress rather than outward expressions of grief <so send them [Adam and Eve] forth, though *sorrowing,* yet in peace – John Milton> <in such literature one learns to *sorrow* for the common griefs and to rejoice in the common satisfactions – Helen C. White> ***ant*** rejoice

grind – see WORK

grip – see HOLD

grit – see FORTITUDE ***ant*** faintheartedness

gross **1** see COARSE ***ant*** delicate, dainty, ethereal
2 see FLAGRANT ***ant*** petty
3 see WHOLE ***ant*** net

grotesque – see FANTASTIC

ground – see BASE

group, cluster, bunch, parcel, lot *shared meaning* **:** a collection or assemblage of separate units. **Group** implies some unifying relationship and ordinarily a degree of physical closeness <a *group* of people waiting for a bus> <a *group* of little islands> <put the books you want to keep in a separate *group*> **Cluster** basically refers to a group of things growing together <a *cluster* of grapes> <a *cluster* of roses> but it is often extended to persons or things that form small groups especially within larger masses <this ... campus ... will consist of a *cluster* of small colleges, each with only about 700 students – F. M. Hechinger> <ten enormous sound stages concealed in industrial-looking buildings and surrounded by a *cluster* of ... shops – Jeremy Bernstein> **Bunch** is likely to imply a natural or homogeneous association of similar things or persons <a *bunch* of bananas> <you never really had a big problem at all; you only had a whole *bunch* of little problems that appeared impossible because the pile was so high – R. J. Bryant> <a *bunch* of boys playing marbles> **Parcel** in this sense is likely to convey an impression of disapproval <the whole story was a *parcel* of lies> <a *parcel* of giddy young kids – Mark Twain> **Lot** applies to persons or things that are associated or that have to be dealt with as a whole <my point was ... that in any such comparison our *lot* just wouldn't be in the running – Malcolm Muggeridge> <the books were sold in *lots*>

grovel – see WALLOW

grudge – see MALICE

gruff – see BLUFF

guard – see DEFEND

guess – see CONJECTURE

guide, lead, steer, pilot, engineer *shared meaning* **:** to direct in a course or show the way to be followed. **Guide** implies intimate knowledge of the way and of all its difficulties and dangers <some heavenly power *guide* us out of this fearful country – Shak.> <the teacher, the parent, or the friend can often do much ... to *guide* the pupil into an enjoyment of thinking – C. W. Eliot> **Lead** implies a going ahead to show the way and often to keep those that follow under control and in order <he longed ... to *lead* his men on to victory – Frederick Marryat> <the law has to *lead* the people sometimes – Burke Marshall> **Steer** implies an ability to keep to a chosen course and stresses a capacity for maneuvering correctly and effectively <fortune brings in some boats that are not *steered* – Shak.> <secure in the faith that his reasoned intelligence will *steer* him correctly at all times – H. N. Maclean> **Pilot** stresses special skill or knowledge used in guiding over a dangerous, intricate, or complicated course <*pilot* a ship through a narrow channel> <*piloting* important bills through the Senate – *Current Biog.*> **Engineer** implies guidance by one who finds ways to avoid or overcome difficulties in achieving an end or carrying out a plan <if society can somehow or other *engineer* a one-point reduction in its total unemployment rate – R. M. Solow> Often the term is somewhat pejorative and tends to suggest slickness and craft more than knowledge and skill <*engineer* an elaborate fraud> <charged his fellow . . . commissioner with having personally *engineered* the plot – J. A. Michener> ***ant*** misguide

guilty – see BLAMEWORTHY ***ant*** innocent
gull – see DUPE
gumption – see SENSE
gush – see POUR
gusto – see TASTE 2
guts – see FORTITUDE

habit 1 habit, habitude, practice, usage, custom, use, wont *shared meaning* : a way of acting that has become fixed through repetition. **Habit** implies a doing unconsciously or without premeditation, often compulsively <she took her religion for granted, accepted it by *habit,* prayed by rote – J. T. Farrell> <trying to break a bad *habit*> **Habitude** suggests a fixed attitude or usual state of mind <the sense of fitness and proportion that comes with years of *habitude* in the practice of an art – B. N. Cardozo> **Practice** describes a method followed with regularity and usually through choice <it was his *practice* to take an early stroll each morning> <what good were the standards and *practices* of such a society, which encouraged savings and investment and solemnly promised a safe return from them and then defaulted? – W. L. Shirer> **Usage** suggests a customary action so generally followed that it has become a social norm <*usage:* The customary use in a language of sounds, words, and grammatical structures by a group or class of speakers of that language – R. A. Peters> <difficult . . . to earn a living in a business community without yielding to its *usages* – W. H. Hamilton> **Custom** adds to *practice* or *usage* the implication of being so firmly fixed in the behavior pattern of an individual or group as to have the force of unwritten law <[they] take the position that there is no difference between right and wrong, justice and injustice, except as the community declares itself upon them through law and *custom* – R. M. Hutchins> **Use** stresses the fact of customary usage <more haste than is his *use* – Shak.> and may imply its distinctive quality <conform to the *uses* of polite society> **Wont** differs little from *use* with which it is frequently coupled as a term of equivalent content <this nice balance between sovereignty and liberty is maintained by use and *wont* – V. L. Parrington> <far more serious and thoughtful than was her *wont* – William Black>
2 see PHYSIQUE

habitual – see USUAL ***ant*** occasional
habitude – see HABIT
hale – see HEALTHY ***ant*** infirm
hallow – see DEVOTE
hallucination – see DELUSION

hamper, trammel, clog, fetter, shackle, manacle *shared meaning* : to hinder or impede in moving, progressing, or acting. **Hamper** implies an encumbering or embarrassing by or as if by an impediment or a restraining influence

<her injured foot *hampered* her progress> <the view is vigorously urged today that rhyme and meter *hamper* the poet's free expression – J. L. Lowes> **Trammel** suggests hindering like an entangling or confining in a net <I doubt that the right ... would be deemed unreasonably *trammeled* by an ordinance protecting local inhabitants – G. H. Gottlieb> <a culture-*trammeled* understanding – B. L. Whorf> **Clog** usually implies a slowing by something extraneous that clings, weighs down, obstructs, or gums up; distinctively it may refer to a channel for movement or action as well as to what is moving or acting <the drain was *clogged* with grease> <the wings of birds were *clogged* with ice and snow – John Dryden> <his mind is *clogged* with the strangest miscellany of truth and marvel – V. L. Parrington> **Fetter** suggests a restraining so severe that freedom to move or progress is almost lost <we reverence tradition, but we will not be *fettered* by it – W. R. Inge> **Shackle** and **manacle** are similar to *fetter* but are more likely to suggest total loss of the power to move, to progress, or to act <the illiterate ... *shackled* by habits of irritability and poor family background – Dixon Wecter> <keep Rome *manacled* hand and foot: no fear of unruliness – Robert Browning> ***ant*** assist (*as a person*), expedite (*as work*)

handle 1 handle, manipulate, wield *shared meaning* : to manage dexterously or efficiently. **Handle** implies the acquirement of skill and its use in attaining an end <knew better than most men how to *handle* a blade – L. C. Douglas> <Richelieu sent Charnacé out to *handle* that situation – Hilaire Belloc> **Manipulate** implies dexterity and adroitness in handling <was a spastic child and found it difficult to *manipulate* a pencil – *Current Biog.*> and often implies crafty or artful and sometimes fraudulent handling for the attainment of one's ends <the political merchandisers ... make no attempt to educate the masses into becoming fit for self-government; they are content merely to *manipulate* and exploit them – Aldous Huxley> **Wield** implies mastery and vigor in handling a tool or a weapon or in exerting influence, authority, or power <*wielded* a pen with clerkly precision – T. B. Costain> <her newborn power was *wielded* ... by unprincipled and ambitious men – Thomas De Quincey> <he *wields* ... a very capable scholarship that gives backbone to his work – N. L. Rothman>

2 see TREAT

3 see TOUCH

handsome – see BEAUTIFUL

hanker – see LONG

haphazard – see RANDOM

happen, chance, occur, transpire *shared meaning* : to come about. **Happen** is the ordinary and general term applying to whatever comes about with or without obvious causation or intention <what has been learned from the experiences undergone – not just what *happened* to the individual but what he did with what *happened* to him – R. F. Lewis> <remembering an incident that *happened* in his childhood> **Chance** regularly implies absence of design or apparent lack of causation <if a bird's nest *chance* to be before thee – *Deut* 22:6 (AV)> <things they themselves *chance* to know – Agnes Repplier> **Occur** stresses presentation to sight or attention <at the last moment ... a complication *occurred* – Jonas Waern> <it hadn't *occurred* to him to borrow ... he had always stolen – Bernard Malamud> **Transpire** in its precise use implies a leaking out so as to become known or apparent <it soon *transpired* that there were two ... conceptions of this problem – C. H. Malik> but through a semantic shift the word has developed a value, deplored by some rigorous purists, in which it is interchangeable with *happen* or *occur* <all memorable events ... *transpire*

in morning time and in a morning atmosphere – H. D. Thoreau>

happy 1 see FIT *ant* unhappy

2 see GLAD *ant* unhappy, disconsolate

3 see LUCKY *ant* unhappy

harass – see WORRY

harbinger – see FORERUNNER

hard 1 see FIRM *ant* soft

2 **hard, difficult, arduous** *shared meaning* : demanding toil and effort. **Hard** implies the opposite of all that is easy <a *hard* lesson> <a *hard* job> <an explanation that is *hard* to follow> <it was *hard* for a gentleman to refuse a lady in distress – George Crout> **Difficult** commonly implies the presence of obstacles to be surmounted or of complications to be removed and is likely to suggest a calling upon special qualities (as skill, knowledge, or endurance) if success is to be attained <[he] has the *difficult* task of following . . . one of the great statesmen of the twentieth century – *Current Biog.*> <men like fly-fishing, because it is *difficult;* they will not shoot a bird sitting, because it is easy – Bertrand Russell> **Arduous** stresses the need of laborious and persevering exertion <made *arduous* forays into fields that few literary minds have the desire or hardihood to investigate – Alan Holder> <determined to save him from a life of *arduous* toil – A. C. Cole> *ant* easy

hardihood – see TEMERITY

hardship – see DIFFICULTY

harm – see INJURE *ant* benefit

harmonize – see AGREE 3 *ant* clash, conflict

harry – see WORRY

harsh – see ROUGH *ant* pleasant, mild

harvest – see REAP

haste, hurry, speed, expedition, dispatch *shared meaning* : quickness in movement or in action. **Haste** implies urgency or precipitancy in persons <out of breath from *haste* – Jane Austen> and may suggest resulting rashness or carelessness in action <*haste* makes waste – *old proverb*> <his tongue, all impatient to speak . . . did stumble with *haste* – Shak.> **Hurry,** often interchangeable with *haste,* can carry a stronger implication of agitation, bustle, or confusion <in the *hurry* of departure she forgot her toothbrush> <the *hurry* and glare of a modern campaign might well obscure a candidate of Lincolnesque qualities – *Springfield* (*Mass.*) *Union*> **Speed** suggests swiftness in movement or action, without bustle and confusion and usually with success <the more haste, the less *speed* – *old proverb*> <the national capital is being built at *speed;* new public buildings are constantly changing the skyline – *Australian Panorama*> *Expedition* and *dispatch* imply both speed and efficiency especially in business or affairs, but **expedition** is likely to stress efficiency in performance, and **dispatch** promptness in bringing matters to a conclusion <they made their plans with *expedition*> <put her things on with remarkable *expedition* – Arnold Bennett> <serious business, craving quick *dispatch* – Shak.> <there was no task in all the household . . . which her mistress could not do far better and with more *dispatch* than she – Thomas Wolfe> *ant* deliberation

hasty – see FAST

hate, detest, abhor, abominate, loathe *shared meaning* : to feel aversion or intense dislike for. **Hate** implies extreme aversion, typically coupled with enmity or malice <she did not *hate* him; she rather despised him, and just suffered him – W. M. Thackeray> **Detest** implies violent or intense antipathy or dislike but usually lacks the active hostility and malevolence implicit in *hate* <I mortally *detest* cards – Henry Fielding> <I have

a horror of the place [New York]. I am constantly afraid the buildings will fall on me, I *detest* elevators – Ludwig Bemelmans> **Abhor** suggests profound shuddering repugnance from or as if from fear or horror <Rome had made herself *abhorred* throughout the world by the violence and avarice of her generals – J. A. Froude> <father was a man who *abhorred* scenes and confusion> **Abominate** implies strong detestation and suggests the effect of something ill-omened or shameful <I *abominate* the kind of writing that ... sets forth to tell the truth ... with no regard to the facts that some of the truth is irrelevant, is uninteresting and can clog the works – Jean Stafford> **Loathe** implies utter disgust or intolerance <except when I am listening to their music I *loathe* the whole race; great stupid, brutal, immoral, sentimental savages – Rose Macaulay> ***ant*** love

hateful, odious, abhorrent, detestable, abominable *shared meaning* : strongly or utterly objectionable. These words are often used with little distinction but they can be applied precisely to present a nice discrimination of feeling. **Hateful** can imply the exciting of actual hatred <why shouldn't we hate what is *hateful* in people, and scorn what is mean? – W. M. Thackeray> <this is a *hateful* book, in the original sense of the word – a book that feels and shows hate, a book literally full of hate – D. F. Schoenbrun> **Odious** stresses disagreeableness or offensiveness or the arousing of repugnance <our blind poet ... stood almost single, uttering *odious* truth – William Wordsworth> <the most pernicious race of little *odious* vermin that nature ever suffered to crawl upon the surface of the earth – Jonathan Swift> **Abhorrent** can describe something that outrages one's sense of what is right, just, honorable, or decent <she [his wife] was his property.... To me it is a view that has always been *abhorrent* – John Galsworthy> **Detestable** implies not merely objectionableness but a capacity to arouse scorn and contempt <unpretending mediocrity is good, and genius is glorious; but a weak flavor of genius in an essentially common person is *detestable* – O. W. Holmes †1894> **Abominable** can effectively describe whatever is so abhorrent as to merit execration <all the living conditions were *abominable* – Willa Cather> ***ant*** lovable, sympathetic

haughty – see PROUD ***ant*** lowly

haul – see PULL

have, hold, own, possess, enjoy *shared meaning* : to keep, control, retain, or experience as one's own. **Have**, the most general term, carries no inherent implication of a cause or reason for regarding the thing had as one's own <he *had* considerable property> <they *have* too many children> <the monopoly which the big oil companies now *have* through their own pipelines and tanker transportation – J. J. Rooney> **Hold** suggests stronger control, grasp, or retention; thus, "to *have* friends" implies a mere amicable relationship but "to *hold* one's friends" implies the retention of their affection; "to *have* an opinion" implies merely existence of that opinion, but "to *hold* an opinion" implies firm grasp and usually assertion of the opinion. Often it additionally suggests continuity or actual occupation as well as ownership <*hold* a job for many years> <*hold* a degree in law> <he *held* considerable land in the western part of the county> **Own** implies a natural or legal right to regard as under one's full control <*own* a house> <when a child is old enough, he should ... be allowed to *own* books – Bertrand Russell> <as if it were in your blood and history not to possess, or if by some miracle to *own* something, to do so on the verge of loss – Bernard Malamud> **Possess** is widely interchangeable with *have;* it is similar to *own* but is applicable more readily to intangibles; thus, one *owns* a car, a book, a jewel, but one *possesses* patience, tolerance, beauty <that astonishingly retentive memory which we *possessed* as little boys – W. R.

Inge> **Enjoy** implies the having of something as one's own or for one's use <*enjoyed* a life estate in her uncle's property> <he *enjoyed* a distinguished reputation for the excellence of his sermons – T. S. Eliot>

havoc – see RUIN *n*

hazardous – see DANGEROUS

haze, mist, fog, smog *shared meaning* : an atmospheric condition that deprives the air of its transparency. **Haze** implies a diffusion of smoke or dust or light vapor sufficient to blur vision but not to obstruct it <the clouds shifted, spread against the sky in a translucent *haze* – William Styron> **Mist** implies a suspension of water droplets, floating and slowly falling through the air, that impairs but does not cut off vision. **Fog** implies a denser suspension than a mist, with power to enshroud and to cut off vision more or less completely <not the thin glassy *mist* of twenty minutes ago, but a thick, dense, blinding *fog* that hemmed in like walls of wadding on every side – Hugh Walpole> **Smog** applies to a fog made thicker and darker by the smoke and fumes of an industrial area <the principal source of toxicity in most pathological *smogs* appears to be sulfur dioxide from the smokestacks – J. N. Myers>

In extended use **haze** suggests vagueness or lack of clear definition <looking back through the *haze* of years – Allen Johnson> **Mist** applies to what can be only dimly apprehended because of its remoteness <times . . . half shrouded in the *mist* of legend – E. A. Freeman> **Fog** implies an obscuring of mental or spiritual vision or of what is perceived by this <you can only see him through a *fog* of ambition and jealousy – Herman Wouk> **Smog** may be chosen to heighten the implications of *fog* <the translators have been too faithful. The meaning is rarely distorted but a dense *smog* of gallicisms reduces visibility – Stanley Hoffmann> <a newspaper whose words would cut the *smog* of apathy, gluttony, dim hatred, glum joy, and the general victory of all that is smug – Norman Mailer>

headlong – see PRECIPITATE

headstrong – see UNRULY

heal – see CURE

healthy, sound, wholesome, robust, hale, well *shared meaning* : enjoying or indicative of good health. **Healthy** implies full strength and vigor as well as freedom from signs of disease or decay <a *healthy* body> <he had a *healthy* color in his cheeks – Charles Dickens> <during a *healthy* and active life – C. W. Eliot> **Sound** emphasizes the absence of disease, weakness, or malfunction <a *sound* mind in a *sound* body> **Wholesome** implies appearance and behavior that indicate soundness and balance <thankful . . . that he had his mother, so sane and *wholesome* – D. H. Lawrence> <the diffuse belief that our predecessors . . . were *wholesomer* and were generally better off – Joseph Bram> **Robust** implies the opposite of all that is delicate or sickly and usually connotes qualities (as muscularity, fresh color, a strong voice) typical of vigorous health <a man in *robust* health> <only the most *robust* people can safely undertake such a climb> **Hale,** a close synonym of *sound,* applies chiefly to older or elderly persons and implies not only soundness of health but unusual retention of youthful vigor <Pete Gurney was a lusty cock turned sixty-three, but bright and *hale* – John Masefield> <a *hale* and hearty old man> **Well,** a rather noncommittal term, implies freedom from actual disease or illness but does not in itself suggest soundness or robustness <father has been very ill but he is getting better and we think he will soon be *well*> <have you kept *well* this winter?> ***ant*** unhealthy

hearsay – see REPORT

heartfelt – see SINCERE

hearty — see SINCERE ***ant*** hollow
heave — see LIFT
heavy, weighty, ponderous, cumbrous, cumbersome *shared meaning* : having great weight. **Heavy** implies possession of greater weight or thickness or sometimes power than the average of a class or kind <a *heavy* stone> <a child *heavy* for his age> and in extended use implies a weighing down or oppressing (as of body, mind, or spirits) <a *heavy* odor of tuberoses lingered in the room> <his son's behavior was a *heavy* burden> **Weighty** implies actual as well as relative heaviness <as *weighty* bodies to the center tend — Alexander Pope> and in extended use implies a momentous or highly important character <a *weighty* decision> <the author was erecting a *weightier* theoretical and analytical edifice than the data warranted — F. J. Sorauf> **Ponderous** implies having great weight because of size and massiveness and in both literal and extended use stresses inertia and clumsiness <the sepulcher . . . hath oped his *ponderous* and marble jaws — Shak.> <his *ponderous* work on the fairy mythology of Europe — George Meredith> **Cumbrous** and **cumbersome** imply such weight and massiveness as makes a thing difficult to move or to deal with <great *cumbrous* oaken chests> <the *cumbersome* old table with twisted legs — Charles Dickens> In extended use both words are applicable to what is at once ponderous and unwieldy <his *cumbersome* archaic terminology confuses more than it enlightens> <take a needlessly *cumbrous* approach to a problem> ***ant*** light
heckle — see BAIT
hector — see BAIT
height, altitude, elevation *shared meaning* : vertical distance whether between the top and bottom of something or between a base and something above it. **Height** may be used of any vertical distance great or small and is interchangeable with, though less explicit than, the remaining words. **Altitude,** often interchangeable with *elevation,* is likely to be preferred in referring to vertical distance above the surface of the earth or above sea level or to the vertical distance above the horizon in angular measurement. **Elevation** is used especially in reference to vertical height above sea level on the surface of the earth. Thus, one would usually refer to the *altitude* of a plane flying above the earth and the *elevation* of a mountain village above sea level.
heighten — see INTENSIFY
heinous — see OUTRAGEOUS ***ant*** venial
help **1 help, aid, assist** *shared meaning* : to supply what is needed to accomplish an end. **Help** carries a strong implication of advance toward an objective <every little bit *helps*> <the danger of taking drugs to *help* one sleep> <how games can *help* children to learn — *Johns Hopkins Mag.*> **Aid** strongly suggests the need of help or relief and often imputes weakness to the one aided and strength to the one aiding <I sat by the side of Miss -- who greatly annoyed me for information during the examination — well I *aided* her — G. C. Catrow> <but this she knows . . . that saints will *aid* if men will call — S. T. Coleridge> **Assist** distinctively suggests a secondary role in the assistant or a subordinate character in the assistance; thus, a deputy *assists* rather than *aids* his superior; a good light *assists* (not *aids*) the eyes in reading <every additional proof that the world is a closely interwoven system . . . *assists* religious belief — W. R. Inge> ***ant*** hinder
2 see IMPROVE
hence — see THEREFORE
herald — see FORERUNNER
hereditary — see INNATE

heritage, inheritance, patrimony, birthright *shared meaning* : something received from a parent or predecessor. **Heritage** may apply to anything (as a right, a tradition, a trade, or the effect of a cause) that is passed on from one generation to another <[Livy] made the average Roman realize the grandeur of the past and the magnitude of his *heritage* – John Buchan> <the war had left its *heritage* of poverty . . . of disease, of misery, of discontent – Rose Macaulay> **Inheritance** applies primarily to what passes from parent to children whether it be money, property, or traits of character or feature <my father's blessing and this little coin is my *inheritance* – Francis Beaumont & John Fletcher> but it may replace *heritage* when the notion of descent is clearly felt <a good man leaveth an *inheritance* to his children's children – *Prov* 13:22 (AV)> <the random brutality that is the *inheritance* of centuries of blackness – Irving Howe> **Patrimony** applies basically to money or property inherited from one's father <to reave the orphan of his *patrimony* – Shak.> or, more broadly, to a material or immaterial inheritance from one's ancestral line or, sometimes, from times past. In the last use it may be indistinguishable from *heritage* <a most important part of the intellectual *patrimony* of Italy – R. A. Hall> **Birthright** can apply to property, rank, or privilege coming by right of birth and especially of primogeniture <Jacob said, Sell me this day thy *birthright*. And Esau said, Behold, I am at the point to die: and what profit shall this *birthright* do to me? . . . and he sold his *birthright* unto Jacob – *Gen* 25:31–33 (AV)>

heroism, valor, prowess, gallantry *shared meaning* : conspicuous courage. **Heroism** implies superlative courage especially in fulfilling a high purpose against odds <*heroism* in battle, bold action which scorned death with a manly calm that was beyond the superb – J. T. Farrell> <it [the desert] is more likely to provoke awe than to invite conquest. The *heroism* which it encourages is the *heroism* of endurance – J. W. Krutch> **Valor** implies illustrious bravery and audacity in fighting. In comparison with *heroism* it carries a weak impression of struggling against odds and a very strong one of mettlesome spirit and of vigor in action against a powerful enemy <the other divisions had had very limited battle experience and had nothing but the *valor* of ignorance – G. S. Patton Jr.> <the Israelis did not have to rely any longer on group *valor* alone – *Collier's Yr. Bk.*> **Prowess** implies combined skill and bravery in arms <warfare was a means of demonstrating tribal *prowess* and superiority to other tribes – G. H. Fathauer> or, more broadly, possession of skill in manly arts and pursuits <the male makes a play for the female . . . by strutting before her, displaying his accomplishments, his *prowess*, his charms – Edmund Wilson> **Gallantry** implies dash and spirit as well as courage and a gay indifference to danger or hardship <the desperate *gallantry* of our naval task forces – G. C. Marshall>

hesitant – see DISINCLINED

hesitate, waver, vacillate, falter *shared meaning* : to show irresolution or uncertainty. **Hesitate** implies pausing or indecision before deciding or acting or choosing <she summoned her voice; to *hesitate* would be fatal; she hoped she appeared calm – H. C. Hervey> <the young second officer *hesitated* to break the established rule of every ship's discipline – Joseph Conrad> **Waver** implies hesitation after seemingly reaching a decision and so connotes weakness or a retreat <let us hold fast . . . without *wavering* – *Heb* 10:23 (AV)> <he'd been *wavering* for years over marrying a girl – Herman Wouk> **Vacillate** implies prolonged hesitation from inability to form a fixed decision and suggests the play of opposing factors that results in indecision <I have *vacillated* when I should have insisted; temporized when I should have taken definite action – Ngaio Marsh> <the

revolt would have to be over – and achieved – within twenty-four hours and the new government firmly installed. Otherwise the *vacillating* generals might have second thoughts – W. L. Shirer> **Falter** implies a wavering or stumbling and often connotes nervousness or lack of courage or outright fear <neither to change, nor *falter,* nor repent – P. B. Shelley>

hide, conceal, screen, secrete, bury *shared meaning* : to withhold or withdraw from sight. *Hide,* the general term, and *conceal* are often interchangeable. But **hide** may or may not suggest intent <let me go, that I may *hide* myself in the field – *1 Sam* 20:5 (AV)> <the snow *hides* the rough ground> <*hid* her purse under the mattress> **Conceal,** on the other hand, ordinarily implies intention and often specifically a refusal to divulge <they will go to great lengths to *conceal* their handicap – William Attwood> <I am glad to be constrained to utter that which torments me to *conceal* – Shak.> <*conceal* a scar with makeup> **Screen** implies an interposing of something which shelters and hides or, sometimes, merely obscures <[he] *screened* himself under a bush and waited – Thomas Hardy> <her garbage cans were *screened* by tall glowing hollyhocks> **Secrete** implies a depositing, often by stealth, in a place screened from view or unknown to others <*secreted* the letter behind a picture> <a hollow tree where squirrels *secreted* their winter hoard of nuts> **Bury** implies a covering with or a submerging in someting that effectively hides or conceals <found the book *buried* under a heap of newspapers> <he *buried* his face in his hands>

hideous – see UGLY ***ant*** fair

high 1 high, tall, lofty *shared meaning* : above the average in height. **High** implies marked extension upward (as from a base) <a *high* hill> <buildings so *high* that they sway in the wind> or placement at a conspicuous height above a lower level <rooms with *high* ceilings> **Tall** applies to what rises or grows high as compared with others of its kind, and usually implies relative narrowness; thus, idiomatically one would refer to a *high* mountain but a *tall* man <that's where the *tall* corn grows – *Iowa Corn Song*> **Lofty** implies great or imposing altitude and is often felt as somewhat poetic <towering mountains . . . raising their superb crests toward the *lofty* skies – Mark Van Doren>

In extended use **high** connotes distinction, elevation, or sometimes arrogance and pride <his *high* attainments made his parents happy> <heaven's *high* king – John Milton> **Lofty** suggests moral grandeur and dignity <to Kennan, the *lofty* ideals of the Soviet revolution were as nothing compared with the baseness of its methods – Walter Mills> <exultation . . . solemn, serene, and *lofty* – P. B. Shelley> or sometimes superciliousness <looked down upon him with the *loftiest* contempt – Charles Dickens> **Tall,** commonly felt as colloquial in extended use, is likely to imply exaggeration or departure from literal truth <given to *tall* stories about his boyhood> <indulging in *tall* talk about the vast mysteries of life – W. A. White> ***ant*** low

2 see DRUNK

hilarity – see MIRTH

hinder, impede, obstruct, block *shared meaning* : to interfere with the action or progress of by or as if by putting obstacles in the way. **Hinder** implies a checking or holding back and usually stresses harmful or annoying interference or delaying <from your affairs I *hinder* you too long – Shak.> <the importance of his church's attitude in helping or *hindering* the solution to the world population explosion – *Current Biog.*> **Impede** implies making forward progress difficult by clogging, hampering, or fettering <the practitioner of the art of politics must learn to minimize the hurdles placed in his path to *impede* or prevent passage of favorable legislation – Jonas

Prager> <peoples were . . . so *impeded* by their different languages from arriving at an understanding – Edmund Wilson> **Obstruct** implies interfering with something in motion or in progress by the often intentional putting of obstacles in the way <the road was *obstructed* by fallen trees> <it may not be an evil conspiracy *obstructing* the University in these tasks so much as sheer ignorance – Rosemary Park> **Block** implies such effective obstructing as to close means of passage or of ingress or egress or as to halt all progress <roads *blocked* by a heavy fall of snow> <a polyglot of diagnostic labels and systems, effectively *blocking* communication and the collection of medical statistics – G. N. Raines> *ant* further

hint – see SUGGEST

hire *n* – see WAGE

hire *vb* **hire, let, lease, rent, charter** *shared meaning* : to engage or grant for use at a price. *Hire* and *let* are usually complementary terms, **hire** implying the act of engaging and **let** the act of granting, for use <we *hired* a house for the summer after having some difficulty in persuading the owner to *let* it> Sometimes, and especially with relation to persons or their services, *hire* may be used in either sense <*hire* a servant> <he *hired* himself out as a servant> **Lease** strictly implies a letting on a contract <the lands . . . are in general not tenanted nor *leased* out to farmers – Adam Smith> but it may also be employed in the sense of to hire on a lease <we found it cheaper to *lease* a car than to buy one> **Rent** stresses the payment of money or an equivalent for the full use of property and may imply either a hiring or a letting. **Charter** applies to the hiring of a ship or public conveyance for exclusive use <*charter* a bus for a school excursion>

history, chronicle, annals *shared meaning* : a written record of events. **History** implies more than a mere recital of occurrences; it regularly implies order and purpose in narration and usually a degree of interpretation of the events recorded <*history* is not a process of chronicling but a gaining of insight into the universal moral order – G. N. Shuster> **Chronicle** applies strictly to a recital of events in chronological order without interpretation <the Anglo-Saxon *Chronicle*> but in less precise usage it is applicable to any essentially chronological account of events <and almost every tale she had told him was a *chronicle* of sickness, death, and sorrow . . . . she had relived each incident in their lives with an air of croaking relish – Thomas Wolfe> **Annals**, otherwise very close to *chronicle*, tends to emphasize the progress or succession of events from year to year; it need not imply a discursive treatment or a continued narrative, for some ancient annals are no more than records of the important events of each year. In the selection of titles for modern historical works these distinctions are often ignored, for *chronicle* and *annals* are sometimes chosen as less pretentious than *history* or because *chronicle* stresses narrative quality and *annals*, the selection of noteworthy events.

histrionic – see DRAMATIC

hit – see STRIKE

hoax – see DUPE

hoist – see LIFT

hold *vb* – see HAVE

hold *n* **hold, grip, grasp, clutch** *shared meaning* : the power of getting or keeping in possession or control. **Hold** is widely applicable and may imply mere possession or control, or possession or control firmly maintained <afraid they may lose their *hold* on the domestic market – *Sydney* (*Australia*) *Bull.*> <lay *hold* on a weapon> <tried to keep a *hold* on his temper> **Grip** regularly suggests a firm or tenacious hold <his books . . . were written

in the *grip* of a terrible fever, a veritable trance – W. L. Shirer> <the *ancien régime* had never really fixed its *grip* on the area – *Times Lit. Supp.*> **Grasp** differs from *grip* chiefly in suggesting a power to reach out and get possession or control of something <success was almost within his *grasp*> **Clutch** implies a seizing and holding with or as if with the avidity or rapacity of a bird of prey <it was frightening to think that only half an inch of walrus hide lay between us and the *clutch* of that glacial water – Berton Roueché> <control of municipal government . . . had fallen into the *clutches* of corrupt political machines – Trevor Armbrister>

hollow – see VAIN

homage – see HONOR

homely – see PLAIN ***ant*** comely, bonny

homogeneous – see SIMILAR

honest – see UPRIGHT ***ant*** dishonest

honesty, honor, integrity, probity *shared meaning* : uprightness of character or action. **Honesty** implies refusal to lie, steal, defraud, or deceive <a man of scrupulous *honesty*> <had the *honesty* to sum up his opponents' arguments in detail, even if he could not successfully refute them – Lewis Mumford> **Honor** adds to *honesty* the notion of an active or anxious regard for the standards of one's profession, calling, or position <business *honor* is the foundation of trade> <a national administration of such integrity . . . that its *honor* at home will ensure respect abroad – D. D. Eisenhower> **Integrity** implies trustworthiness and incorruptibility of such a degree that one is incapable of being false to a trust, responsibility, or pledge <his unimpeachable *integrity* as treasurer of a widows' and orphans' fund – Nathaniel Hawthorne> <so long as the attorney stays within the limits of *integrity* and the facts, he must try to exploit the law to the fullest benefit of his client – *Current Biog.*> **Probity** implies tried and proven honesty or integrity <*probity* in domestic policy and wise judgment in foreign policy – A. E. Stevenson †1965> ***ant*** dishonesty

honor 1 honor, homage, deference, reverence *shared meaning* : respect and esteem shown to another. **Honor** implies justifying and proper but not necessarily exceptional merit on the part of the recipient and carries no implication about the relative rank of donor and recipient <they feel deeply the *honor* of belonging to the Senate, and the necessity of protecting the Senate against dishonorable men – *New Republic*> <old settlers . . . are suddenly superior to newer settlers and entitled to an annual barbecue as befits the *honor* – Mari Sandoz> <no nation is secure whose government does not command respect at home and *honor* abroad – D. D. Eisenhower> **Homage** is likely to apply to praise or tributes of esteem from those who owe allegiance or service and in itself conveys little or nothing about the merit of the recipient <the ostentatious *homage* paid by State officials to bishops – *Times Lit. Supp.*> <the public celebrations in which the Soviet people were to pay continuous *homage* to their absolute ruler – *Springfield (Mass.) Union*> Sometimes it implies no more than flattering attention <the *homage* people paid to money – Mary McCarthy> <turned to look at the young woman . . . and permitted himself the *homage* of a smile – Guy McCrone> **Deference** implies such respect and esteem as courtesy and one's position demand on behalf of a superior or elder <listened with *deference* to the old general's account of the battle> <the somewhat too-elaborate *deference* paid them by their neighbors embarrassed them and caused them to clothe their wealth in muted, simple gray – William Styron> **Reverence** implies a profound respect mingled with love and devotion <in general those parents have the most *reverence* who deserve

it – Samuel Johnson> <a seemly *reverence* may be paid to power – William Wordsworth>
2 see HONESTY

honorable 1 **honorable, honorary** *shared meaning* : attributing honor or serving to honor. **Honorable** in its more general use attributes honor because of merit (as in being noble, high-minded, or highly commendable) <an *honorable* peace> <his *honorable* service in behalf of the league> In its frequent use as a prefix of courtesy to the names of certain persons (as members of Congress or of Parliament) or as a courteous appellation in speaking of an opponent (as in a debate or controversy), it retains the same basic implication, albeit usually in a purely formal manner <I cannot agree with the conclusion of my *honorable* opponent> **Honorary** and less often *honorable* apply to something conferred, awarded, or given as an honor or in recognition of merit <the college conferred an *honorary* degree on its famous alumnus> <his painting received *honorable* mention at the exhibition> *Honorary,* but not *honorable,* when prefixed to the name of an office subordinates the notion of conferring honor and distinctively denotes that the office is held without emolument or without responsibility for service <they named the retiring president *honorary* chairman of the board of directors> <an *honorary* pallbearer>
2 see UPRIGHT ***ant*** dishonorable

honorary – see HONORABLE

hope – see EXPECT ***ant*** despair (*of*), despond

hopeless – see DESPONDENT ***ant*** hopeful

horde – see CROWD

horrendous – see HORRIBLE

horrible, horrid, horrific, horrendous *shared meaning* : inspiring horror or abhorrence. **Horrible** is the general term for what inspires horror <some . . . *horrible* form which might deprive your sovereignty of reason – Shak.> <the love of cruelty for its own *horrible* and fascinating sake – Aldous Huxley> **Horrid,** otherwise very close to *horrible,* can add a stronger implication of inherent or innate offensiveness or repulsiveness <some *horrid* beliefs from which . . . human nature revolts – Walter Bagehot> Both *horrible* and *horrid* are subject in less formal context to a much weakened use in which they become little more than general terms of aversion <the floor was *horrible* with broken dishes and glasses and broken boxes of food – Shirley Jackson> <what have those *horrid* children done now?> <the weather was *horrible*> **Horrific** stresses the power to horrify <television bombards us with communications about the world outside – often unpleasant, often . . . *horrific* – C. P. Snow> <an *horrific* and tragic account of the Quetta earthquake disaster – M. E. Yapp> **Horrendous** is sometimes interchangeable with *horrific* <the history of Asia, like the history of all mankind, is a *horrendous* account of human suffering – F. M. Esfandiary> but often it is used for purely literary effect (as an exaggerated suggestion of extreme frightfulness, an apt rhyme for *tremendous* or *stupendous,* or an onomatopoeic rhythm) <damnings most dreadful . . . execrations *horrendous,* blasphemies stupendous – Edward Hooker> <the Wildcat squad will be sturdier . . . but the schedule is so *horrendous* that a break-even season would be a minor miracle – Anson Mount> ***ant*** fascinating

horrid – see HORRIBLE ***ant*** delightful

horrific – see HORRIBLE

horrify – see DISMAY

hostility – see ENMITY

hound – see BAIT

hue — see COLOR
huff — see OFFENSE
huge, vast, immense, enormous, gigantic, colossal, mammoth *shared meaning* : exceedingly or excessively large. **Huge** indicates extreme largeness, usually in size, bulk, or capacity <*huge* cities grow steadily *huger* – Aldous Huxley> <a sense of community is impossible when the student feels lost in the *huge* complex of the "multiversity" – M. S. Eisenhower> **Vast** denotes extreme largeness or broadness, usually of extent or range <consider the *vast* varieties of religions ancient and modern – M. R. Cohen> <the region's oil reserves are still the *vastest* in the world – *Newsweek*> **Immense** implies an exceeding of usual standards or measurements or accustomed concepts <an *immense* quill, plucked from a distended albatross' wing – Herman Melville> <an *immense* tableland, . . . a tundra swept by a steady, cold, coursing wind – Nathaniel Nitkin> <he seemed to speak all his words with an *immense* wet-lipped relish, as though they tasted good on the tongue – Roald Dahl> **Enormous**, often interchangeable with *immense*, is likely to be preferred when an immensity that exceeds the reasonable, the normal, or the acceptable is to be implied <a straight, simple woman, . . . [who] has taken the *enormous* tragedy of her children with grace and courage – Lillian Hellman> <she absently untied and re-tied her apron strings, taking up what little slack her *enormous* waistline allowed – J. D. Salinger> The remaining terms graphically describe whatever is huge beyond accustomed concepts, **gigantic** calling up the image of the fabled giants of old, **colossal** that of the ancient Colossus, and **mammoth** that of the ponderous prehistoric elephantine mammoth <*gigantic* jewels that a hundred Negroes could not carry – G. K. Chesterton> <the *colossal* speed of 15,000 miles a second – James Jeans> <the *mammoth* hydrogen bomb explosion – *N. Y. Times*> ***ant*** tiny
humble *adj* **humble, meek, modest, lowly** *shared meaning* : lacking all signs of pride, aggressiveness, or self-assertiveness. **Humble** implies the absence of all vanity and arrogance and often an awareness of one's weakness and dependence (as on divine providence) <God resisteth the proud, but giveth grace unto the *humble* – *Jas* 4:6 (AV)> <Knowledge is proud that he has learned so much; Wisdom is *humble* that he knows no more – William Cowper> Sometimes *humble* implies such self-depreciation as verges on abjectness <she is *humble* to abjectness – Thomas DeQuincey> and when applied to a person's circumstances suggests low social rank, poverty, or insignificance <I come from the *humblest* of homes; I depended for my supper upon the catch of a few miserable herrings – Victoria Sackville-West> **Meek** implies the absence of wrath and vindictiveness and a consistent mildness of temper <a *meek* and quiet spirit, which is in the sight of God of great price – *1 Pet* 3:4 (AV)> but, in common and often derogatory use, it can suggest spiritlessness or undue submissiveness <responded [to domination] by submission, moaning, suffering, martyring herself by self-abasement, and by *meek* acceptance of any cruelty – J. T. Farrell> **Modest** stresses moderation and, without any suggestion of abjectness or spiritlessness, is likely to imply absence of conceit and boastfulness and demands for recognition <[he] stood at ease . . . with the *modest* air of a man who has given his all and is reasonably assured it is enough – Thomas Wolfe> As applied to such things as a home, a position, or a price it suggests a reasonable and often unobtrusive medium between extremes <with careful planning they lived very comfortably on a *modest* income> **Lowly** differs from *humble* chiefly in the absence of derogatory connotations; often it stresses lack of pretentiousness <thy heart the *lowliest* duties on herself did lay – William Wordsworth> <the reader never forgets that he is

lowlier-born himself than quite a lot of other people – Glenway Wescott>

humble *vb* – see ABASE

humbug – see IMPOSTURE

humid – see WET

humiliate – see ABASE

humor *n* – see MOOD, WIT

humor *vb* – see INDULGE

humorous – see WITTY

hunger – see LONG

hurl – see THROW

hurry – see HASTE

hurt – see INJURE

hypercritical – see CRITICAL

hypocritical, sanctimonious, pharisaical, canting *shared meaning* : affecting more virtue or religious devotion than one actually possesses. **Hypocritical,** the most inclusive term, implies an assumption of goodness, sincerity, or piety either by one who is deficient in these qualities or by one who is in fact corrupt, dishonest, or irreligious <be *hypocritical,* be cautious, be not what you seem but always what you see – Lord Byron> <the one who really spoiled him was that *hypocritical,* church-going mother of his, always looking sweet as sugar and underneath she was pure vinegar – J. T. Farrell> **Sanctimonious** implies an affectation or merely outward show of holiness or piety <a woman who was religious without being *sanctimonious* – G. S. Stokes> <he never spoke of . . . the Church except in tones of *sanctimonious* respect – H. C. Hervey> **Pharisaical** stresses close adherence to outward forms and a censorious attitude toward others' defects in these respects, coupled with little concern with or interest in spiritual and basic aspects (as of religion) <Northern churchmen were so intent on attacking the obvious sin of their Southern brethren that they did not see their own *pharisaical* sins of self-righteousness and vindictiveness – J. C. Brauer> <where the free man was always in danger from the community straitjackets and from the arrogance and ignorance of his more *pharisaical* neighbors – Stanley Walker> **Canting** implies the use of religious or pietistic language without evidence of underlying religious feeling; often the word suggests the state of mind of one so set in his hypocritical or pharisaical way as to be unaware that he lacks the spirit of true religion <a *canting* moralist> <whining, preposterous, *canting* villain, to murder your uncle . . . then fear to take what he no longer wanted; and bring to me your penury and guilt! – George Lillo> <it is not the dissenters or the papists that we should fear, but the set of *canting* lowbred hypocrites who are wriggling their way in among us – Anthony Trollope>

hypothesis, theory, law *shared meaning* : a formulation of a natural principle based on inference from observed data. **Hypothesis** implies insufficiency of presently available evidence and therefore a tentative formulation that can form a point of departure for further investigation <a scientist says in effect – "Observation shows that the following facts are true; I find that a certain *hypothesis* as to their origin is consistent with them all – James Jeans> **Theory** in general use may mean little more than *hypothesis* or *conjecture* <he had formulated several *theories* about the nature of disease> In precise technical use, however, it presupposes a wider range of evidence and greater probability of truth than does *hypothesis* <that exact verbal expression of as much as we know of the facts, and no more, which constitutes a perfect scientific *theory* – T. H. Huxley> **Law** emphasizes certainty and proof and applies to a statement of an order or relation in phenomena that has been found to be invariable under a particular set of conditions <Grimm's *law* is a statement of the regular changes which the mute consonants of the primitive Indo-European consonant system have undergone in the Germanic languages>

hysteria – see MANIA

idea, concept, conception, thought, notion, impression *shared meaning* : what exists in the mind as a representation (as of something comprehended) or as a formulation (as of a plan). **Idea** may apply to a mental image or formulation of something seen or known or imagined, or to a pure abstraction, or to something assumed or vaguely sensed <our *ideas* of a good time aren't the same, and never will be – Rose Macaulay> <it is doubtful if any of the leaders . . . would have been other than dismayed and frightened at the *idea* of coercion – Gerald Carson> <it is not easy to form an *idea* of a person from letters alone> **Concept** in precise use applies to a generic idea that the mind conceives after acquaintance with instances of a category <the way the child as he grows develops such *concepts* as "chair," "dog," and "house"> but in frequent, though sometimes criticized, use *concept* is applicable to any formulated and widely accepted idea of what a thing should be <we must expand the *concept* of conservation to meet the imperious problems of the new age – J. F. Kennedy> **Conception,** though often interchanged with *concept* in the latter's more general sense, can distinctively stress the process of imagining and formulating and apply to a peculiar or individual idea rather than to one that is purely generic <the *concept* God is the idea of a supreme ruler of the universe. All the religions propose different *conceptions* – Wilson Follett> <too often a writer's *conception* exceeds his powers of execution> **Thought** is likely to suggest the result of reflecting, reasoning, or meditating, rather than of imagining <a child's *thought* about God> <they had not a *thought* about the problem> **Notion** can apply to a vague, tentative, or chance idea <most of us retain the *notion* that all technical change is progress, is necessarily good – R. M. Hutchins> but it can also come close to *concept* in suggesting a general or universal concept <arriving at the *notion* of law – Irving Babbitt> or to *conception* in denoting the meaning content assigned by the mind to a term <have no adequate *notion* of what we mean by causation – Edward Sapir> **Impression** usually implies an idea arising as a result of external stimulation <I had an *impression* that the door opened softly> <his descendants, studying the picture . . . came away with an *impression* of harshness and dishonesty – John Cheever>

ideal – see MODEL

identical – see SAME *ant* diverse

identification – see RECOGNITION

idiom – see PHRASE

idiosyncrasy – see ECCENTRICITY

idiot – see FOOL

idle 1 see INACTIVE *ant* busy

2 see VAIN

ignite – see LIGHT *ant* stifle, extinguish

ignoble – see MEAN *adj* *ant* noble, magnanimous

ignominy – see DISGRACE

ignorant, illiterate, unlettered, untutored, unlearned *shared meaning* : not having knowledge. **Ignorant** may imply a general condition or it may apply to lack of knowledge or awareness of a particular thing <a very superficial

ignorant, unweighing fellow – Shak.> <you're pitifully *ignorant* of the first principles of taste – Herman Wouk> **Illiterate** applies to either an absolute or a relative inability to read and write <*illiterate* in the sense that they could not read or write, or . . . functionally *illiterate* in the sense that they were unable to understand what they read – I. L. Kandel> but is often used as a contemptuous description of one (as a person or an utterance) that shows little evidence of cultivation or education <the expanded school system, while teaching their children to read and write, is turning out political *illiterates* – Claire Sterling> **Unlettered** implies ignorance of the knowledge to be gained from books and may suggest lack of facility in reading and writing <*unlettered* peasants> or general ignorance <his addiction was to courses vain, his companies [companions] *unlettered,* rude and shallow – Shak.> **Untutored** may imply lack of schooling in the arts and ways of civilization <lo, the poor Indian! whose *untutored* mind sees God in clouds, or hears him in the wind – Alexander Pope> **Unlearned** suggests ignorance of advanced and scholarly subjects <the tiny school on the corner served well for its moment. But it was the mark of progress . . . to replace it, along with its *unlearned* ladies, at the earliest possible moment – J. K. Galbraith> ***ant*** cognizant (*of something*), conversant, informed

ignore – see NEGLECT ***ant*** heed (*a warning, a sign, a symptom*), acknowledge

ill – see BAD ***ant*** good

illegal – see UNLAWFUL ***ant*** legal

illegitimate – see UNLAWFUL ***ant*** legitimate

ill-favored – see UGLY ***ant*** well-favored, fair

illicit – see UNLAWFUL ***ant*** licit

illiterate – see IGNORANT ***ant*** literate

illusion – see DELUSION

illusionary – see APPARENT

illusory – see APPARENT ***ant*** factual, matter-of-fact

illustration – see INSTANCE

illustrious – see FAMOUS ***ant*** infamous

ill will – see MALICE ***ant*** goodwill, charity

imaginary, fanciful, visionary, fantastic, chimerical, quixotic *shared meaning* : unreal or unbelievable. **Imaginary** stresses lack of actuality and implies an existence, formation, or ascription by imagination, not fact <*imaginary* ills and fancied tortures – Joseph Addison> <mathematicians tell us we cannot take the square root of a negative number – such a number is purely *imaginary* – J. A. Coleman> **Fanciful** suggests giving free rein to the powers of the imagination <I . . . know how serious he really is, how *fanciful,* how elaborate, his imagination can be – Norman Mailer> <I am not a *fanciful* person, but . . . I seemed to hear Moriarity's voice screaming at me – A. Conan Doyle> **Visionary** applies to something that seems real and practical to its conceiver though in fact impossible of realization or to persons given to such vision <this was a *visionary* scheme . . . a project far above his skill – Jonathan Swift> <planning, as his *visionary* father might have done, to go to Brazil to pick up a fortune – Carl Van Doren> **Fantastic** describes what is or seems extravagantly fanciful or queer and therefore unacceptable to belief <a *fantastic* world inhabited by monsters of iron and steel – Louis Bromfield> <he had lately adopted the *fantastic* trappings of a clown of royalty – Thomas Wolfe> In a common but not universally accepted use *fantastic* loses much of its implication of unbelievableness and becomes little more than an intensive <the shanty town . . . is of *fantastic* squalor – Geoffrey Grigson & C. H. Gibbs-Smith> **Chimerical** applies to what is wildly or fantastically visionary or improbable

<an universal institutional church is as *chimerical* an idea as an universal empire – W. R. Inge> **Quixotic** describes a product of or a person devoted to extravagantly chivalrous and visionary ideals <to insist upon clemency in the circumstances would . . . have required *quixotic* courage – John Buchan> *ant* real, actual

imagination, fancy, fantasy *shared meaning* : the power to form mental images of things not present. **Imagination** is the most general term and the freest from derogatory connotation; it may apply to the representation of what is remembered, or of what has never been experienced in its entirety, or of what is actually nonexistent <her face haunted his *imagination*> <with an understanding of the basic principles, one need only use his *imagination* to discover how the techniques may be applied to the facts – W. K. Goettsche> <musicians who by transcendent powers of execution and *imagination* create an art of their own – Olin Downes> **Fancy** applies especially to the power of inventing the novel and unreal by altering and recombining the elements of reality <like all weak men of a vivid *fancy,* he was constantly framing dramas of which he was the towering lord – G. D. Brown> <Sam even wished himself a priest. For about ten minutes it seemed beautiful to him to surrender his life to God. Such *fancies* are common – Norman Mailer> **Fantasy** may take the place of *fancy* in naming the power of unrestrained and often extravagant or delusive fancy or its exhibition in art <this . . . robot idea has been decidedly overdone in the writings of *fantasy* – C. C. Furnas> <many possibilities beckon once one regards *fantasy* or daydreaming as a dimension of experience and frees it from . . . opprobrium – J. L. Singer>

imagine – see THINK

imbecile – see FOOL

imbibe – see ABSORB *ant* ooze, exude

imitate – see COPY

immediate – see DIRECT *ant* mediate (*knowledge, relation, operation*), distant (*relatives*)

immense – see HUGE

immigrant – see EMIGRANT

immoderate – see EXCESSIVE *ant* moderate

immoral, unmoral, nonmoral, amoral *shared meaning* : not moral. In spite of their common element of meaning these words are rarely interchangeable without serious loss of precision. **Immoral** implies a positive and active opposition to what is *moral* and may designate whatever is discordant with accepted ethical principles or the dictates of conscience or, in a weakened sense, whatever is discordant with accepted social custom or the general practice <for a government to take any part of it [private property], without their consent, for the benefit of other people, is only little less *immoral* than if a mob took it by violent plunder – J. A. Hobson> <a man that cursed and swore and went fishing on Sunday, and he was very *immoral* about other things too – Vance Randolph> *Unmoral, nonmoral,* and *amoral* all, in contrast to *immoral,* imply in one way or another a passive negation of what is moral. Typically, **unmoral** implies a lack of ethical perception and moral awareness <infants and idiots are *unmoral* and without moral responsibility> but sometimes it comes close to *conscienceless* in implying disregard of moral principles <the great *unmoral* power of the modern industrial revolution – F. L. Wright> Occasionally it, along with *nonmoral* and *amoral,* implies that what is so qualified is not a fit subject for ethical judgment. While *nonmoral* and *amoral* are frequently interchangeable <make religion *nonmoral,* a matter of inner experience and personal attitude – J. H. Randall> <science as such is completely *amoral* – W. S. Thomp-

son> **nonmoral** may be preferred when the thing described is patently outside the sphere where moral judgments are applicable, and **amoral** may be applied discriminatively to something not customarily or universally exempted from moral judgment; thus, life in the abstract is a *nonmoral* concept but a particular human life may well be *amoral;* perspective is a *nonmoral* aspect of painting but a painter's approach is likely to be *amoral,* even though some critics consider the result *immoral.* ***ant*** moral

impair – see INJURE ***ant*** improve, amend, repair

impart – see COMMUNICATE

impartial – see FAIR ***ant*** partial

impassioned, passionate, ardent, fervent, fervid, perfervid *shared meaning* : showing intense feeling. **Impassioned** implies warmth and intensity without violence and is especially applicable to utterance or to artistic expression <an *impassioned* plea> <as his *impassioned* language did its work the multitude rose into fury – J. A. Froude> **Passionate** implies vehemence and often violence of emotion sometimes to the point of wasteful diffusion of emotional power <a *passionate* and intemperate denunciation> <*passionate* feeling is desirable, provided it is not destructive – Bertrand Russell> **Ardent** lacks the derogatory connotations of *passionate* and is appropriately used to convey the idea of intense feeling expressing itself in eagerness, zeal, or acts of devotion <an *ardent* supporter of liberal ideas> <gave constant proofs of his *ardent* longing for an education – R. B. Merriman> **Fervent** implies sincerity and stresses steadiness of emotional warmth and zeal; it is especially applicable to prayers, wishes, or hopes that are heartfelt or to an emotion that is deep and constant <offered *fervent* prayers for her daughter's recovery> <*fervent* expressions of goodwill> <Jane's feelings, though *fervent,* were little displayed – Jane Austen> **Fervid,** similar in application to *impassioned,* is likely to suggest warm spontaneity or even febrile urgency of expression <her generous nature, her gift for appreciation, her wholehearted, *fervid* enthusiasm – L. P. Smith> <his *fervid* manner of lovemaking offended her – Arnold Bennett> **Perfervid** implies overwrought or excessive emotion and exaggerated, even insincere, vehemence of expression <some elements are driven primarily by race hatred and anti-Semitism, others by *perfervid* anticommunism – W. W. Turner> <in his *perfervid* flag-waving moments – S. H. Adams> ***ant*** unimpassioned

impassive, stoic, phlegmatic, apathetic, stolid *shared meaning* : unresponsive to something that might normally excite interest or emotion. **Impassive** stresses the absence of any external signs of emotion but implies nothing about the presence or absence of inner reaction <under their *impassive* exterior they preserve . . . emotions of burning intensity – G. P. Lathrop> **Stoic** implies an apparent indifference to pleasure or pain often as a matter of principle or self-discipline <worked on in *stoic* disregard of the cold rain> <a *stoic* atmosphere of fortitude in adversity – Orville Prescott> **Phlegmatic** implies a sluggishness of constitution or temperament that makes arousal difficult and reaction, if attained, modest <the religious mysticism that lurked in the heart of primitive Puritanism found no response in his *phlegmatic* soul – V. L. Parrington> **Apathetic** is likely to imply a puzzling or deplorable indifference or inertness or sometimes one based on preoccupation with another matter (as care, grief, or pain) <rare women who . . . become active instead of *apathetic* as they grow older – Ellen Glasgow> <after his mother's death he became *apathetic* and ceased to interest himself in public affairs> **Stolid** implies an habitual absence of interest, responsiveness, or curiosity about anything outside an accustomed routine and suggests heavy, dull, obtuse impassivity and plodding adherence to routine <*stolid* Saxon rustics in whom the temperature of religious zeal was little

. . . above absolute zero – Aldous Huxley> <no emotion whatsoever was displayed – nothing but *stolid* indifference – V. G. Heiser> ***ant*** responsive

impede – see HINDER ***ant*** assist, promote

impel – see MOVE ***ant*** restrain

imperative – see MASTERFUL

imperious – see MASTERFUL ***ant*** abject

impertinent, officious, meddlesome, intrusive, obtrusive *shared meaning* : inclined to thrust oneself into the affairs of another. **Impertinent** implies exceeding the bounds of propriety in showing interest or curiosity or in offering advice <we were secure from all *impertinent* interference in our concerns – Herman Melville> <approach complete strangers, ask them a battery of *impertinent* questions – S. L. Payne> **Officious** implies the often well-meant offering of services or attentions that are unwelcome or offensive <I cannot walk home from office, but some *officious* friend offers his unwelcome courtesies to accompany me – Charles Lamb> **Meddlesome** stresses an annoying and usually prying interference in the affairs of others <the Africans are learning that the Communist powers . . . are . . . *meddlesome* missionaries whose gospel is even more alien to them than Christianity – William Attwood> <user-oriented systems, in which the programmer provides a basic facility, but does not stand as a *meddlesome* intruder in the transactions of the user with that facility – H. A. Simon> **Intrusive** implies a disposition to thrust oneself into the affairs or company of others or to be unduly curious about what is not one's concern <made an inconspicuous fourth in their small world, always at hand yet never *intrusive* – B. A. Williams> <far too sensitive to be *intrusive* – Mollie Panter-Downes> **Obtrusive** stresses improper or offensive conspicuousness (as of interfering actions) or a thrusting of oneself forward where one has no right to be <why did the two men . . . leave so many *obtrusive* clues to their departure? – Gilbert Highet> <she knelt and watched, quietly, without expressing any *obtrusive* concern for his safety – Floyd Dell>

imperturbable – see COOL ***ant*** choleric, touchy

impetuous – see PRECIPITATE

implant, inculcate, instill *shared meaning* : to introduce into the mind. **Implant** implies teaching that makes for permanence of what is taught <any impulse to share was secondary and acquired, *implanted* only by his sense of justice – Pearl Buck> <the duty of Congress to see that educational institutions *implant* only sound ideas in the minds of students – Elmer Davis> **Inculcate** implies persistent or repeated efforts to impress upon the mind <it is no part of the duty of a university to *inculcate* any particular philosophy of life – Walter Moberly> <the seriousness *inculcated* in men by two cataclysmic world wars – S. P. Lamprecht> **Instill** stresses gradual, gentle imparting of knowledge, usually over a long period of time <those principles my parents *instilled* into my unwary understanding – Sir Thomas Browne> <parental example is the best means of *instilling* social responsibility in children>

implement, tool, instrument, appliance, utensil *shared meaning* : a relatively simple device for performing work. **Implement** may apply to anything necessary to effect an end <tubes, jars, brushes, and shaving *implements* that covered the shelf – Thomas Wolfe> <mathematics is still the necessary *implement* for the manipulation of nature – Bertrand Russell> **Tool** suggests an implement adapted to facilitate a definite kind or stage of work (as by an artisan or craftsman) <a box of carpenters' *tools*> <machine *tools*> <comparison and analysis . . . are the chief *tools* of the critic – T. S. Eliot> **Instrument** applies to a tool or device capable of performing delicate and precise work <surgical *instruments*> or to an implement precisely adapted to the end it serves <the telescope remains the primary astronomical *instrument*> <we must develop new *instruments* of foresight and protection and nurture in order to recover the relationship between man and nature – J. F. Kennedy> **Appliance** is used usually for a device which effects work but which is moved by some power other than or in addition to guidance and control by hand; often it suggests adaptation to a special purpose <the multitude of small electrical *appliances* that open cans, whip cream, dry hair, suck up dust – in fact do everything but put out the cat> **Utensil** chiefly applies to devices, tools, and vessels used in cookery and other household work or at the table, and in other than household applications is likely to mean a vessel with a particular function <the sacred *utensils* of a church>

implore – see BEG

imply **1** see INCLUDE

2 see SUGGEST *ant* express

import – see IMPORTANCE, MEANING

importance, consequence, moment, weight, significance, import *shared meaning* : a quality or aspect (as of a person or thing) that is felt to be of great worth, value, or influence. **Importance** implies a judgment of the mind by which superior value or influence is ascribed to a person or thing and may attribute this superiority either generally or in a particular relationship <an account of Cicero in which . . . some *importance* is given to the historical role of the provincial Italians – *Times Lit. Supp.*> <the *importance* of petroleum to our present way of life> **Consequence** may imply importance in social rank or because of personal distinction <men of *consequence* in the community> but more generally implies importance because of probable outcome, effects, or result <to marry one of the right people . . . is of the greatest *consequence* for a happy life – Rose Macaulay> **Moment** implies conspicuous or self-evident consequence <enterprises of great pith and *moment* – Shak.> <the material inequalities of our worldly life will be found to be of no *moment* in the hereafter – P. G. Waris> **Weight** implies a judgment of the immediately relevant importance and applies to something that must be taken into account or that may seriously affect an outcome <the court's finding that the verdict is against the manifest *weight* of the evidence – L. B. Howard> <the *weight* of a citizen's vote cannot be made to depend on where he lives – Earl Warren> **Significance** and **import,** though often used interchangeably with *importance* or *consequence,* can distinctively imply a quality or character which ought to mark its possessor as of importance or consequence but which may or may not be appreciated or recognized <statistical methods – mainly tests of *significance* and estimations of correlation coefficients – have become commonplace – Philip Burch> <Tom Paine is said not to have grasped the *significance* of industrial revolution – *Times Lit. Supp.*> <careless readers who miss the *import* of a writer's message> <the differences between one variety of man and another, points of negligible *import* in medicine – A. L. Kroeber> *ant* unimportance

importune – see BEG

imposing – see GRAND *ant* unimposing

imposture, fraud, sham, fake, humbug, counterfeit *shared meaning* : a thing imposed on one. **Imposture** applies to any situation in which a spurious object or action is passed off as genuine <its values . . . are an *imposture:* pretending to honor and distinction, it accepts all that is vulgar and base – Edmund Wilson> **Fraud** usually implies a deliberate perversion of the truth <believing that his supposed suicide was but another *fraud* – Justin M'Carthy> but applied to a person it may imply no more than pretense and hypocrisy <like many another literary *fraud*, the writer has been known on occasion to read the preface of a book instead of a book – Norman Mailer> **Sham** applies to a close copy, especially to one that is more or less obviously a fraudulent imitation <he smiled in his worldliest manner. But the smile was a *sham!* – Arnold Bennett> **Fake** applies to an imitation of or substitution for the genuine but in itself implies nothing about the motive <the "bull" catapulted snorting into the ring. It was a remarkably lifelike *fake* – Herman Wouk> <a "reproduction" becomes a *"fake"*... when it is sold as a genuine antique – Ruth W. Lee> <a politically fabricated *fake* – *New Republic*> **Humbug** implies pretense that may be deliberate or may arise in self-deceit <you're a *humbug*, sir ... I will speak plainer, if you wish it. An imposter, sir – Charles Dickens> <what *humbugs* we are, who pretend to live for beauty, and never see the dawn! – L. P. Smith> **Counterfeit** applies especially to the close imitation of something valuable (as a coin or a bond) <the city was flooded with *counterfeits* of five-dollar bills>

impotent 1 see POWERLESS ***ant*** potent
2 see STERILE ***ant*** virile

impoverish – see DEPLETE ***ant*** enrich

impregnate – see SOAK

impress – see AFFECT

impressive – see MOVING ***ant*** unimpressive

improper – see INDECOROUS ***ant*** proper

improve, better, help, ameliorate *shared meaning* : to make more acceptable or bring nearer some standard. **Improve** and **better** apply both to objects and to states or conditions that are not of necessity bad <the faculties of the mind are *improved* by exercise – John Locke> <striving to *better*, oft we mar what's well – Shak.> **Help** implies a bettering that leaves room for further improvement <a coat of paint would *help* that house> <only money could *help* her through the worst of her ordeal – Marcia Davenport> **Ameliorate** implies making more tolerable or acceptable conditions that are hard to endure <abolish feudalism or *ameliorate* its vices – W. O. Douglas> ***ant*** impair, worsen

impudent – see SHAMELESS ***ant*** respectful

impugn – see DENY ***ant*** authenticate, advocate

impulse – see MOTIVE

impulsive – see SPONTANEOUS ***ant*** deliberate

impute – see ASCRIBE

inability, disability *shared meaning* : lack of ability to perform or do something. In spite of their shared meaning element, these words are clearly distinguishable in use. **Inability** implies lack of power to perform usually because of some limiting factor (as mental weakness, lack of means, or lack of training) <deplored ... the *inability* of her undergraduate students to spell *seize* and *siege* – R. W. Chapman> <drift carelessly into a position and somewhat blindly discover their *inabilities* – J. M. Brewer & Edward Landy> <*inability* to beget or bear children is not in itself a bar to marriage – Edward Jenks> **Disability** implies the loss or deprivation of such power (as by accident, illness, or disqualification); the term is applicable both to the resulting inability and to its cause <he lost his right arm, but he overcame this *disability* – O. S. Nock> <a person with even the most tenuous Communist affiliation from years ago may suffer *disabilities* that could ruin his entire future career – A. H. Sulzberger> ***ant*** ability

inactive, idle, inert, passive, supine *shared meaning* : not engaged in work or activity. **Inactive** applies to anyone or anything that is not currently in action, in operation, in use, or at work <bees are *inactive* in cold weather> <an *inactive* charge account> <the chronically unemployed become the *inactive* – Robert Theobald> **Idle** applies to persons who are not busy or occupied or to their powers or their implements <the devil finds mischief for *idle* hands – *old proverb*> <every *idle* miner directly and individually is obstructing our war effort – F. D. Roosevelt> <though his pen was now *idle,* his tongue was active – T. B. Macaulay> **Inert** as applied to things implies inherent powerlessness to move or to affect other things <an *inert* drug> <aimless accumulation of precise knowledge, *inert* and unutilized – A. N. Whitehead> or, as applied to persons, a general indisposition to activity <the *inert* were roused, and lively natures rapt away! – William Wordsworth> <the greatest menace to freedom is an *inert* people – L. D. Brandeis> **Passive** implies an often purposeful immobility or a lack of a positive reaction when subjected to external driving or impelling forces or to provocation <Mao's Red Guards met resistance almost everywhere – *passive* in some areas, violent in others – A. S. Whiting> <whether we look toward future change with foreboding or anticipation depends, in considerable measure, on whether we think of ourselves as the *passive* objects, the victims on whom the change will be worked out, or, alternatively, as agents and shapers of change – H. A. Simon> **Supine** implies abject or cowardly inertia or passivity usually as a result of apathy or indolence <the political order was not merely the *supine* retainer of the economy. Neither the political order nor . . . the economic order was completely closed to the workers – Harvey Wheeler> <the clergy as a whole were . . . obedient and *supine* – G. M. Trevelyan> ***ant*** active, live

inane – see INSIPID

inaugurate – see BEGIN

inborn – see INNATE ***ant*** acquired

inbred – see INNATE

incense – see FRAGRANCE

incentive – see MOTIVE

inception – see ORIGIN ***ant*** termination

incessant – see CONTINUAL ***ant*** intermittent

incident – see OCCURRENCE

incidental – see ACCIDENTAL 2 ***ant*** essential

incisive, trenchant, clear-cut, cutting, biting, crisp *shared meaning* : having or manifesting or suggesting a keen alertness of mind. **Incisive** implies a power to impress the mind by directness and decisiveness <the clear, *incisive* genius which could state in a flash the exact point at issue – A. N. Whitehead> <the writing is *incisive* and the author's enthusiasm . . . is readily apparent – R. N. Sheridan> **Trenchant** implies an energetic cutting or probing that defines differences sharply and clearly or reveals what is hidden <when roused by indignation or moral enthusiasm, how *trenchant* are our reflections! – William James> <[his] high intelligence, *trenchant* powers of analysis, and dedication to the best aims of foreign policy – Walter Mills> **Clear-cut** suggests the absence of any blurring ambiguity or uncertainty of statement or analysis <established a *clear-cut* difference between what is truly important and valid in the youth protest and what is secondary and irrelevant – Tad Szulc> <said the Supreme Court had avoided a *clear-cut* decision on separation of state and church in education – Martin Gansberg> **Cutting** implies a ruthless accuracy or incisiveness without regard to the feelings of an auditor and may suggest sarcasm, harshness, or asperity in presentation <eloquence, smooth and *cutting,* is like a razor whetted with oil – Jonathan Swift> <he prefers the sharpness of the

single word, *cutting* directness, an unembellished door to hard truth – *Current Biog.*> **Biting** suggests a power to grip and deeply impress the mind or memory <the author then turns to a *biting* analysis of the Education Act, 1944, which he not surprisingly regards as humbug – *Times Lit. Supp.*> **Crisp** suggests both incisiveness and vigorous terseness <we are indebted again to Professor Morgenthau for a *crisp* and correct understanding of these relationships – Leo Cherne>

incite, instigate, abet, foment *shared meaning* : to spur to action or to excite into activity. **Incite** stresses stirring up and urging on; often it implies active prompting <the riot was *incited* by subversive agitators> <one of the impressive functions of the cosmic idea is to preside over the birth of possible, new, and good worlds, and to *incite* new wills to make them actual – Scott Buchanan> **Instigate** definitely implies responsibility for initiating another's action and often connotes underhandedness or evil intent <the early persecutions were . . . *instigated* . . . by the government as a safety valve for popular discontent – W. R. Inge> **Abet** implies seconding, and encouraging, and pressing on some action already begun <for the managements . . . more was to be gained by scuttling the merger movement than by *abetting* it – *Forbes*> <talks of cajoling the new Filipino business class into aiding and *abetting* reform – Alex Campbell> **Foment** implies persistent goading, especially of something thought of as already in seething activity <a strategy that seemed bent more on embarrassing the Government and *fomenting* agitation than on seeking a resolution to student grievances – S. T. Wise> *ant* restrain

incline **1** see SLANT

2 incline, bias, dispose, predispose *shared meaning* : to influence one to have or take an attitude toward something. **Incline** suggests the tipping of a balance by which one's interest or liking or favor is directed in one of two or more possible directions <my intellect and my heart and my patriotism and my sense of history *inclined* me toward the Democratic view – J. A. Michener> **Bias** suggests a settled and predictable leaning in one direction <how un*biased* or how precise an estimate need be depends upon the broader purposes of the experiment – E. F. Lindquist> and is likely to connote unfair prejudice <a framework of coherent ideas is a necessary basis for field work; but this should not *bias* the observation or the record of facts – *Notes & Queries on Anthropology*> **Dispose** suggests an affecting of one's mood or temper so as to incline one toward someone or something <I was then sentimentally *disposed* toward the belief that true love knocks but once – Lois B. Wills> <his gentleness with the child *disposed* us to like him> **Predispose** implies the action of a disposing influence well in advance of the opportunity to reveal itself <in the case of a major news story, people have been reading or hearing about it . . . . Then you get a chance to give them information about something when they are *predisposed* to absorb it – Frank McGee> *ant* disincline, indispose

include, comprehend, embrace, involve, imply *shared meaning* : to contain within as part of the whole. **Include** implies that the thing contained forms a constituent, component, or subordinate part <a new study of world fuel reserves, *including* petroleum – M. J. Rathbone> <it would not be argued today that the power to regulate does not *include* the power to prohibit – O. W. Holmes †1935> **Comprehend** implies that the thing in question falls within the scope or range of a whole (as a concept, conception, or view) so that it is held or enclosed therein whether specifically and clearly distinguishable or not <the simple subtends the complex in such a way that the complex may never *comprehend* the simple – Norman Mailer> <philosophy's scope *comprehends* the truth of everything which man may

understand – H. O. Taylor> **Embrace** implies a reaching out and gathering of separate items into a whole <while the zone *embraces* much poor housing, there are also middle-income integrated apartment developments – Bernard Bard> <freedom of speech . . . *embraces* all discussion which enriches human life and helps it to be more wisely led – Zechariah Chafee> **Involve** suggests an intimate entangling of a thing with a whole, often as an essential consequence or antecedent <she knew that when love is not *involved* in a union, any differences are likely to settle into . . . enmity – H. C. Hervey> <a degree in mathematics *involves* much hard study> **Imply,** otherwise close to *involve,* suggests that something's presence can be inferred from a hint, or as a necessary cause or effect, or as a regularly experienced event. The word ordinarily imputes less certainty to a relationship than *involve;* thus, silence is often said to *imply* consent, but it would be rash to say that it *involves* consent <a positive attitude on the part of either parent or teacher does not *imply* an entirely uncritical one – R. K. Corbin> <emergency and crisis *imply* conflict – H. S. Langfeld> ***ant*** exclude

inconstant, fickle, capricious, mercurial, unstable *shared meaning* : lacking firmness or steadiness (as in purpose or devotion) or indicative of such lack. **Inconstant** implies an incapacity for steadiness and an inherent tendency to change <swear not by the moon, the *inconstant* moon, that monthly changes in her circled orb – Shak.> <the children, surging to and fro in their light *inconstant* play – Walker Percy> **Fickle** suggests unreliability because of perverse changeability and incapacity for steadfastness <bitter experience soon taught him that lordly patrons are *fickle* and their favor not to be relied on – Aldous Huxley> **Capricious** suggests motivation by sudden whim or fancy and stresses unpredictability <the *capricious* fluttering of . . . butterflies – Ludwig Bemelmans> <he judged her to be *capricious,* and easily wearied of the pleasure of the moment – Edith Wharton> **Mercurial** implies a rapid changeability of mood, especially between depression and elation and suggests the mobility of spilled quicksilver <I was ardent in my temperament; quick, *mercurial,* impetuous – Washington Irving> <a man of *mercurial* enthusiasms> **Unstable** implies an incapacity for remaining in a fixed position or relationship and when applied to persons suggests a lack of emotional balance <*unstable* as water, thou shalt not excel – *Gen* 49:4 (AV)> <an *unstable* world economy . . . subjected to periods of wars, inflation, and depression – *Farmer's Weekly* (*So. Africa*)> ***ant*** constant

increase, enlarge, augment, multiply *shared meaning* : to become or to make greater or more numerous. **Increase** in the intransitive use implies progressive growth (as in size, amount, numbers, or intensity) <Jesus *increased* in wisdom and stature, and in favor with God and man – *Lk* 2:52 (AV> <Abou Ben Adhem (may his tribe *increase!*) – Leigh Hunt> In transitive use it may imply simple addition and stress the operation of some cause <inflation *increases* the cost of living> <studying new methods to *increase* the participation of minority groups in community life> **Enlarge** implies expansion or extension that makes greater in size or capacity <his own capabilities have been *enlarged* through rigorous exercise of his reasoning power – M. S. Eisenhower> <the house had been *enlarged* several times as his family grew> **Augment** implies a growing greater, more numerous, larger, or more intense of what is already well-developed or well-grown <economists could . . . tell a country . . . what monetary mechanisms it might employ to *augment* purchasing power – Denis Goulet> **Multiply** implies increase in numbers (as by natural generation, by splitting, or by repetition of a process) <commerce *multiplied* wealth and comfort – Stringfellow Barr> ***ant*** decrease

incredulity – see UNBELIEF ***ant*** credulity
inculcate – see IMPLANT
incur, contract, catch *shared meaning* : to bring (as something unwanted) upon oneself. **Incur** is applicable in the presence or absence of foreknowledge of what is to happen <*incur* a debt> <*incur* criticism> but it usually implies responsibility for the acts that bring about what is incurred <an environment containing all the classic elements for *incurring* mental fatigue – H. G. Armstrong> <a couple who adopts a child *incurs* a great responsibility> **Contract** implies more strongly effective acquirement but less often implies definite responsibility for the act of acquiring <each from each *contract* new strength and light – Alexander Pope> <*contract* a disease> **Catch** is the popular term for acquiring infection and in its broader use implies an acquiring through personal contact or association <*catch* a heavy cold> <religion, in point of fact, is seldom taught at all; it is *caught,* by contact with someone who has it – W. R. Inge> <discovered in herself . . . real ability to work and to learn, once her interest was *caught* – Herman Wouk>
incurious – see INDIFFERENT ***ant*** curious, inquisitive
indecent – see INDECOROUS ***ant*** decent
indecorous, improper, unseemly, indecent, unbecoming, indelicate *shared meaning* : not conforming to what is accepted as right, fitting, or in good taste. **Indecorous** suggests a violation of accepted standards of good manners <declared her behaviour was monstrously *indecorous,* reprobated in strong terms the habit of play-acting and fancy dressing, as highly unbecoming a British female – W. M. Thackeray> **Improper** applies to transgressions of rules not only of social behavior but of ethical practice or logical procedure or prescribed method <he was telling her a funny story, probably an *improper* one, for it brought out her naughtiest laugh – Willa Cather> <the problem is to . . . chart the shadowlands of conduct where men of goodwill may have difficulty in deciding whether a course is proper or *improper* – T. E. Dewey> **Unseemly** applies to an indecorum or impropriety that is distinctly offensive to persons of good taste or high principles <Maurice disgraced Amy and himself by joining in an *unseemly* fracas with the police – Rose Macaulay> <an *unseemly* outbreak of temper – Nathaniel Hawthorne> **Indecent** implies great unseemliness or gross offensiveness, especially when referring to sexual matters <buried him with *indecent* haste and without the proper rites – A. M. Young> <guilty of *indecent* exposure> **Unbecoming** applies to behavior or language that is felt to be beneath and unfitting to one's character or status <questioning whether a summer school for the gifted might result in its pupils acquiring an *unbecoming* smugness and conceit – Eleanor McGrath> **Indelicate** implies a lack of modesty or of tact or of refined perception and feeling <an *indelicate* question> <but dying is nearly always *indelicate* and undignified. Its ugliness mocks every beauty – M. S. Mayer> ***ant*** decorous
indelicate – see INDECOROUS ***ant*** delicate, refined
indemnify – see PAY
independent – see FREE *adj* ***ant*** dependent
indifferent 1 indifferent, unconcerned, incurious, aloof, detached, disinterested *shared meaning* : not showing or feeling interest. **Indifferent** implies neutrality of attitude from lack of inclination, preference, or prejudice <*indifferent* to her mother's advice> <the most terrifying fact about the universe is not that it is hostile but that it is *indifferent* – Stanley Kubrick> **Unconcerned** implies such indifference as arises from unconsciousness, insensitiveness, or a selfishness which cuts one off from his fellows <a world completely *unconcerned* with the universe beyond . . . a total absorption

in the lush present – Lester Markel> <the city is teeming with people who go about their business *unconcerned* while the bullets fly – P. T. Chew> **Incurious** implies an inability to take a normal interest due to dullness of mind or to self-centeredness <looked over the square with a blank *incurious* stare> <why . . . are we, as a race, so *incurious,* irresponsive and insensitive – Virginia Woolf> **Aloof** suggests a cool reserve often arising from a sense of superiority or disdain for others or from shyness or suspicion <her manner was correct but icily *aloof*> <each agency at the Washington level is too *aloof* to fully understand and comprehend their individual and common needs – A. H. Quie> **Detached** implies objectivity and a usually commendable aloofness achieved through absence of prejudice or selfishness <he had been *detached* and impersonal about the great facts of life – Mary Webb> <this detailed, scholarly, affectionate yet *detached* biography – John D. Scott> **Disinterested** can imply a circumstantial freedom from concern for personal and especially financial advantage that enables one to judge or advise without bias <no *disinterested* student of our constitutional system . . . could view with complacency the impasse created by a blind and stubborn majority of the Court – Felix Frankfurter> <[St. Francis'] practice of the classical virtues of love, faith, *disinterested* activity and detachment, which he acquired through long periods of disciplined austerity – Francis Hoyland> ***ant*** avid

2 see NEUTRAL

indigence – see POVERTY ***ant*** affluence, opulence

indigenous – see NATIVE ***ant*** naturalized, exotic

indignation – see ANGER

indiscriminate, wholesale, sweeping *shared meaning* : including all or nearly all within the range of choice, operation, or effectiveness. **Indiscriminate** implies lack of consideration of individual merit or worth or deserts (as in giving, treating, selecting, or including) <the risk of a reaction to minority violence in which a community may respond with excessive and *indiscriminate* use of force> <*indiscriminate* praise> **Wholesale** may, but need not, imply indiscriminateness but it regularly stresses extensiveness and action upon all within range of choice, operation, or effectiveness <*wholesale* vaccination of a population> <the continuous battle of this generation against *wholesale* character assassination through the application of indiscriminate labels – R. L. Roy> **Sweeping** suggests a reaching out to draw everyone or everything into one mass and usually carries a strong implication of indiscriminateness <*sweeping* generalizations> <arriving at *sweeping* conclusions based upon false premises, the authors did make their mark . . . spreading concern and confusion – D. J. Murphy Jr.> <an investigation later backed up his findings and led to *sweeping* reforms in the school system – *Current Biog.*> ***ant*** discriminate, selective

individual **1** see CHARACTERISTIC ***ant*** common

2 see SPECIAL ***ant*** general

indolent – see LAZY ***ant*** industrious

induce, persuade, prevail, get *shared meaning* : to move one to act or decide in a certain way. **Induce** implies influencing the reason or judgment often by pointing out the advantages or gains that depend upon the desired decision <conditions which had *induced* many persons to emigrate from the old country – John Dewey> <[he] *induced* Congress to aid his state in building such a canal – C. W. Mitman> **Persuade** implies appealing as much to the emotions as to reason (as by pleas, entreaty, or expostulation) in attempting to win over <deputed . . . to *persuade* her to resume her married life – Anthony Powell> <*persuaded* by his psychiatrist to stop taking the drug – *Trans-action*> **Prevail,** usually with *on* or *upon,* carries a strong implication of overcoming opposition or reluctance with sustained argument or pressure or cogent appeals <I will go now and try to *prevail* on my mother to let me stay with you – G. B. Shaw> <the machinery of positive law . . . is the only means by which newly worked out moral truths can *prevail* against habit and prejudice – R. M. Hutchins> **Get** is the most neutral of these terms and can replace any of them when the method by which a favorable decision is brought about is irrelevant or is deliberately not stressed <finally *got* the boy to do his homework> <succeeded in *getting* the Russians to relinquish certain claims for war damages – *Americana Annual*>

inducement – see MOTIVE

indulge, pamper, humor, spoil, baby, mollycoddle *shared meaning* : to show undue favor to a person or his wishes. **Indulge** implies excessive compliance and weakness in gratifying the wishes of another or of oneself <I would *indulge* her every whim – Thomas Hardy> <punishment temporarily puts a stop to undesirable behavior, but does not permanently reduce the victim's tendency to *indulge* in it – Aldous Huxley> <forgot her diet and *indulged* herself with a rich dessert> **Pamper** implies inordinate gratification of an appetite or taste especially for luxuries or for what is softening in its physical or moral effects <felt wickedly *pampered* and slothful not to have to leave the house for her lessons – H. C. Hervey> <no country can afford to *pamper* snobbery – G. B. Shaw> **Humor** suggests a yielding to a person's moods or whims but need not imply disinterested attention <one must discover and *humor* his weaknesses – H. M. Parshley> <listlessly *humoring* a queasy stomach – William Styron> **Spoil** stresses the injurious effects of persistent indulging and pampering <a *spoiled* ill-mannered child> <the members of the house party, . . . *spoilt* by the surfeits of entertainment that life had always offered them – Victoria Sackville-West> **Baby** suggests excessive and often inappropriate care, attention, and solicitude <if he thinks I'm going to spend my days catering to his whims, *babying* him and watching over him like a child, he's mistaken – Helen S. Rush & Mary Sherkanowski> <the road is steep; *baby* your brakes – Russ Leadabrand> **Mollycoddle** suggests an absurd degree of care and attention to another's health, physical comfort, and security from danger and is likely to attribute effeminacy or infantilism to the willing recipient of such attention <believes we have *mollycoddled* women too much – *N.Y. Times*> <look here, mother dear: I'm as well as ever I was, and I'm not going to be *mollycoddled* any more – Mary E. Braddon> ***ant*** discipline

industrious – see BUSY ***ant*** slothful, indolent

industry – see BUSINESS

inebriated – see DRUNK

inept – see AWKWARD ***ant*** apt, adept, able (*as a result of nature, training*)

inert – see INACTIVE ***ant*** dynamic, animated

inexorable – see INFLEXIBLE ***ant*** exorable

infamous – see VICIOUS ***ant*** illustrious

infamy – see DISGRACE

infer, deduce, conclude, judge, gather *shared meaning* : to arrive at a mental conclusion. **Infer** implies formulation (as of an opinion, a principle, or a decision) from evidence presented or premises accepted <not only must [the teacher] . . . become fully aware of what they want to talk and write about, but he must go . . . further and *infer* what they can think and write about – R. K. Corbin> <reason can note facts and *infer* relations, but it cannot find values – Joseph Fletcher> **Deduce** in general usage adds to *infer* the implication of strong and definite grounds for the inference formed; in more precise use it implies the derivation of an inference from a general principle <as you've probably *deduced* [from his prior statements], I'm really fascinated by UFOs – Stanley Kubrick> <the apprehension of new elements requires a sensitive perception and familiarity with new details and cannot be *deduced* from established principles – M. R. Cohen> **Conclude,** sometimes interchangeable with the more general use of *deduce,* can distinctively imply arriving at a logically necessary inference at the end of a chain of reasoning <do not *conclude* that all State activities will be State monopolies – G. B. Shaw> <he investigated American school texts and teaching on Communism . . . and *concluded* that they were inadequate – *Current Biog.*> **Judge** is close to *conclude* in stressing careful examination of evidence and critical testing of premises <groups of students have organized to protest faults they have *judged* to exist – M. S. Eisenhower> <employees at all levels and in all functional groups *judge* the company in relation to their own aspirations for growth and advancement – Frank Sanfilippo *et al*> **Gather** suggests a direct or intuitive forming of a conclusion from hints or inferences <thereby he may *gather* the ground of your ill will – Shak.> <he lay still, marvelling at the carrying power of the widow's snores. He knew little of the late Mr. Benedetto, but he *gathered* now that he had been either a man of saintly patience, a masochist or a deaf-mute – Theodore Sturgeon>

infertile – see STERILE ***ant*** fertile

infidel – see ATHEIST

inflate – see EXPAND ***ant*** deflate

inflated, flatulent, tumescent, tumid, turgid *shared meaning* : distended by or as if by fluid beyond normal size. **Inflated** implies expansion by or as if by introduction of gas under pressure into an expansive shell <an *inflated* balloon> <caricaturing the *inflated* elegance of Eastern culture as represented in its refined fiction – J. D. Hart> <a very unimportant young man with a very *inflated* opinion of himself> **Flatulent** applies basically to distension of the belly by internally generated gases and in extended use suggests something seemingly full but actually without substance <a score or two of poems, each more feeble and more *flatulent* than the last – A. C. Swinburne> <he was an overornate speaker; at his worst he was a purveyor of *flatulent* claptrap – S. H. Adams> **Tumescent** and **tumid** imply swelling or bloating usually beyond what is normal or wholesome or desirable <they maintained a *tumescent* flow of thought that was mostly feeling and feeling that was mostly imitation – H. G. Wells> <there . . . were the omnipresent reporters, with their *tumescent* microphones – W. F. Buckley> <the genuine scientist would never employ *tumid* phrases or half-baked simplifications – J. E. Gloag> <his face looked damp . . . and slightly *tumid* – J. G. Cozzens> **Turgid** in literal applications is likely to be preferred when normal distension rather than morbid bloating is to be described; thus, one refers to a healthily erect and unwilted plant stem as *turgid* (better than *tumescent* or *tumid*). In extended use *turgid* is likely to suggest vigor manifested in an unrestrained, undisciplined manner and may connote such faults as overemotionalism, bombast, and slovenly thought <the *turgid* intricacies the modern foundation gets itself into in its efforts to spend its millions – Dwight Macdonald> <excursions into *turgid* metaphysical speculations – *Times Lit. Supp.*> <the book is so *turgid,* so repetitive, so full of nearly meaningless tables – Geoffrey Gorer> ***ant*** pithy

inflexible 1 see STIFF ***ant*** flexible

2 inflexible, inexorable, obdurate, adamant *shared meaning* : unwilling to alter a predetermined course or purpose. **Inflexible** implies rigid adherence or even slavish conformance to primly established principles <society's attitude toward drink and dishonesty was still *inflexible* – Edith Wharton>

<more damage to the child's ultimate desire to express his ideas in writing results from the formal, *inflexible* demands of an insensitive teacher . . . to write "correctly" . . . than from any other single cause – R. K. Corbin> **Inexorable** implies relentlessness of purpose and deafness to all entreaty <more fierce and more *inexorable* far than empty tigers or the roaring sea – Shak.> or, as applied to things, inevitability <you and I must see the cold *inexorable* necessity of saying to these inhuman, unrestrained seekers of world conquest . . . "You shall go no further" – F. D. Roosevelt> <the *inexorable* course of human destiny> **Obdurate** stresses hardness of heart and insensitivity to external influences <if when you make your prayers, God should be so *obdurate* as yourselves, how would it fare with your departed souls? – Shak.> <the *obdurate* philistine materialism of bourgeois society – Cyril Connolly> **Adamant** suggests extraordinary strength of will and implies utter immovability in the face of all temptation or entreaty <it seemed to be the face of a man making a last plea to some *adamant,* inquisitional power, and it seemed . . . the face of someone on the verge of apoplexy – William Styron> <the Soviet Union was increasingly *adamant* in its position – Walter Millis> *ant* flexible

influence *n* **influence, authority, prestige, weight, credit** *shared meaning* : power exerted over the minds or behavior of another. **Influence** can imply the effect that one thing or person insensibly has on another <too weak to resist the *influence* of bad companions> or it can imply a conscious use of personal power or, sometimes, of underhanded means to guide or determine a course of action or an effect <perfect competition is defined . . . as . . . the case where no farmer, businessman, or laborer has any personal *influence* on market price – P. A. Samuelson> <those who have survived personal eclipse have been virtually shorn of political power and *influence.* Gone are the . . . organs through which party officials implemented policy – A. S. Whiting> **Authority** implies power (as from personal merit or learning) to compel or to win belief or acceptance <scholars who held that Cicero was an unchallengeable *"authority"* – Gilbert Highet> <his parents . . . were both getting childish and needed care and yet they resented any loss of *authority* – Pearl Buck> <realized that a fantasist's pose of *authority* on such matters is bound to sit ill with a serious and progressive physician – Theodore Sturgeon> **Prestige** implies the ascendancy given by conspicuous excellence or recognized superiority <the almost magical *prestige* that had belonged to the original humanists – Aldous Huxley> <there is usually one form of the language which has higher *prestige* than the others, and which acts as a brake on the divergent tendencies in the language – Charles Barber> **Weight** implies measurable influence, especially in determining the acts of others <your advice carries great *weight* with me> <General de Gaulle put his decisive *weight* on the balance against his restive conservative deputies – J. L. Hess> **Credit** applies to influence arising from one's reputation for inspiring confidence and admiration <Buckingham . . . resolved to employ all his *credit* in order to prevent the marriage – David Hume †1776> <[he] was not slow to perceive his loss of *credit* with the regent – W. H. Prescott>

influence *vb* – see AFFECT

inform, acquaint, apprise, notify *shared meaning* : to make one aware of something. **Inform** implies the imparting of knowledge, especially of facts and occurrences necessary for an understanding of a pertinent matter or as a basis for action <I think that we can *inform* ourselves better than we have about what conditions actually are in South Africa – C. E. Crowther> <*inform* a parent of a boy's truancy> **Acquaint** lays stress on introducing to or familiarizing with <[he] *acquainted* himself with the services and doctrines of many religious denominations – *Current Biog.*> <a man of sorrows, and *acquainted* with grief – *Isa* 53:3 (AV)> **Apprise** implies communication of something of special interest or importance to the recipient <a frantic radio message was sent from the legation to Berlin *apprising* it of the unexpected and unhappy situation – W. L. Shirer> **Notify** implies formal communication (as by a written notice) of something requiring attention or demanding action <the stationmaster *notified* him of the arrival of the package> <*notify* your insurance company at once if you are involved in an accident>

infrequent, uncommon, scarce, rare, sporadic *shared meaning* : not common or abundant. **Infrequent** implies occurrence at wide intervals in space or time <*infrequent* pines dot the hills> <tornadoes are *infrequent* in New England> <his *infrequent* use of the rod may explain unusual tenure [for a schoolmaster] for those times – George Crout> **Uncommon** describes something that occurs or is found so infrequently as to be felt as singular, exceptional, or extraordinary <smallpox has become *uncommon* in the United States> <in certain country districts . . . families of fifteen are not *uncommon* enough to be regarded as extraordinary – G. B. Shaw> <a writer possessing *uncommon* inventive ability – A. C. Ward> **Scarce** implies a falling short of a usual, required, or acceptable abundance <strawberries are *scarce* and very expensive this year> <if skilled labor is *scarce,* American industry can generate a new supply by training – R. M. Solow> **Rare** suggests extreme scarcity or infrequency and often implies a resulting exceptional quality or high value in the thing so qualified <*rare* books and first editions> <on the *rare* occasions that something happens in the world to which I must respond – H. A. Simon> <have you ever realized that things that are remarkable are by definition, *rare?* – Theodore Sturgeon> **Sporadic** implies occurrence in scattered instances or isolated outbursts <*sporadic* outbreaks of malaria still occur> <the lumber industry . . . has dwindled to *sporadic* bursts of activity and lumber mills along the river are idle most of the year – *Amer. Guide Series: Maine*> ***ant*** frequent

infringe – see TRESPASS

infuse, suffuse, imbue, ingrain, inoculate, leaven *shared meaning* : to introduce one thing into another so as to affect it throughout. **Infuse** implies a permeating like that of infiltering fluid, usually of something which imbues the recipient with new spirit, life, or vigor or gives it or him a new cast or a new significance <thou didst smile, *infused* with a fortitude from heaven, when I . . . under my burden groaned – Shak.> <whose work is for the most part *infused* with the spirit of scientific materialism – L. A. White> **Suffuse** implies a spreading through or over of something that imparts a distinctive color, appearance, or quality <when purple light shall next *suffuse* the skies – Alexander Pope> <talking about how one can *suffuse* a feeling of gentleness toward nature and toward the others one meets and make it the permanent context of one's life – J. R. Seeley> **Imbue** implies a permeating like that of a dye so deep and so complete that the very substance and nature of the one affected is altered <thy words, with grace divine *imbued,* bring to their sweetness no satiety – John Milton> <a gentleman farmer *imbued* with a high sense of civic duty – Trevor Armbrister> **Ingrain** suggests an indelible stamping or deep implanting (as of an idea or trait) <*ingrained* prejudice> <acceptance of autocracy, of blind obedience to the petty tyrants who ruled as princes, became *ingrained* in the German mind – W. L. Shirer> **Inoculate** implies an imbuing or implanting with a germinal idea and may suggest surreptitiousness or subtlety <*inoculate* the few who influence the many – *Current Biog.*> <[to the rightist] Communism is Satan personified; it can be faced only in a fight to the death, and only by those properly armed and *inoculated* – I. S. Rohter> **Leaven** implies a transforming or tempering of the whole by something that enlivens, elevates, or disturbs <there was need of idealism to *leaven* the materialistic realism of the times – V. L. Parrington> <wisdom is . . . part integrity, part virtue, part justice, part self-confidence, part experience, part intelligence, all *leavened* with a good measure of courage – Harvey Wheeler>

ingenious – see CLEVER, NATURAL

ingredient – see ELEMENT

inheritance – see HERITAGE

inhibit – see FORBID ***ant*** allow

inimical – see ADVERSE

iniquitous – see VICIOUS ***ant*** righteous

initiate – see BEGIN ***ant*** consummate

injure, harm, hurt, damage, impair, mar *shared meaning* : to affect injuriously. **Injure** implies the infliction of something detrimental, be it material (as a wound) or immaterial (as an injustice) <when have I *injured* thee? when done thee wrong – Shak.> <*injured* in an explosion> <his reputation was *injured* by the scandal> **Harm** may stress the infliction of pain, suffering, or loss <for none of woman born shall *harm* Macbeth – Shak.> <a rumor that greatly *harmed* his business> **Hurt** implies inflicting a wound whether to the body or feelings or to something capable of sustaining injury <a limitless desire to *hurt* and humiliate – H. G. Wells> <he had left her alone . . . feeling . . . that his presence would only *hurt* her, irritate her – William Styron> **Damage** suggests injury that lowers value or impairs usefulness <was his memory failing, or had he so disciplined it in the repression of unpleasant facts that he had *damaged* his sense of truth? – John Cheever> <a late frost *damaged* the crop> **Impair** suggests a making less complete or efficient by deterioration or diminution <his hearing was seriously *impaired*> <a year-long strike greatly *impaired* the university's functions – Gene Currivan> **Mar** suggests disfigurement or maiming that results in loss of perfection or well-being <striving to better, oft we *mar* what's well – Shak.> <too good a book to be *marred* by small defects – R. A. Smith> ***ant*** aid

injury – see INJUSTICE

injustice, injury, wrong, grievance *shared meaning* : an act that inflicts undeserved hurt on a person. **Injustice,** the general term, applies to any act that involves unfairness to another or violation of his rights <Africans who come to the States . . . are almost invariably surprised to discover that there is more equality than *injustice* in our society, imperfect as it may be – William Attwood> <you do me an *injustice* when you claim I deceived you about the worth of the property> **Injury** applies to an injustice that admits of a legal remedy <every person who suffers damage to his person, his property, or his reputation as a result of an infringement of the law suffers a legal *injury* – Ronald Rubenstein> **Wrong** in law applies not only to an injury but to damaging acts punishable under the criminal code; in more general use it differs little from *injustice,* except in carrying a stronger suggestion of seriousness or of flagrancy <we seem to be saying, "Not justice – anything but that. What can we think of that will keep people quiet but that will not require us to right the deep *wrongs* in our society?" – R. M. Hutchins> **Grievance** applies to a circumstance or condition that, in the opinion of those affected, constitutes a wrong or gives just grounds for complaint <in an early state of society any kind of taxation is apt to be looked on as a *grievance* – E. A. Freeman> <*grievances* illegally inflicted upon men by the king's ministers – J. G. Edwards>

innate, inborn, inbred, congenital, hereditary *shared meaning* : not acquired after birth. **Innate** applies especially to qualities or characteristics that are part of one's inner essential nature <Jefferson's rational animals, endowed by nature with inalienable rights and an *innate* sense of justice – Aldous Huxley> but sometimes to elements or qualities that are fundamental to the nature of a nonliving thing <the *innate* defect of a plan> <the *innate* magnetism of the proton – Elmer Davis> **Inborn** applies to a quality or tendency either actually present at birth or so marked and deep-seated as to seem so <to what extent can the *inborn* tendency to be too suggestible for one's own good . . . he neutralized by education? – Aldous Huxley> <the tendency towards schizophrenia was *inborn* – *N.Y. Times*> **Inbred** applies to something acquired from parents, whether by heredity or the effects of nurture, and deeply rooted and ingrained in one's nature <an *inbred* love of freedom> <a methodical man, an *inbred* Yankee – W. A. White> *Congenital* and *hereditary* apply to something present at or before birth; distinctively, **congenital** implies acquirement during fetal development <*congenital* blindness resulting from intrauterine infection> while **hereditary** implies transmission from an ancestor through the germ plasm <the color of one's eyes is a *hereditary* characteristic> or sometimes through social heredity <preventing the perpetuation of an *hereditary* upper class with special privileges and better education – Edmund Wilson>

inordinate – see EXCESSIVE *ant* temperate

inquire – see ASK

inquisitive – see CURIOUS *ant* incurious

insanity, lunacy, psychosis, mania, dementia *shared meaning* : a seriously disordered condition of mind. **Insanity** implies unfitness to manage one's own affairs or to safely enjoy liberty <so ill-adapted to the conditions under which we must live . . . that we are continually falling victim to ailments, *insanities,* deformities, depletions – caused by our failure to cope with these – Edmund Wilson> **Lunacy** may be interchangeable with *insanity* <a *lunacy* commission> but in general usage more often applies to insanity characterized by alternating spells of madness and lucidity <grating so harshly all his days of quiet with turbulent and dangerous *lunacy* – Shak.> **Psychosis** is the general psychiatric term for a profound disorganization of mind, personality, or behavior. Though in content often coextensive with *insanity* and *lunacy* it carries none of the special implications of these terms <drugs like LSD, peyote, and even morning-glory seeds can and do cause *psychosis* – *Trans-action*> **Mania** implies insanity but is often used specifically for a phase marked by sustained and exaggerated elation or excessive activity that is characteristic of some psychoses. **Dementia** implies mental deterioration whether psychogenic in origin or due to structural brain damage. These words, with the exception of *psychosis,* are also used with the implication not of mental disease but of a disordered state suggestive of disease <the *insanity* of failing to enable bloodless entry of blacks into white America – J. L. Perry> <comes too close to the *lunacy* of preventive war to gratify more sensible citizens – *New Republic*> <she had a *mania* for buying and selling land – Thomas Wolfe> <made little effort to remember the day; with its peculiar quality of *dementia* it seemed not a commonplace and civilized social event but a nightmare in vivid technicolor – William Styron> *ant* sanity

inscrutable – see MYSTERIOUS

insert – see INTRODUCE *ant* abstract, extract

insight – see DISCERNMENT *ant* obtuseness

insinuate – see INTRODUCE, SUGGEST

insipid, vapid, flat, jejune, banal, wishy-washy, inane *shared meaning* : devoid of qualities that make for spirit and character. Something **insipid** lacks taste, savor, or pungency <tired of his *insipid* invalid's diet> <happiness is a wine of the rarest vintage, and seems *insipid* to a vulgar taste – L. P. Smith> <all former delights . . . were quite *insipid* when compared with the lawful matrimonial pleasures which of late he had enjoyed – W. M. Thackeray> Something **vapid** is deficient in freshness, spirit, sparkle, or liveliness <the diction is limp, not to say downright *vapid* – Leonard Wolf> <had a genius for making the most interesting things seem utterly *vapid* and dead – Robert Graves> Something **flat** has lost all stimulating qualities and become so dull as to seem lifeless <how weary, stale, *flat* and unprofitable, seem to me all the uses of this world – Shak.> <the story . . . usually sustains its interest. The few *flat* scenes are more than overbalanced by compelling episodes – H. T. Moore> Something **jejune** is incapable of satisfying hunger of body, mind, or emotions; the word commonly connotes barrenness, aridity, or meagerness <literary history without evaluative criteria becomes *jejune* and sterile – C. I. Glicksberg> <the Greeks' colour vocabulary . . . was *jejune* or lacking in substance – *New Scientist*> Something **banal** is so trite and commonplace as to lose all freshness and appeal <a proposed draft of directives for journalists that was as *banal* and old-fashioned as the original decree – Xavier Rynne> <a handsome young man of *banal* mind but of great driving force – W. L. Shirer> Something **wishy-washy** has its essential or striking qualities so weak or diluted as to strike one as utterly insipid or vapid <talent is a *wishy-washy* thing unless it is solidly founded on honest hard work – E. G. Coleman> Something **inane** is devoid of sense, significance, or point <an *inane* remark> <afflict the . . . people with radio programs and motion pictures as *inane* and boring as were the contents of their daily newspapers – W. L. Shirer> *ant* sapid, zestful

insolent – see PROUD *ant* deferential

inspect – see SCRUTINIZE

instance *n* **instance, case, illustration, example, sample, specimen** *shared meaning* : something that exhibits distinguishing characteristics of the category to which it belongs. **Instance** applies to an individual brought forward in support or disproof of a general statement <the *instance* may be rejected, but the principle abides – B. N. Cardozo> <Herodotus is a shining *instance* of the strong Greek bent to examine and prove or disprove – Edith Hamilton> **Case** applies to an instance that directs attention to a situation to be considered or dealt with or that exhibits it in actual operation <such a method . . . would provide *case* studies for motivating the study of an entire region – *NEA Jour.*> <the old *case* of the circus clown who must be the best acrobat of all to appear inept – Pamela Marsh> **Illustration** applies to an instance offered as a means of clarifying or illuminating what is presented for consideration <it may be that the idea is accurate enough but . . . the *illustrations* of it in the author's books are not convincing – *Saturday Rev.*> **Example** applies to a typical, representative, or illustrative instance or case <a most outstanding *example* of a war fought with a purpose was our own American Revolution – W. L. Willkie> <the best of them set an *example* of unselfish endeavour that inspired even the dullest of them with a sense of unconquerable solidarity – *Times Lit. Supp.*> **Sample** denotes a random part or unit taken as representative of the whole to which it belongs <why have sociologists not suggested giving a *sample* of poor people a negative income-tax grant, then studying whether the grant helped them solve some of their other problems? – H. J. Gans> <sent a questionnaire to a random *sample* of students> <a *sample* of wheat for analysis> **Specimen**, often indistinguishable from *sample*, may be the term of choice

when the whole is made up of discrete units that are independent entities or when careful selection (as for typicalness) is to be implied <a *specimen* of the melodramatic fiction of the era – T. S. Eliot> <compare *specimens* of their handwriting>
instance *vb* – see MENTION
instigate – see INCITE
instill – see IMPLANT
instinctive 1 **instinctive, intuitive** *shared meaning* : not based on ordinary processes of reasoning. In spite of their common meaning element these words, as applied to human mentation, are not normally interchangeable because of consistent differences in connotation. **Instinctive** implies a relation to **instinct**, the more or less automatic reactive behavior characteristic of a group (as a species) rather than an individual; as applied to human mental activity or behavior *instinctive* may stress the automatic quality of the reaction <had an *instinctive* dread of snakes> or the fact that it occurs below the level of conscious thought and volition <an *instinctive* response to an emergency> <some of our most inevitable and *instinctive* sentiments . . . cannot be brought directly under logical laws – G. G. Coulton> **Intuitive**, correspondingly, implies a relation to **intuition**, the highly personal intellectual capacity for passing directly from stimulus to response (as from problem to solution or from observation to comprehension) without conscious intervention of reasoning or inferring; as applied to the human mind or products of its activities *intuitive* suggests activity above and beyond the level of conscious reasoning <an *intuitive* mind, passionate in its attempt to capture a great truth in a few words, but impatient of logical sequences – H. S. Canby> <an *intuitive* understanding of the parallelogram of forces – S. F. Mason> *ant* reasoned
2 see SPONTANEOUS *ant* intentional
instruct – see COMMAND, TEACH
instrument – see IMPLEMENT, MEAN *n*
insult – see OFFEND *ant* honor
insure – see ENSURE
insurrection – see REBELLION
intact – see PERFECT *ant* defective
integrity 1 see HONESTY *ant* duplicity
2 see UNITY
intelligent, clever, alert, quick-witted, knowing *shared meaning* : mentally keen or quick. **Intelligent** implies superiority of mind and is likely to stress efficiency in coping with new situations or in solving problems <the vigor of his quick and lucid mind, keenly *intelligent* rather than deeply intellectual – E. M. Lustgarten> **Clever** implies quick native ability or aptness and sometimes suggests a lack of more substantial qualities <I was . . . easily the *cleverest* young fox ever to know how to disguise his ignorance and make a virtue of his limitations – Gore Vidal> **Alert** stresses quickness in perceiving and understanding <an . . . *alert* student, he read widely and at the age of nineteen passed his first teachers' examination – George Crout> **Quick-witted** implies promptness in finding answers or devising expedients <we are not a *quick-witted* race; and we have succeeded . . . by dint of a kind of instinct for improvising the right course of action – W. R. Inge> **Knowing** implies the possession of special knowledge; it is likely to connote sophistication, secretiveness, or cynicism <his work has a distasteful air of pretentious smartness, of being altogether too *knowing* – Herbert Read> <through television . . . the public has become aware of the subtleties of comedy and has grown more sophisticated and *knowing* – *Current Biog.*> *ant* unintelligent

intensify, aggravate, heighten, enhance *shared meaning* : to increase markedly in measure or degree. **Intensify** implies a deepening or strengthening of a thing or of its characteristic quality <an *intensifying* storm moved up the coast> <the final purpose of art is to *intensify* . . . the moral consciousness of people – Norman Mailer> **Aggravate** implies an increasing in gravity or seriousness of something already unpleasant or trying <excessive demands by labor *aggravates* the inflationary trend> <the fact that adolescents have elaborated their own set of stereotypes about adults *aggravates* the misunderstanding – E. J. Anthony> **Heighten** suggests a lifting above the ordinary or expected <the two drinks . . . had *heightened,* rather than suppressed, his sense of fatigue – William Styron> <dances that gave them intense satisfaction and a *heightened* awareness of themselves – Thomas Merton> **Enhance** implies a raising or strengthening above the normal (as in desirability, value, or attractiveness) <show him that by changing his mind, he could *enhance* my image of him – R. L. Foose> <expanding . . . programs where such growth will *enhance* the educational function . . . of the University – M. S. Eisenhower> ***ant*** temper, mitigate, allay, abate

intent – see INTENTION ***ant*** accident

intention, intent, purpose, design, aim, end, object, objective, goal *shared meaning* : what one proposes to accomplish or to attain. **Intention** implies little more than what one intends to do or bring about <it was not his *intention* to criticize the establishment> <the main *intention* of the poem has been to make dramatically visible the conflict – Allen Tate> **Intent** suggests clearer formulation and greater deliberateness <it is the *intent* of this board . . . to give top priority to the activities of the teachers and the learners – Dayton Benjamin> <limits established to guarantee that the legislative *intent* of the Congress is realized – A. H. Quie> **Purpose** implies more settled determination or more resolution than *intention* <the missionary was here for a *purpose,* and he pressed his point – Willa Cather> <a crowd is chaotic, has no *purpose* of its own – Aldous Huxley> **Design** implies a carefully calculated plan and suggests careful ordering of details and sometimes scheming <determine whether the violence in the ghettos has been "instigated and precipitated by the calculated *design* of agitators . . ." – Nat Hentoff> **Aim** adds implications of a clearly directed effort to attain what is proposed <the *aim* of the Elizabethans was to attain complete realism – T. S. Eliot> **End** stresses the intended effect of action often in distinction or contrast to the action or means as such <the pernicious view that the good of the *end* justifies the evil of the means> <you have both had courage and persistence, and the *end* crowns the work – D. C. Gilman> *Object* and *objective* can apply to an end as being that toward which effort or action or emotion is directed <the *object* of a search> <the *objective* of a military action> but distinctively **object** can apply to a distinctly personal aim or end and come close to *motive* in meaning <[the role of] Odette is the *object* of his complete absorption. The role . . . has been transformed into a major one – John Martin> while **objective** is likely to apply to one that is both concrete and attainable <De Gaulle, whose *objective* was to give back to . . . France self-respect, pride, and a world position – S. E. Ambrose> **Goal** suggests something attainable only after prolonged effort and hardship <the Good, which is the *goal* of all moral endeavor – W. R. Inge>

intentional – see VOLUNTARY ***ant*** instinctive

intercalate – see INTRODUCE

intercede – see INTERPOSE

interdict – see FORBID ***ant*** sanction

interfere — see INTERPOSE, MEDDLE
interject — see INTRODUCE
intermeddle — see MEDDLE
intermission — see PAUSE
intermit — see DEFER
intermittent, recurrent, periodic, alternate *shared meaning* : occurring or appearing in interrupted sequence. **Intermittent** stresses breaks in continuity <an *intermittent* correspondence with a distant relative> <in most poets there is an *intermittent* conflict between the poetic self and the rest of the man – C. D. Lewis> **Recurrent** stresses repetition; thus, a *recurrent* fever tends to reappear at more or less regular intervals; a *recurrent* problem is one that can be counted on to come up again and again. **Periodic** implies recurrence at essentially regular intervals <coping with *periodic* shifts of population out of China's swollen cities – A. S. Whiting> <*periodic* appearances of a comet> **Alternate** may apply to two contrasting things appearing repeatedly one after the other <a summer filled with *alternate* fits of false confidence and secret misgivings – Mildred S. Fenner> or to every second member of a series <they divided tasks and waited on *alternate* customers – Bernard Malamud> <the club meets on *alternate* Tuesdays> ***ant*** incessant, continual
interpolate — see INTRODUCE
interpose 1 see INTRODUCE
2 interpose, interfere, intervene, mediate, intercede *shared meaning* : to come or go between. **Interpose** implies no more than this and acquires all its connotations from the context <the tops of the trees . . . *interposed* between him and the sun – C. S. Forester> <tending to *interpose* objects of worship between God and man – W. R. Inge> **Interfere** implies a getting in the way or otherwise hindering (as in movement, vision, or effectiveness) <heavy clouds *interfered* with our view of the mountains> <the R.A.F. . . . and the British Navy were increasingly *interfering* with the concentration of the invasion fleet – W. L. Shirer> **Intervene** may imply an occurring in space or time between two things <an interval for meditation *intervened* between the two parts of the service> or a stepping in for a specific purpose (as settling a quarrel, relieving distress, or clarifying a position) <the fifteen cardinals appealed to . . . [the pope] to *intervene* against possible obstructive tactics – *Current Biog.*> <[the president] had personally *intervened* to persuade the unions and railroads to call off the threatened shutdown – *Current Biog.*> **Mediate** implies intervening between hostile factions or conflicting ideas or principles <humor is a powerful instrument in *mediating* the incongruities of the psyche – Theodore Solotaroff> <I want to *mediate* between the two of you now, because if this breach continues it will be the ruin of us all – Robert Graves> **Intercede** implies intervention on another's and usually an offender's behalf and use of one's good offices for him (as in imploring mercy or forgiveness) <for each at utter need – true comrade and true foeman – Madonna, *intercede!* – Rudyard Kipling> <the captain had a call from the manager of the Palace Hotel, to *intercede* in person for a table for one of his guests – Ludwig Bemelmans>
interpret — see EXPLAIN
interrogate — see ASK
interstice — see APERTURE
intervene — see INTERPOSE
intimate *vb* — see SUGGEST
intimate *adj* — see FAMILIAR
intoxicated — see DRUNK
intractable — see UNRULY ***ant*** tractable

intricate – see COMPLEX
intrigue – see PLOT
introduce, insert, insinuate, interpolate, intercalate, interpose, interject *shared meaning* : to put among or between others. **Introduce** is a general term for bringing or placing a person or thing into a group or body already existing <*introduce* a new topic into a conversation> **Insert** implies a setting of a thing into a fixed space between or among other things <*insert* an empty bottle into a case> <insert a *revolver* into its holster> **Insinuate** implies slow, careful, sometimes artful introduction <slang ... has to *insinuate* itself into the language; it cannot pressure or push its way in – *Saturday Rev.*> <*insinuate* a car through heavy traffic> **Interpolate** applies to the inserting of something extraneous or spurious <*interpolate* a question in the midst of a story> <he has *interpolated* editorial and critical comments – B. R. Redman> **Intercalate** suggests an intrusive inserting of something into an existing series or sequence <lava beds *intercalated* between layers of sedimentary rock> <these vignettes appear to have been *intercalated* into the original story by an early reviser> **Interpose** implies the insertion of something that causes obstruction or delay <[the professor] has simply *interposed* between Euripides and ourselves a barrier more impenetrable than the Greek language – T. S. Eliot> **Interject**, usually concerned with utterances, implies a forced or abrupt introducing of something that breaks in or interrupts <*interject* an impertinent comment> <as they chewed on bones and roots, they paused to *interject* grunts of encouragement for the narrator – F. L. Mott> ***ant*** withdraw, abstract
introductory – see PRELIMINARY ***ant*** closing, concluding
intrusive – see IMPERTINENT ***ant*** retiring, unintrusive
intuition – see REASON ***ant*** ratiocination
intuitive – see INSTINCTIVE ***ant*** ratiocinative
invade – see TRESPASS
invalidate – see NULLIFY ***ant*** validate
invaluable – see COSTLY ***ant*** worthless
invective – see ABUSE
inveigle – see LURE
invent, create, discover *shared meaning* : to bring something new into existence. **Invent** implies fabricating something new and often useful through the exercise of the imagination or of ingenious thinking and experiment <his fund of knowledge seemed inexhaustible, for what he didn't know he *invented* – Alvin Redman> <Gutenberg ... knew about wood engraving, coin stamping, wax seals, and the wine press. Given these elements, the printing press might almost *invent* itself – Sam Glucksberg> **Create** stresses a causing something to come into existence and may suggest a calling into being out of or as if out of nothing <God *created* the heaven and the earth – *Gen* 1:1 (AV)> <we worry about whether our economy can *create* enough jobs to go around – *Trans-action*> <advertising *creates* demand> **Discover** implies preexistence of, but complete lack of knowledge about, something; the term therefore stresses exploration of the unknown and finding of what is hidden, usually through mental or physical effort <*discover* a new chemical element> <William Harvey *discovered* the circulation of the blood>
invert – see REVERSE
inveterate, confirmed, chronic, deep-seated, deep-rooted *shared meaning* : firmly established. **Inveterate** applies to something (as a habit, attitude, or feeling) so fixed by time and usage as to be almost inalterable <an *inveterate* smoker> <the *inveterate* and irrational instinct that impels

human beings to go to war – Edmund Wilson> <an *inveterate* dislike of interruption – Charles Lamb> **Confirmed** implies a growing stronger and firmer with the passage of time so as to increasingly resist change or reform <a *confirmed* bachelor> <like all other *confirmed* habits . . . easier to obey than to break – Ellen Glasgow> **Chronic** implies long duration usually of something undesirable that resists attempts to alleviate or cure <*chronic* tuberculosis> <the commuter's *chronic* problem of getting to work – and home again – *Think*> **Deep-seated** and **deep-rooted** emphasize the extent to which something has entered into the very structure of that in which it has become fixed or embedded <it was suggested that revolution is a permanent *deep-seated* characteristic of human history – Harvey Wheeler> <a *deep-seated* prejudice> <the family was *deep-rooted* in the South – *Current Biog.*> <a *deep-rooted* reverence for truth – John Morley>

invidious – see REPUGNANT

inviolable – see SACRED

inviolate – see SACRED ***ant*** violated

invite, solicit, court *shared meaning* : to request or encourage (as a person) to respond or to do. **Invite** commonly implies a formal or courteous requesting of one's presence or participation <*invite* friends to a picnic> but it may also apply to a tacit or unintended attracting or tempting <security in time of war is one thing, but the 1918 act *invited* a return to the arbitrary repression of 1798 – Nat Hentoff> **Solicit** suggests urgency more than courtesy in encouraging or asking <moral utterances which *solicit* the obedience of children – A. I. Melden> **Court** suggests an endeavoring to win something (as favor or love or success) by suitable acts and words <*court* the favor of her professional associates – Tennessee Williams> <subconsciously . . . men *court* war to escape meaninglessness and boredom – N. F. S. Ferre>

involve – see INCLUDE

involved – see COMPLEX

irascible, choleric, splenetic, testy, touchy, cranky, cross *shared meaning* : easily angered or enraged. **Irascible** implies a tendency to be angered on slight provocation <his proud, *irascible* individualism that went out of its way to pick a quarrel – V. L. Parrington> but sometimes it suggests a superficial weakness of a basically humane character <the *irascible* but kindhearted deity who indulges in copious curses to ease his feelings – M. R. Cohen> **Choleric** may suggest impatient excitability and unreasonableness as well as hot temper <that in the captain's but a *choleric* word, which in the soldier is flat blasphemy – Shak.> <a testy and *choleric* gentleman easily wrought into passion – J. F. Cooper> **Splenetic** suggests moroseness and a bad rather than a hot temper <that *splenetic* temper, which seems to grudge brightness to the flames of hell – W. S. Landor> **Testy** suggests irascibility over small annoyances <he was *testy,* irascible, easily provoked . . . spoke his mind without fear or favor – *Christian Herald*> **Touchy** suggests readiness to take offense and often connotes undue irritability or oversensitiveness <I am not *touchy* under criticism – R. L. Stevenson> <a man who had grown too *touchy* to make judicious decisions – *Time*> *Cranky* and *cross* often mean little more than irritable and difficult to please <a tired *cranky* child> <it's time to go home, the children are getting *cross*> Distinctively, **cranky** can imply the possession of set notions, fixed ideas, or unvarying standards which predispose one to anger when others fail to conform <a *cranky* teacher who had forgotten what it is to be young> <his admissions policies have seemed a little *cranky.* He refused to admit English boys for many years – John McPhee> while

cross usually implies a being temporarily out of sorts that results in ar equally temporary irascibility or irritability <in a burst of indignation, she came forward, *cross* enough ... to slap him – Terry Southern>

ire – see ANGER

irenic – see PACIFIC ***ant*** acrimonious

irk – see ANNOY

ironic – see SARCASTIC

irony – see WIT

irrational, unreasonable *shared meaning* : not governed or guided by reason Both terms are occasionally used in the sense of not having the powe to reason <plants and *irrational* animals – David Hume †1776> <whils his fellowman ... must as the *unreasonable* beast drag on a life of labo – Robert Southey> In more general use **irrational** can imply menta derangement <the patient was *irrational* during the fever> but it more often suggests lack of control by or open conflict with reason <a sudder *irrational* fury revived his ill humor – H. C. Hervey> <this is an *irrationa* world ... and we are living in a continuation of the formalized lunacy ... of war, any war – R. J. Gleason> **Unreasonable** in comparable use is likely to suggest guidance by some force other than reason (as ambition greed, or stubbornness) that makes or shows one deficient in good sense <[he] saw with displeasure, which he recognized as *unreasonable,* that hi younger brother would eventually be ... taller than himself – Pearl Buck> <make *unreasonable* demands on a friend> ***ant*** rational

irregular, anomalous, unnatural *shared meaning* : not according with o explainable by law, rule, or custom. **Irregular** implies a lack of accord with a law or regulation imposed for the sake of uniformity in method, practice or conduct; thus, an *irregular* marriage fails to conform to the regulation of church or state; *irregular* verse departs from an accepted metrical pattern *irregular* behavior deviates from the accepted code of conduct of the com munity <the chicanery was gross, the forgery patent, the procedure *irregula* and illegal – C. V. Woodward> **Anomalous** implies not conforming to what might be expected because of the class to which the thing in questior belongs or the laws that govern its existence <an *anomalous* piece o domestic architecture, combining the small, familiar pleasures of the heartl with the headier excitements of Doomsday – *New Yorker*> and may specifically imply an unclassifiable state or conflict between mutually exclu sive or mutually antagonistic classes <the *anomalous* position of the free Negro in the slave states – E. T. Price> <those who argue ... that i is *anomalous* to expect Communist China to live up to the responsibilitie of international law as long as we are unwilling to recognize it as a membe of the family of nations – D. C. Coyle> **Unnatural** implies a contravening of natural law or of those principles held essential to the well-being o civilized society and is likely to suggest reprehensible abnormality <a daughter who left her father was an *unnatural* daughter; her womanhoo was suspect – Virginia Woolf> <thy deed, inhuman and *unnatural* pro vokes this deluge most *unnatural* – Shak.> <she had been vicious and *unnatural;* she had thriven on hatred – S. S. Van Dine> ***ant*** regular

irritate, exasperate, nettle, provoke, aggravate, rile, peeve *shared meanin* : to excite to angry annoyance. **Irritate** implies an often gradual arousin of angry feeling ranging from mere impatience to open rage <the chatterin crowd, with their rude jokes ... *irritated* him sharply – Sherwood Ander son> **Exasperate** suggests galling annoyance or vexation and the arousa of extreme impatience <an opportunity to ... aggravate his poor patien wife, and *exasperate* his children, and make himself generally obnoxiou – Simeon Ford> **Nettle** suggests a sharp but transitory stinging or prickin

<a touch of light scorn in her voice *nettled* me – W. J. Locke> **Provoke** implies an arousing of strong annoyance or vexation that may incite to action <they were definitely *provoked* to extremity before they did this deed – Rex Ingamells> **Aggravate** implies persistent, often petty, goading that leads to displeasure, impatience, or anger <nothing so *aggravates* an earnest person as a passive resistance – Herman Melville> **Rile** suggests a disturbing of one's peace that agitates as well as angers <the type of unfair and ambiguous statement that ... would *rile* the Justice – E. J. Bander> **Peeve** implies an exciting to petty or querulous fretfulness, especially of one prone to irritation <hadn't seen him for years and was *peeved* to note that he had ... [not] got rid of ... his cavalier attitude – William Styron>

isolation – see SOLITUDE

issue *n* – see EFFECT

issue *vb* – see SPRING

item, detail, particular *shared meaning* : one of the distinct parts of a whole. **Item**, a neutral term, applies to any part that is separable or separately identifiable or listable <meat is an important *item* in our budget> <the dog too went: the most noble-looking *item* in the beggarly assets – Joseph Conrad> **Detail** applies to one of the small component parts of a larger whole (as a building, painting, narration, or process) and may specifically denote one of the minutiae that lends finish or character to the thing of which it is a part <she had her plan clearly in her head, with every *detail* as distinct as though the scheme had already been carried through – Stella D. Gibbons> <his reputation was based largely on his meticulous attention to *details*> **Particular** may imply a relation to something universal or general <foolishly derides the universal, saying that it chooses to consider the *particular* as more important – A. T. Quiller-Couch> but more often it implies relationship to a whole and stresses the smallness, singleness, or concreteness of the part <we know nothing of their language, and only ... minor *particulars* of their social customs and religion – R. W. Murray> <their dissimilarity in every *particular* except shape and size – Scott Fitzgerald>

iterate – see REPEAT

jade – see TIRE ***ant*** refresh

jam – see PREDICAMENT

jargon – see DIALECT

jealous – see ENVIOUS

jeer – see SCOFF

jejune – see INSIPID

jerk, snap, twitch, yank *shared meaning* : to make or move with a sudden sharp quick movement. **Jerk** stresses suddenness and abruptness and is likely to imply a movement both graceless and forceful <*jerked* her head back as if she'd been struck in the face – Dorothy Baker> <we *jerk* along narrow, crazy paths dotted with deep ruts and boulders ... It makes for exciting motoring – Beata Bishop> **Snap** implies a sharp quick action abruptly terminated (as in biting, seizing, locking, or breaking) <his head began to drop, nod by nod, until it hit his chest and he *snapped* awake – Lore Segal> <[the car] *snapped* its occupants up and down and jostled them from side to side – *Consumer Reports*> **Twitch** applies to a light, sudden and sometimes spasmodic movement usually combining tugging and jerking <put out his hand to *twitch* off a twig as he passed – Willa Cather> <it was his face which was so startling, . . . *twitching* all over with emotion – William Styron> **Yank** implies a quick and heavy tugging and pulling <*yank* the bedclothes over one's head> <by means of long blocks and tackle they set to *yanking* out logs – S. E. White>

jest 1 jest, joke, quip, witticism, wisecrack, gag *shared meaning* : a remark, story, or action intended to evoke laughter. **Jest** applies to an utterance not seriously intended whether sarcastic, ironic, witty, or merely playful <continually . . . making a *jest* of his ignorance – J. D. Beresford> <a proper *jest,* and never heard before, that Suffolk should demand a whole fifteenth for costs and charges – Shak.> <the kind of wry *jest* that had sent the ancient gods into peals of ironic laughter – T. B. Costain> **Joke** can apply to a story or remark designed to promote good humor and often depending for its effect on a humorously incongruous ending <the old *joke,* that "black horses eat more than white horses," a puzzling condition which is finally cleared up by the statement that "there are more black horses" – W. J. Reilly> or to an action designed to befool someone sometimes good-humoredly, sometimes maliciously <the human intellect is not some elaborate divine *joke* on Man, leading him astray – *N.Y. Herald Tribune*> **Quip** stresses lightness and neatness of phrase <Kennedy fashioned a *quip:* "I am much happier being the father of nine children and making a hole in one than I would be as the father of one child making a hole in nine" – R. J. Whalen> **Witticism** and **wisecrack** apply to a clever or witty and often a biting or sarcastic remark <in Voltaire, the bright mocking attack is something so completely natural that ironic effects do not need to be built up; the *witticisms* are . . . spontaneous and over in a flash – Edmund Wilson> <sardonic *wisecracks* in which supposedly lofty ideals are mercilessly derided – *Times Lit. Supp.*> **Gag** applies especially to a brief laughter-provoking remark or piece of business interpolated into a public entertainment <*gags* grown venerable in the service of the music halls – *Times Lit. Supp.*>

2 see FUN

jibe – see AGREE 3

job – see POSITION 2, TASK

jocose – see WITTY

jocular – see WITTY

jocund – see MERRY

join, combine, unite, connect, link, associate, relate *shared meaning* : to bring or come together into some manner of union. **Join** implies a bringing into some degree of contact or conjunction of clearly discrete things <asked if he could *join* her and buy her a drink – John Cheever> <once battle was unavoidably *joined,* the losses were terrible – Walter Millis> <imperialism and despotism had *joined* hands – Harvey Wheeler> **Combine** implies such merging or mingling as obscures individual characteristics <*combine* the ingredients for a cake> <a gift for *combining,* for fusing into a single phrase, two or more diverse impressions – T. S. Eliot> **Unite,** too, implies a blending and stresses loss of separate identity <diverse groups throughout the country *united* as a solid majority in support of the exiled royal family – *Current Biog.*> **Connect** suggests a loose or external attachment with little or no loss of identity <*connect* a trailer to a car> <the islands were *connected* by a bridge> and may imply a logical attachment involving relationship <I don't *connect* her with Christmas, but maybe I *connect* her with joy – Robert Henderson> **Link** may imply strong connection or inseparability of elements still retaining identity <attempts to *link* black militancy, antiwar activities and campus protest movements with commu

nism – Nat Hentoff> <a piston *linked* to the driveshaft by a coupling rod> **Associate** stresses the fact of occurrence and existence together in space or in logical relation <the deadly poisonous, green mushroom . . . is *associated* with deciduous trees – Theodor Wieland> <surrealism has been *associated* with psychological and intellectual atmosphere common to periods of war – Bernard Smith> **Relate** implies a natural or logical connection <on his mother's side he was distantly *related* to the president> <*autism* . . . is characterized by an inability on the part of the child to *relate* himself in an ordinary way to the people and situations of his environment – *Johns Hopkins Mag.*> <these seemingly contradictory doctrines are . . . *related* – Guenter Lewy> ***ant*** disjoin, part

joint, articulation, suture *shared meaning* : the place where or the mechanism by which two things are united. **Joint** is the most inclusive term and is freely applicable to either a natural or a man-made structure <the complicated flexible *joint* of the elbow> <the restoration was so carefully done that the *joint* between the old and new wood was imperceptible> **Articulation** is chiefly an anatomical term in this sense and can apply to any joint of the skeleton with particular emphasis on the fitting together of the parts involved. Therefore, it is likely to be the term of choice when the mechanism of a joint or the elements entering into its construction are under consideration <the ball-and-socket structure of highly movable *articulations*> or when the process or method of joining is involved <in the flat bones the *articulations* usually take place at the edges – Henry Gray> **Suture** is used of a joint that suggests a seam (as in linear form or lack of mobility) or that has been formed by sewing <the joints between the two parts of a bean or pea pod are called *sutures*> <the *sutures* of the skull, flexible at birth, become rigid and immovable in the adult> <the surgeon unites severed tissues with a carefully sewn *suture* so that they may grow together anew>

joke – see JEST

jollity – see MIRTH

jolly – see MERRY

jovial – see MERRY

joy – see PLEASURE ***ant*** sorrow (*as emotion*), misery (*as a state of mind*), abomination

joyful – see GLAD ***ant*** joyless

joyous – see GLAD ***ant*** lugubrious

judge – see INFER

judgment – see SENSE

judicious – see WISE ***ant*** injudicious, asinine

junction, confluence, concourse *shared meaning* : an act, state, or place of meeting or uniting. **Junction** is likely to apply to the meeting or uniting of material things (as roads, rivers, or lines) <electricity produced by the *junction* of two dissimilar metals – S. F. Mason> <a town grew up at the *junction* of the two rivers> or occasionally of immaterial things <the *junction* of the Senecan influence with the native tradition – T. S. Eliot> and only rarely of persons or groups <hoped to effect a *junction* of the two armies> **Confluence** usually retains its basic suggestion of a flowing together and is appropriately used when this impression is fitting <the waters that compose the *confluence* of the Hudson and East Rivers – James Purdy> <Toynbee described . . . [our civilization] as a *confluence* of the five or six civilizations which are still extant but are breaking down – Scott Buchanan> **Concourse** places emphasis on a rushing or hurrying together of persons or things to form a great crowd <a *concourse* of people crouched upon the ground forming a rude circle – H. G. de Lisser> <a fortuitous

concourse of atoms> and it may apply to a place where people throng to and fro <everyone hurried across the *concourse* to the gate where the train was waiting>

juncture, pass, exigency, emergency, contingency, pinch, strait, crisis *shared meaning* : a critical or crucial time or state of affairs. **Juncture** stresses a significant concurrence or convergence of events that is likely to lead to a turning point <at this *juncture,* the future looks bright in the extreme – Burt Korall> <this date, apparently, was the *juncture* where relations between father- and son-in-law began to break down – M. A. McCorison> **Pass** implies a bad or distressing situation usually of complex origin <things had certainly come to a pretty *pass* when a lady was insulted in her own front yard> <have his daughters brought him to this *pass?* – Shak.> **Exigency** emphasizes the pressure of necessity or the urgency of demands created by a juncture or pass <they had knowingly made a charter that could be interpreted to meet whatever *exigencies* might arise – R. G. Tugwell> **Emergency** implies a sudden or unforeseen juncture that necessitates quick action to avoid disaster <he became seriously depressed and suicidal, and applied for *emergency* psychotherapy – *Trans-action*> <many wild plants can be used as food in an *emergency*> **Contingency** implies an emergency or exigency that is regarded as possible or even probable but uncertain of occurrence <attempted to provide for every *contingency*> <the *contingencies* of history itself are unpredictable. This is an era of rapid change – M. J. Adler> **Pinch** describes a juncture, especially in personal affairs, that exerts pressure and demands vigorous counteractive action <non-profit organizations today caught in the *pinch* of inflation – Nancy Sandrof> **Strait,** often in its plural **straits,** applies to a troublesome or dangerous situation from which escape is not easy or simple <this disagreeable companion had . . . assisted him in the *strait* of the day – Charles Dickens> <we were in desperate *straits* without food or water and with no way to reach help> **Crisis** applies to a juncture or pass whose outcome will make a decisive difference for better or worse <unless the states enact more effective . . . taxes . . . fiscal *crises* will evolve into fiscal disaster – Trevor Armbrister> <the political situation went into *crisis* stage – Tad Szulc>

junk – see DISCARD

jurisdiction – see POWER 3

just **1** see FAIR *ant* unjust
2 see UPRIGHT

justice, equity *shared meaning* : the act, practice, or obligation of rendering to another what is his or its due. **Justice,** the wider ranging term, may apply to an ideal abstraction <there can be no law and order without *justice* and compassion – Jeanne L. Noble> or to a quality of mind reflecting this <the far-seeing love that punished and praised with that calm *justice* which children so keenly appreciate – Margaret Deland> or to a quality of inherent truth and fairness <pointed out, with equal *justice,* that . . . there are good businesses and bad – D. W. Brogan> or to the treatment due one who has transgressed a law or who seeks relief when wronged or threatened <at the present time . . . there is more danger that criminals will escape *justice* than that they will be subjected to tyranny – O. W. Holmes †1935> or to the system of courts of law <*justice* and administration are directly connected with whatever governs – Hilaire Belloc> **Equity** stresses the notions of fairness and impartiality and implies a justice that transcends the strict letter of the law and is in keeping with what is reasonable rather than with what is merely legal. Thus, a court of *equity* deals with the adjudication and settlement of obscure and unusual cases where abstract justice might not be truly dealt out by strict application of the limitations of the written law <in informal terms, a law case is one where the courts have only to decide who is right; an *equity* case is one where the courts have to decide not only who is right, but go on to say what must be done – *Science*> In its more general use *equity* implies a justice meted out with strict impartiality, be it by law or by the exigencies of circumstances <justice or *equity* and freedom or liberty are the two evidences of human progress and hope – *New Republic*> <the Golden Rule is one [of the great principles], and it is sheer *equity* that it commands – Donald Harrington>

justify **1** see MAINTAIN

2 justify, warrant *shared meaning* : to be what constitutes sufficient grounds (as for doing, using, saying, or preferring something). **Justify** may be preferred when the stress is on providing grounds that satisfy conscience as well as reason; often it implies that in the absence of justification the thing in question would be looked on with disapproval <he deplores what he considers the partially *justified* effeminate public image of the male ballet dancer – *Current Biog.*> <an investment of scarce time can be *justified* in acquiring basic language skills – H. A. Simon> <we know that the pursuit of good ends does not *justify* the employment of bad means – Aldous Huxley> **Warrant** is especially appropriate when the emphasis is on something that requires an explanation or reason rather than an excuse and is likely to suggest support by the authority of precedent, experience, or logic <the deposits have shown enough ore to *warrant* further testing> <the history and appearance clearly *warrant* such assumption – H. G. Armstrong> <they could come out farther [from under the bed] whenever the situation *warranted*, or could retreat wholly out of sight – Robert Francis>

keen **1** see EAGER

2 see SHARP *ant* blunt

keep **1 keep, observe, celebrate, commemorate** *shared meaning* : to notice or honor a day, occasion, or deed. **Keep** is weak in emphasis and may suggest merely a customary or wonted notice without anything untoward or inappropriate <you'll find yourself with . . . no schedules to *keep*, no deadlines to meet – *N.Y. Times*> <his build was all compact, for force, well-knit . . . he *kept* no Lent to make him meager – John Masefield> **Observe** implies punctilious performing of required acts or ceremonies <knowing that the usual ritual would have to be *observed* – T. B. Costain> <his family *observed* Passover with the utmost strictness> **Celebrate** in modern nonreligious context is likely to suggest notice of an occasion by festivity or indulgence <as though he had had a drink or two – which indeed he might have had in reality, to *celebrate* the occasion – Joseph Conrad> <they *celebrated* their anniversary with a family picnic> **Commemorate** implies observances that call to mind the purpose of a celebration; thus, we *celebrate* Christmas by religious ceremonies that *commemorate* the birth of Christ <their six children all died in early youth, and the Bradleys determined to *commemorate* them by founding an educational institution – Marie A. Kasten> *ant* break

2 keep, retain, detain, withhold, reserve *shared meaning* : to hold in one's possession or under one's control. **Keep**, a very general and neutral term, is wide in range of idiomatic use but carries few special implications. Thus, one *keeps* a secret by not sharing it; one *keeps* a house by taking its care under one's control; one *keeps* quiet by controlling one's impulse to talk or make a noise; one *keeps* a car when one owns it and controls its use. **Retain** implies continued keeping, especially as against threatened loss or seizure <Churchill wanted to win the war, *retain* the Empire, restore the balance of power in Europe – S. E. Ambrose> <in the following month's election the Conservatives *retained* power – *Current Biog.*> **Detain** implies a keeping through a delay in letting go <*detain* a ship in quarantine> <[the cat] let the rat run about his legs, but made no effort to *detain* him there – Georgina Grahame> **Withhold** implies restraint in letting go or a refusal to let go, often for good reason <each payday the employer *withholds* money from the pay of each employee and sends it directly to the government – S. E. Dimond & E. F. Pflieger> <forbid who will, none shall from me *withhold* longer thy offered good – John Milton> **Reserve** implies a keeping in store for other or future need that precludes present release <strain off the juice and *reserve* it for use in the sauce> <the force of will which had enabled her to *reserve* the fund intact – Arnold Bennett> <*reserve* the right to change one's mind> ***ant*** relinquish

kick – see OBJECT

kill, slay, murder, assassinate, dispatch, execute *shared meaning* : to deprive of life. **Kill**, a very general term, states the fact and in itself implies nothing about the agency, the method, or the purpose <plants *killed* by an early frost> <sheep-*killing* dogs> <the boy was *killed* by a fall> **Slay** implies killing by force or in wantonness; uncommon in spoken English, the word is often used in writing to suggest a dramatic quality <though he *slay* me, yet will I trust in him – *Job* 13:15 (AV)> <created programs to aid education of Negroes in the *slain* civil rights leader's memory – *Amer. School Board Jour.*> **Murder** implies a motive and, often, premeditation and imputes to the act a criminal character; it is the exact word to use with reference to one person killing another either in passion or in cold blood <*murder* a relative for his money> or with reference to a comparable destroying <the civil war and the foreign one have contrived this summer to *murder* liberalism – Frank Joyce> **Assassinate** applies to deliberate killing openly or secretly but for impersonal motives; it precisely describes the killing of a public person by a hireling or an opponent of his policies <*assassinate* a candidate for office> <hire a man to *assassinate* a rival> **Dispatch** implies speed and directness in putting to death and may replace any of the foregoing terms when this notion is to be stressed <and the company shall . . . *dispatch* them with their swords – *Ezek* 23:47 (AV)> The term is distinctively applicable to the killing of an animal by a human for reasons of necessity or mercy <*dispatched* the injured dog with a single shot> **Execute** specifically applies to the carrying out of a sentence of death <*execute* a convicted assassin>

kind *n* – see TYPE

kind *adj* **kind, kindly, benign, benignant** *shared meaning* : showing or having a gentle considerate nature. *Kind* and *kindly* both imply sympathy and humaneness and interest in the welfare of others; distinctively, **kind** can stress a disposition to be sympathetic and helpful <the human capacity to give and to receive love, to be *kind,* to be empathic – Jeanne L. Noble> <they are . . . not *kind,* only sentimental – G. B. Shaw> while **kindly** is likely to stress the expression of a benevolent, sympathetic, or helpful nature, mood, or impulse <one must be *kindly* to those students who have existed on the pabulum of television and Hollywood – Charles Clerc> <ring in the valiant man and free, the larger heart, the *kindlier* hand – Alfred Tennyson> **Benign** and **benignant** stress mildness, serenity, and mercifulness but are likely to suggest real or assumed superiority when they describe persons or their acts, utterances, or policies <I believe that

the white attitude toward blacks is generally *benign* except when black claims intrude on the majority's privileges or peace of mind – W. H. Ferry> <his face was fatherly and *benign* and his eyes twinkled with friendship – John Steinbeck> <strange peace and rest fell on me from the presence of a *benignant* Spirit standing near – E. R. Sill> ***ant*** unkind

kindle – see LIGHT ***ant*** smother, stifle

kindly – see KIND *adj* ***ant*** unkindly, acrid (*of temper, attitude, comments*)

kindred – see RELATED ***ant*** alien

knock – see TAP

knotty – see COMPLEX

know, believe, think *shared meaning* : to hold something in one's mind as true or as being what it purports to be. These words are often used interchangeably with little thought of their basic signification but it is possible to employ them with discrimination so as to convey quite distinct ideas. In such use **know** stresses assurance and implies sound logical or factual information as its basis; **believe,** too, stresses assurance but implies trust and faith (as in a higher power) rather than evidence as its basis; while **think** suggests probability rather than firm assurance and implies mental appraisal of pertinent circumstances as its basis. Thus, "I *know* he is telling the truth" implies such factual information in the hands of the speaker as fully confirms the questioned statement; "I *believe* he is telling the truth" can imply such knowledge of the character and personality of the one challenged as to inspire perfect trust in his probity; "I *think* he is telling the truth" implies no more than an acceptance of the probability of truth in light of the circumstances <there's always a reason for everything, and if we don't *know* it, we can find it out – Theodore Sturgeon> <it comes down to a matter of subjective reality, or what some people call faith. If you *believe* firmly that the mutilation of a doll . . . will result in your own mutilation, well, that's what will happen – Theodore Sturgeon> <attacking a block of problems once *thought* of as insoluble – Norman Cousins> <while I *think* I have kept myself clean . . . I am struck with the enormous continuing pressures to which politicians are subjected – Paul Douglas> <every man *knows* he must die; many men *believe* in an afterlife; some men *think* life is not worth living>

knowing – see INTELLIGENT

knowledge, learning, erudition, scholarship *shared meaning* : what is known or can be known by the individual or by mankind in general. **Knowledge** applies equally to a body of facts gathered (as by study, observation, or experiment) or to a body of ideas acquired by inference from facts <the inventor of the radio . . . had the advantage of accumulated *knowledge* – J. W. Krutch> <wisdom requires *knowledge,* but . . . does not flow automatically from it . . . *knowledge* is neutral. It may be used for good or evil purposes – R. M. Hutchins> **Learning** specifically applies to knowledge won by long and close application <the books chosen represent significant contributions to *learning* which go beyond narrow interpretations of scholarly disciplines – *Key Reporter*> <help the visitor improve the quality of his *learning* and his appreciation of the American past – Barnes Riznik> **Erudition** appropriately describes the possession of recondite, profound, or sometimes merely bookish knowledge <recall Socrates' irony and humility and Protagoras' blind pride in his own *erudition,* and his flat-footed self-assertion – Stringfellow Barr> <affirmed . . . that a good Christian could not drink the health of a companion, an idea he developed with ponderous *erudition* under seven topical headings – Gerald Carson> **Scholarship** implies possession of the knowledge characteristic of a trained scholar; the term usually suggests deep learning and mastery in detail of a field of study

<although it was widely praised for its *scholarship,* some reviewers felt that the book was too subjective – *Current Biog.*> <*scholarship* in the arts . . . has a surer place among the humanities than even history and philosophy – R. F. Arragon> ***ant*** ignorance

labor – see WORK

lack, want, need, require *shared meaning* **:** to be without something essential or greatly desired. **Lack** may imply either an absence or a shortage in supply <good counselors *lack* no clients – Shak.> <the cheeks were just a trifle *lacking* in color to attain the exacting standards of beauty – Ludwig Bemelmans> **Want** adds to *lack* the implication of needing or desiring urgently <everything was dingy and *wanted* paint – F. W. Crofts> <in sheer courage they were a match for any troops in the world, and . . . it *wanted* the deftest adversary to withstand their terrible swords – G. B. Sansom> **Need** stresses urgent necessity more than absence or shortage <like the hotels of many small towns, the Dorset Hotel is bigger than it *need* be – John Barth> <the kind of writing . . . that lifts fiction onto a plane where it *need* not fear comparison with any other art – Forrest Reid> <all children *need* to succeed – John Holt> **Require** is often interchangeable with *need* but it may heighten the implication of urgent necessity or even suggest imperativeness of needing or desiring <great acts *require* great means of enterprise – John Milton> <the Doctor . . . *required* a few days of complete rest – Charles Dickens>

laconic – see CONCISE ***ant*** verbose

lady – see FEMALE

ladylike – see FEMININE

lag – see DELAY 2

lament – see DEPLORE ***ant*** exult, rejoice

languor – see LETHARGY ***ant*** alacrity

lank – see LEAN

lanky – see LEAN ***ant*** burly

lapse *n* – see ERROR

lapse *vb* **lapse, relapse, backslide** *shared meaning* **:** to fall back from a higher or better state or condition into a lower or poorer. **Lapse** usually presupposes attainment of a high level (as of morals, manners, or habits) or acceptance of a high standard (as of rectitude, accuracy, or accomplishment) and implies an abrupt departure from this level or standard that may reflect culpability or grave weakness or, sometimes, mere absentmindedness <the moment his attention is relaxed . . . he will *lapse* into bad Shakespearean verse – T. S. Eliot> <*lapses* into addiction again at the first temptation – *Time*> **Relapse** presupposes definite improvement or an advance (as toward health or toward a higher state) and implies a severe, often dangerous reversal of direction <the white community tended to *relapse* into complacency after it had accepted the surface requirements of desegregation – H. S. Ashmore> <man's eternal tendency to *relapse* into apathy and atavism – Douglas Stewart> **Backslide,** similar in presuppositions and implications to *relapse,* is restricted almost entirely to moral and religious lapses; consequently, it tends more than the other words to suggest unfaithfulness to duty or to allegiance or to principles once professed <did not I . . . *backslide* into intemperance and folly – Frederick Marryat> <it was unnecessary to apply constant pressure to reform the sinners or to keep the saved from *backsliding* – J. K. Galbraith>

larceny – see THEFT
large, big, great *shared meaning* : above average in magnitude. **Large** may be preferred when dimensions or extent or capacity or quantity or amount is being considered <a *large* hall> <a *large* basket> <a *large* meal> <a *large* allowance> **Big,** on the other hand, is especially appropriate when the emphasis is on bulk or mass or weight or volume <a *big* book> <a *big* pile of hay> <the box is too *big* to carry> <so *big* already – so enormous in fact – that we named him Monstro, and he padded about like a furry whale – *Atlantic*> **Great** may sometimes imply physical magnitude, usually with connotions of wonder, surprise, or awe <the *great* canyon cut by the Colorado River> but it more often implies magnitude in degree <*great* kindness> <a *great* surprise>
In extended use the words are equally discriminable. **Large** tends to stress breadth, comprehensiveness, or generosity <becomes involved in some very *large* questions – Marston Bates> <a man of action and contemplation, capable of sin, *large* enough for good – Norman Mailer> **Big** is more likely to suggest impressiveness or importance than solidity or great worth <it is one of the disadvantages of *big* science . . . that the availability of huge sums attracts a swarm of elbowing and contentious men – L. C. Eiseley> <he didn't expect to work here all his life . . . pretty soon he'd have a new job and would be a *big* man – Harvey Granite> **Great** suggests eminence, distinction, or supremacy< <I never dreamed she had the *great,* soaring, spectacular voice she reveals – Norton Mockridge> <the good qualities and senses of women, which he assumes to be *greater* and quicker than those of men – Bonamy Dobrée> <one of the *greatest* singers of our time – Jule Styne> ***ant*** small
lassitude – see LETHARGY ***ant*** vigor
last *vb* – see CONTINUE ***ant*** fleet
last *adj* **last, final, terminal, eventual, ultimate** *shared meaning* : following all relevant others (as in time, in order, or in importance). **Last** applies to something that comes at the end of a series <the *last* page of a book> but need not imply that the series is ended or stopped <the *last* page I read that night> <fairest of stars, *last* in the train of night – John Milton> **Final** applies to what definitely closes a series, process, or progress <the *final* event on the program> <a *final* decree of divorce> <judgment that is *final,* that settles a matter – John Dewey> **Terminal** may indicate a limiting (as of extension, growth, or development) <the *terminal* stage of a disease> <as fewer and fewer people find solace in religion as a buffer between themselves and the *terminal* moment [of life] – Stanley Kubrick> **Eventual** applies to something bound to occur as the result of causes already in operation and approaches *final* in implying a definite ending of an operative sequence of preliminary events <his task was to evaluate war damage and draw up plans for the *eventual* rebuilding of Greece – *Current Biog.*> **Ultimate** implies either the last element or stage of a long process or a stage beyond which further progress or change is impossible <we pray, we hope that he will prevail in this his *ultimate* struggle [with death] – E. M. Kennedy> <his attitude is . . . to take the answers given . . . as absolute, *ultimate,* and final – J. W. Davis> ***ant*** first
late **1** see DEAD
2 see MODERN
3 see TARDY ***ant*** early, punctual, prompt
latent, dormant, quiescent, potential, abeyant *shared meaning* : not now manifest or showing signs of existence or activity. **Latent** implies concealment and applies to something that is not yet in sight or action but may become

so in the future <his sinister qualities, formerly *latent,* quickened into life> <*latent* heat is heat energy not manifested by a change in temperature> **Dormant** suggests sleeping and describes something once active but now inactive though capable of renewed activity <a *dormant* volcano> <*dormant* plants that will sprout anew when warmed by spring sun and rains> **Quiescent** emphasizes the fact of present inactivity without necessary implications about the past or future <if only we could persuade ourselves to remain *quiescent* when we are happy! – Richard Jefferies> <a flare-up in the now *quiescent* struggle between the two Chinas – *New Republic*> **Potential** applies to something that at the time in question does not show such being, nature, or effect as is indicated but that has the capacity for showing it in the future <technology might be deemed an evil, because evil is unquestionably *potential* in it – E. G. Mesthene> <a growing tendency to disastrously underestimate the *potential* strength of the United States – W. L. Shirer> **Abeyant** (or in common predicate use, **in abeyance**) implies a suspension of activity or active existence and commonly connotes likelihood of recurrence <a lurking and *abeyant* fear – Edith Wharton> <the hereditary strain of Puritan energy was clearly *in abeyance* – George Eliot> ***ant*** patent

laughable, ludicrous, ridiculous, comic, comical, droll, funny *shared meaning* : provoking laughter or mirth. **Laughable** is applicable to anything that excites laughter whether intentionally or not <gave a *laughable* account of the meeting> <you would probably find our misadventure *laughable*> **Ludicrous** suggests such absurdity or preposterousness as incites not only laughter but scorn or sometimes pity <enacted a scene as *ludicrous* as it was pitiable – Charles Kingsley> <history was so falsified in the new textbooks and by the teachers . . . that it became *ludicrous* – W. L. Shirer> **Ridiculous** applies to what excites derision because of extreme foolishness, absurdity, or contemptibility <to be made *ridiculous* before her increased his humiliation – W. S. Maugham> *Comic* and *comical* are sometimes interchangeable, but **comic** may distinctively apply to what calls for consideration and gives rise to thoughtful, or sometimes wry, mirth <he . . . has a remarkable *comic* sense. He can prick the bubble of any illusion – John Erskine †1951> <satire depends for its *comic* effect on the logical development of an illogical situation> while **comical** can describe what evokes spontaneous and unrestrained laughter <references to taboo facts were forgivable and *comical* in children, odious in adults – Herman Wouk> **Droll** suggests laughable qualities arising from oddness or quaintness or deliberate waggishness <some fat friar of their number, looking all the *droller* in his bare feet for the spectacles on his nose – W. D. Howells> **Funny,** interchangeable with any of the other terms, may sometimes suggest queerness or strangeness as the basis of a laughable quality <screaming this stuff about the white devils and the great black man. This was *funny,* because Alley was a very light-skinned guy – Claude Brown>

lavish – see PROFUSE ***ant*** sparing

law 1 law, rule, regulation, precept, statute, ordinance, canon *shared meaning* : a principle governing action or procedure. **Law** implies imposition by a sovereign authority and the obligation of obedience by all subject to that authority <the establishment of settled communities requires the establishment of *law*> **Rule** suggests closer relation to individual conduct and may imply restriction, whether prescribed or self-imposed for the sake of an immediate end <the *rules* of a game> <it's a *rule* in our house that the first one home sets the table> **Regulation** is sometimes equal to *rule* but usually carries a stronger implication of prescription by authority in order

to control an organization or situation; thus, *rules* of the road are an informal body of customs adhered to by sensible drivers in the interests of safety and courtesy, but traffic *regulations* are imposed by a governing body to control the flow and safety of traffic. **Precept** is likely to imply generality in the statement and authority in the source; often it suggests something enjoined by teaching that is advisory rather than obligatory <by *precept* and by practice he proclaimed the lofty solitude of the individual soul – Havelock Ellis> **Statute** applies to a law enacted by a legislative body <the Court . . . makes *statute* law or unmakes it by interpreting what the Congress *meant* to say – R. G. Tugwell> **Ordinance** applies to a local law, especially one enacted by a municipal council <laws enacted by . . . local legislative bodies . . . are called *ordinances,* and such legislation must conform to the federal and state constitutions and state statutes – L. B. Howard> **Canon,** basically applicable to a law of a church, in common use applies to a principle or rule of behavior or procedure generally accepted as a valid guide <a violent reaction against accepted *canons* of decency in life – C. H. Grandgent>
2 see HYPOTHESIS

lawful, legal, legitimate, licit *shared meaning* : being in accordance with law. **Lawful** may imply conformity with law of any sort (as natural, divine, canon, or common) and may come close in meaning to *allowable* or *permissible* <all things are *lawful* unto me, but all things are not expedient – *1 Cor* 6:12 (AV)> or to *rightful* or *proper* <the *lawful* heir> <William desired to reign not as a conqueror but as a *lawful* king – J. R. Green> **Legal** implies a reference to law as it appears in the statute books and is administered by the courts; thus, the *lawful* owner of a piece of property is one whose *legal* right to it is certain. Often *legal* stresses conformity with or sanction by law; thus, a *legal* marriage is one carried out with all the observances called for by law; a *lawful* marriage is one to which no compelling *legal* impediment (as close consanguinity) exists. **Legitimate** implies a legal right (as applied to a child, heir, or successor) or one supported by tradition, custom, or accepted standards (as of authenticity, propriety, or admissibility) <he had seven *legitimate* children and unnumbered bastards> <opinions . . . can differ widely and still be *legitimate* as long as they respect factual truth – Hannah Arendt> <language is a *legitimate* part of the subject matter or content of English – A. H. Marckwardt> **Licit** usually implies strict conformity to the provisions of the law in respect to the way something is to be carried out and therefore applies especially to what is regulated by law <the state is given its right to determine what is *licit* and illicit for property owners in the use of their possessions – *Commonweal*> ***ant*** unlawful

lawyer, counselor, barrister, counsel, advocate, attorney, solicitor *shared meaning* : one authorized to practice law. **Lawyer** applies to anyone in the profession. **Counselor** applies to one who accepts court cases and gives advice on legal problems. **Barrister,** the British equivalent of *counselor,* emphasizes court pleading which in English practice is permitted in higher courts only to barristers. **Counsel** can be equivalent to *counselor* but is typically used collectively to designate a group of lawyers acting for a legal cause in court. **Advocate** is similar in implication to *counselor* and *barrister,* but it is used chiefly in countries (as Scotland) where the legal system is based on Roman law. **Attorney** is often used interchangeably with *lawyer,* but in precise use it denotes a lawyer who acts as a legal agent for a client (as in conveying property, settling wills, or defending or prosecuting a civil law case). **Solicitor** is the British term corresponding to *attorney* with, however, emphasis on the transaction of legal business for a client as distinct from actual court pleading <[he] had two batteries of defense *lawyers,* divided – roughly according to the British distinction between *solicitors* and *barristers* – among *attorneys* and *advocates* – E. J. Kahn>

lax **1** see LOOSE ***ant*** rigid

2 see NEGLIGENT ***ant*** strict, stringent

lazy, indolent, slothful *shared meaning* **:** not easily aroused to action or activity. **Lazy** suggests a disinclination to effort or work and is likely to imply idleness or dawdling, even when supposedly at work <rubbing their sleepy eyes with *lazy* wrists – John Keats> <driving home his points so as to make them plain to the *laziest* coffeehouse reader – Bonamy Dobrée> **Indolent** implies an habitual love of ease and a settled dislike of movement or activity <a whole set of wealthy *indolent* women . . . who got up at noon and spent the rest of the day trying to relieve their boredom – Roald Dahl> **Slothful** implies a temperamental inability to act promptly or speedily when promptness or speed is called for <be not *slothful,* but followers of them who through faith and patience inherit the promises – *Heb* 6:12 (AV)> <not despondency, not *slothful* anguish, is what you now require, – but effort – Nathaniel Hawthorne>

lead – see GUIDE ***ant*** follow

lean *vb* – see SLANT

lean *adj* **lean, spare, lank, lanky, gaunt, rawboned, scrawny, skinny** *shared meaning* **:** thin because of absence of superfluous flesh. **Lean** stresses lack of fat and of rounded contours <*lean* as a greyhound – W. M. Thackeray> <a small, *lean,* wiry man with sunk cheeks weathered to a tan – John Masefield> **Spare** suggests leanness from abstemious living or constant exercise <the *spare,* alert and jaunty figure that one often finds in army men – Thomas Wolfe> **Lank** implies tallness as well as leanness <meager and *lank* with fasting grown, and nothing left but skin and bone – Jonathan Swift> **Lanky** adds a suggestion of loose-jointed awkwardness <a *lanky* youth, all arms and legs> <that tall, blonde, *lanky* girl who had followed him about – Louis Auchincloss> **Gaunt** stresses lack of sufficient flesh to conceal the bones and often connotes undernourishment or overwork <her bony visage – *gaunt* and deadly wan – William Wordsworth> <always a very lean boy, but now he is looking positively *gaunt* – Compton Mackenzie> **Rawboned** is sometimes equivalent to *gaunt,* but more often it is applied to persons of coarse, ungainly frame and without suggestion of undernourishment <a long, gawky, *rawboned* Yorkshireman – Rudyard Kipling> <tall, lean, stooping, *rawboned,* with coarse features – V. L. Parrington> *Scrawny* and *skinny* imply extreme thinness, but **scrawny** is likely to suggest slightness or a shrunken meager quality <a thin, almost *scrawny* little thing, most ungainly and sharp in the face – John Barth> while **skinny** tends to suggest a stringy fleshless condition such as may be associated with a deficiency of vitality or severe malnutrition <those *skinny* hands of his, withered beyond their years – Rex Ingamells> ***ant*** fleshy

leaning, propensity, proclivity, penchant, flair *shared meaning* **:** a strong instinct or liking for something or sometimes someone. One has a **leaning** *toward* something when it exerts a definite but not decisive attraction upon him <he had a *leaning* toward the law but decided to study medicine for practical reasons> One has a **propensity** (usually *toward* or *for* something to *to do* something) when he has an innate or inherent and often uncontrollable longing <all had dangerous, violent, or criminal *propensities* – M. F. A. Montagu> <the inveterate *propensity* of their husbands to linger about the village tavern – Washington Irving> One has a **proclivity** (typically *for* or *towards* something or *to do* something) when he is prone to something, and especially something undesirable or evil, not only by natural inclination but by habitual indulgence <the tragic *proclivity* of each side to fulfill the other's worst prophecies – Robert Scheer> <the French *proclivity* for omitting footnotes that indicate the source of various quotations and pertinent details – Helen A. B. Rivlin> One has a **penchant** *for* something when it has an irresistible attraction for him <he is said to have a bad temper, a *penchant* for getting into fights – *Current Biog.*> <the philosopher's *penchant* for grotesque exaggeration – W. L. Shirer> One has a **flair** *for* something when he has such an instinctive attraction as seems to lead him to it by the very nature of his being <not everyone has a *flair* for style> Often *flair* additionally suggests skill, acumen, and an innate comprehension of the area of interest <his nimble mind, affable manners and *flair* for politics impressed both the generals and the politicians – W. L. Shirer> ***ant*** distaste

learn – see DISCOVER

learned, scholarly, erudite *shared meaning* : possessing or manifesting unusually wide and deep knowledge. **Learned** implies academic knowledge gained by long study and research and is applicable to persons, their associations, or their writings and professional publications <the *learned* journals> <members of a *learned* society> <he is, in the true sense of the term, *learned.* He reads Greek and Latin easily. He can recite poetry in seven languages – *Book-of-the-Month Club News*> **Scholarly** implies learning and applies particularly to persons who have attained mastery of a field of knowledge or to their utterances, ideas, or writings; it carries less suggestion than *learned* of the purely academic context and may connote creativity and advanced critical competence <never academic – still less pedantic – but always *scholarly;* with the effect of profound learning ever so lightly worn – Ronald Storrs> <a *scholarly* study of the causes of war> **Erudite,** sometimes interchangeable with *learned* and *scholarly,* can imply a love of learning for its own sake, a taste for out-of-the-way knowledge, or even mere pedanticism <that odd assortment of *erudite* but unbalanced philosophers, historians and teachers who captured the German mind – W. L. Shirer> <knows about . . . sea fighting in a fashion too informed to be *erudite* – R. J. Purcell>

learning – see KNOWLEDGE

lease – see HIRE

leave *vb* – see GO

leave *n* – see PERMISSION

legal – see LAWFUL ***ant*** illegal

legend – see MYTH

legendary – see FICTITIOUS

legerity – see CELERITY ***ant*** deliberateness, sluggishness

legitimate – see LAWFUL ***ant*** illegitimate, arbitrary (*powers, means*)

lengthen – see EXTEND ***ant*** shorten

lenient – see SOFT ***ant*** caustic

lenity – see MERCY ***ant*** severity

less, lesser, smaller, fewer *shared meaning* : not as great (as in size, number, worth, or significance) as some expressed or implied other. In spite of the common element of meaning these terms are rarely interchangeable without loss of precision. **Less** in its most characteristic use applies to matters of degree, value, or amount, is opposed to *more,* and chiefly modifies collective nouns or nouns denoting a mass or abstract whole <the university guarantees members of the faculty no *less* freedom than that guaranteed them by the nation – W. S. Coffin Jr.> <the moon gives *less* light than the sun> <we always end up with *less* money than we need> *Less* is also applied to matters of number, but the usage is decried by many careful writers and speakers. **Lesser** applies especially to matters of quality, worth, or significance and is opposed to *greater* or *major* <God made ... the *lesser* light to rule the night – *Gen* 1:16 (AV)> <it would assure ... that more urgent needs were met at the expense of *lesser* ones – L. J. Walinsky> In vernacular names of plants and animals *lesser* specifically implies distinction based on relative smallness of size <the *lesser* yellowlegs> <the *lesser* celandine> **Smaller** is applicable especially to matters of size, dimension, or quantity and is opposed to *larger* <the need for *smaller* cars> <use a *smaller* amount of seasoning next time> **Fewer** applies specifically to matters of number and therefore regularly modifies a plural noun. Thus, "he has *fewer* (not *less*) spendable dollars this year," but "he has *less* (not *fewer*) money to spend than he used to." Occasionally the distinction between quantity and number is obscured and either *fewer* or *less* is appropriate <seasonal workers who average *fewer* (or *less*) than six months' work in a year> ***ant*** more

lessen – see DECREASE

lesser – see LESS ***ant*** major

let **1** see HIRE

2 let, allow, permit, suffer *shared meaning* : not to forbid or prevent. **Let** may imply a positive giving of permission but more often implies failure to prevent either through inadvertence and negligence or through lack of power or effective authority <[he] did not awake easily, and so was *let* to snore on – Robert McAlmon> <will your mother *let* you come?> *Allow* and *permit* imply power or authority to prohibit or prevent; but **allow** may imply little more than a forbearing to exert this power, whereas **permit** implies express signification of willingness <the freedom of conscience *allowed* dissenters, the tolerance extended to all creeds – R. A. Billington> <found it necessary ... to apply for episcopal dispensation to *permit* the marriage – W. L. Shirer> **Suffer,** increasingly uncommon in this sense, can be a close synonym of *allow* <*suffer* little children to come unto me – *Lk* 18:16 (AV)> but distinctively it may imply indifference <the eagle *suffers* little birds to sing – Shak.> or reluctance <she *suffered* herself to be led to the tiny enclosure where ... other generations had been buried – S. E. White>

lethal – see DEADLY

lethargic, sluggish, torpid, comatose *shared meaning* : deficient in alertness or activity. **Lethargic** can describe a constitutional, a transitory, or a pathological state of drowsy apathy <the *lethargic* atmosphere of an apathetic people, hopeless and helpless to direct their own destinies – *Atlantic*> <after the huge dinner he dozed in *lethargic* content> **Sluggish** implies conditions which create stagnation or inability to move or function at a normal or expected rate <a *sluggish* market> <the river was very low and *sluggish*> <I want no *sluggish* languor, no bovine complacency – Warren Weaver> **Torpid** suggests a state like the benumbed state of a hibernating animal and is likely to imply loss of power to feel and to exert oneself <Oxford was *torpid* also, droning along in its eighteenth-century grooves – Van Wyck Brooks> <still Richard was *torpid;* could not think or move – Virginia Woolf> **Comatose** basically implies being in a state of profound insensibility from disease or injury <the accident victim remained *comatose* for several days> but it can also imply stultification and lack of intellectual sensibility (as from lethargy or disinterest) <the report seemed to us too woolly and evasive to satisfy any but the most amiably *comatose* inspection – *Times Lit. Supp.*> ***ant*** energetic

lethargy, languor, lassitude, stupor, torpor *shared meaning* : mental and physical inertness. **Lethargy** implies an aversion to activity that may be constitutional or acquired, permanent or transitory, normal or pathological <the state of apathy and *lethargy* into which they had been thrust by their stunning defeat – *Political Science Quarterly*> <the hot moist air of the tropics spreads a feeling of *lethargy* and indolence over everything – G. H. Reed b. 1887> **Languor** usually implies such inertia as results from soft living, an enervating climate, or amorous emotion <certain *languor* in the air hinted at an early summer – James Purdy> <she is characterized essentially by *languor.* Her most familiar posture is on a bed or divan – Wallace Fowlie> **Lassitude** stresses listlessness or indifference and may suggest an underlying fatigue or weakness as a cause <Flora took advantage of her *lassitude* to impose fresh will upon her cousin's flaccid one – Stella D. Gibbons> <reforms are bogged in bureaucratic *lassitude* – *New Republic*> **Stupor** implies a deadening of the mind and senses by or as if by shock, narcotics, or intoxicants <the *stupor* of sleep still deadened his countenance; he looked dense – J. T. Farrell> <had collapsed for the moment in a *stupor* of pain – Marguerite Steen> **Torpor** implies a state of suspended animation (as of a hibernating animal) or a comparable lack of vigor and responsiveness <a weariness of hard lights and empty pavements, a frozen *torpor* broken only occasionally by the footfalls of some prowler – Thomas Wolfe> <a conscience that aches amid widespread moral *torpor* – W. H. Ferry> ***ant*** vigor

level, flat, plane, even, smooth *shared meaning* : having a surface like that of a calm sea. **Level** applies specifically to a horizontal surface conforming to the curvature of the earth or to the line from horizon to horizon <a *level* garden plot> <be sure the clock is perfectly *level*> **Flat** applies to a surface free of prominences or depressions whether it lies in a horizontal plane or not <the sides of a pyramid are all *flat*> <there is little *flat* ground in this mountainous region> **Plane** applies to a real or imaginary flat surface in which a straight line between any two points on it lies continuously in it <the *plane* surfaces of a crystal> **Even** stresses lack of breaks or irregularities in a surface or line but does not imply the horizontal, the straight, or the plane <the frigate was on an *even* keel – Frederick Marryat> <learn to sew an *even* seam> **Smooth** implies a relatively perfect flatness or evenness especially of surface <a *smooth* well-kept lawn> <the typical group learning curve is a *smooth* arc – Tom Trabasso>

levity – see LIGHTNESS ***ant*** gravity

liable **1** see RESPONSIBLE

2 liable, open, exposed, subject, prone, susceptible, sensitive *shared meaning* : being in a position where something stated or implied is likely to happen. **Liable** may be chosen when the thing one may incur is the result of one's obligation to authority, one's state of life, or the action of forces beyond one's control <the pastor must set an example, he must illustrate his morality in public; and this is *liable* to result in hypocrisy – Edmund Wilson> <one of the most horrible diseases to which mankind is *liable* – C. W. Eliot> **Open** stresses ease of access and a lack of protective barriers rather than the probability of the indicated development <the statistical data used are *open* to challenge> <another modern tendency in education ... perhaps somewhat more *open* to question – Bertrand Russell> **Exposed** suggests lack of resistance or powers of protection against something actually present and threatening <*exposed* to temptation> <must do something to protect her *exposed* northeast frontier – Geoffrey Godsell> **Subject** implies an openness to something that must be borne or undergone <a

delicate boy, *subject* to bronchitis – D. H. Lawrence> **Prone** stresses natural tendency or propensity to incur something <the system . . . would necessarily become more and more *prone* to accidents – Harvey Wheeler> <the governments of states, being human, are as *prone* as any other human beings to commit crimes and sins – A. J. Toynbee> **Susceptible** stresses the existence in one's makeup of factors that make one unusually open to something, especially something deleterious <wheat tends to be very *susceptible* to smut – C. C. Turnas> <he was still easily wounded and *susceptible* to jealousy – Pearl Buck> <the destructive potential of a mutant parasite in a *susceptible* host> **Sensitive** implies a readiness to respond to or be influenced by forces or stimuli too slight to affect the average individual <the teacher must be *sensitive* to varying degrees of writing aptitude in his pupils – R. K. Corbin> <a remarkable tutor . . . who . . . imprinted on his receptive mind and *sensitive* soul the glories of militant, conquering Prussia – W. L. Shirer> ***ant*** exempt, immune

liberal **1 liberal, generous, bountiful, munificent** *shared meaning* : giving freely and unstintingly. **Liberal** suggests openhandedness in the giver and largeness in the thing that is given <he is *liberal* in praise to those who try hard> <his will made a *liberal* provision for his widow> **Generous** emphasizes warmhearted readiness to give rather than the size or importance of the gift <she was *generous* in her praise – Norman Mailer> <*generous* beyond the dreary bounds of common sense – Osbert Sitwell> <they are . . . not *generous,* only propitiatory – G. B. Shaw> **Bountiful** suggests lavish or unremitting generosity in providing or giving <he is a worthy gentleman . . . as *bountiful* as mines of India – Shak.> <the school . . . , whose every aspect reflects his *bountiful* temperament – *New Yorker*> **Munificent** suggests splendid or princely lavishness in giving <had been most *munificent* to his soldiers. He had doubled their ordinary pay. He had shared the spoils of his conquests with them – J. A. Froude> ***ant*** close

2 liberal, progressive, advanced, radical *shared meaning* : freed from or opposed to what is orthodox, established, or conservative. **Liberal** implies a greater or less degree of emancipation from convention, tradition, or dogma and may suggest either commendable pragmatism and tolerance or reprehensible extremism and irresponsibility <used his position . . . to keep *liberal* legislation from reaching the floor of the House – T. P. Murphy> **Progressive,** usually a relative term, is likely to imply a comparison with what is backward or reactionary and a readiness to forsake old methods and beliefs for new that hold more promise <until a few decades ago the average American state was an economically sound, politically *progressive* entity – Trevor Armbrister> <one *progressive* publisher is now experimenting with plastic bindings – *Third Degree*> **Advanced** applies to what seems to be ahead of its proper time <a man with *advanced* ideas> <complacency and self-righteousness on the part of "*advanced*" societies – Denis Goulet> **Radical** may replace *advanced,* but it is likely to imply willingness to destroy the institutions which conserve the ideas or policies condemned and then come close to *revolutionary* in meaning <a move . . . to consolidate school districts was firmly resisted by all right-thinking people as *radical* – J. K. Galbraith> <*radical* innovators, challenging the authority of the past – G. C. Sellery> ***ant*** authoritarian

liberate – see FREE *vb*

liberty – see FREEDOM ***ant*** restraint

license – see FREEDOM ***ant*** decorum

licit – see LAWFUL ***ant*** illicit

lick – see CONQUER

lie, prevaricate, equivocate, palter, fib *shared meaning* : to tell an untruth.

Lie is the straightforward word, imputing dishonesty to the speaker <the article ... has deliberately *lied* and distorted facts – *Nation's Business*> **Prevaricate** is commonly used to avoid the insulting bluntness of *lie,* but distinctively it can imply evasion rather than outright lying <he could *prevaricate* no longer, and, confessing to the gambling, told her the truth – Thomas Hardy> **Equivocate** implies evasion by the use of ambiguous words or remarks in an attempt to mislead <by *equivocating,* hesitating, and giving ambiguous answers, she effected her purpose – Harriet Martineau> **Palter** implies a playing fast and loose not only in statements but in dealings <and be these juggling fiends no more believed that *palter* with us in a double sense – Shak.> **Fib,** typically a childish word, applies to the telling of an untruth that is trivial in substance or significance <he didn't like Janet. She *fibbed,* he said, and was a telltale – Ellen Glasgow>

lift, raise, rear, elevate, hoist, heave, boost *shared meaning* : to move from a lower to a higher place or position. **Lift** is likely to carry an implication of effort exerted in or as if in overcoming the resistance of a physical weight <*lift* a stone onto the wall> <the news *lifted* a weight from his mind> but sometimes this implication is lost and the fact of rising high is stressed <high *lifted* up were many lofty towers – Edmund Spenser> **Raise** implies a bringing to the vertical or to a high position; thus, one *raises* a pole by setting it on end, but one *lifts* it by picking it up; one *raises* (better than *lifts*) a price by setting it at a higher level <those arts which were destined to *raise* our Gothic cathedrals – G. G. Coulton> <the most wholehearted attempt ever made to *raise* the individual to his highest power – C. D. Lewis> **Rear** may add to *raise* an element of suddenness <the mast we *rear* – Alexander Pope> <the maypole was *reared* – Washington Irving> but, unlike the latter, it can be used intransitively with the meaning to raise itself or a part <the ... storm clouds *reared* on high – Edna S. V. Millay> <horses, *rearing* and prancing – Sherwood Anderson> **Elevate** may replace *lift* or *raise,* especially when exalting or enhancing is implied <*elevate* a priest to a bishopric> <you could have psychotic civilizations, or decadent civilizations that have *elevated* pain to an aesthetic – Stanley Kubrick> **Hoist** implies lifting something heavy, especially by mechanical means <*hoist* cargo into a ship with a crane and net> **Heave** stresses effort or strain in lifting, usually by impulsion from without <nature's way of creating a mountain peak – first the *heaving* up of some blunt monstrous bulk of rumpled rock – C. E. Montague> **Boost** suggests assisting to climb or advance by or as if by a push and lacks the implication of strain or effort so evident in *hoist* and *heave* <*boost* a boy over a fence> <*boost* prices> <agronomists could help *boost* crop yields – Denis Goulet> *ant* lower

light, kindle, ignite, fire *shared meaning* : to start something to burn. **Light** is likely to imply an end (as illuminating, heating, or smoking) <*light* a lamp> <*light* a fire in the stove> <let me *light* your cigarette> **Kindle** may connote difficulty in setting combustible materials alight and is appropriate when special preparations are needed or when the emphasis is on the fact of successful lighting <it needed kerosene to make the damp wood *kindle*> <we *kindled* the bonfire just after dark> **Ignite** in general use, like *kindle,* stresses successful lighting but is more likely to apply to highly flammable materials <a spark *ignited* the curtains> <*ignite* a firecracker> In technical use it may imply heating of something until it glows or becomes incandescent <the electric current *ignites* the tungsten filament in the light bulb to produce light and heat> or it may imply the placing of a spark (as an electric spark) in contact with a combustible or explosive material so as to produce its combustion <*ignite* the vapor in the cylinder of an internal combustion engine to produce power> **Fire** suggests blazing and rapid combustion and is usually used with respect to something that ignites readily and burns fiercely <*fire* a haystack> <the turnkey *fired* the little pile, which blazed high and hot – Charles Dickens>

All these words have extended use. **Light** in such use is purely a figure of speech <a quick animation *lit* her face – Clarissa F. Cushman> while **kindle** implies an exciting, arousing, or stimulating <his proposal *kindled* their enthusiasm> and **ignite** implies a stirring into activity <that genius for *igniting* others essential to all great teachers – John Mason Brown> **Fire** implies an inspiring (as with passion, zeal, or desire) and is likely to be chosen when the agent or agency induces energetic activity <the subject . . . had *fired* her imagination – Jan Struther> <a combative infielder who can *fire* up a ball club – *Sports Illustrated*>

lighten – see RELIEVE

lighthearted – see GLAD ***ant*** despondent

lightness, levity, frivolity, flippancy, volatility, flightiness *shared meaning* : gaiety or indifference where seriousness and attention are called for. **Lightness** implies a lack of weight and seriousness in character and sometimes instability or careless heedlessness <he spoke . . . with a gentlemanly *lightness,* almost a negligence, as though to cancel any tone of dogmatism . . . in his words – Herman Wouk> <treating with *lightness* what is matter of life and death – Matthew Arnold> **Levity** usually suggests trifling or unseasonable gaiety <her *levity,* her frivolous laughter, her unwomanly jests – J. R. Green> <drunken *levity* at a wake> **Frivolity** suggests irresponsible indulgence in gaieties or in idle or empty speech and conduct <a period of yearly relaxation in London, ordered and increasingly stately as the natural *frivolity* of youth matured into the sobriety of complete matronhood – Victoria Sackville-West> <the extraordinary *frivolity* of much which passes for religious interest – W. R. Inge> **Flippancy** applies especially to unbecoming levity or pertness, especially in respect to grave or sacred matters <the *flippancy* with which my requests for information are treated – Rudyard Kipling> <[he] . . . employs irony well, but the effect is marred by failure to draw the line between irony and *flippancy* – *Williams Alumni Rev.*> <that *flippancy,* which youth sometimes confounds with wit – Sir Walter Scott> **Volatility** implies a lightness or fickleness of disposition that precludes long attention to one thing <*volatility* of character evinces no capabilities for great affections – P. B. Shelley> <the easy *volatility* of the immature mind> **Flightiness** may imply extreme volatility, even to the loss of wholesome mental balance <the *flightiness* of her temper – Nathaniel Hawthorne> or it may suggest gay whimsicality and inability to long fix one's mind or interest <*flightiness* was her infirmity . . . . Little things filled her thoughts – Ellen Glasgow> ***ant*** seriousness

likely – see PROBABLE ***ant*** unlikely

likeness, similarity, resemblance, similitude, analogy, affinity *shared meaning* : agreement or correspondence in details (as of appearance, structure, or quality). **Likeness** commonly implies closer correspondence than **similarity** which often applies to things merely somewhat alike <I should have known you anywhere from your *likeness* to your father – Archibald Marshall> <great works of art have a decided *similarity* to great human beings – they are both three-dimensional – Huntington Hartford> **Resemblance** is likely to suggest correspondence in appearance or in external or superficial qualities <sketches a model of such a [hypothetical] society (bearing a close *resemblance* to modern neo-capitalist actuality) – *Times Lit. Supp.*> **Similitude,** a somewhat bookish term, may be preferred when the abstract idea of likeness is under consideration <all medieval variances of thought show common *similitudes* – H. O. Taylor> **Analogy** implies comparison of things that are basically unlike and is more likely to draw attention to likeness or parallelism in relations than in appearance or qualities <[societies] litter the historical report; their records are the social *analogies* of the fossils of dinosaur, of pterodactyl, of sloth – John Strachey> <as historian he knows that events, like persons, are unique. The likenesses among them are *analogies,* not identities – J. M. Barzun> **Affinity** adds to *resemblance* the implication of a special relationship (as natural kinship, temperamental sympathy, or historical influence) that is responsible for the likeness <a recognizable stylistic *affinity* between the extremes – Herbert Read> <whatever bears *affinity* to cunning is despicable – Jane Austen> ***ant*** unlikeness

limb – see SHOOT

limber – see SUPPLE

limit, restrict, circumscribe, confine *shared meaning* : to set bounds for. **Limit** implies setting a point or line (as in time, space, speed, or capacity) beyond which something cannot or is not permitted to go <*limit* the working day to seven hours> <the Constitution *limits* his [the President's] functions in the law-making process – *Current History*> or it can imply bounds inherent in a situation or in the nature of something <poor soil *limited* their crops> **Restrict** usually connotes a narrowing or tightening or restraining within or as if within an encircling boundary <*restrict* the powers of a court> <alternatively, the jobs will be *restricted* so that the available workers can perform them – R. M. Solow> **Circumscribe** stresses a restricting in every direction and by clearly marked limits <he is a product of his party machine, in which he has had his whole existence and which *circumscribes* his whole ambition – Edmund Wilson> **Confine** usually emphasizes bounds that cannot or must not be passed and often suggests severe restraint and the resulting cramping, fettering, or hampering <*confined* to the house by illness> <we are *confined* to our senses for perceiving the world – K. K. Darrow> <now I am cabined, cribbed, *confined,* bound in to saucy doubts and fears – Shak.> ***ant*** widen

limp, floppy, flaccid, flabby, flimsy, sleazy *shared meaning* : deficient in firmness of texture, substance, or structure. **Limp** implies a lack or loss of stiffness or body and a resulting tendency to droop <[she] has *limp* blond hair and oversized brown eyes – *New Yorker*> <I found its humor strained and its story *limp* – Hollis Alpert> **Floppy** applies to something that sags or hangs limply <the soft *floppy* ears of most hounds> In contrast to *limp* which usually carries such negative connotations as slovenliness, feebleness, or deficiency, *floppy* is likely to suggest flexibility and a natural or intended lack of stiffness <wore a large *floppy* garden hat that shaded her eyes> **Flaccid** applies primarily to living tissues and implies a loss of normal and especially youthful firmness <now, in swift collapse, he was as *flaccid* as a sick hound and as disgusting as an aged drunkard – Arnold Bennett> In extended use the term implies lack of force or energy or substance <took advantage of her lassitude to impose fresh will upon her cousin's *flaccid* one – Stella D. Gibbons> **Flabby** in its application to material things is very close to *flaccid* <her breasts had grown *flabby* and pendulous with many children – Pearl Buck> but in extended use is more likely to imply lack or loss of what keeps a thing in sound condition and suggest a resulting spinelessness, spiritlessness, or lethargy <the *flabby* government which was ... incapable of defending its own interests – Owen Lattimore> <a perfectly horrible film ... an artless and *flabby* attempt as character drama – Dave Fedo> **Flimsy** applies to something of such looseness of structure or insubstantiality of texture as to be unable to stand up under strain <a *flimsy* partition> <girls in *flimsy* summer dresses>

In extended use the term stresses lack of real worth or of capacity for endurance <a *flimsy* excuse> <devourers of all the *flimsier* literature hawked about the streets – Bonamy Dobrée> **Sleazy** implies a flimsiness due to cheap or careless workmanship <thin *sleazy* woolens> and in extended use may stress lack or inferiority of standards <a *sleazy* little gold digger – *New Republic*> <the *sleazier* forms of competition – *Fortune*> or cheap, often shabby, inferiority <reportage, however exact, of *sleazy* trivia can be suffocating when stretched out to novel length – *Times Lit. Supp.*>

limpid – see CLEAR ***ant*** turbid

line, align, range, array *shared meaning* : to arrange in a line or lines. **Line** implies a setting in single file or parallel rows <*line* up prisoners for identification> <parents *line* the sides of the main classroom and applaud as the children . . . dance – Dan Madden> **Align** stresses the bringing of points or parts that should be in a straight line into correct adjustment or into correspondence <*align* the front and rear wheels of an automobile> <the tents were *aligned* in two rows – Norman Mailer> **Range** stresses orderly disposition, sometimes by aligning but often by separating into classes according to some plan <oaken benches *ranged* in seemly rows – William Wordsworth> **Array** applies especially to a setting in battle order and therefore suggests readiness for action or use as well as ordered arrangement <you can imagine the whole labor force *arrayed* in order of desirability to employers. . . . The higher the demand for labor, the farther down the line they will go – R. M. Solow>

lineal, linear *shared meaning* : of or relating to a line or lines. In spite of their common meaning element these words have quite distinct specific applications and are not ordinarily interchangeable. **Lineal** in its usual use is applied to direct line of succession to or from a common physical or spiritual ancestor, is often distinguished from *collateral,* and tends to stress continuity and relationship <a child has a *lineal* relationship to his grandfather and a collateral relationship to his brother> <the businessman, the direct *lineal* descendant of the guild merchant – Roy Lewis & Angus Maude> <our craft was a *lineal* descendant of the old keelboats – R. J. Smith> but it can also apply to something linked to or stemming from such relationship <*lineal* rights> <*lineal* to the throne – John Dryden> **Linear** tends to lay stress on a line other than a line of succession, either in fact or in likeness; often it suggests the presence of a single dimension, usually length; thus, "*linear* measure" denotes a system of measuring length; a *linear* leaf is one so long and slender as to seem to have no breadth; a *linear* relationship between variables is one that can be graphed as a straight line <the longest *linear* structural features on the earth's surface are the east-west fracture zones of the northeast Pacific Ocean – Alexander Malahoff *et al*>

linear – see LINEAL

linger – see STAY

lingo – see DIALECT

link – see JOIN ***ant*** sunder

liquid, fluid *shared meaning* : tending to flow and to take the form of a confining container. Both terms imply an opposition to *solid,* but **liquid** is the more restricted for it applies only to substances that, like water, are but slightly compressible and are capable of conversion, under suitable conditions of pressure and temperature, into gases, while **fluid** is applicable to both liquids and gases; thus, air, oil, and mercury are all *fluid* but only oil and mercury are *liquid* under ordinary conditions.

In extended use the terms are quite distinct. **Liquid** often implies an opposition to *harsh* <thy *liquid* notes that close the eye of day – John

Milton> but it sometimes implies transparency or extreme softness or both <with what *liquid* tenderness she turned and looked back – Arnold Bennett> **Fluid,** on the other hand, can be opposed to *rigid, fixed, unchangeable* and apply to whatever is essentially unstable <emotion, formless, chaotic, *fluid* in itself – J. L. Lowes> <we now know that Africa is *fluid,* volatile and everchanging – William Attwood> or to what tends to flow easily or freely <there appears to be so little easeful, *fluid* continuity today in life between past and present – Michael Arlen> ***ant*** solid, vaporous

lissome – see SUPPLE

lithe – see SUPPLE

lithesome – see SUPPLE

little – see SMALL ***ant*** big

live – see RESIDE

lively, animated, vivacious, sprightly, gay *shared meaning* : keenly alive and spirited. **Lively** is likely to suggest briskness, alertness, and energy <[they] danced like the *liveliest* barefoot angels one could imagine – Allen Hughes> <a *lively* study of political attacks on American school textbooks – L. A. Cremin> **Animated** applies especially to what is spirited, active, and sparkling <the child . . . who is included in *animated* discussion of people, events, and ideas is more likely to write well than the child who experiences only dull silence, or worse, domestic griping and bickering – R. K. Corbin> **Vivacious** suggests an activeness of gesture and wit, often playful or alluring <remember her as very pretty and *vivacious* . . . I never met a girl with as much zip – Ring Lardner> **Sprightly,** very close to *vivacious,* may stress lightness and spirited vigor of manner or wit <this *sprightly* book hails the beauty of the natural world – D. B. Nunis, Jr.> <gradually through the afternoon her step had become less *sprightly* – Douglass Wallop> **Gay** stresses freedom from care and exuberantly overflowing spirits <*gay* carefree children playing by the pool> <the progress of his career . . . had been away from the quieter, more traditional . . . to those forms which were more brilliant and *gay,* filled with the constant excitement of new pleasures and sensations – Thomas Wolfe> ***ant*** dull

livid – see PALE

living, alive, animate, animated, vital *shared meaning* : having or showing life. **Living** and **alive** are opposed to *dead* and are applied to organic bodies which have life as distinguished from those that have lost it; they are distinguished chiefly by the fact that *alive* follows the noun it modifies <among *living* men> <among men still *alive*> <of all it ever was my lot to read, of critics now *alive,* or long since dead – William Cowper> <our appreciations of *living* or dead writers – T. S. Eliot> **Animate,** opposed to *inanimate,* can occasionally replace *living* or *alive,* but typically it describes what is living as contrasted with what never had life <those who ignore the natural world around, *animate* and inanimate – Herbert Spencer> **Animated** is opposed to *lifeless* or *inert* and may apply to something which, once devoid of life, becomes alive or is given motion simulating life <viruses that can behave as *animated* bodies or inert crystals> <an *animated* cartoon> **Vital** applies chiefly to qualities which result from or are specifically associated with life; thus, the *vital* signs (pulse, respiration, temperature, and blood pressure) allow the physician to determine whether life persists; *vital* functions are those without which life cannot persist. ***ant*** lifeless

loath – see DISINCLINED ***ant*** anxious

loathe – see HATE ***ant*** dote on

locution – see PHRASE

logical, analytic, subtle *shared meaning* : having or showing skill in thinking or reasoning. **Logical** may imply a capacity for orderly thinking or, more especially, the power to impress on others that clearness of thought, soundness of reasoning, and freedom from bias underlie the products of one's thinking <he had ... the *logical* as opposed to the intuitive temper. He distrusted emotion for which he could not find a rational basis – C. E. Montague> **Analytic,** often as the variant **analytical,** stresses the power to simplify what is complicated or complex or what is chaotic or confused by separating and recombining the constituent elements in a logical manner <perhaps the critical mind was too *analytical,* too pragmatic, for the creative to be bold enough to assert itself – Helen MacInnes> <science has developed by *analytic* observation, and by interpretations of observed facts on the basis of their relations to one another – John Dewey> **Subtle** basically implies a capacity to penetrate below the surface and perceive fine distinctions and minute relations <these relatively *subtle* differences are most difficult to get across to the inexperienced man – R. F. Lewis> Sometimes the word may imply a criticism (as of being overrefined and difficult to follow) but usually it connotes exceptional skill in reasoning and analysis <his *subtle* sense of political strategy – W. L. Shirer> <the artist ... had thoughts so *subtle* that the average man could comprehend them no more than a mongrel could understand the moon he bayed at – Thomas Wolfe> ***ant*** illogical

logistics – see STRATEGY

loiter – see DELAY 2

lone – see ALONE

lonely – see ALONE

lonesome – see ALONE

long, yearn, hanker, pine, hunger, thirst *shared meaning* : to have a strong desire for something. **Long** implies a wishing with one's whole heart usually for something remote or not easily attainable <ever have I *longed* to slake my thirst for the world's praises – John Keats> <he *longed* for the days when a young man could ... immerse himself in Judaism, renouncing the world – I. B. Singer> **Yearn** implies an eager, restless, or painful longing <but Enoch *yearned* to see her face again – Alfred Tennyson> <she *yearns* so earnestly for understanding that she raises her head and says half a prayer – John Cheever> **Hanker** suggests the uneasy promptings of unsatisfied appetite or desire <she ... still *hankered,* with a natural *hankering,* after her money – Anthony Trollope> <has always *hankered* to do a bit of acting – Bennett Cerf> **Pine** implies a languishing or fruitless yearning for what is impossible of attainment <there were many others who *pined* for advantages that would never be theirs – Catherine Fennelly> <we look before and after, and *pine* for what is not – P. B. Shelley> **Hunger** implies a need like that for food and **thirst** like that for drink; both terms suggest insistency of desire and urgency of need <blessed are they which do *hunger* and *thirst* after righteousness: for they shall be filled – *Mt* 5:6 (AV)> <*hunger* for news of absent friends> <a man *thirsting* for revenge>

look – see EXPECT, SEE, SEEM

loose, relaxed, slack, lax *shared meaning* : not tightly bound, held, restrained, or stretched. **Loose** is widely referable to persons or things freed from a usual or former, material or immaterial restraint <turn cattle *loose* into the pasture> <a book with a *loose* page> <the harm done by *loose* inaccurate gossip> <a person of *loose* morals> or to something not tight between points of contact <drive with *loose* reins> <always wore a *loose* belt> or to a substance or fabric with particles or filaments in open arrangement <a *loose* easily-worked soil> <a *loose*-woven woolen> **Relaxed** implies a lessening of prior tightness, tension, strictness, or rigidity; in comparison with *loose* it is likely to imply an easing of rather than a freeing from what restrains <the *relaxed* discipline of the last few days of school> <a more *relaxed* drawing style – *Current Biog.*> <our grandmother, leaning *relaxed* against the wall – Padma Perera> **Slack,** otherwise close to *relaxed,* may stress lack of firmness and steadiness; thus, *relaxed* control is control deliberately eased for a usually sound reason; *slack* control is irregular control, lacking in sureness and steadiness <shorebirds are notoriously *slack* in regard to the roles of the sexes ... in nesting – Peter Matthiessen> **Lax** stresses lack of steadiness, firmness, and tone <felt the *lax* droop of her shoulder against his arm – Elinor Wylie> or, in respect to immaterial things, may stress lack of needed or proper steadiness and firmness <a *lax* administration> <*lax* supervision of employees> <instead of the careful restrictions of middle-class codes and manners, she breathed the larger air of a *laxer* ease – Victoria Sackville-West> ***ant*** tight, strict

loot – see SPOIL
loquacious – see TALKATIVE
lordly – see PROUD
lorn – see ALONE
lot – see FATE, GROUP
loutish – see BOORISH
lovely – see BEAUTIFUL ***ant*** unlovely, plain
low – see BASE
lower – see FROWN
lowly – see HUMBLE ***ant*** pompous
loyal – see FAITHFUL ***ant*** disloyal
loyalty – see FIDELITY ***ant*** disloyalty
lucid – see CLEAR 2 ***ant*** obscure, vague, dark

lucky, fortunate, happy, providential *shared meaning* : meeting with or producing unforeseen success. **Lucky** stresses the agency of chance in bringing about a favorable result <a discovery that was the result of a *lucky* accident> <a *lucky* sudden combination of chance mutations – Theodosius Dobzhansky> **Fortunate** suggests being rewarded beyond one's deserts or expectations <in friendships I had been most *fortunate* – P. B. Shelley> <a *fortunate* investment> **Happy** combines the ideas of *lucky* and *fortunate* with that of its more common meaning of being blessed or made glad <the three major elements ... form a *happy* partnership, reinforcing and complementing each other – R. R. Lodwig & E. F. Barrett> <found the *happiest* measure for most purposes to be the typically English and infinitely flexible octosyllabic couplet – Bonamy Dobrée> **Providential** can suggest the coming of good fortune or the averting of evil through or as if through the intervention of Providence <what a *providential* return to sanity – W. J. Locke> <this trip will be just what Faith needs at this time. It seems *providential.* – Agnes S. Turnbull> ***ant*** unlucky

ludicrous – see LAUGHABLE
lull – see PAUSE
luminous – see BRIGHT
lunacy – see INSANITY

lure, entice, inveigle, decoy, tempt, seduce *shared meaning* : to draw one from a usual, desirable, or proper course or situation into one considered unusual, undesirable, or wrong. **Lure** implies a strong attracting influence but in itself indicates nothing about its good or evil quality <a manufacturer ..., *lured* by the promise of cheap labor – Pearl Buck> <*lured* into the imperfect world of coarse uncompleted passion – Oscar Wilde> <the magic of a full moon had *lured* me from my laboratory – William Beebe> **Entice**

adds to *lure* a strong suggestion of artfulness and adroitness <materials, . . . concessions, . . . contracts . . . offered in an effort to *entice* economic benefits from the capital-rich countries – Harvey Wheeler> **Inveigle** implies the use of wiles and often of deceit and flattery <with patience and diplomacy, she can eventually *inveigle* him into marrying her – Nellie Maher> **Decoy** implies a luring (as to entrap or lead) by artifice and especially by false appearances <ships which they had skillfully *decoyed* to destruction on the reefs – Thomas Barbour> <the female bird . . . practiced the same arts upon us to *decoy* us away – John Burroughs> **Tempt** usually implies exerting an attraction that overcomes scruples or discretion <*tempted* the young man into kissing her – Sherwood Anderson> <the delicious odor *tempted* him to forget his diet> **Seduce** implies a leading astray by persuasion or false promises <the hideous beast whose craft had *seduced* me into murder – E. A. Poe> <[the government] need not fear that its citizens will be *seduced* by Communism – Claude Julien> ***ant*** revolt, repel

lurk, skulk, slink, sneak *shared meaning* : to behave furtively. **Lurk** is likely to imply a lying in wait in a place of concealment <to the suspicious Fuehrer danger *lurked* everywhere – W. L. Shirer> but often it adds the suggestion of an evil purpose <there . . . ugly treasons *lurk* – Shak.> **Shulk** implies furtive movements and suggests cowardice or fear or sinister intent <disdainful Anger, pallid Fear, and Shame that *shulks* behind – Thomas Gray> <*skulk* up and down with the air of a charity-boy, a bastard, or an interloper – R. W. Emerson> <what bedevilled idiocy *skulks* behind that arrogant mask – Herbert Read> **Slink** implies stealthiness in moving to escape being seen and may connote sly caution <like beasts of prey *slinking* about a campfire – Joseph Conrad> **Sneak** applies to a getting into or out of a place by slinking or into or out of a situation by devious methods <saw modernization as an opportunity to *sneak* their own advantage – *Times Lit. Supp.*> <they keep moiling and fussing and *sneaking* around, making elaborate plans, and building up arsenals – Herman Wouk> <boys *sneaking* behind the barn to smoke>

lush – see PROFUSE

lustrous – see BRIGHT

lusty – see VIGOROUS ***ant*** effete

luxuriant – see PROFUSE

luxurious **1** see SENSUOUS ***ant*** ascetic

2 luxurious, sumptuous, opulent *shared meaning* : ostentatiously rich or magnificent. Something **luxurious** is exceedingly choice and costly <lives in a *luxurious* duplex penthouse – *Current Biog.*> <a *luxurious* cargo of wine, olive oil, and candied tropic fruits – Elinor Wylie> Something **sumptuous** is extravagantly rich, splendid, gorgeous, or luxurious; often the word suggests an overwhelming quality of grandeur or magnificence <the word "wealthy" as he says it, is redolent of a life spiced and *sumptuous,* a tapestry thick to the touch – Walker Percy> <this is surely one of the handsomest and most *sumptuous* books on gardens produced this century – Elizabeth C. Hall> Something **opulent** flaunts or seems to flaunt its luxuriousness or luxuriance or occasionally its costliness <a sprightly oldster in a brand-new suit set off by an *opulent* watch chain – S. J. Perelman> <offered the bribe not only of her person but of an *opulent* and glittering eastern throne – John Buchan>

lying – see DISHONEST ***ant*** truth-telling

machination – see PLOT
magisterial – see DICTATORIAL
magnificent – see GRAND *ant* modest
maim, cripple, mutilate, batter, mangle *shared meaning* : to injure so severely as to cause lasting damage. **Maim** implies the loss of a part or the destruction of its usefulness, usually through violence <people *maimed* by reckless driving> <seems to have been *maimed* psychologically by a brutal father – *N.Y. Times Bk. Rev.*> **Cripple** basically implies such damage to an extremity or part of one as seriously impairs function <hands *crippled* by arthritis> <he was *crippled* by loss of a leg> but it can be used of other damages that gravely impair mobility or function <a battleship, *crippled* by cruisers the night before, lay smoking and floundering within sight – Ira Wolfert> **Mutilate** implies the cutting off of a part essential to completeness, perfection, or functional competence <windows . . . darkened by time and *mutilated* by willful injury – Henry Adams> <savages who *mutilate* captives> *Batter* and *mangle* stress not loss of a part but grave disfiguring injuries. **Batter** implies a pounding that bruises, deforms, or mutilates <at the end of the . . . war, they were *battered* and grisly, demoralized – Edmund Wilson> <so rough were the roads that we were *battered* and pitched about like cargoes in a heavy sea – A. R. Williams> **Mangle** implies a tearing or crushing that produces deep disorganizing wounds <*mangled* with ghastly wounds through plate and mail – John Milton> <people . . . *mangled* by sharks – V. G. Heiser>
maintain, assert, defend, vindicate, justify *shared meaning* : to uphold as true, right, just, or reasonable. **Maintain** stresses firmness of conviction and is likely to suggest persistent or insistent upholding of a cause <*maintained*, with Calvinist passion, their traditional intolerance of evil – William Styron> <against all the evidence he continued to *maintain* both publicly and privately that the senator was innocent> **Assert** strongly implies an intent to make others accept what one puts forward as true and may suggest aggressiveness or obtrusiveness <supporters of Griffin *asserted* that a vote against their candidate would be "a vote for Negroes next door and on the playing fields of Georgia." – *Current Biog.*> <they became estranged when Forbes *asserted* the rule of law and would not tolerate the governor's encroachment into what he deemed the sphere of the judiciary – *Australian Dict. of Biog.*> **Defend** implies maintaining in the face of attack <I have not adopted my faith in order to *defend* my views of conduct – T. S. Eliot> <*defended* his action by saying it was the best and quickest way – S. H. Holbrook> **Vindicate** implies successful defending <arise and *vindicate* Thy Glory; free thy people from their yoke! – John Milton> <the . . . politicians were *vindicated* on all counts – R. H. Rovere> **Justify** implies a showing to be right or acceptable or valid by appeal to a standard or to precedent <a kind of mumbo jumbo to *justify* whatever current policy the government happens to find expedient – Edmund Wilson> <an occasion such as this, he argued, . . . *justified* a car – Pearl Buck>
majestic – see GRAND
majority, plurality *shared meaning* : a number or quantity or part larger than some other expressed or implied. In general applications the two words can be quite comparable <a *majority* of public school students come from a poverty subculture – Susan L. Jacoby> <the individual family is now challenged to new responsibilities toward the *plurality* of families which comprises the nation – *Pilot*> They can differ, however, in their specific application to the excess of votes that determine an election. Both words imply an excess of votes over the next highest candidate, but in an election involving three or more candidates **majority** implies that the winner has

received more votes than the other candidates combined, that is, his vote is in excess of half the votes cast, and his *majority* is the number of votes cast for him in excess of one half the total vote. **Plurality** merely implies that the winner has more votes than any other candidate, whether he had a *majority* of the total or not.

make, form, shape, fashion, fabricate, manufacture, forge *shared meaning* : to cause to come into being. **Make,** the general term, can apply to any action of producing or creating whether by an intelligent agency or blind forces and whether the product has material or immaterial existence <*make* a wheelbarrow> <*make* a promise> <God *made* the world> <we rarely *make* the mistake of hiring someone who is not bright enough to do well with us – R. F. Lewis> **Form** implies a definite outline, structure, or design in the thing produced <*form* a federation of states> <character is partly *formed* by training> <the parade began to *form* in the square> <*form* dough into a loaf> <agreed to *form* a corporation to develop his invention> **Shape,** similar to but more restricted in application than *form,* characteristically connotes an external agent that physically or figuratively impresses a particular form on something <*shape* a timber with an adz> <events that *shaped* his career> <the responsibility of these young people will be to *shape* our nation's future and determine its progress – Thordis K. Danielson> **Fashion** suggests the use of inventive power and ingenuity <*fashion* a lamp out of an old churn> <each university *fashions* its own unique answers in response to these challenges – M. S. Eisenhower> **Fabricate** stresses a uniting of diverse parts or materials into a whole <structural steel shapes . . . *fabricated* in the shop by riveting and welding – W. C. Huntington> It may suggest imaginative skill in construction <*fabricate* a good plot for a novel> or such skill carried to the point of falsehood <*fabricated* an involved explanation of his absence> **Manufacture** usually implies making repeatedly and now usually by a mechanical process <*manufacture* shoes> In extended use it can suggest laboriousness or devising <*manufacture* an excuse> <most students lock-in to the present and struggle to *manufacture* inarticulate dreams – R. E. Kavanaugh> **Forge** implies a making or effecting by great physical or mental effort <the military alliances we have *forged* with nations of Asia – Vera M. Dean> or sometimes specifically the making of a counterfeit <pity was a counterfeit of love, something *forged* in the heart and altered by time and the mind – H. C. Hervey>

make-believe – see PRETENSE

maker, creator, author *shared meaning* : one who brings something new into being or existence. Written with an initial capital letter all three terms designate God or the Supreme Being; without the capital they ascribe similar but not equivalent effects and powers to a person. **Maker** is likely to imply a close and immediate relationship between the one who makes and the thing that is made and an ensuing responsibility for what is turned out; hence, God is often called one's *Maker* (as in hymns and prayers). In many of its human applications (as in king*maker,* a *maker* of men, a *maker* of phrases) *maker* suggests the use of appropriate material as an instrument through which one gives form to one's own ideas <Caxton . . . was not only the father of English printing, but an extraordinarily prolific *maker* of books – Stella Brook> **Creator** stresses a bringing into existence of what the mind conceives; in application to God *Creator* is likely to emphasize omnipotence and the greatness of his works <touched their golden harps, and hymning praised God and his works; *Creator* him they sung – John Milton> In relation to human endeavor *creator* is likely to suggest originality and delving into the unknown <a conservator, call me, if you please, not

a *creator* nor destroyer – Robert Browning> <they are genuine *creators:* they do not describe nor interpret reality as much as construct it – Howard Moss> **Author** applies to one who originates and is the source of something's being and as such wholly responsible for its existence. It is applied to God chiefly in the phrase "*Author* of one's being" when the reference is to the gift of life and its attending circumstances. In application to persons it can be used of a writer <the *author* of several books> or of one who (as a founder, an initiator, or an inventor) brings something into existence <the policy of which he was principally the *author* – Hilaire Belloc>

makeshift – see RESOURCE

maladroit – see AWKWARD ***ant*** adroit

male – see MASCULINE ***ant*** female

malevolence – see MALICE ***ant*** benevolence

malice, ill will, malevolence, spite, malignity, malignancy, spleen, grudge *shared meaning* : a desiring or wishing pain, injury, or distress to another. **Malice** may imply a deep-seated and often unreasonable dislike and a desire to see one suffer <with *malice* toward none; with charity for all ... let us ... bind up the nation's wounds – Abraham Lincoln> or it may suggest a causeless passing mischievous impulse <she was clever, witty, brilliant ...; but possessed of many devils of *malice* and mischievousness – Rudyard Kipling> **Ill will** implies an attitude of enmity that is real but measured and usually lacks any element of mental turmoil <proposed to defend Formosa for Chiang and invite the *ill will* of all the rest of Asia – *Progressive*> **Malevolence** implies a deep and lasting hatred whose rancor colors the whole outlook of the one possessed by it and may suggest inherent evil <appears ... as the incarnation of pure *malevolence* in Pinkie, the boy gangster and murderer – M. D. Zabel> <the frigid *malevolence* with which Wilson denied this strong man's plea – W. A. White> **Spite** suggests active ill will of a mean, petty, and often harassing quality <it was a country of *spite* fences and internecine quarrels – John Cheever> <full of envy, full of *spite* ..., a man who is pleased to find others are as unhappy as he – Norman Mailer> **Malignity** and **malignancy** imply deep passion and relentless driving force <he is cruel with the cruelty of petrified feeling, to his poor heroine; he pursues her without pity or pause, as with *malignity* – Matthew Arnold> <blinded by *malignancy* against the class of manual worker – Cecil Sprigge> **Spleen** implies ill will coupled with bad temper and is likely to suggest wrathful release of latent spite or persistent malice <his countrymen vented their *spleen* at his failure ... by sending the unfortunate naval commander into exile – A. J. Toynbee> <his just fame was long obscured by partisan *spleen* – V. L. Parrington> **Grudge** implies a cherished feeling of resentment or ill will that seeks satisfaction <I will feed fat the ancient *grudge* I bear him – Shak.> <he held no *grudge* against any of the people who had misused him – Willa Cather> ***ant*** charity

malign *adj* – see SINISTER ***ant*** benign

malign *vb* **malign, traduce, asperse, vilify, calumniate, defame, slander** *shared meaning* : to injure by speaking ill of. *Malign* and *traduce* usually imply persecution and suggest intense emotion (as hatred, prejudice, bigotry, or jealousy) as the cause. **Malign** tends to suggest interested misrepresentation but not necessarily conscious and direct lying <the most *maligned* race in history> <gossips had *maligned* the lady – George Meredith> **Traduce** more strongly stresses the resulting ignominy <I am *traduced* by ignorant tongues ... 'tis but the fate of place and the rough brake that virtue must go through – Shak.> **Asperse** implies persistent attack on a reputation often by indirect or insinuated detraction <found their characters assailed and

their motives *aspersed* – V. L. Parrington> **Vilify** implies attempting to destroy a reputation by open and direct abuse <with a malignant insanity, we oppose the measures, and ungratefully *vilify* the persons, of those whose sole object is our own peace and prosperity – Edmund Burke> **Calumniate** imputes malice to the speaker and falsity to his assertions <Asian students *calumniated* the United States as a fat, weary, selfish, illiterate, perverse warmonger, determined to destroy all the world's revolutionary movements – J. A. Michener> *Defame* and *slander* stress the effects on the victim, **defame** implying loss of or injury to reputation <*defaming* and defacing, till she left not even Lancelot brave nor Galahad clean – Alfred Tennyson> and **slander** calling attention to the suffering of the victim <*slandered* to death by villains, that dare as well answer a man indeed as I dare take a serpent by the tongue – Shak.> *ant* defend

malignancy **1** see MALICE *ant* benignity
2 see TUMOR

malignity – see MALICE *ant* benignity

malleable – see PLASTIC *ant* refractory

malodorous, stinking, fetid, noisome, putrid, rancid, rank, fusty, musty *shared meaning* : having an unpleasant smell. **Malodorous** may range from the merely unpleasing to the distinctly offensive <some people find the privet blossom distinctly *malodorous*> <stone castles and *malodorous* hovels – T. B. Costain> **Stinking** and **fetid** suggest the foul or offensive <the *stinking* fish market – Herman Wouk> <trapped in the area's *fetid* tenements – John Kifner> **Noisome** adds a suggestion of being unwholesome or harmful as well as offensive <side streets, long, dark, *noisome,* with gray houses leaning forward to cut out the sky – James Baldwin> **Putrid** applies particularly to organic matter in such a state of decay as to be loathsomely malodorous <a bloated, *putrid,* noisome carcass – Edmund Burke> **Rancid** suggests offensiveness of both taste and odor and typically applies to stale fatty substances that have undergone chemical breakdown <*rancid* bacon> **Rank** implies a strong and unpleasing but not necessarily foul odor <O, my offense is *rank,* it smells to heaven – Shak.> <wreathed in smoke from a *rank* cigar – Ralph Watson> *Fusty* and *musty* suggest staleness and lack of fresh air and sunshine; **fusty** usually stresses the effect of prolonged uncleanliness and an accumulation of dust and dirt, and **musty** such effects of damp and darkness as moldiness <the station bus with its *fusty* smell – Victoria Sackville-West> <the rented coarse black gown she was wearing gave out a *musty* smell, as though it had been lying long disused in a loft – Herman Wouk>

mammoth – see HUGE

manacle – see HAMPER

manage – see CONDUCT

maneuver – see TRICK

manful – see MASCULINE

mangle – see MAIM

mania **1** see INSANITY *ant* lucidity
2 mania, delirium, frenzy, hysteria *shared meaning* : a state marked by loss of emotional, mental, or nervous control. All these terms have technical applications in which they imply pathological disorder of mind but in their frequent use in the general language they usually suggest exaggerated reaction rather than actual abnormality. **Mania** usually implies excessive or unreasonable enthusiasm <has a *mania* for building and transforming – Arnold Bennett> <of all useful *manias,* the compilation of bibliographies is one of the most difficult to understand – *Times Lit. Supp.*> **Delirium** adds the notion of extreme excitement <fame, at last, was knocking at his

door . . . and he lived in a kind of glorious *delirium* – Thomas Wolfe> <a *delirium* of joy> **Frenzy** suggests loss of self-control and violent agitation often manifested in action <a little Negro boy . . . had been kicked by a white man. 'Now,' screamed the white man in a *frenzy* of hate, 'you going to come back to this school again?' – Alex Poinsett> and may refer to things as well as persons when the notion of violent activity is dominant <the *frenzy* of the geysers – Margaret Clarke> **Hysteria** implies emotional instability often marked by swift transition of mood <in a kind of momentary *hysteria,* he began to giggle at the idea of walking in on his mother with a bride – J. T. Farrell> Frequently it stresses a precipitating force <the heady atmosphere of the capital . . . when Chairman Mao . . . lifted into *hysteria* the thousands upon thousands of youths who had poured into the city – A. S. Whiting> <the gradual decline of the *hysteria* the Senator had evoked – R. M. Hutchins>

manifest *adj* – see EVIDENT ***ant*** latent, constructive

manifest *vb* – see SHOW ***ant*** suggest

manipulate – see HANDLE

manlike – see MASCULINE

manly – see MASCULINE ***ant*** unmanly, womanly

manner – see BEARING, METHOD

mannerism – see POSE

mannish – see MASCULINE ***ant*** womanish

manufacture – see MAKE

manumit – see FREE *vb* ***ant*** enslave

many-sided – see VERSATILE

mar – see INJURE

margin – see BORDER

mark – see SIGN

marshal – see ORDER

martial, warlike, military *shared meaning* : of or characteristic of war. **Martial** suggests especially the pomp and circumstance of war <standing in *martial* array> <the army set out to the *martial* strains of a fife and drum corps – *Amer. Guide Series: Calif.*> **Warlike** is more likely to imply the spirit or temper that leads to or accompanies war <the Fuehrer, thirsting for further easy conquests . . . was in one of his *warlike* moods – W. L. Shirer> **Military** may imply reference to war, to arms, or to armed forces or might <a *military* expedition> <the *military* expenditures of a nation> Sometimes, in reference to armed forces, *military* is specifically opposed to *civil* or *civilian* <a *military* governor> <*military* law> or it may be restricted to land, or land and air, forces and is then opposed to *naval* <*military* and naval attachés>

masculine, male, manly, manlike, mannish, manful, virile *shared meaning* : of, characteristic of, or like a male, especially of the human species. **Masculine** applies to qualities or attributes or attitudes characteristic of men and not shared by women <a *masculine* approach to a problem> <radiating pride, love, and *masculine* attraction, the bridegroom in his hour of power – Herman Wouk> **Male** (opposed to *female*) is broadly applicable to plants, animals, and persons and stresses the fact of sex <a *male* tiger> <*male* germ cells> <*male* children> <a *male* choir> **Manly** suggests the qualities of the mature man, especially the finer qualities of a man or the powers and skills that come with maturity <my *manly* pride was wounded – Stringfellow Barr> <what more *manly* exercise than hunting? – Izaak Walton> **Manlike** is more likely to suggest characteristically masculine faults and foibles <exhibited a thoroughly *manlike* disregard for details> but sometimes its reference is nonspecifically to human beings and it suggests resemblance to the human kind <there were a dozen or more of the hairy *manlike* creatures upon the ground – *Blue Bk.*> **Mannish** is often used derogatorily in situations in which womanliness might naturally be expected or wanted <his wife ... withdrawn, formidable, at times disconcertingly *mannish* – Alan Pryce-Jones> <a woman impudent and *mannish* grown – Shak.> but in more neutral use, especially as applied to styles and dress, it carries little more than a suggestion of actual masculinity <the hand-tailored black suit and the *mannish* black hat – Herman Wouk> **Manful** stresses sturdiness and resolution <a *manful* effort to achieve success> **Virile** suggests the qualities of fully developed manhood but is at once stronger in emphasis and more specific in many of its applications than *manly* or *masculine* <[he] came from a line of hardy sailors but he was not as *virile* as his grandfathers – John Cheever> <a man of eighty yet still strong and *virile*> In more general applications it is likely to imply manful vigor <the style is *virile* – Winthrop Sargeant> ***ant*** feminine

mask – see DISGUISE

mass – see BULK

massacre, slaughter, butchery, carnage, pogrom *shared meaning* : a great and usually wanton killing of human beings. **Massacre** implies promiscuous and wholesale slaying, especially of those not in a position to defend themselves <the tyrannous and bloody deed is done, the most arch act of piteous *massacre* that ever yet this land was guilty of – Shak.> **Slaughter** implies extensive and ruthless killing (as in a battle or a massacre) <the chief ... cut his way through the enemy with great *slaughter* – Washington Irving> **Butchery** adds to *slaughter* the implication of exceeding cruelty and complete disregard of the sufferings of the victims <the responsibility of the intellectuals, particularly with respect to the *butchery* in Vietnam, is, according to Chomsky, "to speak the truth and expose lies," – John Wilkinson> <thus was the *butchery* waged while the sun clomb Heaven's eastern steep – P. B. Shelley> **Carnage** stresses bloodshed and great loss of life <a slight resistance was followed by a dreadful *carnage* – Edward Gibbon> <war and all its deeds of *carnage* – Walt Whitman> **Pogrom** describes an organized massacre and looting of defenseless people, carried on usually with official connivance <to turn away the people's attention from their own grievances the government worked up the latent hatred against the Jews, diverting the general malaise into *pogroms* – John Lawrence> <he applauded *pogroms* against the Christians, and later, through a mystical experience, he was converted to Christianity – Charles Neider>

masterful, domineering, imperious, peremptory, imperative *shared meaning* : tending to impose one's will on another. **Masterful** implies a strong virile personality and ability to deal authoritatively with affairs <the major was a *masterful* man; and I knew that he would not give orders for nothing – Rudyard Kipling> <she was ever a *masterful* woman, better fitted to command than to obey – H. O. Taylor> **Domineering** suggests an overbearing or tyrannical manner and an obstinate determination to enforce one's will <he had exaggerated her helpfulness . . . into a horrible false picture of herself as a *domineering* harpy – Herman Wouk> <they are ... not masterful, only *domineering* – G. B. Shaw> **Imperious** applies to one who by position or nature is fitted to command or, often, to one who assumes the manner of such a person; the term is likely to suggest arrogant assurance <she is the cynical, *imperious* guide for the politician's early steps, seething with important and suppressed rage as she watches him grow out of her control – Alton Cook> **Peremptory** implies an abrupt dictatorial manner coupled with an unwillingness to brook disobedience or delay or to entertain objections however valid <his *peremptory* command that she decide at once about his proposal – James Purdy> <two *peremptory* raps at the door – G. B. Shaw> **Imperative** implies peremptoriness arising more from the urgency of the situation than from an inherently domineering nature <he heard her *imperative* voice at the telephone; he heard her summon the doctor – Ellen Glasgow>

match, rival, equal, approach, touch *shared meaning* : to come up to or nearly up to the standard of something else. **Match** implies that one thing is the mate rather than the duplicate of another (as in power, strength, beauty, or interest) <the beauty of his person was *matched* by the grace and dignity of his spirit – John Buchan> **Rival** suggests a close competition (as for superiority or in excellence) <but would you sing, and *rival* Orpheus' strain, the wond'ring forests soon should dance again – Alexander Pope> **Equal** implies such close equivalence (as in quantity, worth, or degree) that no question concerning a difference or deficiency can arise <[a person] whose love and hatred for New York is *equalled* only by his pride in his intimate knowledge of it – *Library Jour.*> **Approach** implies such closeness in matching or equaling that the difference, though detectable, scarcely matters <its mathematics *approaches* mysticism – Theodore Sturgeon> <though some of Shakespeare's songs *approach* purity, there is, in fact, an alloy – Clive Bell> **Touch** suggests close equivalence (as in quality or value) and is typically used in negative constructions <as a chronicle of a man's amorous adventures . . . there was nothing to *touch* it – Roald Dahl> <not another woman there to *touch* her – W. J. Locke>

material – see RELEVANT *ant* immaterial

matter-of-fact – see PROSAIC

mature *adj* **mature, ripe, adult, grown-up** *shared meaning* : fully developed. **Mature** stresses completion of development and as applied to persons implies attainment of the prime of life and powers <a great writer of the past is known by the delight and stimulus which he gives to *mature* spirits in the present – Van Wyck Brooks> <the serious concentration of a *mature* and expert craftsman engaged in an absorbing and exacting labor – Thomas Wolfe> In application to things it is more likely to imply completion (as of a course, process, or period) <the *maturer* concept that virtue is its own reward – A. P. Davies> **Ripe** stresses readiness (as for use and enjoyment or, in much of its extended use, action) <*ripe* for exploits and mighty enterprises – Shak.> <she was full-bosomed and *ripe* rather than plump, like a mango ready for plucking – Budd Schulberg> **Adult** in basic application to living things is very close to *mature* though it may presuppose a clearer demarkation; thus, an *adult* person is one who has passed beyond adolescence or, in law, attained his majority. In extended use *adult* is likely to imply successful surmounting of the weaknesses of immaturity <people supremely *adult* and specially schooled to comprehend ideas and employ logic – Janet Flanner> <an *adult* approach to a problem> **Grown-up** may be preferred to adult when an antithesis to *childish* is desired <adults incapable of *grown-up* behavior> <the only *grown-up* way to keep peace in the world – Leverett Saltonstall> *ant* immature

mature *vb* **mature, develop, ripen, age** *shared meaning* : to come or cause to come to the state of being fit for use or enjoyment. **Mature,** in its basic application to living things, can stress fullness of growth and attainment of adult characteristics <he was *matured* by six years' . . . experience – Robert Lowell> while **develop** stresses the unfolding of what is latent and the attainment of the perfection possible to the species and potential to the individual <the kitten's hunting instinct was not yet *developed* – Bertrand

Russell> and **ripen** emphasizes the approach to or attainment of the peak of perfection <at twenty-three she was still young enough to *ripen* to a maturer beauty – Ellen Glasgow> **Age** may equal *mature* when applied to the young but more often it implies approach to the period of decline or decay <the process of *aging* or deterioration – Susan Sontag>

In extended application to things with a capacity for improving all these terms imply a perfecting with time. **Mature** suggests completing changes <an art that toiling ages have but just *matured* – William Cowper> while **develop** suggests an unfolding of the potential, latent, or nebulous <the sense of fact is something very slow to *develop* – T. S. Eliot> Both *ripen* and *age* imply a becoming fit or more fit for some end over a period of time. Distinctively, **ripen** can suggest addition of desirable characteristics <time had *ripened* his life and mellowed its fruits – Van Wyck Brooks> while **age** tends to suggest elimination of unwanted qualities <*aging* tends toward the restoration of real equilibrium in the metal, and away from any unstable condition induced by a prior operation – S. E. Rusinoff>

meager, scanty, scant, skimpy, exiguous, spare, sparse *shared meaning* : falling short of what is normal, necessary, or desirable. **Meager** can suggest emaciation <*meager* were his looks, sharp misery had worn him to the bones – Shak.> or it can imply lack of fullness, richness, or plenty <a *meager* diet> <how *meager* one's life becomes when it is reduced to its basic facts – Helen MacInnes> **Scanty** emphasizes insufficiency <such a *scanty* portion of light was admitted . . . that it was difficult, on first coming in, to see anything – Charles Dickens> **Scant** implies deficiency, often as a result of deliberate action <a worthwhile addition to the *scant* literature on the subject – O. M. Smolansky> <treated his uninvited guest with *scant* courtesy> **Skimpy** can come close to *meager* <a *skimpy* strapless blue gown – Truman Capote> but distinctively it can suggest niggardliness or penury as the cause of the deficiency <state welfare benefits . . . tend to be *skimpiest* in Southern states – Burt Schorr> **Exiguous** implies a marked deficiency in number or measure that makes the thing described compare unfavorably with others of its kind <trying to ban *exiguous* bathing costumes from fashionable beaches – James Laver> <building ships to supplement his *exiguous* navy – John Buchan> **Spare** implies a falling short of what is fully sufficient and seldom suggests hardship or distress <his accent is slight, his voice even-toned, his gestures *spare* – G. L. Evans> <his story is taut, almost *spare* and tells of the heroism of the Danes – H. U. Ribalow> **Sparse** implies a thin scattering of units, especially where thickness or density is desirable <*sparse* gray hairs tried to cover his pate> <a *sparse* congregation of old women scattered over the church – Bruce Marshall> ***ant*** ample, copious

mean *adj* **mean, ignoble, abject, sordid** *shared meaning* : so low as to be out of accord with normal standards of human decency and dignity. **Mean** stresses inferiority and may suggest poverty or penury or dilapidation <in appearance the city was rather *mean* – Helen Gardner> <intensely *mean* with money – Iris Murdoch> or, as applied to persons, their conduct, or their attitudes, may suggest a repellent or unworthy quality <in his hands the traditional tools and attitudes were always employed toward *mean* ends – Thomas Pynchon> <a decidedly vulgar person, *mean* in his ideals and obtuse in his manners – John Erskine †1951> **Ignoble** suggests a loss or lack of some essential high quality of mind or spirit <if we seek merely swollen, slothful ease and *ignoble* peace . . . then bolder and stronger peoples will pass us by – Theodore Roosevelt> <it is not *ignoble,* nor in any way mean, to embrace the profession of politics – Ernest Barker> **Abject** may imply degradation, abasement, or servility <while the coward stands

aside Doubting in his *abject* spirit, till his Lord is crucified – J. R. Lowell> **Sordid** suggests dirtiness and emphasizes the degrading baseness associated with mental or physical corruption <books filled with *sordid,* filthy statements based on sexual deviations – *U.S. House of Repr. Report*> <*sordid* environments where Jesus Christ and God were only names used in profanity – *Boys' Life*>

mean *n* **1** see AVERAGE

2 mean, instrument, agent, medium *shared meaning* : something or someone necessary or useful in effecting an end. **Mean,** now usually as **means** which may be singular or plural in construction, is very general and may apply to anything (as a person, tool, action, or policy) that serves an end <we know that the pursuit of good ends does not justify the employment of bad *means* – Aldous Huxley> <had no *means* of traveling but his own two feet> **Instrument** as applied to persons, implies a secondary role, sometimes as a tool, sometimes as a dupe <turned on me . . . suspecting perhaps that I only wished to make an *instrument* of him – W. H. Hudson †1922> As applied to things it is likely to suggest a degree of fitness or adaptation for use as a tool and, indirectly, subordination to its user <factors that can make a school an *instrument* either for education or for debasement – Albert Cleage> **Agent** applies to a person who acts to achieve an end conceived by another <you were an unconscious *agent* in the hands of Providence when you recalled me from Tucson – Willa Cather> or to a thing that produces an immediate effect or definite result <an *agent* that turned the insect's own chemistry against itself – Isaac Asinov> **Medium** applies to a usually intangible means of conveying, transmitting, or communicating <when standards of criticism are lacking . . . the press becomes a *medium* of propaganda and entertainment – R. M. Hutchins> <established the validity of choreography as a dramatic *medium* – *Current Biog.*>

meaning, sense, acceptation, signification, significance, import *shared meaning* : the idea which something conveys to the mind. **Meaning** is the general term used of anything admitting of interpretation <I don't know the *meaning* of his behavior> <a dictionary gives the *meanings* of words> <understand a plain man in his plain *meaning* – Shak.> **Sense** denotes the or, more often, a particular, meaning (as of a word or phrase) <some words have many *senses*> In more abstract use it refers to intelligibility in general <speaks things . . . that carry but half *sense* – Shak.> **Acceptation** is used of a sense of a word or phrase as regularly understood <the term . . . will be used in its common *acceptation* – H. O. Taylor> *Signification* and *significance* are often interchangeable, but distinctively **signification** can apply to an established meaning of a term, symbol, or character, usually with the implication that this meaning is uniquely the one called to mind by use of the term, character, or symbol in question <the *signification* of the cross to Christians> while **significance** can apply specifically to a covert as distinct from the ostensible meaning of something <the mood was . . . , I thought, indicative of chinks in the saintly armor. Of course, I tend to see *significances* in everything – John Barth> **Import** may imply momentousness but it denotes the idea or impression conveyed by words <spoke words in her ear that had an awful *import* to her – George Meredith> <a major *import* of this article is that it matters very much indeed if we continue to delude ourselves – W. H. Ferry>

mechanical – see SPONTANEOUS

meddle, interfere, intermeddle, tamper *shared meaning* : to concern oneself with officiously, impertinently, or indiscreetly. One **meddles** *with* or *in* something that is not one's concern; the term suggests officiousness and acting without right or permission of those properly concerned <the driving

spirit of malice which forced him to *meddle* in other people's lives – Carl Van Doren> <the Japanese won't tolerate outside *meddling* in their internal political life – J. A. Michener> One **interferes** *with* someone or something or *in* something when one meddles in such a way as to hinder, interrupt, frustrate, disorder, or defeat; the word need not imply intent or even a conscious agent <a statement ... that he would not *interfere* with the selection of a constitutional government – S. E. Ambrose> <carbon dioxide *interferes* with the liberation of oxygen to the tissues – H. G. Armstrong> One **intermeddles** *with* or *in* something when one meddles impertinently and officiously and in such a way as to interfere <the board of control had no right whatsoever to *intermeddle* with the business – Edmund Burke> <unlearned men *intermeddle* with the practice of physic – G. G. Coulton> One **tampers** *with* someone or something when one seeks to make unwarranted alterations, to perform meddlesome experiments, or to exert an improper influence; the term may but need not suggest corruption or clandestine operation <laws making it illegal to *tamper* with an odometer – *Consumer Reports*> <the goal . . . was fixed; it was sacrilegious and dangerous to *tamper* with the dogmas – Frank Thilly>

meddlesome – see IMPERTINENT

median – see AVERAGE

mediate – see INTERPOSE

meditate – see PONDER

medium – see MEAN *n*

meek – see HUMBLE ***ant*** arrogant

meet *vb* – see SATISFY 3 ***ant*** disappoint

meet *adj* – see FIT ***ant*** unmeet

melodramatic – see DRAMATIC

melody, air, tune *shared meaning* : a clearly distinguishable succession of rhythmically ordered tones. **Melody** stresses the sweetness and beauty of the sound produced <sweetest *melodies* are those that are by distance made more sweet – William Wordsworth> and often suggests the expressiveness or moving power of a carefully wrought pattern <'tis a rich sobbing *melody,* with reliefs full and majestic – John Keats> **Air** is likely to apply to an easily remembered succession of tones which identifies a simple musical composition (as a ballad or waltz) but in technical use it applies to the dominating melody (usually carried by the upper voices) of a piece of vocal music. **Tune** can denote a usually simple musical composition <learned three *tunes* for the recital> or the air that gives it its character <can you remember the *tune* of "America"?>

member – see PART

memorable – see NOTEWORTHY

memory, remembrance, recollection, reminiscence *shared meaning* : the capacity for or act or action of remembering or something remembered. **Memory** stresses the capacity to bring back what one has once experienced or known <a good *memory* for faces> In application to what is remembered it can suggest retentive capacity more than a bringing back <a present moment of comfortable reality was worth a decade of *memories* – Thomas Hardy> **Remembrance** usually applies to the act or process of rather than the faculty for remembering <Roman soldiers . . . keep the restless Jews in *remembrance* of their provincial status – L. C. Douglas> or it may denote the state or fact of being kept in the memory <moments . . . that live again in *remembrance* – W. W. Gibson> **Recollection** adds an implication of consciously bringing back to mind often with some effort <there came to him a slight uneasiness, a movement of the memory, a distant *recollection* of something, somewhere, he had seen before – Roald Dahl> As applied to a product of remembering the term retains this suggestion of effort or even difficulty in remembering <the best that can be done by way of explaining a new kind of art . . . is to evoke *recollections* on the part of the reader which will be analogous to its specific nature – B. H. Hayes, Jr.> **Reminiscence** is likely to suggest the dredging up of what has long been buried in the mind often more or less casually or accidentally <the phenomena of involuntary *reminiscence* fascinate him – B. M. Woodbridge> <an old man's hazy *reminiscence* of his childhood> The term is likely to replace *recollection* in a concrete sense, especially when what is remembered serves as a contribution to a history, a biography, or a narrative <published a book of her grandfather's *reminiscences* of frontier life> ***ant*** oblivion

menace – see THREATEN

mend, repair, patch, rebuild *shared meaning* : to put into good order something that is injured, damaged, or defective. **Mend** basically implies a freeing from faults or defects <*mend* your manners> <the wound *mended* slowly>; in its application to the restoring of what is broken, torn, or damaged (as by use or wear) it may suggest relatively simple tasks calling for no great skill or professional equipment <*mend* a tear in a dress> <*mend* a broken dish with glue> In extended use *mend* is likely to stress the resulting putting in order without much regard to the means <whenever civilization palled upon him, he learned to *mend* his soul by going to sea – John Erskine †1951> **Repair** is likely to be preferred when the damage or dilapidation is such as to require professional assistance or special equipment; thus, one *mends* a leaky hose but, usually, *repairs* a leaking roof <sent his radio to be *repaired*> In extended use *repair* may be quite like *mend* <peace . . . cannot be *mended,* cannot be *repaired,* cannot be restored – Archibald MacLeish> or it may imply a making up for something <will *repair* his ignominious failure – Bernard De Voto> **Patch** can imply a repairing by the application or insertion of new material to close a rent or break <*patch* a torn shirt> Used with *up* it is likely to suggest careless, hasty, or inefficient repairing <try to *patch* the car up enough to get by this year> and this suggestion is present in much of its extended use even in the absence of *up* <*patch* up a disagreement> <thought that I would tinker just a little, try to *patch* a compromise – Norman Mailer> Especially with *together, patch* can imply a putting together of odd pieces in repairing or making <his life must be *patched* together from scattered references in the . . . colonial records – J. T. Adams> **Rebuild** suggests such thorough renovation and repair as make like new without completely replacing <*rebuild* a motor> <decide whether to *rebuild* the old organ or install a new one – *Harvard Alumni Bull.*>

mendacious – see DISHONEST ***ant*** veracious

menial – see SUBSERVIENT

mention, name, instance, specify *shared meaning* : to make clear or specific by referring to something explicitly. **Mention** indicates a calling attention to, either by name or by clear but incidental reference <*mentions* a kind of wine made from persimmons by the Indians – E. L. Core> <I shall *mention* the accident which directed my curiosity originally into this channel – Charles Lamb> **Name** implies clear mention of a name and therefore may suggest greater explicitness <he *names* golf, tennis, and music as his chief means of recreation – *Current Biog.*> **Instance** may indicate clear specific reference or citation as a typical example or special case <examples can be *instanced* from the first to the twentieth century – K. S. Latourette> <is it unfair to *instance* Marlowe, who died young? – A. T. Quiller-Couch> **Specify** implies statement so precise, explicit, and detailed that misunderstanding is impossible <the standards *specify* the names under which these five varieties must be sold – *Americana Annual*>

mercurial – see INCONSTANT ***ant*** saturnine

mercy, charity, grace, clemency, lenity *shared meaning* : a showing or a disposition to show kindness or compassion to others. **Mercy** implies compassion that forbears punishing even when justice demands it or that extends help even to the lowliest or most undeserving <earthly power doth then show likest God's when *mercy* seasons justice – Shak.> **Charity** stresses benevolence and goodwill, not as revealed merely in generous giving but also in broad understanding and kindly tolerance <with malice toward none, with *charity* for all – Abraham Lincoln> **Grace** implies a benign attitude, especially toward one's dependents, and a willingness to grant favors or make concessions <God's *grace* was not an efficacious infusion of a power moving toward the perfection of man; it was the forgiveness of sins, needed newly in each moment – J. M. Gustafson> **Clemency** implies a mild and merciful disposition in one having the responsibility of judging and punishing <*clemency* . . . is the standing policy of constitutional governments, as severity is of despotism – Henry Hallam> **Lenity,** otherwise very close to *clemency,* stresses extreme, even undue, lack of severity and may suggest a weak softness more than a manly compassion <what makes robbers bold but too much *lenity?* – Shak.> <his exceeding *lenity* disposes us to be somewhat too severe – T. B. Macaulay>

meretricious – see GAUDY

merge – see MIX

merry, blithe, jocund, jovial, jolly *shared meaning* : showing high spirits or lightheartedness. **Merry** suggests cheerful, joyous, uninhibited enjoyment of frolic or festivity <let us drink and be *merry,* dance, joke, and rejoice – Thomas Jordan> **Blithe** stresses freshness and lightheartedness and may suggest carefree, innocent, or even heedless gaiety <in the older woman . . . she found the *blithest* gayest fellow rebel and comrade – Walker Percy> <see this lovely child, *blithe,* innocent, and free – P. B. Shelley> **Jocund** applies to gladness marked by liveliness, exhilaration of spirits, and elation <a poet could not but be gay, in such a *jocund* company – William Wordsworth> **Jovial** suggests the stimulation of conviviality and good fellowship or sometimes the capacity for these <singing *jovial* choruses – H. O. Taylor> <his manner became more jaunty, *jovial,* half-jesting – Thomas Wolfe> **Jolly** may go beyond *jovial* in suggesting high spirits and a determination to keep one's companions easy and laughing <*jolly* parties drove to country inns – S. E. Morison> <ran down the street . . . with so *jolly* an air that he set everyone he passed into a good humor – R. L. Stevenson>

metamorphose – see TRANSFORM

meter – see RHYTHM

method, mode, manner, way, fashion, system *shared meaning* : the means or procedure used in attaining an end. **Method** implies orderly, logical, and effective arrangement, usually in steps <the inductive *method* of reasoning> <wrote down her *method* of making pea soup> <the crude *methods* of trial and error – Henry Suzzallo> **Mode** implies an order or course followed by custom, tradition, or personal preference <church architecture in general followed the *modes* of Europe – S. E. Morison> <living . . . with changes in their daily lives wrought by technological innovations, and with new *modes* of expression in the arts – M. S. Eisenhower> **Manner** is close to *mode* but may be preferred when reference is to a personal or peculiar course or procedure or to a distinctive method <mark the *manner* of his teaching – Shak.> <having a nice time. And

having it in an ordinary human *manner* – Stella D. Gibbons> **Way** may be used in place of any of the preceding terms and is found in many familiar idiomatic expressions <the prestige that the Western *way* of life has acquired – A. J. Toynbee> <if there were a single, definable *way* to develop writing skill – R. K. Corbin> **Fashion** may be close to *mode* but often it suggests a superficial or ephemeral origin or source or a motivation less abiding than those connoted by *way* <he will, after his sour *fashion*, tell you – Shak.> <I have been faithful to thee, Cynara! in my *fashion* – E. C. Dowson> **System** suggests a fully developed and often carefully formulated method <his manners, his speech and habits of thought all seemed so prescribed, so intricately connected to one another that they suggested a *system* of conduct – John Cheever>

methodize – see ORDER
meticulous – see CAREFUL
mettle – see COURAGE
mien – see BEARING
might – see POWER
mild – see SOFT ***ant*** harsh, fierce
militant – see AGGRESSIVE
military – see MARTIAL
mimic – see COPY
mind – see OBEY, TEND
mingle – see MIX
miniature – see SMALL
minimize – see DECRY ***ant*** magnify
minute – see CIRCUMSTANTIAL, SMALL
mirage – see DELUSION

mirth, glee, jollity, hilarity *shared meaning* **:** a mood or temper characterized by joy and high spirits and usually manifested in laughter or merrymaking. **Mirth** implies lightness of heart, love of gaiety, and readiness with laughter <there is an absence of *mirth* on today's campus, a lack of humor – R. E. Kavanaugh> <they seem to quiver on the edge of *mirth*, as if some deep continual laughter was repressed – Hallam Tennyson> **Glee** stresses exultation (as over joy, delight, or happiness) often expressed with laughter and smiles but sometimes in malicious gloating (as over the distress of an enemy) <the faces . . . appeared to be animated by some secret and unholy *glee* – Thomas Wolfe> **Jollity** suggests exuberance and lack of restraint in mirth or glee especially when experienced collectively <midnight shout and revelry, tipsy dance and *jollity* – John Milton> **Hilarity** implies exhilaration of spirits <through all the works of Chaucer, there reigns a cheerfulness, a manly *hilarity* – S. T. Coleridge> and may carry added implications of exuberance and boisterousness <the *hilarity* of the last night of carnival>

misanthropic – see CYNICAL ***ant*** philanthropic
miscarriage – see ABORTION
mischance – see MISFORTUNE

miserable, wretched *shared meaning* **:** deplorably or contemptibly bad or mean. **Miserable** implies a state of misery that may arise in extreme distress of body or mind <Gideon has been absolutely *miserable*, and gone about like a man half stunned, ever since it happened – Rose Macaulay> or in pitiable poverty or degradation <a *miserable* creature of a crazed aspect . . . shattered and made drunk by horror – Charles Dickens> In reference to things *miserable*, often used hyperbolically, suggests such meanness or inferiority or unpleasantness as must inflict misery on a person affected or arouse utter dislike or disgust in an observer <worked for a *miserable*

wage> <what *miserable* weather> <the squalor of mean and *miserable* streets – Laurence Binyon> **Wretched** is likely to stress the unhappiness or despondency of a person exposed to a grave distress (as want, grief, oppression, affliction, or anxiety) <it was her unhappy lot to be made more *wretched* by the only affection which she could not suspect – Joseph Conrad> <the *wretched* wife of the innocent man thus doomed to die – Charles Dickens> Applied to things *wretched* stresses extreme or deplorable badness <a *wretched* French cabaret, smelling vilely – George Meredith> <appalled at the *wretched* accident that had ended the afternoon – Herman Wouk> ***ant*** comfortable

miserly – see STINGY

misery – see DISTRESS ***ant*** felicity, blessedness

misfortune, mischance, mishap, adversity *shared meaning* : adverse fortune or an instance of this. **Misfortune** is applicable equally to the event or conjunction of events that causes an unhappy change of fortune <by *misfortune* he fell into bad company> or to the ensuing distress <seemed to him that the tie between husband and wife, even if breakable in prosperity, should be indissoluble in *misfortune* – Edith Wharton> **Mischance** rarely applies to a state of distress and is more likely to refer to a trivial annoyance than to a grave cause of distress <I threw a stone and hit a duck in the yard by *mischance* – W. B. Yeats> **Mishap** in this use is interchangeable with *mischance* <secure from worldly chances and *mishaps* – Shak.> though perhaps more often chosen when the event is felt as portentous <at any great *mishap,* such as . . . a landslide, the Yorubas offered up a human victim to turn away the anger of Oke – W. D. Wallis> **Adversity** denotes the state or an instance of adverse fortune rather than the cause <the Roman empire, though still at its height, was on the eve of falling into *adversity* – A. J. Toynbee> In application to the instance *adversity* is normally used in the plural <the many misfortunes and *adversities* Bolivia has suffered – *Americas*> ***ant*** happiness, prosperity

mishap – see MISFORTUNE

mislay – see MISPLACE

mislead – see DECEIVE

misogynic – see CYNICAL

misplace, mislay *shared meaning* : to put in a wrong place so as to be as unavailable as if lost. **Misplace** basically implies a putting of something in another than its customary or usual place <invoices continually being forgot or *misplaced* by the departments – Terry Southern> but often it suggests a setting or fixing of something where it should not be <her confidence in him was *misplaced*> <the globe and scepter in such hands *misplaced* – William Cowper> **Mislay** usually implies a misplacing in the basic sense but stresses a forgetting of the place in which the thing has been put; it therefore often means to lose, usually temporarily, through misplacing <I have *mislaid* my glasses> and in extended use is scarcely distinguishable from *lose* <some of the literary qualities of *Darkness at Noon* have been *mislaid* in the process of bringing it to the stage – John Mason Brown>

misrepresent, falsify, belie, garble *shared meaning* : to present or represent in a manner contrary to the truth. **Misrepresent** usually implies an intent to deceive and may suggest deliberate lying and often bias, prejudice, or a will to be unfair <*misrepresent* the value of property offered for sale> <presents much from a partisan point of view; yet he never intentionally *misrepresents* – W. H. Allison> **Falsify** implies a tampering with or distorting of facts or reality that is usually, but not necessarily, deliberate and intended to deceive <*falsify* the records of a business to conceal embezzlement>

<history was so *falsified* in the new textbooks . . . that it became ludicrous – W. L. Shirer> <a low-priced sunglass lens said to be completely effective without *falsifying* the colors seen through it – *Newsweek*> **Belie** implies an impression given that is at variance with fact; the word stresses contrast and does not ordinarily suggest intent <his physical carriage and the alert, independent gleam in his eye *belie* his years – Lillian Freedgood> <an air of rural charm . . . *belies* the community's industrial activity – *Amer. Guide Series: Pa.*> **Garble** implies mutilation or distortion (as of facts, reports, testimony, or translations) that may or may not be intentional but that regularly creates a wrong impression of the original and often gravely alters its tone or meaning <their disputes . . . have not been edifying, since both sides have been apt to *garble* the question – Gilbert Ryle> <statements . . . *garbled* into absurdity when copied into the newspapers – Havelock Ellis>

mist – see HAZE

mistake *vb* **mistake, confuse, confound** *shared meaning* : to take one thing to be another. One **mistakes** one thing *for* another when (as by an error of perception or thought) one fails to recognize the thing or to grasp its real nature and therefore identifies it with something not itself <*mistake* gush for vigor and substitute rhetoric for imagination – C. D. Lewis> <could be and often was *mistaken* for a farmer – H. S. Canby> One **confuses** one thing *with* another when one fails to distinguish two things that have similarities or common characteristics <far too intellectually keen to *confuse* moral problems with purely aesthetic problems – Havelock Ellis> <most of our girls look so much alike . . . that they tend to lose their identities and one is prone to *confuse* them – Terry Southern> One **confounds** things, or one thing *with* another, when one mixes them up so hopelessly as to be unable to detect their differences or distinctions; the term usually carries a strong connotation of mental bewilderment or of a muddled mind <the temptation to *confound* accumulated knowledge and experience with intrinsic progress is almost irresistible – W. R. Inge> <they implored Charles not to *confound* the innocent with the guilty – T. B. Macaulay> ***ant*** recognize

mistake *n* – see ERROR

mistrust – see UNCERTAINTY ***ant*** trust, assurance

mitigate – see RELIEVE ***ant*** intensify

mix, mingle, commingle, blend, merge, coalesce, amalgamate, fuse *shared meaning* : to combine or be combined into a more or less uniform whole. **Mix** need not imply loss of identity to the parts but it does imply a relatively homogeneous product <*mix* salt and pepper> <a style that *mixes* erudition and bawdiness – *Saturday Rev.*> <manual and intellectual labor seldom *mix* well – H. S. Canby> **Mingle** is likely to imply that the constituents remain quite identifiable in the product <the evil . . . strangely *mingled* with the good – Irving Babbitt> **Commingle** may suggest greater unity and harmoniousness <*commingled* with the gloom of imminent war, the shadow of his loss drew like eclipse, darkening the world – Alfred Tennyson> **Blend** may be equivalent to *mix* or *mingle* <a tale that *blends* their glory with their shame – Alexander Pope> but usually it implies that the elements as such disappear in enhancing the mixture <our age and . . . modern Christianity need to *blend* a realistic understanding of human nature with idealistic aspiration and an unyielding faith in man's capacity for goodness – Robert Gordis> <a *blended* tea> **Merge** suggests a combining in which one or more elements are lost in the whole <*merge* the private in the general good> <these people did not, however, *merge* anonymously into some homogeneous mass – Oscar Handlin> **Coalesce** implies an affinity in merging elements and usually a resulting organic unity

<when mankind has *coalesced* into a single worldwide society living under a single worldwide government – A. J. Toynbee> <if the right combination of forces had not *coalesced* at the right time – Hubert Humphrey> **Amalgamate** is likely to suggest effective or harmonious union rather than loss of identity <thesis and plot are carefully *amalgamated* – F. B. Millet> <policy of conciliating and *amalgamating* conquered nations – Agnes Repplier> **Fuse,** even more than *blend* and *merge,* stresses loss of identity of the parts and implies oneness and indissolubility of the product <time and history, fact and interpretation of fact, *fuse* here into something not quite poetry, not quite history – Ned O'Gorman> <the real point of a work of art is indeed that it *fuses* and resolves all the forces around it . . . into a unified experience – *Saturday Rev.*>

mob – see CROWD

mobile – see MOVABLE ***ant*** immobile

mock – see COPY, RIDICULE

mode – see FASHION, METHOD

model, example, pattern, exemplar, ideal *shared meaning* : something set or held before one for guidance or imitation. **Model** applies to something taken or proposed as worthy of imitation <there is no poet in any tongue . . . who stands so firmly as a *model* for all poets – T. S. Eliot> <he was the very *model* of what a great captain . . . should be – Thomas Wolfe> **Example** applies to something and especially to a person to be imitated or, in some contexts, on no account to be imitated but to be taken rather as a warning <personal *example* will carry more weight than sage advice or official edict – C. R. Woodward> <let it profit thee to have heard, by terrible *example,* the reward of disobedience – John Milton> <much depends on the *example* parents set their children> **Pattern** suggests a clear and detailed archetype or prototype <a *pattern* for a dress> <the periodicals . . . treated events . . . as an understandable sequence and gave them discernible *pattern* – Terry Southern> **Exemplar** suggests either a faultless example to be imitated or a perfect typification <Christ is the . . . *exemplar* that all preachers ought to follow – Hugh Latimer> <England was the admired *exemplar* of national strength based on ordered liberties within a secure framework of aristocratic power – *Times Lit. Supp.*> **Ideal** implies the best possible exemplification either in reality or in conception <[Livia] embodied in her life the *ideal* of the Roman matron – John Buchan> <the *ideal* of romantic love became the dominating convention. It has always disguised a good deal that is mercenary, prosaic or sordid – Edmund Wilson>

moderate *adj* **moderate, temperate** *shared meaning* : not excessive in degree, amount, or intensity. In many general applications the words are essentially neutral and interchangeable except as idiom dictates a preference <a *moderate* allowance> <*temperate* heat> In certain uses, however, the words are contrasted; in such use **moderate** is likely to connote absence or avoidance of excess and is opposed to *excessive* and *immoderate,* while **temperate** connotes deliberate restraint or restriction and is opposed to *inordinate* and *intemperate.* Thus, "a *moderate* drinker" suggests free but far from excessive indulgence in intoxicants, and "a *temperate* drinker" suggests restrained and cautious indulgence; "*moderate* enthusiasm" suggests lukewarmness, "*temperate* enthusiasm" suggests careful control of one's exhibition of feeling <when they died they died, for the most part, in contentment, shriven of their *moderate,* parochial sins – William Styron> <he was a scholar and a stoic; what *temperate* virtues he owned had been hard won – William Styron> ***ant*** immoderate

moderate *vb* **moderate, qualify, temper** *shared meaning* : to modify so as to avoid an extreme or keep within bounds. **Moderate** stresses reduction of what is excessive without necessarily reaching an optimum <*moderating* his big voice to the dimensions of the room – Clifton Daniel> <the sun *moderated* the chill> **Qualify** emphasizes a restricting that more precisely defines and limits <[he] drew from many critics general praise *qualified* by blame for his final editorial – *Current Biog.*> <statements were explained and *qualified* in the author's lectures – H. O. Taylor> **Temper** strongly implies an accommodating to a special need or requirement and is more likely to suggest a counterbalancing or mitigating addition than a moderating or qualifying <*temper* justice with mercy> <his ancient and Hebraic spirit was *tempered* with a classic sense of moderation – Thomas Wolfe>

modern 1 modern, recent, late *shared meaning* : having taken place, existed, or developed in times close to the present. In spite of the common element of meaning these words are seldom freely interchangeable without loss of exactness. **Modern** may date anything that is not ancient or medieval <the weed-caught wrecks of ancient galleys, medieval ships, and *modern* dreadnaughts – William Beebe> or anything that bears the marks of a period nearer in time than another <ornate mansions of a bygone era mingle with more *modern* concepts of architecture – *N.Y. Times*> or, less clearly, may apply to whatever is felt as new, fresh, or up-to-date <what is *modern* today and up-to-date . . . becomes obsolete and outworn tomorrow – F. D. Roosevelt> In all these uses a change or contrast in character or quality is implicit. **Recent** usually lacks such implication and applies to a date that approximates the immediate past more or less precisely according to the nature of the thing qualified; thus, "*recent* geological ages" may date back millions of years but immediately precede the present geological age; "Shakespeare is a more *recent* author than Chaucer" implies only a comparative statement; "we have all the *recent* books on the subject" implies an absolute relation to a time that can be described as the immediate past <*recent* news> <a *recent* change of plans> **Late** usually implies a series or succession of which the one described is the most recent in time <the *late* war> <his *late* supervisor gave him a strong recommendation> but it can sometimes be less indefinite and equivalent to "not long ago being or serving as" <the firm's new director of research was the *late* professor of chemistry at the state university> ***ant*** antique, ancient

2 see NEW ***ant*** antique, ancient

modest 1 see CHASTE ***ant*** immodest

2 see HUMBLE ***ant*** ambitious

3 see SHY

modify – see CHANGE *vb*

moist – see WET

mollycoddle – see INDULGE

moment – see IMPORTANCE

momentary – see TRANSIENT ***ant*** agelong

monastery – see CLOISTER

monetary – see FINANCIAL

monk – see RELIGIOUS

monopolize, engross, absorb, consume *shared meaning* : to take up completely. **Monopolize,** the most general term, means to possess or control completely <every railroad *monopolizes,* in a popular sense, the trade of some area – O. W. Holmes †1935> <a party that purports to *monopolize* the interests and articulate the ideological wrath of an entire class – Harvey

Wheeler> Occasionally **engross** implies getting a material control of <the sun *engrossed* the east; the day controlled the world – Emily Dickinson> <*engross* a market by buying up available supplies> but more often it implies an unprotested monopolizing of time, attention, or interest <*engrossed* with a new magazine> <political theory has long *engrossed* the Indian mind – H. I. Poleman> **Absorb** is often interchangeable with *engross* but it tends to carry a hint of submission to pressure rather than ready acceptance <I never got accustomed to this question, nor can I yet *absorb* it without anger – J. A. Michener> <petty cares and vexations that *absorb* life's energies – M. R. Cohen> **Consume** in the somewhat extended sense here pertinent implies a monopolization of one's time, interest, or attention <he is *consumed* with the idea of justice – Kay Boyle> <the American conscience today is paralyzed by . . . a *consuming* inner anxiety – M. D. Geismar>

monopoly, corner, pool, syndicate, trust, cartel *shared meaning* : a means of or system for controlling prices. In spite of the common meaning element the terms in precise use are seldom interchangeable. **Monopoly** implies exclusive control of a public service or exclusive power to buy or sell a commodity in a particular market <our modern electric utilities are controlled and regulated *monopolies*> <exceptional scientists, artists, and writers may command *monopoly* rents because of the uniqueness and marketability of their talents. *Monopoly* is an attribute of the uniqueness of any service – R. A. Mundell> **Corner** applies to a temporary effective monopoly of something sold on an exchange so that buyers are forced to pay the price asked <maintained his *corner* on wheat for three days> **Pool** applies to a joint undertaking by apparently competing companies to regulate output and manipulate prices. **Syndicate** in financial circles refers to a temporary association of individuals or firms to effect a particular piece of business (as the marketing of a security issue); in more general use the term applies to a combination (as of newspapers, business firms, or criminals) interested in a common project or enterprise and often carries suggestions of monopoly. **Trust** historically applies to a merger of companies in which control is vested in trustees and stockholders exchange their stock for trust certificates in the new company; but *trust* is often extended to any large or complex combination of business interests especially when felt to represent a threat to healthy competition. **Cartel** commonly implies an international combination for controlling production and sale of one or more products.

monstrous 1 monstrous, prodigious, tremendous, stupendous *shared meaning* : extremely impressive. **Monstrous** implies a departure from the normal (as in size, in form, or in character) and often carries added suggestions of deformity, ugliness, or fabulousness <the imagination turbid with *monstrous* fancies and misshapen dreams – Oscar Wilde> <a *monstrous* mechanized juggernaut such as the earth had never seen – W. L. Shirer> **Prodigious** suggests a marvelousness exceeding belief, usually in something felt as far beyond a previous maximum (as of goodness, greatness, intensity, or size) <men have always reverenced *prodigious* inborn gifts, and always will – C. W. Eliot> <she envied . . . their *prodigious* self-sufficiency, their tacit exclusion of all the world outside their own circle – Victoria Sackville-West> **Tremendous** may imply a power to terrify or inspire awe <the spell and *tremendous* incantation of the thought of death – L. P. Smith> but in more general and much weakened use it means little more than very large or great or intense <a *tremendous* noise> <make a *tremendous* effort> <success gave him *tremendous* satisfaction> **Stupendous** implies a power to stun or astound, usually because of size, numbers, complexity,

or greatness that exceed one's powers of description <all are but parts of one *stupendous* whole, whose body Nature is, and God the soul – Alexander Pope>
2 see OUTRAGEOUS

mood, humor, temper, vein *shared meaning* : a state of mind in which an emotion or set of emotions gains ascendancy. **Mood**, the most general term, imputes pervasiveness and compelling quality to the ascendant emotion and may apply not only to the frame of mind but to its expression (as in art) <he indulged his *moods.* If he were surly, he did not bother to hide it; if he were aggressive, he would swear at her – Norman Mailer> <the language, the stresses . . . are imposed upon the writer by the special *mood* of the piece – Willa Cather> **Humor** implies a mood that is imposed on one by one's special temperament or one's physical or mental condition at the moment <I am not in a *humor* to hear you further. Leave me, please – Thomas Hardy> <victims of nature's cataclysmic *humors* – Julian Dana> **Temper** applies to a mood dominated by a single strong emotion, often that of anger <although he could somehow adapt himself to her *tempers,* it was this sudden change of mood that he felt he could never cope with – William Styron> **Vein** suggests a transitory mood or humor usually without any profound temperamental or physical basis <the merry *vein* you knew me in, is sunk into a turn of reflection – Alexander Pope>

moral, ethical, virtuous, righteous, noble *shared meaning* : conforming to a standard of what is right and good. **Moral** may be opposed to *immoral* in implying conformity to a standard of what is good and right <a man of high *moral* character> or concern with or devotion to such a standard <tragedy . . . hath been ever held the gravest, *moralest,* and most profitable of all other poems – John Milton> or it may contrast with *intellectual* or *aesthetic* as being concerned with character or conduct rather than with achievement, beauty, success, or logical perfection <the whole tendency of modern thought . . . is to extenuate the responsibility of human nature, not merely on the *moral* side, but equally on the spiritual side – Compton Mackenzie> <imperfect . . . competition is the prevailing mode . . . . This is a fact, not a *moral* condemnation – P. A. Samuelson> **Ethical** may suggest the involvement of more difficult or subtle questions of rightness, fairness, or equity; usually it implies existence of or conformance to an elevated code of standards <meanwhile we hear . . . the *ethical* instinct of mankind asserting itself with splendid courage and patience – Henry van Dyke> <search . . . for workable *ethical* tests against which he can measure the degree to which various ventures enhance or dilute human freedom – Denis Goulet> **Virtuous** implies the possession or manifestation of moral excellence <her life had been *virtuous,* her dedication to innocence had been unswerving – John Cheever> **Righteous** stresses guiltlessness or blamelessness <I came not to call the *righteous,* but sinners to repentance – *Mk* 2:17 (AV)> It may imply justifiability and consciousness of rectitude <*righteous* indignation> or, in a worsened sense, an invalid and sanctimonious assumption of the appearance of rectitude <meets the resultant gossip . . . with a *righteous* indifference to . . . his share in it – *Harper's Bazaar*> **Noble** implies moral eminence and freedom from whatever is mean, petty, or dubious in conduct and character <a *noble* aim, faithfully kept, is as a *noble* deed – William Wordsworth>

morally – see VIRTUALLY

moron – see FOOL

morose – see SULLEN

mortal – see DEADLY *ant* venial (*especially of a sin*)

motive *n* **motive, spring, impulse, incentive, inducement, spur, goad** *shared meaning* : a stimulus to action. **Motive** applies chiefly to an emotion or desire operating on the will and causing it to act <always seeking the *motive* of everyone's speech or behavior – W. C. Brownell> <ordinarily his *motive* is a wish to . . . avoid unfavorable notice and comment – Thorstein Veblen> **Spring,** often as the plural **springs,** suggests a basic motive, often not fully recognized <laying open to his view the *springs* of action in both parties – T. L. Peacock> **Impulse** is likely to suggest a driving force arising from personal temperament or constitution <he believed in accepting the human affections and *impulses,* good or bad, in all their power, their uncertainty, their essential tragedy – M. D. Geismar> and may apply specifically to a sudden, unconsidered, and nearly irresistible urge to do something <*impulse* buying inevitably leading to disappointment – Harry Heywood> **Incentive** applies to an external influence (as a hope of reward) inciting to action <money is not the only *incentive* to work, nor the strongest – G. B. Shaw> **Inducement** suggests a motive prompted by the deliberate enticements or allurements of another <his method of holding his followers together by culinary and bibulous *inducements* – L. M. Sears> <promised reward is an *inducement* to effort> **Spur** applies to a motive that stimulates the faculties or increases ardor or energy <fame is the *spur* that the clear spirit doth raise . . . to scorn delights and live laborious days – John Milton> **Goad** suggests a stimulus or motive that keeps one going against one's will or desire <the daily *goad* urging him to the daily toil – T. B. Macaulay>

motive *adj* – see MOVABLE

mount – see ASCEND *ant* dismount

mourn – see GRIEVE

movable, mobile, motive *shared meaning* : capable of moving or of being moved. **Movable** applies to what can be moved or to what is not fixed in position or date; thus, *movable* goods are goods that are not fixed to the land and are capable of being transported; a *movable* feast is one (as Easter) that does not fall on the same day and month each year. **Mobile** stresses facility and ease in moving or, occasionally, in being moved <delicately sniffing the air to the left of him with his *mobile* nose end – Roald Dahl> <they need job skills to become upwardly *mobile* – James Farmer> <a *mobile* radio-transmitting unit> **Motive** applies to an agent capable of causing movement or impelling to action <diesel engines supply the *motive* power for the ship> <his *motive* force is a blissful and naïve faith – Leo Rosten> *ant* immovable, stationary

move, actuate, drive, impel *shared meaning* : to set or keep in motion. **Move** is very general and often implies no more than the fact of changing position <*move* the cat off the table> <the people who are going to *move* and shake the next ten years – Victor Palmieri> <forces that *move* men's lives – Denis Goulet> **Actuate** stresses the communication of power to work or set in motion <most of the hydraulically operated items of equipment are *actuated* by pistons and cylinders – W. R. Sears> <in forming his library . . . [he] was primarily *actuated* by his interest in the history of book production – *Times Lit. Supp.*> **Drive** implies imparting progressive and continuous motion and often stresses the effect rather than the impetus <a machine *driven* by electricity> <*drive* a golf ball down the fairway> <[he] was *driven* by an obsession to find treasure – James Atwater> **Impel** implies great force in the impetus <imitated the action of a man's being *impelled* forward by the butt ends of muskets – Charles Dickens> <a life of adventure . . . was that to which his nature irresistibly *impelled* him – Matthew Arnold>

ıoving, impressive, poignant, affecting, touching, pathetic *shared meaning* having the power to excite deep and usually somber emotion. **Moving** nplies stirring deeply so as to evoke a strong emotional response <a *moving* ppeal for help> <a *moving* revelation of child life in an orphange – lary MacColl> **Impressive** implies such forcefulness as compels a response is of admiration, awe, wonder, or conviction) <his arguments were very *npressive*> <the leader who built the most *impressive* ruling system his ountry has seen for more than a century – A. S. Whiting> **Poignant** iggests an impression so painfully sharp that it pierces one's heart or keenly ffects one's sensibilities <Guevara's death was *poignant* because he was omething of an international folk hero – *Commonweal*> <she left him ith relief and a *poignant* sense of all she had wasted of the night – Bernard lalamud> **Affecting** is close to *moving*, but more often suggests pathos <the scenes of disappointment are quite *affecting* – Walt Whitman> <an *ffecting* exposition of what seems to him a tragic situation – Naomi Bliven> **ouching** implies a capacity to arouse tenderness or compassion <most ıen's *touching* illusion as to the frailness of women and their spiritual fragility - Joseph Conrad> <the music . . . is hair-raising rather than *touching*, nd when one has heard it one is glad that it is over rather than deeply ıoved – Winthrop Sargeant> **Pathetic** implies a capacity to move one pity, whether from compassion <*pathetic* gropings after the fragments f a shattered faith – C. D. Lewis> or in contempt <a *pathetic* attempt make a virtue of necessity – Aldous Huxley> <displaying a *pathetic* ıobbishness born out of a sense of insecurity and confusion – L. E. Hurt>

ıuddy – see TURBID

ıulct – see PENALIZE

ıulish – see OBSTINATE

ıultiply – see INCREASE

ıundane – see EARTHLY *ant* eternal

ıunificent – see LIBERAL

ıurder – see KILL

ıurky – see DARK

ıuse – see PONDER

ıuster – see SUMMON

ıusty – see MALODOROUS

ıutation – see CHANGE *n*

ıutilate – see MAIM

ıutiny – see REBELLION

ıutual – see RECIPROCAL

ıysterious, inscrutable, arcane *shared meaning* : being beyond one's powers discover, understand, or explain. Something **mysterious** excites wonder, ıriosity, or surmise yet baffles attempts to explain it <God moves in a *ıysterious* way his wonders to perform – William Cowper> <brought ack a vivid report on remote and *mysterious* Tibet – W. O. Douglas> omething **inscrutable** defies one's efforts to examine or investigate it or interpret its significance or meaning <great God, thy judgments are *ıscrutable!* – Robert Browning> <most of the time he sat behind a look f bland absorption, now and then permitting himself an *inscrutable* smile H. C. Hervey> Something **arcane** is beyond comprehension because nown or knowable only to the possessor of a restricted key; the word ıay come close to *occult* in meaning but it stresses the reservation of what necessary for comprehension rather than the supranatural character of hat is not understood <his wife, who had her own *arcane* rites such as rranging flowers and cleaning closets – John Cheever> <stories relating

in high drama the *arcane* comings and goings of international bankers an government officials – D. M. Kiefer>

mystery, problem, enigma, riddle, puzzle, conundrum *shared meaning* : some thing which baffles or perplexes. **Mystery** applies to whatever cannot b understood by human reason <the *mystery* of the Holy Trinity> or, les strictly, to whatever attracts curiosity and speculation but resists or defie explanation <no one tradition has all the answers to the *mystery* of existenc and to the challenge of the human condition – Robert Gordis> <it a *mystery* where that boy goes every day> **Problem** applies to any questio or difficulty calling for a solution or causing concern <the way he brok down a major *problem* into a number of relatively minor decisions – F J. Bryant> <she was very bored with the *problems* of being a girl – Herma Wouk> **Enigma** is basically applicable to utterance or behavior that i difficult to interpret <the ancient oracles usually spoke in *enigmas*> bu is often extended to whatever is inscrutable or beyond the range of unaide intelligence <the questions, riddles, aches, and pleasures which surroun the *enigma* of life – Norman Mailer> **Riddle** applies to an enigma or prob lem involving paradox or apparent contradiction <tried to read the *riddl* of this girl's future – John Galsworthy> **Puzzle** applies to an enigma c problem that challenges ingenuity for its solution <hoary old *puzzles* c Ethics and Philosophy – L. P. Smith> **Conundrum** can apply to punnin riddles or to problems whose solution is purely speculative <they rouse him with jam and judicious advice: they set him *conundrums* to guess - Lewis Carroll> <Octavius . . . looked beyond the political *conundrum* t the economic problems of the land – John Buchan>

myth, legend, saga *shared meaning* : a traditional story of ostensibly historic content whose origin has been lost. **Myth** is varied in application an connotation; it can apply to a fanciful explanation (as of a natural phenome non, social practice, or belief) <*myths* of ancient Greece> <the old *my* . . . which represented the cat-moon devouring the gray mice of twilig – Agnes Repplier> or a story, belief, or notion commonly held to be tru but utterly without fact <trying to turn the young from the *myth* th drugs solve everything toward a belief in the active struggle to grow *Look*> <most women are so enslaved to the *myths* of their own inferiori they are unable to see the truth for the *myths* – M. F. A. Montagu> **Legend** typically applies to a story, incident, or notion attached to a particul person or place that purports to be historical though in fact unverifiab or incredible <an American *legend* – that of the poor boy who profi from the hardships of his early life and "makes good" – Thomas Wolfe> <the fabulous Jerry O'Shaugnessy . . . . In the old days . . . they had mad a *legend* of him. All of them with their middle-class origins and their desi to know a worker-hero – Norman Mailer> **Saga** may refer to a lon continued, heroic story that deals with a person or a group and is historic or legendary or a mixture of both <the *Saga* of Burnt Njal> <the buildi of the railroad in the Northwest was one of the great *sagas* of man's enterpri – Meridel Le Sueur> Application of *saga* to any complicated accou or history is common but frowned upon by many precise writers an speakers.

mythical – see FICTITIOUS

naïve – see NATURAL
naked – see BARE
name – see MENTION
narrative – see STORY

asty – see DIRTY
ational – see CITIZEN
ative, indigenous, endemic, aboriginal *shared meaning* : belonging to a ocality. **Native** implies birth or origin in a place or region and may suggest ompatibility with it <a *native* New Yorker> <*native* strawberries are ow on the market> <*native* English speech> **Indigenous** applies especially o species or races and adds to *native* the specific implication of not having een introduced from without <the Spanish began exploiting the natives or gold and destroying the complex *indigenous* culture – Arnold Gordon> <maize, potatoes, and tomatoes are *indigenous* to the Americas> <Afri-aans can perhaps be regarded as an *indigenous* language, since it is the nother tongue of four million South Africans, and is spoken nowhere else - P. L. Van Den Berghe> **Endemic** applies to what is not only indigenous ut is also peculiar to or restricted to its area of origin <edelweiss is *endemic* n the Alps> <that complacency which is an *endemic* disease of academic roups – J. B. Conant> **Aboriginal** typically applies to the earliest known uman race inhabiting a region and is likely to connote a primitive culture <a primitive *aboriginal* race in the southeast of Sumatra – J. G. Frazer>
nt alien, foreign
atural *adj* **1** see REGULAR ***ant*** unnatural, artificial, adventitious
natural, ingenuous, naïve, unsophisticated, artless *shared meaning* : free rom pretension or calculation. **Natural** at once implies freedom from all rtificiality and constraint and an easy spontaneity that suggests nature ather than art <set him to write poetry, he is limited, artificial, and npotent; set him to write prose, he is free, *natural,* and effective – Matthew rnold> <what charming children they both were . . . ; *natural,* unspoilt, nd so good to look at – Victoria Sackville-West> **Ingenuous** stresses nability to hide one's thoughts and feelings and usually implies candid rankness and lack of reserve, often with a hint of childlike simplicity <content to . . . listen to her prattle, contrasting her with other women nd thinking how deliciously *ingenuous* she was, both in her confidences nd in her reservations – Victoria Sackville-West> **Naïve** is likely to stress ck of worldly wisdom which may be the result of a nature untouched y worldly influences <he claimed to himself to be innocent or *naïve,* but is pretense was the thinnest – John Cheever> <a *naïve* prophetic church f puritanical austerity, basing itself on the Word of God, enthusiastically athing the world – Michael Grant> or of one incapable of enlightenment <that *naïve* patriotism which leads every race to regard itself as evidently perior to every other – J. W. Krutch> **Unsophisticated** also stresses lack f worldly wisdom but tends to suggest lack of experience and training s its source; the term often specifically implies lack of competence and noothness or ease in social adjustment <she's not the type of the moment, ot elegant or artificial, too much the *unsophisticated* child of nature – ose Macaulay> **Artless** lays stress on the absence of design and suggests naturalness resulting from unawareness of the effect one is producing <overflowing with . . . *artless* maternal gratitude – Jane Austen>
atural *n* – see FOOL
ature – see TYPE
aughty – see BAD
earest, next *shared meaning* : closest. Though often interchangeable, idiom equently demands their discrimination. In such use **nearest** implies the ighest degree of propinquity (as in space, time, or kinship) and **next** implies nmediate succession, occasionally precedence, in an order, a series, or a equence. Thus, "the *nearest* house" is that house physically closest to the ne under consideration; "the *next* house" is the one just beyond the one

in mind in a row of houses, whether it is closest or not; "the *nearest* gate" may be before or behind one or off one's direct course, but "the *next* gate" is the one toward which one is moving <the *nearest* house is over a mil away> <the *next* house on this road is just around the bend> <you passed the *nearest* gas station, the *next* one is ten miles further on> <in legal use one's *nearest* relative is one's *next* of kin> <pick up the *neares* book> <read the *next* chapter aloud>

nearly, almost, approximately, well-nigh *shared meaning* : within a little o being, becoming, reaching, or sufficing. Their differences in meaning ar often imperceptible. However, **nearly** is suitable when mere proximity i implied <it is *nearly* six o'clock> <we were *nearly* home when the acciden happened> <she was *nearly* hysterical from fright> **Almost** is more explici when the emphasis is on a falling short or deficiency <*almost* out of he mind with grief> <there's *almost* enough meat for another meal> <*almos* too tired to speak> **Approximately** is an appropriate choice when th difference is of no practical importance and a reasonable approach t accuracy is implied <there were *approximately* 10,000 people at the rally> <that boundary of the property is *approximately* 951 feet long> <weathe forecasts cannot be more than *approximately* accurate> **Well-nigh** implie the closest approach short of identity <the acting ... was described b critics as "*well-nigh* perfect" – *Current Biog.*>

neat, tidy, trim, trig *shared meaning* : manifesting care and orderliness. **Nea** in all its uses retains its basic implication of clearness, be it manifeste in freedom from dirt and soil <her house is as *neat* as a pin> <he wa remarkably *neat* in his dress – Samuel Johnson> or in freedom from clutte complication, or confusion <*neat* workmanship> <they were very *nea* stories, very plotted, very "tight" – Nancy Hale> <he has a *neat* gif of expression and a sense of humor always present – *N.Y. Times*> o in freedom from any admixture <a remark is not to be taken *neat,* bu watered with the ideas of common sense – O. W. Holmes †1894> **Tid** suggests pleasing neatness and order diligently maintained <a *tidy* des with everything in its proper place> <persons of Aunt Ada's temperamen were not fond of a *tidy* life. Storms were what they liked; plenty of rows, .. jaws sticking out, and faces white with fury – Stella D. Gibbons> **Trin** implies both neatness and tidiness, but it stresses the smartness and spruce ness of appearance that is given by clean lines and excellent proportion <a *trim* yacht> <his shoes and buckles, too, though plain, were *trim* – Charles Dickens> **Trig,** though close to *trim,* tends to stress compactnes and jaunty neatness <so *trig* in fashionable clothes that he made me fee awkward and uncomfortable – Irving Bacheller> ***ant*** filthy

necessity – see NEED

need *n* **need, necessity, exigency** *shared meaning* : a pressing lack of some thing essential. **Need** implies pressure and urgency <felt the *need* of a education> <children have a *need* for affection> and may suggest distres <collecting supplies for those who were in *need*> or indispensability <orde and discipline were the crying *needs* – Kemp Malone> <the *need* for new water supply> **Necessity** carries less emotional connotation but is likel to stress imperative demand or compelling cause <the present *necessity* t ensure that supply and demand remain in balance – Robert Theobald> <call me only in case of *necessity*> **Exigency** adds the implication of un usual difficulty or restriction imposed by special circumstances <teacher who have spent many years adapting their ideas and personalities to th rigid *exigencies* of Southern Negro schools – Christopher Jencks> <such travel *exigencies* as having to scout around for a room when you're tire – Richard Joseph>

need *vb* – see LACK
nefarious – see VICIOUS
negate – see DENY, NULLIFY
negative *adj* – see NEUTRAL *ant* affirmative
negative *vb* – see DENY
neglect, omit, disregard, ignore, overlook, slight, forget *shared meaning* : to pass over without giving due attention. **Neglect** implies giving insufficient attention to something or someone that has a claim upon one's care or attention <became interested in golf and *neglected* his reading> <appearances must be respected, though morals might be *neglected* – Victoria Sackville-West> <*neglect* to answer a letter> **Omit** can imply a leaving out of a part of a whole <*omit* two stanzas of a hymn> or a neglecting entirely (as from oversight, inattention, or preoccupation) <like many such histories it *omits* to examine the beliefs of primitive societies – *Times Lit. Supp.*> **Disregard** suggests voluntary, sometimes deliberate, inattention <*disregard* petty annoyances> <flouting convention and *disregarding* his own clerical position – Oscar Handlin> **Ignore** implies a failure to regard something obvious and especially an avoidance of what one does not wish to recognize <*ignore* a heckler> <historians are pessimists because they *ignore* the banks for the river – Will Durant> <its theory contains certain impossibilities which are *ignored* in practice – Theodore Sturgeon> **Overlook** implies an omitting or disregarding, sometimes through intention <[he] winced when he heard so young a man call him by nickname, but he *overlooked* this . . . in light of what had happened – James Purdy> but more often through haste or lack of care <the voices of the past . . . *overlooked* the cornucopia of scientific advance and technological change – H. J. Barnett> <*overlook* an error in a sentence> **Slight** is likely to imply contemptuous or disdainful disregarding or neglecting <nothing in the service was *slighted,* every phrase and gesture had its full value – Willa Cather> <they had been *slighted* before, but never had they been completely deprived of everything – Frances P. Egan> **Forget** may suggest a willful ignoring or failure to impress on one's mind <we would be reduced to a simplicity we have *forgot* how to live with – J. W. Krutch> <it was – well, until yesterday – all but *forgotten* – put out of mind, I mean – Walter de la Mare> *ant* cherish
neglectful – see NEGLIGENT *ant* attentive
negligent, neglectful, lax, slack, remiss *shared meaning* : culpably careless or manifesting such carelessness. **Negligent** implies such culpable inattentiveness as is likely to result in imperfection or in damage to others <a careless workman, *negligent* of detail – Edith Hamilton> <injury or property damage due to someone else's *negligent* driving – P. H. Ennis> **Neglectful** carries a strong connotation of laziness or of deliberate and blameworthy inattention <parents *neglectful* of their children's health> <utterly *neglectful* of what we consider the first requirements of decency – Edward Westermarck> **Lax** implies a usually blameworthy lack of needed or normal firmness, severity, or precision <a *lax* parent> <*lax* morals> <we do not intend to leave things so *lax* that loopholes will be left for cheaters – F. D. Roosevelt> **Slack** stresses lack of due or necessary diligence or care and is likely to suggest indolence or sluggishness or indifference as the cause <*slack* standards permitted the misconduct – Charles Mangel> <too many workers are *slack* and interested only in their paycheck> As applied to a result *slack* usually suggests the imperfections resulting from careless disinterest or indolent inattention <a fine nose for what was *slack* in the play or insufficiently developed – Norman Mailer> **Remiss** implies culpable carelessness that shows itself in slackness or forgetfulness or negli-

gence <Congress was shamefully *remiss* about paying them – H. E. Scudder> <called upon President Coolidge to ask for the resignation of his secretary of the navy, on the ground that the latter had been *remiss* in the performance of his official duties – F. A. Ogg & P. O. Ray> <we die, while *remiss* traitors sleep – Shak.>

negotiate, arrange, concert *shared meaning* : to bring about by mutual agreement. *Negotiate* and *arrange* imply exchange of views and wishes and agreement reached by bargaining and compromise. **Negotiate** is especially appropriate when the dealings are carried on by diplomatic, business, or legal agencies, while **arrange** (which retains some notion of its basic idea of putting in order) may be preferred when reference is to dealings tending to the restoration or establishment of order or to those carried out between private persons or their representatives; thus, one *negotiates* a treaty but *arranges* a marriage <nations *negotiate* from strength, but they also *negotiate* from fear; that is, they not only attempt to gain, but they try to prevent possible loss – A. S. Lall> <decided as a matter of wisdom to *arrange* a truce – C. B. Hitchcock> <*arrange* a settlement of a suit out of court> **Concert** implies a planning together and usually a settling upon a joint course of action <their desire to *concert* defensive measures against the enemy was sincere – S. E. Morison>

neighborly – see AMICABLE ***ant*** unneighborly, ill-disposed

neophyte – see NOVICE

neoplasm – see TUMOR

nerve – see TEMERITY

nervous – see VIGOROUS

nettle – see IRRITATE

neutral, negative, indifferent *shared meaning* : lacking decisiveness or distinctness. **Neutral** in the sense pertinent here implies a quality, an appearance, or a reaction that belongs to neither of two opposites or extremes; in many of its applications it connotes vagueness, indefiniteness, indecisiveness, or ineffectualness; thus, a *neutral* character possesses neither positive virtues nor positive vices; a chemically *neutral* substance is neither acid nor basic <knowledge is *neutral.* It may be used for good or evil purposes – R. M. Hutchins> **Negative** carries a stronger implication of absence of positive or affirmative qualities and commonly implies lack of effect, activity, or definite and concrete form <demands that were almost all *negative* and destructive; they were against innumerable aspects of society and Government but not in favor of anything specific – S. T. Wise> <the *negative* happiness that follows the release from anxiety and tension – Aldous Huxley> **Indifferent** implies a quality, a character, or an appearance that is not readily categorized, especially as good or bad, right or wrong, and that, therefore, is unlikely to stir up strong feeling or elicit firm opinions <either one attitude is better than the other, or else it is *indifferent* – T. S. Eliot> <chatting on *indifferent* topics> <she was a hard worker but an *indifferent* student>

new, novel, modern, original, fresh *shared meaning* : having recently come into existence or use or into a particular state or condition. **New** may apply to what is freshly made and unused <*new* brick> <a *new* dress> or to what has not been known or experienced before <a *new* design> <discovered a *new* remedy> <affection was a *new* experience to them> or to a person just taken into a group or association <met *new* boys at school> <her *new* roommate> <no man putteth *new* wine into old bottles – *Mk* 2:22 (AV)> <he was . . . frightened, being *new* to the sight – Charles Dickens> <many *new* and perplexing challenges face higher education today – M. S. Eisenhower> **Novel** applies to what is not only new but strange or unfamiliar <*novel* schemes of salvation – L. P. Smith> <a single courageous state may . . . try *novel* social and economic experiments without risk to the rest of the country – L. D. Brandeis> **Modern** applies to what belongs to or is characteristic of the present time or era <*modern* manners> <*modern* as opposed to classical physics> <societies that are moving from a traditional to a *modern* mode – J. A. Perkins> **Original** applies to what is or produces something not merely new or novel but the first of its kind <the Aztec character was perfectly *original* and unique – W. H. Prescott> <great books are *original* communications. Their authors are communicating what they themselves have discovered, not repeating what they have learned – M. J. Adler> **Fresh** applies to what is or seems new or has not lost its qualities of newness (as liveliness, energy, purity, luster) <young men who brought *fresh* thinking and vitality into the party – *Current Biog.*> <put out *fresh* towels for guests> ***ant*** old

next – see NEAREST

nice 1 nice, dainty, fastidious, finicky, finical, particular, fussy, squeamish *shared meaning* : having or displaying exacting standards. **Nice** implies fine discrimination in perception and evaluation <an appetite for knowledge too eager to be *nice* – Samuel Johnson> <his *nice* sense of form, his restraint and his ironic portraiture – Edmund Wilson> and may apply to things calling for such discrimination <a *nice* point of ethics> **Dainty** suggests a tendency to reject what does not conform to one's delicate taste or sensibility <no shape but his can please your *dainty* eye – Shak.> <*dainty* feeders who expect perfection – A. W. Long> **Fastidious** implies having very high and often capricious ethical, artistic, or social standards <the disorder was almost more than his *fastidious* taste could bear – Willa Cather> <the *fastidious* lady whom it was most difficult to please – L. P. Smith> **Finicky** and the less common **finical** imply an affected or overnice fastidiousness <his voice is too soft, his manners too precise. He is genial, yet he is *finicky* – Norman Mailer> <my grandmother's voracity, so *finical,* so selective, chilled me with its mature sensuality – Mary McCarthy> **Particular** implies an insistence that one's exacting standards be met <they . . . are usually *particular* about grooming because they were brought up in the stricter times – Agnes M. Miall> <his mother was a very *particular* person and always insisted on knowing where he was going and who he was with> **Fussy** may blend the suggestions of *finicky* and *particular,* often with a hint of querulousness <a busy, *fussy* sort of man, much concerned with regulating everything – A. M. Young> **Squeamish** suggests an over-sensitive or prudish readiness to be offended, disgusted, or nauseated <the starved stomach is not *squeamish* – W. H. Hudson †1922> <most psychologists have now abolished the mind and are a little *squeamish* talking about the psyche – A. L. Kroeber> <*ain't,* that perennial *bête noir* of the linguistically *squeamish* – A. H. Marckwardt>

2 see CORRECT

niggardly – see STINGY ***ant*** bountiful

night – see NIGHTLY

nightly, nocturnal, night *shared meaning* : of, relating to, or associated with the night. **Nightly,** opposed to *daily,* may mean no more than this <all is quiet, no alarms; nothing fear of *nightly* harms – A. E. Housman> but more often it carries a strong implication of recurrence and is appropriate when the reference is to something that happens night after night <a fortnight hold we this solemnity in *nightly* revels – Shak.> **Nocturnal,** opposed to *diurnal,* is often interchangeable with *nightly* in its more general application <the changing beauty of *nocturnal* landscapes – Arnold Bennett> but distinctively it can mean active at night <divide birds into the

diurnal which fly by day, and the *nocturnal* which fly by night – R. H. Smythe> <he was now *nocturnal* in habit, café-haunting, and furtively writing his first compositions – *Times Lit. Supp.*> **Night,** often interchangeable with *nocturnal,* may be preferred when a more casual term is desired <*night* noises> <waiting for the *night* train> Distinctively, the term describes a person who works at night <*night* nurses> <ask the *night* clerk> and things that occur or are intended for use at night <*night* baseball> <a bank with a *night* depository> ***ant*** daily

nimble – see AGILE

noble – see MORAL ***ant*** base (*of actions*), atrocious (*of acts, deeds*)

nocturnal – see NIGHTLY ***ant*** diurnal

noise – see SOUND

noiseless – see STILL

noisome – see MALODOROUS ***ant*** **balmy**

nonchalant – see COOL

nonmoral – see IMMORAL

nonplus – see PUZZLE

nonsocial – see UNSOCIAL

norm – see AVERAGE

normal – see REGULAR ***ant*** abnormal

notable – see NOTEWORTHY

note – see SIGN

noted – see FAMOUS

noteworthy, notable, memorable *shared meaning* : having a quality that attracts attention. **Noteworthy** implies a quality, especially of excellence, that merits or attracts attention <made *noteworthy* contributions in diverse fields – M. R. Cohen> <the collection of jade and ceramics is *noteworthy* both for its size and quality – *Amer. Guide Series: Minn.*> **Notable** is likely to connote a special feature (as an excellence, a virtue, a value, or a significance) that makes the thing or person worthy of notice <the clock kept time with *notable* accuracy and pertinacity – *New Yorker*> <a *notable* performance of Hamlet> <since New England has never been *notable* grain country, spirits were distilled from fruits – Gerald Carson> **Memorable** stresses worthiness of remembrance, sometimes as an intrinsic quality, sometimes as a matter personal to the rememberer <a girl with long black hair and a *memorable* figure – Wolcott Gibbs> <his very occasional compliments, steeped in vinegar though they always were, seem more *memorable* than those of others – Osbert Sitwell>

noticeable, remarkable, prominent, outstanding, conspicuous, salient, signal, striking *shared meaning* : attracting notice or attention. **Noticeable** implies that the thing so described is unlikely to escape observation <the meat had a *noticeable* off flavor> <so slight a movement it was barely *noticeable* – Roald Dahl> **Remarkable** adds an implication of an extraordinary or exceptional character that demands attention or comment <they're *remarkable* enough, but have you ever realized that things that are *remarkable* are by definition, rare? – Theodore Sturgeon> <formulated the *remarkable* theory that age improves rather than impairs a man's memory – C. V. Woodward> **Prominent** applies to what stands out clearly against its background or surroundings <feeble gleams . . . served to render sufficiently distinct the more *prominent* objects – E. A. Poe> <the second *prominent* fault in our reading and thinking – F. L. Mott> **Outstanding** implies prominence but is applicable only to what rises above or beyond others of its kind <an *outstanding* performance of an opera> <there are few timbers which can resist teredo attacks; the *outstanding* one is the greenheart of British Guiana – C. J. Taylor> **Conspicuous** applies to what is so obvious or patent that the eye or the mind cannot miss it <*conspicuous* bravery> <his taciturnity was *conspicuous* and disquieting – H. C. Hervey> or to what seizes the attention, often unpleasantly, by its singularity <wear *conspicuous* clothes> <*conspicuous* extravagance> **Salient** suggests a significant quality that thrusts itself into attention <fundamental issues that are still important and *salient* today – David Mechanic> <the *salient* characteristics of cultures other than our own – A. H. Marckwardt> **Signal** applies to what deserves attention as being unusually significant <a *signal* contribution to linguistic theory> <an even more *signal* distinction followed . . . when he became a King's Counsel – *Current Biog.*> **Striking** implies a character that impresses itself vividly or deeply on the sight or mind <*striking* and dramatic achievements of the Maryknoll missionaries in Hong Kong – J. A. O'Brien> <wore a *striking* black costume> <one of the most *striking* and fearful figures in our early fiction – V. L. Parrington>

notify – see INFORM

notorious – see FAMOUS

novel – see NEW

novice, apprentice, probationer, postulant, neophyte *shared meaning* : one who is a beginner (as in a trade, a profession, a career, or a skill). **Novice** stresses inexperience and is widely applicable <her book shows the uneven hand of a *novice* at writing – Rose Feld> <brides who are *novices* in housekeeping> but applies specifically to a new member of a religious order who is undergoing preliminary training before taking binding vows. **Apprentice** applies to a beginner serving under a master or teacher and stresses subordination more than inexperience <while still an *apprentice,* he had made his first attempt at engraving – R. C. Smith> <an *apprentice* teacher> <bricklayers' *apprentices*> **Probationer** applies to a beginner on trial in which he must demonstrate aptitude <the brevity and vanity of this life, in which we are but *probationers* – Samuel Richardson> It finds its most typical application in the case of a student nurse during her introductory period of training. **Postulant** designates a candidate on probation, especially for admission to a religious order <a master in the field of diplomacy but a *postulant* in democratic politics – M. W. Straight> <the reception of *postulant* Joanne Murfey into the Community of the Daughters of the Most Holy Savior – *Gary Post-Tribune*> **Neophyte** usually suggests initiation and is applicable to one newly entered into and learning the ways of something (as an association, a science, or an art). Often the term connotes youthful eagerness and unsophistication <this ardent *neophyte,* who offered to purchase books for him in Europe – Van Wyck Brooks> <the downright despicable manner in which thousands of *neophyte* salesmen are recruited and discarded each year – J. B. Woy> <embraced them with all the feverish enthusiasm of a *neophyte* – W. L. Shirer>

noxious – see PERNICIOUS *ant* wholesome, sanitary

nude – see BARE *ant* clothed

nugatory – see VAIN

nullify, negate, annul, abrogate, invalidate *shared meaning* : to deprive of effective or continued existence. **Nullify** implies counteracting completely the force, effectiveness, or value of something <each of his virtues . . . was *nullified* by some rampant vice – John Buchan> <we are asked to *nullify* legislation as an undue encroachment upon the sphere of individual liberty – B. N. Cardozo> **Negate** implies a nullification of one of two mutually exclusive things by the other <a permanent achievement of the human mind, not likely to be *negated* by future spiritual or intellectual progress – W. W. Wagar> <too often our actions *negate* our principles>

Annul implies a neutralizing or depriving of power to act <they are strange companions, resignation and fear; ordinarily one *annuls* the other – H. C. Hervey> <mystery does not *annul* meaning but enriches it – Reinhold Niebuhr> **Abrogate** is close to *annul* but more consistently implies a legal or official purposeful act <a law that *abrogates* the right of the majority to use their property as they see fit> <the British colonial practice of giving . . . Viceroys the right to *abrogate* colonial laws – W. H. Ferry> **Invalidate** implies a nullifying or making unacceptable by demonstrating a logical or moral or legal unsoundness <let us try to discover how far the facts confirm or *invalidate* this proud claim – Aldous Huxley> <so many reservations, explicit and implicit, as to *invalidate* that pact from the outset – Vera M. Dean>

nun – see RELIGIOUS

nunnery – see CLOISTER

obdurate – see INFLEXIBLE

obedient, docile, tractable, amenable, biddable *shared meaning* : submissive to the control of another. Though typically applied to persons these words are sometimes extended to things. **Obedient** implies compliance with the demands or requests of one in authority <*obedient* to the law> <he seemed to have lost all power of will; he was like an *obedient* child – W. S. Maugham> **Docile** implies a predisposition to submit to control or guidance <behavioral drugs are available that are capable of converting every human being into a *docile* functionary – Harvey Wheeler> <she is a gentle, *docile* person . . . only seventeen. I think she can be moulded into exactly what you would wish her to be – Stella D. Gibbons> **Tractable** suggests adaptability and having a character that permits easy handling or managing but, unlike the otherwise similar *docile,* does not imply a submissive temperament <thou shalt find me *tractable* to any honest reason – Shak.> <their hopes and fears, far less *tractable* than their outward manners, will determine the use their society makes of its prosperity – Oscar Handlin> **Amenable** suggests a willingness to yield to demands, advice, or contrary suggestions <his subjects were . . . under a moral obligation to constrain him to obey the Pope's fiat or, if he refused, to depose him and replace him by a more *amenable* successor – A. J. Toynbee> **Biddable,** a more homely word than *docile,* is used chiefly of children <well-behaved children, *biddable,* meek, neat about their clothes, and always mindful of the proprieties – Willa Cather> ***ant*** disobedient, contumacious

obey, comply, mind *shared meaning* : to follow the direction of another. **Obey** is the general term and implies ready or submissive yielding to authority <the fiercest rebel against society . . . *obeys* most of its conventions – H. J. Muller> <he marks how well the ship her helm *obeys* – Lord Byron> **Comply,** often with *with,* is likely to imply complaisance, dependence, or lack of a strong opinion <should you think ill of that person for *complying* . . . without waiting to be argued into it – Jane Austen> <a new policy was instituted to *comply* with their wishes – Dayton Benjamin> **Mind** as a synonym for *obey* is likely to be used in connection with children or juniors and in admonition or warning <children must *mind* their parents> or in a weaker sense can carry the implication of heeding or attending in order to conform or comply <if your reverence *minds* what my wife says, you won't go wrong – George MacDonald> ***ant*** command

object *n* – see INTENTION, THING

object *vb* **object, protest, remonstrate, expostulate, kick** *shared meaning* : to oppose by arguing against. **Object** stresses dislike or aversion <there's nothing wrong with being painted in the nude.... But our silly husbands have a way of *objecting* – Roald Dahl> **Protest** suggests an orderly presentation of objections in speech or writing <the students carried bright-colored paper posters *protesting* the Viet Nam war – Mary E. Leary> <the residents *protested* the changed zoning to the city council> **Remonstrate** implies protestation but stresses so strongly an intent to persuade or convince that it is more appropriate in intimate than in official or impersonal situations <"Father Joseph," he *remonstrated*, "you will never be able to take all these things back to Denver" – Willa Cather> <*remonstrate* with a child over his bad table manners> **Expostulate** carries a heightened implication of firm, earnest, but friendly reasoning or insistence on the merits of one's stand <reporters at his press conference *expostulated* against playing favorites – *New Republic*> **Kick** implies strenuous protestation and, usually, an exhibition of recalcitrancy <wherefore *kick* ye at my sacrifice and at mine offering – *1 Sam* 2:29 (AV)> <I *kicked* at that and said that Asquith might be limited but he was honest – H. J. Laski> ***ant*** acquiesce

objective *adj* – see FAIR ***ant*** subjective

objective *n* – see INTENTION

obligation, duty *shared meaning* : something that one is bound as a responsible person to do or to refrain from doing. **Obligation** usually implies an immediate constraint imposed by circumstances and a specific reference <a son's *obligation* to care for an aged parent> <the Ralstons fulfilled their *obligations* as rich and respected citizens – Edith Wharton> **Duty**, on the other hand, is likely to imply a more general but greater impulsion on moral or ethical grounds; thus, a person with a strong sense of *duty* is keenly aware of what in general he ought to do; one has a sense of *obligation* only in a particular case and for a particular reason <Paulus, torn between his *duty* to obey the mad Fuehrer and his *obligation* to save his own surviving troops from annihilation, appealed to Hitler – W. L. Shirer>

oblige 1 see FORCE

2 oblige, accommodate, favor *shared meaning* : to do a service or courtesy. **Oblige** implies putting someone into one's debt by doing something that is pleasing to him <most hotels ... will *oblige* if on a particular occasion you wish your meal served at a special time – Charles Roetter> and is commonly used in conventional acknowledgment of small courtesies <there is an oversight ... which I shall be much *obliged* to you to correct – T. B. Macaulay> **Accommodate**, when used of services, can replace *oblige*. Sometimes, especially as the participial adjective, it implies gracious compliance and consideration <a most *accommodating* host> or it may connote the intent to be of assistance <I was willing to *accommodate* you by undertaking to sell the horse – George Eliot> **Favor** implies rendering a service out of goodwill and without imposing an obligation on or expecting a return from the one favored <luck *favored* him in all his enterprises> <students have been called ... one of the most *favored* groups in our society ... "the overfed, overprotected offspring of affluent parents" – C. R. Woodward> Sometimes the term carries a suggestion of gratuitousness or of patronizing <the stupidity with which he was *favored* by nature – Jane Austen> <*favor* a friend with unsought advice> ***ant*** disoblige

obliging – see AMIABLE ***ant*** disobliging, inconsiderate

oblique – see CROOKED

obliterate – see ERASE

oblivious – see FORGETFUL

obloquy — see ABUSE
obnoxious — see REPUGNANT *ant* grateful
obscene — see COARSE *ant* decent
obscure, dark, vague, enigmatic, cryptic, ambiguous, equivocal *shared meaning* : not clearly understandable. **Obscure** implies a hiding or veiling of meaning through some defect of expression or withholding of full knowledge <this sordid, often *obscure* book, without visible motive or meaning — James Purdy> <often the things that we feel are important are very *obscure* and it's hard to develop public interest in them — Frank McGee> **Dark** implies imperfect revelation and, therefore, mysteriousness <I will utter *dark* sayings — *Ps* 78:2 (AV)> <that makes much which was *dark* quite clear to me — John Galsworthy> <made *dark* hints about the plot> **Vague** implies lack of distinct outlines or clear definition often because the matter is imperfectly conceived or thought out <[a book] *vague* enough and inconsistent enough to lend itself to a variety of interpretations — Edmund Wilson> <a *vague* sense of obligation was replaced by an exacting set of rules — R. W. Southern> **Enigmatic** stresses a puzzling mystifying quality <the black-white situation remains as truly *enigmatic* today as it was 107 years ago — W. H. Ferry> <children often teeter between opposing sets of values, . . . they are *enigmatic,* unpredictable — R. G. Frost> **Cryptic** implies a purposely concealed meaning and often an intent to perplex or challenge <you had to intercede, with your *cryptic* innuendoes and mysterious head-waggings — S. S. Van Dine> *Ambiguous* and *equivocal* both imply the use of the same words in different senses, **ambiguous** usually suggesting inadvertence <most words are *ambiguous* as regards their plain sense, especially in poetry — I. A. Richards> and **equivocal** an intent to confuse or evade <nor could he find much pleasure in the subtle, devious, and *equivocal* utterances of Solomon — *Omnibook*> *ant* distinct, obvious
obsequious — see SUBSERVIENT *ant* contumelious
observe — see KEEP *ant* violate
obstinate, dogged, stubborn, pertinacious, mulish *shared meaning* . fixed and unyielding in course or purpose. **Obstinate** is more likely to imply perverseness and unreasonableness than steadfastness <they will not be resolute and firm, but perverse and *obstinate* — Edmund Burke> <so yielding doubtful points that he can be firm without seeming *obstinate* in essential ones — J. R. Lowell> **Dogged** adds an implication of tenacious, even sullen persistence and commonly connotes determination or unwavering purpose <he continued working with *dogged* perseverance> <their *dogged* denial of this enduring fact — Harvey Wheeler> **Stubborn,** often interchangeable with *obstinate* and *dogged,* can distinctively convey an impression of a native fixedness of character or a deeply rooted quality that makes a person immovable or at least sturdily resistant to attempts to change his purpose, course, or opinions or a thing intractable to those who would work with, treat, or manipulate it <there is something *stubborn* in him that makes him follow his own path even though he isn't certain where it goes — Malcolm Cowley> <man and beast joined against *stubborn* nature and her grudging soil — Ann F. Wolfe> **Pertinacious** implies a persistent, even annoying or irksome following of a chosen course <a *pertinacious* mosquito> <a *pertinacious* collector of trivial gossip about his neighbors> **Mulish** implies an obstinacy as settled or as unreasonable as that traditionally ascribed to a mule <a *mulish* determination to make the worst of everything — T. S. Eliot> <a fierce, hot, hard, old, stupid squire . . . small brain, great courage, *mulish* will — John Masefield> *ant* pliant, pliable
obstreperous — see VOCIFEROUS
obstruct — see HINDER

obtain – see GET
obtrusive – see IMPERTINENT ***ant*** unobtrusive, shy
obtuse – see DULL ***ant*** acute
obviate – see PREVENT 2
obvious – see EVIDENT ***ant*** obscure, abstruse
occasion – see CAUSE
occupation – see WORK 2
occur – see HAPPEN
occurrence, event, incident, episode, circumstance *shared meaning* : something that happens or takes place. **Occurrence** is a general and neutral term for something which takes place <violent denunciations of him and his course became everyday *occurrences* – S. E. Ambrose> **Event** applies especially to an occurrence of some importance and often with evident antecedent causes <assassination was an *event* of daily occurrence – T. B. Macaulay> <a seismic *event* can be characterized by its magnitude – E. W. Carpenter> **Incident** can describe a relatively slight event in a course of events that may be trivial <an old man recalling *incidents* of his youth> or disproportionately significant <the *incident* that precipitated the outbreak of war> **Episode** stresses the distinctness or apartness of an incident <the dumb creation lives a life made up of discrete and mutually irrelevant *episodes* – Aldous Huxley> **Circumstance** can replace *incident* when application is to a specific and usually significant detail <all *circumstances* that may transpire respecting . . . my own concerns – John Cheever> <a life every *circumstance* of which is regulated after an unchangeable pattern – Oscar Wilde>
odious – see HATEFUL
odor – see SMELL
offend, outrage, affront, insult *shared meaning* : to cause hurt feelings or deep resentment. **Offend** suggests a violation of the victim's sense of what is proper or fitting that may be either intentional or inadvertent <hurt and *offended* by Ivy's rudeness – Willa Cather> <some people might be *offended* at mentioning a novelist in church – Compton Mackenzie> **Outrage** implies offending beyond endurance and calling forth extreme feelings <her power to make him do things which *outraged* all his upbringing – Victoria Sackville-West> <high praise . . . meted out to books which dismay, and sometimes veritably *outrage* the people who really know the subjects under discussion – R. D. Altick> **Affront** implies treating with deliberate rudeness or contemptuous indifference to courtesy <a moral, sensible, and well-bred man will not *affront* me, and no other can – William Cowper> **Insult** implies a wanton and deliberate offending of another that causes humiliation, hurt pride, or shame <had hardly restrained himself from saying something very bitter, archly *insulting* to his father as the old man stood there – William Styron>
offense 1 offense, resentment, umbrage, pique, dudgeon, huff *shared meaning* : an emotional response to a slight or indignity. **Offense** implies a marked state of displeasure or wounded feelings <he takes *offense* at the least remark> <this tiny breath of genuine criticism had given deep *offense* – E. M. Forster> **Resentment** suggests a longer lasting indignation and often a persistently smoldering ill will <gifted but humble men, conscious of their talent and their mission, but often frustrated and harbouring *resentment* that they had been slighted or inadequately appreciated – *Times Lit. Supp.*> **Umbrage**, chiefly in the phrase *take umbrage*, may imply a feeling of being snubbed or ignored and the resultant resentment <a man took *umbrage* at being called a certain kind of fool – W. F. Hambly> **Pique** applies to a transient feeling of wounded vanity <he had not . . .

allowed his young green jealousy to show itself in words or *pique* – Pearl Buck> **Dudgeon** applies to a fit of angry resentment or indignation, usually provoked by opposition to one's views or wishes <refused to reply and stalked off in a high *dudgeon*> <this offended Mr. Barrow, who retired in *dudgeon* to the remotest part of the field – Dorothy Sayers> **Huff** implies a peevish short-lived spell of anger, usually at a petty cause <half of 'em will be disgusted, and go away in a *huff* – W. F. De Morgan> <read the letter, flew into a rage, and left the country in a *huff* – Virginia Woolf>
2 offense, sin, vice, crime, scandal *shared meaning* : transgression of law or custom. **Offense** is the general term, applicable to any infraction of a law, rule, or code <O, my *offense* is rank, it smells to heaven; it hath the primal eldest curse upon't, a brother's murder – Shak.> Sometimes the term is preferred to denote a minor as contrasted with a grave misdeed <boys charged with petty *offenses* penned up with hardened criminals> **Sin** implies an offense against moral or divine law <all earthly authority was seen as ordained by God, and if a tyrant ruled he was simply God's punishment for man's *sin* – Guenter Lewy> or, in an extended and weakened use, something, whether an overt offense or not, that is felt as highly reprehensible <the grammatical *sins* of modern times – C. E. Reed> <it's a *sin* to waste good food> <it may not have been much of a culture, crude, bloodthirsty, harsh, and worst *sin* of all, different – Seth Agnew> **Vice,** though often applied to transgressions also called *sins,* stresses moral depravity rather than violation of divine law and is especially appropriate to denote a habit or practice that degrades or corrupts <treachery and cruelty, the most pernicious and most odious of all *vices* – David Hume †1776> <suburban *vice,* like a peeling nose, is almost impossible to conceal – William Styron> **Crime** basically implies a serious offense punishable by the law of the state <burglary, arson, murder, and other *crimes*> but, like *sin,* can be extended to something felt as inherently evil or highly reprehensible <the betrayal by a people of itself is the ultimate historical *crime:* the final and the most degrading suicide – Archibald MacLeish> **Scandal** applies to an offense that outrages the public conscience or damages the integrity of an organization or group <*scandal* is an act or omission that is sinful . . . and that is for another an occasion of sin – W. F. Ferrell>
office – see FUNCTION, POSITION 2
officious – see IMPERTINENT
offset – see COMPENSATE
oft – see OFTEN
often, frequently, oft, oftentimes *shared meaning* : again and again in more or less close succession. **Often** tends to stress the number of times a thing occurs without regard to the interval of recurrence <the story . . . has been *often* told – S. E. Ambrose> <significant tax savings most *often* result from a thorough knowledge of the rules of taxation – W. K. Goettsche> while **frequently** usually emphasizes repetition, especially at short intervals <because of her interest in social, political, and economic problems, she was . . . *frequently* compared with Eleanor Roosevelt – *Current Biog.*> <sometimes impatient, more often quietly watchful, *frequently* laughing, he is always the natural man – *London Sunday Times*> *Oft* and *oftentimes* differ little from *often;* **oft,** however, is used chiefly in compound adjectives <an *oft*-told tale> or occasionally in formal discourse <seemingly trifling events *oft* carry in their train great consequences – Calvin Coolidge> and **oftentimes** may be preferred for intonational reasons or as a more florid word <had a sense of humor which was sometimes loud, *oftentimes* lewd, but never deliberately unkind – Grace Metalious> <his bubbling thoughts ran away with him, often leading him into new paths before the old was

cleared of the jungle. This *oftentimes* obscured his ideas – *Dict. of Amer. Biog.*>

oftentimes – see OFTEN

old, ancient, venerable, antique, antiquated *shared meaning* : having come into existence or use in the more or less distant past. **Old,** opposed to *young* or *new,* may imply either relative or actual length of existence, while **ancient,** opposed to *modern,* implies occurrence, existence, or use in the distant past. Thus, one speaks of an *old* (not *ancient*) shoe, but an *ancient* (preferable to *old*> Roman monument <*old* wine> <an *ancient* manuscript> <O heavens, if you do love *old* men – Shak.> <from the *ancient* world those giants came – John Milton> **Venerable** stresses the hoariness and dignity associated with old age <*venerable* as Anglo-Saxon is, and worthy to be studied as the mother of our vernacular speech – A. T. Quiller-Couch> <*venerable* men, you have come down to us from a former generation – Daniel Webster> **Antique** suggests a surviving in knowledge or use from earlier times <an *antique* highboy that had been treasured in the family for seven generations> <undismayed by disaster, he confronted life with *antique* courage – S. E. Morison> **Antiquated** implies being discredited or outmoded or otherwise inappropriate to the present time <the government has . . . reorganized the *antiquated* banking system – *New Republic*> <[they] cherished . . . a stout and defiant loyalty to their *antiquated* limitations – Edmund Wilson> *ant* new

oligarchy, aristocracy, plutocracy *shared meaning* : government by, or a state governed by, the few. The terms are often used of governments or states that are ostensibly republics or monarchies but are, in the opinion of the user, actually governed by a clique. **Oligarchy** is the most inclusive term and is applicable to any government or state in which power is openly or virtually in the hands of a favored few <it is altogether likely that universal suffrage has strengthened the hands of ruling *oligarchies* throughout the world – R. M. Hutchins> <with the failure or discreditation of divinely sanctioned traditions, there are only two remaining sources of value: an anointed elite that monopolizes virtue, or all mankind. Politically, this is the problem of *oligarchy* vs. democracy – Harvey Wheeler> **Aristocracy** basically and historically implies the rule of the best citizens <true *aristocracy* is just this, the government of the best, of a ruling class dedicated to the common well-being – F. G. Wilson> but in its more usual use it implies power vested in a privileged class, often regarded as superior in birth and breeding <revolution was abroad among the people, shifting the basis of our government from *aristocracy* to democracy without destroying its essential republicanism – Clinton Rossiter> <the *aristocracy* of Venice hath admitted so many abuses, through the degeneracy of the nobles, that the period of its duration seems to approach – Jonathan Swift> **Plutocracy** implies concentration of power in the hands of the wealthy and is regularly derogatory <we have been trying to move from a *plutocracy* to a meritocracy through education, so that the most able – no matter what their backgrounds – can rise in the social scale – N. E. Long> <Carthage was a *plutocracy* and the real power of the state lay in the hands of a dozen big shipowners and mineowners and merchants . . . who regarded their common fatherland as a business enterprise which ought to yield them a decent profit – H. W. Van Loon>

ominous, portentous, fateful *shared meaning* : having a menacing or threatening aspect. **Ominous** applies to what has the quality of an omen, especially in forecasting evil; the term regularly suggests a frightening or alarming quality that bodes no good <a statement that can easily be read as the *ominous* conversion of social science into a service industry of the Pentagon

– I. L. Horowitz> <there was something *ominous* about it, and ... one was made to feel that the worst was about to come – Jack London> **Portentous** attributes the character of a portent to what it describes but is more likely to stress a quality of extreme unusualness than one of threatening <his gravity was unusual, *portentous,* and immeasurable – Charles Dickens> <it is *portentous* ... that here at midnight, in our little town a mourning figure walks, and will not rest – Vachel Lindsay> **Fateful** stresses the momentousness and decisive importance of what it describes <it was one of the most *fateful* of Hitler's moves in the war, ... and led to the most humiliating defeat in the history of German arms – W. L. Shirer>

omit – see NEGLECT

omnipresent, ubiquitous *shared meaning* : present or existent everywhere. **Omnipresent** in its precise use is a divine attribute equivalent to *immanent;* in more general use it implies universal or general presence or prevalence <the church is *omnipresent* in an otherwise constantly changing society – Ivan Vallier> <an *omnipresent* sense of social obligation – C. W. Eliot> **Ubiquitous** implies being so active or so numerous as to seem everywhere present; often the word suggests a resulting inescapability or oppressiveness <the *ubiquitous* tourists with their loud shirts and expensive cameras> <the sad, *ubiquitous* spinster, left behind ... by the stampede of the young men westward – Van Wyck Brooks>

onerous, burdensome, oppressive, exacting *shared meaning* : imposing hardship. **Onerous** stresses laboriousness and heaviness and is likely to imply irksomeness or distastefulness <the tyranny of a majority might be more *onerous* than that of a despot – A. N. Whitehead> <the *onerous* burden of finances will be removed ... and their energies will thus be freed for total dedication to things scholastic – P. F. Curran> **Burdensome** usually implies both physical and mental strain but tends to emphasize the latter <*burdensome* government regulations that are a nuisance to everyone – F. D. Roosevelt> <the *burdensome* and invidious job of a formal application to the Board of Trade – *Economist*> **Oppressive** adds to *burdensome* implications of undue harshness or severity and is likely to connote the intolerability of the resulting situation <*oppressive* weather> or the cruelty, tyranny, or utter inconsiderateness of the one responsible for its existence <an *oppressive* dictator> <the belief ... that the white power structure was determined to maintain its *oppressive* rule – Leonard Buder> **Exacting** imputes rigor or sternness or extreme fastidiousness rather than tyranny to the one who demands and extreme care and precision to the one who or the thing that meets these demands <the serious concentration of a mature and expert craftsman engaged in an absorbing and *exacting* labor – Thomas Wolfe> <the *exacting* life of the sea has this advantage over the life of the earth, that its claims are simple and cannot be evaded – Joseph Conrad>

onward, forward, forth *shared meaning* : in the act of advancing (as in a movement, progression, series, or sequence). Though frequently used interchangeably, these words are capable of a degree of discrimination that enhances precision of expression. **Onward** can stress progress or advance toward a definite goal, end, or place <half a league *onward* ... rode the six hundred – Alfred Tennyson> <*onward* into future lives – Emma Hawkridge> while **forward,** opposed to *backward,* more definitely implies movement or advance with reference to what lies before (as in space or time) rather than behind <we should look *forward* to the day when the Soviet Union ... will want to take part in these multilateral endeavors – William Attwood> <Christ the Royal Master leads against the foe; *forward* into battle, see, His banners go! – Sabine Baring-Gould> or in a succession (as of incidents in a narrative or steps in a process) <the center has not yet been rebuilt, though they are . . . getting *forward* with it – A. L. Rowse> **Forth,** often interchangeable with *forward,* in certain idioms may be quite distinctive and imply a bringing forward (as into knowledge, availability, or view) of something previously obscured in some fashion or other; thus, one brings *forth* from or as if from a place of concealment <bring *forth* a gem for appraisal> and one sets *forth* by providing <set *forth* an ample supper> or by making simple and clear <in his charge to the grand jury . . . he set *forth* the democratic basis of the new state government – R. L. Meriwether>

open **1** see FRANK ***ant*** close, closemouthed, close-lipped, clandestine **2** see LIABLE ***ant*** closed

opinion, view, belief, conviction, persuasion, sentiment *shared meaning* : a judgment one holds to be true. **Opinion** implies a conclusion thought out yet open to dispute <I cannot go along with this interpretation. I am of the *opinion* that the price of gold is likely to be unchanged – G. J. Henry> **View** applies to an opinion more or less colored by the feeling, sentiment, or bias of its holder <took . . . the hopeful *view* that there is something positive in a marriage – *Times Lit. Supp.*> **Belief** emphasizes intellectual assent and assurance of truth on the part of the believer <the *belief* that the whole system of nature is calculable in terms of mathematics and mechanics – W. R. Inge> <he sang with *belief* because he was glad and grateful . . . because he lived in faith before and in the shadow of that same Old Rugged Cross – J. T. Farrell> **Conviction** applies to a firmly and seriously held belief <there are those who doubt that he possesses the charismatic warmth, color, and *conviction* essential in a national leader – *Current Biog.*> <most of us retain the *conviction* that economic freedom is maintained by the sovereignty of the consumer – R. M. Hutchins> **Persuasion** implies a belief or opinion based on personal assurance often arising rather from one's feelings or wishes than from evidence or arguments <his strong interest in good government and the proper solution of social problems threw him more and more toward the Democratic *persuasion* – J. A. Michener> <the childish *persuasion* that we have the only rational way of doing things – Gustave Weigel> **Sentiment,** rather infrequent today n this sense, applies to a more or less settled opinion, often involving feelings or emotions <an apparent reversal of his known conservative *sentiments* – A. L. Funk> <when the General decided to answer a letter, he would nform Miss Graves of his *sentiments* and she would translate them into polite and brief answer – Ludwig Bemelmans>

pponent, antagonist, adversary *shared meaning* : one who expresses or nanifests opposition. **Opponent** implies little more than position on the ther side (as in a debate, election, contest, or conflict) <one's *opponent* n an argument> <a stern *opponent* of all reform> **Antagonist** implies harper, often more personal opposition (as in a struggle or combat for upremacy or control) <a swift voracious fish, a formidable *antagonist* for he angler – J. L. B. Smith> **Adversary** ranges in connotation from the dea of mere formal opposition to that of intense hostility <do as *adversaries* o in law, strive mightily, but eat and drink as friends – Shak.> <your *dversary* the devil, as a roaring lion, walketh about, seeking whom he may levour – *1 Pet* 5:8 (AV)>

pportune – see SEASONABLE ***ant*** inopportune

ppose, combat, resist, withstand, antagonize *shared meaning* : to set oneself gainst someone or something. **Oppose** may apply to a range extending from nere objection to bitter hostility or active counteraction (as by civil disorder r warfare) <people who *oppose* fluoridation as forced medication> <*op-*

posed every tendency toward nationalism – Eleanor R. Dobson> **Combat** stresses the actual conflict involved in vigorously active opposition <restrictions designed to *combat* inflation> <nationalist movements in such areas should not be *combated* in ways that drive them toward Moscow or Peking – E. J. Hughes> *Resist* and *withstand* imply answering an offensive action with counter force, but **resist** is likely to imply positive efforts to counteract, repel, or ward off an overtly recognized hostile or threatening force <*resist* aggression> <we are ... not going to *resist* Federal court orders with violence – C. E. Sanders> while **withstand** may suggest a more passive yet often successful resistance <breeding plants better able to *withstand* frost> <having *withstood* the pressure of her parents – Rose Macaulay> **Antagonize** implies an arousing of resistance or hostility in another <*antagonizes* dealers with its arbitrary methods – *Current Biog.*> <they resented his extreme militancy ... he even *antagonized* a few of his fellow workers – John Warner>

opposite, contradictory, contrary, antithetical *shared meaning* : being so far apart as to be or seem irreconcilable. **Opposite,** the inclusive term, may replace any of the others but finds its typical application in description of abstract things that stand in sharp contrast or complete antagonism <*opposite* views on a problem> <attraction and repulsion are *opposite* forces> <a person of the *opposite* sex> <the boys went in *opposite* directions> **Contradictory** applies to two things that completely negate each other so that if one is true or valid the other must be false or invalid <the two suspects made *contradictory* statements to the police> <the real trouble with love is that people want *contradictory* things out of it – Frank O'Connor> **Contrary** can imply extreme divergence (as of opinions, motives, or intentions) or, especially as used in formal logic, diametrical opposition <in logic, *contrary* propositions are those in the relation of affirmative and negative within the same degree of generality – Wilson Follett> <a number of other European faiths had entered New England with their varying creeds and *contrary* forms of church government – Lois B. Wills> **Antithetical** stresses clear and unequivocal diametric opposition <the essential interests of men and women are eternally *antithetical* – H. L. Mencken> <these men were quite right to regard social reform and private investment as often *antithetical* – Michael Harrington>

oppress – see DEPRESS

oppressive – see ONEROUS

opprobrium – see DISGRACE

option – see CHOICE *n*

opulent 1 see LUXURIOUS
2 see RICH *ant* destitute, indigent

oracular – see DICTATORIAL

oral 1 see VOCAL *ant* written
2 oral, verbal *shared meaning* : involving the use of words. **Oral,** the narrower term, implies utterance and speech; it is distinctively applicable to whatever is delivered, communicated, transacted, or carried on directly from one to another by word of mouth <an *oral* examination> <*oral* agreements> <kinds of poetry which exist only in *oral* pre-written tradition – C. L. Wrenn> **Verbal** stresses the use of words and may apply indifferently to what is spoken or written <situations in which signals replace *verbal* communication> <he often loses himself in little trifling distinctions and *verbal* niceties – Thomas Gray> When the idea of speech is prominent, however, *verbal* is better avoided for it cannot convey the precise distinction of *oral* and is likely to suggest unintended or irrelevant distinctions. Thus, one would

choose "an *oral* invitation," "*oral* testimony" when *spoken* is to be implied, because *verbal* would be ambiguous.

order **1 order, arrange, marshal, organize, systematize, methodize** *shared meaning* : to put persons or things into their proper places in relation to each other. **Order** suggests a straightening out so as to eliminate confusion <*order* knickknacks on a shelf> <the Constitution was intended to *order* society while the Declaration of Independence was designed to revolutionize it – W. D. North> **Arrange** implies a setting in a fit, suitable, or right sequence, relationship, or adjustment <*arrange* flowers in a vase> <each of us *arranges* the world according to his own notion of the fitness of things – Joseph Conrad> **Marshal** implies assemblage and arrangement either for ease and advantage in management or for effectiveness in display or exhibition <*marshaled* like soldiers in gay company, the tulips stand arrayed – Amy Lowell> <rose and paced around the small bleak room, as if he were *marshaling* his thoughts with each even step – Helen MacInnes> **Organize** implies arranging so that the whole aggregate works as a unit in which each part has its place and function <*organize* party regulars for effective campaigning> <extensive search parties had been *organized* – John Cheever> <I have a very patient husband and a very well-*organized* mind – Judith Raskin> **Systematize** implies arrangement in accord with a definite and predetermined scheme <the great historic efforts to *systematize* the law> <if grammar was to become a rational science, it had to *systematize* itself through principles of logic – H. O. Taylor> **Methodize** suggests the imposing of an orderly procedure rather than a fixed scheme <developed . . . specialized procedures . . . and *methodized* them – S. E. Hyman> <that art of reasoning . . . which *methodizes* and facilitates our discourse – J. H. Shorthouse> *ant* disorder

2 see COMMAND

ordinance – see LAW

ordinary – see COMMON *ant* extraordinary

organize – see ORDER *ant* disorganize

orifice – see APERTURE

origin, source, inception, root *shared meaning* : the point at which something begins its course or existence. **Origin** applies to the things or persons from which something is ultimately derived and often to the causes operating before the thing itself comes into being <the *origin* of a custom> <opened . . . vast areas of knowledge about the processes of all life on earth, its *origin*, evolution, and future – *Current Biog.*> **Source** applies more often to the point where something springs into being <an ever-present energy, which is the *source* of all cosmical movement – W. R. Inge> <change . . . can be threatening, or it can be the *source* of new excitement and adventure – H. A. Simon> **Inception** stresses the beginning of the actual or material existence of something without implication concerning causes <from its *inception* Judaism has always recognized two purposes in marriage – Robert Gordis> <used the Watt engine from the time of its *inception* – S. F. Mason> **Root** applies to a first, ultimate, or fundamental source that is often not readily discerned <the love of money is the *root* of all evil – *1 Tim* 6:10 (AV)> <the *roots* of all conflict, all sin, suffering, death, are in individual hearts. Jesus exposed these *roots* – hate, lust, greed – R. J. Linnig>

original – see NEW *ant* dependent, banal, trite

originate – see SPRING

ornament – see ADORN

oscillate – see SWING 2

ostensible – see APPARENT
ostentatious – see SHOWY
otiose – see VAIN
oust – see EJECT
out-and-out – see OUTRIGHT
outcome – see EFFECT
outdo – see EXCEED
outer, outward, outside, external, exterior *shared meaning* : being or placed without something. Though sometimes interchangeable these words tend to be restricted in their applications and correspondingly distinct in their implications. **Outer** tends to retain its comparative force and apply to what is farther out from something described as *inner* <the *outer* layer of skin is called epidermis> or is farther than another thing from a center <shed one's *outer* garments> **Outward** commonly implies motion or direction away from, or the reverse of, what is *inward* <given to *outward* display> <an *outward* show of courage belied his inward terror> <give *outward* and objective form to ideas that bubble inwardly – H. L. Mencken> **Outside** usually implies a position on or a reference to the outer parts or surface of a thing <an *outside* shutter covered the window> <the *outside* paint is badly weathered> In extended use it tends to apply to what is beyond some implied limit; thus, the *outside* world is the world beyond a scope of interest (as a family group or social set) or the confines of a place (as a farm, a town, or a state); an *outside* influence is one not originating within the bounds held in mind; *outside* capital is capital obtained from without and not generated by the organization receiving it <the hospital staff has no *outside* practice – J. P. Lyford> *External* and *exterior* come close in meaning to *outside* <*external* appearance> <*exterior* form> but **external** may be preferred when location beyond or away from the thing under consideration is implied <our desires and wills are directed to some object *external* to us – Samuel Alexander> <at this tense moment . . . when *external* wars and internal violence make us so conscious of death – *Pilot*> and **exterior** may be preferred when location on the surface or outer limits of the thing is implied <thou, whose *exterior* semblance doth belie thy Soul's immensity – William Wordsworth> ***ant*** inner
outfit – see FURNISH
outline, contour, profile, silhouette *shared meaning* : the line that bounds and gives form to something. **Outline** applies to a continuous line marking the outer limit or edge of a body or mass <at night, the *outline* of the shore is traced in transparent silver by the moonlight and the flying foam – R. L. Stevenson> **Contour** stresses the effect (as of smoothness, roughness or irregularity) of an outline or bounding surface as indicative of the quality (as of fullness or slenderness, softness or harshness) of what it bounds <the full and flowing *contour* of the neck – P. B. Shelley> <the blurred *contour* of Rainbarrow obstructed the sky – Thomas Hardy> **Profile** applies primarily to a representation of something and especially a face in side view in simple outline <did several *profiles* of his sister> and in more general use may be chosen to describe a varied and sharply defined outline seen against a distinct background <out on the horizon you could see a tanker small and neat in *profile* against the blue sea – Ernest Hemingway> or sometimes a nonmaterial outline (as one built up from bits of data) <asking for . . . a *profile* of the riots – of the rioters, of their environment, of their victims, of their causes and effects – Lyndon Johnson> **Silhouette** basically applies to a likeness cut from dark material and mounted against a light background and in extended use applies to something seen as an outline

ıass without color or internal detail <with a little imagination, he could nd . . . the face of a dead man in the *silhouette* of the mountains – Ludwig emelmans>

utlook – see PROSPECT

utrage – see OFFEND

utrageous, monstrous, heinous, atrocious *shared meaning* : enormously bad r horrible. **Outrageous** implies violation of even the lowest standard of hat is right or decent or going beyond the limits of what one will suffer r tolerate <an *outrageous* practical joke> <his crashing, *outrageous* runkenness – William Styron> <the general conviction that patent and *utrageous* crime would bring divine vengeance – H. O. Taylor> **Monstrous** pplies to what is shockingly wrong, absurd, or horrible or is inconceivably ıntastic, abnormal, or aberrant <a *monstrous* misconception of human esponsibility> <what is disturbing me most . . . is the knowledge that have made a *monstrous* fool of myself – Roald Dahl> <the *monstrous* rchitecture of the city, the phantasmagoric chaos of its traffic – Thomas Volfe> <man's helplessness before *monstrous* and faceless evils – Robert Gordis> **Heinous** implies such flagrance in badness or such conspicuousness ı enormity as inevitably and automatically excites hatred or horror <a ıurder, and a particularly *heinous* murder, for it involves the violation of ospitality and of gratitude – R. P. Warren> **Atrocious** describes something ıat excites condemnation for its savagery or barbarity or contempt of normal uman values <*atrocious* cruelty> <*atrocious* acts which can only take lace in a slave country – C. R. Darwin> These words are frequently ıterchangeable and all lend themselves to hyperbolic description of what for the moment deprecated <*outrageous* prices> <*monstrous* expendiıres> <time divorced from mechanical operations was treated as a *heinous* 'aste – Lewis Mumford> <*atrocious* extravagance>

utright, out-and-out, unmitigated, arrant *shared meaning* : being what is ated without limit or qualification. The words are often used interchangebly as intensives, but they can convey distinct shades of meaning. What **outright** has gone to the extreme and can be made neither better nor 'orse or is past recall <he is an *outright* fool> <called for *outright* ationalization of natural-resource industries> What is **out-and-out** is comletely as described at all times or in every part or from every point of iew <this is an *out-and-out* fraud> <while *out-and-out* looting is strongly ındemned in disaster situations, looters in civil disturbances receive . . . rong social support – Russell Dynes & E. L. Quarantelli> What is **nmitigated** is or seems to be so utterly what it is as to be beyond the ossibility of being lessened, softened, or relieved <an *unmitigated* evil> unrequited affections are in youth *unmitigated* woes – L. P. Smith> Vhat is **arrant** is all that is implied by the term (usually a term of abuse) ıat follows <an *arrant* coward> <this statement . . . is *arrant* nonsense Stanley Kauffmann>

utside – see OUTER ***ant*** inside

utstanding – see NOTICEABLE ***ant*** commonplace

utstrip – see EXCEED

utward – see OUTER ***ant*** inward

utwit – see FRUSTRATE

verbearing – see PROUD ***ant*** subservient

vercome – see CONQUER

verdue – see TARDY

verflow – see TEEM

verlook – see NEGLECT

overreach — see CHEAT
oversight, supervision, surveillance *shared meaning* : a careful watchin
Oversight and *supervision* (and the corresponding verbs, **oversee** and **supe vise**) are often interchangeable; both attribute the power or right to ac to the watcher and imply the intent to assure the good condition or effectiv functioning of what is watched <as President of the whole people, it wa his business to have an *oversight* of all the interests of the young natio — H. E. Scudder> <I have abandoned the *supervision* of public occurrence and given over the helm and pilotage of the Ship of State to other hand — L. P. Smith> But **oversight** is perhaps more likely to be chosen whe the reference is to one in subordinate position or to relatively trivial respon sibilities <in the common fields, the boys tended the cattle together c a hired herdsman had their *oversight* — Oscar Handlin> <each forema is charged with the *oversight* of work done by his crew> <[the] associat superintendent . . . will *oversee* the pupil and staff services — *Johns Hopkin Mag.*> while **supervision** carries a much stronger implication of authoritativ powers and responsibilities <the directors are entrusted with the genera management and *supervision* of the company — McKee Fisk & J. C. Snapp> <he *supervised* the building of bridges and railroads, the reestablishmen of some 3,000 villages — *Current Biog.*> **Surveillance** implies a close, detailed even prying watch kept on something and especially on a person felt likel to require unexpected or immediate attention (as from criminal tendencie or faulty health) <police *surveillance* of known criminals> <defense c North America must include antisubmarine *surveillance* — W. G. Cooper> <a monitor for the continuous *surveillance* of heart-attack patients> bu sometimes the word comes very close to *oversight* or *supervision* <Armagna has only one distillation, while Cognac has two successive ones. In eithe process constant *surveillance* is required — G. G. Weigend>
overthrow — see CONQUER
own **1** see ACKNOWLEDGE *ant* disown, repudiate
2 see HAVE

pacific, peaceable, peaceful, irenic, pacifist, pacifistic *shared meaning* : a fording or promoting peace. **Pacific** applies chiefly to persons or to utte ances, acts, influences, or ideas that tend to maintain peace or concilia strife <seek the settlement of disputes only by *pacific* means — R. I Jackson> <the *pacific* temper, which seeks to settle disputes on ground of justice rather than by force — Bertrand Russell> **Peaceable** stress enjoyment of peace as a way of life <the primitive state of man, *peaceabl* contented, and sociable — William Bartram> and may imply absence c any intent to behave aggressively <the police descended on the *peaceab* . . . middle-class assemblage as if they were invading a black ghetto in revo — Nat Hentoff> **Peaceful** suggests absence of strife or contention as we as of all disturbing influences <and may at last my weary age find ou the *peaceful* hermitage — John Milton> **Irenic,** often used with relatio to religious controversy, may describe attitudes and measures likely to alla dispute <the book . . . is written in an *irenic* rather than polemic sty — *Times Lit. Supp.*> <lived to see his synod adopt a very *irenic* attitud towards its former antagonists — J. M. Rohne> **Pacifist** and **pacifistic** bot stress opposition, and especially active opposition, to war or violence, typ cally on moral or conscientious grounds; the former is more general i application, being equally applicable to persons or organizations or thing <as attitudes, writings, or arguments), while the latter is ordinarily restricte to things <a *pacifist* group on the campus> <*pacifist* critics of the Sta

Department> <the Quakers' *pacifist* philosophy – *Current Biog.*> <a determinedly *pacifistic* outlook> <a *pacifistic* fear that involvement in war ... would produce an interruption in social progress – R. E. Sherwood> ***ant*** bellicose

pacifist – see PACIFIC

pacifistic – see PACIFIC

pains – see EFFORT

palatable, appetizing, savory, tasty, toothsome *shared meaning* : agreeable or pleasant to the taste. **Palatable,** the most neutral term, implies no more than acceptability to the taste and often applies to something that would not ordinarily be expected to be pleasant <the root, when properly cooked, was converted into a *palatable* and nutritious food – W. H. Prescott> or to something offered to the mental taste <as many educators profess, some subject matter can be made more *palatable* with a sprinkling of fun – R. G. Frost> **Appetizing** implies a whetting of the appetite (as by the smell and taste of good food) <the *appetizing* odor of roasting turkey> <a light touch with words, as with pastry, makes for a more *appetizing* dish – Helen R. Cross> **Savory** suggests piquancy and is applicable to well-seasoned foods <poultry is better served with a *savory* stuffing> and other piquantly pleasing things <those engaging books of robust humor were neither autobiography, nor fiction, nor essays, but a *savory* mixture of all three – *N.Y. Times*> **Tasty** implies a marked and appetizing taste <a sharp *tasty* cheese> or quality <gusto and detail that make *tasty* reading – A. L. Coleman> **Toothsome** heightens the implications of agreeableness in *palatable* and may add suggestions of pleasing texture or tenderness <perfectly fried chicken, crisp and *toothsome*> <grandmother's *toothsome* battercakes – S. H. Adams> In extended use it is likely to suggest lusciousness <a *toothsome* blond baggage ... standing there in an unbelievably tight emerald gown – *New Yorker*> ***ant*** unpalatable, distasteful

palate – see TASTE 2

pale, pallid, ashen, ashy, wan, livid *shared meaning* : deficient in natural or healthy color or in vividness or intensity of hue. **Pale** implies relative nearness to white and deficiency of depth and brilliance or color <his face grew *pale*> <her dress was a very *pale* rose> **Pallid** is likely to suggest deprivation of natural color and connote abnormality <his *pallid* face reveals the strain he has been under> <trembling limbs and *pallid* lips – P. B. Shelley> **Ashen** and **ashy** imply a pale grayish color suggestive of ashes and stress an unwholesome or portentous pallor <the *ashen* hue of age – Sir Walter Scott> <oft have I seen a timely-parted ghost, of *ashy* semblance – Shak.> <the skies they were *ashen* and sober – E. A. Poe> **Wan** suggests the blanching associated with waning vitality and is likely to denote a sickly paleness <the blasted stars looked *wan* – John Milton> <her poor *wan* face with its wistful, pitiful little smile – Maurice Hewlett> **Livid** basically means leaden-hued; it is used of things that have lost their normal coloring and assumed a dull grayish tinge <like the *livid* face of a drowned corpse at the bottom of a pool – Joseph Conrad> or of colors so dulled that the basic hue is barely perceptible <his trembling lips are *livid* blue – Sir Walter Scott> <the *livid* red of the sun seen through fog>

pall – see SATIATE

pallid – see PALE

palpable – see PERCEPTIBLE ***ant*** insensible

palpate – see TOUCH

palter – see LIE

pamper – see INDULGE ***ant*** chasten

panegyric — see ENCOMIUM
panic — see FEAR
parade — see SHOW 2
paradox, antinomy, anomaly *shared meaning*: something involving an inherent contradiction. A **paradox** is primarily a statement or proposition which contains a contradiction yet which may be true and in accordance with fact and common sense <the perfectly bred man is born, not bred, if the *paradox* may be permitted — W. C. Brownell> The word may also apply to something that exists but when put into words seems incredible because it involves a logical contradiction <the colonel . . . is a *paradox* — a well-known secret agent — John Kobler> An **antinomy,** basically, is a contradiction between two laws, principles, or conclusions both of which are logically arrived at or inferred from the same facts or premises <the apparent *antinomy* between materialist and idealist interpretations of history — Robert Redfield> <there is no beginning to art: it belongs with Kant's other *antinomies,* whereby the world had and had not a point of origin in time — J. M. Barzun> In more general use the word implies a conflict (as of principles, beliefs, or aspirations) irresolvable in the light of present knowledge <every dogma is but one side of an inevitable *antinomy* — H. W. Cushing> <writers . . . who so symbolize . . . the fundamental *antinomies* of experience that they give grounds for endless speculation — R. G. Davis> An **anomaly** is something that is contrary to what it should be; the term may imply exception to a rule, or monstrous quality, or irreconcilability (as with surroundings, conditions, or pertinent beliefs) <there is no greater *anomaly* in nature than a bird that cannot fly — C. R. Darwin> <the *anomaly* of a war fought to preserve freedom by a people enslaved by prejudice — Quentin Anderson>
parallel *adj* — see SIMILAR
parallel *n* **parallel, counterpart, analogue, correlate** *shared meaning* : one that corresponds to or closely resembles another. **Parallel** is especially appropriate when the two being compared are so like that their lack of divergence suggests parallel lines <none but thyself can be thy *parallel* — Alexander Pope> <like the Biblical Israelites — with whom the Ibos share striking cultural *parallels* — Biafra's predominant tribe is individualistic, clannish and enterprising — Lloyd Garrison> **Counterpart** suggests a complementary and sometimes an obverse relationship <the mincing airs and graces of such a fellow, his antics and his gibes . . . were the exact *counterparts* of the malicious quips of ancient clowns — Thomas Wolfe> <they are not all troubled in the same way. . . . Yet, the hippie's most conservative *counterpart* who volunteers for Vietnam is still troubled — Jeanne L. Noble> **Analogue** usually implies a more remote likeness and may involve a comparison made to clarify, enlighten, or demonstrate <in the political sphere, the basic expectation is an *analogue* of that in the economic realm. A strong central government is assumed to give the nation direction and purpose — R. A. Bauer *et al*> <the wing of a bat (a modified hand) is an *analogue* of that of a bird (a modified forelimb)> **Correlate** applies to what corresponds to something else from another point of view or in another order of viewing <words are the mental *correlates* of direct experience — A. T. Weaver> <works of art that are the objective *correlate* of his inner emotional tensions — Herbert Read>
paramount — see DOMINANT
parcel — see GROUP
pardon *n* **pardon, amnesty, absolution** *shared meaning*: a remission of penalty or punishment. **Pardon** is often ambiguous; it denotes a release not from guilt but from a penalty imposed by secular or spiritual law. Thus, in civil

and military affairs *pardon* usually implies release from a sentence of death, from imprisonment, or from a fine, typically as an act of executive clemency or in the undoing of a judicial wrong. When a pardon is extended to a whole class (as an insurgent group) or to a community, it is called an **amnesty** <a royal *pardon* later freed him from a death sentence – *Amer. Guide Series: Md.*> <a proclamation of universal *amnesty* . . . finally restored the civil rights of Jefferson Davis and a handful of others – A. D. Kirwan> <the . . . Library announced a one-day *amnesty* during which overdue library books could be returned without paying of fines – *N.Y. Times*> When in ecclesiastical and especially Roman Catholic use a pardon is extended for sins confessed and atoned for, it is specifically called **absolution** when it implies that the eternal punishment for sin has been remitted in the sacrament of penance.

pardon *vb* – see EXCUSE *ant* punish

pardonable – see VENIAL

parody – see CARICATURE

parsimonious – see STINGY *ant* prodigal

part *n* **part, portion, piece, member, division, section, segment, fragment** *shared meaning*: something less than the whole to which it belongs. **Part** is a general and neutral term capable of replacing any of the others <give me *part* of the paper> <*part* of the time they fished and *part* of the time they loafed> **Portion** need not presuppose a compact or integral whole for its referent may be an existing or available or possible stock <he is a *portion* of the loveliness which once he made more lovely – P. B. Shelley> In much of its use it implies an assigned or allotted part <cut a pie in six equal *portions*> **Piece** stresses separateness and applies to a part or portion in some way separated from an expressed or implied whole; thus, one cuts a *piece* of bread from a loaf; one works a *piece* of iron at the forge with the implication that a larger mass exists; one tells a *piece* of news with the implication that one knows other news <bought a big *piece* of land> **Member** applies to one of the functional units composing a body <the club has 500 *members*> <the body can be no healthier than its *members*> <the saddle seat is a distinctive *member* of a Windsor chair> *Division* and *section* apply to a part made by or as if by cutting, **division** usually suggesting a larger or more diversified and **section** a smaller or more typical part; thus, one would speak of the graduate *division* of the university but of the several *sections* of the freshman English class. **Segment** applies to a part separated or marked out by or as if by natural lines of cleavage <the *segments* of an orange> <[they] made up the small Jewish *segment* of this gentile community – Bernard Malamud> **Fragment** applies to a random bit and especially to one left after the rest has been used, eaten, worn away, or lost <they took up of the *fragments* . . . twelve baskets full – *Mt* 14:20 (AV)> <remembered a *fragment* of her religious training – Herman Wouk> *ant* whole

part *vb* – see SEPARATE *ant* cleave

partake – see SHARE

participate – see SHARE

particular *adj* **1** see CIRCUMSTANTIAL

2 see NICE

3 see SINGLE *ant* general

4 see SPECIAL *ant* general, universal

particular *n* – see ITEM *ant* universal, whole, aggregate

partisan – see FOLLOWER

pass – see JUNCTURE

passion **1** see FEELING

2 passion, fervor, ardor, enthusiasm, zeal *shared meaning* : intense emotion compelling action. **Passion** implies an overwhelming or driving emotion <the *passion* and frenzy of the Children's Crusade of the Middle Ages – Gerald Carson> <the idea of mankind may be destined to attract the consideration it deserves, not only as a concern of the mind but as a *passion* of the heart – W. W. Wagar> *Fervor* and *ardor* both imply the kindling of emotion to a high degree of heat, but **fervor** more often suggests a steady glow or burning and **ardor** a restless or leaping flame <Mao's . . . concern for the loss of revolutionary *fervor* among present-day Chinese youth – A. S. Whiting> <traditionalist individuals . . . who believe with almost religious *fervor* that the true value of gold will never decline – B. K. Thurlow> <an intense sympathy with youth, with its shyness, its tremulous *ardors* – Laurence Binyon> <the raptures and *ardors* of sudden conversion to any cause – H. V. Gregory> **Enthusiasm,** otherwise close to *ardor,* is likely to stress rational grounds and a definitive object or objective for the emotion <they are . . . still radicals out of habit, but without *enthusiasm* and without a cause – Norman Mailer> **Zeal** implies energetic and unflagging pursuit of an end or devotion to a cause <[he] worked in almost silent *zeal* and entire absorption – Pearl Buck> <with all the *zeal* which young and fiery converts feel – Lord Byron>

passionate – see IMPASSIONED

passive – see INACTIVE ***ant*** active

pastoral – see RURAL

pat – see SEASONABLE

patch – see MEND

patent – see EVIDENT ***ant*** latent

pathetic – see MOVING ***ant*** comical

pathos, poignancy, bathos *shared meaning* : a quality that moves one to pity or sorrow. **Pathos,** common in critical and literary use, typically suggests the detachment of an observer and the arousal of aesthetic rather than acute and personal emotional response <*pathos* she has, the nearest to tragedy the comedian can come – W. B. Yeats> <*pathos* is the luxury of grief; and when it ceases to be other than a keen-edged pleasure it ceases to be *pathos* – C. K. D. Patmore> **Poignancy** may be preferred when the genuineness of the thing's emotional quality and of the emotions it arouses need to be stressed <all the terrible *poignancy* of spring, its hope, its pain, its blossoming – Edith Sitwell> <it was not in my nature, as it was in hers, to feel the acute sudden *poignancy* of love in emergency – Havelock Ellis> **Bathos** is often applied to a false or pretentious pathos and typically implies a maudlin sentimentality more likely to arouse disgusted contempt than the emotion it seeks to elicit <the *bathos* of the "my old mammy" theme – Lillian Smith>

patrimony – see HERITAGE

pattern – see MODEL

pause, recess, respite, lull, intermission *shared meaning* : a temporary cessation. **Pause** stresses the fact of stopping and ordinarily implies an expectation of resumption (as of movement or activity) <between the dark and the daylight . . . comes a *pause* in the day's occupations, that is known as the Children's Hour – H. W. Longfellow> <there is no *pause* in the invention of new and appalling weapons – Grenville Clark> **Recess** implies a temporary suspension of work or activity <children playing during the morning school *recess*> <the justices adjourned for their summer *recess* – *N.Y. Times*> **Respite** implies a period of relief (as from labor, suffering, or war) or of delay (as before being sentenced or before having to pay money due) <there were a few years of *respite* from repression of dissent – Nat Hen-

toff> **Lull** implies a temporary cessation or, more often, marked decline (as in the violence of a storm or in business activity) <there was a *lull* in the noises of insects as if they ... were making a devotional pause – Stephen Crane> **Intermission** basically implies a break in continuity and is especially applicable to an interval available for some new or special activity; thus, an *intermission* of an entertainment (as a theatrical performance) is a brief pause during which spectators may move about, relax, and take refreshments; an *intermission* of a disease is a period in which the affected person is more or less completely free from symptoms <no one should work day after day without *intermission*>

paw – see TOUCH

pay *vb* **pay, compensate, remunerate, satisfy, reimburse, indemnify, repay, recompense** *shared meaning* : to give money or an equivalent in return for something. **Pay** implies the discharge of an obligation incurred <*pay* regular wages> <*pay* one's bills on time> **Compensate** may be chosen when it is desired to stress a counterbalancing payment (as for services rendered or loss incurred) <*compensate* a neighbor for damage done to his property> <the immense costs of a war could never be *compensated* by any economic gains that came from it – Max Lerner> **Remunerate** usually implies discharge of an obligation, especially for services rendered and may suggest a reward <promised to *remunerate* the searchers handsomely> <the party always *remunerates* its faithful workers> **Satisfy** implies paying what is demanded or required by law <death duties had been paid and the demands of creditors *satisfied* – Stella D. Gibbons> **Reimburse** implies a return of money expended (as by oneself in search of a profit or by another on one's behalf) <*reimburse* an agent for traveling expenses> <his profit did not *reimburse* him for the capital he had kept tied up so long> **Indemnify** implies promised or actual reimbursement for loss, injury, or damage <the basic purpose for which insurance exists is to *indemnify* persons subject to loss when such loss occurs – J. E. Hedges> **Repay** stresses paying back an equivalent in kind or amount <*repay* a loan> <*repay* her scorn for scorn – John Keats> **Recompense** suggests due return in amends, friendly repayment, or reward <*recompense* these people, and especially the priest, for their great kindness – Rudyard Kipling>

pay *n* – see WAGE

peaceable – see PACIFIC ***ant*** contentious, acrimonious

peaceful **1** see CALM ***ant*** turbulent
2 see PACIFIC

peak – see SUMMIT

peculiar – see CHARACTERISTIC, STRANGE

pecuniary – see FINANCIAL

pedantic, academic, scholastic, bookish *shared meaning* : too narrowly concerned with learned matters. **Pedantic** implies ostentation in learning and stodginess in expression and may connote absorption in scholarly minutiae to the point of exclusion of truly significant issues <much *pedantic* mistaking of notions for realities – Aldous Huxley> <that *pedantic* attention to detail which so annoyed all with whom he negotiated – W. L. Shirer> **Academic** is likely to stress abstractness and such lack of practical experience and interests as deprives one of the ability to deal with realities <there is so much bad writing ... because writing has been dominated by ... the *academic* teachers and critics – Havelock Ellis> <the *academic* economist's primary concern seems to be not with the real problems of our time ... but with esoteric model-building – Walter Adams> **Scholastic** is likely to imply aridity, formalism, adherence to the letter <it is very able, but harsh and crabbed and intolerably *scholastic* – H. J. Laski> **Bookish** may suggest learning derived from books rather than actualities <the gestures of Mr. Lutyens's heroes are a trifle *bookish,* too seldom of the dusty streets – *Times Lit. Supp.*> or, less pejoratively, it may imply a decidedly literary or rhetorical quality or interest <a too *bookish* vocabulary> <his father, whom he has described as being lively, *bookish,* and intelligent – *Current Biog.*>

peer – see GAZE

peeve – see IRRITATE

pellucid – see CLEAR

penalize, fine, amerce, mulct *shared meaning* : to punish by depriving of something. **Penalize,** most general in meaning and broadest in applicability, usually presupposes violation of an order, rule, or law intended to maintain discipline or ensure propriety: it implies exaction by an authority of a penalty (as forfeiture of money or an advantage or privilege or imposition of a handicap) <*penalize* late taxpayers by adding interest to their bills> <*penalize* a boxer for a low blow> *Fine* and *amerce* occur chiefly in technical legal language but retain their basic implications in their occasional extended use. **Fine** implies a monetary penalty fixed within certain limits by law <violators of minor traffic ordinances are *fined* from one to ten dollars> <the library *fines* careless borrowers a few cents a day to encourage prompt return of books> **Amerce** implies a penalty left to the discretion of the judge <he was compelled to ask pardon, and heavily *amerced* in costs – Thomas De Quincey> and in extended use may refer to a nonpecuniary penalty <millions of spirits for his fault *amerced* of heaven – John Milton> **Mulct** implies subjection to a superior power that can legally or illegally enforce penalties and especially monetary penalties for failure to conform to its discipline or edicts; in this as in its other senses *mulct* is likely to stress the helplessness of the victim and the arbitrariness of the penalizing power <an additional fee had to be paid by a member of the company to join the "Acception," and any not belonging there was *mulct* in twice the sum – *Encyc. Britannica*> <gentlemen of the jury, this is simply the barefaced attempt to bleed and *mulct* a poor impecunious Indian – T. A. Guthrie>

penchant – see LEANING

penetrate – see ENTER

penetration – see DISCERNMENT

penitence, repentance, contrition, compunction, remorse *shared meaning* : regret for sin or wrongdoing. **Penitence** implies humble realization of and regret for one's wrongdoing <the majority . . . took the attitude that no sin is beyond forgiveness if it is followed by true *penitence* – K. S. Latourette> **Repentance** suggests additionally an awareness of one's general moral shortcomings and a resolve to change <I came not to call the righteous, but sinners to *repentance* – *Lk* 5:32 (AV)> **Contrition** stresses the sorrow and regret that accompanies true penitence <the tears of my *contrition* . . . repentance for things past – Edmund Spenser> **Compunction** implies a painful sting of conscience for past or anticipated sin or wrong <they no longer felt *compunctions* about replacing men with machines – J. S. Vandiver> <would not have hurt a gnat unless his party . . . told him to do so , and then only with *compunction* – Sir Winston Churchill> **Remorse** suggests prolonged and insistent self-reproach and mental anguish for past wrongs and especially for those whose consequences cannot be escaped <*remorse* that makes one walk on thorns – Oscar Wilde> <O, that the vain *remorse* which must chastise crimes done, had but as loud a voice to warn, as its keen sting is mortal to avenge! – P. B. Shelley>

penurious – see STINGY

penury – see POVERTY ***ant*** luxury

perceptible, sensible, palpable, tangible, appreciable, ponderable *shared meaning* : apprehensible as real or existent. **Perceptible** applies to whatever can be discerned by the senses <*perceptible* sounds> <something strange was in the air, *perceptible* to a little boy but utterly beyond his understanding – H. G. Wells> Often it describes specifically what just crosses a borderline (as of visibility or audibility) <a *perceptible* change in her tone> <the ship was just *perceptible* through the mist> **Sensible** may describe whatever is clearly apprehended by the senses <*sensible* perspiration> or impresses itself on the mind through the medium of sensations <his embarrassment was *sensible* in his manner> <*sensible* of the gathering storm they gathered up their toys and hurried home> **Palpable** applies either to what has physical substance <a *palpable* grit blew in through the cracks and settled on everything> or to what is obvious and unmistakable <dangers must be *palpable* before a remedy will be forthcoming – B. L. Felknor> **Tangible** implies a capacity for being grasped, literally or figuratively, and on a physical or a mental level <something held her back, something almost as *tangible* as a restraining touch upon her shoulder – H. C. Hervey> <plant, inventory, and other *tangible* assets> **Appreciable** applies to what is distinctly apparent to the senses or definitely measurable <there was an *appreciable* cooling of the air after sundown> <a satellite must be launched above the *appreciable* atmosphere – H. E. Newell> **Ponderable** is applicable to whatever can be weighed either physically or mentally but is used typically of what is significant in terms of weight or significance as distinguished from what is so intangible as to elude such weighing <exert a *ponderable* influence on the events of his time> ***ant*** imperceptible

perception – see DISCERNMENT

peremptory – see MASTERFUL

perennial – see CONTINUAL

perfect, whole, entire, intact *shared meaning* : not deficient, defective, or faulty in any respect. **Perfect** implies the soundness and the excellence of every part, element, or quality <a *perfect* set of teeth> <he is the most *perfect* writer of my generation, he writes the best sentences word for word, rhythm upon rhythm – Norman Mailer> Sometimes the term implies exact conformance to a type <a *perfect* hexagon> and then may be a close synonym of *utter* or *complete* <a *perfect* fool> <much of the record of Christian benevolences is besmirched by being inept, imperfectly timed or by being a *perfect* mistake – D. A. Redding> **Whole** is likely to imply perfection especially in moral or physical matters <daughter, be of good comfort; thy faith hath made thee *whole* – *Mt* 9:22 (AV)> <the Sikhs puzzled and attracted me. They were among the few *whole* men in India . . . They had . . . energy – V. S. Naipaul> **Entire** implies perfection derived from completeness, integrity, or soundness <an *entire* horse is an adult uncastrated male> <oh grant me, Phoebus, calm content, strength unimpaired, a mind *entire* – John Conington> **Intact** implies retention of an original or natural perfection that might easily have been lost <that high courage which enabled Fielding . . . to keep his manly benevolence and love of truth *intact* – W. M. Thackeray> ***ant*** imperfect

perfervid – see IMPASSIONED

perfidious – see FAITHLESS

perform, execute, discharge, accomplish, achieve, effect, fulfill *shared meaning* : to carry out or into effect. **Perform**, sometimes interchangeable with *do,* can imply action that follows established patterns or procedures or fulfills agreed-upon requirements and often connotes special skill or experience in the performer <*perform* a play> <*perform* a piece on the violin> <a

solemn sacrifice, *performed* in state – Alexander Pope> **Execute** stresses the carrying out of what exists in design or intent <the escape was planned meticulously and *executed* boldly – Edmond Taylor> <we came to the conclusion that the [State] Department was either so inefficient that it could not *execute* a policy, or so dull that it did not have one – R. M. Hutchins> **Discharge** implies execution and completion of appointed duties or tasks <I had *discharged* my confidential duties as secretary . . . to the general satisfaction – Thomas De Quincey> **Accomplish** stresses the successful completion of a process rather than the means by which it is carried out <it took us twenty-three days to *accomplish* the return journey – W. H. Hudson †1922> **Achieve** adds to *accomplish* the implication of conquered difficulties <neither could *achieve* anything more than his first aim of winning the war, partly because it was the only aim the two leaders really agreed on – S. E. Ambrose> **Effect** adds to *achieve* an emphasis on the inherent force in the agent capable of surmounting obstacles <prepared to undertake . . . the task of *effecting* economic and social changes in developing nations – Vera M. Dean> **Fulfill** implies a complete realization of what exists potentially or hitherto in conception, or is implicit in the nature or sense of responsibility of the agent <the role of the university president, as . . . [he] conceives it and tries to *fulfill* it, combines the skills of a scholar and a teacher with those of an administrator and a fund raiser – *Current Biog.*> <*fulfill* a promise>

perfume – see FRAGRANCE

perilous – see DANGEROUS

perimeter – see CIRCUMFERENCE

period, epoch, era, age *shared meaning* : a portion or division of time. **Period,** the generic term, can designate an extent of time of any length and for whatever purpose delimited <they had a half-hour lunch *period*> <was returned for eight successive Congresses – a *period* of seventeen years – W. C. Ford> **Epoch** may designate the beginning of a period, especially a striking or remarkable beginning <this is an *epoch* . . . the end and the beginning of an age – H. G. Wells> but more often designates such a new period <[his] milieu is war; he was fortunate to have lived in an *epoch* whose stages of destruction correspond so closely to his inner needs – M. D. Geismar> **Era** applies to a period characterized especially by some new order of things <a better intellectual *era* is dawning for the working men – Charles Kingsley> <the Christian *era*> **Age,** often interchangeable with *era,* may be chosen to denote an era dominated by a central figure or prominent feature <the Bronze *Age*> <the *age* of Pericles> or may quite specifically imply a long period of time <not for an *age* had he lived a whole day in the open . . . in America, he rarely saw the sky – Bernard Malamud>

periodic – see INTERMITTENT

periphery – see CIRCUMFERENCE

perjure, forswear *shared meaning* : to violate one's oath or make a false swearer of (oneself). **Perjure,** in general as distinct from technical legal use, implies making a liar of oneself whether under oath or not <he thanked her, with as much enthusiasm as he could muster without actually *perjuring* himself – Archibald Marshall> **Forswear** regularly implies a violation of an oath, promise, or vow <he swore a thing to me on Monday night, which he *forswore* on Tuesday morning – Shak.> <thou shalt not *forswear* thyself, but shalt perform unto the Lord thine oaths – *Mt* 5:33 (AV)> or sometimes of something (as one's principles or beliefs) as sacred as an oath <Shelley indignantly refused to "*forswear* his principles" by accepting "a proposal so insultingly hateful" – Matthew Arnold>

permission, leave, sufferance *shared meaning* : sanction to act or do something granted by one in authority. **Permission** implies the power or authority to grant or refuse <refused strangers *permission* to hunt on his land> <applied to the courts for *permission* to sell the library, and this was granted – A. G. Thomas> **Leave** may be preferred to *permission* in conventionally courteous phrases <ask *leave* to arrive late> <by your *leave*, we'll be going now> or in official (as military) reference to permission to absent oneself from one's duties <he was given *leave* to take care of emergency business> <a soldier absent without *leave* is subject to severe discipline> **Sufferance** implies a neglect or refusal to forbid or interfere and therefore suggests a tacit permission that may be withdrawn without notice either for cause or arbitrarily <most [Vietnamese] businessmen have the uneasy feeling that they exist on *sufferance* of the enemy – *Newsweek*> <he comes among us on *sufferance*, like those concert singers whom mamma treats with so much politeness – W. M. Thackeray> *ant* prohibition

permit – see LET *ant* prohibit, forbid

permutation – see CHANGE *n*

pernicious, baneful, noxious, deleterious, detrimental *shared meaning* : exceedingly harmful. *Pernicious* and *baneful* apply to what is irreparably harmful, but **pernicious** is more likely to imply the action of evil or of an insidious corrupting or undermining, and **baneful** that of a poisoning or destroying influence <the effects of false and *pernicious* propaganda cannot be neutralized – Aldous Huxley> <*pernicious* social institutions which stifle the nobler impulses – V. L. Parrington> <the *baneful* notion that there is no such thing as a high, correct standard in intellectual matters – Matthew Arnold> <he felt that some *baneful* secret in his life might be exposed – John Cheever> **Noxious** applies to what is both offensive and harmful to health of body or mind <*noxious* insects> <the impression that inflation, like some *noxious* gas, is seeping into every nook and cranny – L. H. Clark, Jr.> **Deleterious** is applied to what has an unanticipated or obscure harmful effect, especially on the living body <the controversial question as to whether prolonged weightlessness has *deleterious* effects on the human skeleton – *The Sciences*> <my books have no social significance, except a *deleterious* one – Ian Fleming> **Detrimental** applies to something obviously, though not necessarily extremely, harmful to the thing it affects <foreign policy should be left to professionals . . . and . . . decisions should not be entirely governed by a desire to reform or reprove if it is *detrimental* to American interest – *Current Biog.*> <the *detrimental* effect of overnutrition> *ant* innocuous

perpendicular – see VERTICAL *ant* horizontal

perpetual – see CONTINUAL *ant* transitory, transient

perplex – see PUZZLE

persevere, persist *shared meaning* : to continue in a course in the face of difficulty or opposition. **Persevere** implies an admirable determination and suggests both refusal to be discouraged (as by failure, doubts, or difficulties) and a steadfast pursuit of an end or undertaking <I will *persevere* in my course of loyalty, though the conflict be sore between that and my blood – Shak.> <for, strength to *persevere* and to support, and energy to conquer and repel – these elements of virtue, that declare the native grandeur of the human soul – William Wordsworth> **Persist** may imply a virtue <this is the poetry within history, this is what causes mankind to *persist* beyond every defeat – Jean S. Untermeyer> but it more often suggests a disagreeable or annoying quality, for it stresses pertinacity more than courage or patience and is likely to imply self-willed opposition to advice, remonstrance, disapproval, or conscience <disregarding the objections of

his family and his teachers . . . [he] *persisted* in learning to play the guitar – *Current Biog.*> <*persist* in a bad habit>

persist 1 see CONTINUE *ant* desist
2 see PERSEVERE *ant* desist

personality – see DISPOSITION

perspicacious – see SHREWD *ant* dull

perspicuous – see CLEAR 2

persuade – see INDUCE *ant* dissuade

persuasion – see OPINION

pert – see SAUCY *ant* coy

pertinacious – see OBSTINATE

pertinent – see RELEVANT *ant* impertinent, foreign

perturb – see DISCOMPOSE

perverse – see CONTRARY

pervert – see DEBASE

pessimistic – see CYNICAL *ant* optimistic

pester – see WORRY

pet – see CARESS

petite – see SMALL

pharisaical – see HYPOCRITICAL

phase, aspect, side, facet, angle *shared meaning* : one of the possible ways of viewing or of being presented to view. **Phase** implies a change in appearance, either literal or figurative, often without clear reference to an observer <the red fox occurs in several color *phases*> <the *phases* of the moon> <describes development as a coordinated series of changes . . . from a *phase* of life perceived . . . as being less human to a *phase* perceived as more human – Denis Goulet> **Aspect** may stress the point of view of the observer and its limitation of what is seen or considered <the north *aspect* of the house was very bleak> <Stalin, who feared all *aspects* of France, much as the Persians feared all *aspects* of ancient Greece – S. E. Ambrose> <the healthy, constructive, normal, ethical *aspects* of this political society – N. B. Brown> **Side**, sometimes interchangeable with *phase* or *aspect*, is used typically with reference to something felt as having two or more faces and so not fully apprehensible unless it or its observer shifts position <see life only on its pleasant *side*> <if you get on the wrong *side* of authority, you are executed or exiled – Edmund Wilson> **Facet** implies the presence of a multiplicity of sides similar to the one singled out for attention <noticed the different shades of green on the planes and *facets* of each clipped tree – Roald Dahl> <another *facet* of the teacher's personality that his profession threatens is his sense of humor – Joseph Crescimbeni & R. J. Mammarella> **Angle** denotes an aspect seen from a very restricted or specific point of view <examines the contemporary American musical scene from various *angles* – *Current Biog.*>

phlegm – see EQUANIMITY

phlegmatic – see IMPASSIVE

phrase, idiom, expression, locution *shared meaning* : a group of words which together express a notion and which may be used as part of a sentence. **Phrase** is applicable to any group of words that recurs frequently but is likely to suggest some such distinctive quality as triteness <to use the *phrase* of all who ever wrote upon the state of Europe, the political horizon is dark indeed – William Cowper> or pithiness or pointedness <I summed up all systems in a *phrase* – Oscar Wilde> **Idiom** applies to a combination of word elements which is peculiar to the language in which it occurs either in grammatical relationships or in its nonliteral meaning; thus, "to keep house," "to catch cold," "to strike a bargain" are examples of English *idioms.*

Expression and *locution* are sometimes used in place of *phrase* when the idea of a way of expressing oneself is uppermost. **Expression** may be preferred when accompanied by a qualifying adjective, phrase, or clause <that's an odd *expression*> <an *expression* that has gone out of use> and **locution,** a somewhat bookish word, may be chosen when reference is to phrases that are idiomatically peculiar to a language or a group <she missed some of the richest parts on account of the language – the west Georgia *locutions* were sometimes too much for her – R. G. Tugwell>

physical – see BODILY

physique, build, habit, constitution *shared meaning* : bodily makeup or type. **Physique** applies to the structure, appearance, or strength of the body as characteristic of an individual or a race <a people of sturdy *physique*> <tall of stature, slender in *physique* – H. W. H. Knott> **Build,** freely interchangeable with *physique,* may stress the geometrically determinable qualities of a physique <a horse of chunky *build*> <his *build* was square and sturdy, his physique rugged> **Habit** implies reference to the body as the outward evidence of characteristics that determine one's physical and mental capabilities and condition; thus, a full *habit* suggests a fleshy build and the ruddy congested look of a self-indulgent person; a consumptive *habit* suggests the slender feeble-seeming body of one subject to lung disorders <like many persons of active mind and dominating will, [she was] sedentary and corpulent in her *habit* – Edith Wharton> **Constitution** applies to the makeup of the body as affected by the complex of physical and mental conditions which collectively determine its state <buy them horses to ride, if you want them to enjoy good health and sound *constitutions* – Richard Jefferies> <the key to her nature lay, I think, largely in her fragile *constitution* – Havelock Ellis>

picked – see SELECT

pickle – see PREDICAMENT

pictorial – see GRAPHIC

picturesque – see GRAPHIC

piece – see PART

pierce – see ENTER

pietistic – see DEVOUT

piety – see FIDELITY ***ant*** impiety

pilfer – see STEAL

pillage *n* – see SPOIL

pillage *vb* – see RAVAGE

pilot – see GUIDE

pinch – see JUNCTURE

pine – see LONG

pinnacle – see SUMMIT

pious – see DEVOUT ***ant*** impious

piquant – see PUNGENT ***ant*** bland

pique *n* – see OFFENSE

pique *vb* – see PRIDE *vb,* PROVOKE

pitch – see PLUNGE, THROW

piteous – see PITIFUL

pithy – see CONCISE

pitiable – see CONTEMPTIBLE, PITIFUL

pitiful, piteous, pitiable *shared meaning* : arousing or deserving pity or compassion. **Pitiful** applies especially to what actually excites pity or sometimes commiseration because it is felt to be deeply pathetic <a long line of *pitiful* refugees> <*pitiful* is the case of the blind, who cannot read the face; *pitiful* that of the deaf, who cannot follow the changes of the voice

– R. L. Stevenson> but it can also apply to what excites pitying contempt <she is a *pitiful* housekeeper> <a *pitiful* excuse> **Piteous** implies not so much the effect on the observer as the quality in the thing that has the potential capacity for exciting pity <the *piteous* cries of the appliance dealers who are shedding such copious tears because of the activities of discount houses – *Wall Street Jour.*> <Muriel sought to excite his pity; he was deaf to her *piteous* entreaties – W. S. Maugham> **Pitiable,** otherwise very close to *pitiful,* almost always implies a contemptuous commiseration, though contempt may be weakly or strongly connoted <felt a tender pity . . . mixed with shame for having made her *pitiable* – Bernard Malamud> <a sure, disciplined actress; she knows how to take a *pitiable* kind of indignity and give it a dignified . . . interpretation – R. M. Coles> <its glory was won at the expense of a helpless foe, for enemy resistance was *pitiable* – Allan Nevins & H. S. Commager> ***ant*** cruel

pittance – see RATION

pity – see SYMPATHY

place – see POSITION 2

placid – see CALM ***ant*** choleric (*of persons*), ruffled (*of things*)

plague – see WORRY

plain **1** see EVIDENT ***ant*** abstruse

2 plain, homely, simple, unpretentious *shared meaning* : free from all ostentation or superficial embellishment. **Plain** stresses lack of anything (as ornamentation or affectation) likely to catch the attention <a *plain* house on a quiet street> Additionally it may suggest elegance <the furnishings were *plain* with very simple classic lines> or frugality <she set a *plain* but abundant table> or, with reference to personal appearance, lack of positive beauty that does not go to the extreme of ugliness <he looked round for his tidy miss. He pitched upon the dullest, nicest, and *plainest* girl he could find – Victoria Sackville-West> **Homely** may suggest comfortable informality without ostentation or easy familiarity <reassuringly *homely* against this puissant background, sound a . . . peddler's horn, a carpenter's hammer – J. M. Flagler> <a book-learned language, wholly remote from anything personal, native, or *homely* – Willa Cather> Especially in American use in application to personal appearance *homely* is likely to imply something between *plain* and *ugly* <she was gaunt and *homely,* with no breasts to speak of, and she probably would never get married – William Styron> **Simple,** very close to *plain* in its references to situations and things, may stress volition as the source of the quality described <what was then called the *simple* life . . . is recognizable as the austere luxury of a very cultivated poet – Agnes Repplier> and regularly connotes lack of complication or ostentation <the somewhat too-elaborate deference paid them by the neighbors embarrassed them and caused them to clothe their wealth in muted, *simple* gray – William Styron> **Unpretentious** stresses lack of vanity or affectation and may praise a person <soft-spoken and *unpretentious,* he inclines to the simple and austere in his personal life – *Current Biog.*> but in reference to a thing may convey either praise <*unpretentious,* informative, and trifling in cost though not in content, this handbook should be afforded a cordial welcome – Bernard Lowy> or depreciation <an *unpretentious* and battered old car> ***ant*** lovely

3 see FRANK

4 see COMMON

plan, design, plot, scheme, project *shared meaning* : a method devised for making or doing something or achieving an end. **Plan** regularly implies mental formulation of a method or a course of action <make *plans* for a summer holiday> <she had her *plan* clearly in her head, with every

detail . . . distinct – Stella D. Gibbons> and it may imply graphic representation of such a method or course <drew *plans* for a new home> **Design** adds to *plan* a suggestion of defined pattern and of achieved order or harmony <the most wonderful and delicate *design* composed entirely of flowers – Roald Dahl> <work out a *design* for a piece of embroidery> **Plot** implies a laying out in clearly distinguished sections with attention to their relations or proportions <make a *plot* of the course for a cross-country race> Specifically, it can apply to the fundamental framework of a literary work <there is plenty of action in this play, but no clearly developed *plot*> **Scheme** stresses calculation of the end in view <work out a *scheme* for the care of disaster victims> and may apply to a plan motivated by craftiness and self-seeking <a lurking suspicion that our work was . . . a *scheme* to superimpose American economic control upon ingenuous foreign countries – V. G. Heiser> **Project**, basically close to *scheme*, is more likely to stress enterprise, imaginative scope, or vision <sanguine schemes, ambitious *projects*, pleased me less – William Wordsworth> <such were my *projects* for the city's good – Robert Browning> but sometimes suggests ponderous or needless extension <we have done a great deal concerning this matter without making too much of a *project* of it – R. D. Patterson>

plane – see LEVEL ***ant*** solid

plastered – see DRUNK

plastic, pliable, pliant, ductile, malleable, adaptable *shared meaning* **:** susceptible of being modified in form or nature. Something **plastic** has the quality (as of wax, clay, or plaster) of being soft enough to be worked or molded yet capable of hardening into a final form <life is *plastic:* it will assume any shape you choose to put on it – O. S. J. Gogarty> <two contrasting concepts of human nature, either as innately corrupt or as *plastic*, malleable, either for good or for evil – Robert Gordis> Something **pliable** or **pliant** has the quality (as of willow twigs) of being supple enough to be bent or manipulated without breaking or permanent deformation. In extended use *pliable* usually suggests submission to the will of another <I flatter myself that I have some influence over her. She is *pliable* – Thomas Hardy> while *pliant* is more likely to suggest flexibility or a yielding quality than submissiveness <many fathers and mothers tend to vacillate: they are *pliant* and permissive one week, stern and demanding the next – Stanley Jacobs> <this sober, *pliant* prose, with its easy movement between homely imagery and terms of abstract praise – Stella Brook> Something **ductile** has the quality of a tensile metal (as copper) of being drawn out into a filament or, in extended use, of being easily drawn or led <a vast portion of the public feels rather than thinks, a *ductile* multitude drawn easily by the arts of the demagogue – Amy Loveman> Something **malleable** is literally or figuratively capable of being beaten into shape <tempers . . . rendered pliant and *malleable* in the fiery furnace of domestic tribulation – Washington Irving> <behavior is *malleable* and is shaped by the rewards and punishments in the environment – *Trans-action*> Something **adaptable** is capable of modification to suit other conditions, other needs, or other uses <have proved themselves an uncommonly *adaptable* people – *Amer. Guide Series: Ariz.*> <in spite of, or perhaps because of, the complexity of his inner workings, man is a very *adaptable* creature – C. C. Furnas>

plausible, credible, believable, colorable, specious *shared meaning* **:** outwardly acceptable as true or genuine. **Plausible** implies reasonableness at first sight or hearing usually with some hint of a possibility of being deceived <a *plausible* excuse> <the most *plausible* and persuasive confidence man of his day – S. H. Adams> **Credible** implies apparent worthiness of belief especially because of support by known facts or sound reasoning <his story is perfectly *credible* to one who knows his background> <a *credible* witness> **Believable** can apply to what seems true because within the range of known possibility or probability <a down-to-earth, rat-chasing, thoroughly *believable* wharf cat – Shirley Camper> **Colorable** stresses credibility on merely outward grounds <any *colorable* pretext for refusing – Bertrand Russell> and often implies an intent to deceive <a *colorable* compliance with the law – Joseph Wright> **Specious** stresses plausibility usually with a clear implication of dissimulation or fraud <*specious* piety> <the thousands of pages of the transcript of evidence form an interesting but often *specious* chronicle – J. M. Bennett> <a dated and *specious* ideology but one which holds great attraction for masses of people – G. F. Kennan> ***ant*** implausible

play – see FUN ***ant*** earnest

plea – see APOLOGY

pleasant, pleasing, agreeable, grateful, gratifying, welcome *shared meaning* : highly acceptable to the mind or senses. *Pleasant* and *pleasing* are often indistinguishable; however, **pleasant** is more likely to stress a quality inherent in an object, and **pleasing** the effect that something has on one; thus, *pleasant* weather is *pleasing* to one exposed to it <it was a *pleasant* bright winter day and he found the warmth of the sun *pleasing*> <a *pleasant* garden> <a *pleasing* arrangement of colors> **Agreeable** applies to what is in accord with one's tastes or liking <an *agreeable* companion> <if I was obliged to define politeness, I should call it the art of making oneself *agreeable* – Tobias Smollett> **Grateful** implies a satisfaction or relief yielded by what is pleasing or agreeable <lay down . . . under the *grateful* shade of the tall cottonwoods – Willa Cather> <expertly composed in full romantic vein, lavish with melody, *grateful* to the voices – Herbert Weinstock> **Gratifying** implies mental pleasure arising usually from a satisfying of one's hopes, desires, conscience, or vanity <the *gratifying* feeling that our duty has been done – W. S. Gilbert> <having been given a free hand by the paper, he was able to keep City Hall in a *gratifying* turmoil with his denunciations – Bernard Taper> **Welcome** is stronger than *pleasing* and *grateful* in stressing the pleasure given by satisfying a prior need or longing <as *welcome* as rain after a long drought> <a strange but *welcome* silence settled over the Continent for the first time since September 1, 1939 – W. L. Shirer> ***ant*** unpleasant, distasteful

pleasing – see PLEASANT ***ant*** displeasing, repellent

pleasure, delight, joy, delectation, enjoyment, fruition *shared meaning* : the agreeable emotion accompanying the possession or expectation of what is good or greatly desired. **Pleasure** stresses satisfaction or gratification rather than visible happiness <when these wild ecstasies shall be matured into a sober *pleasure* – William Wordsworth> <the ordinary face of an ordinary man, a mixture of small worries and *pleasures,* hopes and disappointments – Helen MacInnes> <take *pleasure* in one's possessions> **Delight** usually reverses this emphasis and stresses lively expression of obvious satisfaction <man's *delight* in the arts and with the kind of entertainment which feeds the spirit – August Heckscher> <the *delight* of grandparents in a new grandchild> **Joy** may replace *pleasure* or *delight* or it may imply a more deep-rooted rapturous emotion than either <and all its aching *joys* are now no more, and all its dizzy raptures – William Wordsworth> <bright, eager students can be a *joy* to teach – M. S. Eisenhower> <fiddling a little song which is his pride and *joy* in a mediocre way, and so pleased with himself he could explode – Herman Wouk> *Delectation* and *enjoyment* imply reaction to pleasurable experience; distinctively **delectation** suggests amusement, diversion, or entertainment <revived ancient, joyful customs for the *delectation* of islanders and visitors – Ernest Gruening> while **enjoyment** stresses a resulting gratification or happiness <just as backbiting and gossip could be a source of *enjoyment,* so could friendliness and ... the indulgence in sentimentality – J. T. Farrell> **Fruition,** increasingly uncommon in this sense, implies pleasure in possession or enjoyment in attainment <the *fruition* of the 'glorious Godhead' is the enjoyment of the glorious presence of God – Stella Brook> <the sweet *fruition* of an earthly crown – Christopher Marlowe> ***ant*** displeasure

plenary – see FULL ***ant*** limited

plentiful, ample, abundant, copious *shared meaning* : more than sufficient without being excessive. **Plentiful** implies a great or rich supply, often of something that is not regularly or universally available <peaches are *plentiful* this year> <it is also a zone of *plentiful* food and therefore able to support an extensive fauna – W. H. Dowdeswell> **Ample** implies generous sufficiency to satisfy a particular requirement <there is *ample* meat for another meal> <*ample* apologies indeed for fifteen years of persecution – T. B. Macaulay> **Abundant** suggests an even larger or richer supply than *plentiful* <his *abundant* vitality – Arnold Bennett> <the production evoked a whole ... riotous manner of living; so *abundant* and compelling was the life on the stage that I could not wait to find out what happened next – Kenneth Tynan> **Copious** stresses largeness of supply rather than fullness or richness <*copious* eating and still more *copious* drinking – Aldous Huxley> <I found our speech *copious* without order, and energetic without rules – Samuel Johnson> ***ant*** scanty, scant

pliable – see PLASTIC ***ant*** obstinate

pliant – see PLASTIC

plight – see PREDICAMENT

plot 1 see PLAN

2 plot, intrigue, machination, conspiracy, cabal *shared meaning* : a plan secretly devised to accomplish an evil or treacherous end. **Plot** implies careful foresight in planning positive action <there is a *plot* against my life, my crown – Shak.> <the great Jesuit *plot* for the destruction of Protestant England – S. M. Crothers> **Intrigue** suggests secret underhand maneuvering in an atmosphere of duplicity <[his] tortuous *intrigues* had at last brought him to the highest office – W. L. Shirer> <only a person with a candid mind, who is usually bored by *intrigues,* can appreciate the full fun of an *intrigue* when they begin to manage one for the first time – Stella D. Gibbons> **Machination,** usually in the plural, imputes hostility or treachery to the makers and usually suggests craftiness in devising annoyances, injuries, or evils <tortured by some black trouble of the soul, and given over to the *machinations* of his deadliest enemy – Nathaniel Hawthorne> <the devilish *machinations* of an enchanter masquerading as a pious hermit – J. L. Lowes> **Conspiracy** implies a secret agreement among many persons not necessarily for positive action <there's been a *conspiracy* of silence as regards state needs – John Bebout> <these people he has been taking for granted are all part of an insidious *conspiracy* to undermine the world as he knows it – Edmund Wilson> **Cabal** applies to an intrigue, often among highly placed individuals, in which a group acts jointly to accomplish some end favorable to its members but injurious or disastrous to the one or ones affected <the *cabal* against Washington found supporters exclusively in the north – George Bancroft> <that moment ... when a senatorial *cabal,* the most venal since the days of President Grant, nominated Warren G. Harding for the Presidency – Irving Stone>

pluck – see FORTITUDE

plumb — see VERTICAL
plume — see PRIDE *vb*
plunder — see SPOIL
plunge, dive, pitch *shared meaning* : to throw oneself or to throw or thrust something forward and downward into or as if into deep water. **Plunge** stresses the force of the movement and may imply entry into any penetrable medium or into a state or condition in which one is overwhelmed or immersed or into a course which works a deep descent, a complete change, or a distinct involvement <*plunge* bodily into the water after a forty-foot drop — C. S. Forester> <we are *plunged* once more into the war of nerves — *Times Lit. Supp.*> <he *plunged* eagerly into the new course of studies> **Dive** suggests intent and may imply more deliberateness and more skill than *plunge* <a . . . pilot . . . *dove* at supersonic speed to within 8000 feet of the ground — John Lear> <an enormous water rat *dived* down from the bank — J. C. Powys> <they read the documents and then . . . *dived* for the nearest telephones — Richard Harris> **Pitch** is likely to stress lack of all intent or design <she caught her heel in a crack and *pitched* to the ground> <my anxiety to own the ducks caused me to *pitch* into the water with all my clothes on — Owen Wister> or may imply complete disregard of the fate of the thing pitched <we decided it would be better to have the study guides sent to me, because . . . students getting them from the bookstore might think them just advertising and *pitch* them — F. R. McLeod>
plurality — see MAJORITY
plutocracy — see OLIGARCHY
pogrom — see MASSACRE
poignancy — see PATHOS
poignant **1** see MOVING
2 see PUNGENT *ant* dull (*reaction, sensation*)
poise — see TACT
poison, venom, virus, toxin, bane *shared meaning* : material that when present in or introduced into a living organism produces a deadly or seriously injurious effect. **Poison,** the most general term, is applicable to any deadly or noxious substance (as strychnine, arsenic, or carbon monoxide) or to anything felt as having a comparable effect <the subtle *poison* of racist thinking by 'decent' men who deny that they are racists — John Hersey> **Venom** basically applies to a poison-containing fluid secreted by an animal (as a snake, bee, or spider) and injected into another animal in defensive or predatory action; in extended use it implies a malignant hostility <academic economists . . . greeted the book's appearance with undisguised *venom* and vitriol — Walter Adams> <biting his tongue, while others trod upon him, or worse, discharged subtle *venom* in the guise of wit — H. C. Hervey> **Virus,** once equivalent to *venom,* retains this value only in extended use and then applies to what is felt to have a corrupting quality poisonous to mind and spirit <the force of this *virus* of prejudice — V. S. Waters> and in more literal use applies to a submicroscopic agent of infection working with insidious deadliness or deleteriousness <the *virus* of infantile paralysis> **Toxin** basically denotes a complex organic poison produced by the metabolic processes of a living organism, especially a bacterium or virus <the *toxins* of plague and anthrax bacilli — A. W. Bernheimer> In its occasional extended use it suggests an insidious undermining effect like that of a bacterial toxin <the nation was young, hopeful, essentially healthy, having begun to throw off the *toxins* of civil hate and the ulcer of slavery — Dixon Wecter> <the emotions, feeding only on themselves, turn into *toxins* — H. A. Overstreet> **Bane** may apply to any cause of ruin, destruction,

or tribulation <the red cotton bug, the *bane* of India's cotton crop – Isaac Asimov> <heresy is a fighting word.... To the rebel, just because it is the *bane* of orthodoxy, it signifies a proclamation of truth – W. R. Miller> Its literal use is now mostly in compounds naming plants with poisonous principles <rats*bane*> <hen*bane*>

polite – see CIVIL ***ant*** impolite

politic – see EXPEDIENT, SUAVE

politician, statesman, politico *shared meaning* : a person actively engaged in politics or the affairs of government. **Politician** regularly implies a personal and professional interest and party affiliation and stresses to varying degrees the resulting bias. **Statesman,** except in eulogistic partisan discourse, implies an elevation above party conflict and a mind able to view objectively the needs and problems of the state and its citizens and to concern itself with the long-term greatest good of the greatest number <they were *statesmen, not politicians;* they guided public opinion, but were little guided by it – Henry Adams> <the scornful may say that "a *statesman* is a dead *politician,*" but it is more truly said that a *statesman* lives by his principles and a *politician* is ruled by his interest – P. P. Van Riper> <every day ... *politicians,* of which there are plenty, swear eternal devotion to the ends of peace and security.... And every day *statesmen,* of which there are few, must struggle with limited means to achieve these unlimited ends, both in fact and in understanding – A. E. Stevenson †1965> **Politico** is virtually interchangeable with *politician* but perhaps more likely to stress concern with partisan political activity than with the actual business of government <his strength rests on the support of veteran *politicos* throughout the State – W. V. Shannon> <some sharp *politicos* still think the President won't run again – *Wall Street Jour.*> Like *politician,* it can be highly derogatory <Machiavelli's *The Prince,* in which the individual *politico* is shown how to succeed by ignoring all moral, social, and religious restraints on his own action – Gilbert Highet> <not a game to be played so publicity-mad *politicos* can build fame for themselves – B. J. Sheil>

politico – see POLITICIAN

pollute – see CONTAMINATE

ponder, meditate, muse, ruminate *shared meaning* : to consider or examine attentively and deliberately. **Ponder** implies a careful weighing of a problem or prolonged, often inconclusive thinking about a matter <*pondering* over the best style in which to address the unknown and distant relatives – Stella D. Gibbons> <study its organization, reflect on its psychology and political techniques and *ponder* the results – W. L. Shirer> **Meditate** adds to *ponder* an implication of a definite directing or focusing of one's thought <*meditate* upon these things; give thyself wholly to them – *1 Tim* 4:15 (AV)> In transitive use it may imply such deep concentration on a plan or project as to approach *intend* or *purpose* in meaning <he was *meditating* a book on Shakespearian questions – H. J. Oliver> **Muse,** otherwise close to *meditate,* is likely to suggest a persistent but languid and inconclusive turning over in the mind <Cabot *mused* over the fact that the old bastard considered himself ... one of the eminences of the great metropolis – James Purdy> <ever since man first *mused* about his own nature, it has been the gift of language that has surprised him most – E. H. Lenneberg> **Ruminate** implies going over the same matter in one's thoughts again and again, often by way of casual reasoning or rambling speculation <sit at home and *ruminate* on the qualities of certain little books ... which I can read and read again – L. P. Smith> <forty years of *ruminating* on life, of glimpsing it in its simplest forms through microscopes – Waldemar Kaempffert>

ponderable – see PERCEPTIBLE
ponderous – see HEAVY
pool – see MONOPOLY
popular – see COMMON ***ant*** unpopular, esoteric
portentous – see OMINOUS
portion – see FATE, PART
pose *vb* – see PROPOSE
pose *n* **pose, air, affectation, mannerism** *shared meaning* : an adopted way of speaking or acting. **Pose** implies an attitude deliberately assumed to impress others or call attention to oneself <if De Gaulle's public *pose* was that France was a great power, his policy for the war gave that *pose* the lie – S. E. Ambrose> <realized that a fantasist's *pose* of authority on such matters is bound to sit ill with a serious and progressive physician – Theodore Sturgeon> **Air** may come close to demeanor <listened with an *air* of alert interest> but, especially in the plural, it often implies artificiality and the intent to give a false appearance and usually also implies a vulgar pretense (as of breeding or superiority) <heaped ridicule on the academic "gentry," their degrees and diplomas and their pedagogical *airs* – W. L. Shirer> <their grown-up sons and daughters, usually a joking and irreverent band of ordinary young Americans, wore awkward company *airs* – Herman Wouk> **Affectation** applies to a trick of speech or behavior that strikes the observer as insincere <an *affectation* of girlish innocence> <his *affectation* of ease fooled no one> **Mannerism** designates an acquired peculiarity of behavior or speech that has become a habit <said to resemble his father-in-law in physical appearance as well as in speech and *mannerisms* – *Current Biog.*> <those little *mannerisms* of hers . . . especially the way she has of pointing a finger at me to emphasize a phrase – Roald Dahl>
position **1 position, stand, attitude** *shared meaning* : a point of view or way of regarding something. *Position* and *stand* both imply reference to a question at issue or a matter about which there is a difference of opinion. **Position** is the milder term since it, unlike **stand**, rarely connotes aggressive expression or defiance of a generally held or popular opinion <the candidate discussed his *position* on the war> <he took the *stand* that the national interest required continuance of the war> **Attitude** is likely to apply to a point of view colored by personal or party feeling and as much the product of temperament or emotion as of thought or conviction <he took a humorous *attitude* toward life> <it was their *attitude* of acceptance . . . their complaisance about themselves and about their life – Thomas Wolfe>
2 position, place, situation, office, post, job *shared meaning* : employment for wages or salary. **Position** and **place** mean little more than this though the former may be preferred where the employment suggests higher status or more dignity in the work involved <my brother has a *position* as research director in the new company> <she has lost her *place* as a cook> **Situation** adds an emphasis on a place needing to be filled <obtained a *situation* as clerk to the city council> **Office** applies to a position of trust or authority especially in public service <he has held the *office* of county treasurer for many years> <men in public *office*> **Post** suggests a position involving some degree of responsibility <took a *post* as governess in an aristocratic household> or sometimes onerous duties <teaching *posts* in our colleges – E. J. Simmons> **Job,** a very general term, stresses the work involved <his first *job* was in public-school teaching> and is especially appropriate when physical labor is in question <*jobs* for manual laborers> <seasonal *jobs*>
positive – see SURE ***ant*** doubtful
possess – see HAVE

possible **1 possible, practicable, feasible** *shared meaning* : capable of being realized. **Possible** implies that a thing may certainly exist or occur given the proper conditions <one of the duties of regulative wisdom is to trace the limits of the *possible* – Denis Goulet> <the regime of religious toleration has become *possible* only because we have lost the primal intensity of religious conviction – M. R. Cohen> **Practicable** applies to what is not only possible but may be easily or readily effected by available means or under current conditions <trial by jury – an institution in which . . . we have the very abstract and essence of all *practicable* democratic government – W. H. Mallock> **Feasible** applies to what is likely to work or be useful in attaining an end desired <they debated whether it would be *feasible* and if *feasible,* desirable, to attempt to make a national assessment of education – Helen Rowan> <cheap iron and steel made it *feasible* to equip larger armies and navies than ever before – Lewis Mumford>
2 see PROBABLE

post – see POSITION 2

postpone – see DEFER

postulant – see NOVICE

potential – see LATENT *ant* active, actual

pother – see STIR

pour, stream, gush, sluice *shared meaning* : to send forth or come forth copiously. **Pour** suggests abundant emission <it never rains but it *pours*> <*pour* men and money into the Netherlands – Stringfellow Barr> and may sometimes imply a coming in a course or stream from or as if from a spout <workers *poured* from the subway exits> **Stream** suggests a flow limited by issuance through a channel or from an opening <tears *streamed* from her eyes> <light *streamed* through the open door> <thousands of Moslems *streamed* along the narrow alleys of the ghettos – *Hadassah Mag.*> **Gush** implies a sudden and copious outpouring of or as if of something released from confinement <blood *gushed* from the wound> <he . . . suddenly *gushed* forth in streams of wondrous eloquence – Leslie Stephen> **Sluice** implies the operation of something like a sluice or flume for the control of the flow of water and regularly suggests a sudden abundant stream <[he] was awakened . . . by a cold spit of sea which, clearing the bow, *sluiced* down across the foredeck – Peter Matthiessen> <the boiling broth is *sluiced* over cuts of coarse, grainy bread that is first rubbed with oil and garlic – Silas Spitzer>

poverty, indigence, penury, want, destitution *shared meaning* : the state of one who is poor or without enough to live on. **Poverty** may cover a range from extreme want of necessities to a falling short of having comfortable means <today about one fifth of all the people in this affluent country live in *poverty* – H. J. Geiger> <this ugly, barren *poverty* on the Spanish land was his first view of some men's helpless fate – Janet Flanner> Often it suggests detachment from the mainstream of society <we have been drawn to a conception of *poverty* as a lack of power to command events in one's life . . . as the incapacity to consume resources and to exploit available opportunities – Martin Rein> **Indigence** suggests straitened circumstances and the concomitant hardships and lack of comforts <many historic dwellings remain, sinking stage by stage from *indigence* to squalor, from squalor to grimy destitution, like old pensioners, too decrepit to perform any offices but the most menial ones – Lewis Mumford> **Penury** suggests a cramping or oppressive lack of resources and especially money <she has to take anything she can get in the way of a husband rather than face *penury* – G. B. Shaw> but distinctively it may imply the appearance of poverty that results from stinginess or penuriousness <her relatives

considered that the *penury* of her table discredited the Mingott name, which had always been associated with good living – Edith Wharton> **Want** and **destitution** imply an extreme poverty that deprives one of the basic necessities of life; both terms, but especially the latter, often imply such an utter lack of resources as threatens life unless relieved <here to the homeless child of *want* my door is open still – Oliver Goldsmith> <in poverty, morality and even a touch of happiness was possible, never in *destitution* – R. A. Schermerhorn> <a time of utter misery and *destitution* for the . . . young man – W. L. Shirer> *ant* riches

power 1 power, force, energy, strength, might *shared meaning* : the ability to exert effort. **Power** may imply latent or exerted, physical, mental, or spiritual ability to act or be acted upon <the productive *power* of the nation> <declining purchasing *power* of the dollar> <the precious *power* to lift the minds and hearts of children – R. H. Wittcoff> **Force** implies the actual and efficacious exercise of power <a society crowded by almost every other *force* toward like-mindedness and conformity – Oscar Handlin> <by gradually increasing the *force* on the bar he pried open the stuck window> **Energy** implies stored-up power releasing or seeking to release itself in work <the prodigious *energy* put forth by industry in time of war – A. C. Morrison> <the man was a dynamo of *energy* and could perform the labors of a Titan – Thomas Wolfe> **Strength** applies to the quality or property of a person or thing that permits the exertion of force or the withstanding of strain, pressure, or attack <a man of exceptional *strength*> <the bridge collapsed because of deficient *strength* in its structure> <social scientists . . . sometimes emphasize, without sufficient qualification, the *strengths* more than the vulnerabilities of the poor – Nat Hentoff> **Might** suggests great or superhuman power or force <protect us by thy *might*, Great God, our King – S. F. Smith> <let us have faith that right makes *might* – Abraham Lincoln> *ant* impotence

2 power, faculty, function *shared meaning* : ability of a living being to perform in a given way or capacity for a particular kind of performance. **Power**, the general term, may apply to any such ability or capacity whether acting primarily on a physical or a mental level <the *power* to digest food> <our human *powers* of speech> <*power* to think clearly> **Faculty** is applicable to those powers which are the possession of every normal human being <man . . . how infinite in *faculty* – Shak.> and especially to those that arise in or are associated with the mind <sensory *faculties*> <her *faculty* for moral perception had withdrawn into that dim neutrality – H. C. Hervey> **Function** applies to any special ability or capacity of a body part or system or of the mind that contributes to the normal and natural economy of a living organism <the primary *function* of the eye is vision> <thought is a *function* of mind>

3 power, authority, jurisdiction, control, command, sway, dominion *shared meaning* : the right to govern or rule or determine. **Power** implies possession of ability to wield coercive force, permissive authority, or substantial influence <for thine is the kingdom, and the *power*, and the glory, for ever – *Mt* 6:13 (AV)> <we are looking for the control of education, the transfer of *power* from white educators to black educators, the *power* of the black community to educate its own children – Albert Cleage> **Authority**, often interchangeable with *power*, is more likely to refer to power resident in or exercised by another than oneself; thus, one may have *power* (rather than *authority*) to determine one's course of action, but a parent or master or ruler has *authority* (better than *power*) to determine the actions of those under him; children are obedient to *authority* rather than *power*. *Authority* may also denote power granted for a specific purpose and with specified limits <the additional *authority* that the new law gave to the Food and Drug Administration led to the creation of an investigational drug branch, whose function is to regulate the testing of new drugs – *Current Biog.*> **Jurisdiction** applies to official power exercised within prescribed limits <a court can give no judgment for either party, where it has no *jurisdiction* – R. B. Taney> **Control** stresses the power to direct and restrain <the fire burned out of *control*> <he was at last in triumphant *control* of his destiny – Thomas Wolfe> **Command** implies the power to make arbitrary decisions and compel obedience <the responsibilities of officers in direct *command* of troops> <how, in one house, should many people, under two *commands,* hold amity? – Shak.> **Sway** suggests the extent or scope of exercised power or influence <the law of compensation rules supreme in art, as it holds *sway* in life – J. L. Lowes> **Dominion** stresses sovereign power or supreme authority <God of our fathers ... beneath whose awful Hand we hold *dominion* over palm and pine – Rudyard Kipling> <states may appear godlike on account of their formidable power ... but this power is ... merely collective human power, and there are limits to its *dominion* over individual human beings – A. J. Toynbee>

powerless, impotent *shared meaning* : unable to effect one's purpose, intention, or end. **Powerless** denotes merely lack of power or efficacy which is often temporary or relative to a specific purpose or situation <became entangled in the marsh ... and was *powerless* to make the attack – *Amer. Guide Series: La.*> <I hope that the luxuries of this palatial mansion are *powerless* to corrupt your heart – G. B. Shaw> **Impotent** implies powerlessness coupled with persistent weakness or inherent ineffectiveness <an angry little spitfire sea ... thrashes with *impotent* irascibility – R. L. Stevenson> <*impotent* aristocrats talking about the code of chivalry but unable to bring it to life – *Time*> *ant* powerful, efficacious

practicable **1** see POSSIBLE *ant* impracticable

2 practicable, practical *shared meaning* : capable of being used or turned to account. In spite of the common element of meaning these terms are not true synonyms and are not interchangeable without loss of precision of expression. **Practicable** applies chiefly to something immaterial (as a plan, project, or design) which has not been tested in practice or to something material (as a new machine or implement) that has not been proved in service or use; in each situation the term implies expectation rather than assurance of successful testing or proving <it was the "control" rather than the elimination of the great weapons systems which thereafter offered the only *practicable* avenue of advance – Walter Millis> <a serviceable concept on which to base a *practicable* policy – J. A. Hobson> **Practical** stresses opposition to all that is *theoretical, speculative, ideal, unrealistic,* or *imaginative* and implies a relation to the actual life of man, his daily needs, or conditions that must be met. In the present relation the term emphasizes actual established usefulness rather than discovered or theoretical usableness; thus, the modern low-slung high-speed automobile was *practicable* long before improved roads and fuels made it *practical;* a *practicable* expedient is one that seems to meet the needs of a case in point, but a *practical* expedient is one that has been proved effective in identical past situations <in everything he undertook he demanded a utilitarian purpose and a *practical* result – John Buchan>

practical – see PRACTICABLE

practically – see VIRTUALLY

practice *vb* **practice, exercise, drill** *shared meaning* : to perform or make perform repeatedly. **Practice** may imply a doing habitually or regularly <*practice* what you preach> <*practice* one's profession> or a doing over and over for the sake of acquiring proficiency or skill <*practice* on the piano each day> **Exercise** implies a keeping at work and often suggests the resulting strengthening or developing <*exercise* muscles by active play> <they are . . . unlikely soon to recover their self-confidence and sense of authority – to take personal responsibility and *exercise* initiative – A. S. Whiting> **Drill** fundamentally connotes an intent to fix as a habit and stresses repetition as a means of training and discipline <*drill* a squad of soldiers> <*drill* schoolchildren in pronunciation>

practice *n* – see HABIT

precarious – see DANGEROUS

precedence – see PRIORITY

preceding, antecedent, foregoing, previous, prior, former, anterior *shared meaning* : being before. **Preceding** usually implies being immediately before in time or place <the *preceding* day> <the *preceding* clause of the document> **Antecedent** applies to order in time and may imply a causal or logical relation or suggest an indefinite intervening interval <a conclusion based on a chain of *antecedent* inferences> <the people . . . were possessed of a certain entirety of development, in which the component elements of culture and *antecedent* human growth and decadence were blended – H. O. Taylor> **Foregoing** applies to what has preceded, especially in a discourse <the *foregoing* statements are all open to challenge> *Previous* and *prior* imply existing or occurring earlier but **previous** is less likely to stress the importance of what is in question than is **prior** <change *previous* plans for a meat loaf and instead have a chowder – L. A. Harlow> <*prior* to independence, African political leaders saw such problems as unemployment, . . . ethnic conflict, and the like, as prospectively soluble – V. T. LeVine> **Former** implies a definite comparison or contrast with something that is *latter;* thus, there can be a *former* engagement only when there is also a later one, but there can be a *prior* or *previous* engagement that prevents the making of a later one <has a charm and graciousness suggestive of a *former* era – *Current Biog.*> **Anterior** applies to position ahead of, usually in space <the *anterior* surface of the brain> or less often in time or order <organization must presuppose life as *anterior* to it – S. T. Coleridge> ***ant*** following

precept – see LAW ***ant*** practice, counsel

precious – see COSTLY

precipitate, headlong, abrupt, impetuous, sudden *shared meaning* : showing undue haste or unexpectedness. *Precipitate* and *headlong* imply rashness and lack of foresight, **precipitate** applying usually to actions or decisions <the crisis . . . appears to have resulted from the *precipitate* withdrawal of the United Nations Emergency Force – *Saturday Rev.*> and **headlong** serving to describe persons or their acts or the qualities exhibited by such persons or acts <the *headlong* torrent of her feelings scared her – Herman Wouk> <talented people whom she writes of in a *headlong* Celtic manner – H. T. Moore> <the *headlong* affair of a young Swedish lieutenant who, enamored of a beautiful circus girl, deserts the army to be with her – Arthur Knight> **Abrupt** may suggest complete lack of warning or even unceremoniousness <an *abrupt* change in soil conditions may cause a sudden change in the vegetation – C. J. Taylor> <made an *abrupt* departure> or, in application to manners or words, curtness <an *abrupt* refusal> **Impetuous** is likely to suggest impulsiveness or extreme impatience, especially with whatever hampers or delays <they had been *impetuous* and daring, making up their minds in a couple of flashes – J. T. Farrell> <all the *impetuous* restlessness of her girlhood had left her and she had bloomed into a quiet half-indolent calm – Pearl Buck> **Sudden** stresses unexpectedness and impetuous abruptness of action <now and then an access of . . . *sudden* fury . . . would lay hold on a man or woman – Rudyard Kipling> <the *sudden* rush of a fresh, strong, exhilarating, and unpredictable wind – B. R. Redman> ***ant*** deliberate

precipitous – see STEEP

précis – see COMPENDIUM

precise – see CORRECT *adj* ***ant*** loose

preciseness – see PRECISION

precision, preciseness *shared meaning* : the quality or state of being precise. In spite of their fundamentally identical denotation the terms are rarely interchangeable because of marked differences in their suggestions and connotations. **Precision** regularly suggests a desirable or sought-for quality and connotes such contributory factors as exactitude, care, devoted workmanship, or thoughtful choice; thus, *precision* in the use of language involves careful choice of words with due consideration of their implications and appropriateness as well as their denotations; a *precision* instrument is one made by the carefullest workmanship to the closest tolerances in order to serve accurately some exact function <defining words with utmost care, they fashioned their statements of doctrine with meticulous *precision* – C. A. Dinsmore> <like a fine watch, he is not only made of good stuff, he functions efficiently. He keeps good time, and he does all of this with balance and *precision* – R. J. Bryant> **Preciseness** more often suggests a less than desirable quality and is likely to connote such contributory factors as rigidity, severity and strictness, or overnicety in observance (as of rules, proprieties, or a code) <savoring of Puritanism and overstrict *preciseness* – William Prynne> <there was a certain amount of *preciseness* about the young man, and his approach to Texas was in the best striped-trousers tradition – T. D. Clark>

preclude – see PREVENT 2

precursor – see FORERUNNER

predicament, dilemma, quandary, plight, fix, jam, pickle *shared meaning* : a situation from which one does or can extract oneself only with difficulty. **Predicament** suggests a difficult situation, usually with no satisfactory or at least no ready and easy solution <the *predicament* of Great Britain was indeed grim, more dangerous than it had been since the Norman landings nearly a millennium before – W. L. Shirer> <the *predicament* with which our civilization now finds itself confronted – the problem, namely, how to find healthy, happy leisure for all the working millions who are now being liberated by machines – L. P. Smith> **Dilemma** implies a predicament presenting a choice between equally unpleasant or unacceptable alternatives <the tragic *dilemma* of the Western liberal world, confronted by two brutal and regressive dictatorships neither one of which it could overcome without the help of the other – Walter Mills> **Quandary** stresses the puzzlement and perplexity of one faced by a dilemma <problems of adjustment that not infrequently are resolved by ruthless determination to escape from *quandaries* into action – Harold Lasswell> <all his *quandaries* terminated in the same catastrophe, a compromise – Benjamin Disraeli> **Plight** suggests an unfortunate or trying situation <the *plight* of reluctant students is even more hopeless, because they lack the will to learn even when study conditions are ideal – R. K. Corbin> **Fix** and **jam** are somewhat casual equivalents of *plight* that often suggest involvement as a result of one's folly or wrongdoing <the Administration is in a grave *fix* over Vietnam – *New Republic*> <as though he himself were dazed at the *fix* he had got himself into and felt a little desperate about it – W. L. Shirer> <they get sick and it puts them in a *jam* and they end up under a pile of bills – Hamilton Basso>

Pickle applies to a particularly distressing or sorry plight <when I was left ashore in Melbourne I was in a pretty *pickle.* I knew nobody, and I had no money – G. B. Shaw>

predict – see FORETELL

predilection, prepossession, prejudice, bias *shared meaning* : an attitude of mind that predisposes one to choosing, or judging, or taking a stand without full consideration or knowledge. **Predilection** implies a strong liking deriving from one's temperament or experience rather than from investigation or testing <a *predilection* for the strange and whimsical – S. T. Coleridge> <his *predilection* for urban themes is rooted in his own youth in New York City – *Current Biog.*> **Prepossession** implies a fixed idea or conception likely to preclude objective judgment of anything that seems counter to it <the *prepossessions* of childhood and youth – Dugald Stewart> <his moral *prepossessions* held his sensibility in check – C. I. Glicksberg> **Prejudice** basically implies a usually unfavorable judgment made before evidence is available or adequately and honestly considered; the term in such use regularly connotes a feeling rooted in suspicion and marked by fear and intolerance <their beliefs, attitudes, and *prejudices* were a crowd of inconsistencies and contradictions, but they were happy in their blindness to their own muddle – J. T. Farrell> <all the preposterous *prejudices* and hates then rife among its German-speaking extremists – W. L. Shirer> **Bias** implies an unreasoned and unfair distortion of judgment in favor of or against a person or thing <the most pernicious kind of *bias* consists in falsely supposing yourself to have none – Walter Moberly> <discover some of our own peculiarities, our own particular slant or *bias* – A. J. Toynbee> *ant* aversion

predispose – see INCLINE

predominant – see DOMINANT

preempt – see APPROPRIATE *vb*

preen – see PRIDE *vb*

prefatory – see PRELIMINARY

preference – see CHOICE *n*

prejudice – see PREDILECTION

preliminary, introductory, preparatory, prefatory *shared meaning* : serving to make ready the way for something else. **Preliminary** suggests reference to what must be done or made ready or acquired before entrance into some definitive state or activity becomes possible <prepared a *preliminary* sketch of the machine to be built> <held a *preliminary* discussion to set up the agenda for the meeting> **Introductory** implies reference to the first steps in a process and applies usually to what sets something (as an action, a work, or a process) going <the speaker's *introductory* remarks established his point of view> **Preparatory** comes close to *preliminary* in denotation but lays emphasis on preparation for or against what is expected to ensue <take *preparatory* protective measures against a predicted hurricane> <a note on sources and a bibliography . . . indicate the wide range of the author's *preparatory* reading – Geoffrey Bruun> **Prefatory** usually implies a desire on the part of someone to prepare others (as for hearing, for action, or for understanding) <introduces each of them with a really distinguished little group of *prefatory* passages – Robert Bierstedt>

preparatory – see PRELIMINARY

prepare, fit, qualify, condition, ready *shared meaning* : to make someone or something ready. **Prepare** implies an often complicated process of making or getting ready <*prepare* ground for a crop> <in time of peace *prepare* for war> <made a few notes for a paper I was *preparing* – Roald Dahl> <*prepare* dinner for the family> **Fit** is more limited in scope and implies a making fit for or suitable to a particular end or objective <accomplishments, *fitting* him to shine both in active and elegant life – Washington Irving> <parents whose duty it is to *fit* children for carrying on life – Herbert Spencer> **Qualify** stresses the implication that fitness for a particular situation (as an office, duty, function, or status) requires the fulfillment of necessary conditions (as the taking of a course of study, an examination, or an oath) <his extensive knowledge of foreign languages specially *qualified* him for such service – A. P. Wills> <the village doctor . . . goes away to Liverpool or to Edinburgh to *qualify* – Cledwyn Hughes> **Condition** implies a getting into or a bringing to the condition that is proper or necessary to satisfy a particular purpose or use <*condition* cattle for show or market> or sometimes merely a condition that is the inevitable result of past events and impacts <the public is *conditioned* to see the student in terms of revolt, dope, sex, or the image transmitted by the mass media – R. E. Kavanaugh> **Ready** emphasizes a putting or getting into order especially for use or action <*ready* a room for a committee meeting> <the expedition *readied* itself during the summer – Oscar Handlin>

preponderant – see DOMINANT

prepossession – see PREDILECTION

prerequisite – see REQUIREMENT

prescribe, assign, define *shared meaning* : to fix arbitrarily or authoritatively. **Prescribe** implies an intent to provide explicit direction or clear guidance to those who accept or are bound by one's authority <the Constitution *prescribes* the conditions under which it may be amended> <the natural law sets the standards in a general way . . . it provides guidance; it does not *prescribe* a particular statute or judicial decision – R. M. Hutchins> **Assign** implies arbitrary but not despotic determination, allotment, or designation for the sake of some such end as harmonious functioning, smooth routine, or proper or efficient operation <*assign* a worker to the late shift> <the senior press association man *assigned* to the White House – Merriman Smith> <the clause, *assigning* original jurisdiction to the supreme court – John Marshall> **Define** stresses an intent to mark boundaries so as to prevent confusion, conflict, or overlap <these sites are *defined* as dwelling places of the Ertebolle people by a whole range of finds of typical objects – Liam de Paor> <joined the radicals to work for change from within the newly *defined* student society – Xandra Kayden> <the Constitution of the United States *prescribes* the powers of the government, *assigns* the limits of each, and *defines* the function of each governmental branch>

prescription – see RECEIPT

present – see GIVE

presently, shortly, soon, directly *shared meaning* : after a little while. **Presently** is a term of rather vague implications as to the time indicated <the doctor will be here *presently*> <I shall forget you *presently,* my dear, so make the most of this, your little day – Edna S. V. Millay> **Shortly** is less vague about the time interval and typically implies a following quickly or without avoidable delay <he finished the last volume *shortly* before he retired> <questions of vital importance came up for solution *shortly* after his appointment – H. W. H. Knott> <you will receive the report *shortly* after the tests are completed> **Soon** may imply that the thing narrated or predicted happened or will happen without much loss of time; otherwise the term is indefinite and may suggest any length of time that seems short within the pertinent frame of references <I will not *soon* forget the understanding and clarity which you gave to millions of others and myself – Hubert Humphrey> <father should be home very *soon*> **Directly** in this relation implies with little or a minimum of delay <I shall be back

directly after sundown – Robert Hichens> <*directly* after graduation he joined the family business>
preserve – see SAVE
pressure – see STRESS
pretend – see ASSUME
pretense, pretension, make-believe *shared meaning* : the offering of something false or deceptive as real or true. **Pretense** may denote false show or the evidence of it <a woman utterly devoid of *pretense*> <there is too much *pretense* in his piety> or it may apply to something (as an act, an appearance, or a statement) intended to convince others of the reality of something that in fact lacks reality <rushing away from the discussion on the transparent *pretense* of quieting the dog – Joseph Conrad> **Pretension** is often used in the sense of false show or evidence of this; in this use it differs from *pretense* in implying not hypocrisy or intentional deceit but an unwarranted assumption of one's possession of desirable qualities or powers that arises in conceit or self-deception <his disdain of affectation and prudery was magnificent. He hated all *pretension* save his own *pretension* – H. L. Mencken> <annoyed with . . . the *pretensions* of simplicity and homeliness in her parlor – John Cheever> **Make-believe** applies chiefly to pretenses that arise not so much out of a desire to give a false impression to others as out of a strong or vivid imagination (as of a child or poet) <content with desultory chatter and *make-believe* occupation throughout the long hours of an idle day – Victoria Sackville-West> <most children have *make-believe* retreats from the hazardous business of growing up. Occasionally, however, things go wrong and the *make-believe* begins to serve as a total substitute for reality – *Times Lit. Supp.*>
pretension – see AMBITION, PRETENSE
pretentious – see SHOWY *ant* unpretentious
pretext – see APOLOGY
pretty – see BEAUTIFUL
prevail – see INDUCE
prevailing, prevalent, rife, current *shared meaning* : general (as in circulation, acceptance, or use) in a given place or at a given time. **Prevailing** stresses predominance <the *prevailing* winds are westerly> <*prevailing* opinion in the trade> **Prevalent** implies frequency without suggesting predominance <though the *prevailing* winds are westerly sharp northerly breezes are *prevalent* in late fall> <so *prevalent* is urban blight that the nickname "Garden State" seems a macabre joke – Trevor Armbrister> **Rife** implies a growing prevalence or rapid spread <when the whole educational enterprise . . . is *rife* with inequities and imbalances – N. M. Pusey> <the wildest rumors of what might happen were *rife* in the capital – W. L. Shirer> **Current** applies to what is subject to change and stresses prevalence at a particular time or at the moment <the *current*, but presumably corrigible, defects of governmental machinery – R. M. Hutchins> <a custom *current* during earlier years of the century> <Shakespeare used the *current* language of his day – J. R. Lowell> <had enough money to meet *current* expenses>
prevalent – see PREVAILING
prevaricate – see LIE
prevent 1 prevent, anticipate, forestall *shared meaning* : to deal with beforehand. **Prevent** implies taking advance measures against something possible or probable <the use of vaccination to *prevent* smallpox> <who stands safest? tell me, is it he? . . . whose *preventing* care in peace provides fit arms against a war? – Alexander Pope> **Anticipate** stresses more the foreseeing of something that will or may eventuate <*anticipate* cooler

weather after the storm> but it, like *prevent*, may imply a frustrating by prior action <he would probably have died by the hand of the executioner, if the executioner had not been *anticipated* by the populace – T. B. Macaulay> and distinctively it may imply dealing with (as by using, providing, or spending) before the proper or expected time; thus, one *anticipates* a need by providing what is needed before it is asked for; one *anticipates* a payment on a loan by making it before it is due; one *anticipates* one's salary by spending its equivalent before it is earned. **Forestall** basically implies a getting ahead so as to stop or interrupt something in its course <something you were not in the least prepared to face, something you hurried to *forestall* – Mary Austin> but often it loses the suggestion of intercepting and then stresses a rendering of something ineffective or harmless by forehanded action <to *forestall* every risk and retain every advantage – *New Republic*> <the President announced a high-priority employment . . . program for District youths . . . . The hope is that it will *forestall* a major racial explosion – Andrew Kopkind & James Ridgeway>

2 prevent, preclude, obviate, avert, ward off *shared meaning* : to stop something from coming or occurring. **Prevent** implies the placing or the existence of an insurmountable obstacle <zoning ordinances *prevent* the establishment of businesses in residential areas> <factional fights among the crews *prevented* maintenance – A. S. Whiting> <illness *prevented* his attendance at the meeting> **Preclude** stresses the existence of some factor that shuts out every possibility of a thing's happening or taking effect <his death *precluded* the completion of his mission> <the adoption of one choice often necessarily *precludes* the use of another – C. I. Glicksberg> **Obviate** suggests the use of forethought to avoid the necessity for disagreeable or unwelcome steps or measures <[the hostess] had thoughtfully ordered 400 two-horse carriages from O'Toole the liveryman to *obviate* the inconvenience to her guests of keeping their own coachmen up until all hours – Lucius Beebe> **Avert** and **ward off** both presuppose an approaching or oncoming evil and imply the taking of immediate and effective measures in the face of what threatens; the former is more likely to suggest the use of active measures to turn aside or force back the evil before it is actually encountered <built a series of dams to *avert* the threat of floods> <faculty members tried frantically . . . to find some way of *averting* what appeared to be the inevitable confrontation between the student protesters and the police – Sylvan Fox> while the latter implies a close encounter and the use of defensive measures <*ward off* a blow with a raised forearm> <[wore] a cowboy hat to *ward off* the rain – Jon Jacobson> <our nation has *warded off* all enemies – D. D. Eisenhower> ***ant*** permit

previous – see PRECEDING ***ant*** subsequent, consequent

prey – see VICTIM

price, charge, cost, expense *shared meaning* : what is given or asked in exchange for something. *Price* and *charge* in their general use designate what is asked – in the case of **price,** especially for goods or commodities; in the case of **charge,** especially for services <the *price* of meat has risen sharply> <what is the *charge* for hauling away a load of brush?> In technical economic use *price* refers to the quantity or number of units of one thing exchangeable in barter or sale for another <labor was the first *price*, the original purchase money that was paid for all things – Adam Smith> *Charge*, especially in accounting use, can apply additionally to what is imposed on one as a financial burden; thus, a person who is a public *charge* is a pauper living at public expense; fixed *charges* of a business are those items (as rent, taxes, interest, or liens) that are items of expense whether the business is actively productive or not. *Cost* and *expense* in their general use apply to what is given or surrendered for something – **cost** often implying specifically the payment of a price asked and **expense** often designating the aggregate amount actually disbursed for something <they found the *cost* of new furniture a heavy drain on their resources> <sold his home to meet the *expense* of his wife's long illness> <the *expense* of converting from coal to gas heat> <our *expenses* were higher last month> Occasionally *cost* applies to what would have to be given or surrendered and then may replace *price* though with quite different connotations and a different point of view in the user; thus, the *price* of an article is what a seller is prepared to accept, but the *cost* of an article can be either what a buyer will pay or what has already been paid <the *prices* of loss leaders is often less than the *cost* of their production>

priceless – see COSTLY

pride *n* **pride, vanity, vainglory** *shared meaning* **:** the quality or feeling of a person who is firmly convinced of his own excellence or superiority. The same distinctions in implications and connotations are found in the corresponding adjectives **proud, vain, vainglorious. Pride** and **proud** may imply either justified or unjustified self-esteem both insofar as the merit or superiority is real or imagined and insofar as the feeling manifests itself in proper respect of one's self and one's standards or in blatant and arrogant conceit. Unjustified pride is a sin or vice and the antithesis of humility <those that walk in *pride* he is able to abase – *Dan* 4:37 (AV)> <recall Socrates' irony and humility and Protagoras' blind *pride* in his own erudition – Stringfellow Barr> but justified pride is a virtue or at least a commendable quality that is the antithesis of shame <the solemn *pride* that must be yours to have laid so costly a sacrifice upon the altar of freedom – Abraham Lincoln> <*proud* of an excellent school record> **Vanity** and **vain** imply an excessive desire to win notice, approval, or praise; both connote self-centeredness and may suggest concentration on trivia <had . . . not the gay, tail-spreading peacock *vanity* of his son – Thomas Carlyle> <he was conceited and *vain,* and he was endlessly trying to enjoy what he thought he appeared to be in the eyes of others – J. T. Farrell> **Vainglory** and **vainglorious** imply excessive boastful pride often manifested in arrogant display of one's vaunted qualities <*vainglorious* boastings – Washington Irving> <having blockaded their minds behind . . . walls of nationalistic egoism and *vainglory,* symptoms of collective paranoia – *Yale Rev.*> *ant* humility, shame

pride *vb* **pride, plume, pique, preen** *shared meaning* **:** to congratulate (oneself) because of something one is, has, or has done or achieved. **Pride** usually implies a taking of credit for something that redounds to one's honor or gives just cause for pride <he *prides* himself on his ancestry> <Mark *prided* himself upon maintaining outwardly a demeanor that showed not the least trace of overstrung nerves – Compton Mackenzie> **Plume** adds to *pride* the implication of obvious, often vain display of one's satisfaction and commonly suggests less justification than does *pride* <the Viceroy *plumed* himself on the way in which he had instilled notions of reticence into his staff – Rudyard Kipling> <artist though he was in prose Defoe never pretended to any artistry in that medium, *pluming* himself rather upon his verse – Bonamy Dobrée> **Pique** differs from *plume* chiefly in carrying a hint of stirred-up pride, usually in some special accomplishment <every Italian or Frenchman of any rank *piques* himself on speaking his own tongue correctly – Horace Walpole> **Preen** occasionally replaces *plume,* sometimes with a slight suggestion of adorning oneself with one's virtues or accomplishments <he *preened* himself upon his sapience – Amy Lowell>

<*preened* himself on having put across another sharp deal – David Walden>
prior – see PRECEDING
priority, precedence *shared meaning* : the act, the fact, or the right of preceding another. **Priority** is the usual term in law and the sciences and chiefly concerns an order of time. In questions involving simple time relations of events the term implies antecedence in occurrence <the right to inherit a title depends mainly on *priority* of birth> <they disputed *priority* of invention of the regenerative electron-tube circuit – C. B. Fisher> but in questions involving a number of things (as debts or cases or needs to be met) which cannot be taken care of at one time and must be arranged in an order of time, *priority* suggests a rule of arrangement that determines the order of procedure <in payment of debts he must observe the rules of *priority* – William Blackstone> In much current use the notion of time has been subordinated to or even replaced by that of relative importance <teaching ... must be restored to its rightful *priority* among the many diverse aims which universities have come to serve – M. S. Eisenhower> <in assigning *priorities* to the tasks he must do, the effective manager begins with the question, "What results do we need?" – R. J. Bryant> **Precedence** in its general use is often close to the last-mentioned use of *priority* <it is the intent of this board ... to give curriculum matters *precedence* over less imperative business – Dayton Benjamin> but its most typical application is as a term of formal etiquette where it implies an established order which gives preference to those of superior rank, dignity, or position <the order of *precedence* was very rigidly observed, for the visiting maids and valets enjoyed the same hierarchy as their mistresses and masters – Victoria Sackville-West>
priory – see CLOISTER
prize *vb* – see APPRECIATE
prize *n* – see SPOIL
probable, possible, likely *shared meaning* : such as may be or may become true or actual. **Probable** applies to what is supported by evidence that is strong but not conclusive; the term regularly suggests consideration of evidence and often the weighing of alternatives in the mind. Thus, one weighs one's *probable* enjoyment of a trip abroad against its cost; the *probable* villain in a play is the character toward whom most of the evidence seems to point <it is not *probable* that any enemy would ... attack us by landing troops in the United States – F. D. Roosevelt> **Possible** applies to what lies within the known limits of performance, attainment, nature, or mode of existence of a thing or person regardless of the chances for or against its actuality <it is *possible* that she went home without telling us> <once it was not thought *possible* to fly an airplane across the Atlantic> Sometimes the term specifically suggests improbability <his election is *possible* but not at all probable> **Likely** differs from *probable* in implying more superficial or more general grounds for judgment or belief and from *possible* in imputing much greater chance of being true or occurring to the thing qualified <the *likely* result of their quarrel is continued bickering> <no one is *likely* to succeed in squaring the circle> <the poor are *likelier* to be sick. The sick are *likelier* to be poor. The poor get sicker and the sick get poorer – H. J. Geiger> ***ant*** certain, improbable
probationer – see NOVICE
probe – see ENTER
probity – see HONESTY
problem – see MYSTERY ***ant*** solution

problematic — see DOUBTFUL
procedure — see PROCESS
proceed — see SPRING
proceeding — see PROCESS
process, procedure, proceeding *shared meaning* : the series (as of actions, operations, or motions) involved in the accomplishment of an end. **Process** is particularly appropriate when progress from a definite beginning to a definite end is implied and the sequence of events is divisible into a sequence of steps or stages <the *process* of digestion> <I have always liked the *process* of commuting; every phase of the little journey is a pleasure to me – Roald Dahl> **Procedure** stresses the method followed or the routine to be followed <the rules and *procedures* that academic institutions have evolved as central to the teaching-learning process – J. A. Perkins> <this Byzantine court, which is trying to adapt its *procedure* to the ideals of its Western education – Edmund Wilson> **Proceeding** applies not only to the sequence of events, actions, or operations directed to the attainment of an end but also to any one of these events, actions, or operations. The term throws more stress on the items involved than on their closely knit relation or the end in view and often means little more than an instance or course of conduct or action <the law ... stepped in to prevent a *proceeding* which it regarded as petty treason to the commonwealth – J. A. Froude> <the precise habits, the incredible *proceedings* of human insects – L. P. Smith> <legislative *proceedings* frequently veer off into areas of somewhat less than momentous significance – Trevor Armbrister>
proclaim — see DECLARE
proclivity — see LEANING
procrastinate — see DELAY 2 ***ant*** hasten, hurry
procure — see GET
prodigal *adj* — see PROFUSE ***ant*** parsimonious, frugal
prodigal *n* — see SPENDTHRIFT
prodigious — see MONSTROUS
profanation, desecration, sacrilege *shared meaning* : a violation or misuse of something normally held sacred. **Profanation** implies irreverence or contempt as shown especially by vulgar intrusion or vandalism <these sages attribute the calamity to a *profanation* of the sacred grove – J. G. Frazer> <turned America into a cultural wasteland characterized by the *profanation* of almost everything that might ennoble human existence – Harvey Wheeler> **Desecration** implies loss or impairment of sacred character, typically through defilement that is often malicious or malign and culpable <an unbelievable flaunting of opulence, with several holy images to complete the *desecration* – H. C. Hervey> <*desecration* of temples by barbarian invaders> **Sacrilege** may apply to technical violations (as improper reception of sacraments or theft of sacred objects) not intrinsically outrageous or to an outrageous profanation <the execution was not followed by any *sacrilege* to the church or defiling of holy vessels – Willa Cather>
proficient, adept, skilled, skillful, expert *shared meaning* : having (or manifesting) the knowledge and experience needed for success in a skill, trade, or profession. **Proficient** implies a thorough competence derived from training and practice <*proficient* in the art of self-defense – G. B. Shaw> <he became *proficient* in paperhanging, painting, ... and even broom-making – George Crout> **Adept** implies special aptitude as well as proficiency <so *adept* at the lovely polishing of every grave and lucent phrase – Stella D. Gibbons> **Skilled** stresses mastery of technique; thus, a *skilled* worker is one who has mastered the techniques of a trade <[he] is a photographer

with a *skilled* lens and a writer with a gift of words – Mary Darrah> **Skillful** implies individual dexterity in execution or performance <managed to keep the city's buses and trains running through his *skillful* handling of labor-management disputes – *Current Biog.*> <a *skillful* teacher> **Expert** implies extraordinary proficiency and often connotes knowledge as well as technical skill <explaining at length, but with an *expert* lucidity, some basic point of law or government – Edmund Wilson> <to acquire *expert* craftsmanship, the necessity of good teachers and good schools is obvious – Henry Mancini>

profile – see OUTLINE

profitable – see BENEFICIAL ***ant*** unprofitable

profligate – see SPENDTHRIFT

profound – see DEEP ***ant*** shallow

profuse, lavish, prodigal, luxuriant, lush, exuberant *shared meaning* : giving out or given out in great abundance. What is **profuse** seems to pour or be poured forth in abundance, without restraint, or in a stream <*profuse* apologies> <pourest thy full heart in *profuse* strains of unpremeditated art – P. B. Shelley> <a land where life was great . . . and beauty lay *profuse* – Robert Browning> What is **lavish** is so profuse as to suggest munificence or extravagance or the absence of all stint or moderation <*lavish* gifts> <the *lavish* attentions of his mother – George Meredith> <*lavish* expenditures> What is **prodigal** gives or is given so lavishly as to suggest waste or the ultimate exhaustion of resources <the table spread with opulent hospitality and careless profusion . . . a *prodigal* feast – V. L. Parrington> <the *prodigal* expenditures of the recent war – M. W. Childs> What is **luxuriant** produces or is produced in great and rich abundance; the term usually connotes not only profusion but excellence or splendor in what is produced <his powerful *luxuriant* voice filled the auditorium with incredible ease – Winthrop Sargeant> <rich and *luxuriant* beauty; a beauty that shone with deep and vivid tints – Nathaniel Hawthorne> What is **lush** is not only luxuriant but has reached the peak of its perfection <how *lush* and lusty the grass looks! how green! – Shak.> or, in depreciatory use, passed slightly beyond this point <the recording is appealing, romantic, and simple (not *lush* or overdone) – P. T. Jackson> What is **exuberant** produces or is produced so abundantly or luxuriantly as to suggest great vigor, vitality, or creative power <to restrain my too *exuberant* gesture – Mary Austin> <an *exuberant* sense of the perfectibility of the American social order – Gerald Carson> <dahlias and roses are in *exuberant* bloom – David Weber> ***ant*** spare, scanty, scant

prognosticate – see FORETELL

progress, progression *shared meaning* : movement forward. In spite of the common element of meaning the words are seldom interchangeable without loss of precision. **Progress** usually applies to a movement considered as a whole and may stress such aspects as the distance covered, the change or changes taking place, or the amount of improvement made <the expectation . . . that *progress* can be made in resolving the inextricable mix of urban and racial questions confronting the United States – J. D. Carroll> <the *progress* of a disease> <while the meeting was in *progress*> <modesty would not halt nor even delay her *progress* – John Cheever> **Progression** commonly applies to a movement in itself or in its detail and may imply a series of stages or steps or degrees toward an objective or sometimes little more than a moving on more or less continuously <no constitutional amendment had acknowledged the *progression* from competition to mutuality – R. G. Tugwell> <every generation . . . adds . . . its own discoveries

in a *progression* to which there seems no limit – T. L. Peacock> <all the events and *progressions* of life were gathered up and recorded – Victoria Sackville-West>
progression – see PROGRESS
progressive – see LIBERAL 2 ***ant*** reactionary
prohibit – see FORBID ***ant*** permit
project – see PLAN
projection, protrusion, protuberance, bulge *shared meaning* : an extension beyond a normal line or surface. **Projection** implies a jutting out, especially at a sharp angle <tore her skirt on a sharp *projection* on the gate> <the appendix is a small fingerlike *projection* from the large bowel – Morris Fishbein> **Protrusion** suggests a thrusting out so that the thing in question seems an excrescence or a deformity <a gnarled windswept tree with many rough *protrusions* on its twisted branches> <the fantastic gables, pinnacles, and *protrusions* which intercepted the light – Samuel Lucas> **Protuberance** applies to something that swells or pushes out from a surface often as a rounded mass <horns first appear as skin-covered bony *protuberances* of the frontal bone> <balconies, bay windows and *protuberances* which make their fronts look like bemedaled chests – E. O. Hauser> **Bulge** applies to a local swelling of a surface caused usually by pressure from within or below <he was a man with no *bulges,* only angles, and he still had hair, though few teeth – R. G. Tugwell> <there was a *bulge* in the tire where it had struck the curb>
prolific – see FERTILE ***ant*** barren, unfruitful
prolix – see WORDY
prolong – see EXTEND ***ant*** curtail
prominent – see NOTICEABLE
promote – see ADVANCE ***ant*** impede
prompt – see QUICK
promulgate – see DECLARE
prone 1 see LIABLE
2 prone, supine, prostrate, recumbent *shared meaning* : lying down. **Prone** implies a position with the front of the body turned toward a supporting surface <Her Majesty, *prone* but queenly, stretched out on the deck . . . to try her hand at target shooting – *Time*> **Supine** implies a position with the back of the body turned toward a supporting surface <not a sound from the Trojans, *supine* along the walls, tired out, in the embrace of sleep – C. D. Lewis> and often suggests lethargy, abjectness, or inertness, especially in extended use <people lolling *supine* in carriages – G. B. Shaw> <that lachrymose music . . . that is so limpid in its amorousness, so *supine* and wistful in its statement of passion that it will offend the ears of a man in love – John Cheever> **Prostrate** implies a horizontal position <an attractive shrub with slender *prostrate* branches> and especially a lying full-length (as in submission, defeat, or physical collapse) <*prostrate* in homage, on her face, silent – Gordon Bottomley> <a bad cold . . . laid him low, *prostrate* and helpless, for a week afterward – William Styron> **Recumbent,** the most general term, can describe any position of lying at ease or in comfortable repose <*recumbent* upon the brown pine-droppings – George Meredith>
propel – see PUSH
propensity – see LEANING ***ant*** antipathy
proper – see FIT ***ant*** improper
property – see QUALITY
prophesy – see FORETELL
propinquity – see PROXIMITY

propitious — see FAVORABLE ***ant*** unpropitious, adverse

proportional, proportionate, commensurate, commensurable *shared meaning* : duly proportioned to something else. *Proportional* and *proportionate* are often interchangeable but **proportional** may be preferred when a constant or mathematically precise ratio between corresponding aspects (as number, amount, size, or length) of related things is under consideration; thus, a *proportional* tax is one assessed as a constant percentage of the value being taxed <the circumference of a circle is *proportional* to the length of its radius> <a detailed plan for *proportional* . . . disarmament to be achieved by stages — Grenville Clark> **Proportionate** is more likely to be chosen to imply the sometimes deliberate adjustment by which reciprocally related things are held in keeping with each other or with what is right, fair, or just <the punishment should be *proportionate* to the crime> <most state taxes produce a yield *proportionate* . . . to general economic growth — Trevor Armbrister> **Commensurate** and **commensurable** carry a stronger implication of equality between related things each of which has a value (as of measure, degree, or intensity) that is intimately related to that of the other <psychedelic drugs . . . offer great promise of unleashing perceptions, but they also hold *commensurate* dangers of causing withdrawal and disengagement from life — Stanley Kubrick> <the two punishments must be perfectly *commensurable* — Jeremy Bentham> or they may imply a scale of values by which outwardly dissimilar things may be shown to be equal or proportionate in some significant way <if two magnitudes can both be expressed in whole numbers in terms of a common unit, they are *commensurable* — W. G. Shute *et al*> <the largest use for industrial diamond is in abrasive grinding wheels. Crushed bort and powder in the coarsest grit size *commensurate* with the finish desired are used — P. M. Ambrose>

proportionate — see PROPORTIONAL ***ant*** disproportionate

proposal, proposition *shared meaning* : something proposed for consideration. **Proposal** usually carries a clear suggestion of an act of proposing; thus, one receives a *proposal,* or entertains a *proposal,* or listens to a *proposal.* The term commonly implies an offer (as of oneself for a husband or of a sum of money in exchange for a piece of property) or the suggestion of a scheme, a plan, or a project which may be accepted or rejected at the will of the one to whom it is proposed <the steel industry refused to make any wage *proposals* until it obtained federal clearance for higher steel prices — *Current History*> <this *proposal* was distinctly treasonable, but Burr probably never seriously intended to carry it out — I. J. Cox> **Proposition** basically applies to a usually affirmative statement that is propounded for discussion, argument, proof, or disproof <the fanatical and ordered mobs . . . proved, if the *proposition* needed proof, that in a time of crisis men will act from passion — Archibald MacLeish> The term is also applicable to an implied or expressed principle that is or may be questioned or is regarded from the point of view of its truth or falsity <the often-disputed *proposition* that all men are created equal> or it may replace *proposal* either in the sense of a formal proposal of some course of action <parking meters for Bakersfield again will be a *proposition* on the . . . ballot — *Los Angeles* (*Calif.*) *Examiner*> or, more generally, in that of an act of proposing <if you want to buy this land, make me a *proposition*> but in such use it and the corresponding verb **proposition** commonly carry a hint of irregularity or impropriety that *proposal* lacks; thus, one offers a *proposal* of marriage, but makes a *proposition* of a more irregular sexual relation.

propose, propound, pose *shared meaning* : to set before the mind for consideration. **Propose** fundamentally implies an invitation to consider, discuss, settle, or agree upon some clearly stated question or proposition <in the last chapter I *proposed* the hypothesis that a pure poetry exists – C. D. Lewis> or an offering of someone as a candidate or aspirant or of something by way of a suggestion <*proposed* his brother for attorney general> <with a swarm of fantastic reforms being every day suggested . . . perhaps we may *propose* one as fantastic as any other – W. L. Sullivan> **Propound** implies the stating of a question or proposition for discussion usually without personal bias or without any attempt to prove or disprove on the part of the propounder <*propound* the thesis that the great artist is an unconscious artist – T. S. Eliot> <the student picks up such attitudes. It is not that professors *propound* these views and students learn them. Rather, they are in the air and students absorb them – J. W. Gardner> **Pose,** very close to *propound,* is likely to imply that no attempt will be or can be made to seek an immediate answer <I shall try at least to *pose* basic issues that underlie all our political problems – <Felix Frankfurter> <the mysteries *posed* by Mars – *N.Y. Times Mag.*> <parents and pupils *posed* as many problems for the nineteenth-century teacher as do those of today – George Crout>

proposition – see PROPOSAL

propound – see PROPOSE

propriety – see DECORUM

prorogue – see ADJOURN

prosaic, prosy, matter-of-fact *shared meaning* : having a plain, practical, unimaginative quality or character. **Prosaic** basically implies an opposition to *poetic* in the extended sense of that word, and usually attributes a commonplace unexciting quality and the absence of everything that would stimulate feeling or awaken great interest to the thing or person it describes <a record of mediocrities, of the airless *prosaic* world of a small college town – E. K. Brown> <the ideal of romantic love . . . has always disguised a good deal that is mercenary, *prosaic* or sordid – Edmund Wilson> **Prosy** stresses dullness or tediousness <he groped for something meaningful – but his thoughts dwindled off into a *prosy* and confused prayer which he left half-completed – William Styron> and in application to persons usually implies a tendency to talk or write at length in a boring and uninviting manner <all *prosy* dull society sinners, who chatter and bleat and bore – W. S. Gilbert> **Matter-of-fact** implies a disinterest in the imaginative, speculative, visionary, romantic, or ideal; it may connote down-to-earth practicality and accuracy in detail <this might have been another nightmare, except that it was too coherent, too vivid, too *matter-of-fact.* It was really happening – Herman Wouk> <a *matter-of-fact* account of their adventure> but often it suggests preoccupation with the obvious and a neglect of more subtle values <faced with this *matter-of-fact* skepticism you are driven into pure metaphysics – G. B. Shaw> <Lilly, who was *matter-of-fact* and in whom introspection, poetry or contemplation had no place – Ethel Wilson>

proselyte – see CONVERT

prospect, outlook, anticipation, foretaste *shared meaning* : an advance realization of something to come. **Prospect** is used chiefly of particular expected events or situations, especially those that interest one personally and evoke an emotional response <the *prospect* of a quick, easy conquest of Greece . . . proved too big a temptation for the strutting Fascist Caesar to resist – W. L. Shirer> <his *prospect* for the duration of the war was a dull cryptographic job – *Current Biog.*> **Outlook** suggests an attempt to forecast the future and its reference is as often general as personal <uncertainties that cloud the business *outlook*> <the *outlook,* domestic and international,

was still what those who think in terms of color call black – Rose Macaulay> **Anticipation** implies a prospect or outlook that involves advance suffering or enjoyment of what is foreseen <Lord Beaconsfield once said that the worst evil one has to endure is the *anticipation* of the calamities that do not happen – A. C. Benson> <began rolling her eyes in *anticipation* of their customary exchange of banter – H. C. Hervey> **Foretaste** implies a brief or partial experiencing of something that will or may come later in full force <giving me amid the fretful dwellings of mankind a *foretaste* . . . of the calm that Nature breathes among the hills and groves – William Wordsworth> <we are now getting a *foretaste* of the problems presented by the desires of militant black students to fill their psychological and physical needs – D. E. Pentony>

prosper – see SUCCEED

prostrate – see PRONE

prosy – see PROSAIC

protect – see DEFEND

protest **1** see ASSERT

2 see OBJECT ***ant*** agree

protract – see EXTEND ***ant*** curtail

protrusion – see PROJECTION

protuberance – see PROJECTION

proud **1 proud, arrogant, haughty, lordly, insolent, overbearing, supercilious, disdainful** *shared meaning* : showing or feeling superiority toward others. **Proud,** the most neutral of these terms, implies a feeling of pleased satisfaction in oneself, one's accomplishments, or one's status that may or may not be justified and that may or may not be manifested offensively <she might grieve . . . but she was gallant, she was *proud;* she would not whine – Victoria Sackville-West> <she's a stuck-up *proud* girl, and she hasn't a proper decency – Pearl Buck> **Arrogant** implies a claiming for oneself more consideration or importance than is warranted and often suggests an aggressive domineering manner <they have a rather *arrogant* assurance that they are so right, that they are above the law – Mary J. White> <slumped in their seats fidgeting nervously, they no longer resembled the *arrogant* leaders of old. They seemed to be a drab assortment of mediocrities – W. L. Shirer> **Haughty** suggests a more or less blatantly displayed consciousness of superior birth or position <pride goeth before destruction, and an *haughty* spirit before a fall – *Prov* 16:18 (AV)> <his *haughty,* indifferent manner spoke his scorn for the two . . . men who accompanied him – H. C. Hervey> **Lordly** implies pomposity or an arrogant display of power <a *lordly* indifference to making money by his writings – Leslie Stephen> <replied with *lordly* condescension> **Insolent** implies insultingly contemptuous haughtiness <vile food . . . slapped down before their sunken faces by *insolent* waiters – Katherine A. Porter> <searching the crowd until he found the face from which the *insolent* jeering came – O. E. Rölvaag> **Overbearing** suggests a bullying tyrannical disposition or intolerable insolence <whose temper was so *overbearing,* that he could not restrain himself from speaking disrespectfully of that young lady – Charles Dickens> **Supercilious** implies a cool patronizing haughtiness <they have no blood these people. Their voices, their *supercilious* eyes that look you up and down – John Galsworthy> **Disdainful** implies a more contemptuous and more manifest scorn than *supercilious* and is more likely to suggest a justifiable attitude <a lovelorn swain chasing a *disdainful* paramour – *Current Biog.*> <many college students have, of late, been clearly *disdainful* of business careers – *Think*> ***ant*** humble, ashamed

2 see under PRIDE ***ant*** ashamed, humble

provide, supply, furnish *shared meaning* : to give or get what is desired by someone or needed for something. These words are often freely interchangeable <*provide* what is needed for an army> <*supply* regular rations> <*furnish* supplies for an expedition> but each can stress different implications and connotations that make it peculiarly appropriate in particular situations. **Provide** suggests foresight and stresses the idea of making provision for the future <*provide* for the common defense – *U.S. Constitution*> <*provide* schools and teachers to all children and illiteracy goes down dramatically – Peter Rossi> **Supply** may stress the idea of replacing, of making up what is needed, or of satisfying a deficiency <cards . . . and the polished die, the yawning chasm of indolence *supply* – William Cowper> <*supply* the defects of nature by providing the . . . homeless child with the nearest possible approach to life and training in a family setting – *Pilot*> <supplements that *supply* needed protein and vitamins to the diet> **Furnish** may emphasize the idea of fitting with whatever is needed or, sometimes, normal or desirable <the southeast trade winds and the tropical foliage *furnish* alleviating coolness – H. A. Chippendale> <'tis now but four o'clock. We have two hours to *furnish* us – Shak.>

providential – see LUCKY

province – see FUNCTION

provisional, tentative *shared meaning* : not final or definitive. Something **provisional** is adopted only for the time being and will be discarded when the final or definitive form is established or when the need that called it into being comes to an end; the term appropriately describes something made or used while its permanent successor is in process of formation <a *provisional* government> or when circumstances prevent introduction of a corresponding permanent or definitive thing; thus, a *provisional* order of a government agency is one subject to review and revision by the legislative branch; a *provisional* teacher's certificate is one that can be replaced by a permanent certificate upon fulfilling specified requirements. Something **tentative** is of the nature of a trial or experiment or serves as a test of practicability or feasibility <her *tentative* approval . . . settled into awed respect; such devoutness was indeed a sign of superior character – H. C. Hervey> <our plans are still *tentative* – subject to change without notice> *ant* definitive

provoke 1 provoke, excite, stimulate, pique, quicken *shared meaning* : to rouse one into doing or feeling or to produce by so rousing a person. **Provoke** directs attention to the response called forth and often applies to an angry or vexed reaction <his candor *provoked* a storm of controversy – *Times Lit. Supp.*> <inoculate you with that disease . . . in order to *provoke* you to resist it as the mud *provokes* the cat to wash itself – G. B. Shaw> **Excite** implies a stirring up or moving profoundly <the curiosity *excited* by his long absence burst forth in . . . very direct questions – Jane Austen> <the questions that trouble, *excite,* and motivate youth – Jeanne Noble> <the litigation *excited* much public concern – Bernard Taper> **Stimulate** suggests a provoking by or as if by a spur or goad and often connotes a rousing out of lethargy or indifference or an activating of something that is latent or quiescent <a demanding, long-range, and scholarly approach . . . that sometimes *stimulated* readers by irritating them – *Current Biog.*> <the stupidity of the opposition *stimulated* him and made him resolute – H. L. Mencken> **Pique** suggests stimulating by mild irritation or challenge <no ailurophile could pass up such a curiosity-*piquing* item as an ugly cat – Tessa B. Unthank> **Quicken** implies beneficially stimulating and making active or lively <the mistress which I serve *quickens* what's dead – Shak.> <the political literature of Greece and Rome was a positive

and *quickening* influence on the Convention debates – S. E. Morison> **2** see IRRITATE ***ant*** gratify

prowess – see HEROISM

proximity, propinquity *shared meaning* : nearness. **Proximity** usually implies simple, often temporary nearness in space <affected much as he might have been by the *proximity* of a large dog of doubtful temper – G. B. Shaw> <such apparent games [of chimpanzees] are nonce-events; they are dependent upon physical *proximity* . . . , and they never achieve the status of time-transcending, traditional culture – Weston La Barre> **Propinquity** can replace *proximity* but is then likely to suggest a more intimate or perceived closeness or even contact <they are jammed into such *propinquity* with one another in their new suburbia – W. H. Whyte> <the mere *propinquity* of that supple youthful body and those clinging idealizing glances, was something that restored him to his lost place in the centre of his universe – J. C. Powys> But more often *propinquity* implies closeness of relationship <here I disclaim all my paternal care, *propinquity,* and property of blood – Shak.> or in association, in age, or in tastes <environment and *propinquity* make for a desire to graduate from marijuana to opiates – D. W. Maurer & V. H. Vogel> <thereby was declared the *propinquity* of their desolations, and that their tranquility was of no longer duration than those soon decaying fruits of summer – Sir Thomas Browne> ***ant*** distance

prudent **1** see WISE ***ant*** imprudent

2 prudent, prudential *shared meaning* : characterized or dictated by prudence. **Prudent** applies to persons or their acts, plans, or utterances and implies such qualities of mind or character as caution, circumspection, and thrift or as wisdom in practical affairs <there are considerations that deter *prudent* college presidents from speaking out their judgments – W. S. Coffin, Jr.> <Marsh pointed out a century ago that greed and shortsightedness were the natural enemies of a *prudent* resources policy – J. F. Kennedy> <a *prudent* . . . businessman who never does anything except for a useful end – M. R. Cohen> **Prudential** may apply to habits, motives, policies, or considerations that are dictated by prudence, forethought, business sense, or practical wisdom <they have been taught to avoid their white neighbors for *prudential* reasons – N. V. Sullivan> In this use the word often suggests expediency and sometimes selfishness <'We must love one another or die. . . . Just what would a love vamped up on such *prudential* considerations be really worth? – G. S. Fraser> <hedonism is at best a statement of certain *prudential* limits within which ethical theories must function – Joseph Margolis> *Prudential* also applies, and without prejudicial suggestion, to groups or associations having charge of or exercising discretionary or advisory powers in regard to practical affairs <a *prudential* investment society> <the *prudential* committee of a church>

prudential – see PRUDENT 2

prying – see CURIOUS

psychosis – see INSANITY

publish – see DECLARE

pugnacious – see BELLIGERENT ***ant*** pacific

pull, draw, drag, haul, tug *shared meaning* : to cause to move toward or after an applied force. **Pull,** the general term, may emphasize the force exerted more than the resulting motion <the engine *pulled* a long line of freight cars> <we'll *pull* his plumes – Shak.> <[he] went outside to *pull* in the two milk cases – Bernard Malamud> **Draw** implies a smoother steadier motion and generally a lighter force than pull <*draw* a chair to the fireside> <*draw* off one's gloves> <the superintendent of the building

where I have an office *drew* me aside – Nat Hentoff> <*draw* wood for winter's firing> **Drag** suggests effort in pulling and the overcoming of active or passive resistance <*drag* an unconscious man from a burning building> <he uses the camera as a means of *dragging* the audience through the screen into the reality of the action – Michael Roemer> **Haul** implies sustained pulling or dragging, typically in the transporting of bulky or heavy materials <trucks *hauling* gravel for the new road> <that dangling figure was *hauled* up forty feet above the fountain – Charles Dickens> <began to kiss all the girls . . . until his wife . . . *hauled* him aside and calmed him down – William Styron> **Tug** implies a strenuous, usually spasmodic pulling that may or may not produce effective movement <*tugged* at the chains with the aid of two husky comrades – T. B. Costain> <he gripped the boxes but they were like rocks, so he let one go and *tugged* at the other – Bernard Malamud> <two kittens *tugging* apart a catnip mouse>

punch – see STRIKE

punctilious – see CAREFUL

pungent, piquant, poignant, racy *shared meaning* : sharp and stimulating to the mind or senses. **Pungent** implies a stinging or biting quality, especially of odors <the *pungent* reek of a strong cigar – A. Conan Doyle> <he has a neat gift of expression and a sense of humor always present and often *pungent* – *Current Biog.*> **Piquant** suggests a power to whet the appetite or interest through a pleasingly pungent or provocative quality <*piquant* with the tart-sweet taste of green apples and sugar – Silas Spitzer> <those *piquant* incongruities, which are the chief material of wit – C. E. Montague> **Poignant** suggests a power to enter deeply as if by piercing or stabbing <an avenue solidly arched and walled with blooming lilacs. The smell, sweet and *poignant* beyond imagining, saturated the air – Herman Wouk> <there was something . . . *poignant* about her face . . . the face of one whose essential innocence could not be dissipated by maturity, even tragedy – H. C. Hervey> **Racy** implies possession of a strongly marked natural quality, fresh and unimpaired <fruit . . . which had a *racy* tartness in delicious proportion to its ample sugars – John McPhee> <a rare and *racy* sense of humor – W. S. Maugham> and sometimes carries a hint of going beyond good taste <if men yawn . . . the singers will sweep into an especially *racy* and obscene offering – Julian Dana> *ant* bland

punish, chastise, castigate, chasten, discipline, correct *shared meaning* : to inflict a penalty on in requital for wrongdoing. **Punish** implies imposing a penalty for violation of law, disobedience of authority, or intentional wrongdoing <if ye will not . . . hearken unto me, then I will *punish* you – *Lev* 26:18 (AV)> **Chastise** usually implies corporal punishment, sometimes in anger but more often with a view to reformation <my father hath *chastised* you with whips, but I will *chastise* you with scorpions – *1 Kings* 12:11 (AV)> **Castigate** implies a severe and often public lashing with words <fellow citizens were *castigated* as immoral or evil – Mary J. White> <those poems in which he *castigates* man's general inhumanity and lack of sincerity – J. G. Southworth> **Chasten** implies a subjecting to distress or suffering in order to make morally stronger or more perfect; the term presupposes imperfection or defect and stresses the improving of the one acted upon <for whom the Lord loveth he *chasteneth* . . . If ye endure *chastening*, God dealeth with you as with sons – *Heb* 12:6–7 (AV)> **Discipline** implies a punishing or chastising to bring under control <*discipline* a disobedient child> Often it implies a course of action intended to maintain control of oneself or another <feeling . . . the rush of old jealousy he had thought long since *disciplined* from him – Pearl Buck> <helped

. . . to persuade governmental investigators that the industry could be trusted to *discipline* itself – *Current Biog.*> **Correct** implies punishment intended to reform an offender <his faults lie open to the laws; let them, not you, *correct* them – Shak.> and is appropriately used with reference to chastening punishment of small children by their parents. ***ant*** excuse, pardon

pure – see CHASTE ***ant*** impure, immoral

purloin – see STEAL

purpose – see INTENTION

pursue – see FOLLOW 2

pursuit – see WORK 2

push, shove, thrust, propel *shared meaning* **:** to use force on so as to cause to move ahead or aside. **Push** implies the application of force by a body already in contact with the thing to be moved <*push* a wheelbarrow> <*push* a door open> <*push* one's chair from the table> **Shove** implies a strong and often fast, sudden, or rough pushing that forces something along or aside <*shove* a child out of the path of a car> <*shove* one's way through a crowd> <they *shoved* the furniture against the wall> **Thrust** suggests less steadiness and greater violence than *push* and is peculiarly appropriate when a sudden or abrupt single movement or action is involved <as gamblers will stake a fortune on some moment's whimsey of belief, *thrusting* their money into a stranger's hand and bidding him to play – Thomas Wolfe> <*thrust* a knife into the back of an enemy> <[he] *thrust* the old man out of his tent – Jeremy Taylor> **Propel** implies a driving forward or onward by a force or power that imparts motion <the flow of air which *propels* the slow-sailing clouds – J. L. Lowes> <how many times have the best things been done in the worst way – a despicable thought *propelling* a beautiful deed – D. A. Redding>

pushful – see AGGRESSIVE

pushing – see AGGRESSIVE

pushy – see AGGRESSIVE

putrefy – see DECAY

putrid – see MALODOROUS

puzzle *vb* **puzzle, perplex, bewilder, distract, nonplus, confound, dumbfound** *shared meaning* **:** to disturb and baffle mentally. **Puzzle** implies presenting a problem difficult to solve <the prison sentence handed down by a court that was more *puzzled* than vindictive was mild – James Purdy> <a malignant fever which *puzzled* the doctors – John Buchan> **Perplex** adds a suggestion of worry and uncertainty especially about making a required decision <many new and *perplexing* challenges face higher education today – M. S. Eisenhower> <[he] was greatly *perplexed* to know what to do – H. E. Scudder> **Bewilder** often implies perplexity but it stresses a confusion of mind that makes clear and decisive thinking almost impossible <the former saddlemaker, still *bewildered* by the day's events which had suddenly thrust into his unwilling hands whatever political power remained in a crumbling Germany – W. L. Shirer> <the *bewildering* confusion of our times – Matthew Arnold> **Distract** implies agitation or uncertainty arising from conflicting preoccupations or interests <for if we are *distracted* by war, divided by race, deflected from our proper course, we remain a people of great and enduring promise – E. M. Kennedy> <that conflict of races and religions which had so long *distracted* the island – T. B. Macaulay> **Nonplus** implies a bafflement causing complete blankness of mind <the Israeli capacity for doing the unexpected in a way likely to *nonplus* a conventionally-minded enemy – *Times Lit. Supp.*> **Confound** implies temporary mental paralysis caused by astonishment or profound abasement <so spake the son of God; and Satan stood a while as mute, *confounded*

– John Milton> **Dumbfound** suggests a strong but momentary confounding <he captured the public and *dumbfounded* the critics – J. A. Macy> Often the idea of astonishment is so stressed that *dumbfound* becomes a near synonym of *astound* <I was *dumbfounded* to hear him say that I was on a quixotic enterprise – William Lawrence>

puzzle *n* – see MYSTERY

quail – see RECOIL

qualified – see ABLE *ant* unqualified

qualify – see MODERATE, PREPARE

quality 1 quality, property, character, attribute *shared meaning* : one of the marks or indications by means of which a thing may be identified or its constitution understood. **Quality** can designate any such mark, material or immaterial, individual or generic <there was only one *quality* in a woman that appealed to him – charm – John Galsworthy> <the persistent contemporariness that is a *quality* of all good art – Aldous Huxley> **Property** applies to a quality that belongs to something as part of its essential nature and that, therefore, distinguishes it from related things <testing chemicals for insecticidal *properties*> <the eye has this strange *property:* it rests only in beauty – Virginia Woolf> <viscosity is undoubtedly the most important single physical *property* of lubricating oils – S. W. Rein> **Character** applies to a peculiar and distinctive quality, typically of a class, sometimes of an individual <the institutions that frame the *character* of American life – Victor Palmieri> <the myth is that there are 'pure races,' when in fact, all human groups for whom we have accurate information turn out to have a mixture of *characters* – Charles Barber> **Attribute** denotes a quality ascribed to a thing or being and may imply a lack of definite knowledge of the thing in question; thus, the *attributes* of God are not known qualities but are those that man in his ignorance ascribes to divinity. Often the term denotes a quality that, though ascribed, is felt as an essential concomitant of the nature of the thing <mercy is . . . an *attribute* to God himself – Shak.> <his chief *attribute* was persistence; his chief strength, his belief in France and all that she stood for – S. E. Ambrose>

2 quality, stature, caliber *shared meaning* : distinctive merit or superiority. **Quality,** used in the singular, implies a complex of qualities (sense 1) that together conduce to a high order of excellence, virtue, or worth <they're all made by machinery now. The *quality* may be inferior, but that doesn't matter. It's the cost of production that counts – Roald Dahl> <splendid writing, of course, but to no purpose . . . . It's not *quality* we look for in a novel, but mileage – James Purdy> **Stature** is likely to suggest height reached or development attained and to connote considerations of prestige and eminence <[he] deserves credit for the *stature* that Turkey has achieved among the nations of the free world – *Current Biog.*> <I concluded that his *stature* had diminished [and] that his social philosophy was out of date even while he was preaching it – H. J. Laski> <every piece of work you do adds something to your *stature,* increases the power and maturity of your experience – Thomas Wolfe> **Caliber** suggests unusual but measurable extent or range of quality or powers (as of ability or intellect) or sometimes of deviation from a norm or standard <a man of very low moral *caliber*> <the exceptionally intelligent and highly motivated youngsters who are college *caliber* – A. H. Quie> <it is disturbing to note how few

people you can name today of the *caliber* of our first generation of statesmen, even though our population is over sixty times as great as it was then – W. S. Coffin, Jr.>

qualm, scruple, compunction, demur *shared meaning* : a misgiving about what one is doing or is going to do. **Qualm** implies an uneasy fear that one is not following his conscience or better judgment and may emphasize personal aversion to an act offensive to taste or morals <how few little girls can squash insects and kill rabbits without a *qualm* – Rose Macaulay> <we go on spreading culture as if it were peanut butter ... but we feel *qualms* about the results – J. M. Barzun> **Scruple** is likely to stress the involvement of principle rather than personal feeling <the Germans had ... no moral *scruples* against aggression – W. L. Shirer> and it may imply an overnice conscience <overconscientiousness ... has wrecked many a promising career; I honor *scruples* but they ... have their place and should be kept there – Elinor Wylie> **Compunction** basically denotes a spontaneous feeling of personal responsibility often accompanied by compassion for a prospective victim <Lady Macbeth ... had the *compunction* which he lacked – she could not kill ... the king – S. L. Gulick b. 1902> but often in current use implies no more than a passing concern or superficial prick of conscience <[she] agreed to keep the book, but quickly saw it was not a good idea. It released Marsha of all *compunctions* about borrowing – Herman Wouk> **Demur** suggests resistance to or protest against an outside influence and usually implies delay in acceptance of something offered or proposed <fashion is accepted by average people with little *demur* – Edward Sapir> <rather than be brought into court he will pay without *demur* – G. B. Shaw>

quandary – see PREDICAMENT

quarrel, wrangle, altercation, squabble, spat, tiff *shared meaning* : a dispute marked by anger or discord. **Quarrel** usually implies a heated verbal clash followed by strained or severed relations <make concessions to avoid a family *quarrel*> <she hated any kind of *quarrel* ... she shuddered at raised voices and quailed before looks of hate – Jean Stafford> **Wrangle** implies undignified, acrimonious, and often futile disputing with noisy insistence on each participant's point of view <spent three hours in an inconclusive *wrangle* over what was to be included in the communiqué – J. P. Lash> <matters stood rather awkwardly between her and George. Their last date had ended in a long *wrangle* – Herman Wouk> **Altercation** implies noisy heated controversy chiefly with words <I have an extreme aversion to public *altercation* on philosophic points – Benjamin Franklin> <fights and violent *altercations* which grew out of impassioned discussion of the day's doings – Herbert Asbury> **Squabble** applies to childish and unseemly wrangling over a petty matter <now we run scared; we stay polite, not sure how an open, slam-bang *squabble* would end – Arthur Mayse> **Spat** implies a trivial cause and suggests an angry outburst and a quick ending without hard feelings <a childish *spat* over sharing a favorite toy> **Tiff**, close to *spat*, is more likely to imply a disagreement manifested in ill humor or temporarily hurt feelings <tell myself that this was just a passing *tiff* and that matters would speedily adjust themselves – P. G. Wodehouse>

quarrelsome – see BELLIGERENT

quarry – see VICTIM

query – see ASK

question – see ASK *ant* answer

questionable – see DOUBTFUL *ant* authoritative, unquestioned

quick 1 see FAST

2 **quick, prompt, ready, apt** *shared meaning* : able to respond without delay

or hesitation or manifesting such ability. **Quick** stresses instancy of response and is likely to connote native rather than acquired power <very *quick* in perception> <even as a child she had had a *quick* mind, a gift of mimicry, an excellent memory – Herman Wouk> **Prompt** is more likely to connote training and discipline that fits one for instant response <*prompt* insight into the workings of complex apparatus – F. H. Garrison> **Ready** suggests facility or fluency in response <a calm man with a dignified manner but a *ready* smile> <reading maketh a full man, conference a *ready* man – Francis Bacon> **Apt** stresses the possession of qualities (as high intelligence, a particular talent, or a strong bent) that make quick effective response possible <most children are more *apt* at some activities than others> <*apt* as he was in attack or report . . . [he] was readier still to give mercy – Maxwell Anderson> ***ant*** sluggish

quicken 1 quicken, animate, enliven, vivify *shared meaning* : to make alive or lively. **Quicken** stresses a sudden renewal of life or activity, especially in something inert <it is the Spirit that *quickeneth* . . . the words that I speak unto you, they are spirit, and they are life – *Jn* 6:63 (AV)> <the time when Yeats and company were about to *quicken* their country with great art in English – Frank O'Brien> **Animate** emphasizes the imparting of motion or activity or vivacity to what was previously deficient in such quality <isolated by their frozen fixity from the vibrant ever-growing intellectual life that *animates* the secular city – Robert Gordis> <a dynamism and excitement that *animates* education both as an academic subject and an arena for action and social change – Wallace Roberts> **Enliven** suggests a stimulating influence that kindles, exalts, or brightens from a prior state of dullness, depression, or torpidity <the sun . . . was wonderfully warm and *enlivening* – D. H. Lawrence> <a barrel of home brew on a sledge to *enliven* the occasion – Roderick Finlayson> **Vivify** can imply either a renewal of life or a giving of the appearance of life and in either case suggests a freshening or energizing through renewal of vitality <the room was dead. The essence that had *vivified* it was gone – O. Henry> <[he] recounts Singapore's . . . development, then *vivifies* expansionist rivalries dominating twentieth-century Southeast Asia – *Booklist*> ***ant*** deaden

2 see PROVOKE ***ant*** arrest

quick-witted – see INTELLIGENT

quiescent – see LATENT

quiet – see STILL ***ant*** unquiet

quip – see JEST

quit – see CEASE, GO

quixotic – see IMAGINARY

quote, cite, repeat *shared meaning* : to speak or write again something already said or written by another. **Quote** usually implies precise repetition of the words of another for a particular purpose (as adornment or illustration) <illustrate the use of a word by *quoting* classical and modern authors> but sometimes *quote* is applied to a more general referral to someone as author or source of information without implication of precise reproduction of the original <in one sense we are *quoting* all the time. To whistle Tin Pan Alley's latest inanity is to *quote* . . . . To transmit the tired gag of a television comic is to *quote* – Clifton Fadiman> **Cite** is likely to stress the idea of mentioning for a particular reason (as proof of a thesis or substantiation of a position taken) with or without the idea of quoting another's exact words <[she] is one of the best examples observers of show business can *cite* to disprove the cliché that marriages and professional careers do not mix very well – *Current Biog.*> <his analysis of the causes of student unrest has been *cited* in several recent judicial opinions> **Repeat**

stresses the mere fact of saying or writing again the words or presenting the ideas of another often with no reference to the source and little concern for precision <*repeat* a scandalous story told one in confidence> <unrealistic to go on *repeating* phrases about the connection of industry with personal independence – John Dewey>

quotidian – see DAILY

rack – see AFFLICT

racy – see PUNGENT

radiant – see BRIGHT

radical – see LIBERAL 2

rage – see ANGER, FASHION

rail – see SCOLD

raise – see LIFT

rally – see RIDICULE

rampant – see RANK

rancid – see MALODOROUS

rancor – see ENMITY

random, haphazard, casual, desultory *shared meaning* : determined by accident rather than design. **Random** stresses chance and lack of definite aim, fixed goal, or regular procedure <[in 1912] for the first time in human history, a *random* patient with a *random* disease consulting a doctor chosen at random stood better than a 50-50 chance of benefiting from the encounter – Lawrence Henderson> <mutations are *random,* not in the sense that all kinds of change are possible and equally probable, but *random* in the sense of being adaptive only by chance – G. G. Simpson> **Haphazard** suggests a lack of concern for regularity or fitness or ultimate consequence <the disorder . . . the *haphazard* scattering of stray socks, shirts and collars – Thomas Wolfe> <ability to gather, organize, and express ideas in an orderly, rather than a *haphazard,* way will be of crucial value – R. K. Corbin> **Casual** implies a leaving or a seeming to leave things to chance; the term can suggest a lack of deliberation and care (as in acting or working) <[he] was . . . *casual* about peculation and inefficiency among minor officials, which he regarded as regrettable but inevitable in a new settlement – R. Hetherington> or a carefully planned effect <he can extract powerful emotional meaning from the most *casual* pose or gesture – Stuart Preston> **Desultory** implies a lack of system or method or an erratic skipping from one thing to another <apparently content with *desultory* chatter and make-believe occupation throughout the long hours of an idle day – Victoria Sackville-West>

range – see LINE

rank **1 rank, rampant** *shared meaning* : growing or increasing at an immoderate rate. **Rank** applies primarily to vegetation and implies vigorous, luxuriant, and often unchecked or excessive growth <behold, seven ears of corn came up upon one stalk, *rank* and good – *Gen* 41:5 (AV)> <the paths of other days were *rank* with tangled growth – Samuel Beckett> The term is common in metaphoric extension <weed your better judgments of all opinion that grows *rank* in them – Shak.> **Rampant** is more widely applicable than *rank;* it implies rapid and often wild or unrestrained spreading and is applicable both to what literally grows and to what extends or increases as if by physical growth <the impression is easily created that student discontent is *rampant* and that American higher education is in deep trouble

– M. S. Eisenhower> <tumors destroy man . . . as flesh of his own flesh, which has somehow been rendered proliferative, *rampant,* predatory, and ungovernable – Peyton Rous>
2 see MALODOROUS ***ant*** balmy
3 see FLAGRANT
ransom – see RESCUE
rant – see BOMBAST
rap – see TAP
rapacious – see VORACIOUS
rapid – see FAST ***ant*** deliberate, leisurely
rapture – see ECSTASY
rare – see CHOICE *adj,* INFREQUENT
rash – see ADVENTUROUS ***ant*** calculating
rate – see ESTIMATE
ration, allowance, dole, pittance *shared meaning* **:** the amount of food, supplies, or money allotted to an individual. **Ration** implies apportionment and, often, equal sharing; basically, it applies to the daily supply of food provided for one individual (as a prisoner or a milk cow) but it is freely extended to things in short supply that are made available either equally or equitably in accord with need <gasoline *rations* in wartime vary with the special needs of different individuals> **Allowance,** though often interchangeable with *ration,* is wider in its range of applications for it stresses granting, rather than sharing what is available in restricted supply <provided a weekly *allowance* of tobacco for each of the old men> <each child was given an *allowance* as soon as he became old enough to handle money> **Dole** tends to imply a grudging allowance to needy or grasping recipients <cold charity's unwelcome *dole* – P. B. Shelley> In modern, and especially British, use *dole* applies to a public payment to the needy or unemployed <people who are eligible yet not on welfare, who in some cases don't know about it, who in other cases are ashamed to ask for the *dole* – Frances F. Piven> **Pittance** stresses meagerness or miserliness and may apply indifferently to a ration, an allowance, an alms, a dole, or a wage <and gained, by spinning hemp, a *pittance* for herself – William Wordsworth> <one half only of this *pittance* was ever given him in money – T. B. Macaulay>
rational, reasonable *shared meaning* **:** having or manifesting the power to reason or being in accordance with the dictates of reason. **Rational** usually implies a latent or active power to make logical inferences and to draw conclusions that enable one to understand the world about him and to relate such knowledge to the attainment of ends; in this use the term is often opposed to *emotional* or *animal* <most students are *rational,* and intensely dislike facing decisions that are apparently capricious or silly – J. W. Moscow> <we are *rational;* but we are animal too – William Cowper> In applications to things conceived or formulated *rational* stresses satisfactoriness to the reason or actuation by reason <were there no Revelation nor religion, civilization itself would require *rational* discipline of the sexual instinct – *Pilot*> **Reasonable** lays a much weaker stress on the power to reason in general or of use of such power in conception or formulation; its emphasis, rather, is on the possession or use of practical sense, justice, and fairness and the avoidance of needless error <*reasonable* men do not find it easy to recommend courses of action that might seem "impractical" or "utopian" to their *reasonable* colleagues – W. W. Wagar> <the [Supreme] Court . . . makes constitutional law by saying what is a *reasonable*

interpretation of the Constitution in present circumstances – R. G. Tugwell> **ant** irrational, animal (*of nature*), absurd (*as of behavior*)

rattle – see EMBARRASS

ravage, devastate, waste, sack, pillage, despoil *shared meaning* **:** to lay waste by plundering or destroying. **Ravage** implies violent, severe, and often cumulative destruction, be it by hostile human agency or the forces of nature <forests *ravaged* by fire> <an Indian hunt was never a slaughter. They *ravaged* neither the rivers nor the forest – Willa Cather> <four major disasters had *ravaged* the country – L. S. B. Leakey> **Devastate** stresses the ruin and desolation which follows upon ravaging <the ruins of a city, shattered, *devastated*, crumbled piles of concrete and stone – William Styron> <a fire broke out ... which thoroughly *devastated* the front of the building before it was brought under control – Michael Murray> **Waste** tends to suggest a less complete destruction or one produced more gradually or less violently <he fell suddenly on the Nervii ..., seized their cattle, *wasted* their country – J. A. Froude> <land *wasted* by kaolinite mining ... is being reclaimed – *Technical Survey*> **Sack** basically applies to the looting and destroying of a captured place or of one likely to fall into the hands of an enemy <the retreating Federals *sacked* and burned as they went, leaving scarcely a cabin in their wake – *Amer. Guide Series: La.*> It may be extended to nonmilitary activities <a crowd sympathetic with the employees *sacked* the newspaper's offices – Irving Dilliard> **Pillage** stresses ruthless plundering but carries a weaker implication of devastation than *sack* <the houses, first *pillaged*, were then fired – W. H. Prescott> and in nonmilitary use implies ruthlessness in appropriating to one's own use what belongs to another (as by fleecing, plagiarizing, or embezzling) <humbugged by their doctors, *pillaged* by their tradesmen – G. B. Shaw> **Despoil**, like *sack*, implies a stripping of valuables, sometimes violently but more often under a guise of legality or through heedless destruction <the English buccaneers ... fell upon their cities and *despoiled* them – F. J. Haskin> <magnificent stands of pine ... *despoiled* by naval-stores operators and loggers – *Amer. Guide Series: Fla.*> <*despoiled* of innocence, of faith, of bliss – John Milton>

ravening – see VORACIOUS

ravenous – see VORACIOUS

ravish – see TRANSPORT

raw – see RUDE

rawboned – see LEAN

reach, gain, compass, achieve, attain *shared meaning* **:** to arrive at a point or end by effort or work. **Reach**, the general term, may be used with reference to anything arrived at by any degree of effort <television, through which for the first time in the history of any civilized society every home can be *reached* – Victor Palmieri> <*reach* an agreement through arbitration> <after a long climb we *reached* the top of the hill> **Gain** is likely to imply a struggle to reach a contemplated or desired goal or end <to *gain* its own legitimate or illegitimate ends, each was ready to sacrifice the ideal of a people governing themselves by majority rule – Mary J. White> <where technical competence is required it will, in view of the rapidity of change, have to be *gained* on the job – R. M. Hutchins> **Compass** implies efforts to get around difficulties and transcend limitations; often it connotes skill or craft in management <if you can *compass* it, do cure the younger girls of running after the officers – Jane Austen> <in the case of married women the ... [headdress] might be of diamonds, or any

gems they fancied, or could *compass* – Frederic Hamilton> **Achieve** can stress the skill or endurance as well as the effort involved in reaching an end <some are born great, some *achieve* greatness – Shak.> **Attain** stresses the spur of aspiration or ambition and suggests a reaching for the extreme, the unusual, or the difficult <the first Englishman to have *attained* to full possession of all that was then known . . . of linguistics – C. L. Wrenn>

readiness, ease, facility, dexterity *shared meaning* : the power of doing something without evidence of effort. **Readiness** emphasizes the quickness or promptitude with which something is done <acquired *readiness* and accuracy in writing – J. S. Reeves> **Ease** implies absence of strain or care or hesitation with resulting smooth efficiency in performance <answer a series of questions with *ease*> <true *ease* in writing comes from art, not chance – Alexander Pope> **Facility** is often very close to *ease* <I loathed algebra at first, although afterwards I had some *facility* in it – Bertrand Russell> but sometimes it suggests a slick superficiality rather than true ease <his *facility* in language has been fatal only too often to his logic and philosophy – J. C. Van Dyke> <the *facility* in these brilliant coloured pictures has about it just a hint of the facile – *Times Lit. Supp.*> **Dexterity** implies proficient skill such as results from training and practice <absorbed in his own *dexterity* and in the proposition of trying to deceive a fish with a bird's feather and a bit of hair – John Cheever>

ready *adj* – see QUICK

ready *vb* – see PREPARE

real, actual, true *shared meaning* : corresponding to known facts. As compared here in their general rather than their technical philosophical, aesthetic, or critical use these words are often interchangeable, but each can stress different aspects of their common meaning. **Real** is likely to stress genuineness and especially correspondence or identity between appearance and essence <a *real* diamond> <the difference between *real* and sham enjoyment – G. B. Shaw> <opera . . . achieves the *real* function of art without becoming realistic – Jess Thomas> **Actual** stresses the fact of existence or of fidelity to the existent as opposed to the nonexistent, abstract, hypothetical, or conjectural <most men are potential autocrats, the strong and capable may become *actual* autocrats – V. L. Parrington> <the possible world envisioned needs God's as well as man's will to make it *actual* – Scott Buchanan> **True** can stress conformity to the real especially as a model or standard <the ladybug is not a *true* bug but a beetle> or to the actual through correspondence to what exists or to the pertinent facts that are known or knowable <is any given truth any the less *true* for having been uttered more than once? – Theodore Sturgeon> ***ant*** unreal, apparent, imaginary

realize – see THINK

reap, glean, gather, garner, harvest *shared meaning* : to do the work or a particular part of the work of collecting ripened crops. **Reap** basically applies to the cutting down and usually collecting of ripened grain; in extension, it usually suggests a return or requital <the success of civil service employes in gaining their objectives through strikes has encouraged teachers to try to *reap* the fruits of militancy – F. M. Hechinger> **Glean** basically implies a stripping of a field or plant that has already been gone over once; in extension, it applies to any gathering up of useful bits from here and there and especially of such as have been overlooked or missed by others <the Sophy, homebound, had *gleaned* excursionists from a dozen islands – Arthur Mayse> <she had *gleaned* all the information the library contained – Robertson Davies> **Gather** applies to any collecting or bringing together of the produce of farm and garden; in extension, it stresses amassing or accumulating <when Dr. Weizmann's movement to establish a Jewish homeland in the Middle East was *gathering* momentum – Andrew Hamilton> **Garner** implies the storing of produce reaped or gathered; in extension, it can apply to any laying away of a store <a forty-man computation team responsible for collating the information *garnered* by these far-flung tracking stations – *Current Biog.*> **Harvest,** the general and inclusive term, may imply any or all of these agricultural practices or may be extended in meaning to apply to any gathering in or husbanding <he had sown pain and *harvested* regret – Maurice Samuel> <a delightful restaurant . . . [that] specialized in everything . . . *harvested* from the sea – *New Yorker*>

rear – see LIFT

reason *n* **1** see CAUSE

2 reason, understanding, intuition *shared meaning* **:** the power of the intellect by which man attains to truth or knowledge. **Reason** centers attention on the faculty for order, sense, and rationality in thought, inference, and conclusion about perceptions <the maintenance of *reason* – the establishment of criteria, by which ideas are tested empirically and in logic – Dorothy Thompson> **Understanding** may widen the scope of *reason* to include both most thought processes leading to comprehension and also the resultant state of knowledge <*understanding* is the entire power of perceiving and conceiving, exclusive of the sensibility; the power of dealing with the impressions of sense, and composing them into wholes – S. T. Coleridge> <philosophy is said to begin in wonder and end in *understanding* – John Dewey> **Intuition** stresses quick knowledge or comprehension without evident orderly reason, thought, or cogitation <the exact relation of reason and *intuition* is not clear. Some persons think that *intuition* is a way of knowing distinct from reason and the senses, and that it furnishes us with an insight into a supernatural reality which is inaccessible to both reason and the senses. Others think of *intuition* as a supplement to both, a kind of funding of one's past experience and thinking – J. W. Davis>

reason *vb* – see THINK 2

reasonable – see RATIONAL *ant* unreasonable

rebellion, revolution, uprising, revolt, insurrection, mutiny *shared meaning* **:** an armed outbreak against a government or against powers in authority. **Rebellion** implies open, organized armed resistance to constituted authority; the term is usually applied after the event to an instance of such resistance that has failed of its intent. **Revolution** applies to a rebellion that has succeeded to the extent that the old government is overthrown and a new one substituted; thus, the American War of Independence is commonly called "the American *Revolution*" and Northerners for many years referred to the American Civil War as "the War of the *Rebellion*." *Revolution,* however, may stress success and overturning to the virtual exclusion of warlike notions <the opposition effected a *revolution* by a bloodless coup d' etat> **Uprising** is applicable to an act of popular violence in defiance of an established government; it is typically used of a small or localized and ineffective movement that flared up suddenly or of the initial phases of a more general action <an Indian *uprising* drove him and his family from home – W. J. Ghent> but in much current use the term means little more than vigorous, often disorderly or violent protest against the Establishment <long before the new student *uprisings* . . . life on campus had become intensely grim – R. E. Kavanaugh> *Revolt* and *insurrection* apply to an armed uprising that is either immediately successful or more often quickly suppressed. **Revolt,** however, is more likely to suggest a firmness of purpose and a refusal to accept conditions, while **insurrection** may suggest more truculent intransigance and less organized purpose <a premature

revolt of some 200 native soldiers . . . had resulted in the deaths of their officers and in lusty shouts for independence – C. A. Buss> <the Negro is in *revolt* today not to change the fabric of our society . . . but to enter into partnership in that society – W. M. Young> <*insurrections* of base people are more furious in their beginnings – Francis Bacon> **Mutiny** applies chiefly to an insurrection against military or especially maritime or naval authority <*mutiny* imports collective insubordination and necessarily includes some combination of two or more persons in resisting lawful military authority – *U.S. Manual for Courts-Martial*>

rebuild – see MEND

rebuke – see REPROVE

rebut – see DISPROVE

recalcitrant – see UNRULY *ant* amenable

recall – see REMEMBER, REVOKE

recede, retreat, retrograde, retract, back *shared meaning*: to move backward. **Recede** implies a withdrawing, often slowly or gradually, from some fixed or definite forward point (as in space, time, or attitude) by or as if by moving backward <the floodwaters continued to *recede*> <Mexico's student strike has loosed a flood of political disquiet that may not *recede* for a long time – S. T. Wise> <he was far too self-willed to *recede* from a position, especially as it would involve humiliation – Thomas Hardy> **Retreat** implies withdrawal from a point or position reached typically in response to some pressure <the result was economic chaos, and Mao was forced to *retreat* – A. S. Whiting> <as we *retreated* across the town, they flowed out . . . and marched behind us . . . shouting insults – Norman Mailer> **Retrograde** basically applies to a moving backward rather than in an expected forward course and can imply the reverse of progress (as in a course of development) <in his Latin and Greek he was *retrograding* – George Meredith> <where one man advances, hundreds *retrograde* – T. L. Peacock> **Retract** implies a literal or figurative drawing backward or inward from a forward or outward position <a cat *retracting* its claws> <*retracted* his statement and apologized> <throwing out and *retracting* their left fists like pawing horses – G. B. Shaw> **Back,** often qualified by an adverb (as *up, out,* or *down*), applies to any retrograde or reversed motion <*back* a car out of a driveway> or, especially with *out* or *down,* to a receding (as from a stand or attitude taken) or retreating (as from a promise) <*backed* down on his promise to treat them to dinner> <[the President] temporarily *backed* away from a previous pledge for a tax cut – M. D. Reagan> *ant* proceed, advance

receipt, recipe, prescription *shared meaning* : a formula or set of directions for the compounding of ingredients especially in cookery and medicine. **Receipt** often denotes a formula for a homemade or folk medical remedy <a family *receipt* for a cough syrup> Though used in reference to cookery formulas, the term in this use is commonly felt as old-fashioned or dialectal and is being gradually replaced by *recipe.* **Recipe** is broadly applicable and can denote not only a formula or set of instructions for doing or making something but a method or procedure for attaining some end <*recipes* are used in making steel, and each ingredient is measured to a fraction of one percent – *Hot-Metal Magic*> <reading good books . . . is the *recipe* for those who would learn to read – M. J. Adler> In application to medical formulas *recipe* is likely to suggest an old-fashioned empirical remedy as distinct from a modern pharmaceutical product <some of his *recipes* are printed in pharmacopoeias of today – Norman Douglas> In cookery *recipe* is the usual and standard English term for a set of directions for preparing a made dish <tried a new *recipe* for scalloped oysters> The usual term for a physician's instruction to a pharmacist for the compounding or dispensing of a medicine is **prescription.** The term also applies to a medicine compounded or dispensed according to such a direction and is occasionally extended to other formulas or formulations with a suggestion of the precision expected in medical directions and their products <the *vignerons* of Tavel make their famous *rosé* in many ways . . . . Two white grapes and two red is a common *prescription* in set and ordered proportions – A. L. Simon> <the problem . . . awaits a theoretical formulation and a systematic policy *prescription* – Walter Adams>

receive, accept, admit, take *shared meaning* : to permit to come into one's possession, presence, group, mind, or substance. **Receive** can imply a welcoming recognition <*receive* guests with open arms> but more often it implies that something comes or is allowed to come (as into one's possession or presence) while one is passive <the barrel *receives* excess rainwater> <*received* the news without comment> <*receive* mail from home> **Accept** adds to *receive* an implication of some degree of positive acquiescence or consent even if tacit <refused to *accept* a valuable gift from a comparative stranger> <gradually she *accepted* her frustrating and ambiguous role – . . . content to be sole woman companion of the great man – W. L. Shirer> **Admit** carries strong implications of permission, allowance, or sufferance; thus, a judge *admits* evidence only after its admissibility has been questioned and he has allowed its entrance <the king *admitted* the ambassador to his presence> <*admit* new members to a club> The situation remains the same when the subject is impersonal <a door wide enough to *admit* a small car> **Take** carries the notion of accepting or at least of making no positive protest against receiving, often of almost welcoming on principle, what is offered, conferred, or inflicted <a man who *took* whatever fortune sent him> <learn to *take* weather as it comes – Helen R. Cross> <you don't have to *take* anything from him, or to stand his bad manners – Willa Cather>

recent – see MODERN

recess – see PAUSE

recipe – see RECEIPT

reciprocal, mutual, common *shared meaning* : shared, experienced, or shown by each of those concerned. **Reciprocal** implies an equal return or counteraction by each of two sides toward or against or in relation to the other <the *reciprocal* feelings of man and woman towards each other – T. S. Eliot> **Mutual** is likely to apply to feelings or actions shared by two and then may imply an accompanying reciprocity, equality, or interaction or may stress the fact of a shared experience or emotion <a devoted attachment and *mutual* admiration between aunt and niece – George Eliot> <there was a long pause during which their eyes held and the air was eloquent of *mutual* suspicion – H. C. Hervey> **Common** carries no suggestion of reciprocity but implies sharing with others <death and other incidents of our *common* fate – M. R. Cohen> <the pale-blue abstracted eyes *common* to most people who have flaming red hair – William Styron>

reciprocate, retaliate, requite, return *shared meaning* : to give back, usually in kind or in quantity. **Reciprocate** is likely to imply a more or less equivalent exchange or a paying back of what one has received <he . . . is peevish and sensitive when his advances are not *reciprocated* – G. B. Shaw> <the love of Lavinia for the hero, most correctly *reciprocated* by him – H. O. Taylor> **Retaliate** usually applies to a paying back of an injury and usually implies return in exact kind by way of vengeance <the students charged the police with brutality and *retaliated* with some brutality of their own – S. T. Wise> **Requite** can imply simply paying back, often reciprocally, but additionally it can imply a paying back according to what one considers the merits of the case and then need not imply mutual satisfaction <hospitality should be *requited* in kind – Agnes M. Miall> <thought . . . incumbent on a man to *requite* injuries – Henry Sidgwick> <his servility was *requited* with cold contempt – T. B. Macaulay> **Return** stresses a paying back whatever has been given, sometimes in kind, sometimes by way of contrast <*return* blow for blow> <*return* good for evil> <he *returns* my envy with pity – Richard Steele>

reckless – see ADVENTUROUS *ant* calculating

reckon – see RELY

reclaim – see RESCUE *ant* abandon

recognition, identification, assimilation, apperception *shared meaning* : a form of cognition that relates a perception of something new to knowledge already acquired. **Recognition** implies that the thing now perceived (as by seeing, smelling, hearing) has been previously perceived in itself or in kind and that the mind is aware of the fact that the two perceptions are of the same thing or identical things. **Identification** adds to *recognition* the implication of such prior knowledge as permits one to recognize the thing as a member of a class <one of the key concerns in anthropological . . . research . . . is the *identification* of the unit of mankind being studied – be it a caste, a class, a tribe, or an ethnic group – N. R. Crumrine> **Assimilation** implies that the mind responds to new ideas, facts, and experiences by interpretation in light of the previously known, thereby making them an integral part of one's body of knowledge <programs can . . . be made progressive so that each "subscriber" climbs the ladder of cultural excellence according to his capacity for *assimilation* – Harvey Wheeler> <*assimilation* . . . involves the internalization of knowledge, attitudes, norms, statuses, and roles . . . one assimilates a foreign language and uses it in communication – W. E. Cole> **Apperception** implies that the mind responds to new facts, ideas, or situations when and only when it can relate them to what is already known <as artists have always been, these are people who actually *see* the immediate environment and who devise meanings from their *apperceptions* of the present . . . the artist takes up common objects . . . and places them within a framework of imaginative consciousness – William Jovanovich>

recoil, shrink, flinch, wince, blench, quail *shared meaning* : to draw back through fear or distaste. **Recoil** is likely to stress the physical signs of shock, fear, or disgust and may imply a physical starting or swerving away or a like emotional withdrawal <had so great a dread of snakes that he instinctively *recoiled* at the sight of one – T. B. Costain> <she was principally aware of the sentiment of fear. She *recoiled* from the future – Arnold Bennett> **Shrink** implies an instinctive recoil (as from something painful or horrible); it often suggests cowardice, but may also suggest extreme sensitiveness or scrupulousness <guilt and misery *shrink,* by a natural instinct, from public notice – Thomas De Quincey> <we should not *shrink* from responsibility . . . we should welcome it – W. H. Hebert> **Flinch** implies a failure to endure pain or face what is dangerous or distressing with resolution <he looked his fate in the face without *flinching* – John Burroughs> and may indicate a slight physical recoiling <cannot bear the slightest touch without *flinching* – Tobias Smollett> **Wince** implies a slight involuntary physical recoiling from what pains, frightens, or disgusts <his features seemed to *wince,* as if his face were too close to a hot fire – Henry Roth> <he *winced* as though she had uttered blasphemy – W. J. Locke> **Blench,** sometimes indistinguishable from *flinch,* is likely to carry a stronger suggestion of faintheartedness or of signs of fear <though his

death seemed near he did not *blench* – John Masefield> **Quail** implies a cowering cringing recoil (as from something that strikes one with terror or fills one with dread) <I am never known to *quail* at the fury of a gale – W. S. Gilbert> <the strongest *quail* before financial ruin – Samuel Butler †1902> ***ant*** confront, defy

recollect – see REMEMBER

recollection – see MEMORY

recompense – see PAY

reconcile – see ADAPT

recrudesce – see RETURN

rectify – see CORRECT *vb*

recumbent – see PRONE ***ant*** upright, erect

recur – see RETURN

recurrent – see INTERMITTENT

redeem – see RESCUE

redound – see CONDUCE

redress – see CORRECT *vb*

reduce – see CONQUER, DECREASE

redundant – see WORDY ***ant*** concise

reel, whirl, stagger, totter *shared meaning* : to move or seem to move uncertainly and irregularly or with such loss of control as occurs in extreme weakness, in vertigo, or in intoxication. **Reel** usually suggests a turning round and round or a sensation of so turning or being turned <for, while the dagger gleamed on high, *reeled* soul and sense, *reeled* brain and eye – Sir Walter Scott> but it may also imply a being thrown off balance <giddy and restless, let them *reel* like stubble from the wind – John Milton> <the flying wedge of policemen sent the crowd *reeling* back in disorder – Nat Hentoff> **Whirl** is often used like *reel* <the dim brain *whirls* dizzy with delight – P. B. Shelley> but it more frequently implies swiftness or impetuousness of movement <flights of mallards . . . *whirl* back and forth in search of some unfrozen spring where they can feed – Geoffrey Grigson & C. H. Gibbs-Smith> **Stagger** stresses loss of control and resulting uncertainty of movement, typically of a person walking while weak, giddy, intoxicated, or heavily burdened but sometimes of whatever meets with difficulty or adverse conditions <made for her bungalow, almost *staggering* under a sudden wave of fatigue – Herman Wouk> <at whose immensity even soaring fancy *staggers* – P. B. Shelley> **Totter** implies not only weakness or unsteadiness that causes uncertain movement but often also hints the approach of complete collapse <feudalism *tottered* slowly but surely to its grave – J. R. Green> <his ideals are like monuments: they are hard to shake, but, once they *totter,* they fall fast – E. H. Erikson>

refer **1** see ASCRIBE

2 see RESORT

3 refer, allude, advert *shared meaning* : to call or direct attention to something. **Refer** usually implies intentional introduction and distinct and specific mention <we may here again *refer,* in support of this proposition, to the plain and unequivocal language of the laws – R. B. Taney> **Allude** suggests indirect mention (as by a hint, roundabout expression, or figure of speech) <fruit . . . gives him that intestinal condition I *alluded* to – Jean Stafford> <proposals . . . always *alluded* to slightingly as innovations – Compton MacKenzie> **Advert** in this relation usually implies a slight or glancing reference interpolated in a text or utterance <will be *adverted* to here, but will be dealt with more fully in other chapters – T. E. May>

reflect – see THINK 2

reflection – see ANIMADVERSION

reform – see CORRECT *vb*
refractory – see UNRULY ***ant*** malleable, amenable
refrain, abstain, forbear *shared meaning* : to keep oneself from doing or indulging in something. **Refrain** is likely to suggest the checking of a passing impulse <*refrain* from laughter in church> **Abstain** usually implies deliberate renunciation or self-denial on principle and often permanency of intent; thus, a person trying to lose weight may *refrain* (better than *abstain*) from eating a rich dessert at a dinner party because he has decided to *abstain* (not *refrain*) from all sweets until his weight is where he wants it <early Christians ... *abstained* from the responsibilities of office – J. E. E. Dalberg-Acton> **Forbear** usually implies self-restraint rather than self-denial, be it from patience, charity, or clemency, or from discretion, or from stoicism <wherever he has not the power to do or *forbear* any act according to the determination or thought of the mind, he is not free – Frank Thilly> <he was so poison-mean that the marsh mosquitoes *forbore* to bite him – S. H. Adams> but sometimes it is scarcely distinguishable from *refrain* <I cannot *forbear* quoting what seems to me applicable here – O. W. Holmes †1935>
refresh – see RENEW ***ant*** jade, addle
refuse – see DECLINE
refute – see DISPROVE
regard, respect, esteem, admire *shared meaning* : to recognize the worth of a person or thing. **Regard** is at once colorless and formal in feeling; often it requires qualification to reinforce and orient its meaning <he was highly *regarded* as a mechanic> <among the least *regarded* of all Elizabethan kinds of verse is the long poem – *Times Lit. Supp.*> **Respect** adds implications of careful evaluation or estimation as the basis of recognition of worth <one must *respect* their views even if one cannot agree with them> Often, *respect* implies a show of deference or veneration <a hunted fugitive ... but faithfully protected by the tribesmen, who *respected* his blood and pitied his misfortunes – *Encyc. Americana*> <failure to practice democracy and *respect* human rights cannot be concealed – Vera M. Dean> or observance of what is fitting <*respect* one's parents' wishes> or recognition of something as inviolable <*respect* the privacy of a house guest> **Esteem** adds implications of a high valuation and a consequent prizing and warmth of feeling or attachment <crying babies were often quieted with hot toddy, then *esteemed* an infallible remedy for wind – Caroline L. Rice> <in the Renaissance, no Latin author was more highly *esteemed* than Seneca – T. S. Eliot> **Admire** implies a recognition of superiority but is likely to stress connotations of enthusiastic but often uncritical appreciation <*admire* the beauty of the coastal scenery> <small boys, noses pressed to the glass, *admiring* puppies in a pet shop>
regret – see SORROW
regular, normal, typical, natural *shared meaning* : being of the sort or kind that is expected as usual, ordinary, or average. **Regular** stresses conformity to a rule, standard, or pattern <living staid existences, dull, *regular*, unexciting and without adventure – J. T. Farrell> <a *regular* boy, full of mischief and energy> <their action was made *regular* and legal – J. R. Green> **Normal** suggests falling within the limits of a norm <save the student part of his college costs by helping him to graduate in less than the *normal* four years – E. M. Gerritz> <her intensity ... would leave no emotion on a *normal* plane – D. H. Lawrence> **Typical** implies conformance to a type (as a class, species, or group) and may suggest lack of marked individuality <his feeling that he was not wholly accepted made him more prone to talk about diplomatic matters than the *typical* career ambassador

– J. A. Michener> <peculiar to himself, not *typical* of Greek ideas – G. L. Dickinson> **Natural** applies to what conforms to a thing's essential nature, function, or mode of being <it's *natural* for children to be noisy> <unless rapid action is taken, irreparable imbalances will result from uncontrolled technological disturbance of *natural* systems – Denis Goulet> ***ant*** irregular

regulation – see LAW

reimburse – see PAY

reiterate – see REPEAT

reject – see DECLINE ***ant*** accept, choose, select

rejoin – see ANSWER

rejuvenate – see RENEW

relapse – see LAPSE

relate – see JOIN

related, cognate, kindred, allied, affiliated *shared meaning* : connected by or as if by close family ties. **Related** in application to persons can imply consanguinity or connection by marriage; in application to things it implies a correspondingly close connection <it is as impossible to think of an idea which is not *related* to other ideas as it is to find a person who is not and never has been *related* to any other person. And ideas are *related* – Olive S. Niles> <these two modern masters created separate but *related* parts of a single work – *Current Biog.*> **Cognate** applies to things that are generically alike, have a common ancestor or source, or derive from the same root or stock <*cognate* words in various languages, such as *pater, Vater, father*> <action engendered in regard to drugs may spill over into the *cognate* problem of the alcoholic – *New Republic*> **Kindred** in its primary relation stresses consanguinity <an isolated community most of whose members were more or less closely *kindred*> but in more common extended applications is likely to stress community (as of interests or tastes) and congeniality <he would never be popular . . . but he might appeal to a little circle of *kindred* minds – James Joyce> <they and their fellow officials . . . , along with *kindred* souls on Capitol Hill, are still doing business at the same old doctrinaire stand – *Barron's*> **Allied** is likely to imply connection by union and especially by marriage or voluntary association rather than by origin or blood <*allied* through his wife with several prominent English families> where blood or biological relationship is implied it is likely to be remote <earthworms and the *allied* clam worms and leeches> In its extended use the term is likely to stress relationship based on common characters, qualities, aims, or effects <*allied* physical types> <DDT and *allied* insecticides> **Affiliated**, often close to *allied*, distinctively tends to stress a dependent relation like that of a child to a parent <favored federal aid to private colleges, including those that are church-*affiliated* – *Current Biog.*> and may connote a loose union in which the associated elements are more or less independent <the CIO and its *affiliated* unions>

relaxed – see LOOSE ***ant*** stiff

release – see FREE *vb* ***ant*** detain (*as a prisoner*), check (*as thoughts, feelings*), oblige

relegate – see COMMIT

relent – see YIELD

relevant, germane, material, pertinent, apposite, applicable, apropos *shared meaning* : relating to or bearing upon the matter in hand. **Relevant** implies a traceable, significant, logical connection <great books are universally *relevant* . . . they deal with the common problems of thought and action that confront men in every age and every clime – M. J. Adler> **Germane** can additionally imply a fitness for, or appropriateness to, the situation or occasion <the passionate cravings which are *germane* to the hermit life – H. O. Taylor> **Material** implies a relation of such closeness that it cannot be altered without evident, usually deleterious effect <the appeals court's definition says that anything that "may affect the desire of investors to buy, sell or hold the company's securities" is *material – Wall Street Jour.*> **Pertinent** stresses a clear and decisive relevance <develop efficient means for rapid access to information that is transient, but *pertinent* to their immediate concerns – H. A. Simon> **Apposite** implies a marked and felicitous relevance <analyzing their programs of instruction in hope of improving them and making them more *apposite* – N. M. Pusey> <whatever she did she made her circumstances appear singularly *apposite* and becoming – Victoria Sackville-West> **Applicable** applies to something that may be brought to bear upon or used fittingly in reference to a particular case, instance, or problem <a basic technique of musical rendition that is *applicable* to any piece – Virgil Thomson> **Apropos** implies being both relevant and opportune <a tale extremely *apropos* – Alexander Pope> <she had often told herself how *apropos,* in a ghastly way, Kate's suicide had been. Their life together had come to its logical conclusion; it could never be the same again – I. V. Morris> ***ant*** extraneous

relieve, alleviate, lighten, assuage, mitigate, allay *shared meaning* : to make less grievous or more tolerable. **Relieve** implies a lifting of enough of a burden to make it endurable or even temporarily forgotten <drugs that *relieve* pain> <indolent women . . . who got up at noon and spent the rest of the day trying to *relieve* their boredom – Roald Dahl> **Alleviate** stresses the temporary or partial nature of the relief <the Indians applied the juice to *alleviate* the sting of the nettle and the itching of poison ivy – E. L. Core> **Lighten** implies reduction in the weight of what burdens or depresses and often connotes a cheering influence <married women . . . whose home responsibilities have *lightened* as their children move into . . . school grades – *Conn. Teacher*> <*lightened* the spirits of her co-workers whenever they betrayed any dissatisfaction – F. E. Pitkin> **Assuage** implies softening or sweetening what is harsh or disagreeable <the good gods *assuage* thy wrath – Shak.> <this will not *assuage* the resentment of the have-nots – Hedley Bull> **Mitigate** suggests a moderating or countering of the effects of something inflicting or likely to inflict pain or distress <*mitigate* the barbarity of the criminal law – W. R. Inge> <Luther *mitigated* his own doctrine; its social implications were found to be too radical – N. F. Cantor> **Allay** implies an effective calming or soothing, especially of fears and alarms <his suspicions were *allayed* by her confident account of the day> <the encyclical . . . foreshadowed a program not merely of ending the cold war, which for a while it did *allay,* but also of organizing the world – R. M. Hutchins> ***ant*** intensify

religious *adj* – see DEVOUT ***ant*** irreligious

religious *n* **religious, monk, friar, nun** *shared meaning* : a member of a religious order bound by vows of poverty, chastity, and obedience. **Religious** is the general term applicable to either a man or a woman. **Monk** in general use may designate any male religious, but in more precise use it applies to a member of a religious order for men whose members live an ascetic life in a cloistered community and devote themselves mainly to contemplation, prayer, and liturgical observances and to some assigned work. **Friar** applies to a man who is a member of a mendicant order or to an order patterned after the historic mendicant orders, whether he lives as a mendicant or in a cloistered community and whether he serves as a pastor, a curate, a missionary, a preacher, or a teacher <this obscure German *friar* [Martin

Luther] had recaptured the central message of the Christian faith – N. F. Cantor> **Nun** applies to any female religious.

relinquish, yield, resign, surrender, abandon, waive *shared meaning* : to give up completely. **Relinquish** is likely to be chosen for use in contexts that imply some regretful emotion as involved in the giving up <the research scholar, reluctant to *relinquish* to another the tasks which he has performed unaided – Mary L. Bundy & Paul Wasserman> <he had let something go . . . : something very precious, that he could not consciously have *relinquished* – Willa Cather> **Yield** implies concession or compliance or submission to force <*yield* not thy neck to fortune's yoke – Shak.> <argues that the left-outs must unite to fight for things which the Establishment will not otherwise *yield* them – *New Republic*> **Resign** emphasizes voluntary relinquishment or sacrifice without a struggle <in her face . . . was that same strange mingling of *resigned* despair and almost eager appeal – John Galsworthy> <half the original teachers *resigned*, feeling they could not work with the proposed plan – D. E. Rosenbaum> **Surrender** implies the existence of an external compulsion or demand and commonly suggests submission after a greater or lesser degree of resistance <she had rallied her forces for a month of energetic . . . obstructing, only to *surrender* with queer docile suddenness a week before Marjorie's departure – Herman Wouk> **Abandon** stresses finality and completeness in giving up <after dinner, they *abandoned* Mickey Mouse for Houston and Tuesday night's All-Star Game – Mark Mulvoy> <*abandoning* standards that are not really relevant to the job – R. M. Solow> **Waive** implies conceding or foregoing with little or no compulsion or pressure <*waive* one's right to a jury trial> <if art can enthrall him, he is willing to *waive* all question of logic or rationality – Irving Babbitt> ***ant*** keep

relish – see TASTE 1, 2

reluctant – see DISINCLINED

rely, trust, depend, count, reckon *shared meaning* : to place full confidence. **Rely** (with *on* or *upon*) implies a judgment based on experience or association <a man one can *rely* on in an emergency> <to figure out precisely what is going on . . . they are forced to *rely* on their own reasoning and inventiveness – M. S. Eisenhower> **Trust** (with *in* or *to*) implies assurance based on faith that another will not fail one <take short views, hope for the best, and *trust* in God – Sydney Smith> **Depend** (with *on* or *upon*) implies a resting on someone or something for support or assistance and often connotes lack of self-sufficiency <the captain of the ship at sea is a remote, inaccessible creature . . . *depending* on nobody – Joseph Conrad> **Count** and **reckon** (each with *on*) imply a taking into one's calculations as certain or assured <he had 1,500 votes, but if something went wrong he did not know if he could *count* on a single one of them – they could all wash away in the night – Norman Mailer> <the Oriental writer *reckons* largely on the intellectual cooperation of his reader – T. K. Cheyne> or, in weakened use, may mean little more than *expect* <did not *reckon* on such heavy expenses> <they *counted* on staying with friends>

remain – see STAY ***ant*** depart

remark, comment, commentate, animadvert *shared meaning* : to make observations or pass judgment. **Remark** implies little more than to notice and call attention to something <a metropolitan newspaper *remarked* that no one today hopes for progress – Robert Bierstedt> <*remark* on a friend's taste in dress> **Comment** stresses often critical interpretation <there's no such thing as a comic strip that doesn't *comment*. *Blondie* is *commenting* savagely on a vexing problem that I would never dare tackle: Twentieth

Century marriage – Al Capp> **Commentate** is sometimes substituted for *comment* to suggest a purely expository or interpretive intent <*commentating* upon and collating of the works of former times – H. E. Cushman> **Animadvert** implies a remarking or commentating usually of scholarly caliber or based on careful judgment <I went to an old-fashioned school. All who wish to *animadvert* on education ought to be able to begin that way – Hortense Calisher> but this basic implication is often obscured by an emphasis on passing an adverse judgment <we talked of gaming, and *animadverted* on it with severity – James Boswell>

remarkable – see NOTICEABLE

remedy – see CORRECT *vb,* CURE

remember, recollect, recall, remind, reminisce *shared meaning* : to bring an image or idea from the past into the mind. **Remember** may so stress the fact of receiving back from the store of memory as to imply no conscious effort or willing <years – so many of them that no one *remembered* the exact number – Roark Bradford> <down all the seasons to the hours of her old age, I would be the one she would be forced to *remember* – Norman Mailer> **Recollect** implies a bringing back to the mind what has been lost or scattered <trying to *recollect* a friend's address> <beasts and babies remember, that is, recognize: man alone *recollects* – S. T. Coleridge> **Recall** differs from *recollect* chiefly in implying a summoning rather than a mental collecting; often, also, it connotes a telling of what is brought back <let me *recall* a case within my own recent experience – H. L. Mencken> <he had told the story simply.... Probably it was a true memory, *recalled* because he happened to be feeling lonely – Bernard Malamud> **Remind** suggests a jogging of one's memory by an association or similarity <the country became fatter and richer-looking.... In spots it *reminded* of New England – Kaj Klitgaard> <we don't want any ad that *reminds* the reader that he is growing fat or old or is inadequate – H. W. Lederer> **Reminisce** implies a casual, often nostalgic, recalling of experiences long past and gone <she liked ... to *reminisce* about her experiences as a samaritan – John Cheever> <would take an evening off to *reminisce* ... on the stupidity of the teachers he had had in his youth – W. L. Shirer> ***ant*** forget

remembrance – see MEMORY ***ant*** forgetfulness

remind – see REMEMBER

reminisce – see REMEMBER

reminiscence – see MEMORY

remiss – see NEGLIGENT ***ant*** scrupulous

remonstrate – see OBJECT

remorse – see PENITENCE

remote – see DISTANT ***ant*** close

removed – see DISTANT

remunerate – see PAY

rend – see TEAR

renew, restore, refresh, renovate, rejuvenate *shared meaning* : to make like new. **Renew** implies a replacing of what is damaged, decayed, or depleted <each spring the trees *renew* their foliage> <they that wait upon the Lord shall *renew* their strength – *Isa* 40:31 (AV)> or sometimes a making of a fresh start <*renew* one's efforts to escape> **Restore** stresses a return to an original or perfect state after damage, dilapidation, or depletion <in many of our universities, teaching ... must be *restored* to its rightful priority among the many diverse aims which universities have come to serve – M. S. Eisenhower> <*restore* one's energy by rest> **Refresh** implies a supplying of what restores lost strength, animation, or power <this afternoon

the thirsty earth was *refreshed* with a most charming shower – John Cheever> **Renovate** can replace *renew* when cleansing, repairing, or rebuilding is implied <*renovate* an old house> <the rebellions . . . acted as a safety valve that helped *renovate* political authority even as it attacked a particular ruler – Guenter Lewy> **Rejuvenate** implies a literal or figurative restoration of youthful vigor, powers, and appearance <had the air of an old bachelor trying to *rejuvenate* himself – Washington Irving> <outworn themes may be *rejuvenated* by taking on contemporary garb – J. L. Lowes>

renounce – see ABDICATE ***ant*** arrogate, covet

renovate – see RENEW

renowned – see FAMOUS

rent – see HIRE

renunciation, abnegation, self-abnegation, self-denial *shared meaning* : voluntary forgoing of something desired or desirable. **Renunciation** commonly connotes personal sacrifice for a higher end <a life of complete *renunciation* . . . as a nun – C. C. Cregan> **Abnegation** and the increasingly common **self-abnegation** imply a high degree of unselfishness as a capacity for putting aside personal interest or desires <the distinctive ethics of the New Testament is an "ethics of *self-abnegation,*" which regards as the highest form of human conduct the surrender of one's self and the suppression of one's impulses and desires – Robert Gordis> <cold lines, but penned by what heartbroken *abnegation* – George Meredith> **Self-denial** usually applies to an act or a practice and implies a forbearance from gratifying one's desires, whatever the motive <the *self-denial* involved in following a rigid diet> <*self-denial* is not a virtue: it is only the effect of prudence on rascality – G. B. Shaw>

repair – see MEND

repartee – see WIT

repay – see PAY

repeal – see REVOKE

repeat 1 repeat, iterate, reiterate *shared meaning* : to say or do again. **Repeat,** the general term, centers attention on the fact of uttering, presenting, or doing again one or more times <the *repeated* disruption of the railroad service – A. S. Whiting> <falsehoods and half-truths . . . uncritically *repeated* from writer to writer – R. D. Altick> **Iterate** and **reiterate** usually imply one repetition after another (though the former can apply to single repetitions), especially of something that is said, and are sometimes combined for emphasis <a leader, who traced a theme, while the rest, from time to time, *iterated* his phrases – E. K. Chambers> <over and over again, in a somber, bullfrog voice, he *reiterates* his favorite theme: A legislature cannot be the expressive arm of government until it is independent – Trevor Armbrister> <scientific research *iterates* and *reiterates* one moral . . . the greatness of little things – *Sat. Rev.* (*London*)>
2 see QUOTE

repellent – see REPUGNANT ***ant*** attractive, pleasing

repentance – see PENITENCE

replace, displace, supplant, supersede *shared meaning* : to put a person or thing out of his or its place or into that of another. **Replace** usually implies a filling of a place once occupied by something lost, destroyed, or no longer adequate or usable <the general survey of . . . the science is often *replaced* by an approach to depth in one or two fields – A. H. Marckwardt> <*replace* a leaky faucet> **Displace** may imply a dislodging, ousting, or crowding out <*displaced* young intellectuals – university graduates who had been unable to find suitable jobs – W. L. Shirer> often as a prelude to replacement <protection for those *displaced* by personnel changes is . . . an obliga-

tion of the city – J. V. Lindsay> or it may stress the notion of replacing <the general tendency will be for service functions . . . to *displace* subsistence, productive, and clerical functions – Harvey Wheeler> **Supplant** basically implies a displacing by devious means and the taking over of the place and prerogatives of the one displaced <you three from Milan did *supplant* good Prospero – Shak.> but the notion of deviousness is often lost <a pastime that threatens to *supplant* baseball as the national sport – Helen Rowan> **Supersede** implies replacing a person or thing that is felt to be superannuated, obsolete, or otherwise inferior <the original aim was soon *superseded* by other, more spectacular, student campaign targets – David Binder> <the horse, *superseded* for transport, was now bred entirely for hunting – S. E. Morison>

replete – see FULL

replica – see REPRODUCTION

reply – see ANSWER

report, rumor, gossip, hearsay *shared meaning* : common talk or an instance of it that spreads rapidly. **Report,** the most general and least explicit of these terms, is likely to suggest some ground for belief unless specifically qualified (as by *false, untrue,* or *wild*) <my brother Jaques he keeps at school and *report* speaks goldenly of his profit – Shak.> <evil *report* beset him early and pursued him throughout his active life – S. H. Adams> <it was common *report* that they were living together> **Rumor** applies to a report that flies about, often gains in detail as it spreads, but lacks both an evident source and clear-cut evidence of its truth <we make our blunders . . . as *rumor* has it that you make your own – B. N. Cardozo> <the impact of *rumor* and reality on a group of men living in complete isolation from reliable news – *Times Lit. Supp.*> **Gossip** applies primarily to the idle, often personal, chatter that is the chief source and means of propagating rumors or reports <*gossip* about the party leader and his beautiful blonde niece was inevitable – W. L. Shirer> <but *gossip,* thank goodness, needed no brains beyond a certain shrewdness in human affairs – Victoria Sackville-West> <wrote a *gossip* column for the local paper> **Hearsay** stresses the source of a rumor or report as what is heard rather than what is seen or known directly <the qualifications and doubts that distinguish critical science from *hearsay* knowledge – M. R. Cohen> <while some hold for certain facts the most precarious *hearsays,* others turn facts into falsehood – Robert Graves> and in its application to evidence retains this implication of indirect and imperfect knowledge of the facts <evidence is called *"hearsay"* when its probative force depends in whole or in part, on the competency and credibility of some person other than the witness who produces it – *U.S. Dept. of Justice Board of Immigration Appeals*>

reprehend – see CRITICIZE

repress – see SUPPRESS

reprimand – see REPROVE

reproach – see REPROVE

reprobate – see CRITICIZE

reproduction, duplicate, copy, facsimile, replica *shared meaning* : something that closely resembles a thing previously made, produced, or written. **Reproduction** implies a fundamentally correct and readily identifiable imitation that may or may not differ from the original in significant matters (as size, material, or quality) <each original print remains an authentic expression of the artist's intent . . . . A *reproduction* . . . may vary from the original in color, size, medium, texture, or any of a number of other factors – R. E. Cain> **Duplicate** applies to a double or counterpart, exactly corresponding to an original in all significant respects <a *duplicate* of a bill

of sale> <sold several *duplicates* from his coin collection> **Copy** applies distinctively to one of a number of things produced mechanically (as from the same type format, die, or mold) <modern *copies* of sixteenth-century chess sets – *New Yorker*> <the book sold over a million *copies*> In more general use it suggests adaptation with retention of the identifying details of an original <made a dress for her daughter and a *copy* of it for her little granddaughter> **Facsimile** applies to a close reproduction and implies as close an imitating (as in scale, materials, or details) as is possible or feasible <employed ... to convert Sherry's ballroom into a reasonable *facsimile* of a wing of the Palace of Versailles – Lucius Beebe> **Replica** emphasizes closeness of likeness and is specifically used of a reproduction (as of a work of art) made exactly like the original (as in scale, materials, and details) by or under the direction of the maker of the original <the confusing tendency of some Renaissance painters to make *replicas* of their paintings> In less precise use this restriction is lost <collection of miniature sports cars. Tiny, Swiss-made *replicas,* they were precision machined and finely detailed, all scaled to perfection – Terry Southern>

reprove, rebuke, reprimand, admonish, reproach, chide *shared meaning* : to criticize adversely. **Reprove** implies an often kindly intent to correct a fault <husband and wife ... may *reprove* each other for acts that each would tolerate without comment from strangers – C. A. Kiesler> <the Court later on *reproved* them for exceeding their powers – R. G. Tugwell> **Rebuke** implies sharp or stern reproof <[he] was *rebuked* for using longshoreman's language in the presence of women – Andrew Hamilton> <must *rebuke* this drunkenness of triumph – P. B. Shelley> **Reprimand** implies a formal and often public or official rebuking <this member was found guilty ... and voted by the House to be *reprimanded* – D. G. Hitchner> **Admonish** stresses the implication of warning or counsel <count him not as an enemy, but *admonish* him as a brother – *2 Thess* 3:15 (AV)> <*admonish* speakers ... to stay within the time allotted to them – H. E. Kaplan> **Reproach** and **chide** suggest displeasure or disappointment expressed in mild scolding or expostulation <they urged themselves to improve their minds and they *reproached* themselves for idleness, sloth, lewdness, stupidity and drunkenness – John Cheever> <his wife ... who was forever *chiding* him for his grammatical lapses – William Styron>

repudiate – see DECLINE ***ant*** adopt

repugnant, repellent, abhorrent, distasteful, obnoxious, invidious *shared meaning* : so alien or unlikable as to arouse antagonism and aversion. **Repugnant** applies to something so incompatible to one's tastes, ideas, or principles as to stir up resistance and loathing <a law *repugnant* to the Constitution is void – R. G. Tugwell> <a tiny fraction of the population ... uses ... a disproportionate percentage of the world's resources.... This inequity is morally *repugnant* – Denis Goulet> **Repellent** suggests a generally forbidding or unattractive quality that causes one to back away <*repellent* materials ... make foliage distasteful to rabbits – *Boston Sunday Herald Traveler*> <the mediocre was *repellent* to them; cant and sentiment made them sick – Rose Macaulay> **Abhorrent** implies a repugnance causing active antagonism <dictatorial methods *abhorrent* to American ways of thinking – *Forum*> **Distasteful** implies dislike based on personal taste rather than inherent quality of the thing in question <finds it *distasteful* to think of using the personal belongings of ... previous occupants – Kenneth Roberts> **Obnoxious** suggests an objectionableness, often on personal grounds, too great to tolerate with equanimity <nothing can be more *obnoxious* than the facts to someone who has already made up his mind – H. A. Gleason> **Invidious** applies to what cannot be used or made or undertaken without creating ill will, odium, or envy <a despotism resulting from *invidious* discriminations, which divides the populace into a favored Establishment and a mass of culturally deprived – Harvey Wheeler> <the *invidious* word usury – David Hume †1776> ***ant*** congenial

request – see ASK 2

require – see DEMAND, LACK

requirement, requisite, prerequisite *shared meaning* : something regarded as necessary. **Requirement** may imply something more or less arbitrarily demanded, especially by those with a right to lay down conditions <college entrance *requirements*> <two *requirements* are necessary . . . for a material to rate as an insulation – P. D. Close> or it may be interchangeable with **requisite** which is the customary term for something indispensable for the end in view or otherwise essential and not arbitrarily demanded <the first *requisite* of literary or artistic activity, is that it shall be interesting – T. S. Eliot> <a ceiling fan . . . for use in areas where quietness is a *requisite* – *Amer. School Board Jour.*> <permit agriculturists to buy their *requirements* upon favorable conditions – *Nineteenth Century*> **Prerequisite** applies to a requisite that must be available in advance or acquired as a preliminary <peace in the labor market is the foremost *prerequisite* for an expanding economy – Arne Geijer> <we are emotionally free to make justice the *prerequisite* of law and of order – C. E. Crowther>

requisite – see REQUIREMENT

requite – see RECIPROCATE

rescind – see REVOKE

rescue, deliver, redeem, ransom, reclaim, save *shared meaning* : to set free (as from confinement or risk). **Rescue** implies freeing from imminent danger by prompt or vigorous action <we are beset with thieves; *rescue* thy mistress – Shak.> <his career was *rescued* from decline by the success of one song – *Current Biog.*> **Deliver** implies a setting free from something (as confinement, suffering, or temptation) that distresses <lead us not into temptation, but *deliver* us from evil – *Mt* 6:13 (AV)> **Redeem** stresses the giving up of an equivalent in order to set a person or thing free <let me *redeem* my brothers both from death – Shak.> <faced with major obstacles in pushing through the legislation he needed to *redeem* his campaign pledges – T. P. Murphy> <Christ died to *redeem* mankind> **Ransom** specifically applies to a buying out of captivity <*ransom* a kidnapped child> or in religious use is a close equivalent of *redeem* <his brethren, *ransomed* with his own dear life – John Milton> **Reclaim** implies a bringing back to a former state (as of something debased, gone wild, or laid waste) <realizing that existing practices in architecture and community planning could not *reclaim* Greece from devastation – *Current Biog.*> **Save** can replace any of the foregoing terms; it is likely to add to the notion of setting free that of preserving or maintaining for future usefulness or in continued existence <*save* a boy from drowning> <the city's last hope to *save* these children from a wasted life – K. B. Clark>

resemblance – see LIKENESS ***ant*** difference, distinction

resentment – see OFFENSE

reserve – see KEEP 2

reserved – see SILENT ***ant*** affable, expansive, blatant

reside, live, dwell, sojourn *shared meaning* : to have as one's habitation or domicile. **Reside** may be preferred to express the idea that a person keeps or returns to a particular place as his fixed, settled, or legal abode while **live,** the more general term, may stress the idea of actually spending one's time and carrying out the activities of one's family life <the senator *resides* in San Francisco but most of the year he *lives* in Washington> <as soon

as school was out we left the city where we *resided* all winter to *live* in the country> **Dwell**, a close synonym of these words, is likely to appear in elevated language <she *dwelt* among the untrodden ways beside the springs of Dove – William Wordsworth> **Sojourn** distinctively implies a temporary habitation or abode or a more or less uncertain place or way of living <artists who *sojourned* for a time amidst the western scene – *Amer. Guide Series: Oregon*> <the right . . . to *sojourn* there as long as they pleased – R. B. Taney> <for what purpose . . . was the world created, and immortal spirits sent to *sojourn* in it? – W. R. Inge>

resign – see ABDICATE, RELINQUISH

resilient – see ELASTIC

resist – see OPPOSE ***ant*** submit, abide

resolute – see FAITHFUL

resolution – see COURAGE

resolve 1 see ANALYZE ***ant*** blend
2 see DECIDE

resort *n* – see RESOURCE

resort *vb* **resort, refer, apply, go, turn** *shared meaning* : to have recourse (to something) when in need of help or relief. **Resort** may imply that one has encountered difficulties impossible to surmount without help and then connotes an approach to desperation <a devout Catholic who still *resorts* to prayer in moments of personal and family stress – *Current Biog.*> <found he could get no relief unless he *resorted* to the courts> **Refer** suggests a need for authentic information or authoritative action and recourse to a source of this <whenever you come to an unfamiliar word, *refer* to your dictionary> <made it a practice to *refer* students to more competent authorities who can deal directly with the problem – J. W. Moscow> **Apply** suggests having direct recourse (as in person or by letter) to one able to supply what is needed <*apply* to a bank for a loan> <*apply* to the authorities for abatement of a nuisance> **Go** and **turn** are more general but often more picturesque or more dramatic terms that directly suggest action or movement in seeking aid or relief <the president *went* directly to the people with his plan> <she had taken fright at our behavior and *turned* to the captain pitifully – Joseph Conrad>

resource, resort, expedient, shift, makeshift, stopgap *shared meaning* : something one turns to in the absence of the usual means or source of supply. **Resource** and the less common **resort** apply to whatever one falls back upon when in need of support, assistance, or diversion <he has exhausted every *resource* he can think of> <this clear, accurate, and highly readable introduction . . . is . . . a useful *resource* for inquisitive laymen seeking factual information – K. F. Mather> <some . . . Negroes have responded to the black-power concept in a sometimes . . . emotionally charged manner – because it seemed the only available *resource* with which they could confront white American society – Joyce Ladner> <he would borrow only as a last *resort*> <a simple . . . answer . . . is to avoid . . . problem areas of behavior . . . . This *resort* may be necessary where children are concerned – Louis Chapin> **Expedient** may apply to a simple substitute or, sometimes, to something that eases or simplifies a difficult task <rules of thumb generally . . . are a lazy man's *expedient* for ridding himself of the trouble of thinking and deciding – B. N. Cardozo> <had to learn all sorts of *expedients* and prepare for all sorts of emergencies – V. G. Heiser> **Shift** implies a tentative or temporary and often imperfect expedient; often it suggests dubiousness or trickery <the usual *shifts* and dodges of a businessman clipping corners to make more money – Herman Wouk> <the staff were put to extraordinary *shifts* to keep the programs on the air –

T. O. Beachcroft> **Makeshift** implies an inferior expedient adopted because of urgent need or countenanced through indifference <*makeshifts* may for a while suffice – W. H. Ferry> **Stopgap** applies to something or someone temporarily filling an emergency need <she discovered that she was only a *stopgap;* a search for a man to fill the job had been in progress all along – Eulah C. Laucks> <until such comes along the present offering will form a worthwhile *stopgap* – Elizabeth C. Hall>

respect – see REGARD *ant* contempt

respite – see PAUSE

resplendent – see SPLENDID

respond – see ANSWER

responsible, answerable, accountable, amenable, liable *shared meaning* : subject to an authority that may punish default. *Responsible, answerable,* and *accountable,* although often used interchangeably, are capable of distinction based on their typical applications. **Responsible** may center attention on a formal organizational role, function, duty, or trust <while held *responsible* for the bank's operation, the president has powers considered largely nominal – *Current Biog.*> <the ideally free individual is *responsible* only to himself – Henry Adams> **Answerable** is likely to stress the presence both of a moral or legal responsibility and of a judge or tribunal qualified to appraise its handling <men in business, who are *answerable* with their fortunes for the consequences of their opinions – William Hazlitt> <there was something ineradicably corrupt inside her for which her father was not *answerable* – E. K. Brown> **Accountable** may be used in situations involving imminence of retribution for unfulfilled trust or violated obligation <the Russian leaders . . . are not *accountable* to their people – *Reporter*> <[the General Assembly] can hold the Security Council morally *accountable* for its acts of commission and omission – Walter Lippmann> **Amenable** and **liable** stress the fact of subjection to review, censure, or control by a designated authority under certain conditions <scholar and teacher alike ranked as clerks . . . *amenable* only to the rule of the bishop – J. R. Green> <the present United States . . . took nothing by succession from the Confederation . . . was not *liable* for any of its obligations – R. B. Taney>

restful – see COMFORTABLE

restive – see CONTRARY

restore 1 see RENEW

2 **restore, revive, revivify, resuscitate** *shared meaning* : to regain or cause to regain signs of life and vigor. **Restore** implies a return to consciousness, to health, or to vigor often by the use of remedies or treatments <hearing can sometimes be *restored* by surgery> <it took months of rest and care to *restore* his health> **Revive** may imply recovery from a deathlike state (as a stupor or faint) <*revive* a swooning miss with cold water> but is widely applicable to restoration to a flourishing state <the showers *revived* the withering crops> <If history has any lesson at all, it is that never have men accomplished anything great by trying to *revive* a dead past – M. R. Cohen> **Revivify** tends to suggest adding of new life and carries a weaker suggestion than *revive* of prior depletion <a good night's sleep *revivifies* the strongest person> <one of the American ladies who had given *revivifying* injections of new American millions to ancient European families – J. D. Scott> **Resuscitate** commonly implies a restoration to consciousness by arduous efforts to overcome a serious impairment <*resuscitate* a nearly drowned person with artificial respiration> In extended use it can suggest a restoring to vitality of someone or something in which life seems nearly or wholly extinct <the zoo languished until it was *resuscitated* by a federal grant – Elizabeth Thalman> <the peoples of the world

... were *resuscitated* by the inauguration of the Roman peace – A. J. Toynbee>
restrain, check, curb, bridle *shared meaning* : to hold back from or control in doing something. **Restrain,** the comprehensive term, suggests holding back by force or persuasion from acting or from going to extremes <to produce in the child the same respect for the garden that *restrains* the grown-ups from picking wantonly – Bertrand Russell> <he had hardly *restrained* himself from saying something very bitter, archly insulting – William Styron> **Check** implies restraining or impeding a progress, activity, or impetus <*check* for a time the inward sweeping waves of melancholy – Louis Bromfield> <the ambition of churchmen to shine in worldly contests is disciplined and *checked* by the broader interests of the Church – Henry Adams> **Curb** can imply either a sharp, drastic bringing under control <they deplore the excesses but deny society's responsibility to *curb* them – Mary J. White> or a restraining influence that tends to moderate or restrict <the sober scientific method does not stimulate the imagination; it *curbs* it – S. M. Crothers> **Bridle** stresses a bringing and keeping under control (as by subduing, moderating, or holding in) <*bridle* one's curiosity> <endowed ... with zest, with abundance, with romping blood. She had never been *bridled* in mind or body – Francis Hackett> ***ant*** impel, incite, activate, abandon (*oneself*)
restrict – see LIMIT
result – see EFFECT
resuscitate – see RESTORE
retain – see KEEP 2
retaliate – see RECIPROCATE
retard – see DELAY ***ant*** accelerate, advance, further
reticent – see SILENT ***ant*** frank
retire – see GO
retort – see ANSWER
retract – see RECEDE ***ant*** protract
retreat – see RECEDE
retrench – see SHORTEN
retrograde – see RECEDE
return **1 return, revert, recur, recrudesce** *shared meaning* : to go or come back. **Return** may imply a going back to a starting place or a source <they *returned* as wolves *return* to cover, satisfied with the slaughter that they had done – Rudyard Kipling> or a coming back to a former or proper place or condition <now shall the kingdom *return* to the house of David – *1 Kings* 12:26 (AV)> <after this residence they can *return* to their own teaching with a deeper appreciation of current work in all the areas of humanistic study – M. S. Eisenhower> **Revert** is likely to imply a going back to a former, often a lower, condition <the conception of a lordly splendid destiny for the human race, to which we are false when we *revert* to wars and other atavistic follies – Bertrand Russell> but it can also apply to a returning after interruption <at the end of a lease property *reverts* to the lessor> <after careful consideration he *reverted* to his first decision> **Recur** implies a return, often repeated returns, of something that has happened or been experienced before <the fundamental philosophic belief which has *recurred* consistently in human history – that each individual has a right to a minimal share in the production of his society – Robert Theobald> <suffered from *recurring* headaches> **Recrudesce** implies a returning to life or activity especially as a breaking out anew of something that has been suppressed or kept under control <after an initial subsidence the epidemic *recrudesced* with renewed vigor> <the

general influence . . . which is liable every now and then to *recrudesce* in his absence – Edmund Gurney>
2 see RECIPROCATE
reveal, discover, disclose, divulge, tell, betray *shared meaning*: to make known what has been or should be concealed. **Reveal** may imply an unveiling of what is not clear to human vision <in laws divine, deduced by reason, or to faith *revealed* – William Wordsworth> or may apply to simple disclosure (as of information or a secret) <a foreboding crept into him that if he said nothing now, he would someday soon have a dirtier past to *reveal* – Bernard Malamud> or even inadvertent disclosure <his slovenly speech *revealed* his lack of education> **Discover** implies an uncovering of matters kept secret or not generally known <go draw aside the curtains and *discover* the several caskets to this noble prince – Shak.> <he *discovered* to his friend the sorry state of his finances> **Disclose** may imply a discovering but more often it implies an imparting of information previously held back or kept secret <[he] began to *disclose* his annual income and its sources when he first held political office – Charles Mandel> **Divulge,** otherwise close to disclose, often carries a suggestion of impropriety or breach of confidence <his voice became secretive and confidential, the voice of a man *divulging* fabulous professional secrets – Roald Dahl> **Tell** may come close to *divulge* in implying indiscretion <gentlemen never *tell*> but more often it implies the giving of necessary or helpful information <why didst thou not *tell* me that she was thy wife? – *Gen* 12:18 (AV)> <she never *told* her love – Shak.> **Betray** implies a disclosing that represents a breach of faith <*betray* the secret of a friend> or an involuntary or unconscious revealing <speech will *betray* a man's origins, his education, his outlook on life, his very nature – Eric Malpass> ***ant*** conceal
revenge – see AVENGE
revengeful – see VINDICTIVE
revere, reverence, venerate, worship, adore *shared meaning* : to regard with profound respect and honor. **Revere** stresses deference and tenderness of feeling <that makes her loved at home, *revered* abroad – Robert Burns> <one of the few fictional masterpieces of the age . . . it has been more *revered* than read – Conrad Knickerbocker> **Reverence** presupposes an intrinsic merit and inviolability in the thing, or less often person, honored and a corresponding depth of feeling in the one who reverences <sincerity and simplicity! if I could only say how I *reverence* them – A. C. Benson> <pledged to *reverence* the name of God – F. B. Steck> **Venerate** implies a regarding as holy or sacrosanct because of character, associations, or age <those who *venerate* . . . Dante and Shakespeare and Milton – Havelock Ellis> <you will *venerate* ideas and institutions because they have remained for a long time in force . . . . That is real atrophy of the soul – Victoria Sackville-West> **Worship** implies homage in word or ceremony to or as if to a divine being; in other than divine application it is likely to impute exalted character or outstanding merit to the one worshiped or weakness (as of judgment or sense) to the worshiper <he had the wildness we all *worshiped* – Eudora Welty> <admire the poetry and *worship* the memory of the poet – William DuBois> <foolish mothers *worshiping* and indulging their already spoiled children> **Adore,** otherwise close to *worship,* may stress the notion of an individual and personal approach or attachment <[Satan] said to him: all these will I give thee, if falling down thou wilt *adore* me – *Mt* 4:9 (DV)> <his staff *adored* him, his men worshiped him – W. A. White> ***ant*** flout
reverence *n* **1** see HONOR
2 reverence, awe, fear *shared meaning* : the emotion inspired by something

that arouses one's deep respect or veneration. **Reverence** stresses a recognition of the sacredness or inviolability of the person or thing which stimulates the emotion <a profound *reverence* for and fidelity to the truth – H. L. Mencken> <Richelieu's *reverence* for the throne was constant – Hilaire Belloc> **Awe** fundamentally implies a sense of being overwhelmed or overcome by great superiority or impressiveness and may suggest such varied reactions as standing mute, adoration, profound reverence, terror, or submissiveness <my heart standeth in *awe* of thy word – *Ps* 119:161 (AV)> <make me as the poorest vassal is that doth with *awe* and terror kneel – Shak.> **Fear** in the sense here considered occurs chiefly in religious use and implies awed recognition of divine power and majesty <the *fear* of the Lord is the beginning of wisdom – *Ps* 111:10 (AV)> <calm with *fear* of God's divinity – William Wordsworth>

reverence *vb* – see REVERE

reverse 1 **reverse, transpose, invert** *shared meaning* : to change to the opposite position. **Reverse**, the most general term, may imply change in order, side, position, or meaning; thus, to *reverse* a coin is to turn it upside down; to *reverse* a process is to follow the opposite order or sequence; to *reverse* a judgment is to replace it with another contrary to it; to *reverse* an automobile is to make it go backward instead of forward. **Transpose** implies a change in order or relative position of units often through exchange of positions <had *transposed* economy and security in his table of priorities – *Atlantic*> **Invert** basically implies a change from one side to another, typically by turning upside down but sometimes by turning inside out or end for end <*invert* a bowl> <*invert* a piece of type> but in its more general use comes very close to *reverse* <both poems *invert* the original affective situation, turning despair into success – Malcolm Brown>
2 see REVOKE

revert – see RETURN

revile – see SCOLD *ant* laud

revise – see CORRECT *vb*

revive – see RESTORE

revivify – see RESTORE

revoke, reverse, repeal, rescind, recall *shared meaning* : to undo something previously done. In legal context these terms though similar in basic meaning are rarely interchangeable without loss of precision. **Revoke** implies a calling back that annuls what was previously done; thus, a testator may *revoke* a will and make a new one; a benefactor may *revoke* a gift to an institution; the registrar *revokes* the operator's license of a drunken driver. **Reverse** usually applies specifically to a high court's action in overthrowing a disputed law, decree, or court decision <the court of appeals *reversed* the opinion of the circuit court> **Repeal** usually implies revocation of a law or ordinance by the legislative body that made it but may be extended to other nullifications of something firmly in effect <when automation has thrown most people out of work and the curse of Adam is at last *repealed* – R. M. Hutchins> **Rescind** implies the exercise of proper authority in abolishing or making void <the council . . . had . . . power over the senate and other magistrates, *rescinding* their decisions – Henry Hallam> **Recall**, a less technical term, can replace any of the others <they *recalled* the hasty decree – Edward Gibbon>

revolt – see REBELLION

revolution – see REBELLION

rhapsody – see BOMBAST

rhythm, meter, cadence *shared meaning* : the more or less regular rise and fall in intensity of sounds that is associated especially with poetry and music.

Rhythm implies movement and flow as well as an agreeable succession of rising and falling sounds and the recurrence at fairly regular intervals of a stress (as a prolonged syllable or an accented note) <the wavering, lovely *rhythms* of the sea – Rose Macaulay> **Meter** implies the reduction of rhythm to system and measure and the establishment of a definite rhythmical pattern <the only strict antithesis to prose is *meter* – William Wordsworth> **Cadence** may be equivalent to *rhythm* or to *meter* or may stress variety in ordered sequence, often with falling or rising effects <I could hear the *cadence* of his voice and that was all, nothing but the measured rise and fall of syllables – J. P. Marquand>

ribald – see COARSE

rich, wealthy, affluent, well-off, well-to-do, opulent *shared meaning* : having goods, property, and money in abundance. **Rich** implies having more than enough to gratify normal needs and desires <our increasingly *rich* citizenry> <the *richest* nation in the world> **Wealthy** stresses the abundant possession of property and intrinsically valuable things and more often than *rich* suggests luxury and a way of life in keeping with one's wealth and position <she was indeed *rich,* according to the standards of the Square; nay, *wealthy!* – Arnold Bennett> <the word *"wealthy,"* as he says it, is redolent of a life spiced and sumptuous – Walker Percy> **Affluent** implies prosperity; beyond this, it may suggest constantly increasing material possessions <this is an *affluent* society. In 1955 only 40% of the U.S. families had annual incomes in excess of $5,000. By 1963, 63% were making over $5,000 – R. W. O'Neill> or it, like **well-off** and **well-to-do,** may apply to a level of prosperity above the average but below that usually implied by *rich* or *wealthy* <the *rich* man enjoys total economic freedom, whereas the merely *affluent* one depends on others to a certain degree – J. K. Hutchens> <a favorite early-day stopping place for *well-to-do* travelers. The less *affluent* parked their wagons in the yard, and slept . . . on the floor of the wagon house – *Amer. Guide Series: Texas*> <let their daughter break her engagement to a *well-off* butcher – Henry Hewes> **Opulent,** applied less often to persons than to things, is likely to stress ostentatious display of prosperity; thus, a person in *affluent* circumstances may or may not maintain an *opulent* establishment, for *affluent* suggests the inflow of money and *opulent* lavish expenditure <the food is *opulent* and priced accordingly – Clementine Paddleford> <an *opulent* entertainment> ***ant*** poor

ridicule, deride, mock, taunt, twit, rally *shared meaning* : to make an object of laughter. **Ridicule** implies either deliberate and often malicious or quite impersonal belittling <the man who wants to preserve his personal identity is *ridiculed* as an eccentric or resented as a snob – S. J. Harris> <death and disease *ridicule* man's petty arrogance – Harriet Zinnes> **Deride** implies a bitter or contemptuous spirit <he took his revenge on the fate that had made him sad by fiercely *deriding* everything – Aldous Huxley> **Mock** stresses scornful decision and the expression of defiance and contempt <a joke was a good way to *mock* reality, to dodge an issue, to escape involvement – Helen MacInnes> <he never spoke of . . . the Church except in tones of sanctimonious respect, nor did he openly *mock* her devoutness – H. C. Hervey> **Taunt** implies both mockery and reproach, typically by means of jeering insults <the mill foreman so *taunted* the workers, so badgered them and told them that they dared not quit – Sinclair Lewis> **Twit** may come close to *taunt* and imply a mocking or cruel casting up of something distressing or embarrassing <the absence of ideas with which Matthew Arnold *twits* them – W. R. Inge> but it, like **rally,** usually implies good-natured raillery or friendly ridicule <the paper delights in *twitting* new laws – *Newsweek*><a useful place for getting away from the cheery *rallying* of . . . the English governess – Nancy Hale>

ridiculous – see LAUGHABLE

rife – see PREVAILING

right – see CORRECT *adj* ***ant*** wrong

righteous – see MORAL ***ant*** iniquitous

rigid **1** see STIFF ***ant*** elastic

2 rigid, rigorous, strict, stringent *shared meaning* : extremely severe or stern. **Rigid** implies uncompromising inflexibility <*rigid* discipline> <a proud, bitter, and *rigid* man whom his children were never glad to see come home – *Current Biog.*> <a *rigid,* totalitarian structure, altogether unadapted to the 20th century – J. L. Hess> **Rigorous** implies the imposition of hardship and difficulty <he liked good food and knew that he did and he was *rigorous* with himself about his waistline – Pearl Buck> <a *rigorous* climate> <maintain a *rigorous* work schedule> **Strict** emphasizes undeviating conformity to rules, standards, or requirements <a *strict* disciplinarian> <*strict* vegetarians> <conducted their business under a system of control that was *strict* and even paternalistic – Gerald Carson> **Stringent** suggests restrictions or limitations that curb or coerce <the *stringent* limitations on the power of the Hebrew kings – Robert Gordis> <colleges with the most *stringent* admissions requirements – N. O. Frederiksen> ***ant*** lax

rigor – see DIFFICULTY ***ant*** amenity

rigorous – see RIGID

rile – see IRRITATE

rim – see BORDER

rip – see TEAR

ripen – see MATURE

rise – see SPRING ***ant*** abate

risky – see DANGEROUS

rival **1** see MATCH

2 rival, compete, vie, emulate *shared meaning* : to strive to equal or surpass. **Rival** usually suggests an attempt to outdo each other <a work . . . which contending sects have *rivaled* each other in approving – Reginald Heber> **Compete** stresses a struggle for an objective that may be conscious but is typically a quite impersonal striving <the student must be free of concerns which *compete* with open-minded intellectual curiosity – M. S. Eisenhower> <the important point is that the teen-agers learn to share the parent's time, rather than *compete* for it – C. E. Phillips> **Vie** suggests less intense effort but more conscious awareness of an opponent than *compete* <the calypso singers who . . . *vie* with one another in duels of lyrical improvisation – *Lamp*> <in our nationalistic propaganda, we have lately been *vying* with the Russians in an ostrich-like and naïve absurdity – Edmund Wilson> **Emulate** implies a conscious effort to equal or surpass one that serves as a model <a simplicity *emulated* without success by numerous modern poets – T. S. Eliot> <in order to outdo, we first imitate, then *emulate.* If greatness is any part of our projected lives, then we are born imitators and competitors of the classic – William Arrowsmith>

rive – see TEAR

robbery – see THEFT

robust – see HEALTHY ***ant*** frail, feeble

rock – see SHAKE

roily – see TURBID

root – see ORIGIN

rot – see DECAY
rotate, alternate *shared meaning* : to succeed or cause to succeed each other in turn. **Rotate,** which may be used of two or more, implies indefinite repetition of the order of succession; thus, a *rotating* shift is one in which each worker passes a set period on the first, second, and third shifts again and again; one *rotates* crops who grows different things in a regular succession on the same land, usually to maintain or improve fertility. **Alternate,** which is referable only to two, implies repetition but does not carry as strong a suggestion of continuity as *rotate* <*alternate* heat and cold in treating a sprain> <the weather *alternated* between blinding sandstorms and brilliant sunlight – Willa Cather>
rough 1 rough, harsh, uneven, rugged, scabrous *shared meaning* : not smooth or even. **Rough** implies the presence of detectable inequalities (as points, bristles, projections, or ridges) <*rough* ground> <a *rough* tweed> <*rough* chapped skin> **Harsh** implies a surface or texture distinctly unpleasant to the touch <a *harsh* cotton towel> **Uneven** implies a lack of regularity in height, breadth, or quality <an *uneven* floor> <an *uneven* hem> **Rugged** implies irregularity or roughness of land surface and connotes difficulty of travel <touched down on the *rugged* lunar surface – Irwin Stambler> <even on *rugged,* rutted byroads, earthbound trucks today can offer shippers the smoothness of an air ride – *Dupont Mag.*> **Scabrous** basically implies roughness of surface <a *scabrous* leaf> <cold sand *scabrous* with cockles – J. M. Brinnin> and may often connote an unwholesome, decayed, or diseased appearance <patches of darker plaster, of *scabrous* paint – Edith C. Rivett> <the yellowed, *scabrous* flesh, which looked only too much like pictures she had once seen in a medical book – William Styron>
ant smooth
2 see RUDE ***ant*** gentle
rout – see CONQUER
rude, rough, crude, raw, callow, green *shared meaning* : lacking in social refinement. **Rude** implies ignorance of or indifference to good form; it may suggest intentional discourtesy <a *rude,* domineering, arrogant type of man, without cultivation or culture – W. L. Shirer> <he was *rude* to his . . . hosts, especially in public – S. E. Ambrose> **Rough** is likely to stress lack of polish but it need not imply positively unpleasant qualities <a plain, *rough,* honest man, and wise, tho' not learned – Joseph Addison> **Crude** may emphasize a predisposition to the gross, simple, obvious, or primitive and an ignorance of the amenities <the marks of the thoroughbred were simply not there. The man was blatant, *crude,* overly confidential – H. L. Mencken> **Raw** suggests being untested, inexperienced, or unfinished <compared with her, he felt vague and *raw,* incapable of coming to terms with life – Victoria Sackville-West> **Callow** applies to the immature and suggests such youthful qualities as naïveté, simplicity, and lack of sophistication <an embarrassingly *callow* master of ceremonies – *New Yorker*> <what had amused me in the *callowest* days of my youth – Babette Deutsch> **Green** implies inexperience and lack of assurance, especially in a new or complex situation <he has taken me for a *green* country girl, impressed with him because he is from the city – Sherwood Anderson>
rugged – see ROUGH ***ant*** fragile
ruin *n* **ruin, havoc, devastation, destruction** *shared meaning* : the bringing about of or the results of disaster. **Ruin** suggests collapse and is applicable to whatever has through decay, corruption, neglect, or loss given way or fallen apart <the old house had fallen to *ruin*> <cases of hopeless *ruin* . . . in which the body has first been ruined through neglect or vice – C.

W. Eliot> **Havoc** suggests an agent that pillages, destroys, or ravages and the resulting confusion and disorder <appalled by the *havoc* and loss of life caused by the earthquake – F. J. Crowley> <hookworms live a long, long time in the small intestine, creating *havoc* all the while – V. G. Heiser> **Devastation** basically implies a widespread laying waste (as by war or a natural catastrophe) <the terrible *devastation* wrought by the great tidal wave – T. H. Huxley> but it is also applicable to something that overwhelms an individual with comparable decisiveness <the *devastation* in her health that was soon to be revealed – Havelock Ellis> **Destruction** suggests utter undoing by or as if by demolition or annihilation <an unjust society wreaks cruel if subtle imprisonments and *destructions* of personal energy – Norman Mailer> <with economic and social *destruction* as the penalty for dissent – Archibald MacLeish>

ruin *vb* **ruin, wreck, dilapidate** *shared meaning* **:** to subject to forces that are destructive of soundness, worth, or usefulness. **Ruin** usually suggests the action of destructive agencies and the ending of the integrity, value, beauty, or well-being of something or someone or the loss of something vital (as to happiness or success) <those sins of the body which smear and sully, debase and degrade, destroy and *ruin* – J. T. Farrell> <a reputation *ruined* by rumor> <too much rain *ruined* the crops> **Wreck** implies a ruining by or as if by crashing or being shattered and, especially in extended uses, is likely to suggest damage that is beyond repair <courts ... have in the past understood that this [the academic] community is something special and might be easily *wrecked* if the law were insensitively applied – J. A. Perkins> <health *wrecked* by dissipation> **Dilapidate** historically implies ruin resulting from neglect or abuse <the church ... was ... shamefully suffered to *dilapidate* by deliberate robbery and frigid indifference – Samuel Johnson> but in more general use it implies a shabby, run-down, or tumbledown condition without direct suggestion of culpability <the ... furniture is *dilapidated* by use, by having frequently been moved from house to house – Janet Flanner> <the Englishman ... who had totted up too many years in the Orient, a *dilapidating* cynic, who had seen too much of life to give a damn any longer – Vanya Oakes>

rule *n* – see LAW

rule *vb* – see DECIDE, GOVERN

ruminate – see PONDER

rumor – see REPORT

rural, rustic, pastoral, bucolic *shared meaning* **:** of or characteristic of the country. **Rural,** the comprehensive term, implies a contrast to *urban* and may refer to open country with or without a suggestion of agricultural pursuits and the pleasures of country life <they were well-off by *rural* standards> <a peaceful *rural* scene> **Rustic** is often interchangeable with *rural* but somewhat more likely to be chosen to describe less pleasing aspects of country life <rude carts, bespattered with *rustic* mire – Charles Dickens> or to stress a contrast with the refinements of city or town <if education had not meddled with her *rustic* nature – Jean Stafford> **Pastoral** implies an idealized simplicity and peacefulness and apartness from the bustling world <to *pastoral* dales, thin-set with modest farms – William Wordsworth> <a land of prim *pastoral* fences, virgin timber, grazing sheep and Anglo-Saxons – William Styron> **Bucolic,** a curiously dichotomous word, may on the one hand be a close synonym of *pastoral* in stressing the charm of rural environment and life <there is here a *bucolic* atmosphere of peculiar beauty and inspiration – Sacheverell Sitwell> <like a man from the city who longs for the *bucolic* pleasures – Kenneth Roberts> or on the other come close to *rustic* in application to the crudity and lack of refinement of rural life or people <huge, mulish, with a gargantuan smile and the *bucolic* talk of the country lawyer – Marya Mannes> <to give up all the city's life . . . for the *bucolic* tedium of a Pennsylvania farm – he couldn't do it – Thomas Wolfe>

ruse – see TRICK

rustic – see RURAL

ruth – see SYMPATHY

sack – see RAVAGE

sacred, sacrosanct, inviolate, inviolable *shared meaning* : protected (as by law, custom, or human respect) against abuse. **Sacred** implies either a setting apart (as for a special use) <middle-class people, with their almost *sacred* conception of private property – Russell Dynes & E. L. Quarantelli> <the battered chair by the fireside that was *sacred* to father> or a special quality that leads to an almost religious reverence <majority rule, which is *sacred* to Western democracy, is often offensive to the African tradition of decision by consensus – William Attwood> **Sacrosanct** in general use may retain its religious implication of the utmost of sacredness <the strikers . . . respected the *sacrosanct* character of the mails, and were willing to undertake their delivery to the pier – V. G. Heiser> or it may take on an ironic quality and suggest an imputed rather than a real sacredness <those who feel that all socially critical art is unpatriotic, that established figures and institutions are *sacrosanct* – *Times Lit. Supp.*> *Inviolate* and *inviolable* apply to things (as laws, agreements, institutions, or persons) that for one reason or another are secure from abuse or injury; distinctively, **inviolate** stresses the fact of not having been violated while **inviolable** implies a character that does not admit of violation; thus, one holds a vow *inviolable* but keeps his vow *inviolate* <desired the Italian culture to be *inviolate* and predominant – John Buchan> <thinking of conscience as an *inviolable* source of moral certitude – Lucius Garvin>

sacrilege – see PROFANATION

sacrosanct – see SACRED

safe, secure *shared meaning* : free from danger or risk. These terms, though sometimes interchangeable and often applicable to the same things, are likely to be quite distinct in their typical implications. **Safe** can imply that a risk has been run without incurring harm or damage <the rocks were to windward on our quarter, and we were *safe* – Frederick Marryat> or can stress freedom from risk <let the great world rage! We will stay here *safe* in the quiet dwellings – P. B. Shelley> or can suggest a character that eliminates or minimizes risk <a strong *safe* bridge> <*safe* investments> **Secure** usually stresses a freedom from apprehension or anxiety of danger or risk based on grounds that appear sound and sufficient <a provident, rather thoughtful people, who made their livelihood *secure* by raising crops and fowl – Willa Cather> <reached a *secure* harbor before the storm broke> <their manner so *secure* from any conceivable bewilderment or confusion – Victoria Sackville-West> *ant* dangerous, unsafe

safeguard – see DEFEND

saga – see MYTH

sagacious – see SHREWD

sage – see WISE

salary – see WAGE

salient — see NOTICEABLE

same, selfsame, very, identical, equivalent, equal *shared meaning* : not different from another or others or not differing from each other. **Same** may imply, and **selfsame** invariably implies, that the things under consideration are in reality one and not two or more different things <they take their children to the *same* doctor that they went to as children> <this is the *selfsame* book I borrowed from you> But *same* may also be applied to things actually distinct but without appreciable difference <eat the *same* rations as the captain – H. A. Chippendale> **Very,** like *selfsame,* implies identity <that is the *very* thing that I was saying – P. B. Shelley> <at that *very* moment United States shipping was suffering – C. S. Forester> **Identical** may imply either selfsameness <we went back to the *identical* spot where we had stopped before> or absolute agreement in all details <a block-long rectangle of nearly *identical* backyards – J. T. Farrell> **Equivalent** implies amounting to the same thing (as in worth or import) <[organized] protest . . . may lead the way to the moral *equivalent* for riots – Harvey Wheeler> <barter involves the exchange of one thing for another of *equivalent* value> **Equal** implies complete correspondence (as in number, size, or value) and therefore equivalence but not selfsameness <the right to receive *equal* salaries for *equal* work> <before the academic bar, all students are not *equal.* Five minutes with a bright student may be *equal* to an hour with a slow one – J. A. Perkins> ***ant*** different

sample — see INSTANCE

sanctimonious — see DEVOUT, HYPOCRITICAL

sanction — see APPROVE ***ant*** interdict

sand — see FORTITUDE

sane — see WISE ***ant*** insane

sangfroid — see EQUANIMITY

sanitize — see STERILIZE

sap — see WEAKEN

sapient — see WISE

sarcasm — see WIT

sarcastic, satiric, ironic, sardonic *shared meaning* : marked by bitterness and a power or intent to cut or sting. **Sarcastic** implies an intent to wound by deriding, taunting, or making ridiculous <although he is ordinarily affable . . . he can be sharp and *sarcastic* in committee hearings – *Current Biog.*> <*sarcastic* comments on an actor's performance> **Satiric** implies an intent to censure by holding up to ridicule and reprobation <all this comedy was filled with bitter *satiric* strokes against a certain young lady – W. M. Thackeray> **Ironic** implies an amusing, piquant, startling, or surprising difference between what is said and what is intended <a wryly *ironic* dissertation on how man is rapidly developing . . . ways to render himself extinct – *Playboy*> or between what is given out and accepted and what is really true <how exquisitely *ironic* is the entertainment we can derive from our disillusions – L. P. Smith> **Sardonic** implies a disbelief in or doubt about values that manifests itself in scorn, mockery, and derision <*sardonic* laughter> <an eccentric, gangling man, whose *sardonic* wit somewhat compensated for his shallow mind – W. L. Shirer>

sardonic — see SARCASTIC

sate — see SATIATE

satellite — see FOLLOWER

satiate, sate, surfeit, cloy, pall, glut, gorge *shared meaning* : to fill to repletion. Both **satiate** and **sate** can imply either a complete satisfying or, more often, an overfilling or overfeeding to the point of distaste <the ordinary Roman . . . *satiated* alike with the fervors of the democrats and the rigidity of the

conservatives – John Buchan> <so overwhelmed by information . . . that curiosity becomes *sated,* discrimination dulled – W. R. Parker> **Surfeit** implies a feeding or supplying to the point of nausea or disgust <if music be the food of love, play on; give me excess of it, that, *surfeiting,* the appetite may sicken, and so die – Shak.> **Cloy** stresses the disgust or boredom that results from a surfeiting <poetic wit itself is a rarity . . . . Large indiscriminate doses of it tend to *cloy* – H. V. Gregory> **Pall** stresses the loss of all power to attract or interest on the part of something with which one is surfeited <there anguish does not sting; nor pleasure *pall* – John Keats> <the rooms of portraits of famous Americans . . . *palled* upon me after a while – John Canaday> **Glut** suggests a full supply or oversupply that chokes or impedes <professors are *glutting* the highways in their Flight From Teaching – W. R. Hutchison> <markets *glutted* with produce> or one that is avidly consumed in a constantly renewed greed, limited only by physical necessity <*glutted,* but not sated with blood – Jane Porter> **Gorge** implies glutting to the point of bursting or choking <fell upon eggs and bacon and *gorged* till he could *gorge* no more – Rudyard Kipling> <the more she heard, the more she wanted to know; there was no *gorging* her to satiety – Samuel Butler † 1902>

satire – see WIT

satiric – see SARCASTIC

satisfied – see under SATISFY 1

satisfy **1 satisfy, content** *shared meaning* : to appease one's desires or longings. Their distinctions in implications are shared by their corresponding adjectives **satisfied** and **content** or **contented.** **Satisfy** implies full appeasement not only of desires or longings but of needs or requirements <*satisfy* the desire for power – W. G. Walter> <the *satisfied* look of a child when it regards in silence some object of its love . . . and finds it good – Thomas Wolfe> <[he] was scrupulous, and certain accepted conventions had forced him to *satisfy* his conscience – Victoria Sackville-West> **Content** implies appeasement to the point where one is not disquieted or disturbed even though every wish is not fully gratified <my own garden must *content* me this year – A. T. Quiller-Couch> <when I was at home, I was in a better place: but travelers must be *content* – Shak.> <I go to him consistently with knotty problems and . . . he always has . . . an answer with which I am *contented* – H. A. Smith> ***ant*** tantalize

2 see PAY

3 satisfy, fulfill, meet, answer *shared meaning* : to measure up to a set of criteria or requirements. **Satisfy** implies adequacy to an end or need in view and often suggests a standard of comparison <he will *satisfy* Newman's famous definition of a gentleman as one who never inflicts pain – C. E. Montague> <a culture which will *satisfy* our needs – J. B. Conant> **Fulfill,** often interchangeable with *satisfy,* may imply more abundance or richness of qualification and a need less calculable, more immeasurable <a son who *fulfilled* his father's fondest hopes> <complementary opposites that balanced and *fulfilled* each other – Thomas Merton> **Meet** implies an exactness of agreement between a requirement and what is submitted to fill it <we must expand the concept of conservation to *meet* the imperious problems of the new age – J. F. Kennedy> <the company has *met* the challenges of competition in a rapidly shifting world scene – *Lamp*> **Answer** usually implies the simple satisfaction of a demand, need, or purpose often in a temporary or expedient manner that may fall short in completeness or adequacy or produce less than complete content <she could ask herself now . . . if any other reasonably attractive man would have *answered* as

well in his place – Ellen Glasgow> <in teaching the young to think hard, any subject will *answer* – C. W. Eliot> <if peace did not serve his purposes, war might *answer* them – Francis Hackett>

saturate – see SOAK

saucy, pert, arch *shared meaning* : flippant and bold in manner or attitude. **Saucy** is likely to stress a piquant levity with a hint of smartness or amusing effrontery <Mencken was no social reformer but a *saucy* iconoclast who had something amusing to say about every region, class, and profession in America – S. E. Morison> and may be applied to birds and small animals on similar grounds <some *saucy* puppies on their hind legs – John Ruskin> **Pert** implies a saucy freedom that may verge on presumption or affectation <a *pert* jackanapes, full of college petulance and self-conceit – Tobias Smollett> and sometimes also suggests sprightliness or cleverness <she spoke in a slightly *pert,* shrill voice, provocative, and answered questions with a certain flare – Arturo Vivante> **Arch** usually implies coquettish or roguish audacity <sly wit, which he delivers in a modest, although *arch* manner – *Current Biog.*> <the [letter] ... was sweetly girlish, and just a wee bit *arch;* it hinted that she was only a poor little orphan – Stella D. Gibbons>

saunter, stroll, amble *shared meaning* : to walk slowly and more or less aimlessly. **Saunter** suggests a leisurely pace and an idle and carefree mind <*sauntering* about the streets, loitering in a coffeehouse – Henry Fielding> **Stroll** implies an objective (as sight-seeing or exercise) pursued without haste and often without predetermined path <then we *strolled* for half the day through stately theaters – Alfred Tennyson> <you can hunt mushrooms, pick wild berries, *stroll* hills and visit the site of an old Indian village – Alfred Balk> **Amble** can replace either *saunter* or *stroll* but distinctively it suggests an easy effortless gait like that of an ambling horse <you were just *ambling* around that party, eating, drinking, carefree as a bird – Herman Wouk> <the way he walked ... – that slow, almost a delicate *ambling* walk with a lot of give at the knees – Roald Dahl>

savage – see BARBARIAN, FIERCE

save **1** see RESCUE ***ant*** lose, waste, damn (*in theology*)

2 save, preserve, conserve *shared meaning* : to keep secure from injury, decay, or loss. **Save** in this connection can imply measures taken to protect against danger of loss, injury, or destruction <thou hast ... quitted all to *save* a world from utter loss – John Milton> <if experiments ... prove successful, many of the plantations might be *saved* and Ecuador might return to the list of leading cacao producers – P. E. James> **Preserve** stresses resistance to destructive agencies and implies methods and efforts to keep something intact or in existence <*preserve* food for winter use> <there's nothing like routine and regularity for *preserving* one's peace of mind – Roald Dahl> <develop realistic policies to *preserve* those legal rights already ours and to acquire those legal rights we need – W. D. North> **Conserve** suggests keeping sound and unimpaired (as by the avoidance of undue use or of waste or loss or damage) <one can *"conserve"* an unpolluted river .... But one can only "restore" a legal sewer – S. L. Udall> <the air is recirculated within the cabin in order to *conserve* heat – H. G. Armstrong> ***ant*** spend, consume

savoir faire – see TACT

savor – see TASTE

savory – see PALATABLE ***ant*** bland (*to taste*), acrid (*in taste and smell*)

say, utter, tell, state *shared meaning* : to put into words. **Say** basically means to articulate words <the baby *said* his first word today> <*say* each word carefully and clearly> but it may be used in reporting something voiced <he *said* he would be home soon> or in implying the fact of putting in speech or writing <be careful what you *say* to that man> <pay attention to what I *say*> <someone must *say* what is needed> **Utter** stresses the use of the voice and the act of putting into spoken words <he formed this speech with his lips many times before he could *utter* it – Charles Dickens> and is the one of these terms appropriate for reference to vocal sounds other than words <*utter* a hoarse laugh> <the meadowlark *uttered* her strong but tender note – John Burroughs> **Tell** stresses the imparting of an idea or information rather than the method and may refer to either spoken or written communication or other method that clearly presents an idea to the mind <the book reveals as much as the authors dare *tell* – R. D. Franklin> <priorities *tell* the story. In the last seven years we have spent $384 billion on war, $27 billion on space, and less than $2 billion on community development and housing – W. H. Ferry> **State** may replace *say* when the added implication of clearness and definiteness is needed <one should know what one thinks and what one means, and be able to *state* it in clear terms – Rose Macaulay> <*state* one's objections to a proposal>

scabrous – see ROUGH *ant* glabrous, smooth

scale – see ASCEND

scan – see SCRUTINIZE

scandal – see OFFENSE 2

scant – see MEAGER *ant* plentiful, profuse

scanty – see MEAGER *ant* ample, plentiful, profuse

scarce – see INFREQUENT *ant* abundant

scatter, disperse, dissipate, dispel *shared meaning* : to cause to separate or break up. **Scatter** implies a force that drives parts or units irregularly in different directions <the whip – in fancy he cracked it aloft and sent his adversaries *scattering* – H. C. Hervey> or sometimes a throwing or casting so that the things thrown fall at random <*scatter* grain for chickens> **Disperse** implies a wider separation of units and a complete breaking up of the mass or assemblage <the courts are simply moving into a vacuum left by a *dispersed* and weakened community – J. A. Perkins> <a sea where all the ships in the world might be so *dispersed* as that none should see another – William Cowper> **Dissipate** stresses complete disintegration or dissolution and final disappearance <the sun *dissipated* the morning mist> <had a small patrimony . . . that he *dissipated* before he left college – George Meredith> <protests . . . tends to *dissipate* the sense of frustration felt among students – James Feron> **Dispel** stresses a driving away or getting rid of by or as if by scattering <the rising sun *dispelled* the darkness> <only by admitting our own errors . . . can we . . . *dispel* lingering suspicions of our motives – William Attwood>

scent – see FRAGRANCE, SMELL

scheme – see PLAN

scholarly – see LEARNED

scholarship – see KNOWLEDGE

scholastic – see PEDANTIC

school – see TEACH

scoff, jeer, gibe, fleer, sneer, flout *shared meaning* : to show contempt in derision or mockery. **Scoff** stresses insolence, disrespect, or incredulity as motivating the derision <fools, who came to *scoff*, remained to pray – Oliver Goldsmith> <*scoffed* at the idea that modern man might have developed before Neanderthal – L. C. Eiseley> **Jeer** suggests a coarser, more undiscriminating derision <they would laugh at his warning. They

would *jeer* him and, if practicable, pelt him with missiles – Stephen Crane> **Gibe** implies taunting, either good-naturedly or in sarcastic derision <you . . . with taunts did *gibe* my missive out of audience – Shak.> <teasingly *gibe* a boy over his loss of a girl friend> **Fleer** emphasizes derisive grins, grimaces, and laughter <listened with a *fleering* mouth to his father's long dogmatic grace before meat – Joseph Hergesheimer> **Sneer** strongly implies ill-natured contempt and stresses insulting by facial expression, phrasing, or tone of voice <it has become . . . fashionable to *sneer* at economics and emphasize "the human dilemma" – Norman Mailer> <that's a woman's love, he would *sneer* contemptuously at his wife when he had just humiliated her – J. T. Farrell> **Flout** adds to the implications of the preceding terms one of refusal to heed or denial of a thing's truth or power <people who *flout* convention> <for the past eight years they had watched an administration purposely *flout* the intellectual life – J. A. Michener>

scold, upbraid, berate, rail, revile, vituperate *shared meaning* : to reproach angrily and abusively. **Scold** implies rebuking in irritation or ill temper justly or unjustly <[he] pleaded, cajoled and *scolded* in a vain effort to end the feuding – A. S. Whiting> **Upbraid** stresses censuring on more definite grounds and usually with justification <I think he'd meant to *upbraid* me for sneaking off, but he didn't – Willa Cather> **Berate** suggests prolonged and often abusive scolding <for years, Anne had heard her mother *berate* and condemn men. They were no good. They were all like the beasts of the field – J. T. Farrell> **Rail** (with *at* or *against*) implies an unrestrained berating <enemies . . . *rail* at him for crimes he is not guilty of – *Junius*> <*rail* against humanity for not being abstract perfection – T. L. Peacock> **Revile** suggests a scurrilous abusive attack prompted by anger or hatred <the two brothers . . . had *reviled* one another and had thought of the world as a place where the other would be exposed as an evil-tempered fraud – John Cheever> **Vituperate**, close to *revile*, may stress even more the violence and abusiveness of the censure or attack <he *vituperated* from the pulpit the vices of the court – J. A. Froude> <how the sage reviled and *vituperated* the horrors of city life – A. C. Benson>

scorn – see DESPISE

Scotch, Scottish, Scots *shared meaning* : constituting, belonging to, or deriving from Scotland or its people. **Scotch** is more widely used outside Scotland and is likely to occur in casual context or in the spoken language <we referred to ourselves as *Scotch* and not Scots. When, years later, I learned that the usage in Scotland was different it seemed to me rather an affectation – J. K. Galbraith> <a *Scotch* painter> **Scottish** has a more literary, less casual flavor and use <*Scottish* universities> <she left for Edinburgh the following year to assume the *Scottish* crown – Geoffrey Bruun & H. S. Commager> **Scots**, otherwise interchangeable with *Scottish*, may be preferred in reference to law and in historical references to money <a pound *Scots*> In Scotland itself *Scottish* and *Scots* are often preferred to *Scotch* <a delegation of *Scottish* editors – *Scotsman*> <the *Scots* community in New York – *Scotsman*> but *Scotch* is also used <I'm pure *Scotch* . . . . My father was pure *Scotch*. The correct term is *Scottish*, but that sounds so pompous – Margaret, Duchess of Argyll>

Scots – see SCOTCH

Scottish – see SCOTCH

scout – see DESPISE

scowl – see FROWN

scrap – see DISCARD

scrawny – see LEAN ***ant*** brawny, fleshy, obese

screen — see HIDE
scruple — see QUALM
scrupulous **1** see CAREFUL *ant* remiss
2 see UPRIGHT *ant* unscrupulous
scrutinize, scan, inspect, examine *shared meaning*: to look at or over carefully and usually critically. **Scrutinize** implies close observation and attention to minute details <scores of plain-dress detectives closely *scrutinized* the bidden guests as they arrived – Lucius Beebe> <immigration officials carefully *scrutinized* the passengers' entry permits – Robert Sherrod> **Scan** implies a point-to-point survey that may involve careful scrutiny or may be cursory <stooping over as he went, his eyes *scanning* every foot of the ground – O. E. Rölvaag> <*scanned* . . . yesterday's . . . paper that he had already thoroughly read – Bernard Malamud> **Inspect** is likely to imply a searching scrutiny for possible errors, defects, flaws, or shortcomings <he enacted a series of sweeping reforms after *inspecting* every prison in the country – *Current Biog.*> **Examine** implies a close scrutiny or investigation in order to determine the nature, condition, or quality of a thing <he will have to *examine* his own attitudes to avoid tripping over his own doubts – Harry Levinson> <undying trivialities which the public find romantic without seeking to *examine* them for truth – J. F. Gore>
scurrility — see ABUSE
scurvy — see CONTEMPTIBLE
seasonable, timely, opportune, pat *shared meaning* : being appropriate to the time or situation. **Seasonable** implies appropriate to the season or perfectly fitted to the occasion or situation <*seasonable* weather> <his caution was . . . *seasonable,* and his advice . . . good – Daniel Defoe> **Timely** applies to what occurs or appears at the time or moment when it is most useful or valuable <to me alone there came a thought of grief: a *timely* utterance gave that thought relief – William Wordsworth> <saved from the flames by *timely* aid – Charles Dickens> **Opportune** describes something that comes, often by chance, at the best possible moment and invites being capitalized on <this was not the fulfillment of any program but the result of *opportune* variations . . . which . . . enabled the animals to cope with unpredictable changed conditions – G. G. Simpson> **Pat** may apply to what is notably apt, ready, or well-timed to the occasion <this *pat* tale got a big laugh – Dorothy Barclay> or to what is so very apt as to be suspect <he has . . . acquired a tolerance of viewpoints not his own and a wariness of ideological clichés and *pat* solutions – M. S. Eisenhower> *ant* unseasonable
seclusion — see SOLITUDE
secret, covert, stealthy, furtive, clandestine, surreptitious, underhand, underhanded *shared meaning* : existing or done in such a way as to evade attention or observation. **Secret** implies concealment on any grounds and from any motive <a beautiful woman . . . shrewd, mature, *secret,* betraying her real self to none – Victoria Sackville-West> <a *secret* passage in an old castle> <he imagined his father's *secret* dismay as he found himself less able . . ., his strength fading, his mind less alive – Pearl Buck> **Covert** stresses the fact of not being open or declared <his *covert* alliance against the House of Austria – Hilaire Belloc> **Stealthy** suggests taking pains to avoid being seen or heard, especially in some misdoing <murder . . . with his *stealthy* pace . . . towards his design moves like a ghost – Shak.> <in contrast to the *stealthy* looting that occasionally occurs in disaster situations, looting in civil disturbances is quite open and frequently collective – Russell Dynes & E. L. Quarantelli> **Furtive** implies a sly or timid stealthiness <the *furtive* sex fumbling that all boys her own age considered natural and in

fact obligatory – Herman Wouk> **Clandestine** implies secrecy usually for an evil or illicit purpose <[they] kept open a *clandestine* pipeline to the seats of power – Frank Graham> <Germany's *clandestine* rearmament – W. L. Shirer> **Surreptitious** applies to actions done, emotions cherished, or things held or enjoyed secretly, often with opportune cleverness and against usage or authority <enjoying a *surreptitious* cigarette – P. G. Wodehouse> <glancing at the clock with a *surreptitious* eye – H. S. Scott> **Underhand** and **underhanded** stress mean or dishonest intent more than the mere fact of secrecy <he had suspected his agent of some *underhand* dealings – Jane Austen> <a coward with an *underhand* streak of cruelty – G. J. Becker> <he did not look quite like a professional gambler, but something . . . suggested an *underhanded* mode of life – Willa Cather>

secrete – see HIDE

secretive – see SILENT

section – see PART

secure *adj* – see SAFE ***ant*** precarious, dangerous

secure *vb* – see ENSURE, GET

sedate – see SERIOUS ***ant*** flighty

sedition, treason *shared meaning* : a serious breach of allegiance. **Sedition** implies conduct leading to or inciting commotion or resistance to authority but without overt violence or betrayal <*sedition* is . . . a matter of expressing opinions, not of committing acts – *Reporter*> **Treason** implies overt action aiming at the overthrow of one's government or its betrayal to an enemy <one cannot commit *treason* simply by talking or conspiring against the government; he must actually do something, and there must be witnesses – F. A. Ogg & P. O. Ray> <*sedition* . . . is traitorous behavior that falls short of *treason* because it does not actively levy war . . . or give aid to an enemy. . . . It stirs up resistance to law or encourages conduct that may become *treason* – M. T. Smelser & J. G. Kerwin>

seduce – see LURE

sedulous – see BUSY

see, look, watch *shared meaning* : to perceive something by use of the eyes. **See** stresses the fact of receiving visual impressions <she *sees* well with her new glasses> <one cannot *see* in the absence of light> **Look** stresses the directing of the eyes to or the fixing of the eyes on something <Indians with curious pointed straw hats *looked* in and out again – Graham Greene> <I sit up in bed beside him and *look* and *look* my eyes out at him – R. P. Jhabvala> **Watch** implies a following of something with one's eyes so as to keep it under constant observation <*watching* the clock as closely as a cat *watches* a mouse>

seem, look, appear *shared meaning* : to give the impression of being as stated without necessarily being so in fact. These terms are often used interchangeably without evident difference <*seem* happy> <*look* contented> <*appear* at ease> But **seem** is likely to suggest an opinion based on subjective impressions and personal reaction <she had *seemed* a capable woman, intent on work. Now, as we sat in her own parlor, she was formidable – R. G. Tugwell> <those attending the Meriden seminar . . . *seemed* receptive and tried hard to get into the spirit of things – W. E. Burrows> while **look** implies an opinion based on general visual impression <her . . . lips *looked* parched and unnatural – Ellen Glasgow> <[he] *looks* a playwright; his appearance fits the part – Alan Rosenthal> **Appear** may convey the same implications as *look* but often it suggests an obviously distorted impression <his tongue . . . could make the worse *appear* the better reason – John Milton> <children and infants engage in behaviors that on a physical level *appear* sexual – William Simon & J. H Gagnon>

<the old case of the circus clown who must be the best acrobat of all to *appear* inept – Pamela Marsh>
seeming – see APPARENT
segment – see PART
seize – see TAKE
select, elect, picked, exclusive *shared meaning* : set apart by some superior character or quality. **Select** refers to one chosen with discrimination in preference to others of the same class <the hotel caters to a *select* clientele> <this weighty enterprise in *select* bibliography for the general reader – *Times Lit. Supp.*> or may be used in the sense of *superior* or *exceptional* with little or no suggestion of choice <persecution . . . which bows down and crushes all but a very few *select* spirits – T. B. Macaulay> **Elect** in all its senses stresses the notion of being chosen and in the present relation carries a strong implication of admission to a restricted or inner circle and often one of special privilege <that delicious phantom of being an *elect* spirit . . . unlike the crowd – Charles Kingsley> **Picked** commonly applies to what is conspicuously superior and may suggest the best available <the candidates were all *picked* men> **Exclusive** basically implies a character that sets apart or rules out whatever is not compatible or congruous <*exclusive* concepts – animal and vegetable, for instance – Francis Bowen> <didacticism and a sense of humor are mutually *exclusive* qualities – J. L. Lowes> but in respect to persons, groups, or institutions is likely to suggest a feeling of superiority as the basis for ruling out what is felt as beneath imposed standards or fastidious and critical requirements <the *exclusive* caste system of a rigid feudalism – Laurence Binyon> <the sense of authority in a public official tends to become arbitrary and *exclusive* – *Vineyard Gazette*> <an *exclusive* social set> ***ant*** indiscriminate
selection – see CHOICE *n* ***ant*** rejection
self-abnegation – see RENUNCIATION
self-assertive – see AGGRESSIVE
self-denial – see RENUNCIATION
self-possession – see CONFIDENCE
selfsame – see SAME ***ant*** diverse
sensation, sense, feeling, sensibility *shared meaning* : the power to respond or the capacity for or act of responding to stimuli. **Sensation** may center attention on the fact of perception through or as if through the sense organs, with or without comprehension <tapped her left foot on the porch boards in rhythm, and had the illusion of a *sensation* of the nerves in her right leg quivering to the rhythm of a fast fox trot – J. T. Farrell> <the visual impression is a *sensation* and is derived from past experience – Adelbert Ames, Jr.> **Sense** may differ little from *sensation* <as the fire burned lower a *sense* of chill crept over them> or it may be applied specifically to any one of the basic perceptive powers <the *sense* of smell> but in its typical application to the power or act of responding to stimuli it tends to stress intellectual awareness and full consciousness <a deep *sense* of loss . . . – a *sense* of loss and unbelief such as one might feel to discover suddenly that some great force in nature had ceased to operate – Thomas Wolfe> <there is . . . an underlying *sense* of pathos and human feeling which is irresistible – Lionel Collier> <the *sense* of frustration felt among students – James Feron> **Feeling** may apply to sensations (as touch, heat, cold, pressure) that are perceived through the skin <so cold she had no *feeling* in her fingers> <a *feeling* of gentle warmth> or to a complex response to stimulation involving sensation, emotion, and a degree of thought <the *feeling* that there was something to be gained by every personality in the group – W. J. Pelton> or to the power to respond <profoundly

feeling as she was, she shrank with physical distaste from emotionalism – Pearl Buck> **Sensibility** often replaces *feeling* in this last use, especially when a keenly impressionable nature is to be implied <the extreme *sensibility* to physical suffering which characterizes modern civilization – W. R. Inge> or excessive or affected responsiveness suggested <the nerveless sentimentalist and dreamer, who spends his life in a weltering sea of *sensibility* – William James>

sense **1** see SENSATION

2 see MEANING

3 sense, common sense, gumption, judgment, wisdom *shared meaning* : ability to reach intelligent conclusions. **Sense** implies a reliable ability to judge and decide with soundness, prudence, and intelligence <the only one that has any *sense* in that family – Margaret Deland> <seems to have read every writer of importance . . . and he talks about them with clarity and sound *sense* – Dudley Fitts> **Common sense** suggests ordinary good judgment and prudence, often with native shrewdness but without sophistication, learning, or special knowledge <taking the dramatically symbolic step of working as a labourer. But he had the *common sense* to do it for only six months in each year – *Times Lit. Supp.*> <the *common sense* of common men . . . has not been seriously affected by these still academic aberrations of our alleged wise men – Reinhold Niebuhr> **Gumption** suggests a readiness to use or apply common sense and is likely to stress initiative or drive <a man's common sense means his good judgment, his freedom from eccentricity, his *gumption* – William James> <the pioneer had *gumption* enough to unpack once he had arrived – George Ade> **Judgment** implies sense tempered and refined by experience, training, and maturity <the *judgment* and recommendation of the professional are not open to question or debate by the layman. The professional knows – Mary L. Bundy & Paul Wasserman> **Wisdom** implies sense and judgment far above the average <common sense in an uncommon degree is what the world calls *wisdom* – S. T. Coleridge> <tradition . . . is the accumulated *wisdom* of the race . . . : it is those works of the mind which illuminate or are likely to illuminate human life under any conditions that may arise – R. M. Hutchins>

sensibility – see SENSATION

sensible **1** see AWARE ***ant*** insensible (*of* or *to*)

2 see PERCEPTIBLE ***ant*** insensible

3 see WISE ***ant*** absurd, foolish, fatuous, asinine

sensitive – see LIABLE ***ant*** insensitive

sensual – see CARNAL, SENSUOUS

sensuous, sensual, luxurious, voluptuous, epicurean *shared meaning* : relating to or providing pleasure through gratification of the senses. Both *sensuous* and *sensual* apply to things of the senses as opposed to things of the spirit or intellect; distinctively **sensuous** tends to suggest an aesthetic gratification (as in beauty of color, sound, or artistic form) without the implication of grossness or carnality in indulgence of the appetites that is regularly present in **sensual** <Chinese painters are not, like the Persians, absorbed in expressing their *sensuous* delight in the wonder and glory of the world – Laurence Binyon> <arise and fly the reeling faun, the *sensual* feast – Alfred Tennyson> <[his] *sensuous* descriptive prose, which sets a scene in terms of emotional response – *Newsweek*> <not that food which entereth into the mouth defileth a man, but the appetite with which it is eaten. It is neither the quality nor the quantity, but the devotion to *sensual* savors – H. D. Thoreau> **Luxurious** implies indulgence in sensual or sensuous pleasures and often suggests a resulting pleasant languor, delightful ease, or grateful peace of mind <gave a cautious sniff, and then a *luxurious* one – Jan

Struther> <the fatuous air of *luxurious* abandon . . . as she danced with the prince – Cyril Connolly> <looked like something Picasso might have turned out in a particularly *luxurious* mood – Joseph Alsop> **Voluptuous** implies more definitely an abandonment to sensual or sensuous pleasure for its own sake <fair fallacious looks . . . softened with pleasure and *voluptuous* life – John Milton> <sat and concentrated upon it with an enjoyment that was little short of *voluptuous* – H. C.. Hervey> **Epicurean** suggests catering to or indulging in the satisfaction of a refined and fastidious taste in usually physical pleasures <any pretext to get this *epicurean* young pianist to play here again would be welcome – Howard Klein> <a people possessed of the *epicurean* rather than the ascetic ideal in morals – W. C. Brownell> <*epicurean* cooks sharpen with cloyless sauce his appetite – Shak.>

sentiment – see FEELING, OPINION

separate *vb* **separate, part, divide, sever, sunder, divorce** *shared meaning* : to become or cause to become disunited or disjoined. **Separate** may imply a putting or keeping apart <*separate* the sheep from the goats> <the Atlantic *separates* Europe from America> <the generations that *separate* us from the pioneers> or a scattering or dispersion of units <families *separated* during the war> or a removal of one thing from another <*separate* a troublemaker from a group of children> **Part** may suggest a definitive separation of two persons or things from close association or union <if aught but death *part* thee and me – *Ruth* 1:17 (AV)> <the cable *parted* under the added strain> **Divide** is likely to stress the idea of the parts or groups resulting from a literal or figurative cutting, breaking, or branching <he that will *divide* a minute into a thousand parts – Shak.> <*divide* existing assets among creditors in proportion to the debts they hold – Jacques Rueff> **Sever** often adds the idea of violence, suggesting forced separation especially of a part from a whole or of individuals joined by close ties <*severed* from thee, can I survive? – Robert Burns> <Columbia has *severed* its institutional ties with the Institute – Sylvan Fox> <*sever* an artery in a fall> **Sunder** is likely to imply a violent tearing or wrenching apart <even as a splitted bark, so *sunder* we – Shak.> <the dearest ties of friendship and of blood were *sundered* – T. B. Macaulay> **Divorce** usually suggests a separating of things so closely associated that they interact upon each other or work well only in union with each other <its academic tendency to *divorce* form from matter – C. D. Lewis> <he had become *divorced* from . . . the capacity to see, to feel as others – H. C. Hervey> In its specific reference to the legal dissolution of a marriage *divorce* contrasts with *separate* which implies a mutually agreed ending of cohabitation. ***ant*** combine

separate *adj* – see DISTINCT, SINGLE

serene – see CALM

serious, grave, solemn, sedate, staid, sober, earnest *shared meaning* : not light or frivolous. **Serious** implies a concern for what really matters <serve the complete cultural needs of the family, furnishing everything from light amusements to *serious* intellectual endeavors – Harvey Wheeler> <a fantasist's pose of authority on such matters is bound to sit ill with a *serious* and progressive physician – Theodore Sturgeon> **Grave** implies both seriousness and dignity in expression or attitude <his air was *grave* and stately, and his manners were very formal – Jane Austen> <so adept at the lovely polishing of every *grave* and lucent phrase – Stella D. Gibbons> **Solemn** is likely to heighten the suggestion of impressiveness or awesomeness often present in *grave* <perhaps it was natural . . . to mistake *solemn* dignity for sullenness – W. L. Shirer> <their talk was . . . touched

with a synthetic exaltation, and its sadness and its mood of fatality gave them a *solemn* sort of joy – William Styron> **Sedate** implies a composed and decorous seriousness <good sense alone is a *sedate* and quiescent quality – Samuel Johnson> <a sowing of wild oats followed by a *sedate,* conservative middle age – Michael Stern> **Staid** suggests a settled, accustomed sedateness and prim self-restraint <living *staid* existences, dull, regular, unexciting and without adventure – J. T. Farrell> **Sober** may stress seriousness of purpose <if our pupils are to devote *sober* attention to our instruction – C. H. Grandgent> but it typically implies gravity attained by habit or the practice of self-discipline <come, pensive Nun, devout and pure, *sober,* steadfast, and demure – John Milton> <a group of *sober* merchants who detested the leveling tendencies – V. L. Parrington> **Earnest** adds to *serious* an implication of zeal or sincerity of purpose <set out on an *earnest* and grim quest for the dollar – Herman Wouk> <nowhere but in the state capitols are able men quite so *earnest* or scoundrels quite so base – Trevor Armbrister> ***ant*** light, flippant

servile – see SUBSERVIENT ***ant*** authoritative

servitude, slavery, bondage *shared meaning* : the state of being subject to a master. **Servitude,** often vague or rhetorical in application, implies in general lack of liberty to do as one pleases <I am as free as Nature first made man, ere the base laws of *servitude* began, when wild in woods the noble savage ran – John Dryden> or, more specifically, lack of freedom to determine one's course of action or way of life <a man sentenced to penal *servitude*> **Slavery** implies subjection to a master who owns one's person and may treat one as property <taken by the insolent foe and sold to *slavery* – Shak.> or sometimes a comparable subservience to something that dominates like a master <deliverance of mankind from the long *slavery* of want, fear and cruelty – Leslie Rees> **Bondage** implies a being bound by law or by other, usually physical, constraint in a state of complete subjection <the *bondage* of the Hebrews in Egypt> <the revolt of a man against the pure footlessness which had held him in *bondage* for half a lifetime – William Styron>

set *vb* **set, settle, fix, establish** *shared meaning* : to put securely in position. **Set** stresses the fact of placing in a definite, often final position or situation or relation <*set* food on the table> <*set* a new hedge> <a ring *set* with a large diamond> <*set* the terms of a contract> <the patristic system of dogma with the antique philosophy *set* the forms of medieval expression – H. O. Taylor> **Settle** carries a stronger suggestion of putting in a place or condition of stability, ease, or security <*settle* an invalid in an easy chair> <*settled* themselves gradually in their new home> <*settle* down to sleep> <the tendency to *settle* standards on the level of the "common man" – Edmund Wilson> and may imply decisiveness or finality (as in ordering or adjusting something previously disturbed or unsettled) <*settle* an upset stomach> <*settle* a man's doubts with a clear explanation> <there's nothing will *settle* me but a bullet – Jonathan Swift> **Fix** stresses permanence and stability <his resolution was already *fixed* – John Buchan> <Greene and his fellows evolved the style of what was to become Shakespearean drama, and . . . Marlowe *fixed* it – W. B. Adams> **Establish** is likely to give less stress to the fact of putting something in place than to subsequent fostering and care that helps it become stable and fixed <do not transplant a tree once it is *established*> <sculptors . . . whose reputation was already *established* – Edith Wharton> <distinguishing what the author assumes from what he *establishes* through arguments – M. J. Adler>

set *n* **set, circle, coterie, clique** *shared meaning* : a more or less closed and exclusive group of persons. **Set** applies to a comparatively large, typically social, group of persons bound together by common interests or tastes <the hunting *set*> <a solid citizen of the fast and frantic international *set* – Kenneth Fearing> <this was the way people in our *set* did things – Claude Brown> **Circle** implies a common center of interest (as a person, an activity, or a cause) that holds a group together <the sewing *circle* of the church> <a peaceful family *circle*> <the aristocratic little court *circle* surrounding the royal governor – Gerald Carson> **Coterie** applies to a small exclusive circle with a binding common interest or purpose <we three formed a little *coterie* within the household – J. A. Symonds> <the aristocratic *coterie* finally got the upper hand – Edith Hamilton> **Clique** is likely to suggest a selfish or arrogant exclusiveness <the corruption and debauchery of the homosexual *clique* – W. L. Shirer> and is especially applicable to a small inner or dissident group within a larger set or circle <the best English society – mind, I don't call the London exclusive *clique* the best English society – S. T. Coleridge>

settle **1** see DECIDE

2 see SET *vb* ***ant*** unsettle

sever – see SEPARATE

several – see DISTINCT

severe, stern, austere, ascetic *shared meaning* : given to or marked by strict discipline and firm restraint. **Severe** implies standards enforced without indulgence or laxity <*severe* impartiality> <a *severe* teacher, but just> and may suggest a preference for the hard, plain, or meager <*severe* in dress> or, more often, harshness <a *severe* penalty for a minor fault> <*severe* discipline> **Stern** adds to *severe* an implication of inflexibility or inexorability of temper or character; thus, a *severe* judge may appear kindly though dispassionately just, but a *stern* judge shows no disposition to mercy or mildness. **Austere** stresses absence of warmth, color, or feeling and is likely to imply rigorous restraint and self-denial <the *austere* dignity and simplicity of their existence – Walter Pater> <my common conversation I do acknowledge *austere,* my behavior full of rigor – Sir Thomas Browne> **Ascetic** implies abstention from whatever comforts or pleases as a measure of self and especially spiritual discipline and may suggest a positive seeking of the painful or disagreeable <strong-willed and *ascetic,* he discovered in discipline the chief end for which the children of Adam are created – V. L. Parrington> <the monastic profession was then a little more than a vow of celibacy and his devotion took no *ascetic* turn – J. R. Green> ***ant*** tolerant, tender

shackle – see HAMPER

shade – see COLOR

shadow – see SUGGEST 2

shake, agitate, rock, convulse *shared meaning* : to cause to move up and down or to and fro with some degree of violence. **Shake** is likely to add to the basic notion an implication of purpose; thus, one *shakes* a rug to free it from dust, one *shakes* a tree to bring down its fruit, one *shakes* a person's hand in greeting him, one *shakes* a stick at a naughty child in warning. **Agitate** suggests a tossing or a violent stirring <the dasher of a churn *agitates* the cream in making butter> <the leaves on the trees were *agitated* as if by a high wind – W. H. Hudson †1922> **Rock** suggests a swinging or swaying motion <*rock* a cradle> but is likely to connote violent upheaval (as from the action of a potent natural force) <wind *rocked* the house> <stood there, letting the sound *rock* him like waves at sea – David Madden> **Convulse** suggests a violent pulling or wrenching (as of the body in a paroxysm or the earth in a seismic disturbance) <she writh'd

about, *convuls'd* with scarlet pain – John Keats> <the world is *convulsed* by the agonies of great nations – T. B. Macaulay>

shallow – see SUPERFICIAL

sham *n* – see IMPOSTURE

sham *vb* – see ASSUME

shame – see DISGRACE ***ant*** glory, pride

shameless, brazen, barefaced, brash, impudent *shared meaning* : characterized by boldness and a lack of a sense of shame. **Shameless** implies a lack of effective restraints (as modesty, an active conscience, or a sense of decency) <fiend and *shameless* courtesan – Shak.> <makes such *shameless* use of patriotic feelings to advertise his product – Virgil Thomson> **Brazen** adds to shamelessness an implication of defiant insolence <solicited praise and power with the *brazen,* businesslike air of a streetwalker on the prowl for clients – R. H. Rovere> <a *brazen* minister of state, who bore for twice ten years the public hate – Jonathan Swift> **Barefaced** implies absence of all efforts to disguise or mask one's transgressions; it connotes extreme effrontery <a *barefaced* liar> <the whole deal was a *barefaced* double cross – *Time*> **Brash** stresses impetuousness and may replace *shameless* to imply that heedlessness and temerity are responsible for indifference to the claims of conscience or decency <deeply I repented of *brash* and boyish crime – Vachel Lindsay> <the frequent complaint of aristocrats that Athenian slaves were too *brash* for the city's good – John Stambaugh> **Impudent** adds to *shameless* implications of bold or pert defiance of considerations of modesty or decency <conduct so sordidly unladylike that even the most *impudent* woman would not dare do it openly – G. B. Shaw> <has a passion for *impudent* adventure – Robert Payne>

shape *vb* – see MAKE

shape *n* – see FORM

share, participate, partake *shared meaning* : to have, get, or use in common with another or others. **Share** may imply that one as the original holder grants to another the partial use, enjoyment, or possession of something or it may imply merely mutual use and possession <*share* a treat with a friend> <all the tenants *shared* one bathroom> <though men do different things, they can all *share* in understanding – R. M. Hutchins> **Participate** implies a having or taking part (as in an undertaking, activity, or discussion) <prepare individuals to meet their responsibilities as *participating* citizens in a changing democratic society – Dayton Benjamin> <*participate* in active sports> **Partake** implies accepting or acquiring a share of something <both *partook* of salted bread that a slave proffered – H. C. Hervey> <adventurers who were willing to *partake* his fortunes – A. W. Kinglake>

sharp, keen, acute *shared meaning* : possessing or marked by alert competence and clear understanding. **Sharp** is likely to suggest an incisive self-centered quality, sometimes manifest in alert rationality, sometimes in devious cunning <his ability for *sharp* analysis, might have carried him far – Herman Wouk> <a man whose *sharp* face . . . seemed wholeheartedly dedicated to chicanery – John Cheever> <his sense of politics and timing remains *sharp* – Jay Walz> **Keen** usually stresses quick penetrating character of mind, often with a suggestion of enthusiasm and clear-sightedness <[his] work on Cornwall was always both exact and *keen* – C. L. Wrenn> <now hath the child grown greater, and is *keen* and eager of wit and full of understanding – William Morris †1896> but it may imply no more than shrewd astuteness <*keen* bargainers> **Acute,** too, may imply a penetrating quality of mind but it is likely to stress sensitivity of perception and depth of insight <I was *acute* at sensing other people's inadequacies

– *New Yorker*> <an *acute,* sometimes heartrending documentary about race relations – Brendan Gill> <the *acutest* philosophers have succeeded in liberating themselves completely from the narrow prison of their age and country – Aldous Huxley> ***ant*** dull, blunt

shed – see DISCARD

sheer – see STEEP

shield – see DEFEND

shift – see RESOURCE

shimmer – see FLASH

shoot, branch, bough, limb *shared meaning* : one of the members of a plant that are outgrowths from a crown or from a main base or one of its divisions. **Shoot** stresses actual growing and is applicable chiefly to new growth, be it from a sprouting crown or from established members. **Branch** suggests a spreading out by dividing and subdividing and applies typically to a matured member arising from a primary stem or trunk or from a division or subdivision of one of these. *Bough* and *limb* apply to members of a tree or shrub. **Bough** may replace *branch,* especially when the notion of the presence of foliage or blossom or fruit is more prominent than that of ramification <pine *boughs* for Christmas decoration> <naked *branches* whipped by autumn winds> <superfluous *branches* we lop away, that bearing *boughs* may live – Shak.> **Limb** is likely to apply to a main branch arising directly from a trunk <the knotty *limbs* of an enormous oak – P. B. Shelley>

shorten, curtail, abbreviate, abridge, retrench *shared meaning* : to reduce in extent. **Shorten** implies reduction in length or duration, real or apparent <*shorten* a rope> <*shorten* one's life by dissipation> <have tried to *shorten* or to enliven the tedium of waiting – C. E. Montague> **Curtail** adds an implication of cutting that in some way deprives of completeness or adequacy <the freedom of the person to pursue his own life in his own way, so long as he does not *curtail* the freedom of others – W. W. Wagar> **Abbreviate** implies a making shorter usually by omitting some part or cutting off some normally following part; thus, one *abbreviates* a word or phrase by cutting out or cutting off letters in such a way that the remaining part stands for the whole <a marriage *abbreviated* by the lures of a slick . . . seaman . . . who owned a cleverer tongue than he [the husband] – William Styron> <a . . . man of great physical strength and energy, though of *abbreviated* intelligence – W. L. Shirer> **Abridge** may imply reduction in compass or scope <I feel that you do not fully comprehend the danger of *abridging* the liberties of the people – Abraham Lincoln> or it may imply a shortening that retains essential elements and relative completeness of the result <an *abridged* edition of a book> <*abridge* a course of study for an accelerated program> **Retrench** stresses reduction in extent of something (as costs) felt to be excessive <a long speech . . . but I could be glad you would *retrench* it – Thomas Gray> <must *retrench* on the expenses of her household – Edith Sitwell> ***ant*** lengthen, elongate, extend

short-lived – see TRANSIENT ***ant*** agelong

shortly – see PRESENTLY

shove – see PUSH

show 1 show, manifest, evidence, evince, demonstrate *shared meaning* : to reveal outwardly or make apparent. **Show,** the general term, may distinctively imply a revealing to the mind by presenting evidence from which inferences can be drawn <the purely economic impact of technological progress . . . will inescapably *show* itself in the conventional statistics on productivity – R. M. Solow> <experience has *shown* that the economy does not

immediately respond to changes in monetary policy – *Monthly Economic Letter, First National City Bank, NYC*> **Manifest** implies a plainer, more direct, and more immediate revelation <[he] *manifested* his spirit of adventure early in life when he toured Europe by bicycle at the age of twelve – *Current Biog.*> **Evidence** may suggest serving as proof of the existence or actuality of something <that neither . . . accepted this particular annoyance as suicidal is *evidenced* by their both still walking the earth – John Barth> **Evince** implies a showing by outward marks or tokens <[her] acceptance of the proposal may also be thought to have *evinced* courage – Richard Garnett> <[his] writings *evince* that kind of classical scholarship which springs only from great study – H. O. Taylor> Its use as a general equivalent for *show* or *indicate* is common but frowned on by purists. **Demonstrate** implies a showing by action or by a display of feelings or of evidence <*demonstrated* their approval by loud applause> <the Exodus *demonstrated* that the king of Egypt was a human figure and only God is sacred – Robert Gordis> <the experiments *demonstrated* the effects of marijuana on mice>
2 show, exhibit, display, expose, parade, flaunt *shared meaning* : to present in such a way as to invite notice or attention. **Show** may imply no more than presenting to view <*show* one's tongue to the doctor> <*show* interest in a school project> or, especially with *off*, it may imply an insistent calling attention to something <[chosen to] *show* off his abilities in a great variety of music – Winthrop Sargeant> **Exhibit** implies a putting forward prominently or openly, typically with the intent to attract attention <artists *exhibiting* their work in a joint show> <*exhibiting* the synthesis of water to Queen Victoria – E. C. Large> **Display** stresses a placing so as to be seen to advantage <his aquiline profile, both views of which he *displayed* without modesty – William Styron> <the degree of courage we *display* in the face of cowardly tendencies outside and within us will be the measure of our worth – Edwin Castagna> **Expose** implies a bringing out of concealment and displaying <the tide was low and the mudbanks were *exposed* – John Cheever> <leave no stone unturned to discover and *expose* the awful truth – Rose Macaulay> often with a suggestion of unmasking <a vitriolic joy in *exposing* their pretensions and their hypocrisy – Van Wyck Brooks> **Parade** implies ostentatious or arrogant displaying <even if some people here are better off than others, they do not *parade* the difference – Mollie Panter-Downes> **Flaunt** implies a shameless, often boastful and offensive parading <it is understandable that people who have no hope of enjoying the *flaunted* fruits of this society may be driven to burn down the trees – Walter Goodman> <a Russian minister in Washington could afford to *flaunt* a mistress, but hardly the American ambassador in London – *Times Lit. Supp.*> ***ant*** disguise

showy, pretentious, ostentatious *shared meaning* : given to or making excessive outward display. **Showy** implies an imposing or striking appearance but often suggests cheapness, inferiority, or lack of taste <*showy* brass ware – G. B. Shaw> <a *showy* design> <the *showy* talents, in which the present age prides itself – J. H. Newman> **Pretentious** implies an appearance of importance not justified by the thing's value or the person's standing <his works are neither *pretentious* nor esoteric; . . . they present the beautiful ordinariness of everyday things – J. W. Foster> <his sense of character is nil, and he is as *pretentious* as a rich whore – Norman Mailer> **Ostentatious** stresses conspicuous or vainglorious display that may or may not involve showiness or pretentiousness <embarrassed by the too *ostentatious* piety of our family – R. M. Lovett> <thought their cortege *ostentatious* . . . slaves marching ahead with drums, porters bearing food and . . . gifts, and an armed escort – H. C. Hervey>

shrewd, sagacious, perspicacious, astute *shared meaning* : acute in perception and sound in judgment. **Shrewd** implies native cleverness and stresses the possession or effect of hardheaded acumen and the ability to see below the surface and judge wisely, albeit sometimes selfishly <a *shrewd* observer> <drive a *shrewd* bargain> <the *shrewd* wisdom of an unlettered old woman – Walter Pater> **Sagacious** stresses wisdom, penetration, and farsightedness and, especially, mature keenness of judgment <his strength was in his *sagacious* sifting of practical ideas from the mass of suggestions proffered – T. D. McCormick> <an important book, *sagacious* yet entertaining> **Perspicacious** implies unusual power to see into and understand what is dark, mysterious, or puzzling <a sound, critical, and *perspicacious* account of Planck's ... contributions to the very foundations of physics – W. Yourgrau> <those blind spots which are found in the most *perspicacious* mortals – L. P. Smith> **Astute** implies a combination of shrewdness with perspicacity or sagacity and often suggests artfulness and craft (as in managing) <savages ... are often as ... *astute* socially as trained diplomatists – William James> <the man who can make millions by an *astute* business deal – J. A. Hobson>

shrink 1 see CONTRACT *ant* swell
2 see RECOIL

shrivel – see WITHER

shun – see ESCAPE *ant* habituate

shy, bashful, diffident, modest, coy *shared meaning* : disinclined to obtrude oneself. **Shy** implies a timid reserve and a shrinking from contact or familiarity with others <*shy* in the presence of strangers and bold with people she knew well – Sherwood Anderson> <radiating a direct warmth that heartens the *shiest* and melts the stiffest – Mildred Adams> **Bashful** applies to a frightened or hesitant shyness characteristic of immaturity <he hesitated, awkward and *bashful,* shifted his weight from one leg to the other – Jack London> **Diffident** implies a self-distrust that causes hesitation in acting or speaking <conservative and *diffident* by nature ... he felt tongue-tied in the presence of those stricken by grief – William Styron> **Modest** may imply an absence of all undue self-confidence <the most *modest,* silent, sheepfaced and meek of little men – W. M. Thackeray> or it may stress a manner free from all marks of brashness, boldness, or self-assertion <a truly *modest* person admires the works of others with eyes full of wonder, and with a joy that leaves him no time to deplore his own – John Ruskin> **Coy** implies an assumed or affected shyness and often suggests coquetry <without being in the least *coy,* ... [she] displayed a certain half-smiling modesty – Terry Southern> <she ignored this surliness, hoping by *coy* persuasion to make him be nice – William Styron> *ant* obtrusive

side – see PHASE

sidereal – see STARRY

sign 1 **sign, mark, token, note, symptom** *shared meaning* : a sensible indication of what is not directly perceptible. **Sign** applies to any indication (as a symbol, a trace, an indication, or a device) to be perceived by the senses or the reason <good manners are *signs* of good breeding> <saw the *signs* of their passage> <there were *signs* of an early spring> <watch for a road *sign*> **Mark** may be chosen when the distinguishing or revealing indication is felt as impressed upon or inherent in a thing, often in contrast to something outwardly evident <courtesy is the *mark* of a gentleman> <the *mark* of a man is not how much he accumulates, but the quality of his relationships and his response to human suffering – Jeanne L. Noble> or it may apply to a visible trace (as a scar or stain) or to an identifying sign <a laundry *mark*> **Token** applies to something that serves as proof or offers evidence of the existence of something intangible; thus, a bus *token,* essentially valueless in itself, is accepted as fare because it evidences the fact of money previously paid <demanded that the bereaved . . .give some small *token* of distress, if only pale, drawn lips trying bravely to smile – William Styron> **Note** suggests a distinguishing mark or characteristic given out by a thing <the grand manner that is the *note* of great poetry> <a fertile oasis possesses a characteristic color scheme of its own . . . . The fundamental *note* is struck by the palms – Aldous Huxley> <her perfume had a delicate woodsy *note*> **Symptom** basically applies to a change, and especially a subjectively detectable change from normal that constitutes evidence of disease <the *symptoms* that she reported caused her doctor to look for signs of heart disease> and in more general use applies to an outward indication of change <war is a *symptom* of human unhappiness – N. F. S. Ferre>

2 sign, signal *shared meaning* : something (as a gesture or action) by which a command or wish is expressed or a thought made known. **Sign** is applicable to any means (as a shrug, a beckoning, or a pantomime) by which one conveys information without verbal communication <put a finger to her lips as a *sign* for quiet> <made a *sign* to the others to wait while he reconnoitered> <Indians of different tribes communicated with a complicated language of *signs*> **Signal** usually applies to a conventional and readily recognizable sign that conveys a command, a direction, or a warning <she was startled by a ring at the door, the certain *signal* of a visitor – Jane Austen> or it may apply to a mechanical device that performs a comparable function <waiting for a traffic *signal* to change to green>

signal *n* – see SIGN 2

signal *adj* – see NOTICEABLE

significance – see IMPORTANCE, MEANING

signification – see MEANING

silent 1 silent, taciturn, reticent, reserved, secretive *shared meaning* : showing restraint in speaking. **Silent** implies a habit of saying no more than is actually needed <a stern, *silent* man, long a widower – Willa Cather> <the stubborn, *silent* anger of the poor against the rich – Thomas Wolfe> **Taciturn** implies a temperamental disinclination to speech and usually connotes unsociability <[he] was . . . a *taciturn* hater of woman – George Meredith> <the farmer was *taciturn* and drove them speechlessly to the house – Pearl Buck> **Reticent** implies a reluctance to speak out or at length, especially about one's own affairs <he had been characteristically *reticent* regarding the details of his own financial affairs – J. P. Marquand> **Reserved** implies reticence and suggests the restraining influence of caution or formality in checking easy familiar conversational exchange <even the *reserved* Washington wrote caustically of their bad manners – Allan Nevins & H. S. Commager> <a certain vulgar gusto . . . that divided him from the *reserved,* watchful rest of the family – D. H. Lawrence> **Secretive** implies reticence and usually carries a disparaging suggestion of deficiency of frankness or openness or of an often ostentatious will to conceal what might properly or reasonably be made known <you're so excessively *secretive* that I can't help being curious – Dashiell Hammett> <the king was a *secretive* child, and showed little of his mind – Edith Sitwell> ***ant*** talkative

2 see STILL

silhouette – see OUTLINE

silly – see SIMPLE

similar, alike, akin, analogous, parallel, homogeneous, uniform *shared meaning* : closely resembling each other. **Similar** implies such likeness as allows the possibility of being mistaken one for the other <Virginia creeper or the

deceptively *similar* poison ivy – *Amer. Guide Series: Md.*> **Alike** implies having close resemblance even though obviously distinct <their resemblance as brother and sister . . . they looked utterly *alike* – Sinclair Lewis> **Akin** suggests essential rather than apparent likeness <science . . . is *akin* to democracy in its faith in human intelligence and cooperative effort – H. J. Muller> **Analogous** applies to things susceptible of comparison even though belonging to different categories <the wing of an airplane can be viewed as *analogous* to the wing of a bird> **Parallel** stresses the fact of similarities over a course of development <the almost *parallel* growth of the Twin Cities – *Amer. Guide Series: Minn.*> or of resemblances permitting a setting together as though side by side <black students are still caught in the dream of *parallel* subcultures on the campus – Max Lerner> **Homogeneous** implies likeness of a number of things in kind, sort, or class <a *homogeneous* population> <at the time of its founding, Israel was a *homogeneous* society – nearly all its citizens came from European countries – Shirley M. & Sol Kolack> **Uniform** implies consistent likeness and lack of variation in something, wherever it exists or operates <one of the most fundamental social interests is that the law shall be *uniform* and impartial – B. N. Cardozo> ***ant*** dissimilar

similarity – see LIKENESS ***ant*** dissimilarity

similitude – see LIKENESS ***ant*** dissimilitude, dissimilarity

simple 1 see PLAIN

2 simple, foolish, silly, fatuous, asinine shared meaning : actually or apparently deficient in intelligence. **Simple** implies a degree of intelligence inadequate to cope with anything complex or involving mental effort <this poor, *simple* boy. Half-witted, they call him; and surely fit for nothing but to be happy – Nathaniel Hawthorne> Used critically of normal people or their acts the term implies a failure to use one's intelligence <he forgot where he was to meet her and felt utterly *simple* to have to inquire> **Foolish** implies the character of being or seeming unable to use judgment, discretion, or good sense <oh, *foolish* youth! Thou seek'st the greatness that will overwhelm thee – Shak.> <in his younger days he had been very *foolish*. He had flirted and giggled – Virginia Woolf> **Silly** suggests failure to act as a rational being, whether by showing lack of common sense or by behaving in a ridiculous manner <man is surely the *silliest* of animals . . . full of postures and pufferies that appear to have no relation whatever to the requirements of surviving – K. T. Erikson> <the women talked woman talk which, to the men, was mostly incomprehensible or *silly*, or both – J. T. Farrell> **Fatuous**, distinctly a term of contempt, suggests foolish inanity and a disregard of reality <a *fatuous* answer to a reasonable question> <the serenely *fatuous* looks of store-window mannequins – William Styron> <a *fatuous* and at the same time arrogant epistle, abounding in nonsense and lies and subterfuge – W. L. Shirer> **Asinine**, with its implied comparison to a donkey, is also a term of contempt; it suggests inexcusable failure to exercise intelligence or rational perception <an *asinine* excuse> <a man so *asinine* that he looks for gratitude in this world – H. L. Mencken> ***ant*** wise

simpleton – see FOOL

simulate – see ASSUME

simultaneous – see CONTEMPORARY

sin – see OFFENSE 2

sincere, wholehearted, heartfelt, hearty, unfeigned *shared meaning* : genuine in feeling. **Sincere** stresses absence of hypocrisy, simulation, or any falsifying embellishment or exaggeration <in spite of her confusion, something strong and *sincere* and questing emanated from her – William Styron> <I always

promised to mend my bad ways. I was always *sincere* and usually kept the promise for about a week – Claude Brown> **Wholehearted** suggests sincerity arising from a deep and moving response to something <expressed her *wholehearted* sympathy with their plight> <the service they one and all gave . . . was *wholehearted* and even passionate – Victoria Sackville-West> **Heartfelt** suggests depth of genuine feeling outwardly expressed <our sympathy for you therefore is *heartfelt,* for we are sharing the same sufferings – Sir Winston Churchill> **Hearty** is likely to suggest honesty, warmth, and sometimes exuberance in the display of feeling <a *hearty* laugh> <a *hearty* assumer of its full share of . . . responsibilities – F. S. C. Northrop> **Unfeigned** may replace *sincere,* especially when the lack of all simulation is to be stressed <an *unfeigned* interest in people and scenes – Geoffrey Bruun> ***ant*** insincere

single, sole, unique, separate, solitary, particular *shared meaning* : one as distinguished from two or more or all others. Something **single** is not accompanied or supported by, or combined or united with, another <a revolutionary sentiment . . . channeled in the *single* direction of preserving national freedom – Tad Szulc> <a problem with no *single* solution> Something **sole** is the only one that exists, acts, has power or relevance, or should be considered <California is not the *sole* repository of political virtue in the United States – Trevor Armbrister> <I remain convinced that . . . we shall resort to the *sole* simple solution, concrete and well-tested – increasing the price of gold – Jacques Rueff> Something **unique** stands alone as the only one of its kind or character <[he] considers it *unique* and says there will never be another like it – *Harvard Alumni Bull.*> <the *unique* character of the English conquest of Britain – Kemp Malone> Something **separate** is not only single, but disconnected from or unconnected with any of the others in question <turning over in his thoughts every *separate* second of their hours together – Edith Wharton> <group consciousness . . . makes the individual think lightly of his own *separate* interests – M. R. Cohen> Something **solitary** is both single and isolated <the *solitary* sin of an otherwise blameless life> <a sentry kept *solitary* vigil – J. H. Cutler> Something **particular** is the singular or numerically distinct instance, member, or example of a whole or class considered <reality is a succession of concrete and *particular* situations – Aldous Huxley> <it was . . . necessary to distinguish the *particular* species of fungi associated with specific plant diseases – E. C. Large> <the *particular* edition in which the quoted passage occurs>

singular – see STRANGE

sinister, baleful, malign *shared meaning* : seriously threatening evil or disaster. **Sinister** applies to what threatens by appearance or reputation to be formidably troublesome or dangerous, sometimes in an obvious but often in an obscure or insidious manner <some of the customers did look *sinister* enough – scar-faced toughs in ragged caps and sweaters – Herman Wouk> <denouncing the *sinister* aims and wicked conduct of those in high places – C. L. Becker> **Baleful** imputes perniciousness or destructiveness and carries a strong suggestion of hovering menace <deceit contrived by art and *baleful* sorcery – Shak.> <the *baleful* power of fanaticisms and superstitions – Edmund Wilson> **Malign** applies to what is inherently evil or harmful <[he] is . . . *malign,* evasive, always ready to use his friends' abject confessions against them – E. M. Potoker> <a struggle between two forces, the one beneficent, the other *malign* – James Bryce>

situation – see POSITION 2, STATE

skeleton – see STRUCTURE

skepticism – see UNCERTAINTY

sketch — see COMPENDIUM
skill — see ART
skilled — see PROFICIENT *ant* unskilled
skillful — see PROFICIENT *ant* unskillful
skimpy — see MEAGER
skinny — see LEAN *ant* fleshy
skulk — see LURK
slack — see LOOSE, NEGLIGENT
slacken — see DELAY *ant* quicken
slander — see MALIGN
slang — see DIALECT
slant, slope, incline, lean *shared meaning* : to diverge from the vertical or horizontal. **Slant,** the comprehensive term, implies merely a noticeable physical divergence <she had . . . long, jet-black hair, and *slanted* eyes — Claude Brown> <the strips were *slanted* against the sides as a promenade — Isaac Asimov> **Slope,** often interchangeable with *slant,* may be preferred when reference is made to a gradual divergence of a side or surface <the land *slopes* to the east> <a *sloping* roof> <enjoyed their wide *sloping* lawns with the sprinklers idly turning — Louis Auchincloss> **Incline** is likely to suggest the intervention of an external force (as in bending or tipping) <just as the twig is bent, the tree's *inclined* — Alexander Pope> <graciously *inclined* her head in response to the cheers> **Lean** may stress a definite directing of an inclination <the old man *leaned* the mast . . . against the wall — Ernest Hemingway> or a literal or figurative resting or intent to rest against a support <*lean* back in an easy chair> <both items *lean* heavily on nostalgia, both bring happy memories of an era unfortunately ended — Bennett Cerf>
slap — see STRIKE
slatternly, dowdy, frowzy, blowsy *shared meaning* : deficient in neatness, freshness, and smartness, especially in dress or appearance. **Slatternly** stresses notions of slovenliness, unkemptness, and sordidness <tatterdemalion, *slatternly,* slipshod women — E. C. Clayton> <streets terribly shabby and *slatternly* and badly paved — Arnold Bennett> **Dowdy** is likely to suggest a blend of the untidy, drab, and tasteless <so dreadfully *dowdy* that she reminded one of a badly bound hymnbook — Oscar Wilde> **Frowzy** may describe a lazy lack of neatness, order, and cleanliness <a dumpy, *frowzy* woman, clad in old dress and apron — A. J. Coutts> or it may apply to a natural and not unwholesome disorder <white spruce, and the *frowzy,* slender jack pine thrive on the high land — J. J. Rowlands> or it may suggest drab misery and squalor <women . . . by circumstances reduced to a daily diet of *frowzy* economy — F. A. Swinnerton> <the only slightly *frowzier* parade of eateries, drinkeries and sleeperies — J. W. Krutch> **Blowsy** implies dishevelment or disorder <her hair, so untidy, so *blowsy* — Jane Austen> to which is often added a notion of crudity or coarseness or grossness <and Galatea joined the throng — a *blowsy,* apple-vending slattern — E. C. Stedman> <that *blowsy* hoyden of an America that existed when Grant was accounted a statesman and Longfellow an epic poet — Sinclair Lewis>
slaughter — see MASSACRE
slavery — see SERVITUDE
slavish — see SUBSERVIENT
slay — see KILL
sleazy — see LIMP
sleepy, drowsy, somnolent, slumberous *shared meaning* : affected by or inducing a desire to sleep. **Sleepy** applies to whatever seems about to fall

asleep or to whatever conduces to such a state <away, you rogue, away! I am *sleepy* – Shak.> <a *sleepy* little town> <the yellowhammer trills his *sleepy* song in the noonday heat – L. P. Smith> **Drowsy** carries a stronger implication of the heaviness or loginess or languor associated with sleepiness than of an actual need for sleep <would grow *drowsy* . . . and go off to take a nap – Margaret Deland> <*drowsy* wine which fills the veins with soft contentment – Lafcadio Hearn> **Somnolent** is likely to suggest the sluggishness or inertness accompanying sleepiness more than the actual impulse to sleep <a *somnolent* want of interest – Thomas De Quincey> or sometimes the capacity for inducing this <the *somnolent* pages of a volume of ancient sermons> **Slumberous** may replace any of the other terms; distinctively it may connote quiescence or the repose of latent powers <forgetting that white men once left the *slumberous* feudal world and eagerly took the risks of, as William James phrased it, an "unguaranteed existence" – Richard Wright> <I . . . heard the mountain's *slumberous* voice – P. B. Shelley>

slender – see THIN

slight *adj* – see THIN

slight *vb* – see NEGLECT

slim – see THIN ***ant*** chubby (*of persons*)

sling – see THROW

slink – see LURK

slip – see ERROR

slope – see SLANT

slothful – see LAZY ***ant*** industrious

slow – see DELAY ***ant*** speed

sluggish – see LETHARGIC ***ant*** brisk, expeditious, quick (*of mind*)

sluice – see POUR

slumberous – see SLEEPY

sly, cunning, crafty, tricky, foxy, artful *shared meaning* : attaining or seeking to attain one's ends by devious means. **Sly** implies furtiveness, lack of candor, and skill in concealing one's intentions and methods <peeking around with a *sly* look on his face to see if any of the watchdogs of the law were in sight – Thomas Wolfe> <with knowing leer and words of *sly* import – Washington Irving> **Cunning** suggests the effective use of sometimes limited intelligence in evading or circumventing <his *cunning* made him seem formidable and intelligent – John Cheever> <all gods are cruel . . . but women-gods are mean and *cunning* as well – Gordon Bottomley> **Crafty** implies clever cunning and subtlety of method <he disappointeth the devices of the *crafty,* so that their hands cannot perform their enterprise – *Job* 5:12 (AV)> <as a *crafty* envoy does his country's business by dint of flirting and conviviality – C. E. Montague> **Tricky** is more likely to suggest shiftiness and unreliability than skill in deception and maneuvering and stresses unscrupulousness <he avoided the mean and *tricky:* he was always an honorable foe – W. C. Ford> **Foxy** implies a shrewd and wary craftiness usually based on experience in devious dealing <this *foxy* publicity man turned fumbling poet – Sherwood Anderson> <this time the lecherous Alsatian uses a *foxier* gambit to achieve his ends – S. J. Perelman> **Artful** implies insinuating or alluring indirectness in dealing and is likely to connote sophistication or coquetry or cleverness <oddly enough, they stayed sober. The *artful* Henry had told them that all the wine in Panama was poisoned – D. B. Chidsey>

smack – see TASTE 1

small, little, diminutive, minute, petite, tiny, miniature, wee *shared meaning* : noticeably below average in magnitude. *Small* and *little* are often used without distinction; but **small** applies more often to relative size especially as determined by capacity, value, or number <a *small* box> <a *small* estate> <the audience was *small*> and is preferred to qualify such words as *size, quantity,* or *amount* <had only a *small* sum of money left> while **little** is more absolute in implication and may connote less magnitude than is usual, expected, or desirable <the alert, experienced teacher has *little* difficulty distinguishing the child who is doing his own work from the child who is not – R. K. Corbin> <he enjoyed the *little* vices and luxuries – coffee, fresh water, and women – T. E. Lawrence> *Little* is also appropriate in the sense of a small amount, a small quantity, or a small extent; thus, one may have a *small* amount of money or a *little* money; one finds the garden too *little,* or of too *small* extent, for convenience. **Diminutive** implies exceptional or abnormal smallness <a *diminutive* financial wizard, who looked like a Kewpie doll – J. D. Hart> **Minute** implies extreme smallness on an absolute and typically a near-microscopic scale <ants that marched their *minute* columns over the floor – H. C. Hervey> <the tremendous forces imprisoned in *minute* particles of matter – W. R. Inge> **Petite** applies chiefly to girls and women and implies marked but not abnormal smallness and trimness of figure <a *petite* blonde, a scant 80 pounds, with large, brilliant eyes and fine skin – Martin Cohen> **Tiny** is a less formal equivalent of *minute* <prominent eyes yellowed with *tiny* red veins – Avram Davidson> or it may imply notable smallness within the range of a class <a *tiny* child lisped a grave answer> **Miniature** applies to something complete in itself but built or made on a very small scale <we may thus picture an atom as a *miniature* solar system – A. S. Eddington> <one of the *miniature* Italian cities . . . all compact and complete, on the top of a mountain – L. P. Smith> **Wee** is a homely or dialectal equivalent of *small* or *little* <a *wee* drop of whiskey> <a *wee* lad> or in more general use an equivalent of *diminutive* <the combination permits a *wee* penumbra of healthy vanity – Martin Mayer> ***ant*** large

smaller – see LESS

smell, scent, odor, aroma *shared meaning* **:** a quality that makes a thing perceptible to the olfactory sense. **Smell** implies solely the sensation without suggestion of quality or character or source unless qualified <the air seemed to sink under its burden of tobacco smoke and mingled *smells* – Stella D. Gibbons> <the fresh river *smell,* rank and a little rotten – Thomas Wolfe> **Scent** is likely to stress the source of the sensation <the *scent* of the first wood fire upon the keen October air – Walter Pater> <a *scent* came from it, dank and pervasive. It was the must of the forest – H. C. Hervey> <the dog caught the *scent* of a rabbit> and from its use as a synonym of *perfume* often suggests a pleasant quality <the rich, vital *scents* of the plowed ground – Ellen Glasgow> **Odor** is likely to imply a stronger or more readily distinguished scent <the sharp *odor* of hot vinegar> <gave off a kind of sweetish rich animal-vegetable *odor,* such as one associates with the tropics – James Purdy> **Aroma** usually adds to *odor* an implication of a penetrating, pervasive, or, sometimes, pungent quality that suggests something to be savored <spiced among these odors was the sultry *aroma* of strong boiling coffee – Thomas Wolfe> <the rich *aromas* of a holiday kitchen>

smite – see STRIKE 1

smog – see HAZE

smooth **1** see LEVEL ***ant*** rough
2 see SUAVE ***ant*** bluff

smother – see SUFFOCATE

snap – see JERK

snare — see CATCH
snatch — see TAKE 1
sneak — see LURK
sneer — see SCOFF
snug — see COMFORTABLE
soak, saturate, drench, steep, impregnate *shared meaning* : to permeate or be permeated with or as if with water. **Soak** implies a usually prolonged exposure or immersion that results in thorough wetting, softening, or dissolving <*soak* a sponge> <stayed out in the rain and got *soaked*> <*soak* the dirt from soiled clothes> and in extended use stresses permeating by something comparable to water <the shadowy copse was *soaked* in piny sweetness — Rose Macaulay> <old ladies *soaked* in religion — J. T. Farrell> **Saturate** stresses absorption to the point where no more can be held <a *saturated* solution of salt in water> <the air was *saturated* with moisture> <a culture that is *saturated* with respect for and faith in the "scientific process" — R. K. Corbin> <the city . . . was *saturated* with fear — *Kerner Report*> **Drench** basically implies a thorough wetting (as by rainwater) <they were in an open buggy and were *drenched* to the skin — Willa Cather> and in extended use suggests being soaked or saturated by something that pours down <[they] . . . have *drenched* the rebel towns with bombs — *Atlanta* (*Ga.*) *Jour.*> <the new life with which it *drenches* the spirits — P. B. Shelley> **Steep** implies immersion and soaking, usually in order to extract an essence <*steep* tea in boiling water> In extended use it is likely to imply the acquisition of qualities by a process analogous to soaking or suggest their abundant presence <sensational headlines were followed by articles *steeped* in redundancy and disjointed rhetoric — D. J. Murphy, Jr.> <the world was all *steeped* in sunshine — D. H. Lawrence> **Impregnate** implies the thorough interpenetration of one thing by another <*impregnate* fence posts with creosote to prevent decay> <this poem, everywhere *impregnated* with original excellence — William Wordsworth>
sober 1 sober, temperate, continent, unimpassioned *shared meaning* : having or manifesting mastery of oneself and one's appetites. **Sober** basically implies moderation in the use of food and especially drink; in more general application it may suggest composure under stress and freedom from emotional excess <a *sober* book, written without hysteria or excitement — A. T. Steele> <a calm *sober* man well-fitted to function in an emergency> **Temperate** stresses moderation and implies such control that one never exceeds the bounds of what is right or proper <his compassion is *temperate,* is unassuming, is staunch, is kind — R. G. Frost> <for Socrates . . . music made the soul gentle and *temperate* — Stringfellow Barr> **Continent** stresses deliberate self-restraint <my past life hath been as *continent,* as chaste, as true, as I am now unhappy — Shak.> <not . . . a subject of irregular and interrupted impulses of virtue, but a *continent,* persisting, immovable person — R. W. Emerson> **Unimpassioned** may imply a subduing of feeling or passion by rationality <his manner resembled their manner, reserved, logical, *unimpassioned,* and intelligent — W. C. Ford> but often it connotes a resulting coldness or hardness of heart <when love is not involved in a union, any differences are likely to settle into . . . *unimpassioned* enmity — H. C. Hervey> ***ant*** excited, drunk
2 see SERIOUS ***ant*** gay
sobriety — see TEMPERANCE ***ant*** drunkenness, excitement
sociable — see GRACIOUS ***ant*** unsociable
soft, bland, mild, gentle, lenient *shared meaning* : devoid of harshness, roughness, or intensity. **Soft** implies a subduing of all that is vivid, intense, or forceful until it is agreeably soothing <as sweet as balm, as *soft* as air,

as gentle – Shak.> <a *soft* answer turneth away wrath – *Prov* 15:1 (AV)> <ever, against eating cares, lap me in *soft* Lydian airs – John Milton> **Bland** implies the absence of anything that might disturb, stimulate, or irritate and may suggest insipidness; thus, a *bland* climate is free from all extremes and neither stimulates nor depresses; foods and beverages that are not unpleasant but that lack all marked flavor or pungency or richness are *bland* <the whole shabby performance . . . the *bland* reassurances instead of the hard dichotomies – J. A. Michener> **Mild** and **gentle** stress moderation or restraint of force or intensity <*mild* weather> <a *gentle* rain> <a man of *mild* and simple character – Roald Dahl> <O *gentle* sleep, nature's soft nurse – Shak.> **Lenient** in this use stresses an emollient, relaxing, softening, or calming influence <earthly sounds, though sweet and well combined, and *lenient* as soft opiates to the mind – William Cowper> ***ant*** hard, stern

sojourn – see RESIDE
solace – see COMFORT
sole – see SINGLE
solemn – see SERIOUS
solicit – see ASK 2, INVITE
solicitor – see LAWYER
solicitude – see CARE ***ant*** negligence, unmindfulness
solid – see FIRM ***ant*** fluid, liquid
solidarity – see UNITY
solitary – see ALONE, SINGLE

solitude, isolation, seclusion *shared meaning* **:** the state of one who is alone. **Solitude** stresses aloneness and implies lack of contact, literal or figurative, physical or mental with others of one's own kind; thus, one may be in *solitude* in the midst of a city if one knows no one there; one is in *solitude* when one loses touch with the ideas and activities that matter to most people. Sometimes the term suggests the resulting loneliness <suffer in *solitude*> <aye, *solitude,* black *solitude* indeed, to meet a million souls and know not one – W. H. Davies> **Isolation** stresses detachment from others, often because of circumstances not under one's control <brought American linguistics out of the scholarly *isolation* from which it suffered for a time – W. G. Moulton> <we are exposed to *isolation* imposed on us from the outside by unfriendly powers – Max Ascoli> **Seclusion** suggests a shutting away or keeping apart from others and often connotes a withdrawal from the active life of the busy world <he lived in *seclusion* while planning his novel> <even in the *seclusion* of the convent, Sister had heard the rumors – Ruth Park>

somatic – see BODILY
somnolent – see SLEEPY
soon – see PRESENTLY
sordid – see MEAN *adj*

sorrow *n* **sorrow, grief, anguish, woe, regret** *shared meaning* **:** distress of mind. **Sorrow,** the most general term, may imply a sense of loss or of guilt and remorse <when you depart from me, *sorrow* abides and happiness takes his leave – Shak.> <felt a deep *sorrow* as he thought of the opportunities he had neglected> **Grief** implies deep and poignant sorrow for an immediate cause <*grief* over the death of a child> or sometimes a merely mundane distress of mind <a thankless job that gave him a great deal of *grief* and little reward> **Anguish** implies a torturing often persistent grief or dread <lived in *anguish* at the thought of her husband's return> <to learn again, and to suffer, the cleansing *anguish* of responsibility of decision – E. J. Hughes> **Woe** implies a deep or inconsolable misery or distress (as from grief or privation) <outcast from God ... condemned to waste eternal days in *woe* – John Milton> <their concern was the weal and *woe* of their own people – Robert Gordis> **Regret** implies pain caused by deep disappointment, fruitless longing, or unavailing remorse <if Moses had any *regrets* or hints of *regrets* they were lost in the confusion of his feelings – John Cheever> <that expression of mildly cynical *regret* and acceptance that one often notices in people who have seen much of life, and experienced its hard and seamy side – Thomas Wolfe> ***ant*** joy

sorrow *vb* – see GRIEVE

sorry – see CONTEMPTIBLE

sort – see TYPE 2

soul, spirit *shared meaning* : an immaterial entity distinguishable from and superior to the body. **Soul** may be preferred when emphasis is on the entity as having functions, responsibilities, aspects, or destiny, while **spirit** may be chosen when the stress is upon the quality, the constitution, or the activity of the entity <pray for the *souls* of the dead> <a man fervent in *spirit*> <for what shall it profit a man, if he shall gain the whole world, and lose his own *soul* – *Mt* 8:36 (AV)> <the *spirit* indeed is willing, but the flesh is weak – *Mt* 26:41 (AV)> *Soul* in both its basic and extended senses emphasizes a relation to or connection to a material entity to which it gives life or power; *spirit* in corresponding use is likely to suggest an antithesis to the material or even a repugnance to the latter <the *soul* of wit may become the very body of untruth – Aldous Huxley> <these students are not struggling for themselves alone. They are seeking to save the *soul* of America – M. L. King, Jr.> <the judges are willing now to look to the *spirit* of the law much more than to its letter – Francis Heisler> <the national states ... are still girding for conflict and still committing crimes without number against the *spirit* and the body of mankind – W. W. Wagar> ***ant*** body

sound *adj* **1** see HEALTHY

2 see VALID ***ant*** fallacious

sound *n* **sound, noise** *shared meaning* : a sensation or effect resulting from stimulation of the auditory receptors. **Sound** is applicable to anything that is heard and in itself is completely neutral in implication <the *sound* of a crowd> <loud *sounds* of laughter> **Noise** basically applies to the confused and disordered sounds emanating from a crowd and usually suggests a clamor of mingled voices calling and shouting; in more general use the term applies to a disagreeably loud or harsh sound <the terrific *noise* of the explosion> or to one constantly or irritatingly perceptible <the constant *noise* and bustle of the city> <they could not trace the *noise* to its source> or to one inappropriate to the situation and therefore disturbing <wakened by a *noise* at the door late at night> <a *noise* like that from just one stringy throat must be an impossibility – Theodore Sturgeon> Occasionally *noise* loses its suggestions of unpleasantness and discordance and then differs little from *sound* <still the sails made on a pleasant *noise* till noon, a *noise* like of a hidden brook – S. T. Coleridge>

sour, acid, acidulous, tart *shared meaning* : having a taste devoid of sweetness. *Sour* and *acid* are often interchangeable, but **sour** is preferred in reference to something that has lost its natural sweetness through fermentation or decay, while **acid** is appropriately used of something naturally lacking sweetness, usually due to the presence of chemical acids; thus, *sour* milk is milk fermented by bacteria; *sour* milk is *acid* because of the lactic acid formed in it by bacteria. Sometimes the choice depends on whether the emphasis is on lack of sweetness <*sour* apples make tastier pies> or on the presence of acid <it's easier to make jelly with *acid* fruits> **Acidulous**

implies a moderate degree of acidity <a pleasantly *acidulous* mineral water> and **tart,** a marked but not usually unpleasing acidity <*tart* fruit is better for cooking than for eating raw>

In extended use **sour** implies crabbedness or morosity <a man with a prim *sour* mouth and an expression of eternal disapproval – Roald Dahl> **Acid** implies a biting or caustic quality <his wit became *acid,* his letters are filled with caustic comment – V. L. Parrington> <Tom Sawyer's Aunt Polly was the only *acid* lady in the lot – Zena Sutherland> **Acidulous** and **tart** imply asperity, pungency, or sharpness <a memorial to the fallen of the area. An *acidulous* relative . . . said it was the only proof that they had not died in vain – J. K. Galbraith> <he is *tart* as a grandaunt, but . . . he is the most perfect writer of my generation – Norman Mailer>

source – see ORIGIN ***ant*** termination, outcome

sovereign – see DOMINANT, FREE *adj*

spacious, commodious, capacious, ample *shared meaning* : larger in extent than the average. **Spacious** implies limits enclosing abundant space <*spacious* gardens> <the whole interior . . . a dim, *spacious,* fragrant place, afloat with golden lights – Walter Pater> <one great *spacious* golden morning followed another – J. C. Powys> **Commodious** stresses roominess and freedom from hampering constriction <many doors among the bookshelves, anyone of which will lead you from one *commodious* room to another – John Cheever> **Capacious** stresses capacity and an ability to hold or, sometimes, receive or retain in exceptional quantity or to an exceptional degree <fumbled in a *capacious* pocket of the old-fashioned sort – Dorothy Sayers> <the dull girls, with their slow but *capacious* memories – Mavis Gallant> **Ample** basically means more than adequate (as in space, size, or amount) <*ample* funds> <an *ample* supply of food> and may suggest fullness or bulk <draped in an *ample* cloak> <an imposing creature, tall and stout, with an *ample* bust – W. S. Maugham> or, especially in extended use, freedom to expand or from cramping restrictions <a government entrusted with such *ample* powers – John Marshall>

spare **1** see LEAN ***ant*** corpulent
2 see MEAGER ***ant*** profuse

sparing, frugal, thrifty, economical *shared meaning* : careful in the use of one's money or resources. **Sparing** stresses abstention or restraint <the English are *sparing* in their use of . . . [gesture] – David Abercrombie> <had always been a *sparing* eater of plain foods – Pearl Buck> **Frugal** implies simplicity and temperance and suggests the absence of all luxury and display <Roman life was a *frugal* thing, sparing in food, temperate in drink, modest in clothing, cleanly in habit – John Buchan> **Thrifty** implies industry, good management, and prosperity as well as frugality <a *thrifty* people – *thrifty* of property, of speech, of their emotions above all – H. S. Commager> <had been a prudent and *thrifty* wife to him – W. M. Thackeray> **Economical** may replace *thrifty* with reference to the careful use of money and goods <an *economical* housewife> but often it stresses efficiency and prudence in the use of resources and is, therefore, more widely applicable than *thrifty* <her prose is powerful, *economical,* and elegant – Naomi Bliven> <historically, sea power is the most mobile and therefore the most *economical* form of military force – *Time*> ***ant*** lavish

sparkle – see FLASH

sparse – see MEAGER ***ant*** dense

spasmodic – see FITFUL

spat – see QUARREL

speak, talk, converse *shared meaning* : to articulate words so as to express one's thoughts. **Speak** may refer to any utterance, however coherent or disconnected, and with or without reference to hearers <*speak* to a boy about his manners> <too hoarse to *speak* clearly> <a . . . man who *speaks* fluently but without flamboyance – Ben Hibbs> **Talk** usually implies one or more auditors and connected colloquy or discourse <you don't *talk* nonsense as a rule – John Barth> <*talk* over a problem with an adviser> **Converse** implies an interchange in talk of thoughts and opinions <in the press conference the president can *converse* with the public rather than preach to it – Douglass Cater> <don't ever remember hearing my parents *converse* . . . . My father would expound on law and ritual, my mother would listen – S. N. Behrman>

special, especial, specific, particular, individual *shared meaning* : of or relating to one thing or class. **Special** implies differences that give the thing qualified its distinctive quality, character, identity, or use <a *special* soap for dry skin> and may additionally imply superiority and then come close to *uncommon* or *exceptional* in meaning <preventing the perpetuation of an hereditary upper class with *special* privileges and better education – Edmund Wilson> **Especial** may add implications of preeminence or preference <his *especial* friend in that group> <a matter of *especial* importance> **Specific** basically implies unique and peculiar relationship to a kind or category or individual <*specific* nutritional needs of the aged> <*specific* virtues of this system> but in much of its use stresses uniqueness often to the point of obscuring the notion of relationship <whether the *specific* freedoms we know and cherish . . : can be maintained – Sidney Hook> or even means no more than explicitly mentioned or brought into consideration <if such injuries . . . result in any of the following *specific* losses – *insurance policy*> **Particular** may replace *specific* in the last use and then stresses the distinctness of the thing as an individual; thus, one gives a *specific* illustration of a word's normal use but describes the *particular* applications of the word <we get a sense for *particular* beauties of nature, rather than a sense for Nature herself – Laurence Binyon> In much of its use *particular* stresses an opposition to *general* (or sometimes to *universal*) <one is apt to amplify a *particular* judgment into a general opinion – Compton Mackenzie> **Individual** unequivocally refers to one of a class or group as distinct <it was not the magnitude or multiplicity of burdens that created martyrs and saints; it was the *individual* capacity to bear suffering – H. C. Hervey>

specific **1** see EXPLICIT ***ant*** vague
2 see SPECIAL ***ant*** generic

specify – see MENTION

specimen – see INSTANCE

specious –see PLAUSIBLE

speculate – see THINK 2

speculative – see THEORETICAL

speed – see HASTE

speedy – see FAST ***ant*** dilatory

spend, expend, disburse *shared meaning* : to pay out for something received or expected. **Spend,** the ordinary term, recites the fact of paying out and leaves details to the context <*spend* a nickel for candy> <*spends* more than she can afford on clothes> <the Pentagon *spends* so wastefully that we could cut our military budget at least 25 percent – Bruce Catton> In nonmonetary applications the term is more likely to suggest a draining or depleting than to imply a direct return <man after man *spends* himself in this cause – Thomas Carlyle> <*spent* months trying to find a satisfactory house> **Expend** is likely to be chosen with reference to public or business rather than private spending and to imply largeness of outlay <the social

services upon which public revenue is *expended* – J. A. Hobson> and in extended use retains this idea of large outlay and often of depleting of resources <we have *expended* our resources – both human and natural – without stint – Harry S Truman> **Disburse** basically implies a paying out of money from a fund, but it may imply distribution (as to pensioners or heirs) and often stresses an acting under authority in such paying <our time and our money, even though *disbursed* by governmental authority – W. F. Hambly> <waiting for the teller to *disburse* those complex payroll accounts – Christopher Morley> In extended use the term usually stresses distribution <uranium ... designated for research only, and ... to be *disbursed* under strictly bilateral agreements – John Lear> ***ant*** save

spendthrift, prodigal, profligate, waster, wastrel *shared meaning* : a person who dissipates his resources foolishly and wastefully. **Spendthrift** stresses lack of prudence in spending and usually implies imbalance between income and outgo <to *spendthrifts* ... there is only one limit to their fortune, – that of time – R. L. Stevenson> In legal application the term implies such a degree of imbalance as is likely to leave the spendthrift and his dependents public charges. **Prodigal** suggests such lavish expenditure as can deplete the most abundant resources <the Irish produce great writers because they're temperamentally *prodigals*... willing to squander their lives on the gratuitous work that great art demands – Edmund Wilson> In legal application the term denotes specifically one held legally incompetent to manage his own affairs or contract debts because of demonstrated incapacity. **Profligate** may imply the habits of a spendthrift but it stresses dissipation of resources and powers and suggests debauchery and dissoluteness more than waste <the wretched *profligate* found himself again plunged into excesses – J. R. Green> **Waster** may come close to *spendthrift* but carries a stronger implication of worthlessness and often suggests an idle ne'er-do-well or frivoler <he who will not work, must ... leave the town, as they will not sweat themselves for an healthy, idle *waster* – James Adair> **Wastrel** stresses disreputable worthlessness and typically applies to one who has become a drain on the community through profligate and dissolute habits <the danger of so shaping them that they shall be mere mechanisms in working hours, and mere *wastrels* in the rest – C. H. Grandgent> <was regarded as essentially a *wastrel* and, given the opportunity, a Grade A guttersnipe – Stanley Walker>

spirit – see COURAGE, SOUL

spite – see MALICE

spleen – see MALICE

splendid, resplendent, gorgeous, glorious, sublime, superb *shared meaning* : extraordinarily or transcendently impressive. Although often interchangeable in hyperbole or in general expressions of admiration or satisfaction, these adjectives are capable of being used to convey quite distinctive impressions. **Splendid** can imply an outshining of the usual or an impressing of the observer <a fine – yea even a *splendid* room, of great height, and carved grandeur – John Galsworthy> <one of those *splendid* individuals occasionally produced by an aristocratic society – a curious blend of pragmatic rationalist and incorruptible saint – C. W. Griffin, Jr.> **Resplendent** implies a glowing or blazing splendor <had shown how great and *resplendent* a thing love could be – J. W. Krutch> <the stars of early evening were *resplendent* – Erle Stanley Gardner> **Gorgeous** is likely to stress display or color, often splendid, sometimes merely showy or elaborate <this *gorgeous* combination of all the hues of Paradise – Henry Adams> <a quite meaningless but quite *gorgeous* archway ... covered and festooned with

pink roses – Herman Wouk> **Glorious** implies a being radiant with light or beauty or a standing out as being eminently worthy of admiring attention <now is the winter of our discontent made *glorious* summer by this sun of York – Shak.> <I never dreamed she had the great, soaring, spectacular voice she reveals . . . . Listening to her is a *glorious* experience – Norton Mockridge> **Sublime** implies an elevation or exaltation almost beyond human comprehension <there is in man's soul a flowing equilibrium between good and evil, the noble and the base, the *sublime* and the ridiculous – Eric Hoffer> <the *sublime* but also terrible and sombre experiences and emotions of the battlefield – Sir Winston Churchill> **Superb** implies attainment of the highest possible degree of competence, brilliance, excellence, grandeur, or splendor <the author's style is brilliant, his command of words and images *superb* – Harrison Smith> <*superb* figures, breathing health and strength – Laurence Binyon>

splenetic – see IRASCIBLE

split – see TEAR

spoil *n* **spoil, pillage, plunder, booty, prize, loot** *shared meaning* : something taken from another by force or craft. **Spoil,** usually as the plural **spoils,** applies to what belongs by right or custom to the victor (as in war or a political contest) <fire the palace, the fort, and the keep – leave to the foeman no *spoil* at all – Rudyard Kipling> <claim . . . colonies in Africa as its share of the *spoils* of war – Vera M. Dean> or sometimes to what can be gained (as by skill and effort or by casual collection) <the *spoils* of a conservative industrial life – Van Wyck Brooks> <showing the *spoils* from her bridal shower> **Pillage** stresses often violence and lawlessness in taking <hiding *pillage* taken during a riot> **Plunder** implies open violence and robbery <often the pirates were glad to accept money instead of *plunder* – C. S. Forester> **Booty** implies plunder accumulated and awaiting disposal or distribution <if they shared the *booty,* why should they not share the blame? – W. L. Shirer> **Prize** applies to spoils captured on the high seas or in the territorial waters of an enemy <a Latin treatise on the right of seizing *prizes* at sea – Stringfellow Barr> **Loot** is a highly condemnatory synonym for *plunder, booty,* or *spoils,* and may be applied specifically to what is taken from one who is helpless to protect his property (as by reason of death, catastrophe, or riot) <believed that the revolution which they had fought by brawling in the streets would bring them *loot* and good jobs – W. L. Shirer> <prowlers seeking *loot* after a disaster> In more general use the term applies to any ill-gotten gains <corrupt officials enriched by the *loot* of years>

spoil *vb* – see DECAY, INDULGE

spontaneity – see UNCONSTRAINT

spontaneous, impulsive, instinctive, automatic, mechanical *shared meaning* : acting or activated without deliberation. **Spontaneous** further implies lack of prompting and connotes naturalness <a *spontaneous* burst of applause> <the *spontaneous* wish to learn, which every normal child possesses – Bertrand Russell> **Impulsive** implies acting under stress of feeling or spirit of the moment, seemingly without thought or volition <an *impulsive* act of generosity> <my heart, *impulsive* and wayward – H. W. Longfellow> **Instinctive** stresses spontaneous action involving neither judgment nor will <her attitude was . . . as *instinctive* as the humping-up of a cat at a dog – Herman Wouk> <clung to their candles with an *instinctive* feeling that these . . . were . . . more to be trusted than the miracles of science – Thomas Wolfe> **Automatic** and **mechanical** apply to action seeming to engage neither the mind nor the emotions and connote uniformity and predictability of response <the responses of well-trained soldiers to commands are *automatic*> <engaged in futile and *mechanical* lovemaking, compulsive drinking, and considerations of suicide – J. W. Aldridge> ***ant*** studied

sporadic – see INFREQUENT

sport – see FUN

sprain – see STRAIN 2

sprightly – see LIVELY

spring *vb* **spring, arise, rise, originate, derive, flow, issue, emanate, proceed, stem** *shared meaning* : to come up or out of something into existence. **Spring** stresses surprising or rapid emergence <plants *springing* up after rain> <freedom of the mind, the basic freedom from which all other freedoms *spring* – Elmer Davis> *Arise* and *rise* may both convey the fact of coming into existence or notice, but **arise** may convey either no suggestion of a prior state or one of causation <a rumor *arose* and was widely circulated> <mistakes often *arise* from carelessness> <the right never existed, and the question whether it has been surrendered cannot *arise* – John Marshall> while **rise** often stresses gradual growth or ascent <the Gothic cathedrals *rose* in England in the first half of the thirteenth century – O. Elfrida Saunders> **Originate** implies a definite source or starting point <isn't it logical that a Supreme Being who is divine Truth *originates* honesty and justice? – R. J. Linnig> **Derive** implies a prior existence in another form <most of the value of a world constitution as symbol will *derive* from its principles – W. W. Wagar> <a basic sentence type may be transformed into a large variety of *derived* constructions – W. G. Moulton> **Flow** adds to *spring* the idea of abundance or ease of inception <ideas *flow* from him like water> <praise God from whom all blessings *flow* – Thomas Ken> **Issue** suggests emerging from confinement or a receptacle <the Court . . . *issues* no advisory opinions – it decides only actual cases and controversies – A. J. Goldberg> <three conclusions at least *issue* from the perusal – T. S. Eliot> **Emanate** suggests the passage of something immaterial and carries less suggestion of a causal force than *issue* <the house . . . was Carrie's and it was from her that *emanated* the atmosphere of a home – James Purdy> <though he is not given a chance to voice his tragedy, he manages to *emanate* it silently – Henry Hewes> **Proceed** may stress place of origin or derivation or cause <no public benefit which you receive but it *proceeds* or comes from them to you – Shak.> <his seeming inattention had only *proceeded* from his being involved in a profound meditation – T. L. Peacock> **Stem** implies originating by branching off from something as an outgrowth or subordinate development <[his] concern . . . in the problems of human settlements *stems* from his own early experience as a refugee – *Current Biog.*> <[school] decentralization *stemmed* from legislation and city policy – D. E. Rosenbaum>

spring *n* – see MOTIVE

springy – see ELASTIC

spry – see AGILE ***ant*** doddering

spur – see MOTIVE

spurn – see DECLINE ***ant*** crave, embrace

squabble – see QUARREL

squalid – see DIRTY

squander – see WASTE 2

square – see AGREE 3

squat – see STOCKY ***ant*** lanky

squeamish – see NICE

stagger – see REEL

staid – see SERIOUS ***ant*** jaunty

stain – see STIGMA

stalwart – see STRONG

stammer, stutter *shared meaning*: to speak stumblingly. **Stammer** more often implies a temporary inhibition (as from fear, embarrassment, or shock) <the eloquent tongue forgot its office. Cicero *stammered,* blundered, and sat down – J. A. Froude> **Stutter** is more likely to suggest a habitual defect characterized by involuntary repetition of sounds <this gentleman has . . . a small natural infirmity; he *stutters* – Samuel Foote> but it may apply to a similar manifestation due to a temporary cause <he has a tendency to get excited, and when he does he *stutters* – Jack Olsen> or even (as may *stammer*) to something suggesting the speech pattern of a stutterer <climbed into his Ford and *stuttered* down the hill – John Steinbeck> <her pen sometimes *stammers* with the intensity of the emotion that she controlled – Virginia Woolf>

stand *vb* – see BEAR

stand *n* – see POSITION

standard, criterion, gauge, yardstick, touchstone *shared meaning* : a means of determining what a thing should be. **Standard** applies to an authoritative rule, principle, or measure by which the qualities, worth, or nature of something can be measured <each generation . . . has its own ideals and its own *standards* of judgment – S. M. Crothers> <[she] was scrupulous about upholding *standards,* particularly the ones her husband wished enforced – R. J. Whalen> **Criterion** denotes the thing (whether formulated into rule or principle or not) by appeal to which one reaches a decision or judgment <the sole *criterion* of the truth of illusion is its inner congruity – J. L. Lowes> <these . . . recommendations . . . stand as ethical *criteria* for the federal government's relationship to social scientists – I. L. Horowitz> **Gauge** applies to a device for measuring a particular dimension or a distinguishable quality <a *gauge* for measuring the diameter of wire> <the fact that The Bomb exists becomes an absolute *gauge,* an ultimate proof, by which to consider our leaders misguided at best, and, at worst, sick – S. B. Chickering> **Yardstick,** basically a measuring stick a yard long, is often extended to standards or criteria for intangibles <the consumption of petroleum products, an accurate *yardstick* of economic growth – *Lamp*> **Touchstone** implies something (as a superior exemplar) by which the authenticity or value of an intangible can be tested <consistency is a *touchstone* by which the basic doctrine can often be distinguished from the propaganda line – L. C. Stevens> <a person's attitude to Hitler's persecution of the Jews during the 1930s was a *touchstone* by which one could judge much else about him – Henry Fairlie>

stare – see GAZE

stark – see STIFF

starry, stellar, astral, sidereal *shared meaning* : of, relating to, or suggesting a star or group of stars. **Starry** is nontechnical in status and general in application <a *starry* night> <our *starry* flag> <*starry* eyes> <here are the skies, the planets seven, and all the *starry* train – A. E. Housman> **Stellar** equally general in application is more likely to derive its suggestions from astrological lore and astronomical studies than, as *starry,* directly from the appearance of the celestial stars; thus, one tends to speak of a *stellar* (rather than *starry*) influence or aspect; one refers to a *stellar* (better than *starry*) eclipse or nebula <these soft fires . . . shed down their *stellar* virtue on all kinds that grow on Earth – John Milton> **Astral,** in much of its use a technical term in theosophy and related cults, tends in more general use to bear connotations (as of spirituality, mysticism, and remoteness from the fleshly) that derive largely from concepts of the stars as abodes of higher, rarer, superhuman beings <an *astral* myth> <an *astral* and most impractical thinker> <enchantments that unlock a crystal cage; an alphabet with *astral* fire seasoned – Elinor Wylie> **Sidereal** may replace any of the other terms but usually and distinctively it is used in opposition to *solar,* especially as applied to periods of time measured by the rotation of the earth with respect to a chosen star <a *sidereal* day>

start – see BEGIN

state *n* **state, condition, situation, status** *shared meaning* : the way in which a person or thing manifests existence or the circumstances under which he or it exists or by which he or it is given character. **State** may imply a mode of existence <[Dante's Inferno] reminds us that Hell is not a place but a *state* – T. S. Eliot> but more often implies the sum of the qualities involved in an existence at a particular time and place <in the present *state* of the art a semantic count ... is beyond the reach of computer technology – Henry Kucera & W. N. Francis> <remained in a feeble *state* for many months> **Condition** more distinctly imputes the effect of immediate or temporary influences <the present *condition* of the country> <under the best *conditions,* a voyage is one of the severest tests to try a man – R. W. Emerson> **Situation** applies to a state or condition that represents a combination of definite concrete circumstances; it implies an arrangement of these circumstances both with respect to each other and to the one involved that makes for a particular resulting condition (as of embarrassment, advantage, or difficulty) <there was a dizzy succession of events and of constantly changing *situations* for a politician to watch – W. L. Shirer> <while the French *situation* seemed to be following the classic Marxist pattern of a revolutionary *situation,* it was in reality something else – Irving Howe> **Status** applies to one's state or condition as determined with some definiteness, especially for legal administrative purposes or by social or economic considerations <his *status* as a university officer allows him access to university files that otherwise would be closed to him – *N.Y. Times*> <slave and citizen were separable and distinct legal *statuses,* but these merged and blurred in practice – Maurice Zeitlin>

state *vb* – see SAY

stately – see GRAND

statesman – see POLITICIAN

stature – see QUALITY 2

status – see STATE

statute – see LAW

staunch – see FAITHFUL

stay **1 stay, remain, wait, abide, tarry, linger** *shared meaning* : to continue in a place. **Stay** stresses continuance in a place or sometimes a situation and may connote the status of a visitor <[she] was *staying* over to do some shopping – *New Yorker*> <*stayed* for the evening meal – Sherwood Anderson> <*stayed* in the same job for over forty years> **Remain** is likely to suggest a staying after others have left <a little verse my all that shall *remain* – Thomas Gray> often for a usually specified purpose <he *remained* at Harvard for graduate study> **Wait** implies a staying in expectation or in readiness <*wait* for an answer to a letter> <[they] have learned to expect his verbal thunderstorms and *wait* them out – Andrew Hamilton> **Abide** implies prolonged staying or waiting and suggests either settled residence or patiently attending on some outcome <the foundations of a culture whose influence will *abide* while the world stands – Edward Clodd> <I will *abide* the coming of my lord – Alfred Tennyson> <repented my rashness in venturing to *abide* in town – Daniel Defoe> **Tarry** suggests failing to proceed when it is time to do so <he had *tarried* too

long abroad whooping it up with the international set – Arthur Knight & Hollis Alpert> **Linger,** often very close to *tarry,* may add an implication of deliberate delay or unwillingness to depart <he had walked the streets ... hoping to find the slave still *lingering* about – H. C. Hervey> <there still *lingers* some absurd prejudice against living on one's friends – Stella D. Gibbons>
2 see DEFER
steadfast – see FAITHFUL ***ant*** capricious
steady, even, equable *shared meaning* : not varying throughout a course or extent. **Steady** in general suggests regularity and lack of deviation (as in movement or course) <drove at a *steady* 40 miles an hour> <walk at a *steady* pace> but it may imply fixity in position <*steady* as a rock> or consistency in character <a *steady* workman> <maybe she'd marry the first nice and good *steady* fellow with a *steady* job who'd be a *steady* provider – J. T. Farrell> **Even** stresses lack of irregularity or variation and often connotes a dead level (as in quality or character) <had a monotonous *even* voice> <the child . . . was naturally of an *even* temper – Samuel Butler †1902> <able to compete on *even* terms> **Equable** usually implies an inherent quality that makes for invariability, such as uniformity <an *equable* pulse> or freedom from extremes or sudden changes <an *equable* climate> or a temperamental calmness <she won and lost, with the same *equable* sangfroid – Rose Macaulay> ***ant*** unsteady, nervous, jumpy
steal, pilfer, filch, purloin *shared meaning* : to take another's possession without right and without his knowledge or permission. **Steal,** the commonest and general term, may apply to any such act, though it is likely to suggest furtiveness and secrecy <it hadn't occurred to him to borrow . . . he had never borrowed, he had always *stolen* – Bernard Malamud> <Wagner *stole* liberally from Schubert as he did from other, often less exalted, figures – Harvey Gross> **Pilfer** suggests stealing with cautious stealth usually in small amounts and often again and again <the pantry mouse that *pilfers* our food – A. F. Gustafson *et al*> <*pilfer* the secret files of the foreign office – H. J. Morgenthau> **Filch,** close to *pilfer,* may stress the use of active though surreptitious means (as quick snatching) <I would fix drinks for us, often lacing them with rum or whiskey *filched* from the butler's pantry – John Barth> <a lot of fellows were too hungry to wait, and so some of the rations were *filched* – Asa Autry> **Purloin** stresses removing or carrying off for one's own use or purposes <had *purloined* $386,920 from the . . . firm for which he worked, then absconded – *Time*> <I hope to quote him is not to *purloin* – John Dryden>
stealthy – see SECRET
steep *adj* **steep, abrupt, precipitous, sheer** *shared meaning* : having an incline approaching the perpendicular. **Steep** implies such sharpness of pitch that ascent or descent is difficult <the trail . . . then struck up the side of the mountain, growing *steeper* every foot of the way – H. D. Quillin> **Abrupt** implies a sharper pitch and usually a sudden break in a level <high *abrupt* banks in places become hanging cliffs – *Amer. Guide Series: N.C.*> **Precipitous** suggests extreme steepness and an abruptness like that of a precipice <a deep gorge, with *precipitous,* volcanic walls which no man could scale – Jack London> **Sheer** implies precipitousness approaching the perpendicular and showing no break in its line <*sheer* cliffs that fell from the summit to the plain, more than a thousand feet – Willa Cather>
steep *vb* – see SOAK
steer – see GUIDE
stellar – see STARRY
stem – see SPRING

sterile, barren, impotent, unfruitful, infertile *shared meaning* : lacking the power to produce offspring or bear fruit. **Sterile** implies inability to reproduce or to bear literal or figurative fruit through or as if through an organic defect <the workers among ants and bees are *sterile*> <the way our culture makes the middle class safe, polite, obedient, and *sterile* – W. S. Coffin, Jr.> <a *sterile* parliamentary opposition – William Attwood> **Barren,** basically applicable to a sterile female, in more general use implies a lack of normal or expected return or profit <a *barren* conquest which brought him no special repute – John Buchan> **Impotent** applies to the male and implies inability to copulate or reproduce. **Unfruitful** may replace *barren* in any of its applications with the emphasis on not bearing fruit <an *unfruitful* tree> <an *unfruitful* enterprise> <this unsavory and *unfruitful* piece of research – Douglass Cater> **Infertile** is often interchanged with *sterile* <an *infertile* egg> but it may imply deficiency rather than absence of fertility <an *infertile* strain of beef cattle> <has our history shown that liberty is so *infertile* a principle that with it we are unable to compete in the world struggle . . . ? – W. L. Chenery> ***ant*** fertile

sterilize, disinfect, sanitize, fumigate *shared meaning* : to treat so as to destroy living organisms and especially germs. **Sterilize** suggests the use of drastic methods (as the use of intense heat or strong chemicals) with the intent of destroying all microorganisms, whether harmful or not. **Disinfect** implies an intent to free from all infective materials and suggests the use of strong methods on things likely to be contaminated. **Sanitize** is likely to be preferred with reference to preventive measures affecting the health of a community (as in the care and treatment of water supplies) or in cases when *sterilize* (because of its implication of killing all microorganisms) and *disinfect* (because of its suggestion of probable contamination) seem inappropriate. **Fumigate** implies the use of smoke or fumes to destroy microorganisms or, more often in modern use, insects and other arthropod pests.

stern – see SEVERE ***ant*** soft, lenient

stick, adhere, cohere, cling, cleave *shared meaning* : to become closely attached. **Stick** implies attachment by affixing or by or as if by being glued <marriage . . . was nothing more than a token that a couple intended to *stick* to each other – F. M. Ford> <the Council . . . could never hope to make its decisions *stick* – John Fischer> **Adhere** is narrower in idiomatic range and more formal in tone than *stick* but is the usual term when attachment results from or as if from growth of parts normally distinct or separate <abdominal tissues sometimes *adhere* after surgery> In reference to persons *adhere* usually implies deliberate acceptance and firm fealty <when he had made a plan he liked to *adhere* to it – Victoria Sackville-West> **Cohere** suggests a sticking together of parts or items to form a unified whole <good mortar *coheres* readily with the bricks> <he constructs a set of thematic embellishments which consistently develop and *cohere* into a unity – Henry Woodfin> **Cling** implies attachment by or as if by hanging on (as with arms, tendrils, or roots) <[they] *cling* stubbornly to their hopes of being saved . . . by a miracle – W. L. Shirer> <the traditional liberal . . . is still *clinging* to a concern for personal liberties and respect for personal rights – J. P. Lyford> **Cleave** implies closeness and strength of attachment <my tongue *cleave* to my roof within my mouth, unless a pardon ere I rise or speak – Shak.> <even if there were no children, he would probably *cleave* to her – Norman Mailer>

stiff, rigid, inflexible, tense, stark *shared meaning* : difficult or impossible to bend or enliven. **Stiff** may apply to any degree of this condition <a *stiff* taffeta> <egg whites beaten *stiff*> In extended application to persons or their ways it may suggest either extreme coldness and formality <[he]

is gracious without being *stiff* – *N.Y. Herald Tribune*> or a lack of ease in dealing with others <Brutus had . . . a *stiff* ungracious character – John Buchan> In application especially to things to be dealt with, or submitted to, or overcome it is likely to suggest severity or difficulty or the need for special effort <a *stiff* task> <a *stiff* sentence> <*stiff* controls> **Rigid** applies to something so stiff it cannot be bent or flexed without damaging or breaking it <an airplane with a *rigid* hull> <*rigid* iron gates – Aharon Appelfeld> **Inflexible** stresses lack of suppleness or pliability <snakes . . . with portions of their bodies still numb and *inflexible,* waiting for the sun to thaw them out – H. D. Thoreau> **Tense** suggests a straining or stretching to the point where elasticity or flexibility is lost <*tense* nerves> <his *tense* movements, the rather rigid way he held himself . . . showed excessive nervousness – Herman Wouk> <so frightened by his driving that she couldn't enjoy the night . . . . She was *tense,* taut, and curdling up inside – J. T. Farrell> **Stark** implies a stiffness associated with loss of life or warmth and often connotes desolation, barrenness, death, or present worthlessness <many a nobleman lies *stark* and stiff – Shak.> <all the surfaces *stark* and unyielding, thin and sharp – George Santayana> but often *stark* is little more than an intensive (often an adverb) <stood in *stark* terror> ***ant*** relaxed, supple

stifle – see SUFFOCATE

stigma, brand, blot, stain *shared meaning* : a mark of shame or discredit. **Stigma** may imply dishonor or public shame <the *stigma* of personal cowardice – William Peden> but more often it applies to a mark (as a charge or judgment) affixed to one in order to bring discredit <they can attach a social *stigma* to the relief by taking away the pauper's vote – G. B. Shaw> <mental illness . . . no longer carries a numinous *stigma* – *Times Lit. Supp.*> **Brand** carries stronger implications of disgrace and infamy and may suggest impossibility of removal or concealment or resulting social ostracism and public condemnation <for the sorrow and the shame, the *brand* on me and mine, I'll pay you back in leaping flame – Rudyard Kipling> <segregation, however "equal" the physical facilities, does put the *brand* of inferiority on Negro pupils – *N.Y. Times*> **Blot** and **stain** imply a blemish that diminishes but does not extinguish the honor of a name or reputation <thou noteless *blot* on a remembered name – P. B. Shelley> <to have loved one peerless, without *stain* – Alfred Tennyson>

still, stilly, quiet, silent, noiseless *shared meaning* : making no stir or noise. **Still** applies to what is motionless or at rest with the added implication of hush or absence of sound <ha! no more moving? *still* as the grave – Shak.> <the crowd remained *still,* quietly stupefied, and with a shaky reverence – William Styron> **Stilly** emphasizes the absence of sounds but usually implies also the absence of stir or motion <oft, in the *stilly* night, ere Slumber's chain has bound me – Thomas Moore> **Quiet,** like *still,* may imply absence of perceptible motion or sound or of both but it is likely to stress absence of excitement or turbulence and connote tranquillity, serenity, or repose <through the green evening *quiet* in the sun – John Keats> <a *quiet* town filled with people who lived *quiet* lives and thought *quiet* thoughts – Sherwood Anderson> *Silent* and *noiseless* can both apply to motion or stir that is unaccompanied by sound; in such use **silent** carries a stronger impression of silence <the Earth . . . from West her *silent* course advance[s] – John Milton> whereas **noiseless** usually connotes absence of commotion or of sounds of activity or movement <along the cool sequestered vale of life they kept the *noiseless* tenor of their way – Thomas Gray> ***ant*** stirring, noisy

stilly – see STILL

stimulate — see PROVOKE *ant* unnerve, deaden

stingy, close, niggardly, parsimonious, penurious, miserly *shared meaning* : being unwilling or showing unwillingness to share with others. **Stingy** implies a marked lack of generosity and regularly suggests an illiberal spirit <was he *stingier* than he dreamed, more lacking in the true if exorbitant demand for compassion without measure . . . ? — Norman Mailer> **Close** suggests keeping a tight grip on one's money or possessions <he was a little bit *close.* So the bargain hung fire — Dashiell Hammett> <a *close* buyer and a good marketer — W. A. White> **Niggardly** implies grudging giving or spending or, sometimes, being provided with the smallest amount possible <hated to part with even the most *niggardly* sum to charity> <tried to live on a *niggardly* pension> <he was close but not *niggardly;* he wasted nothing but he met his responsibilities ungrudgingly> **Parsimonious** suggests a frugality so extreme as to lead to stinginess <had spent a lonely bachelor life in caring for his property and in adding to it by *parsimonious* living — A. W. Long> **Penurious** implies niggardliness so great as to give the appearance of poverty <a grudging master . . . a *penurious* niggard of his wealth — John Milton> **Miserly** implies penuriousness, but it stresses obsessive avariciousness as the motive <a *miserly* man who hoards money out of avarice — William Empson> *ant* generous

stinking — see MALODOROUS

stint — see TASK

stipend — see WAGE

stir, bustle, flurry, pother, fuss, ado *shared meaning* : signs of excitement or hurry accompanying an act, action, or event. **Stir** suggests brisk or restless movement or reaction usually of a crowd <his denigration of traditional philosophy . . . caused a great *stir* in academic circles — *Current Biog.*> <as some messenger arrived . . . a *stir* would pass through the throng — Osbert Sitwell> **Bustle** implies a noisy, obtrusive, often self-important activity <the meaningless and vulgar *bustle* of newspaper offices — Stella D. Gibbons> **Flurry** stresses nervous agitation and undue haste <the reporter . . . sent the panel into a *flurry* by asking a question about clerical celibacy — John Leo> *Pother* and *fuss* imply flurry and fidgety activity; distinctively, **pother** may stress commotion or confusion and **fuss** needless worry or effort <it had made a dreadful *pother* and was still remembered uneasily — H. L. Mencken> <invited her parents to come on the fiesta weekend, calculating that the excitement and *fuss* would distract their attention from herself — Herman Wouk> **Ado** may suggest fussiness or waste of energy <go to work without more *ado*> or it may imply trouble or difficulty to be overcome <let's follow to see the end of this *ado* — Shak.> *ant* tranquillity

stocky, thickset, thick, chunky, stubby, squat, dumpy *shared meaning* : being or having a body that is relatively compact in form. **Stocky** suggests broad compact sturdiness <a *stocky,* round-faced man in a blue suit — Murray Schumach> **Thickset** implies a thick, solid, burly body <too *thickset* for jockeying — John Masefield> **Thick** is more often used for body parts than of body build <*thick* lips> <a small, stocky man, broad-shouldered and *thick* about the girth — W. F. Starkie> **Chunky** applies to a body type that is ample but robust and solid <short and *chunky,* not quite fat — H. A. Sinclair> **Stubby** stresses lack of height or length and real or apparent breadth <splay *stubby* fingers that looked incapable of such delicate precision in action> <a *stubby* little fellow with a broad smile on his broad face> **Squat** is likely to suggest an unshapely lack of height <the *squat* misshapen figure that flattened itself into the shadow — Oscar Wilde> **Dumpy** is likely to suggest short, lumpish gracelessness of body

<stumpy, *dumpy* girls with their rather coarse features, big buttocks and heavy breasts – Arthur Koestler>

stoic – see IMPASSIVE

stolid – see IMPASSIVE ***ant*** adroit

stoop, condescend, deign *shared meaning* : to descend from one's level (as of rank or dignity) to do something. **Stoop** may imply a descent in dignity or from a higher to a lower moral plane and often suggests a debasing of one's standards or principles for an unworthy end <to turn Federal stipends into a device to regulate student views and behavior is to *stoop* to methods generally associated with totalitarian states – *N.Y. Times*> **Condescend** may imply a gracious stooping of one exalted in power, rank, or dignity to facilitate intercourse with inferiors <Spain's mighty monarch, in gracious clemency, does *condescend,* on these conditions, to become your friend – John Dryden> but often it implies an assumed superiority and an affrontingly patronizing manner <those who thought they were honoring me by *condescending* to address a few words to me – F. W. Robinson> **Deign** suggests a reluctant condescension, especially of one temperamentally haughty, arrogant, or contemptuous <a scientific community which, insisting on its purity, will not *deign* to communicate with the public and justify itself, but prefers to believe that its virtues are so self-evident that a right-minded society must necessarily support it on its own terms – D. F. Hornig>

stop, cease, quit, discontinue, desist *shared meaning* : to suspend or cause to suspend activities. **Stop** applies primarily to action or progress or to what is thought of as moving or progressing; **cease** applies primarily to states and conditions or to what is thought of as being or having existence; thus, a train *stops* but does not *cease;* the noise it makes both *stops* and *ceases;* one *stops* a car but may *cease* driving a car <when I have fears that I may *cease* to be – John Keats> **Quit** may suggest either finality or abruptness in stopping or ceasing <*quit* smoking> <a few came, straggling and reluctant . . . : most *quit* after the first day – Thomas Pynchon> **Discontinue** implies the suspension of an accustomed activity or practice <*discontinue* a correspondence> <rural bus service was first curtailed and then *discontinued* entirely> **Desist** may stress forbearance or restraint as a motive for stopping or ceasing <*desisted* in his effort to press love upon her – Sherwood Anderson> or it may imply the futility of one's efforts <swindler and murderer *desisted* because they felt the latent strength of his personality – Osbert Sitwell>

stopgap – see RESOURCE

storm – see ATTACK

story, narrative, tale, anecdote, yarn *shared meaning* : a recital of happenings that is less elaborate than a novel. **Story** is the most general term, applicable to legendary lore <snowy summits old in *story* – Alfred Tennyson> or to an oral or written, factual or fictitious, prose or verse account, typically designed to inform or entertain and characteristically dealing with a series of related incidents or events <repeat the *story* of an opera> <*stories* tell of the wife . . . shouting at the old chief in a most unseemly manner – Mari Sandoz> **Narrative** is more likely to imply factual than imaginative content <an historical *narrative*> <his journal is the only surviving *narrative* of the expedition> **Tale** may suggest a leisurely and loosely organized recital often of legendary or imaginative happenings <*tales* based on folklore, legends of great men and small – Jane G. Mahler> **Anecdote** applies to a brief story featuring a small discrete and often humorous incident that may illustrate some truth or principle or illuminate some matter <relates . . . examples of satiric *anecdote* from the diatribes of Callimachus to the barbed witticisms of Mort Sahl – *Current Biog.*> **Yarn** is likely to suggest a rambling and rather dubious tale of exciting adventure, often marvelous or fanciful and without clear-cut outcome <the uncle, a wild or renegade sundowner, would arrive from Australia . . . bringing no gifts but his wonderful *yarns.* As far as Victoria remembered, he'd never repeated himself – Thomas Pynchon>

stout – see STRONG

straightforward, forthright, aboveboard *shared meaning* : free from all that is dishonest or secretive. Something **straightforward** is consistently direct and free from deviations or evasiveness <a *straightforward* answer> <he is a man; with clear, *straightforward* ideas, a frank, noble presence – Benjamin Disraeli> Something **forthright** goes straight to the point without swerving or hesitating <there should be no confusion about this University's dedication and *forthright* activity in the area of civil rights – M. S. Eisenhower> Something **aboveboard** is free of all traces of deception or duplicity <if his disobedience is ethical . . . he will be open and *aboveboard* about it – Joseph Fletcher> <the peace of mind that comes from being completely honest and *aboveboard* – R. J. Haupt> All three words are also used adverbially with the same implications and connotations. *ant* devious, indirect

strain **1** see STRESS

2 strain, sprain *shared meaning* : an injury to a part of the body through overstretching. **Strain,** the more general and less technical term, usually suggests overuse, overexercise, overexertion, or overeffort as a cause and implies injury that may vary from slight soreness or stiffness to a disabling damage; thus, eye*strain* is a condition of the eye or its muscles involving fatigue and pain and occurring especially in those who do close work with their eyes or have uncorrected visual defects; *charley horse* is a familiar term for stiffness resulting from a *strain* in an arm or leg <slipped and got a bad *strain* in his back> Sometimes *strain* specifically implies an injury resulting from a wrench or twist and involving overstretching of muscles and ligaments; in such use it is nearly interchangeable with, though usually suggesting less severe injury than, **sprain** which regularly implies injury to a joint, usually from a wrenching that stretches and tears its ligaments or enclosing membrane, resulting in swelling, pain, and disablement of the joint.

strait – see JUNCTURE

strange, singular, unique, unparalleled, peculiar *shared meaning* : varying from what is ordinary, usual, or to be expected. **Strange** stresses unfamiliarity; it may apply to what is foreign, unnatural, inexplicable, or new <it was *strange* to be having snow in April – Herman Wouk> <to most of us the art of China and Japan, however much it may attract and impress, is *strange* – Laurence Binyon> <lacked sympathy for *strange* customs – Agnes Repplier> **Singular** implies difference from all others of the same kind and stresses individuality <a distinguished and *singular* excellence – H. L. Mencken> often with a suggestion of a strangeness that puzzles or piques <his brain, in which everything was *singular,* hallucinatory, painfully distinct with that first impression of an utterly new world – Alfred Kazin> **Unique** implies an absence of peers but lacks the suggestion of a strange or baffling quality so often found in *singular* <the . . . Hope Diamond, a *unique* sapphire-blue gem – *Current Biog.*> <hardly a student passes through our schools and colleges who hasn't his *unique* expectations for self-discovery and fulfillment – J. A. Perkins> **Unparalleled** may be very close to *unique* <[his] experience and *unparalleled* ability in advertising – Mabel F. Hale> <his reputation was *unparalleled* in his day – Vincent Starrett> **Peculiar** may describe what exhibits marked or conspicuous distinctiveness in quality or character <a *peculiar* destiny had been in her blood, waiting for the proper time to crop out, and disturbing her with premonitory sensations – Herman Wouk> sometimes to the point of being singular or unique <the problems *peculiar* to the cities and the slums or most exacerbated there – M. A. Farber> ***ant*** familiar

strangle – see SUFFOCATE

stratagem – see TRICK

strategy, tactics, logistics *shared meaning* : an aspect of military science. Though sometimes used without clear distinction these words are capable of exact application and precise differentiation. In such use **strategy** applies to the art or science of fundamental military planning for the overall effective use of forces in war while **tactics** applies to that of handling forces in the field or in action; distinctively it suggests not only the actual presence of an enemy force but the immediate direction of a commanding officer on the scene <the theater of war is the province of *strategy*, the field of battle is the province of *tactics* – E. B. Hamley> <for the Germans everything went according to the book . . . in the unfolding both of *strategy* and of *tactics* – W. L. Shirer> **Logistics** is the art or science of military supply and transportation; the term covers both planning and implementation in all their aspects <*logistics* is the science of transportation and supply in war. It is the art of getting the right number of the right men to the right place with the right equipment at the right time – B. B. Somervell>

stream – see POUR

strength – see POWER

strenuous – see VIGOROUS

stress, strain, pressure, tension *shared meaning* : the action or effect of force exerted upon or within a thing. *Stress* and *strain,* the comprehensive terms, are sometimes interchangeable in application to a force tending to deform a body <put *stresses* and *strains* on parts of the body that were not constructed to bear that burden – Morris Fishbein> **Stress,** especially in physics, may also apply to the force by which a body resists deformation <a weight suspended from a rod tends to pull the rod apart. The *stress* developed in the rod to resist being pulled apart is called tensile *stress* – Samuel Slade & Louis Margolis> while **strain** in similar use may denote the deformation of a body resulting from applied force <a new device . . . measures *strain* in vulcanized rubber . . . after application of a predetermined stress – *Technical News Bull.*> **Pressure** commonly applies to a stress characterized by a weighing down upon or a pushing against a surface <the normal atmospheric *pressure* is about 14.7 pounds per square inch – *Van Nostrand's*> **Tension** applies to either of two balancing forces causing or tending to cause elongation of an elastic body or to the stress resulting in the body <*tension* is the stress that resists the tendency of forces acting in opposite directions to pull a body apart – *U.S. Technical Manual*>

strict – see RIGID ***ant*** lax, loose, lenient, indulgent

stricture – see ANIMADVERSION ***ant*** commendation

strident – see VOCIFEROUS

strife – see DISCORD ***ant*** peace, accord

strike 1 strike, hit, smite, slap, swat, punch *shared meaning* : to come or bring into contact with a sharp blow. *Strike, hit,* and *smite* are general in application and have broad possibilities of extension. **Strike** basically may imply aiming and dealing a blow with the hand or with a weapon or tool and usually with moderate or heavy force <*strike* a nail with a hammer> <*strike* a man down with a heavy blow> <the mixture of emotions that had convulsed him was now a vivid anger that *struck* at a single object – David Madden> **Hit** is likely to stress the impact of

the blow or the reacting of the target aimed at <*hit* a snake with a stick> <he held a club over my head – well, not literally, but if I didn't practice, I got *hit* – Henry Mancini> <life had never *hit* her very hard – Nevil Shute> **Smite,** a somewhat rhetorical or bookish word, is likely to stress the injuriousness or destructiveness of the contact and to suggest such motivations as hot anger or a desire for vengeance <with the hammer she *smote* Sisera, she *smote* off his head – *Judg* 5:26 (AV)> <the military settlement . . . had been *smitten* by a hurricane – A. H. Chisholm> **Slap** primarily applies to a striking with the open hand and implies a sharp or stinging blow with or as if with the palm of the hand <*slap* a naughty child> <waves *slapped* against the boat> <*slapped* the coverlet angrily – Kenneth Roberts> **Swat** suggests a forceful slapping blow with an instrument (as a flyswatter or a bat) <in off moments he would *swat* the regiments of cockroaches – Paul de Kruif> **Punch** implies a quick sharp blow with or as if with the fist <*punch* a man in the nose> <*punched* in the back by a shopper's umbrella> <we then pushed and *punched* our way into the . . . bus – J. D. Salinger>
2 see AFFECT
striking – see NOTICEABLE
stringent – see RIGID
strive – see ATTEMPT
stroll – see SAUNTER
strong, stout, sturdy, stalwart, tough, tenacious *shared meaning* : showing power to resist or to endure. **Strong** may imply power derived from muscular vigor, large size, structural soundness, or intellectual or spiritual resources <a community . . . is *strong* only to the extent that its members make the effort required to sustain and nourish it – J. A. Perkins> <with its wingspan of two feet or more, the black-bellied plover is a *strong* flier – Peter Matthiessen> **Stout** suggests an ability to endure without giving way <the Southerners cherished still . . . a *stout* and defiant loyalty to their antiquated limitations – Edmund Wilson> <our forebears in Virginia and New England . . . were indeed *stout* fellows – S. E. Morison> **Sturdy** implies strength derived from healthy vigorous growth, close, solid construction, or a determined spirit <this rash act against a *sturdy* foe . . . threatened to upset the applecart in the Balkans – W. L. Shirer> <our people are . . . conspicuous for a *sturdy* independence – W. R. Inge> **Stalwart** stresses an unshakable dependability and implies outstanding strength of body, mind, or spirit <[he] brings his *stalwart* common sense to bear upon the problem, and clarifies the issue – J. L. Lowes> <a *stalwart* man, limbed like the old heroic breeds – J. R. Lowell> **Tough** suggests the strength that comes from a firm unyielding texture that resists injury; it, then, stresses effective resistance and great resilience more than active defense <physically fragile, she was spiritually *tough* – Victoria Sackville-West> <learned . . . what a *tough,* cynical and opportunistic bargainer he was – W. L. Shirer> **Tenacious** adds to *tough* a suggestion of strength in seizing, retaining, clinging to, or holding together <he had always held with *tenacious* devotion to one of the ancient traditions of his race – Thomas Wolfe> <bold and *tenacious* as the bamboo shooting up through the hard ground of winter – Laurence Binyon> ***ant*** weak
structure, anatomy, framework, skeleton *shared meaning* : the parts of or the arrangement of parts in a whole. **Structure,** the most general term, is referable to any whole, natural or man-made, material or immaterial; thus, study of the *structure* of a fruit involves consideration of the several parts or layers of which it consists, their makeup and interrelations, and their source. Sometimes the term is used specifically of the parts or arrange-

ments that give a whole its characteristic form or nature; thus, the *structure* of a poem includes those features (as meter, verse form) that underlie and give form to the expression of the ideas it contains. **Anatomy** applies basically to the structure of an organism or any of its parts <study human *anatomy*> <the *anatomy* of the heart> but in its increasingly frequent extended use it is likely to stress examination of parts and study of their relation to a whole <a noted authority on the *anatomy* of the American government – Henry Brandon> *Framework* and *skeleton* apply to an underlying or supporting structure forming part of a whole. **Framework** is used chiefly with reference to an artificial construction that serves as a prop or guide in building but is not visible in the finished whole <the *framework* of a sofa> In extended and nonmaterial reference the same implications are usually present <teachers . . . can use it as a *framework* for the elaboration of exercises to suit their own classes – David Abercrombie> **Skeleton** basically applies to the bony framework of the animal body and is used in the building trades of a rigid supporting framework (as of steel). In its common extension to literary constructions it may imply either a carefully developed and articulated design or a sketchy conception of the whole that serves as a starting point; in either case it usually further implies that the elaboration of detail and actual writing remains to be done.

struggle – see ATTEMPT

strut, swagger, bristle, bridle *shared meaning* : to assume an air of dignity or importance. **Strut** suggests a pompous affectation of dignity, especially in gait or bearing <a poor player that *struts* and frets his hour upon the stage – Shak.> **Swagger** implies an ostentatious conviction of one's own superiority, often manifested in insolent gait and overbearing manner <what a *swaggering* puppy must he take me for – Oliver Goldsmith> <I'd noted a solitary jay *swaggering* among the fruit and almond trees – Jack Smith> **Bristle** implies an aggressive manifestation sometimes of anger or of zeal but often of an emotion that causes one to show one's sense of dignity or importance <all the time he stuck close to her, *bristling* with a small boy's pride of her – D. H. Lawrence> **Bridle** usually suggests an awareness of a threat to one's dignity or state and a reaction (as of hostility or resentment) typically expressed by a lofty manner and tokens of physical withdrawal (as a raised head and drawn-in chin) <the Negro hash house on the corner where the bucks *bridled* a little when I came in, and then ignored me – Norman Mailer> but it may suggest other motives (as coyness or self-importance) for a similar display <[she] *bridled* with pleasure when she saw me – Victoria Holt>

stubborn – see OBSTINATE

stubby – see STOCKY

study – see CONSIDER

stupendous – see MONSTROUS

stupid, dull, dense, crass, dumb *shared meaning* : lacking in or exhibiting a lack of power to absorb ideas or impressions. **Stupid** implies a slow-witted or dazed state of mind that may be either inborn or temporary <pouting one minute, charming the next, smart as a whip today, *stupider* than the most idiotic clerk tomorrow . . . the most aggravating man – Herman Wouk> <it was the worst period of my life, an extremely bleak, dreary, and *stupid* period – Jack Tworkov> **Dull** suggests a slow or sluggish mind such as results from disease, depression, or shock <had a warm spot in his heart for this *dull,* stupid, fumbling man – W. L. Shirer> **Dense** implies a thickheaded imperviousness to ideas or impressions <a woman may be a fool, . . . and she may even be simply stupid. But she is never *dense* – Joseph Conrad> <human error's *dense* and purblind faith – P. B. Shelley>

Crass suggests a grossness of mind precluding discrimination or delicacy <he resented him as a *crass* and stupid person who had fallen through luck into flowing prosperity – Bernard Malamud> **Dumb** may replace any of the other terms as a contemptuous designation but characteristically applies to an exasperating obtuseness and lack of articulateness <too *dumb* to do things in the right way – W. J. Reilly> <striking layouts attract the eye to fatuous articles and *dumb* stories – Walter Goodman> ***ant*** intelligent

stupor – see LETHARGY

sturdy – see STRONG ***ant*** decrepit

stutter – see STAMMER

style – see FASHION

suave, urbane, diplomatic, bland, smooth, politic *shared meaning* : ingratiatingly tactful and well-mannered. **Suave** suggests a specific ability to encourage easy and frictionless dealings with others <what gentle, *suave,* courteous tones! – Helen M. H. Jackson> <a man fashionably at ease, urbanely social . . . informed, alert, *suave* . . . the very model of what a great captain of finance, letters, arts, and enlightened principles should be – Thomas Wolfe> **Urbane** implies high cultivation and poise coming from wide social experience <writes with fluent charm, in the easy, *urbane,* richly allusive manner of an Oxford and Cambridge savant – Dixon Wecter> **Diplomatic** stresses an ability to deal with ticklish situations tactfully and effectively <the *diplomatic* manner . . . of a government official whose career depended on politeness to his equals and deference to his superiors – Helen MacInnes> **Bland** emphasizes mildness of manner and absence of irritating qualities <most of the time he sat behind a look of *bland* absorption, now and then permitting himself an inscrutable smile – H. C. Hervey> <his manners were gentle, complying, and *bland* – Oliver Goldsmith> **Smooth** tends to be derogatory and may imply an excessive, often assumed suavity <the words of his mouth were *smoother* than butter, but war was in his heart – *Ps* 55:21 (AV)> or an excess of tactfulness and craft <they . . . disguised their feelings . . . beneath masks of *smooth* feminine guilelessness – William Styron> **Politic** is likely to suggest a capacity for gaining one's ends or avoiding friction that may amount to a proper suavity or diplomaticness or may involve artful craft and deviousness <an attendant lord . . . deferential, glad to be of use, *politic,* cautious, and meticulous – T. S. Eliot> ***ant*** bluff

subdue – see CONQUER ***ant*** awaken, waken

subdued – see TAME ***ant*** intense, barbaric (*of taste*), bizarre (*of effects*), effervescent (*of character and temperament*)

subject *n* – see CITIZEN ***ant*** sovereign

subject *adj* – see LIABLE ***ant*** exempt

subjugate – see CONQUER

sublime – see SPLENDID

submission – see SURRENDER ***ant*** resistance

submissive – see TAME ***ant*** rebellious

submit – see YIELD 2 ***ant*** resist, withstand

subscribe – see ASSENT ***ant*** boggle

subservient, servile, slavish, menial, obsequious *shared meaning* : showing extreme compliance or abject obedience. **Subservient** stresses subordination and the associated state of mind and may connote a cringing or truckling attitude <he figured . . . as a certainty that she would always worship him and be nice and *subservient* – J. T. Farrell> **Servile** suggests an attitude of mean cringing submissiveness <in no country . . . did the clergy become by tradition so completely *servile* to the political authority – W. L. Shirer>

<they are not loyal, they are only *servile* – G. B. Shaw> **Slavish** suggests abject or debased servility, more fitting to a slave than a free man <fear took hold on me from head to foot – *slavish* superstitious fear – R. L. Stevenson> <she also became increasingly assiduous in her *slavish* attentions, until ... one would almost have thought that her duty toward him was her very life – Thomas Wolfe> **Menial** stresses humbleness and degradation of or like that of one bound to an economically and socially inferior occupation by lack of skill or intelligence <most *menial* of stations in that aristocratic old Boston world – V. L. Parrington> <life for each man had become a *menial* thing – Robert Lowry> **Obsequious** implies fawning or sycophantic compliance and exaggerated deference of manner <I slowed down so as not to burst in on him and so heighten the aversion my person inspired even in its most abject and *obsequious* attitudes – Samuel Beckett> <a duteous and knee-crooking knave ... doting on his own *obsequious* bondage – Shak.> ***ant*** domineering, overbearing

subside – see ABATE

substantiate – see CONFIRM

subterfuge – see DECEPTION

subtle – see LOGICAL ***ant*** dense (*in mind*), blunt (*in speech*)

succeed **1** see FOLLOW ***ant*** precede

2 succeed, prosper, thrive, flourish *shared meaning* : to attain or be attaining a desired end. **Succeed** implies an antithesis to *fail* and is widely applicable to persons and things <it is at the local level that innovations *succeed* or fail – Elton Hocking> <the little man had *succeeded* in disturbing the boy with his absurd proposal – Roald Dahl> **Prosper** carries an implication of continued or long-continuing and usually increasing success <*prosper* in business> <most whites and some Negroes outside the ghetto have *prospered* to a degree unparalleled in the history of civilization – *Kerner Report*> **Thrive** adds the implication of vigorous growth often because of or in spite of specified conditions <like most great revolutionaries he could *thrive* only in evil times – W. L. Shirer> <the creative personality, which *thrives* on conflict and on the clash and ferment of ideas – Stanley Kubrick> **Flourish** implies a state of vigorous growth and expansion without signs of decadence or decay but without any suggestion of how long this state will be maintained and sometimes with a hint of future decline <a Sudanese kingdom that *flourished* one thousand years before the Christian era – *Current Biog.*> <like all scholarship, the sciences cannot fully *flourish* ... in a society which gives an increasing share of its resources to military purposes – *Science*> ***ant*** fail, attempt

successive – see CONSECUTIVE

succinct – see CONCISE ***ant*** discursive

succumb – see YIELD 2

sudden – see PRECIPITATE

suffer – see BEAR, LET

sufferance – see PERMISSION

suffering – see DISTRESS

sufficient, enough, adequate, competent *shared meaning* : being what is requisite or desirable. **Sufficient** is likely to refer to a quantity or scope that meets the demands of a specific situation <an ample sum, one *sufficient* to supply those wants of hers – Thomas Hardy> <have not *sufficient* information to state the exact damage – F. D. Roosevelt> **Enough** differs little from *sufficient* except in being somewhat more approximate and less exact in its suggestion <my country! and 'tis joy *enough* and pride for one hour's perfect bliss to tread the grass of England once again – William Wordsworth> <for about eighty cents a day ... [he] ate *enough* to live

– Tex Maule> <after they burn their hands *enough* times on a hot stove, they learn to avoid the stove – R. K. Corbin> **Adequate** may imply barely meeting a requirement (as in quantity or quality) <there are many occasions when school textbooks are not *adequate* to the purpose – A. H. Marckwardt> <we can never have too many wise citizens or good men. The future of civilization depends on our having a more *adequate* supply of both – R. M. Hutchins> **Competent** implies measuring up to all requirements without question or being adequately adapted to an end <a *competent* person is one who has the legal and mental capacity to make a contract enforceable against him at law – L. B. Howard> <this is a *competent* review of the interaction of the police and the citizen – E. J. Bander> ***ant*** insufficient

suffocate, asphyxiate, stifle, smother, choke, strangle *shared meaning* : to interrupt the normal course of breathing. **Suffocate** is likely to imply the impossibility of effective breathing (as from the absence of oxygen, the presence of noxious gases, or interference with the passage of gases to and from the lungs) <*suffocating* under the sand which had fallen upon him> **Asphyxiate** is likely to refer to situations involving lack of oxygen or presence of toxic gas <several people were *asphyxiated* by chlorine escaping from the wrecked train> **Stifle** is appropriately used to refer to situations where breathing is difficult or impossible because of inadequate fresh air <a room dimly lighted by a few tiny oil lamps, the air heavy with a *stifling* sweet odor – Stanley Karnow> **Smother** is usable in situations in which the supply of oxygen is or seems inadequate for life; it often suggests a deadening pall of smoke, dust, or impurities in the air <a smell of soot which *smothered* the scent of wistaria and iris – Louis Bromfield> <I walked out into the *smothering* summer weather – *New Yorker*> **Choke** suggests positive interference with breathing (as by compression, obstruction, or severe inflammation of the throat) <*choke* on a bit of apple> <*choked* to death by a brutal marauder> **Strangle,** used in similar situations to *choke,* more consistently implies a serious or fatal interference <fingers itched to *strangle* him – R. W. Buchanan>

suggest 1 suggest, imply, hint, intimate, insinuate *shared meaning* : to convey an idea indirectly. **Suggest** may stress putting into the mind by association of ideas, an awakening of a desire, or an initiating of a train of thought <indirectly *suggest* the desired attitude – Dorothy Barclay> <he can *suggest* in his work the immobility of a plain or the extreme action of a bolt of lightning, without showing either – Dale Nichols> **Imply** is close to *suggest* but may indicate a more definite or logical relation of the unexpressed idea to the expressed <the philosophy of Nature which is *implied* in Chinese art – Laurence Binyon> <obscuring fundamental principles of democracy and *implying* that, in the immediate crisis, they were of only secondary importance – Mary J. White> **Hint** implies the use of slight or remote suggestion with a minimum of overt statement <looking for a minute at the soft *hinted* green in the branches against the sky – Shirley Jackson> <as thou with wary speech . . . hast *hinted* – John Keats> **Intimate** stresses delicacy of suggestion without connoting any lack of candor <from what he *intimated* to me the action . . . constituted a classic example of how beleaguered democracies can defend themselves – J. A. Michener> **Insinuate** applies to the conveying of a usually unpleasant or depreciatory idea in a sly underhanded manner <he could quietly *insinuate* the most scandalously hilarious things – Theodore Sturgeon> <the *insinuated* scoff of coward tongues – William Wordsworth> ***ant*** express

2 suggest, adumbrate, shadow *shared meaning* : to give an indication or impression of something stated. **Suggest** implies a quality in one thing that conveys to the senses or mind an impression of another <the flavor of allspice *suggests* that of nutmeg to many people> <his manners, his speech and habits of thought all seemed so prescribed ... that they *suggested* a system of conduct – John Cheever> <the fleur-de-lis *suggests* the royal power of France> **Adumbrate** implies a faint, obscure, or sketchy suggestion <such attitudes are only faintly *adumbrated* in the Conservative manifesto – Henry Fairlie> and is especially appropriate in reference to something felt as beyond full and perfect comprehension by man <both in the vastness and the richness of the visible universe the invisible God is *adumbrated* – Isaac Taylor> **Shadow** (often with *forth*) implies an obscure or indirect or sketchy representation (as by a symbol) <my theory of right conduct which these pages *shadow* forth – Herbert Spencer> <a statement could be delicately *shadowed* by an illusion – A. L. Guérard> ***ant*** manifest

suitable – see FIT ***ant*** unsuitable, unbecoming

sulky – see SULLEN

sullen, glum, morose, surly, sulky *shared meaning* : showing a forbidding or disagreeable mood. **Sullen** implies a silent ill humor and an unwillingness to be sociable or cooperative <he shuns the bellicose, *sullen* demeanor of many militants – T. J. Bray> <hordes of *sullen* slave laborers – W. L. Shirer> **Glum** suggests a dismal silentness either from low spirits or depressing circumstances <the two of you ... sitting there as *glum* as a pair of saints in hell – Mary Deasy> <a temporary *glum* period that's part of the ups and downs of daily life – *Consumer Reports*> **Morose** is likely to suggest a habitual mood of glumness coupled with an austere sour bitterness <life in a metropolitan center is a *morose* demonstration of the failure of otherwise intelligent men to manage their environment – Norman Cousins> <should there be any cold-blooded and *morose* mortals who really dislike this book – James Boswell> **Surly** implies a sullen mood accompanied by gruffness or churlishness of manner or speech <he indulged his moods. If he were *surly,* he did not bother to hide it; if he were aggressive, he would swear at her – Norman Mailer> **Sulky** suggests childish resentment expressed in peevish sullenness <we were a precious pair: I *sulky* and obstinate, she changeable and hot-tempered – G. B. Shaw>

sum, amount, aggregate, total, whole *shared meaning* : the quantity or number present in a group or mass. **Sum** applies to the result of addition of numbers or particulars <the family is ... much more than the *sum* of its problems – *Pilot*> **Amount** implies the result of combining sums into a whole <no limits are set ... to the *amount* one may impose upon one's relatives – Stella D. Gibbons> <the *amount* of cotton raised last year> **Aggregate** implies a counting or considering together all the distinct individuals or particulars of a group or collection <it is not true that a social force or effort is the mere *aggregate* of individual forces and efforts – J. A. Hobson> <minds which were expert on the *aggregate* and so had senses too lumpy for the particular – Norman Mailer> *Total* and *whole* suggest the completeness or inclusiveness of the result; distinctively, **total** may stress magnitude in the result, and **whole** unity in what is summed up <students in 2,086 high schools took a *total* of 37,829 examinations for college credit – E. M. Gerritz> <in the years to come the groups of buildings ... will all form a symmetrical *whole* – R. B. Keyser>

summary – see CONCISE ***ant*** circumstantial

summit, peak, pinnacle, climax, apex, acme, culmination *shared meaning* : the highest point attained or attainable. **Summit** implies the topmost level attainable <quickly rose to the *summit* of his profession> <certain com-

munity developers . . . have circumvented *summit* planners and rejected planning from the top down – Denis Goulet> **Peak** suggests the highest among other high points <this event was the *peak* of his career> <[he] considered physics . . . the *peak* of knowledge – G. T. Hellman> **Pinnacle** suggests a dizzying and often insecure height <a *pinnacle* of happiness – Van Wyck Brooks> <never achieved the *pinnacle* of public life, the presidency – Eric Sevareid> **Climax** implies the highest point in an ascending series <the quarrel had been only the *climax* of a long period of increasing strain – Elmer Davis> <the prophet Ezekiel, who describes the four sides of the heavenly chariot . . . is struck with silence when he reaches the *climax,* "the image of the glory of God" – Robert Gordis> **Apex** applies to the highest point (as in time or accomplishment) to which everything (as in a career or system of ideas) ascends and in which everything is concentrated <men who are at or near the *apex* of the business pyramid – J. P. Getty> <a point where it [textual criticism] reaches an *apex* of intellectual virtuosity, of self-enclosed sterility – M. D. Geismar> **Acme** applies to that high level which represents the perfection of a thing <he was the *acme* of courtesy> <that psychological stalwart, T. H. Huxley, seemingly the *acme* of self-confidence – R. K. Merton> **Culmination** may imply an apex that represents the necessary or logical outcome of a process of growth or development <his distinguished career found its *culmination* in the new appointment> or it may stress a coming to a head that may or may not suggest an apex <war is a *culmination* of evils, a sudden attack on the very existence of the body politic – F. D. Roosevelt>

summon, call, cite, convoke, convene, muster *shared meaning* : to demand the presence of. **Summon** implies authoritative action and may suggest a mandate, an imperative order, or urgency <I *summon* your grace to his Majesty's parliament – Shak.> <she could *summon* tears and delights as one *summons* servants – H. G. Wells> **Call** may replace *summon,* especially when less formality is implied, when imperativeness is not stressed, or when literal shouting is to be indicated <*call* men to arms> <*call* a servant> <I can *call* spirits from the vasty deep – Shak.> **Cite** may occasionally replace *summon,* especially in legal context <he hath *cited* me to Rome, for heresy – Alfred Tennyson> **Convoke** implies a summons to assemble, especially for legislative or deliberative purposes <he *convoked* the chiefs of the three armed services . . . and laid down the law – W. L. Shirer> **Convene** is close to *convoke* but often weaker in its suggestions of the exercise of authority and imperativeness <the principal *convened* the students in the high-school auditorium> <Mlle. Boulanger, who *convened* her bright young composers . . . in Paris – H. W. Wind> **Muster** basically applies to a summoning together of a body of persons (as a body of troops or a ship's company) for a particular purpose (as exercise, parade, or inspection) and in extended use may imply the assembling of a number of items for some purpose <*muster* a few pounds to buy some seed corn – Adrian Bell> or it can replace *summon* with certain immaterial objects <couldn't *muster* courage to pop the question – Agnes S. Turnbull>

sumptuous – see LUXURIOUS

sunder – see SEPARATE *ant* link

superb – see SPLENDID

supercilious – see PROUD

superficial, shallow, cursory, uncritical *shared meaning* : lacking in depth, solidity, and comprehensiveness. **Superficial** implies a concern with obvious or surface aspects or an avoidance of more fundamental matters <made a *superficial* inspection of the premises before writing his report> <critics complained that the exposition was more *superficial* than they had expected

from a sophisticated, literate diplomat – *Current Biog.*> <a *superficial* burn> **Shallow** is more generally derogatory in implying lack of depth (as in knowledge, reasoning, or character) <their interests are large, if *shallow* – Norman Mailer> <the poem . . . aims at a far *shallower* level of apprehension – Bonamy Dobrée> **Cursory** suggests haste and casualness that leads to a lack of thoroughness and neglect of details <the coffeehouse must not be dismissed with a *cursory* mention – T. B. Macaulay> <the Colonial Office found Wilmot slapdash in administrative procedures, . . . *cursory* in describing local affairs – Michael Roe> **Uncritical** implies a superficiality or shallowness unbefitting to a critic or a sound judge <*uncritical* acceptance would at best be transient and without conviction – H. C. White & J. W. Lee> <a wholly *uncritical* evaluation of the original analytical data – Cesare Emiliani> ***ant*** radical

supersede – see REPLACE

supervene – see FOLLOW

supervision – see OVERSIGHT

supine **1** see INACTIVE ***ant*** alert

2 see PRONE

supplant – see REPLACE

supple **1** see ELASTIC ***ant*** stiff

2 supple, limber, lithe, lithesome, lissome *shared meaning* : showing freedom and ease in bodily movements. **Supple** stresses flexibility of muscles and joints and perfect coordination and ease in movement <in good condition – not fat, like grass-fed cattle, but trim and *supple,* like deer – John Burroughs> **Limber** implies flexibility and ease and quickness in moving but does not stress excellence of coordination or grace <*limber* boys scrambling over the rocks> <her long *limber* fingers moved over the keyboard> **Lithe** suggests a slender supple body and nimble graceful movements <a *lithe* movement of her apparently boneless little figure – F. T. Jesse> <saw the *lithe* mechanic's body . . . flex like a drawn bow – Waldo Frank> **Lithesome** may suggest a strength and vigor that makes for sure graceful movement <the warlike carriage of the men, and their strong, *lithesome,* resolute step – A. W. Kinglake> **Lissome** may imply a light easy supple grace in bearing or movement <she only wanted wings to fly away, easy and light and *lissome* – J. C. Ransom>

supplicate – see BEG

supply – see PROVIDE

suppress, repress *shared meaning* : to hold back more or less forcefully one that seeks an outlet. **Suppress** implies a putting down or keeping back completely, typically by the exercise of great or oppressive power or violence; thus, one *suppresses* a revolt by taking vigorous steps to disorganize the group that supports it (as by military action, arrest of leaders, and restrictive legislation); one *suppresses* a foolish impulse by a strong, stern act of self-control <the bishop was purple with *suppressed* wrath – S. P. Sherman> <agreed to institute . . . a reign of terror designed to brutally *suppress* Polish freedom, culture, and national life – W. L. Shirer> **Repress** implies little more than a checking or restraining (as by keeping within bounds) and often suggests that the thing restrained may break out anew or in a different way <had difficulty in *repressing* his curiosity> <could not *repress* a smile at the comical figure – Ellen Glasgow> <developed psychic interests . . . but . . . these were *repressed* by her parents – A. G. N. Flew>

supremacy, ascendancy *shared meaning* : the position of being first (as in rank, power, or influence). **Supremacy** implies superiority over all others (as in utility, quality, desirability, or prestige) that is usually perfectly apparent or generally accepted <in the Sahara, the automobile has begun

to challenge the *supremacy* of the camel – Aldous Huxley> <the *supremacy* of Shakespeare among English dramatists> **Ascendancy** sometimes implies supremacy but its chief idea is either that of emerging domination or of autocratic use of power <the whole system of oppression and cruelty by which dominant castes seek to retain their *ascendancy* – Bertrand Russell> <the growing *ascendancy* of brains and skills over capital power – Bud Wilson> <gradually developed such an *ascendancy* over the old man that she could alienate him from his family>

sure, certain, positive, cocksure *shared meaning* : having no doubt or uncertainty (as of an opinion or conclusion). **Sure** is more likely to suggest an intuitive or subjective assurance <wonderful how she managed that light note when you were *sure* she couldn't be feeling it – Mary Austin> <they were *sure* . . . , forever wrong, but always confident . . . they confessed no ignorance or error, and they knew no doubts – Thomas Wolfe> **Certain** tends to stress the presence of definite grounds or indubitable and objective evidence as support for a position or conviction <whether slavery could have been abolished short of war is questionable, but it is *certain* that the methods employed by the radicals stirred public passions to the point that leaders who tried to work through to a peaceable . . . solution were cut off – Mary J. White> <knowledge of the briefness of man's days . . . and the *certain* dark that comes too swiftly and that has no end – Thomas Wolfe> **Positive** carries an intense implication of sureness or certainty <[they] turned up such evidence of the Abominable Snowman as part of a scalp and a mummified and skeletal hand, they found no *positive* proof – *Current Biog.*> and, as applied to persons, implies an absence of all uncertainty or doubt that may or may not be justified <so much more *positive* than most of his customers, and he impressed his convictions on them so determinedly, that he had his own way – H. E. Scudder> **Cocksure** implies careless or presumptuous positiveness <not being *cocksure* of my position [I] have often lacked the passionate conviction – W. A. White> <a pert *cocksure* answer to a question> ***ant*** unsure

surfeit – see SATIATE ***ant*** whet

surly – see SULLEN ***ant*** amiable

surmise – see CONJECTURE

surmount – see CONQUER

surpass – see EXCEED

surprise 1 surprise, waylay, ambush *shared meaning* : to attack unawares. **Surprise** in technical military use may imply strategic planning and secrecy in operations intended to catch an enemy unawares <R.A.F. bombers *surprised* a large invasion training exercise and inflicted heavy losses – W. L. Shirer> In more general use it is more likely to suggest a chance catching unawares <housemaids must vanish silently if *surprised* at their tasks – Victoria Sackville-West> <police *surprised* a burglar leaving the house> **Waylay** commonly implies a lying in wait along a public way, often in concealment <many a family coach was *waylaid* and its occupants robbed – F. W. Burgess> but sometimes it contains no hint of an evil intent and merely implies an intercepting and detaining <a group of seniors *waylaid* the president and asked if something couldn't be done about one of the boys who could not graduate – Josephine Y. Case> **Ambush** tends to evoke the image of would-be attackers concealed in a thicket; it is often used with reference to guerrilla warfare <he had been *ambushed* by Indians on nearby Wolf Run – *Amer. Guide Series: Pa.*> but is equally applicable to other situations where the primary image is pertinent <the nymphs feed by *ambushing* lesser insects . . . grabbing them with a pinching lower lip that can shoot out faster than the eye can see – R. H. Boyle> <the same

kind of feeling *ambushed* me a few weeks ago – Jan Struther>
2 surprise, astonish, astound, amaze, flabbergast *shared meaning* : to impress forcibly through unexpectedness, startlingness, or unusualness. **Surprise** can apply to a coming upon another unexpectedly and startlingly <Susannah *surprised* in her bath by the elders> or to any unexpected development that tends to startle or cause wonder <*surprised* at the way the children had grown during the summer> <he . . . frequently *surprises* by the contrast between the strength of his imagination and the awkwardness of his technique – Ian Scott-Kilvert> **Astonish** applies to a surprising so greatly as to seem incredible <the former corporal showed an *astonishing* grasp of military strategy and tactics – W. L. Shirer> <this sense of political identity . . . has . . . instilled an *astonishing* notion of self-discipline – Tad Szulc> **Astound** stresses the stunning or overwhelming emotional effect especially of something unprecedented <as Americans approached the latter part of the twentieth century the older ones among them could look back on some *astounding* changes – R. G. Tugwell> <*astounded* his congregation by putting up for sale a mulatto slave girl – *Amer. Guide Series: N.Y. City*> **Amaze** usually stresses bewilderment, perplexity, or wonder more than astonishment <she went through agonies of jealousy and remorse, and fantasies of revenge, which *amazed* her with their violence – Herman Wouk> <that he should even speak to her was *amazing!* – but to speak with such civility – Jane Austen> **Flabbergast** is a picturesque and often hyperbolic synonym of *astonish* or *amaze* that suggests a visible and sudden dumbfounding <all said . . . that when . . . they didn't know the answer they were scared half to death. I was *flabbergasted* – to find this in a school which people think of as progressive; which does its best not to put pressure on little children – John Holt>
surrender *vb* – see RELINQUISH
surrender *n* **surrender, submission, capitulation** *shared meaning* : the yielding up of one's person, forces, or possessions to another person or power. **Surrender** in both military and general use is likely to imply a complete yielding and a dependence on the mercy or humanity of a stronger power <Dreiser will derive his creative energy from a kind of fascinated *surrender* to the mysterious forces that in the City destroy freedom – Richard Poirier> <believed that a *surrender* to necking marked a dramatic turn in one's emotions – Herman Wouk> **Submission** stresses the acknowledgment of the power or authority of another and often suggests loss of independence <the hierarchical system . . . protects and perpetuates itself through its demands for *submission,* obedience, and acceptance – Mary L. Bundy & Paul Wasserman> <*submission,* Dauphin! 'tis a mere French word; we English warriors wot not what it means – Shak.> **Capitulation** may stress conditions elaborated between parties to a surrender <after Lee's surrender . . . Buckner . . . negotiated terms of *capitulation* . . . for the trans-Mississippi armies – E. M. Coulter> but, especially in general applications, it is likely to stress completeness or finality of yielding <Hilter, reassured of the strength of his position, now forced a complete *capitulation* on the other leaders – W. L. Shirer> <it was not the story which amazed her so much as Mrs. Holt's startling *capitulation* to the impulse to tell it – Marcia Davenport>
surreptitious – see SECRET
surveillance – see OVERSIGHT
survey – see COMPENDIUM
susceptible – see LIABLE ***ant*** immune
suspend – see DEFER, EXCLUDE
suspicion – see UNCERTAINTY

suture – see JOINT
swagger – see STRUT
swarm – see TEEM
swarthy – see DUSKY
swat – see STRIKE 1
sway *vb* – see AFFECT, SWING 2
sway *n* – see POWER 3
sweeping – see INDISCRIMINATE
sweet, engaging, winning, winsome *shared meaning* : distinctly pleasing or charming and free of all that is irritating or distasteful. **Sweet** is likely to be a term of mild general approbation for what pleases or attracts without stirring deeply <what a *sweet* little cottage> <twilight, *sweet* with the smell of lilac and freshly turned earth – Corey Ford> <has been very *sweet.* He wants to help – Louis Auchincloss> but in this use, as in its primary application to a taste sensation, it can sometimes suggest a cloying excess of what is pleasing in moderation <the flaw in her book is the *sweet* side, the Pollyanna note – Rosemary Benét> **Engaging** is likely to stress the power of attracting and often of holding favorable attention <affectionate, cheerful, happy, his sweet and *engaging* personality drew all men's love – H. O. Taylor> <an able and *engaging* history of the relationship between American political and educational thought – L. A. Cremin> **Winning,** otherwise close to *engaging,* is likely to stress the power of a person to please or delight <a nobler and more *winning* appearance – Edmund Wilson> <a girl with a ready smile and very *winning* ways> **Winsome** implies a generally pleasing and engaging quality and often a childlike charm and innocence <misled by ill example and a *winsome* nature – Francis Jeffrey> <he rarely gave offense. His drawing-room conversation was such an artless dance of bad words that he was considered at his *winsomest* when he was at his bawdiest – Alva Johnston> ***ant*** sour, bitter
swell – see EXPAND ***ant*** shrink
swerve, veer, deviate, depart, digress, diverge *shared meaning* : to turn aside from a straight course. **Swerve** may suggest a usually somewhat abrupt physical, mental, or moral turning <at this point the road *swerves* to the left> <if I be false, or *swerve* a hair from truth – Shak.> **Veer** is likely to imply a change or series of changes of course, often under an outside influence <[the ship] plunged and tacked and *veered* – S. T. Coleridge> <his thought, *veering* and tacking as the winds blew – V. L. Parrington> <legislative proceedings frequently *veer* off into areas of somewhat less than momentous significance – Trevor Armbrister> **Deviate** stresses the fact of turning from a customary or prescribed course and often suggests irregularity <in reality [he] lives in a climate where nonconformity is forbidden, . . . where he does not dare to express a *deviating* opinion – *AAUP Bull.*> <when the aesthetic sense *deviates* from its proper ends to burden itself with moral intentions – Havelock Ellis> **Depart** stresses leaving an old, customary, or accepted way <*departed* from the path to short-cut through the woods> <conditions of actual practice in virtually every profession *depart* . . . from the professional ideal – Mary L. Bundy & Paul Wasserman> **Digress** implies a usually voluntary departure that is typically intended to be transitory <*digress* from one's main theme to explain a point of usage> **Diverge** may imply departure <*diverging* from his direct path – Thomas Hardy> <traditions recorded there *diverge* from those that my mother handed down – George Santayana> but more typically it suggests division of one course or path into two that lead away from each other <proceeded along the road together till . . . their paths *diverged* – Thomas Hardy>

swift — see FAST
swindle — see CHEAT
swing **1 swing, wave, flourish, brandish, thrash** *shared meaning* : to move or move something repetitively or in an orderly pattern. **Swing** implies regularity or periodicity of usually to-and-fro motion <*swing* the lantern to warn of danger> <the road ran along by the sea . . . *swinging* gently up and down — D. H. Lawrence> **Wave** usually implies smooth or continuous movement <a flag *waving* in the breeze> <then grave Clarissa graceful *waved* her fan; silence ensued — Alexander Pope> **Flourish** implies triumph, ostentation, or bravado in swinging or waving something held in the hand <with their swords *flourished* as if to fight — William Wordsworth> **Brandish** adds a suggestion of menace or threat <I shall *brandish* my sword before them — *Ezek* 32:10 (AV)> <the men, *brandishing* . . . pistols, took their loot from a teller — *Gary Post-Tribune*> **Thrash** suggests a noisy vigorous abrupt swinging <everyone went to the woods and *thrashed* out some new blaze — Mary H. Vorse> <*thrashing* his arms about his body to keep warm>
2 swing, sway, oscillate, vibrate, fluctuate, waver, undulate *shared meaning* : to move to and fro, up and down, or back and forth. **Swing** implies movement through an arc of something attached at one end or one side <the door *swung* open> <the red amaryllises . . . *swung* in heavy clusters — Stark Young> **Sway** implies a slow swinging or teetering movement <he remained standing there for at least four or five seconds, gently *swaying*. Then he crashed to the carpet — Roald Dahl> <camels, *swaying* with their padded feet across the desert — L. P. Smith> **Oscillate** stresses a usually rapid alternation between extremes <the psychological poles between which the generations since Rousseau have *oscillated* — Judith N. Shklar> <the motion of the [atomic] nucleus will be negligible compared with that of the electrons, so that the latter may be considered to *oscillate* about a fixed position — John W. Gardner> **Vibrate** suggests the rapid oscillation of an elastic body under stress or impact <at any temperature above absolute zero, atoms *vibrate* — *U.S. Atomic Energy Commission*> <they could share nothing but a secret knowledge, a shadowy terror which *vibrated* between them — H. C. Hervey> **Fluctuate** suggests constant irregular changes of level, intensity, or value <markets operate most efficiently when prices are allowed to *fluctuate* in response to conditions of supply and demand — *Monthly Economic Letter, First National City Bank (NYC)*> **Waver** implies unsteadiness or uncertainty suggestive of reeling or tottering <his plump hands *wavering* uncertainly away from his body as he tripped, and caught up and tripped, trying desperately not to fall behind — Norman Mailer> <a very effective lever in swaying a *wavering* legislator confronted with a decision on a controversial law — *Amer. Labor*> **Undulate** implies a wavelike motion <a snake *undulating* through the grass> and is likely to suggest a continuous rolling or rippling <the ripe corn under the *undulating* air *undulates* like an ocean — P. B. Shelley>
syllabus — see COMPENDIUM
symbol, emblem, attribute, type *shared meaning* : a perceptible thing that stands for something unseen or intangible. *Symbol* and *emblem*, often interchangeable, can be so used as to convey clearly distinguishable notions; in such use **symbol** is applicable to an outward sign of something spiritual or immaterial; thus, the cross is to Christians the *symbol* of salvation because of its connection with the Crucifixion <a king's crown is the *symbol* of his sovereignty and his scepter the *symbol* of his authority> <a flock of sheep is not the *symbol* of a free people — *New Republic*> **Emblem**, on the other hand, may apply to a pictorial device or representation chosen

as the symbol of one (as a person, a nation, a royal line, or an office) who has adopted it; thus, the spread eagle, the usual *emblem* of the United States is found on its coat of arms and on some of its coins and postage stamps <the fleur-de-lis is the *emblem* of French royalty> <remembering this flower . . . as the feminine *emblem* of the big college football games – Edmund Wilson> *Emblem* may also, like **attribute,** apply to an object that is conventionally represented in art as an accompanying symbol of a character (as a saint) or of a personified abstraction; thus, the balance appears as the *emblem* or *attribute* of Justice; the turning wheel, of Fortune; the spiked wheel, of Saint Catherine of Alexandria. **Type,** chiefly in theological use, applies to one that prefigures or foreshadows another to come and serves as a symbol of the latter in the interim <concludes that the whole of the Old Testament is one great prophecy, one great *type* of what was to come – A. J. Maas>

sympathetic – see CONSONANT

sympathy **1** see ATTRACTION *ant* antipathy

2 sympathy, pity, compassion, ruth, empathy *shared meaning* : a feeling for or a capacity for sharing in the interests or distress of another. **Sympathy** is the most general term, ranging in meaning from friendly interest or agreement in taste to emotional identification <in immediate *sympathy* with my desire to increase my . . . knowledge – David Fairchild> <*sympathy* involves similar feelings. What affects one person affects another similarly. A man feels bad because a friend is hurt or sick – Harry Levinson> **Pity** implies tender or sometimes slightly contemptuous sympathy or sorrow for one in distress <he felt a tender *pity* for her, mixed with shame for having made her pitiable – Bernard Malamud> <for those who walk out on a great book I have only *pity* – Stringfellow Barr> **Compassion** implies tenderness and understanding and a desire to aid or spare <with understanding, with *compassion* (so different from pity) she shows the sordid impact . . . on the lives of the natives – Sarah Campion> but *compassion* can be quite impersonal in its reference <there can be no law and order without justice and *compassion* – Jeanne L. Noble> **Ruth** is likely to suggest pity or compassion resulting from the softening of a stern or indifferent spirit <is there no pity, no relenting *ruth* – Robert Burns> <look homeward, Angel, now, and melt with *ruth* – John Milton> **Empathy** implies a capacity for vicarious feeling, but the feeling need neither be one of sorrow nor involve agreement; thus, *empathy* is used as a synonym for some senses of *sympathy* but is essentially opposed to *sympathy* in other uses <what he lacks is not *sympathy* but *empathy,* the ability to put himself in the other fellow's place – G. W. Johnson>

symptom – see SIGN

synchronous – see CONTEMPORARY

syndicate – see MONOPOLY

synopsis – see ABRIDGMENT

synthetic – see ARTIFICIAL

system – see METHOD

systematize – see ORDER

taciturn – see SILENT *ant* garrulous, clamorous (*especially of crowds*), convivial (*of habits*)

tact, address, poise, savoir faire *shared meaning* : skill and grace in dealing with others. **Tact** implies delicate and sympathetic perception of what is fit or considerate under given circumstances <of political wisdom ... Elizabeth had little or none; but her political *tact* was unerring – J. R. Green> <without the *tact* to perceive when remarks were untimely – Thomas Hardy> **Address** stresses dexterity and grace in approach to or coping with new and difficult situations and may imply success in attaining one's ends <to bring the thing off as well as Mike has done requires *address* – Herman Wouk> **Poise** often implies both tact and address but stresses self-possession and ease in meeting trying situations <the appearance of self-possession or *poise* that comes from an habitual attention to what is graceful and becoming – D. C. Hodges> **Savoir faire** may stress worldly experience and resulting awareness of what is proper or expedient in various situations <the inexperience and want of *savoir faire* in high matters of diplomacy of the Emperor and his ministers – C. C. F. Greville> ***ant*** awkwardness

tactics – see STRATEGY

taint – see CONTAMINATE

take 1 take, seize, grasp, clutch, snatch, grab *shared meaning* : to get hold of by or as if catching up with one's hand. **Take** is a very general term applicable of any method of getting into one's possession <*take* meat from the platter with a fork> <*take* a city after a long siege> <*take* a prize by winning a contest> **Seize** implies a sudden and forcible effort in getting hold of something tangible or in apprehending something fleeting and elusive <the hungry cat *seized* the fish head> <*seize* an opportunity> <let every hope be *seized* – John Ciardi> **Grasp** stresses a laying hold of so as to have firmly in possession <thy hand is made to *grasp* a palmer's staff – Shak.> <there is nothing harder to *grasp* than the tone of a word or phrase – Susie I. Tucker> **Clutch** suggests haste or avidity or anxiety in seizing or grasping and often failure to take or hold <they *clutch* childishly at straws of optimism – Herman Wouk> <I . . . *clutched* desperately at the twigs as I fell – W. H. Hudson †1922> **Snatch** can apply to sudden, hurried, often stealthy <*snatch* a purse> <*snatch* a kiss> <*snatch* a free moment for writing a letter> or sometimes aggressive action <*snatched* a book from her sister's hand> <the Gestapo *snatched* him as he was leaving the courtroom – W. L. Shirer> **Grab** usually implies more roughness and rudeness than *snatch* and often suggests arrogant or vulgar disregard for the rights of others <[he] was the first to *grab* the phone, which he refused to release to the other reporter – *Current Biog.*> <*grab* the best piece of meat> <he *grabbed* his hat and ran> <hastened to California . . . to *grab* rich mineral and timber lands – *Amer. Guide Series: Minn.*> **2** see RECEIVE

tale – see STORY

talisman – see FETISH

talk – see SPEAK

talkative, loquacious, garrulous, voluble *shared meaning* : given to talk or talking. **Talkative** may imply a readiness to engage in talk or a disposition to enjoy conversation <a *talkative* boy learns French sooner in France than a silent boy – Sydney Smith> <he was *talkative,* he had a natural curiosity – William Styron> **Loquacious** may imply fluency and ease in speech or an undue talkativeness <the briskness of the mountain atmosphere, or some other cause, made everyone so *loquacious* – Nathaniel Hawthorne> **Garrulous** implies prosy, rambling, or tedious loquacity <a fond *garrulous* old man, who loved to indulge his mind in reminiscences – Anthony Trollope> **Voluble** suggests a free, flowing, and seemingly unending loquacity <realizing that she had made a faux pas, was uneasy and *voluble* – S. H. Adams> <in his open, *voluble* way, . . . [he] launched

into a story tangential to the matter we had been discussing – R. G. Tugwell> *ant* silent
tally – see AGREE 3
tame, subdued, submissive *shared meaning* : docilely tractable or incapable of asserting one's will. **Tame** in application to persons or their acts or utterances implies a lack of independence and spirit that permits or results from domination by others <the tribunal lately so insolent, became on a sudden strangely *tame* – T. B. Macaulay> <the *tamest,* the most abject creatures . . . they seem to have no will or power to act but as directed by their masters – William Bartram> **Subdued** generally implies a loss of vehemence, intensity, or force; in reference to persons or their activities it may suggest the quietness or meekness of one dependent, chastised, or timorous <in such a man, so gentle and *subdued* . . . a race illustrious for heroic deeds, humbled, but not degraded, may expire – William Wordsworth> <[his] manner . . . was well-trained deception, a *subdued* mockery – J. T. Farrell> **Submissive** implies the state of mind of one who has yielded his will to control by another <man wants woman to be neither *submissive* nor aggressive but an equal combination of the two – Eulah C. Laucks> *ant* fierce
tamper – see MEDDLE
tang – see TASTE 1
tangible – see PERCEPTIBLE *ant* intangible
tantalize – see WORRY *ant* satisfy
tap, knock, rap, thump, thud *shared meaning* : to strike audibly. As nouns all apply to the resulting sounds. **Tap** implies a light blow usually repeated (as to attract attention) <*tap* on the window to attract a friend's attention> **Knock** implies a firmer blow, sometimes amounting to a pounding or hammering, and a correspondingly louder sound <the messenger *knocked* loudly to awaken us> **Rap** suggests a smart vigorous striking on a hard surface that produces a sharp quick sound or series of sounds <they heard the woodpecker *rapping* away on the old apple tree> <the chairman *rapped* for order> **Thump** implies a solid pounding or beating that produces a dull booming sound <fell head first down the stairs of the bungalow, with tremendous *thumping* and banging – Herman Wouk> <everybody's heart was *thumping* as hard as possible – W. M. Thackeray> **Thud** places more emphasis on the sound and often implies the result of something falling or striking rather than of something being struck <they could hear the soft *thudding* of the hoofs on the ground – Elizabeth Spencer> <a bullet *thudded* into the wall – Hubert Wales>
tardy, late, behindhand, overdue *shared meaning* : not arriving or doing or occurring at the set, due, or expected time. **Tardy** implies a lack of promptness or punctuality that may result from slowness in progress but more often is due to delay in starting <ten years is a long time for a courtship, and she summons courage to spur her *tardy* swain – Seamus Kelly> <the *tardier* indicators of business activity have . . . begun to turn down – *Fortune*> **Late,** opposed to *early,* usually stresses a failure to come or take place at the time due and may or may not imply culpability <he was *late* for work most mornings> **Behindhand** usually applies directly or indirectly to persons who are in arrears (as in paying debts) or who are in some respect slower than the usual or normal person <a whole class who were *behindhand* with their lessons – Nathaniel Hawthorne> <in a big house . . . one is always *behindhand.* The days aren't long enough – George Moore> **Overdue** may apply to what has become due but not been dealt with <an *overdue* library book> or what has been expected or scheduled but has not arrived <our guests are long *overdue*> or to what might logically

have occurred or appeared long before <this impulse has shaken up the educational establishment, produced *overdue* educational reform – J. A. Perkins> ***ant*** prompt

tarry – see STAY 1

tart – see SOUR

task, duty, job, chore, stint, assignment *shared meaning* : a piece of work to be done. **Task** applies to a specific piece of work or service usually imposed by authority or circumstances <[he] is often summoned to *tasks* outside the . . . campus – *Current Biog.*> <there was no *task* in all the household range of duties . . . which her mistress could not do – Thomas Wolfe> **Duty** implies an obligation to perform or responsibility for performance <complain of the inefficient way the nurses and tutors carried out their *duties* – Victoria Sackville-West> <all agreed that . . . it was Goering's clear *duty* under the decree to take over – W. L. Shirer> **Job** is a general term wide in suggestion, ranging from voluntary undertaking of some signal service down to an assigned bit of menial work <he was on his way to France for a four-week vacation combined with a *job* of writing – Helen MacInnes> <it was his *job* to polish the brass every Saturday> <took on the thankless *job* of committee chairman> **Chore** may apply to a minor routine activity essential to functioning (as of a home or office) <every high calling has its *chore* work – David Poling> or it may stress the drabness of such routine work or activity <when you travel every day it becomes a *chore* – A. C. Ingersoll> **Stint** stresses carefully measured or timed apportionment of work <journalists who, in their daily *stints* . . . played . . . with the vagaries of the American language – Richard Bridgman> <widespread awareness among Americans of the importance of a *stint* in Vietnam for professional advancement – R. J. Lifton> **Assignment** implies a definite limited task assigned by one in authority <the teacher gave the class a long *assignment* in arithmetic> <it is not our *assignment* to settle specific questions of territories – Harry S Truman>

taste 1 taste, flavor, savor, tang, relish, smack *shared meaning* : that property of a substance which makes it perceptible to the gustatory sense. **Taste** merely indicates the property <the fundamental *tastes* are acid, sweet, bitter, and salt> **Flavor** suggests the interaction of the senses of taste and smell <a head cold seems to spoil the *flavor* of most foods> <the *flavor* of a fine tea has been described as "a bouquet which can be tasted"> **Savor** suggests delicate or pervasive flavor appealing to a sensitive palate <sipping slowly to get the full *savor* of the wine> **Tang** implies a sharp penetrating flavor or savor <there was a *tang* of thyme in the dressing> **Relish** may come close to *savor* and then imply enjoyment of the taste <a Laplander . . . has no notion of the *relish* of wine – David Hume †1776> **Smack** applies especially to an added or unexpected flavor <ale with an odd musty *smack*> <there's a good *smack* of pepper in the stew>

2 taste, palate, relish, gusto, zest *shared meaning* : a liking for or enjoyment of something because of the pleasure it gives. **Taste** implies a specific liking or interest natural or acquired <she had a *taste* for melancholy – for the smell of orange rinds and wood smoke – John Cheever> <his *taste* was for something either very lowbrow or very highbrow – Rex Warner> **Palate** implies a liking based on pleasurable sensation <in the midst of such beauty . . . one's body is all one tingling *palate* – John Muir †1914> <the discriminating *palate* of a tea taster> **Relish** suggests a capacity for keen gratification <a man of . . . a quick *relish* for pleasure – T. B. Macaulay> <he turns with *relish* to the death scenes of the victims of strong drink – Gerald Carson> **Gusto** implies a hearty relish that goes with high spirits and vitality <the pagans had the advantage: they could sin with *gusto* and abandon

– A. C. Guild> <they ... kissed with ... *gusto* and began to speak of their marriage as a thing settled – Herman Wouk> **Zest** implies eagerness and avidity in doing, making, encountering, or experiencing or a quality that stimulates these <[he] can still recall in detail, and recount with *zest*, the improbable details of some of those transactions – Bernard Taper> <there is a *zest* and sparkle in writing and pictures alike which is most stimulating – *Times Lit. Supp.*> ***ant*** antipathy

tasty – see PALATABLE ***ant*** bland

taunt – see RIDICULE

taut – see TIGHT 1

tawdry – see GAUDY

tawny – see DUSKY

teach, instruct, educate, train, discipline, school *shared meaning* : to cause to acquire knowledge or skill. **Teach** applies to any manner of imparting information or skill so that others may learn <*teach* a child to read> <that same prayer does *teach* us all to render the deeds of mercy – Shak.> **Instruct** suggests methodical or formal teaching <schoolmasters will I keep within my house, fit to *instruct* her youth – Shak.> <*instruct* a group in first-aid procedures> **Educate** stresses the bringing out and developing of latent qualities <*educate* the masses into becoming fit for self-government – Aldous Huxley> and is likely to imply complex schedules of instruction and plans of teaching designed to this end <there is no reason to believe that an automated economy ... could not be built around ... a level of educational attainment which is considerably lower than our own. However, since we have the *educated* they are hired in preference to the uneducated – R. M. Solow> **Train** stresses instruction and drill with a specific end in view <troops ... equipped and *trained* to fight in the bitter cold and the deep snow – W. L. Shirer> <*train* a dog to point game> **Discipline** stresses subordination to a master or subjection to control, often self-control <[she] writes like a jet-propelled butterfly – an impression of light ... absent-mindedness masking her *disciplined* prose – Pamela Marsh> <*disciplined* thinkers> **School** usually implies training or disciplining especially in what is hard to master or to bear <they would tell him they had detected in the book some slight traces of a talent which, with careful nursing, could be *schooled* to produce, in time, a publishable book – Thomas Wolfe> but occasionally it is interchangeable with *educate* <some of them have been *schooled* at Eton and Harrow – G. B. Shaw> or with *teach* or *instruct* <*schooled* by my guide, it was not difficult to realize the scene – S. C. Hall>

tear, rip, rend, split, cleave, rive *shared meaning* : to separate forcibly. **Tear** implies pulling apart or away by or as if by main force and often suggests jagged rough edges or laceration <*tore* his coat on a nail> <*tore* a chunk from the loaf of bread> <flood *tore* a ... gorge through the township – *Amer. Guide Series: Vt.*> **Rip** implies a forcible pulling or breaking apart typically along a line of juncture <Macduff was from his mother's womb untimely *ripped* – Shak.> <*rip* the shingles from a roof> **Rend,** somewhat rhetorical in tone, implies a violent and ruthless severing or sundering <*rend* your heart, and not your garments – *Joel* 2:13 (AV)> <the black volume of clouds ... *rent* asunder by flashes of lightning – Washington Irving> **Split** suggests a forceful but often precise separation in the direction of natural grain or layers <*split* wood for kindling> and in extended use implies force sufficient to split <let sorrow *split* my heart, if ever I did hate thee – Shak.> **Cleave,** often close to *split*, may convey the notion of laying open by or as if by a powerful blow of an edged weapon or tool <struck the final blow, *cleaving* the Archbishop's skull – E. V. Lucas> <his acumen

clove clean to the heart of a piece of writing – D. G. Mandelbaum> **Rive** implies a violent splitting <when the Presbyterians were *riven* by the Great Schism – J. K. Galbraith> <blunt wedges *rive* hard knots – Shak.>

tease – see WORRY

tedium, boredom, ennui, doldrums *shared meaning* : a state of dissatisfaction and weariness. **Tedium** is likely to suggest dullness and lowness of spirits resulting from irksome inactivity or sameness or monotony of occupation <incessant recurrence without variety breeds *tedium* – J. L. Lowes> <a natural *tedium* inherent in a solid week of broadcasting a big political assembly – R. L. Tobin> **Boredom** adds suggestions of listlessness, dreariness, and unrest that accompany an environment or situation or company that fails to stimulate or challenge <she failed bookkeeping because of *boredom,* preferring to write poetry on the ledger – *Current Biog.*> <he often made her smile and gave her a little distraction from the *boredom* of housework – J. T. Farrell> **Ennui** stresses profound dissatisfaction or weariness of spirit and often suggests physical depression as well as boredom <is there really any writer . . . who cares to have miserable readers, with loathing and *ennui* in their hearts – Lesley Conger> <that *ennui,* that terrible taedium vitae, that comes on those to whom life denies nothing – Oscar Wilde> **Doldrums** applies to a period of depression marked by listlessness, lagging spirits, and despondency <Lotharioism is simple monogamy's *doldrums* multiplied, and with thrice monogamy's duties – G. J. Nathan> In more general applications the term implies a dull inactive state <the stock market has been in the *doldrums* lately>

teem, abound, swarm, overflow *shared meaning* : to be plentifully supplied (*with*) or rich (*in*). Though often interchangeable these words are capable of carrying quite distinct implications. **Teem** implies productiveness or fecundity <the rivers *teemed* with fish and the woods with game> <[he] lounged . . . outwardly inert but *teeming* inside with sad and philosophical reflections – Thomas Pynchon> **Abound** implies plenitude in numbers or amount and usually stresses profusion <the fine restaurants with which the town *abounds* – John Weld> <explanations of his behavior *abound,* but most are unsatisfactory – S. E. Ambrose> **Swarm** usually stresses motion and thronging <a marketplace *swarming* with buyers and sellers – T. B. Macaulay> but it may suggest infestation <tenements that *swarmed* with rats and other vermin> **Overflow** adds to *abound* the notion of exceeding capacity to contain or use <built up a supposition . . . about cartons in a closet *overflowing* with valuable material – R. G. Tugwell> <a black beehive of a woman, *overflowing* with flesh and . . . good humor – H. C. Hervey>

tell – see REVEAL, SAY

telling – see VALID

temerity, audacity, hardihood, effrontery, nerve, cheek, gall *shared meaning* : conspicuous or flagrant boldness. **Temerity** implies a contempt of danger and consequent rashness or presumptuousness <the *temerity* of those whites who . . . are willing to prescribe . . . self-genocide for blacks, which is precisely how unrelenting black versus white violence must end – J. L. Perry> **Audacity** implies a bold disregard of usual or normal restraints <[he] had the *audacity* to make a synthesis of the antithetical creeds of impressionism and cubism – Duncan Phillips> <the moral *audacity,* the sense of spiritual freedom, that one gets from certain scenes in the Gospels – Edmund Wilson> **Hardihood** stresses firmness of purpose and may imply considered defiance (as of conventions); it is commonly used with critical intent and then may come close to *insolence* or *impudence* <no historian or astronomer will have the *hardihood* to maintain that he commands this God's-eye view

– A. J. Toynbee> **Effrontery** implies a flagrant arrogant disregard of propriety or courtesy <he had the damnable *effrontery* to tell me my father's delay was occasioned by . . . his addiction to immoral practices – John Cheever> *Nerve, cheek,* and *gall* are close synonyms of *effrontery;* distinctively, **nerve** may stress hardihood, **cheek** impudent self-assurance, and **gall** outrageous insolence <had the *nerve* to think that the federal government could be of help to its very poorest citizens – Robert Coles> <the *cheek* of him . . . imagine a miserable-looking leprechaun like Pat Dolan to be having notions of a fine girl like Maria – Maura Laverty> <the small stockholder who . . . has the *gall* to ask questions about the management – D. L. Cohn> ***ant*** caution

temper *vb* – see MODERATE *vb* ***ant*** intensify

temper *n* – see DISPOSITION, MOOD

temperament – see DISPOSITION

temperance, sobriety, abstinence, abstemiousness, continence *shared meaning* : self-restraint in the gratification of appetites and desires. Basically **temperance** implies habitual moderation and the exercise of discretion in any activity; but it may be used specifically in reference to the use of intoxicating beverages and then implies not moderation but abstention; thus, a *temperance* hotel is one where no alcoholic drinks are sold. **Sobriety** suggests avoidance of excess, often specifically of the excess of drinking that leads to intoxication; in its general applications it may connote seriousness and the avoidance of ostentation <the natural frivolity of youth matured into the *sobriety* of complete matronhood – Victoria Sackville-West> <he lived in *sobriety* . . . and gave all outward appearance of godliness – Gerald Carson> **Abstinence** implies voluntary deprivation <the Cynic preached *abstinence* from all common ambitions, rank, possessions, power, the things which clog man's feet – John Buchan> **Abstemiousness** implies habitual self-restraint, moderation, and frugality, especially in eating or drinking <four years, or so, of *abstemiousness* enable them to stand an election dinner – Sir Walter Scott> **Continence** emphasizes the fact of self-restraint in regard to impulses and desires <he knew what to say, so he knows also when to leave off, a *continence* which is practiced by few writers – John Dryden> and finds its typical application in regard to sexual indulgence where it may imply, according to circumstances, either complete chastity or avoidance of excess.

temperate **1** see MODERATE *adj* ***ant*** intemperate, inordinate
2 see SOBER 1

tempt – see LURE

tenacious – see STRONG

tenacity – see COURAGE

tend, attend, mind, watch *shared meaning* : to take charge of or look after someone or something. All these words can apply to a responsibility that constitutes an occupation or to one that is a duty imposed by authority or one's circumstances. **Tend** suggests the need for constant or recurring attention; though often used in reference to menial, unskilled, or routine activities it typically takes as its object something that requires attention; thus, one who *tends* a lock must be ready to adjust the water level when a boat approaches; a shepherd *tends* a flock of sheep by seeing that they get good grazing, do not stray, and are protected from predators; one *tends* a fire by seeing to its fuel supply and adjusting its draft as needed; to *tend* a sick person or a child one provides watchful ministering personal care. **Attend** is more likely to stress a taking charge and is, therefore, appropriate when a professional service or skilled activity is involved <the doctor who *attended* his mother> **Mind,** otherwise close to *tend,* distinctively suggests a guarding or protecting (as from injury or harm) <when more scholarships took him abroad . . . she stayed home *minding* the children – Padma Perera> **Watch,** often close to *mind,* may imply a more constant or more professional relationship or suggest an actual need to forestall danger <wilt thou receive this weighty trust when I am o'er the sea? To *watch* and ward my castle strong, and to protect my land – Sir Walter Scott>

tendency, trend, drift, tenor, current *shared meaning* : a movement or course having a particular direction and character. **Tendency** implies an inclination that may amount to a driving force sending a person or thing in a particular direction <a growing *tendency* to . . . underestimate the potential strength of the United States – W. L. Shirer> <the whole *tendency* of evolution is towards a diminishing birthrate – Havelock Ellis> **Trend** applies to the general direction maintained by a winding or irregular course <the *trend* of the market has been downward for some months> <the *trend* in contemporary Christian thought that seeks to reduce . . . its traditional preoccupation with God – Robert Gordis> **Drift** may apply to a tendency whose direction or course is determined by external influences (as a wind or a fashion or a state of public feeling) <arguing . . . for national unity, trying to end the *drift* towards civil war – *Current Biog.*> <the universal *drift* towards violence, bureaucracy, irrationality – Jack Newfield> or it may apply to an underlying inferable meaning <I see the whole *drift* of your argument – Oliver Goldsmith> **Tenor,** often close to *drift* in this latter use, carries a stronger implication of clearness of meaning or purport <the general *tenor* . . . of the talks – Bernard Smith> In this as well as its more common application to a course or movement with a clearly perceptible direction, the word stresses continuity and absence of deviation from a course or plan <wrote a letter of very bellicose *tenor*> <along the cool sequestered vale of life they kept the noiseless *tenor* of their way – Thomas Gray> **Current** implies a clearly defined but not necessarily unalterable course or direction <no *current* should be yielded to merely because it is strong – R. M. Hutchins> <he has not . . . changed the *current* of our constitutional law – M. R. Cohen>

tenet – see DOCTRINE

tenor – see TENDENCY

tense 1 see STIFF *ant* expansive
2 see TIGHT 1

tension – see STRESS

tentative – see PROVISIONAL *ant* definitive

tenuous – see THIN *ant* dense

terminal – see LAST *ant* initial

terminate – see CLOSE *vb*

termination – see END *ant* inception, source

terminus – see END *ant* starting point

terrestrial – see EARTHLY *ant* celestial

terrible – see FEARFUL 2

terrific – see FEARFUL 2

terse – see CONCISE

testy – see IRASCIBLE

thankful – see GRATEFUL *ant* thankless

theatrical – see DRAMATIC

theft, larceny, robbery, burglary *shared meaning* : the act or crime of stealing. In spite of the common meaning element these words are precisely and distinctively applicable to specific situations. **Theft** implies the taking and removing another's property without his consent and usually by stealth; it is the broadest of these terms and is applicable to such varied acts as pilfering, purloining, swindling, embezzling, or plagiarizing <the *theft* of an idea may hurt far more than the *theft* of money> **Larceny,** chiefly in legal use, applies to simple direct theft in which the property of one person is taken into the possession of another <the shoplifter was watched and only arrested after she left the store with the stolen jewelry in order that there be complete proof of *larceny*> <*larceny* is divided into "grand" and "petty" categories according to the value of the goods taken> **Robbery** in strict use implies violence or the threat of violence employed in taking another's property from his person or in his presence <highway *robbery*> <the messenger was attacked and seriously injured in the course of a *robbery*> **Burglary** implies a forced and unlawful entering of enclosed premises for the purpose of committing a felony, usually that of larceny or robbery.

then – see THEREFORE

theoretical, speculative, academic *shared meaning* : concerned principally with abstractions and theories. **Theoretical** may apply to branches of learning which deal with the inferences drawn from observed facts and the laws and theories which explain these <the distinguishing feature of *theoretical* science is the anticipation of facts from experience – G. H. von Wright> and in such use is often opposed to *applied* <the discoveries of *theoretical* physics that form the bases for applied physics> But *theoretical* may often imply a divorce from reality or actuality that gives one a distorted view of things or a lack of testing and experience in actual use and is then opposed to *practical* <the book does have great practical importance in spite of its predominantly *theoretical* character – M. G. White> <[he] is familiar with both the *theoretical* and practical aspects of the problems his bank now faces – *Forbes*> **Speculative** may go beyond *theoretical* in stressing a concern with theorizing and often implies a daring use of the imagination in the manipulation of ideas <the strength of much Catholic theology and philosophy . . . is its *speculative* boldness, its willingness to bear and even revel in total uncertainty – Daniel Callahan> **Academic** in this use is likely to be depreciatory; it regularly stresses a tendency to concentrate, often overconcentrate, on the abstract to the neglect of reality or practical concerns <professionalism . . . not in abstract *academic* terms but rather in the real world – Mary L. Bundy & Paul Wasserman> <an inept *academic* urge to technical accuracy – C. L. Wrenn>

therefore, hence, consequently, then, accordingly *shared meaning* : as a result or concomitant. The terms vary in the degree of closeness of relation suggested as well as in the kind of logical sequence implied. *Therefore* and *hence* usually indicate that what follows is a necessary deduction from what has preceded. **Therefore** stresses the conclusion that it introduces <half of our new recruits . . . were substandard . . . and, *therefore,* offered less than the best educational opportunity to their students – *Conn. Teacher*> **Hence,** though often interchangeable with *therefore,* is more likely to stress the importance of what precedes <implicit in the few studies . . . that have been made . . . is a feeling that the psychological variables are intangible and *hence* not amenable to analysis – Deborah Tanzer> **Consequently** in introducing a deduction need not imply necessity in the inference; rather, it tends to suggest good and reasonable grounds or imply a strong antecedent possibility <he said he would come; *consequently* we will wait for him> <the majority are impatient for freedom from adult control. . . . *Consequently,* many give the bulk of their interest and energy to peer-group activities – *Johns Hopkins Mag.*> **Then,** when used to indicate logical sequence, is employed chiefly in the consequent clause or conclusion in a conditional sentence <if A and B are mutually exclusive possibilities

and A is true, *then* B is false> <if the angles are equal, *then* their complements are equal> **Accordingly** usually indicates logical or causal sequence but connotes naturalness or usualness in the consequence rather than necessity or inevitability <he also knew that their support was essential to the success of his legislative program. *Accordingly,* he took steps to solidify their positions with their constituents – T. P. Murphy>

thick 1 see CLOSE *adj*

2 see STOCKY ***ant*** thin

thickset – see STOCKY

thin, slender, slim, slight, tenuous *shared meaning* : not thick, broad, abundant, or dense. **Thin** may imply comparatively little extension between surfaces or in diameter <a *thin* sheet of glass> <*thin* wire> or it may imply lack of substance, richness, or abundance <a *thin* soup> <*thin* reedy voices> <*thin* gray hair> **Slender** implies leanness or spareness, often with grace and good proportion <a clump of *slender* birches swaying in the breeze> <*slender* white hands – Sherwood Anderson> **Slim,** often very close to *slender,* may, especially in extended use, stress meagerness or scantiness or lack of substance <he has only a *slim* chance to recover> <a *slim* attendance at the party> <even if the black African nations' military resources were not *slim,* South Africa's forces would be more than adequate to deal with any conceivable African alliance – Anthony Delius> **Slight** in most of its use stresses smallness more than thinness <of *slight* stature, . . . [he] is five feet two inches tall – *Current Biog.*> and often implies a failure to come up to a level of what is adequate, significant or desired <a charming though *slight* novel – Dorrie Pagones> <a *slight* and transient fancy – Matthew Arnold> **Tenuous** implies extreme thinness, sheerness, or lack of substance and firmness <sheer hose, *tenuous* as cobwebs> <the *tenuous* alliances developing here and there between African nations and black Americans – W. H. Ferry> <the *tenuous* Martian atmosphere – E. J. Öpik> ***ant*** thick

thing, object, article *shared meaning* : something considered as having actual, distinct, and demonstrable existence. In spite of their shared element of meaning these terms vary considerably in their range of application. **Thing** may apply not only to whatever can be known directly through the senses but to something the existence of which is inferred from its signs and effects; thus, one thinks of the state, the church, literature, health, and the law as *things* rather than abstractions; one's affection for one's family is as real a *thing* as one's body or one's house; one distinguishes a word from the *thing* it names. In more restricted use *thing* can distinguish an entity existing in space and time from one existing only in thought <virtue is not a *thing* but an attribute of a *thing*> or an inanimate entity (as a material possession) from living beings and especially persons <she treasures each *thing* she buys> Idiomatically, *thing* may be used also to mention without specifically identifying an item whose nature is implicit in the context; thus, in "be sure to wear warm *things,*" clothing is implied; in, "bring in the tea *things,*" the needed dishes, implements, and food is implied. **Object** stresses existence separate from the observer and typically applies to something that is or can be set before one to be viewed, considered, or contemplated <a student may make an abstraction an *object* of thought> or that has body and usually substance and shape <stumbled over some unseen *object* in the dark room> **Article** is used chiefly of objects that are thought of as members of a group or class <the high cost of meat and other food *articles*> <picked up several *articles* of clothing that the boy had dropped>

think 1 think, conceive, imagine, fancy, realize, envisage, envision *shared meaning* : to form an idea of something in the mind. **Think** implies the entrance of an idea into the mind, with or without deliberate consideration or reflection <*think* of a plan to get out of work> <the children *thought* the clown very amusing> <I would make a little mistake and that would be all I could *think* about – Don Drysdale> **Conceive** implies the bringing forth of an organized product of thought and often suggests the growth and development that ensues as the mind dwells on it <they're philosophers . . . . They can't help *conceiving* the highest good in terms of intelligence and morality – Herman Wouk> <he shivered with pleasure as he *conceived* robberies, assaults – murders if it had to be – Bernard Malamud> **Imagine** stresses visualization <he . . . *imagined* seeing her in the things that were hanging on the line – Bernard Malamud> **Fancy** suggests an imagining more or less unrestrained by factual reality <expressed his daydreams in drawings of himself as a cowboy and other *fancied* figures – *Current Biog.*> <the Center . . . ought not to be carried away and *fancy* itself as a behind-the-scenes formulator of governmental policy – R. M. Hutchins> **Realize** implies a vivid conception or imagination through which the significance of a thing is attained <*realize* one's limitations> <on the whole the novel, though small in scope, is well *realized* – Cecil Hemley> <why couldn't they *realize* certain obvious truths – William Styron> **Envisage** and **envision** imply a conceiving or imagining that is especially clear or detailed <education . . . as Hitler *envisaged* it, was not to be confined to stuffy classrooms but to be furthered by a Spartan, political and martial training – W. L. Shirer> <in his youth he had *envisioned* the starred face of the night with high exaltation – Thomas Wolfe>

2 think, cogitate, reflect, reason, speculate, deliberate *shared meaning* : to use one's powers of conception, judgment, or inference. **Think** is general and may apply to any mental activity or, when used alone, may suggest attainment of clear ideas or conclusions <when I was a child, I spake as a child, I understood as a child, I *thought* as a child: but when I became a man, I put away childish things – *1 Cor* 13:11 (AV)> <she talks too much. She reads too little. She *thinks* not at all. Her mind is hysterically hidebound – Theodore Sturgeon> <colleges are places where at least some men learn to *think* – Walter Lippmann> **Cogitate** stresses depth and intentness of thinking more than productivity <a number of the delegates had been *cogitating* for years, and discussing among themselves the content of a desirable constitution – R. G. Tugwell> **Reflect** suggests unhurried consideration of something called or recalled into the mind <stood *reflecting* on the circumstances of the preceding hours – Thomas Hardy> **Reason** implies consecutive logical thinking <where all is uncertain, we must *reason* from what is probable – A. T. Quiller-Couch> <he has seen the great capabilities of the human mind . . . and his own capabilities have been enlarged through rigorous exercise of his *reasoning* power – M. S. Eisenhower> **Speculate** implies reasoning about theoretical or problematic matters <the two women *speculated* with deep anxiety on whether or not little Pamela had died of exposure – John Cheever> <in times of peace the specialists of war . . . may only *speculate* about the effect of new weapons – S. L. A. Marshall> **Deliberate** suggests slow or careful reasoning and consideration of various aspects in an attempt to reach a conclusion or form an idea <he allows no digressions, he dispenses with ornaments . . . . All his effects are *deliberated,* not chanced – *Times Lit. Supp.*> <please you, *deliberate* a day or two – Shak.>

3 see KNOW

thirst – see LONG

though, although, albeit *shared meaning* : in spite of the fact that. All introduce subordinate clauses stating something that is or may be true notwithstanding what is asserted in the main clause. **Though,** the most widely used of these words, can introduce a clause that states an established fact <*though* philology was Bede's chief interest and concern, he by no means stopped there – Kemp Malone> or one that offers a hypothesis or admission of possibility or probability <they decided to go on, *though* rain seemed likely> and is the usual term to introduce a contrary-to-fact or imaginary condition <*though* he slay me, yet will I trust in him – *Job* 13:15 (AV)> It is also likely to be preferred when inverted order is chosen for its effect <modest *though* his needs were, he found he must add to his slender income> **Although,** in most uses interchangeable with *though,* may be chosen to introduce an assertion of fact <[he] has lived in England almost continuously . . . , *although* he has remained an American citizen – *Current Biog.*> and is sometimes preferred when the subordinate clause precedes the main clause <*although* they worked hard . . . their movements seemed painfully slow – C. S. Forester> **Albeit** is especially appropriate when the idea of admitting something that seems or suggests a contradiction is to be stressed <a worthy fellow, *albeit* he comes on angry purpose now – Shak.> <try . . . to see economics as a great and continuing, *albeit* constantly altering, concern of mankind – R. L. Heilbroner>

thoughtful, considerate, attentive *shared meaning* : mindful of others. **Thoughtful** usually implies unselfish concern for others and a capacity for anticipating another's needs or wants <a *thoughtful* hostess> <in his *thoughtful* wish of escorting them through the streets of the rough, riotous town – Elizabeth C. Gaskell> **Considerate** stresses concern for the feelings or distresses of others <the French poor people are very *considerate* where they see suffering – George Meredith> **Attentive** emphasizes continuous thoughtfulness often shown by repeated acts of kindness <Emmy had always been good and *attentive* to him. It was she who ministered to his comforts – W. M. Thackeray> ***ant*** thoughtless

thrash – see SWING 1

threaten, menace *shared meaning* : to announce or forecast impending danger or evil. **Threaten** basically implies an attempt to dissuade or influence by promising punishment for failure to obey <*threaten* a child with a spanking if he teases the baby> or it may apply to an impersonal warning or presage of something dire, disastrous, or disturbing <a single locust somewhere commenced a loud chatter . . . *threatening* death and rain – William Styron> <prolongation of the . . . war . . . *threatens* not only the lives of millions, but the humanitarian values and goals which we are striving to maintain – *Science*> **Menace** stresses a definitely hostile or alarming quality in what portends <conditions that *menace* the stability of society> <the devastating weapons which are at present being developed may *menace* every part of the world – Clement Attlee>

thrifty – see SPARING ***ant*** wasteful

thrill, electrify, enthuse *shared meaning* : to fill with emotions that stir or excite or to be so stirred. **Thrill** suggests pervasion by usually agreeably stimulating emotion that sets one atingle (as with pleasure, horror, or excitement) <a *thrilling* detective story> <by carefully copying what other people did, she would manage to get through . . . this *thrilling,* agonizing, exquisite ordeal – Victoria Sackville-West> <the custom . . . of assigning one's daughter to a good *parti,* no matter how little he might *thrill* her – Edmund Wilson> **Electrify** suggests a sudden, violent, startling stimulation comparable to that produced by an electric current <the paper had an *electrifying* impact on his fellow-scientists – *Current Biog.*> <the news *electrified* the community> **Enthuse** implies an arousing or experiencing of enthusiasm <a salesman shouldn't sell a product he doesn't believe in.

He must be *enthused* about it . . . . Without enthusiasm any job can be more difficult – N. V. Peale>
thrive – see SUCCEED 2 ***ant*** languish
throng – see CROWD
through – see BY
throw, cast, toss, fling, hurl, pitch, sling *shared meaning* : to cause to move swiftly through space by a propulsive movement or a propelling instrument. **Throw,** often interchangeable with the other terms, may imply a distinctive propelling movement of the arm and wrist but in practice is applicable to almost any propulsive action <boys *threw* stones through the windows of the old house> <this gun *throws* a large shell a long distance> <the hose *threw* a strong stream of water> **Cast** usually implies lightness in the thing thrown and sometimes scattering <*cast* a net to catch fish> <*cast* dice> <*cast* seed in sowing> and may apply when the throwing is figurative <these clouds *cast* an intangible pall over everything and made the day gray and cold – Nathaniel Nitkin> **Toss** suggests a light or careless or aimless throwing either literal or figurative <he . . . *tossed* me some pieces of money – Charles Dickens> <they . . . discussed a doubt and *tossed* it to and fro – Alfred Tennyson> **Fling** is likely to imply much vigor and slight aim or control in throwing <*fling* away a bone> and may suggest a strong motivating emotion <the opening pages irritated him . . . in the end, in exasperation, he *flung* them aside – Bernard Malamud> **Hurl** stresses driving and impetuous force in throwing <him the Almighty Power *hurled* headlong flaming from the ethereal sky – John Milton> **Pitch** may imply lightness and casualness in throwing <*pitch* out old papers> but distinctively it is likely to suggest a definite objective and a careful aiming <*pitch* horseshoes> <*pitching* matchbooks at a crack . . . was the favorite sport – James Jones> **Sling** suggests propelling with a swirling or sweeping, usually sudden and forceful, motion <*slung* an inkwell at a fellow senator – *Time*> <*slung* his coat about his shoulders>
thrust – see PUSH
thud – see TAP
thump – see TAP
thwart – see FRUSTRATE
tidy – see NEAT ***ant*** untidy
tie, bind *shared meaning* : to make fast or secure. Although often used interchangeably these two words carry such fundamentally distinct connotations in both their basic and extended senses that greater precision in their use is often possible. **Tie** basically implies the use of a line (as a rope or chain or strap) to attach one thing that may wander or move to another that is stable <I'll *tie* them [horses] in the wood – Shak.> **Bind,** in corresponding use, implies use of a band or bond to attach two or more things firmly together <gather ye together first the tares, and *bind* them in bundles – *Mt* 13:30 (AV)> <a fillet *binds* her hair – Alexander Pope> In extended use, especially when what is tied or bound is a person, both terms imply an imposed restraint that deprives of liberty. *Tie* suggests a being held down by something stronger than oneself or from which one cannot escape <*tied* to a boring job> <*tied* down by family responsibilities> *Bind* may suggest a being held together in close union (as for mutual support) <and vows of faith each to the other *bind* – P. B. Shelley> or a being held down or back by something (as a pledge or duty) that hampers like a physical bond <when you have your own script, you can ad lib . . . more smoothly . . . than when you are *bound* to someone else's material – Frank McGee> <you may unwittingly barter away some of your rights and then be legally *bound* by your actions – *Catholic Digest*> ***ant*** untie

tiff — see QUARREL

tight **1 tight, taut, tense** *shared meaning* : drawn or stretched to the limit. **Tight** commonly implies a drawing together or around something in such a way that there is little or no slack or a binding or constricting results <a *tight* belt> <Tom has eaten . . . till his little skin is as *tight* as a drum – Thomas Hughes> In extended use it commonly stresses the idea of squeezing or restraining unmercifully <even when *tight* restrictions do exist there . . . is usually a little latitude reserved to the board – T. A. Shannon> <a *tight* employment market> **Taut** suggests the pulling of a rope or fabric until there is no give or slack <he is *taut* as one of the hawsers of his own boat – Van Wyck Brooks> <*taut,* white cotton on the walls stretched almost infinitely upward – J. A. Murray> In extended use it is likely to stress strain <she was formidable and astringent, with hands that seemed forever *taut* – H. C. Hervey> especially nervous strain <she . . . tense, *taut,* and curdling up inside – J. T. Farrell> **Tense** may be preferred when tightness or tautness that results or manifests itself in severe physical or mental tension or strain is in question <the rat was crouching, very *tense,* sensing extreme danger, but not yet frightened – Roald Dahl> <during the *tense* period that followed . . . [they] continued to irritate each other – S. E. Ambrose> <could see the *tense* look on her face – Helen MacInnes> ***ant*** loose

2 see DRUNK

timely — see SEASONABLE ***ant*** untimely

timid, timorous *shared meaning* : so fearful and apprehensive as to hesitate or hold back. **Timid** stresses lack of courage and daring and implies a fear of venturing into the unfamiliar or the uncertain <realized he was in a far, alien land, without familiar signs and sights to succor his essentially *timid* heart – H. C. Hervey> <loyal to the Republic they were . . . but . . . too *timid* to take the great risks which alone could have preserved it – W. L. Shirer> <a *timid* investor impairing his capital in a vain search for complete security> **Timorous** stresses a usually habitual domination by fears and apprehensions of often imaginary risks that leads one to shrink terrified from any exhibition of independence or self-assertion <*timorous* and fearful of challenge – H. L. Mencken> <a *timorous* incompetent who was lucky to have good men under him – W. A. Swanberg>

timorous — see TIMID ***ant*** assured

tinge — see COLOR

tint — see COLOR

tiny — see SMALL

tipsy — see DRUNK

tire, weary, fatigue, exhaust, jade, fag *shared meaning* : to make or become unable or unwilling to proceed because of loss of strength or endurance. **Tire** implies a draining of one's strength or patience (as by exertion or boredom) <she was too *tired,* too shaken . . . to take the trouble to argue with him – Herman Wouk> <the day's work had *tired* him more than he expected> **Weary** suggests tiring until one is unable to do or endure more <ah, I am worn out – I am *wearied* out – it is too much – I am but flesh and blood, and I must sleep – Edna S. V. Millay> <*wearied* of her husband's infidelities, and could not bear them any more – Rose Macaulay> **Fatigue** implies great lassitude due to overstrain or extreme effort and usually incapacity for further strain or effort <I rested . . . being, in my enfeebled condition, too *fatigued* to push on – H. G. Wells> <the sense of smell can be *fatigued* (i.e., with continuous stimulation, the sensation of odor fades) – W. R. Roderick> **Exhaust** implies completely drained strength or worn-out state of mind or body <they are *exhausted* and addled

by the frustration of their failures – Norman Mailer> <France was *exhausted* and incapable of doing anything to rescue herself – S. E. Ambrose> <too *exhausted* to sleep> **Jade** implies weariness or fatigue that deprives of all freshness and eagerness <revitalizes contemporary mankind's *jaded* perception of the Christ who taught in parables – N. P. Hurley> <to the *jaded* . . . eye it is all dead and common . . . flatness and disgust – William James> **Fag** implies a drooping with weariness or fatigue <I worked . . . at correcting manuscript, which *fags* me excessively – Sir Walter Scott> <the long march . . . had *fagged* them brutally; overtired, the rest periods did them little good – Norman Mailer>

toady – see FAWN

toil – see WORK 1 ***ant*** leisure

token – see SIGN

tolerate – see BEAR

tool – see IMPLEMENT

toothsome – see PALATABLE

torment – see AFFLICT

torpid – see LETHARGIC ***ant*** agile

torpor – see LETHARGY ***ant*** animation

torture – see AFFLICT

toss – see THROW

total *adj* – see WHOLE

total *n* – see SUM

totalitarian, authoritarian *shared meaning* : of, relating to, or being a government or state in which power is narrowly and closely held. Although often applicable to the same states the terms carry quite different emphases. **Totalitarian** implies an undivided state in which all power is vested in the government and in which the people as a unit sanction and support and obey this government. Practically, it implies a one-party system and concentration of authority in the hands of an individual or group, that theoretically speaks with the voice of the people. **Authoritarian** implies a government organization in which professedly as well as actually all political power is ultimately concentrated in the hands of an individual (as a sovereign or a dictator) and not in the people or their chosen representatives. Practically, an *authoritarian* government, though professing political power, often extends its control as completely over the economic and cultural life of its people as does one called *totalitarian* <Formosa under Nationalist rule is not so heavy-handed in its suppression of political dissidence as Russia or Communist China; it is *authoritarian* but not *totalitarian*. An analogy with Spain or Portugal would be closer to the truth – D. H. Mendel, Jr.>

totter – see REEL

touch 1 touch, feel, palpate, handle, paw *shared meaning* : to get or produce or affect with a sensation by or as if by bodily contact, often in examining or exploring. **Touch** stresses the act and may imply bodily contact or the use of an implement <*touch* paint with a finger to see if it is dry> <*touch* the strings of a violin with the bow> or it may imply immaterial contact <it is essential that the College . . . be strengthened in its enduring task of *touching* creatively the lives of those many who will study here – N. M. Pusey> **Feel** stresses the sensation induced or experienced <come near . . . that I may *feel* thee, my son – *Gen* 27:21 (AV)> <the Court saw the issue clearly and in the same human terms in which [the Negro] had *felt* it – K. B. Clark> **Palpate** stresses the feeling of the surface of a body as a means of examining its internal condition <the doctor *palpated* the abdomen and detected a swollen mass> <having probed and prodded and *palpated* that tortured . . . flesh until it was as familiar as his own –

William Styron> **Handle** implies examination or exploration with hands or fingers to determine qualities (as texture, weight, or condition) <heavier fabrics can be appreciated better by actually *handling* them, feeling the substance and texture> <*handle* me, and see; for a spirit hath not flesh – *Lk* 24:39 (AV)> **Paw** is likely to imply clumsy or offensive handling <inspectors ... *pawing* through his papers, consulting dusty books of regulations – W. S. Burroughs> <kept trying to kiss and hug and *paw* her – Herman Wouk>
2 see AFFECT
3 see MATCH
touching – see MOVING
touchstone – see STANDARD
touchy – see IRASCIBLE ***ant*** imperturbable
tough – see STRONG ***ant*** fragile
toxin – see POISON
toy – see TRIFLE
trace, vestige, track *shared meaning* : a perceptible sign left behind. **Trace** basically applies to a line or rut made by something that has passed <follow the *traces* of a deer in snow> <when the hounds of spring are on winter's *traces* – A. C. Swinburne> but is often extended to material or immaterial evidence of something past <the stimulation of violent emotions may leave permanent *traces* on the mind – W. R. Inge> <the kitten licked the last *trace* of cream from his chin> **Vestige** applies to a tangible reminder such as a fragment or remnant of what is past and gone <of this ancient custom no *vestige* remained – Edward Gibbon> <the *vestiges* of some knowledge of Latin still appear ... in his sentences – *Nation*> **Track** often replaces *trace* in the sense of a continuous line (as of scent or footprints) <the hounds soon got back on the *track* of the fox> <on the two strips of soft mud were the *tracks* of birds' feet – Ludwig Bemelmans>
track – see TRACE
tractable – see OBEDIENT ***ant*** intractable, unruly
trade – see BUSINESS
traduce – see MALIGN
traffic – see BUSINESS
trail – see FOLLOW 2
train – see TEACH
traitorous – see FAITHLESS
trammel – see HAMPER
tranquil – see CALM ***ant*** troubled
transcend – see EXCEED
transfer, convey, alienate, deed *shared meaning* : to make over property from one owner to another. **Transfer,** the general term, is applicable to any such act in which the ownership of real or personal property passes by a lawful means (as sale, gift, or foreclosure) from one owner to another. **Convey** stresses the legalistic aspects of transferring and is the precise term when a sealed writing or deed plays an essential part in the transfer (as of real estate or a ship). **Alienate,** sometimes interchangeable with *transfer* or *convey,* in precise use implies the passing of a title by the act of an owner rather than its passing by the operation of the law (as in the case of inheritance by descent). In this and in related uses the term suggests diversion from a prior or normal relationship <he pleaded for the resumption by clerics of Church revenues *alienated* into lay hands – Hilaire Belloc> **Deed** specifically applies to a conveying or transferring by deed and is more common in popular than in legal use.
transfigure – see TRANSFORM

transform, metamorphose, transmute, convert, transmogrify, transfigure *shared meaning* : to change a thing into another or from one form into another. **Transform** may imply a mere change in outward seeming <a Hunter senior *transformed* into a bride floating in a white brilliant mist – Herman Wouk> or it may imply a basic changing of character, nature, or function <*transform* electrical energy into light> <too much organization *transforms* men and women into automata – Aldous Huxley> **Metamorphose,** basically close to *transform,* may add such implications as the action of a magical or supernatural agency <men were by the force of that herb *metamorphosed* into swine – Richard Steele> or the proceeding of a process of natural development <butterflies and other insects that *metamorphose* from larval to adult stages of development – R. M. Davidson> and in more general use is likely to stress the abruptness, violence, or extremity of the change <the little song . . . later *metamorphosed* into one of the noblest chorales – P. L. Miller> **Transmute** implies a fundamental change usually of a lower into a higher element or thing <still valuable elements of our old religions and philosophies can be *transmuted* . . . into the gold of a new world culture – W. W. Wagar> <the harrowing experiences of those days had been *transmuted* into warm memories – H. S. Ashmore> **Convert** stresses, not fundamental change in nature, but such modification and alteration as fits a thing for use or especially for a new use or function <*convert* grain into flour> <a sofa that *converts* into a bed> **Transmogrify** implies an extreme, often grotesque or preposterous, metamorphosis <the car gave to the democratic cavalier his horse and armor and haughty insolence in one package, *transmogrifying* the knight into a misguided missile – Marshall McLuhan> **Transfigure** may replace *transform* but typically it suggests an exhaltation or glorification of outward appearance <for this hope . . . that they will be *transfigured,* women will pay ten or twenty times the value of the emulsion – Aldous Huxley> <Jesus . . . was *transfigured* before them: and his face did shine as the sun – *Mt* 17:1–2 (AV)>

transient, transitory, ephemeral, momentary, fleeting, fugitive, evanescent, short-lived *shared meaning* : lasting or staying only a short time. **Transient** applies to what is short in duration and passes quickly <a *transient* breeze> <*transient* sorrows – William Wordsworth> <uncritical acceptance would at best be *transient* and without conviction – H. C. White & J. W. Lee> **Transitory** applies to what is bound by its nature or essence to pass, change, or come to an end <because so many [birds] are migratory their presence is often *transitory* with the seasons – C. H. Buckner> <barter the *transitory* pleasures of the world for the heavenly hope – Nathaniel Hawthorne> **Ephemeral** may imply existence for only a day <*ephemeral* insects> or in more general use stress shortness of life or duration <not local and *ephemeral* . . . but universal and timeless – J. P. Boyd> **Momentary** suggests coming and going quickly, often as a brief interruption of a settled state or course <a *momentary* irritation – Thomas Hardy> **Fleeting** and **fugitive** apply to what passes swiftly and is gone; the former may stress the difficulty or impossibility of holding back from flight, and the latter the difficulty of catching or fixing <a *fleeting* wisdom told her that . . . one does not love another for his good character – H. C. Hervey> <the *fleeting* fantasy or distracting image we call the daydream – J. L. Singer> <both crucifix and river . . . offered . . . poignant, *fugitive* hints of another world – William Styron> **Evanescent** implies momentary existence and quick vanishing and usually connotes a delicate, fragile, or airy quality <*evanescent* visitations of thought and feeling . . . arising unforeseen and departing unbidden – P. B. Shelley> **Short-lived** implies extreme brevity of life or existence, often of what might be expected to persist <the *short-lived* panic of 1857 – S. E. Morison> <*short-lived* fame> ***ant*** perpetual

transitory – see TRANSIENT ***ant*** everlasting, perpetual

translucent – see CLEAR

transmogrify – see TRANSFORM

transmute – see TRANSFORM

transparent – see CLEAR ***ant*** opaque

transpire – see HAPPEN

transport *vb* **1** see CARRY

2 transport, ravish, enrapture, entrance *shared meaning* : to carry away by strong and usually pleasurable emotion. **Transport** implies the fact of being intensely moved by an emotion (as delight or rage) that exceeds ordinary experience and agitates or excites <the test of greatness in a work of art is . . . that it *transports* us – Herbert Read> <children *transported* with delight at the thought of Christmas> **Ravish** can imply a seizure by emotion and especially by joy or delight <a young, handsome woman with a very slight tendency toward plumpness and a voice of *ravishing* richness – Winthrop Sargeant> <his eye was *ravished* by a thin sunshine of daffodils spread over a meadow – Clemence Dane> **Enrapture** implies putting into a state of rapture and usually suggests an intense, even ecstatic, delight, often in one of the arts <he is *enrapturing* us with his extraordinary powers to make us see and feel beauty – Eudora Welty> but sometimes it stresses the bemusing aspects of rapture and then suggests a bedazzling or suppressing of the powers of clear thinking <[his] personality simply has not *enraptured* the voters – Rowland Evans & Robert Novak> **Entrance** usually suggests being held as spellbound as if in a trance by something that awakens an overmastering emotion <the beauty of the land *entranced* them – Joe Baily, Jr.> <as a ruthless village spinster [she] . . . *entrances* and convulses the house every moment she is on the stage – J. E. Agate>

3 see BANISH

transport *n* – see ECSTASY

transpose – see REVERSE

trap – see CATCH

travail – see WORK 1

travesty – see CARICATURE

treacherous – see FAITHLESS

treason – see SEDITION ***ant*** allegiance

treasure – see APPRECIATE

treat, deal, handle *shared meaning* : to have to do with in a specified manner. **Treat** in the sense of doing about, serving, or coping with is usually accompanied by context indicating attitude, temperament, or point of view that determines behavior or manner <*treat* a subject realistically in an essay> <*treat* subordinates with consideration> <*treat* a cut with antiseptic to prevent infection> **Deal,** used with *with,* may suggest managing, controlling, or authoritative disposing <she *dealt* with moral problems as a cleaver *deals* with meat – James Joyce> <efforts to *deal* with the race crisis – Bernard Weissbourd & Herbert Channick> **Handle** as a substitute for *treat* or *deal* usually suggests manipulation and a placing, using, directing, or disposing with or as if with the hand <*handle* an ax skillfully> <he wondered – if and when they were married – how on earth he would *handle* her – William Styron> <learned to *handle* the language enough to get by>

tremendous – see MONSTROUS

trenchant – see INCISIVE

trend – see TENDENCY

trepidation — see FEAR

trespass, encroach, entrench, infringe, invade *shared meaning* : to make inroads upon the property, territory, or rights of another. **Trespass** implies a usually unwarranted intrusion that is often also unlawful and offensive <students *trespassing* on the rights of other students.... Individual rights were trampled on by both sides – J. P. Lyford> <*trespass* on a friend's good nature by bringing a stranger to dinner> **Encroach** suggests gradual and stealthy intrusion on territory or usurpation of rights or possessions <groups of houses *encroaching* ... upon the desolation of the marshland – William Styron> <the telephone has probably done more to *encroach* on managers' time than any other invention of the past century – R. J. Bryant> **Entrench** suggests establishing and maintaining oneself in a position of advantage, typically at the expense of others <saw the principle of unity being employed to *entrench* the authority of a despotic, counterrevolutionary clique – Harvey Wheeler> <brave the opposition ... of *entrenched* greed – P. H. Douglas> **Infringe** implies an encroachment that clearly violates the law or the rights of another <*infringe* a patent> <he was *infringing* upon the liberties of a man who had never done him any injury – Maria Edgeworth> **Invade** suggests aggressive action and usually implies a definite and hostile entry into the territory or rights of another <the infection *invaded* nearby healthy tissues> <where there is a legal right, there is also a legal remedy ... whenever that right is *invaded* – William Blackstone>

tribute — see ENCOMIUM

trick *n* **trick, ruse, stratagem, maneuver, artifice, wile, feint** *shared meaning* : an indirect means to gain an end. **Trick** implies cheating and deceiving and often an evil intent <*tricks* and devices to conceal evasions and violations of ethical principles – H. A. Wagner> but it may also imply nothing more than roguishness or playfulness and then denote an antic, a prank, a hoax, a joke <the *tricks* of circus clowns> or a dexterous device that pleases, deludes, or amazes <illusions produced by *tricks* of lighting> **Ruse** implies an attempt to mislead by giving a false impression <used the old *ruse* of oxen dragging trees to create a dust that would give the English the impression of a large force moving – Stuart Cloete> **Stratagem** applies to a ruse used to entrap, outwit, circumvent, or surprise <some women ... are driven to every possible trick and *stratagem* to entrap some man into marriage – G. B. Shaw> **Maneuver** implies adroit and dexterous manipulation of persons or things in attaining an objective <unless indeed, all her talk of flight had been a blind, and her departure no more than a *maneuver* – Edith Wharton> <unable to meet the *maneuvers* of the speculative railroad wrecker – W. C. Ford> **Artifice** implies ingenious contrivance or invention not necessarily designed to deceive or overreach <the *artifices* by which friends endeavor to spare one another's feelings – G. B. Shaw> **Wile** suggests an attempt to entrap or deceive with false allurements <he was no longer a mild old man to be worked on by the *wiles* of engaging youth, but a stern-spoken person in high authority – Archibald Marshall> <the Devil ... made him sly and foxier than the fox with all the *wiles,* and the cunning – J. T. Farrell> **Feint** implies a distraction or diversion of attention from one's real objective <believed the dropping of parachutists was merely an Allied *feint* to cover their main landings – W. L. Shirer> <I love to think the leaving us was just a *feint* – Robert Browning>

trick *vb* — see DUPE

trickery — see DECEPTION

tricky — see SLY

trifle, toy, dally, flirt, coquet *shared meaning* : to deal with or act toward without serious purpose. **Trifle** can replace any of the other words and may imply such varied attitudes as playfulness, unconcern, indulgent contempt, or light amorousness <dabbled in poetry, delivered ironical orations . . . *trifled* with some of the radical doctrines then current – Max Lerner> <[he] is friendly and charming, but no one can *trifle* with him. He knows what he wants and usually gets it – *N.Y. Herald Tribune*> **Toy** implies acting without full attention or serious exertion of one's powers <*toyed* with the idea of moving to the country> <he lapsed into becoming an observer of life, *toying* on the margin of women and politics – Marvin Lowenthal> **Dally** stresses indulgence in something as a pastime rather than seriously and may suggest frivolity or deliberate dawdling (the notion predominant in another of its senses) <*dallying* with a glass of wine – Victoria Sackville-West> <*dallied* with a young Mexican girl – Green Peyton> <poetry . . . is not a mere exercise in fancy, not a *dallying* with pretty little nothings – C. S. Kilby> **Flirt** stresses vagrancy and superficiality of interest, attention, or liking <German leaders were *flirting* with the idea of a deal with Russia – *Time*> <the bright young people *flirting* with new isms – Walter O'Hearn> **Coquet** primarily refers to a trifling in love, such as is characteristic of a flirtatious woman <she *coquetted* with the solid husbands of her friends – Dorothy Parker> but may apply when a similar lack of seriousness in other matters is to be indicated <he *coquetted* with the idea, discussing it . . . , but rejecting it – G. D. H. Cole>

trig – see NEAT

trim – see NEAT *ant* frowzy

triumph – see VICTORY

trouble *vb* **trouble, distress, ail** *shared meaning* : to cause to be uneasy or upset. **Trouble** suggests loss of tranquillity and implies a disturbing element that is responsible <'tis not my speeches that you do mislike, but 'tis my presence that doth *trouble* ye – Shak.> <let not your heart be *troubled:* ye believe in God, believe also in me – *Jn* 14:1 (AV)> <*troubled* by sleeplessness> **Distress** implies subjection to strain or pressure and resulting tension, pain, worry, or grief <a hard *distressing* cough> <often *distressed* by gas in her stomach> <he was *distressed* by the pressure of his job – Harry Levinson> <the sight of blood . . . always *distressed* him – Charles Lee> **Ail**, used in reference to unspecified causes, regularly implies that something has gone wrong and often suggests a will to find the cause with an eye to aid or correction <the book continued to be a mess . . . . Something *ailed* my prose and all my rhythms were off – Jean Stafford> <what *ails* that naughty child?>

trouble *n* – see EFFORT

truckle – see FAWN

true – see REAL *ant* false

trust *n* – see MONOPOLY

trust *vb* – see RELY

truth, veracity, verity, verisimilitude *shared meaning* : the quality or property of keeping close to fact and avoiding distortion or misrepresentation. **Truth** is broadly applicable, ranging in use from a transcendent idea to an indication of conformity with fact and avoidance of error, misrepresentation, or falsehood <*truth* as the opposite of error and of falsehood – C. W. Eliot> <stick to the *truth* and you will have done your duty> <he has an eye for *truth;* he sees it in the tiniest details – H. S. Resnik> **Veracity** usually implies rigid and unfailing adherence to, observance of, or respect for truth <this . . . slur at his mother's *veracity* made Coverly feel sad and homesick and annoyed – John Cheever> <his passion for *veracity* always kept him from taking any unfair rhetorical advantages – Aldous Huxley> **Verity**

usually designates the quality of a state or thing that is exactly what it purports to be or is in complete accord with the facts <most . . . religions have . . . started out, naturally enough, with the assumption of their own *verity* and importance – A. L. Kroeber> <trying to test the *verity* of his recollections> or it may designate what is felt as lasting, ultimate, or fundamental truth <I do not believe in a set of eternal *verities* – some fixed set of moral injunctions or final truths . . . to be used as a guide to all the puzzles of life – Daniel Bell> **Verisimilitude** describes the quality of a representation that causes one to accept it as true or valid <the dialogue is too abstract and self-conscious for *verisimilitude* – Paul Pickrel> <*verisimilitude* is not just a trick of the trade, a set of rules which give the poet a chance to show his ingenuity; it is the body of the fiction's life, without which the vision becomes a ghost – Arthur Mizener> ***ant*** untruth, lie, falsehood

try – see AFFLICT, ATTEMPT

tug – see PULL

tumescent – see INFLATED

tumid – see INFLATED

tumor, neoplasm, malignancy, cancer *shared meaning* **:** an abnormal growth or mass of tissue. **Tumor,** the most general term, is applicable to any such growth on or in the body of a person, animal, or plant and to various other enlargements <*tumor* literally means a swelling, and thus has been applied to the prominence caused by an overdistended bladder, to the enlargement of pregnancy, to the swelling produced by an abscess, to the overgrowth of tissue (hyperplasia) associated with injury and consequent inflammation, and to numerous other phases of tissue enlargement directly connected with recognized disease processes – J. R. Mohler> **Neoplasm** is likely to replace *tumor,* especially in technical use, when reference is to a more or less unrestrained growth of cells without evident function or to a mass formed by such growth <a *neoplasm* is an uncontrolled new growth of tissue – Shields Warren> **Malignancy** applies to a neoplasm that because of unrestrained proliferation and tendency to invade tissues constitutes a menace to life. This use, though deplored by some purists, is common in medical literature and often used euphemistically in discussion with a patient or his associates. **Cancer** is the usual popular and technical term for a malignant neoplasm, though sometimes it is restricted to such neoplasms arising in epithelial tissues (as skin or membrane) which are often distinguished as *carcinomas* from the other great class of cancers, the *sarcomas,* which arise in nonepithelial tissues (as bone, muscle, or connective tissue).

tune – see MELODY

turbid, muddy, roily *shared meaning* **:** not clear or translucent but clouded with or as if with sediment. **Turbid** describes something (as a liquid, an idea, or an affair) which is stirred up and disturbed so that it becomes opaque, or obscured, or confused <the *turbid* water of a river in flood> <the *turbid* ebb and flow of human misery – Matthew Arnold> <*turbid* feelings, arising from ideas not fully mastered, had to clarify . . . themselves – H. O. Taylor> **Muddy** describes something turbid as a result of being mixed with or as if with mud <*muddy* coffee> <a *muddy* pond> or something which suggests this state (as in color or in dull, heavy, muddled character) <a *muddy* complexion> <a *muddy* thinker, but a superb artist – J. D. Adams> <on strongly modulated signals the tone became somewhat *muddy – Consumer Reports*> **Roily** describes something which is turbid and agitated <where the *roily* Monongahela meets the clear Allegheny – J. M. Weed> <human rubble . . . washed up by the *roily* wake of the war – John Woodburn> ***ant*** clear, limpid

turgid – see INFLATED
turn – see CURVE, RESORT
twist – see CURVE
twit – see RIDICULE
twitch – see JERK
type **1** see SYMBOL *ant* antitype
2 type, kind, sort, nature, description, character *shared meaning* : a number of individuals thought of as a group because of a common quality or qualities. **Type** may suggest strong, marked, or obvious similarities so that the distinctiveness of the group cannot be overlooked <that most dangerous *type* of critic: the critic with a mind which is naturally of the creative order – T. S. Eliot> <creating new *types* of cereal grains tailored to particular climates> **Kind** may be very indefinite and involve any criterion of classification whatever <each *kind* of mental or bodily activity – Herbert Spencer> <the *kind* of fear here treated of is purely spiritual – Charles Lamb> or it may suggest natural or intrinsic criteria <search for the real essences of natural *kinds* – Stuart Hampshire> <four *kinds* of taste sensation are usually recognized> **Sort** is often very close to *kind* <the *sort* of culture I am trying to define – J. C. Powys> but, distinctively, may carry a note of disparagement <what *sort* of idiots have you got around here? – A. W. Long> **Nature** may suggest inherent essential characteristics rather than obvious or superficial resemblances <the few hitherto known phenomena of a similar *nature* – *Amer. Jour. of Science*> **Description** may suggest a grouping marked by agreement in all salient details <all embargoes are not of this *description.* They are sometimes resorted to . . . with a single view to commerce – John Marshall> **Character** may stress distinguishing or individualizing criteria <the black is perceived as belonging to a different order of humanity. This perception is not Southern or Northern but white in *character* – W. H. Ferry>
typical – see REGULAR *ant* atypical, distinctive
tyro – see AMATEUR

ubiquitous – see OMNIPRESENT
ugly, hideous, ill-favored, unsightly *shared meaning* : neither pleasing nor beautiful, especially to the eye. **Ugly,** the comprehensive term, may apply not only to what is not pleasing to the eye but to what offends another sense or gives rise to repulsion, dread, or moral distaste in the mind <a street of small drab *ugly* houses> <[her] neglect of her son makes *ugly* reading – George Steiner> <the *ugly* state of race relations – *Wall Street Jour.*> **Hideous** stresses personal reaction and the horror or loathing induced by something felt as outwardly or inwardly extremely ugly <an altogether *hideous* room – expensive but cheesy – J. D. Salinger> <under their *hideous* rule personal ends were subordinated . . . by a mixture of violence and propaganda – Aldous Huxley> <wild leeks which were delicious and left everyone with a *hideous* breath – J. K. Galbraith> **Ill-favored** applies especially to personal appearance and implies ugliness to the sense of sight without in itself suggesting a resulting distaste or dread <an *ill-favored* thing, sir, but mine own – Shak.> <a scrawny, *ill-favored* little girl – Margaret Mead> **Unsightly** is likely to refer to a material thing on which the eye dwells with no pleasure and is somewhat less positive in its suggestion of distaste than *ugly* <an *unsightly* swamp and dump grounds – *Amer. Guide Series: Minn.*> *ant* beautiful

ultimate **1** see LAST
2 ultimate, absolute, categorical *shared meaning* : so fundamental as to reach the extreme limit of actual or possible knowledge. Something **ultimate** represents the utmost limit attained or attainable either by analysis or synthesis <that lofty musing on the *ultimate* nature of things – Aldous Huxley> Something **absolute** has the character of being above imperfection because original rather than derived, complete rather than partial, unlimited rather than qualified, self-sufficient rather than dependent; often the term implies ideal existence and an opposite in actuality that lacks the marks of absoluteness <*absolute,* as opposed to human, justice> <the prohibition of idolatry in the Decalogue denies *absolute* value to any ideal except the ultimate – Robert Gordis> <any principle, when it becomes *absolute,* brings other principles into question – Nathan Glazer> Something **categorical** is so fundamental that human reason cannot go beyond it in search for generality or universality; the term therefore implies an affirmative, undeniable character; thus, the *categorical* concepts (often called *categories*) are the few concepts (as quantity, quality, and relation) to which human knowledge can be ultimately reduced <social scientists investigate *what is* in contrast to *what ought to be* (the *categorical* in contrast to the normative) – J. U. Michaelis & A. M. Johnston>
umbrage – see OFFENSE
unbecoming – see INDECOROUS
unbelief, disbelief, incredulity *shared meaning* : the attitude or state of mind of one who does not believe. **Unbelief** stresses absence of belief especially in respect to something above or beyond one's experience or capacity <a sense of loss and *unbelief* such as one might feel to discover suddenly that some great force in nature had ceased to operate – Thomas Wolfe> **Disbelief** implies a positive rejection of something stated or advanced <if she was not wholly disenchanted, she now regarded everything Marsha said with caution or downright *disbelief* – Herman Wouk> **Incredulity** suggests a disposition to refuse belief or acceptance <there is a vulgar *incredulity,* which . . . finds it easier to doubt than to examine – Sir Walter Scott> ***ant*** belief
unbeliever – see ATHEIST
unbiased – see FAIR ***ant*** biased
uncanny – see WEIRD
uncertainty, doubt, dubiety, skepticism, suspicion, mistrust *shared meaning* : lack of sureness about someone or something. **Uncertainty** stresses lack of certitude that may range from a mere falling short of this to a nearly complete lack of knowledge or conviction, especially about a result or outcome <if you are really in love, there is no *uncertainty* – Helen MacInnes> <waited in eagerness and impatience, and then in *uncertainty,* in anxiety, in hurt pride, in anger – J. T. Farrell> **Doubt** implies both uncertainty and inability to make a decision <there crept into the diary . . . signs of *doubt* and then of despair – W. L. Shirer> <when *doubt* exists about the propriety of a certain practice, it is often best to seek . . . advice – *NEA Jour.*> **Dubiety** stresses a lack of sureness that leads to a wavering between conclusions <cannot escape the *dubieties* and problems of his day and . . . finds himself swerved from his certainties and confronted with the tenuousness of his preconceptions – *Saturday Rev.*> **Skepticism** implies unwillingness to believe without conclusive evidence and is likely to refer to a habitual state of mind or customary reaction <an easy and elegant *skepticism* was the attitude expected of an educated adult; anything might be discussed, but it was a trifle vulgar to reach very positive conclusions – Bertrand Russell> <the African is entitled to view with deserved *skep-*

ticism our verbal concern for his political emancipation – C. E. Crowther> **Suspicion** stresses lack of faith in the truth, reality, fairness, or reliability of someone or something <seized with unwonted *suspicion* of his own wisdom – George Meredith> <any outsider was regarded with *suspicion* and disdain – Victoria Sackville-West> **Mistrust** implies a genuine doubt that is based on suspicion <man is only weak through his *mistrust* and want of hope – William Wordsworth> ***ant*** certainty

uncommon – see INFREQUENT ***ant*** common

unconcerned – see INDIFFERENT ***ant*** concerned

unconstraint, abandon, spontaneity *shared meaning* : free and uninhibited expression or a mood or style marked by this. **Unconstraint** expresses the fact and can replace either of the other terms though it is less positive in implication <living with the *unconstraint* of a slattern who has no plans – Hortense Calisher> <the old red blood and stainless gentility of great poets will be proved by their *unconstraint* – Walt Whitman> **Abandon** may add an implication of loss of self-control <weep with *abandon*> or of the absence or impotence of any check on full, free, or natural expression of feeling <concluded that the pagans had the advantage: *they* could sin with gusto and *abandon; we* are cramped by "guilt complexes" – A. C. Guild> **Spontaneity** suggests an unstudied naturalness and may connote freshness or abandonment to the impulse of the moment <[they] manage to retain a youthful *spontaneity* in their approach to life – N. L. Gerrard> <the straightforward *spontaneity* of a love letter – D. A. Redding>

uncritical – see SUPERFICIAL ***ant*** critical

underhand – see SECRET ***ant*** aboveboard

underhanded – see SECRET ***ant*** aboveboard

undermine – see WEAKEN ***ant*** reinforce

understand, comprehend, appreciate *shared meaning* : to have a clear or complete idea of. *Understand* and *comprehend* both imply an obtaining of a mental grasp of something, but **understand** may stress the fact of attained grasp and **comprehend** the process by which it is attained; thus, one *understands* a decision when he knows what it involves even though he fails to *comprehend* the reasoning process by which it was reached <for well on a thousand years there have been universities in the Western world; to *understand* the present institutions, we must therefore *comprehend* something of their history – J. B. Conant> **Appreciate** implies a just estimation of a thing's value and is often used in reference to what is likely to be misjudged <you are of an age now to *appreciate* his character – George Meredith> <local leaders could come to know, understand, and *appreciate* one another – G. W. Corrigan>

understanding – see REASON

undulate – see SWING 2

unearth – see DISCOVER

uneven – see ROUGH ***ant*** even

unfeigned – see SINCERE

unfruitful – see STERILE ***ant*** fruitful, prolific

ungovernable – see UNRULY ***ant*** governable, docile

uniform – see SIMILAR ***ant*** various

unimpassioned – see SOBER 1 ***ant*** impassioned

union – see UNITY

unique – see SINGLE, STRANGE

unite – see JOIN ***ant*** divide, alienate

unity, solidarity, integrity, union *shared meaning* : a combining of parts or elements or individuals into an effective whole or the quality of character of that whole. **Unity** implies oneness, especially of what is varied and diverse in its elements or parts <the indispensable *unity* of a beautiful design – Samuel Alexander> <science may be defined as the reduction of multiplicity to *unity* – Aldous Huxley> **Solidarity** implies a unity (as in a group or class) that makes for strength and ability to exert a unified influence <groups . . . intent on promoting black *solidarity* – *Trans-action*> <[they] built their classic cities spontaneously, freely, as a communal expression of *solidarity* – Thomas Merton> **Integrity** stresses completeness and unity based on the perfection of the parts and the exactitude of their association and interaction <guarantee the *integrity* of the British Empire – Upton Sinclair> <facts and laws which are revelations of the *integrity* of nature – Kenneth Rexroth> **Union** implies a thorough integration and harmonious cooperation of the parts <such harmony alone could hold all Heaven and Earth in happier *union* – John Milton> <no longer thinking there was a conflict between *union* and freedom, [he] became a staunch unionist – J. S. Rosenberg> <a . . . delicate face of noble beauty . . . in its mobile features there was a strange *union* of child and woman – Thomas Wolfe>

universal, general, generic *shared meaning* : characteristic of, relating to, comprehending, or affecting all or the whole. **Universal** implies reference to every one without exception in the class, category, or genus considered <prolongation of the . . . war, with its increasing danger of *universal* catastrophe – *Science*> <Schweitzer was a *universal* man, whose allegiance was to all the world – Hallowell Bowser> **General** is usually used with less precise boundaries and tends to imply reference to all or nearly all <ethylene has come into *general* but not yet universal favor – A. C. Morrison> <his new suit attracted *general* attention> In reference to such things as words, language, ideas, and notions it is likely to suggest lack of precision <he worked in a sombre *general* key, which made his strong colors glow richly – *Current Biog.*> <some rather weak cases must fall within any law which is couched in *general* words – O. W. Holmes †1935> <gave a *general* sketch of their plans> **Generic** implies reference to every member of a genus and is applicable especially to items (as qualities, characteristics, or likenesses) that serve as identifying guides; thus, the use of words is a *general* characteristic of writing but the use of meter is a *generic* characteristic of poetry <Sanskrit . . . shows close *generic* resemblance to its modern European cousins – Margaret Schlauch> <the novel has always had a *generic* habit of reaching out to the extremes of literary expression – Mark Schorer> ***ant*** particular

universe – see EARTH

unlawful, illegal, illegitimate, illicit *shared meaning* : not being in accordance with law. Otherwise than this negation in character, the words in general exhibit the same differences in implications and connotations as the affirmative adjectives discriminated at LAWFUL. There are, however, a few differences. **Illegitimate** tends to be narrower in reference than *legitimate;* its usual application is to children born out of wedlock or to a relation leading to such a result <their union was *illegitimate*> but it may refer to something that is not proper according to rules (as of logic) or to authorities or to precedent <an *illegitimate* inference> <riots are illegal but not *illegitimate* – Jesse Jackson> <it is *illegitimate* to suppose a chasm between the brute facts of physical nature . . . and the most abstract principles – Samuel Alexander> **Illicit** is used much more widely than *licit;* it may imply lack of conformance with a regulatory law <*illicit* distilling> <an *illicit* slaughterhouse> but it is also applied to something obtained, done, or maintained unlawfully, illegally, or illegitimately <the tradition that *illicit* love affairs are at once vicious and delightful – G. B. Shaw> <the . . . monk who

loved Virgil had to study him with an *illicit* candle – A. T. Quiller-Couch> *ant* lawful

unlearned – see IGNORANT

unlettered – see IGNORANT

unman – see UNNERVE

unmindful – see FORGETFUL *ant* mindful, solicitous

unmitigated – see OUTRIGHT

unmoral – see IMMORAL

unnatural – see IRREGULAR *ant* natural

unnerve, enervate, unman, emasculate *shared meaning*: to deprive of strength or vigor and the capacity for effective action. **Unnerve** implies marked often temporary loss of courage, self-control, or power to act <government was *unnerved,* confounded, and in a manner suspended – Edmund Burke> <he did not *unnerve* her any more; he stimulated her – Herman Wouk> **Enervate** suggests a gradual physical or moral weakening, usually under the influence of debilitating factors (as climate, disease, luxury, or self-indulgence), to the point that one is too feeble to make an effort <those unhappy people whose tender minds a long course of felicity has *enervated* – H. S. J. Bolingbroke> <the constant wet heat *enervated* him to the point that he had to give up his appointment> **Unman** implies a loss of manly vigor, fortitude, or spirit <what, quite *unmanned* in folly? . . . . Fie, for shame! – Shak.> <to this day . . . the sight of lightning *unmans* him – C. F. Saunders> **Emasculate** implies a loss of essential or effective power especially by the removal of something that has made for strength <many states *emasculate* such civil rights statutes as exist – W. F. Swindler> <Hellenism . . . was not destroyed, though it was *emasculated,* by the loss of political freedom – W. R. Inge>

unparalleled – see STRANGE

unpretentious – see PLAIN

unreasonable – see IRRATIONAL *ant* reasonable

unruffled – see COOL *ant* ruffled, excited

unruly, ungovernable, intractable, refractory, recalcitrant, willful, headstrong *shared meaning* : not submissive to government or control. **Unruly** stresses unwillingness to submit to discipline whether from lack of experience with discipline or from a turbulent wayward nature <*unruly* children> <whatever my *unruly* tongue may say – J. R. Green> <the *unruly* passions – T. S. Eliot> <a . . . man . . . [with] an *unruly* shock of coarse white hair – *Current Biog.*> **Ungovernable** implies incapacity for or escape from guidance or control <that . . . *ungovernable* wonder, the wind – Nathaniel Hawthorne> <an *ungovernable* temper> <genius was as valuable and as unpredictable, perhaps as *ungovernable,* as the waves of the sea – Pearl Buck> **Intractable** suggests stubborn resistance to guidance or control <his rough, *intractable* spirit – John Wesley> or to handling or working <our final solution for an *intractable* racial problem – W. H. Ferry> <an *intractable* metal> **Refractory** stresses resistance to attempts to manage or mold <it becomes my duty to struggle against my *refractory* feelings – Fanny Burney> <the boy was solitary and *refractory* to all education – F. J. Mather> **Recalcitrant** implies active and violent resistance or obstinate rebellion and may suggest deliberate thwarting of the will of another <his father became *recalcitrant* and cut off the supplies – R. L. Stevenson> <our most *recalcitrant* source of despotism, which is cultural deficiency – Harvey Wheeler> **Willful** implies obstinate and often capricious self-will <the Grand Inquisitor, ancient and *willful,* the embodiment of ruthless dogmatism – Roland Gelatt> **Headstrong** suggests self-will impatient of restraint, advice, or suggestion <proffering advice to the *headstrong*, flamboyant monarch – W. L. Shirer> <they are testy and *headstrong* through an excess of will and bias – R. W. Emerson> ***ant*** tractable, docile

unseemly – see INDECOROUS ***ant*** seemly

unsightly – see UGLY

unsocial, asocial, antisocial, nonsocial *shared meaning* : opposed to what is social. In spite of their common meaning element these words are rarely interchangeable. **Unsocial** implies a distaste for the society of others or an aversion to close association and interaction with others <he is a withdrawn, *unsocial* person> <a very *unsocial* temperament> **Asocial** applies more often to behavior, thoughts, or acts viewed objectively and implies a lack of all the qualities conveyed by the word *social*. Typically it stresses a self-centered individualistic orientation <dreaming is an *asocial* act> <his interests are predominantly *asocial*> **Antisocial** applies to things (as acts, ideas, or movements) that are felt as harmful to or destructive of society or the social order <anarchists are *asocial* in their thinking and *antisocial* in their propaganda> <*antisocial* or sociopathic personalities . . . . These people are hostile, immature, and emotionally unstable – F. D. Harris> **Nonsocial** applies to what cannot be described as *social* in any relevant sense <a man's *nonsocial* correspondence – Elizabeth L. Post> <*nonsocial* bees> ***ant*** social

unsophisticated – see NATURAL ***ant*** sophisticated

unstable – see INCONSTANT ***ant*** stable

untangle – see EXTRICATE

untruthful – see DISHONEST ***ant*** truthful

untutored – see IGNORANT ***ant*** tutored

upbraid – see SCOLD

upright, honest, just, conscientious, scrupulous, honorable *shared meaning* : having or exhibiting a strict regard for what is morally right. **Upright** implies a firm adherence to high moral principles <he lies with a simplicity and quick confidence which will stifle the breath of any *upright* citizen who encounters it innocently for the first time – Norman Mailer> <we shall exult, if they who rule the land be men . . . wise, *upright*, valiant; not a servile band – William Wordsworth> **Honest** implies recognition of and adherence to solid virtues (as candor, sincerity, and fairness) <the *honest* heart that's free frae . . . fraud or guile – Robert Burns> <he has demanded of himself and his musicians *honest* perfection, uncluttered by histrionic poses – *Current Biog.*> **Just** may stress conscious choice and regular practice of what is right or equitable <a *just* man, and one that feareth God, and of good report among all the nation – *Acts* 10:22 (AV)> *Conscientious* and *scrupulous* imply an active moral sense governing one's actions; distinctively, **conscientious** stresses painstaking efforts to follow that guide <*conscientious* and incorruptible and right-minded, a young man born to worry – William Styron> while **scrupulous** stresses meticulous attention to details of morality or conduct <finished the work with *scrupulous* care> <a more *scrupulous* court would disqualify itself – H. L. Ickes> **Honorable** suggests a firm holding to codes of right behavior and the guidance of a high sense of honor and duty <did this vile world show many such as thee, thou perfect, just, and *honorable* man – P. B. Shelley> <a man *honorable* in all his dealings>

uprising – see REBELLION

uproot – see EXTERMINATE ***ant*** establish, inseminate

upset – see DISCOMPOSE

urbane – see SUAVE ***ant*** rude, clownish, bucolic

usage – see HABIT

use *n* **1 use, usefulness, utility** *shared meaning* : capacity for serving an end or purpose. **Use,** the most general and least specific term, implies little more than suitability for employment for some purpose specified or implied <she hated to throw away anything that might have some *use*> <our gymnasium . . . is of excellent *use,* and all my girls exercise in it – George Meredith> **Usefulness** is employed chiefly with reference to definite concrete things that serve or are capable of serving a practical purpose <her [the cat's] sacred character was in no wise impaired by her *usefulness* – Agnes Repplier> <the reforms . . . have too limited a *usefulness* – R. G. Tugwell> **Utility** may differ from *usefulness,* especially in technical use, by implying a measurable property or one that can be viewed as an abstraction <the extent to which the price of motorcars per unit of *utility* has fallen – J. A. Schumpeter> <whether or not social *utility* is the proximate purpose of those who pursue knowledge, the search for truth . . . [has] a positive long-range effect on human understanding and human life – J. A. Perkins> **2** see HABIT

use *vb* **use, employ, utilize** *shared meaning* : to put into service to some end or in such a way as to give a practical value to. **Use** implies an availing oneself of something material or immaterial as a means or instrument <*use* a hoe in cultivating> <*use* careful English to make a good impression> <*use* patience in dealing with children> <*use* discretion in investing> **Employ** implies using a person or thing that is idle or inactive by putting him or it to work or into the way of profitable activity <she had . . . *employed* her leisure in reading every book that came in her way – G. B. Shaw> <the new enterprise will *employ* several hundred workers> **Utilize** usually implies a putting to practical use of something that might easily be overlooked or wasted <charged . . . that he *utilized* his military office for private gain – R. G. Adams> <*utilize* wasted ability of ghetto youths> <prolonging a man's life, he believes, entails the responsibility of enabling him fully to *utilize* his added years – *Current Biog.*>

usefulness – see USE *n* 1

usual, customary, habitual, wonted, accustomed *shared meaning* : familiar through frequent or regular repetition. **Usual** stresses the absence of strangeness and is applicable to whatever is normally expected or happens in the ordinary course of events <paid the *usual* fee> <open for business as *usual*> <the darkness caused them to speak much louder than *usual* – Roald Dahl> **Customary** applies to what accords with the practices, conventions, or usages of an individual or community <having her *customary* cup of tea before walking down the road to the bus stop – J. D. Salinger> <rolling her eyes in anticipation of their *customary* exchange of banter – H. C. Hervey> **Habitual** suggests a practice settled or established by much repetition <his evening clothes were as *habitual* as his breath and hung on him with a weary and accustomed grace as if he had been born in them – Thomas Wolfe> <a *habitual* drunkard> **Wonted,** a somewhat bookish word, stresses habituation, especially to something purposefully cultivated <in revolutionary times when all our *wonted* certainties are violently called in question – Walter Moberly> <his nerve steadied itself back into its *wonted* control – C. G. D. Roberts> **Accustomed** is less emphatic than *habitual* or *wonted* in suggesting fixed habit or invariable custom <make my *accustomed* weekly visits to the . . . Library – H. R. Mayes> <government offices where decisions are endlessly delayed because no one is *accustomed* to taking the responsibility of making them – William Attwood>

utensil – see IMPLEMENT

utility – see USE *n* 1

utilize – see USE *vb*
utter – see EXPRESS, SAY

vacant – see EMPTY
vacillate – see HESITATE
vacuous – see EMPTY
vagary – see CAPRICE
vague – see OBSCURE *ant* definite, specific, lucid
vain 1 **vain, nugatory, otiose, idle, empty, hollow** *shared meaning* : devoid of worth or significance. **Vain** implies either absolute or relative absence of value or worth <*vain* pomp and glory of this world – Shak.> <*vain* pleasures of luxurious life, forever with yourselves at strife – William Wordsworth> **Nugatory** applies to what is trifling or insignificant or, especially in legal use, inoperative <a literary work . . . likely to be despised as ephemeral and *nugatory* – J. W. Clark> <limiting the right to pass laws for the execution of the granted powers, to such as are indispensable, and without which the power would be *nugatory* – John Marshall> **Otiose** suggests a lack of excuse for being as serving no purpose and often constituting an encumbrance <wide, empty, modern highways at whose pretentious crossings an occasional rickshaw waits for the *otiose* traffic lights to change to green – Ian Fleming> <*otiose* dogmas that have long lost their vitality – W. R. Inge> **Idle** implies a lack of capacity for a worthwhile effect often because of lack of substantialness or base or ground <*idle* musings> <it would be *idle* to discuss the point further in view of our fundamentally different outlooks> **Empty** and **hollow** suggest a deceiving lack of real substance or soundness or genuineness <an *empty* show> <a *hollow* farce> <in itself unreal, *empty,* of no importance and discardable overnight – Herman Wouk> <the music was loud and *empty* . . . like a malediction in which not even those who hated most deeply any longer believed – James Baldwin> <they were married with the bright *hollow* panoply attending such military affairs – William Styron> <nothing is more *hollow* than the air of sanctimony worn to cover a mean act – Barbara Tuchman>
2 see FUTILE
3 see under PRIDE *n*
vainglorious – see under PRIDE *n*
vainglory – see PRIDE *n*
valid, sound, cogent, convincing, telling *shared meaning* : having such force as to compel serious attention and usually acceptance. **Valid** implies being supported by objective truth or generally accepted authority <a *valid* argument> <a *valid* marriage> <established a clear-cut difference between what is truly important and *valid* in the youth protest and what is secondary and irrelevant – Tad Szulc> <a contract which satisfies all the requirements for enforceability by a court is termed a *valid* contract – L. B. Howard> **Sound** implies being based on flawless reasoning or on solid grounds <a *sound* argument> <he has a *sound* claim against the estate> <sacrifice a *sound* curriculum in order to bask in the prestige of offering courses for the elite – C. R. Haywood> <he seems to have read nearly every writer of importance . . . and he talks about them with clarity and *sound* sense – Dudley Fitts> **Cogent** may stress either weight of sound argument or evidence or lucidity of presentation <a soul-searching melancholia through which he was to create a *cogent* universality of form

and meaning – J. A. Dennis> <his argument is *cogent,* and the conclusion he reaches sound> **Convincing** suggests a power to overcome doubt, opposition, or reluctance to accept <the very lack of planning . . . is *convincing* proof that there was no conspiracy – Sylvan Fox> <[his] casual ease builds a completely *convincing* portrait of the reluctant hero – Alton Cook> **Telling** stresses an immediate and crucial effect striking at the heart of a matter and may or may not imply soundness and validity <certainly makes some *telling* points . . . with a deftness that will disarm orthodox heresy-hunters – M. R. Cohen> <a *telling* attack, made with skill and shrewd insight – V. L. Parrington> ***ant*** invalid, fallacious, sophistic

validate – see CONFIRM ***ant*** invalidate

valor – see HEROISM

valuable – see COSTLY

value *n* – see WORTH

value *vb* – see APPRECIATE, ESTIMATE

vanity – see PRIDE *n*

vanquish – see CONQUER

vapid – see INSIPID

variance – see DISCORD

various – see DIFFERENT ***ant*** uniform, cognate

vary – see CHANGE *vb*

vast – see HUGE

vaunt – see BOAST

veer – see SWERVE

vein – see MOOD

venerable – see OLD

venerate – see REVERE

vengeful – see VINDICTIVE

venial, pardonable *shared meaning* **:** not warranting punishment or the imposition of a penalty. **Venial** usually implies an opposition to *grave, serious,* or *grievous* <he had learned to see what was really criminal in what he had done, and what was *venial* – Anthony Trollope> or, in theological use, to *mortal;* consequently, it applies to what is trivial, harmless, or unwitting <the *venial* indiscretions of youth – Robert Southey> <the public interest . . . covers a multitude of sins, from the *venial* to the deadly – *Barron's*> <the faults of this book . . . are few and *venial* – Dudley Fitts> **Pardonable** implies that there is excuse or justification that makes the fault unworthy of consideration <her heart innocent of the most *pardonable* guile – Joseph Conrad> <spoke with *pardonable* pride of his son's success> ***ant*** heinous, mortal

venom – see POISON

vent – see EXPRESS ***ant*** bridle

venturesome – see ADVENTUROUS

veracity – see TRUTH

verbal – see ORAL

verbose – see WORDY ***ant*** laconic

verge – see BORDER

verify – see CONFIRM

verisimilitude – see TRUTH

veritable – see AUTHENTIC ***ant*** factitious

verity – see TRUTH

vernacular – see DIALECT

versatile, many-sided, all-around *shared meaning* **:** marked by or showing skill or ability or capacity or usefulness of many kinds. Applied to persons, **versatile** stresses variety of aptitude and facility that allows one to turn from one activity to another without loss of effectiveness or skill; applied to things, it stresses their multiple and diverse qualities, uses, or possibilities <a bewildering variety of *versatile* helicopters . . . including one with the unique capability of flying upside down – W. D. Patterson> <[he] is a *versatile* performer, often providing the piano accompaniment for one of his own compositions while conducting the orchestra from the bench – *Current Biog.*> **Many-sided** applied to persons stresses breadth or diversity of interests or accomplishments; applied to things, diversity of aspects, attributes, or uses <a *many-sided* scholar, critically aware of yesterday, today, and tomorrow> <we are surrounded by the products of our *many-sided* genius – C. E. Crowther> <a *many-sided* agreement – *Manchester Guardian Weekly*> **All-around** implies completeness or symmetry of development, either general or within a single activity with many phases; the term implies general competence more often than special or outstanding ability <an *all-around* athlete and sportsman> <the *all-around* adaptability and quality of our men – A. B. Vosseller>

vertical, perpendicular, plumb *shared meaning* : being at a right angle with the plane of the horizon. **Vertical** suggests a line or direction rising upward toward or approximately toward the zenith <*vertical* threads in a tapestry> <walls not quite *vertical*> *Vertical* is the most common of these terms in application to abstractions and in extended use <[he] divides thought processes into logical and reasoned, which are "*vertical,*" and unconventional, which are "lateral" – *Brit. Bk. News*> <besides the *vertical* gap between this generation and the last there is a horizontal gap between students of the far left and their middle-of-the-road peers – R. E. Kavanaugh> **Perpendicular** normally applies to things that extend upward or downward or both from the horizontal; it is appropriately used to suggest steepness or precipitousness <a *perpendicular* cliff> <the water fell in *perpendicular* sheets> or, sometimes, rigid erectness <a stiff *perpendicular* old maid – Mary R. Mitford> **Plumb** stresses exact verticality and implies its determination by or as if by a plumb line <the walls were *plumb*> ***ant*** horizontal

very – see SAME

vestige – see TRACE

vex – see ANNOY ***ant*** please, regale

vibrate – see SWING 2

vice 1 see FAULT

2 see OFFENSE 2 ***ant*** virtue

vicious, villainous, iniquitous, nefarious, flagitious, infamous, corrupt, degenerate *shared meaning* : highly reprehensible or offensive in character, nature, or conduct. **Vicious** may directly oppose *virtuous* in implying moral depravity <acquire *vicious* habits> or may connote malignancy, cruelty, or destructive violence <the horseman delivered one last *vicious* cut with his whip – Rudyard Kipling> or it may imply a debasing or vitiation by faults or defects <a *vicious* system of financing> <discriminate between thoroughly *vicious* ideas and those which should have a chance to be heard – Zechariah Chafee> **Villainous** applies to any evil, depraved, or vile conduct or disposition <*villainous* abuse of privilege> <dreams bizarre and frantic, *villainous* beyond men's wildest imaginings – William Styron> **Iniquitous** usually implies absence of all signs of justice or fairness <the *iniquitous* Population Registration Act – which defines who is white and who is not – Noel Mostert> **Nefarious** suggests flagrant breaching of time-honored laws and traditions of conduct <race prejudice is most *nefarious* on its politer levels – H. E. Clurman> <believed herself the victim of a *nefarious* plot> **Flagitious** and **infamous** suggest shameful and scandalous wickedness <in

the beginning, the common law applied only to acts that all men, everywhere, admitted were *flagitious* – G. W. Johnson> <forced and *flagitious* bombast – T. S. Eliot> <the *infamous* Astor set which tried to buy peace for England by encouraging Hitler to acquire an Eastern empire – Henry Pachter> <[she] would have scouted as *infamous* any suggestion that her parent was more selfish than saintly – G. B. Shaw> **Corrupt** stresses a loss of moral integrity or probity causing betrayal of principles or obligations <cities . . . fallen into the clutches of *corrupt* political machines – Trevor Armbrister> <leaders who are *corrupt,* disruptive, or hostile to African stability – William Attwood> **Degenerate** suggests having sunk from a higher to a lower and usually a peculiarly corrupt and vicious state <the governments . . . have become corrupt, immoral, and *degenerate* structures – W. W. Wagar> <strutted before the mirror . . . experimenting with various *degenerate* leers and wiggles. It seemed to her that she made quite a fetching and vicious whore – Herman Wouk> ***ant*** virtuous

vicissitude – see CHANGE *n,* DIFFICULTY

victim, prey, quarry *shared meaning* : one killed or injured for the ends of the one who kills or injures. **Victim** basically applies to a living being killed as a sacrifice to a divinity but in more general use it applies to one killed, injured, ruined, or badly treated either by a ruthless person or by an impersonal power that admits of no effective resistance <*victims* of wars and disasters> <spent much time . . . complaining of his poverty as if it were a new invention and he its first *victim* – Bernard Malamud> <all are *victims* of circumstances; all have had characters warped in infancy and intelligence stunted at school – Bertrand Russell> **Prey** basically applies to animals hunted and killed for food by other animals and is often extended to a victim of something suggestive of a rapacious predator <we are tolerant of nonsense, a notoriously easy *prey* to slogans, in both our political and our economic life – A. H. Marckwardt> <ill fares the land, to hastening ills a *prey* – Oliver Goldsmith> **Quarry** basically applies to a victim of the chase; in this and in its more general use it may apply to one pursued intensely as well as to one actually taken by the hunter or pursuer <the startled *quarry* bounds amain, as fast the gallant greyhounds strain – Sir Walter Scott> <sometimes a man has to stalk his *quarry* with great caution, waiting patiently for the right moment to reveal himself – Roald Dahl>

victory, conquest, triumph *shared meaning* : a successful outcome in a contest or struggle. **Victory** stresses the fact of winning against an opponent or against odds <the purpose of the program was to translate the civil rights *victories* into actual conditions of equality in the daily lives of Negro citizens – *Current Biog.*> <won an upset *victory* in the election> **Conquest** stresses the subjugation or mastery of a defeated opponent, be it a personal antagonist or a difficult undertaking <the *conquest* of space> <men have accelerated the *conquest* of nature by means of science – Liam de Paor> <the prospect of a quick, easy *conquest* of Greece – W. L. Shirer> **Triumph** suggests a brilliant or decisive victory or an overwhelming conquest and usually connotes the acclaim and personal satisfaction accruing to the winner <the battle . . . marked the beginning of final Union *triumph* – A. P. James> <another great oratorical *triumph* – A. C. Cole> <the *triumph* of industrialism – C. I. Glicksberg> ***ant*** defeat

vie – see RIVAL

view – see OPINION

vigilant – see WATCHFUL

vigorous, energetic, strenuous, lusty, nervous *shared meaning* : having great vitality and force. **Vigorous** adds the implication of undiminished capacity for further activity, development, or use <seemed as *vigorous* as a youth

half his age> <a *vigorous* fast-growing tree> <a *vigorous* argument – Edmund Wilson> <[she] was a bold, *vigorous* thinker – Sherwood Anderson> **Energetic** suggests a display of or capacity for great activity, sometimes a bustling or forced activity that has little to do with real strength <to be counted among the strong, and not the merely *energetic* – J. R. Lowell> <they were capable and *energetic* women, as fit to intimidate local government boards as to control the domestic economy of their own homes – Victoria Sackville-West> **Strenuous** applied to persons suggests a preference for coping with the arduous or the challenging; applied to things, it can imply a making of constant demands on one's vigor <he taught . . . that there existed an operative providence always at hand to help those *strenuous* to help themselves – Bonamy Dobrée> <to hustle and to be *strenuous* . . . seem to be prominent American virtues – M. R. Cohen> <relaxing . . . after a *strenuous* day's work – Hervey Allen> **Lusty** implies exuberant vigor and energy freely manifested <therefore, my age is as a *lusty* winter, frosty, but kindly – Shak.> <Pete Gurney was a *lusty* cock turned sixty-three, but bright and hale – John Masefield> <a *lusty* appetite> **Nervous**, in this sense applicable to things (as qualities or expression) rather than persons, implies a keen vigor of mind or feeling or style <enjoying the sharp *nervous* rhythm of the band> <vivid pages in simple, *nervous*, racy language – Carl Van Doren> <the *nervous* alertness of youthful brains, and the stamina of youthful bodies – *Amer. Guide Series: Mich.*> *ant* languorous, lethargic

vile – see BASE

vilify – see MALIGN *ant* eulogize

villainous – see VICIOUS

vindictive, revengeful, vengeful *shared meaning* : showing or motivated by a desire for vengeance. The terms are often used interchangeably but are capable of more precise use in which they convey distinctive notions. In such use **vindictive** tends to stress the reaction as inherent in the nature of the individual and is appropriate when no specific motivating grievance exists <there was nothing *vindictive* in his nature; but, if revenge came his way, it might as well be good – R. L. Stevenson> Sometimes the term implies a persistent emotion, based on real or fancied wrongs, that may manifest itself in implacable malevolence or in mere spiteful malice <a *vindictive* man will look for occasions of resentment – James Martineau> <hunted by . . . gangsters [who] . . . harbor *vindictive* grudges – *Boston Spectator*> **Revengeful** and **vengeful** are more likely to suggest the state of one specifically provoked to action and truculently ready to seek or take revenge <no creature is so *revengeful* as a proud man who has humbled himself in vain – T. B. Macaulay> <Africans are far less racist than the colonialists had thought. With so many reasons to be bitter, they have surprised their former white masters by being forgiving instead of *vengeful* – William Attwood> Either term may also apply to an agent or weapon by which vengeance can be attained <may my hands . . . never brandish more *revengeful* steel – Shak.>

virile – see MASCULINE *ant* effeminate, impotent

virtually, practically, morally *shared meaning* : not absolute or actually, yet so nearly so that the difference is negligible. Though often used interchangeably these terms are capable of nice discrimination. **Virtually** may imply a merely apparent difference between outward seeming and inner reality <the prime minister is *virtually* the ruler of his country> <[he] assumed the post of rector with the university *virtually* under siege by students, many of whom threatened his life – S. T. Wise> **Practically** implies a difference between what meets ordinary or practical demands and what qualifies in some formal or absolute way <a practically worthless stretch of barren eroded hillside is still subject to taxation> <the road is *practically* finished; cars can use it all the way> <she'd . . . felt sorry for me in college, and sometimes she *practically* kept me from starving – Roy Shivers> **Morally** implies a difference between what satisfies one's judgment and what constitutes legal or logical proof <the jurors were *morally* certain of the defendant's guilt but the lack of conclusive evidence demanded a verdict of "not guilty"> <the claim to sovereignty is a claim by the members of a community . . . to be at liberty, not only de facto but de jure, and *morally* too – A. J. Toynbee>

virtuous – see MORAL *ant* vicious

virus – see POISON

visionary – see IMAGINARY

visit, visitation, call *shared meaning* : a coming to stay with another temporarily and usually briefly. **Visit,** the general term, applies to any such coming, be it long or short, and whatever its nature or cause or purpose <pay a *visit* to a housebound friend> <a *visit* to the dentist> <spent the summer on a *visit* to her English cousins> <planned a *visit* to Washington> **Visitation** applies chiefly to a formal or official visit made by one in authority often for a special purpose (as inspection or counseling) <parochial *visitations* of a bishop> or it may apply to something that comes to one by or as if by the will of a superior power <the nun was as elated as if she had had a blessed *visitation* – H. C. Hervey> or that is visited upon one, especially as an affliction <an illness, a maiming accident or some other *visitation* of blind fate – Joseph Conrad> **Call** applies to a brief, usually formal visit for social or professional purposes <afternoons given up to a round of *calls* on friends and acquaintances> <the doctor made several house *calls* before seeing the patients at his office> <the salesmen were expected to make at least ten *calls* each day>

visitation – see VISIT

vital – see ESSENTIAL, LIVING

vitalize, energize, activate *shared meaning* : to arouse to activity, animation, or life. **Vitalize** may stress the arousal of something more or less inert or lifeless, often by communicating an impetus or force <local investment has joined foreign in *vitalizing* Cartagena's economy – Robert Collins> or an imparting of significance or interest to something or a making one aware of its inherent significance <a power of description that *vitalizes* his words – *Christian Science Monitor*> **Energize** implies an arousing to activity or a readying for activity (as work) by an imparting of strength or a providing with a source of energy <the use of electromagnetic energy transmitted to *energize* a passive transmitter – L. A. Geddes> <Liberalism has lost its *energizing* purity – Jack Newfield> **Activate** implies a passing from an inactive to an active state and stresses the influence of an external agent in arousing to activity <the report has done much to crystallize and *activate* . . . opinion – Walter White> <a switch in the office *activates* all the outdoor lights> *ant* atrophy

vitiate – see DEBASE

vituperate – see SCOLD

vituperation – see ABUSE *ant* acclaim, praise

vivacious – see LIVELY *ant* languid

vivid – see GRAPHIC

vivify – see QUICKEN

vocal, articulate, oral *shared meaning* : uttered by the voice or having to do with such utterance. **Vocal** implies the use of the voice, but not necessarily of speech or language; thus, *vocal* sounds are those produced by a creature that has *vocal* organs; *vocal* music is contrasted with instrumental music because the sounds are produced by the voice rather than an instrument. **Articulate** implies the use of distinct intelligible language; thus, speech is the uttering of *articulate* sounds; *articulate* cries are expressed in meaningful words <Constance nodded her head in thorough agreement. She did not trouble to go into *articulate* apologies – Arnold Bennett> **Oral** implies the use of the voice rather than the hand (as in writing or signaling) in communication <an *oral* examination> <give *oral* directions simply and accurately> <legend is the *oral* transmission of tradition>

vociferous, clamorous, blatant, strident, boisterous, obstreperous *shared meaning* : so loud or insistent as to compel attention. **Vociferous** may imply loud and vehement cries or shouts <watermen, fishwomen, oysterwomen, and . . . all the *vociferous* inhabitants of both shores – Henry Fielding> or it may imply insistent urgent presentation (as of requests, excuses, or demands) <his dislikes are many and *vociferous,* in print if not in conversation – Katherine Scherman> <the Northern press and people were *vociferous* for action – S. E. Morison & H. S. Commager> **Clamorous** may be chosen to stress insistence in vociferous demanding or protesting <it was impossible to yield to her *clamorous* demands – Agnes Repplier> but often stresses the notion of sustained din or confused turbulence <stood and peered into the *clamorous* living room – Herman Wouk> **Blatant** implies a tendency to bellow or to be conspicuously, offensively, or vulgarly noisy or clamorous <they were heretics of the *blatant* sort, loudmouthed and shallow-minded – *Expositor*> <their *blatant* rudeness was a nightmare. They booed and yelled – Rex Reed> **Strident** basically implies a harsh discordant quality distressing to the ear <[her] voice struck me as being particularly *strident* – Roald Dahl> and may describe something that forces itself on the attention <while . . . embittered Negroes turned in frustration to the *strident* slogans of black nationalists – *Progressive*> **Boisterous** suggests the rowdy high spirits that go with noisy turbulence and release from restraint <lament the decadence of a once *boisterous* port – John Cheever> <*boisterous* spring winds – Willa Cather> **Obstreperous** suggests unruly and aggressive noisiness, typically occurring in resistance to or defiance of authority <the most careless and *obstreperous* merriment – Samuel Johnson> <a post-midnight demonstration on the [convention] floor which became progressively more *obstreperous* – Norman Mailer>

vogue – see FASHION

voice – see EXPRESS

void – see EMPTY

volatility – see LIGHTNESS

voluble – see TALKATIVE ***ant*** curt

volume – see BULK

voluntary, intentional, deliberate, willful *shared meaning* : done or brought about of one's own will. **Voluntary** implies deciding by one's free choice and without intervention of an effective outside influence <a *voluntary* renunciation of an inheritance> <a *voluntary* confession> Sometimes it stresses spontaneity <large *voluntary* contributions to the fund> or subjection to or regulation by the will <*voluntary* movement> or prior consideration leading to choice <*voluntary* taking of life> or absence of any legal compulsion <*voluntary* bankruptcy> or valuable consideration <*voluntary* conveyance of property> **Intentional** stresses an awareness of an end to be attained <the insult was plainly *intentional*> <not one in a thousand . . . perpetrates any *intentional* damage – Richard Jefferies> **Deliberate** implies full consciousness of the nature of one's act and its consequences <a *deliberate* falsehood> <we ask . . . that . . . there be a

deliberate and massive effort to include the Negro citizen in the mainstream of American life – W. M. Young> **Willful** adds to *deliberate* implications of a refusal to be taught, guided, or restrained and of an obstinate determination to follow one's planned course <*willful* blindness to ascertained truth – W. R. Inge> <*willful* murder> ***ant*** involuntary, instinctive

voluptuous – see SENSUOUS ***ant*** ascetic

voracious, gluttonous, ravenous, ravening, rapacious *shared meaning* **:** excessively greedy. **Voracious** implies habitual gorging with what satisfies an appetite <a *voracious* reader> <*voracious* birds, that hotly bill and breed, and largely drink – John Dryden> **Gluttonous** stresses covetous delight, especially in food, and acquiring and consuming past need or to the point of satiety <he was *gluttonous* for jewels – John Gunther> <his *gluttonous* appetite for food, praise, pleasure – A. L. Guérard> **Ravenous** implies extreme hunger and suggests violence and grasping in satisfying it <she was so *ravenous* to talk to him that it was quite impossible to stop herself – Penelope Gilliatt> **Ravening** may replace *ravenous* <the hordes of *ravening* ants – William Beebe> but more often it, like **rapacious,** suggests a violent tendency to seize and appropriate in the manner of a predaceous animal <if the mess isn't settled ... the voters will be *ravening* for a scapegoat – *New Republic*> <beware of false prophets, which come to you in sheep's clothing, but inwardly they are *ravening* wolves – *Mt* 7:15 (AV)> <*rapacious* animals we hate – John Gay> Often *rapacious* loses its connection with natural appetites and suggests excessive and utterly selfish acquisitiveness and cupidity <the *rapacious* ambition of the palace eunuchs – H. D. Lasswell> <a *rapacious* divorcee on the prowl – Helen Howe>

vouchsafe – see GRANT

vulgar – see COARSE, COMMON

wage, salary, stipend, pay, fee, hire, emolument *shared meaning* **:** the price paid for services or labor. **Wage,** often as the plural **wages,** applies to an amount paid usually on an hourly basis and chiefly at weekly intervals especially for mostly physical labor <a gardener's *wages*> <dirty and difficult jobs should command a higher *wage*> **Salary** and **stipend** usually apply to compensation at a fixed, often annual, rate that is paid in installments at regular (as weekly) intervals; both terms, and particularly the latter, are likely to suggest that the services performed require training or special ability, but only the latter is used of a regular income (as a pension or scholarship) paid without concurrently performed service. **Pay** can replace any of the foregoing and is the one of these four terms freely used in combination and attributively <cash one's *pay*check> <waiting for *pay*day> <lost his *pay* envelope> **Fee** applies to the price asked, usually in the form of a fixed charge, for a specific professional service <a pianist's *fee* for a concert> <the doctor raised his *fee* for house calls> **Hire,** which basically denotes payment for the temporary use of something (as the property or money of another) may sometimes be used of compensation for labor or services and is then equivalent to *wage* or *salary* <the laborer is worthy of his *hire* – *Lk* 10:7 (AV)> **Emolument,** usually as the plural **emoluments,** may apply to the financial reward of one's work or office <the *emoluments* of a profession – Edward Gibbon> or sometimes to rewards and perquisites other than wages or salary <*emoluments* of value, like pension and insurance benefits, which may accrue to employees – C. W. Boyce>

wait – see STAY 1
waive – see RELINQUISH
wallow, welter, grovel *shared meaning* : to move heavily or clumsily because or as if impeded or out of control. In application to persons the notion of movement is often replaced by one of existence. **Wallow** basically implies a lurching or rolling to and fro (as of a hog in the mire or a ship in a troubled sea) <a jeep came *wallowing* through the mud – Norman Mailer> In extended use the term suggests the state of an animal wallowing in mud and may imply complete self-abandonment <*wallowing* in self-pity> or absorption <enjoyed sitting . . . and *wallowing* in the sensual melodies – Osbert Sitwell> or helpless involvement <the economic catastrophe in which they were . . . *wallowing* – J. P. O'Donnell> or, especially, sensual enjoyment and disregard of defilement <publicly *wallowed* in his infamies – Merle Miller> <in port . . . [he] would roar off to the fleshpots, in which he would *wallow* noisily until an hour before takeoff – Theodore Sturgeon> **Welter** may replace *wallow* but is likely to carry a stronger implication of being helplessly at the mercy of outside forces <the mass of the people were *weltering* in shocking poverty whilst a handful of owners wallowed in millions – G. B. Shaw> <survivors . . . *weltered* in the sea for four days – *Time*> **Grovel** implies a crawling or wriggling close to the ground (as in abject fear, self-abasement, or utter degradation) <upon thy belly *groveling* thou shalt go, and dust shalt eat all the days of thy life – John Milton> <before the wrath of the former Austrian corporal, its . . . [the German army's] leaders fawned and *groveled* – W. L. Shirer>
wan – see PALE
wane – see ABATE ***ant*** wax
want *vb* – see DESIRE, LACK
want *n* – see POVERTY
ward off – see PREVENT 2 ***ant*** conduce to
warlike – see MARTIAL
warn, forewarn, caution *shared meaning* : to let one know of approaching or possible danger or risk. **Warn** may range in meaning from simple notification of something to be watched for or guarded against to admonition of threats of violence or reprisal <the weather bureau *warned* coastal areas to prepare for a hurricane> <*warned* him of the consequences of his folly> <the priestly brotherhood . . . prompt to persuade, expostulate, and *warn* – William Cowper> <*warn* a trespasser off one's land> **Forewarn** stresses timeliness and regularly implies warning in advance of a foreseen risk or danger <I will arm me, being thus *forewarned* – Shak.> <he knew not one *forewarning* pain – William Wordsworth> **Caution** stresses giving advice that puts one on guard or suggests precautions against either a prospective or a present risk or peril <the doctor *cautioned* him against overeating> <*caution* the children about a dangerous place>
warp – see DEFORM
warrant – see JUSTIFY
wary – see CAUTIOUS ***ant*** foolhardy, brash (*of persons*)
waste **1** see RAVAGE ***ant*** conserve
2 waste, squander, dissipate, fritter, consume *shared meaning* : to spend or expend futilely or without gaining a proper or reasonable or normal return. **Waste** usually implies careless or prodigal expenditure <the younger son . . . took his journey into a far country, and there *wasted* his substance with riotous living – *Lk* 15:13 (AV)> but it may imply fruitless or useless expenditure <some ironist once observed that education is too precious to be *wasted* on children – J. W. Ramsey> <why *waste* time trying to help people who want no help?> **Squander** stresses reckless and lavish

expenditure that tends to exhaust resources <we the people of the United States, in order to form for ourselves a more profitable existence, have *squandered,* exploited, and polluted our natural environment – L. J. Bakanowsky> <tumbling yellow cassias *squandering* their petals down our dusty road – Padma Perera> **Dissipate** implies loss by extravagance as though scattered to the four winds and commonly stresses exhaustion of the store or stock <to see the sense of this life *dissipated,* to see our reason for existence disappear, that is what is intolerable – W. S. Coffin, Jr.> <we have *dissipated* much of the international trust and respect that was once ours – F. W. Neal> **Fritter,** usually with *away,* implies expenditure on trifles, bit by bit, or without commensurate return <a natural resource as complex and valuable as the Red River ought not to be *frittered* away – *N. Y. Times*> <the friend had lost $300,000 and Lasker had *frittered* away almost as much – Bennett Cerf> **Consume** can imply a wasting or squandering as entirely as if by devouring <having then *consumed* all his estate he grew very melancholy – Anthony Wood> ***ant*** save, conserve

waster – see SPENDTHRIFT

wastrel – see SPENDTHRIFT

watch – see SEE, TEND

watchful, vigilant, wide-awake, alert *shared meaning* : being on the lookout, especially for danger or opportunity. **Watchful** is the general word <the five *watchful* senses – John Milton> <be *watchful,* and strengthen the things which remain, that are ready to die – *Rev* 3:2 (AV)> <his ... mother ... *watchful,* never disapproving, but saddened by the pleasures of her only son – John Cheever> **Vigilant** implies keen, courageous, often wary, watchfulness <eternally *vigilant* against attempts to check the expression of opinions that we loathe – O. W. Holmes †1935> <be sober, be *vigilant;* because your adversary the devil, as a roaring lion, walketh about, seeking whom he may devour – *1 Pet* 5:8 (AV)> **Wide-awake** stresses keen awareness, more often of opportunities and developments than of dangers <merchants who ... were ... *wide-awake* and full of energy – H. W. van Loon> <listened with *wide-awake* interest – A. C. Whitehead> **Alert** stresses readiness or promptness in apprehending and meeting a problem, an opportunity, or an emergency <not only watchful in the night, but *alert* in the drowsy afternoon – Walter Pater> <silent and *alert,* like a sentinel on duty – J. G. Frazer>

wave – see SWING 1

waver – see HESITATE, SWING 2

way – see METHOD

waylay – see SURPRISE 1

wayward – see CONTRARY

weaken, enfeeble, debilitate, undermine, sap, cripple, disable *shared meaning* : to lose or cause to lose strength, vigor, or energy. **Weaken** may imply loss of physical strength, health, soundness, or stability or of quality, intensity, or effective power <the illness had *weakened* him> <the timbers were *weakened* by decay> <the batteries in my radio are *weakening*> <wearing down the *weakening* defenders in battles of attrition – W. L. Shirer> <his actions ... harm not only the British and the Americans but also *weaken* France herself – S. E. Ambrose> **Enfeeble** implies an obvious and pitiable condition of weakness or helplessness <a country crushed and *enfeebled* by war> <poverty ... *enfeebles,* aborts, ... and numbs those qualities we deem most highly human – Kenneth Keniston> **Debilitate** is likely to suggest a less marked or less permanent impairment than *enfeeble* <old people crippled and *debilitated* by chronic diseases – Edith M. Stern> <the fears and the rages that *debilitate* – H. A. Overstreet> **Undermine**

and **sap** imply a weakening by something working surreptitiously and insidiously that may lead to collapse <persuaded that these people he has been taking for granted are all part of an insidious conspiracy to *undermine* the world as he knows it – Edmund Wilson> <expressing his fear that the traditional function of the colleges is being *sapped* away – Morris Keeton> **Cripple** implies causing a serious loss of functioning power through damaging or removing an essential part or element <the . . . armies had been *crippled* but not destroyed – W. L. Shirer> <a shy girl *crippled* both physically and emotionally – Elaine L. Lawrence> **Disable** is likely to imply an intervention (as an injury or an event) that deprives of strength or competence <a siren that can *disable* people merely with its sound – Nat Hentoff> <these consoling yet nonetheless *disabling* illusions – M. W. Straight> ***ant*** strengthen

wealthy – see RICH ***ant*** indigent

wean – see ESTRANGE ***ant*** addict

weary – see TIRE

wee – see SMALL

weigh – see CONSIDER

weight – see IMPORTANCE

weighty – see HEAVY

weird, eerie, uncanny *shared meaning* : mysteriously strange or fantastic. **Weird** may imply an unearthly or preternatural strangeness <when night makes a *weird* sound of its own stillness – P. B. Shelley> <*weird* whispers, bells that rang without a hand – Alfred Tennyson> or it may mean little more than strangely or absurdly queer <frantically he contrived – anything to keep her with him – the *weirdest* blandishments – William Styron> **Eerie,** used chiefly to create atmosphere, suggests an uneasy or fearful consciousness that mysterious and usually malign powers are at work <smiles which were pitched, with an *eerie* precision, between longing and contempt – James Baldwin> <the girl found awe creeping over her as her brother's voice filled the vault of the temple, chanting words thousands of years old, in an *eerie* melody from a dim lost time – Herman Wouk> **Uncanny** may imply an uncomfortable strangeness or an unpleasant mysteriousness <the *uncanny* bridges that history builds between past and present – R. L. Shayon> <he tried quickly to think of something else, lest with her *uncanny* intuition she discern the cloud of death in his mind – Pearl Buck> or, in common though often criticized use, may mean little more than *exceptional, unusual,* or *surprising* <an *uncanny* amount of luggage was mislaid by the airlines>

welcome – see PLEASANT ***ant*** unwelcome

well – see HEALTHY ***ant*** unwell, ill

well-nigh – see NEARLY

well-off – see RICH

well-to-do – see RICH

welter – see WALLOW

wet, damp, dank, moist, humid *shared meaning* : more or less covered with or permeated by liquid. **Wet** may imply saturation <the game was postponed because of *wet* grounds> <we were *wet* to the skin by a sudden shower> or describe a surface covered with liquid <*wet* pavements> <cheeks *wet* with tears> or apply to something not or not yet dry <touched the paint to see if it was still *wet*> **Damp** implies a slight or partial covering or permeating <streets still *damp* from last night's rain> and often suggests unpleasant or disagreeable wetness <a *damp* chilly day> <the house was *damp* and smelled musty> **Dank** implies a more distinctly disagreeable or unwholesome dampness and often connotes lack of fresh air and sunshine <*dank* clouds of fog wallowed round the two men – Chris Somersett> <his forehead . . . was *dank* with clammy sweat – Oscar Wilde> **Moist,** a usually neutral term, is likely to suggest a not unpleasant dampness or an absence of positive dryness <kept the sandwiches *moist* in a plastic wrapper> <the air was *moist* and cool> **Humid** usually implies the presence of oppressive amounts of moisture in warm air <the *humid* prairie heat, so nourishing to wheat and corn, so exhausting to human beings – Willa Cather> <a *humid* little fitting room [in a tailor's shop] – John Cheever> ***ant*** dry

while, wile, beguile, fleet *shared meaning* **:** to pass idle or leisure time without being bored. One **whiles** or **wiles** *away* a space of time by causing it to be filled with something pleasant, diverting, or amusing <[he] had *whiled* away a good part of the winter in sunny Italy – W. L. Shirer> <attempt to *wile* away the long days . . . telling a story to his sister – Virginia Woolf> One **beguiles** a space of time or its tedium or irksomeness by occupying that time with some agreeable employment <others . . . *beguiled* the little tedium of the way with penny papers – Nathaniel Hawthorne> <to *beguile* his enforced leisure, I tried to teach him sundry little tricks – C. H. Grandgent> One **fleets** the time by causing it to pass quickly or imperceptibly <many young gentlemen . . . *fleet* the time carelessly – Shak.> <*fleeting* the quiet hour in observation of his pets – G. H. Lewes>

whim – see CAPRICE

whirl – see REEL

whiten, blanch, bleach *shared meaning* **:** to change from an original or natural color to or nearly to white. **Whiten** implies a making white or whiter, often by a surface application <*whiten* soiled shoes with pipe clay> <the snow fell softly, *whitening* the roofs and streets> **Blanch** implies a whitening either by the removal of color <the general *blanched* as he regarded the squalor – Robert Standish> <an injection of nicotinic acid *blanches* the rash – *Therapeutic Notes*> or by preventing it from developing <plants *blanched* by lack of light> <*blanch* celery by covering the stalks with earth> **Bleach** implies the action of light or chemicals in removing or reducing color <*bleach* hair with peroxide> <linen spread on the grass to *bleach* in the sunlight> ***ant*** blacken

whole *adj* **1** see PERFECT

2 whole, entire, total, all, gross *shared meaning* **:** including everything or everyone without exception. **Whole** implies that nothing has been omitted, ignored, abated, or removed <the *whole* country is affected> <*whole* milk> <a *whole* industry may be able to increase its sales by general price reduction, but less easily than a single firm can – R. M. Solow> **Entire** may replace *whole* <his *entire* career> <the *entire* State was up in arms> but it can also, as *whole* cannot, imply literal completeness or perfection from which nothing has been taken or to which nothing has been added <an *entire* stallion> <whom to obey is happiness *entire* – John Milton> **Total** may imply that everything has been taken into account (as by weighing, measuring, or counting) <the *total* output of a factory> <our *total* expenses on the trip were higher than we had planned> or it may imply the absence of all reservation, especially when qualifying something that is often incomplete <a *total* eclipse> <listening with *total* attention and devotion – Edith Oliver> **All** may equal *whole* <*all* the city was in an uproar> or come close to *entire* <*all* their affection was centered on their children> or be interchangeable with *total* <*all* their earnings were insufficient for their needs> **Gross** may replace *total* (as in financial statements) with the added implication that ultimately necessary deductions from a whole have not been made <most taxes are charged against net, not *gross,* income>

<*gross* national product is one measure of economic progress> ***ant*** partial
whole *n* – see SUM ***ant*** part, constituent, particular
wholehearted – see SINCERE
wholesale – see INDISCRIMINATE
wholesome – see HEALTHY
wicked – see BAD
wide – see BROAD ***ant*** strait
wide-awake – see WATCHFUL
wield – see HANDLE
wile *n* – see TRICK
wile *vb* – see WHILE
willful 1 see UNRULY ***ant*** biddable
2 see VOLUNTARY
win – see GET ***ant*** lose
wince – see RECOIL
wink, blink *shared meaning* : to move one's eyelids. **Wink** may mean to close and open the eyelids rapidly and usually involuntarily <houses so white that it makes one *wink* to look at them – Charles Dickens> or it may apply to a deliberate partial closing of one eye (as in mischievous or teasing communication, in flirtation, or as a hint or command) <he grinned and *winked* knowingly> **Blink** implies an involuntary and often repeated winking with eyes half-shut as if dazzled, half-asleep, or nearly blind <he was . . . hauled up . . . *blinking* and tottering . . . into the blessed sun – R. L. Stevenson> <she creates the impression that no detonation could make her *blink* – *Time*> In extended use *wink* implies connivance <in William Penn's absence his governor *winked* at a surreptitious trade with the Dutch – S. E. Morison> and *blink* suggests evasion or shirking <both major parties successfully *blinked* the issue for a decade – S. E. Morison>
winning – see SWEET
winsome – see SWEET
wipe out – see EXTERMINATE
wisdom – see SENSE ***ant*** folly, injudiciousness
wise, sage, sapient, judicious, prudent, sensible, sane *shared meaning* : having or showing ability to choose sound ends and appropriate means. **Wise** suggests great understanding of people and situations and unusual discernment and judgment in dealing with them and may imply a wide range of experience or knowledge or learning <prudent and conservative, Edward was *wise* enough to know that these two qualities . . . were not enough – Pearl Buck> <it is *wise* to be cautious in condemning views and systems which are now out of fashion – W. R. Inge> **Sage** suggests wide experience, great learning, and wisdom <the natural crown that *sage* Experience wears – William Wordsworth> or sometimes a mere affectation of these <answered only with *sage* smiles and knowing glances> **Sapient** may apply to one exhibiting the utmost sagacity <the *sapient* leader who shall bring order out of the wild misrule – V. L. Parrington> but more often is used ironically to imply a hollow sham of such sagacity <the generals . . . put on expressions of *sapient* authority – Eric Linklater> <a *sapient,* instructed, shrewdly ascertaining ignorance – Walter Pater> **Judicious** stresses a capacity for weighing and judging and for arriving at wise decisions or just conclusions <the imaginative and *judicious* use of research evidence – E. P. Torrance> <he is noble, wise, *judicious,* and best knows the fits o' the season – Shak.> **Prudent** suggests exercise of the restraint of sound practical wisdom and discretion <the *prudent* man looketh well to his going – *Prov* 14:15 (AV)> <people who are both dissolute and *prudent.* They

want to have their fun, and they want to keep their position – Victoria Sackville-West> **Sensible** implies the guidance and restraint of good sense and rationality <the *sensible* use of leisure – R. M. Hutchins> <if we go about our business, which is helping *sensible* governments solve their problems, the Communists will eventually trip over themselves – William Attwood> **Sane** stresses mental soundness and levelheaded prudent sense <thankful in his heart and soul that he had his mother, so *sane* and wholesome – D. H. Lawrence> <his ... school reports were models of *sane* educational thinking – Caroline Ticknor> ***ant*** simple

wisecrack – see JEST

wish – see DESIRE

wishy-washy – see INSIPID

wit, humor, irony, sarcasm, satire, repartee *shared meaning* **:** a mode of expression intended to arouse amused interest or evoke laughter or a quality of mind that predisposes to such expression. **Wit** suggests the power to evoke laughter by remarks showing verbal felicity or ingenuity and swift perception especially of the incongruous <true *wit* is nature to advantage dressed, what oft was thought, but ne'er so well expressed – Alexander Pope> **Humor** implies an ability to perceive the ludicrous, the comical, or the absurd in human life and to express them meaningfully to others; regularly it suggests keen insight and deep, usually sympathetic, understanding <the modern sense of *humor* is the quiet enjoyment and implicit expression of the fun of things – Louis Cazamian> **Irony** applies to a manner of expression in which the intended meaning is the opposite of the expressed meaning <*irony* properly suggests the *opposite* of what is explicitly stated, by means of peripheral clues – tone of voice, accompanying gestures, stylistic exaggeration .... Thus, for "Brutus is an honorable man" we understand "Brutus is a traitor" – Jacob Brackman> **Sarcasm** applies to savagely humorous expression, frequently in the form of irony, intended to cut and wound by ridiculing its victim <the arrows of *sarcasm* are barbed with contempt – Washington Gladden> **Satire** primarily applies to writing intended to hold up vices or follies for ridicule and reprobation often by use of irony, parody, or caricature <*satire,* which holds up to ridicule conduct, beliefs, or institutions disapproved of by the author, may be seriously corrective in purpose – K. T. Rowe> **Repartee** applies to the power or art of responding quickly, smoothly, pointedly, and wittily or to an interchange of such response <as for *repartee* ..., as it is the very soul of conversation, so it is the greatest grace of comedy – John Dryden>

with – see BY

withdraw – see GO

wither, shrivel, wizen *shared meaning* **:** to lose or cause to lose freshness and smoothness of appearance. **Wither** implies a loss of vital moisture (as sap or tissue fluids) with consequent fading or drying up <*withered* leaves> <[blossoms] which fall before they *wither* – Laurence Binyon> In extended use it implies a comparable loss of vigor, vitality, or animation <age cannot *wither* her, nor custom stale her infinite variety – Shak.> <we arrived broken, weary, and *withered* by the long flight – Horace Sutton> **Shrivel** carries a stronger impression of becoming wrinkled or crinkled or shrunken <her face popped out of the shadows, *shrivelled* and sagging – Theodore Sturgeon> <poverty ... undermines, *shrivels,* flattens and numbs those qualities we deem most highly human – Kenneth Keniston> **Wizen** may be preferred when the notions of shrinking in size and accompanying wrinkling of the surface are to be stressed; often the term adds such suggestions as aging, deprivation, or failing vitality <the parched lips of the babies, sucking on the *wizened,* dry breasts of their mothers – J. K.

Sale> <his plump features *wizened*, and his rosy cheeks grew white – D. C. Murray>

withhold – see KEEP 2

withstand – see OPPOSE

witticism – see JEST

witty, humorous, facetious, jocular, jocose *shared meaning* : provoking or intended to provoke amusement or laughter. **Witty** suggests cleverness and quickness of mind and often a caustic tongue <she was clever, she was *witty*, and by the use of a few English words and the dramatic facility to express complex thoughts in pantomime, she was quite capable of carrying on extended conversations – Norman Mailer> **Humorous** applies broadly to anything that evokes usually genial laughter; the term may contrast with *witty* in suggesting sensibility rather than intellect and whimsicality more than quickness of mind <whose *humorous* vein, strong sense, and simple style may teach the gayest, make the gravest smile – William Cowper> **Facetious** may apply to clumsy or inappropriate jesting or to attempts at wittiness that please their maker more than others <her lines were weak *facetious* echoes of a style of college slang ten years outmoded – Herman Wouk> **Jocular** implies habitual fondness for jesting and joking and usually suggests a naturally jolly mood or a temperament delighting in the amusing of others <his more solemn and stately brother, at whom he laughed in his *jocular* way – W. M. Thackeray> <the . . . lesson enlivened by the *jocular* conversation of the kindly, humorous old man was always great fun – Joseph Conrad> **Jocose** suggests waggishness or sportiveness in jesting that is often clumsy or inappropriate <sundry *jocose* proposals that the ladies should sit in the gentlemen's laps – Charles Dickens>

wizen – see WITHER

woe – see SORROW

woman – see FEMALE

womanish – see FEMININE *ant* mannish

womanlike – see FEMININE

womanly – see FEMININE *ant* unwomanly, manly

wont – see HABIT

wonted – see USUAL

wordy, verbose, prolix, diffuse, redundant *shared meaning* : using more words than necessary to express thought. **Wordy** may carry an additional suggestion of garrulousness or loquacity <a *wordy*, prolegomenous babbler – R. L. Stevenson> <the whole *wordy* story is unwholesome, unreal, and confused – Donald Wasson> **Verbose** suggests a resulting dullness, obscurity, or lack of effectiveness <a thoughtful work marred by a heavy *verbose* style> <his arguments, clear, logical, never *verbose* – H. W. H. Knott> **Prolix** suggests unreasonable and tedious dwelling on details <very *prolix*, and bursting with subordinate sentences and clauses – Arnold Bennett> <the belief, so prevalent abroad, that it is typical of Russian literature to be formless, *prolix* and hysterical – Edmund Wilson> **Diffuse** implies verbosity but stresses lack of the organization and compactness that makes for pointedness of expression and strength of style <a sprawling, formless, *diffuse*, and unselective book – Orville Prescott> <though Seneca is long-winded, he is not *diffuse;* he is capable of great concision – T. S. Eliot> **Redundant** can suggest superfluity resulting from needless repetition or overelaboration and is applicable both to utterances and style and to persons guilty of producing these <the court may order stricken from any pleading . . . any *redundant*, immaterial, impertinent, or scandalous matter – *U.S. Code*> <at the risk of being *redundant*, I return to my original proposition – J. B. Conant>

work **1 work, labor, travail, toil, drudgery, grind** *shared meaning* : activity involving effort or exertion. **Work** may imply activity of body, of mind, or of a machine or it may apply to effort expended or to the product of such effort <six days shalt thou labor, and do all thy *work* – *Exod* 20:9 (AV)> <this sculpture is the *work* of an unknown artist> <tired out by a hard day's *work*> <machines that accomplish more *work* than a hundred men> **Labor** applies usually to work performed by human beings and suggests the mental or physical effort involved, often stressing its strenuous, onerous, or fatiguing quality <*labor* is doing what we must; leisure is doing what we like – G. B. Shaw> <the backbreaking physical *labor* of the old quarry workers – R. K. Massie> **Travail,** increasingly bookish, stresses painful effort or exertion to the point of suggesting suffering rather than labor <the sentimentalist escapes the stern *travail* of thought – J. L. Lowes> **Toil** implies prolonged and fatiguing labor <the labor of sifting, combining, constructing, expunging, correcting, testing: this frightful *toil* is as much critical as creative – T. S. Eliot> **Drudgery** implies dull, irksome, and distasteful labor <*drudgery* can be cut down. Most men have had to dig for their lives since Adam, but this is now avoidable – Francis Hackett> **Grind** suggests dreary monotonous repetition of burdensome or taxing work <tried to adjust to the daily *grind* of a routine job> <the long *grind* of teaching the promiscuous and preoccupied young – Henry James †1916> ***ant*** play

2 work, employment, occupation, calling, pursuit, business *shared meaning* : a specific sustained activity engaged in, especially in earning one's living. **Work** may apply to any purposeful activity whether remunerative or not <the distress of men out of *work*> <made a life's *work* of collecting rare butterflies> <he is at *work* on a new book> <a miner's *work* is both hazardous and difficult> **Employment** may stress work that occupies one's time and attention <her baby will give her *employment* enough now – Rachel Henning> but usually it implies work engaged in for wages or salary at the behest of another <I . . . went from town to town, working when I could get *employment* – Oliver Goldsmith> **Occupation** implies work in which one engages regularly or preferentially, often as a result of training or experience; thus, one seeks *employment* but normally follows a particular *occupation* <by *occupation* he is a teacher> **Calling** usually applies to an occupation that can be described as a vocation or profession and to which one is likely to have been called by one's nature or tastes or special aptitudes <the learned *callings*> <[she] had received that luckiest of fairy gifts, a *calling* . . . something that she loved to do – L. P. Smith> **Pursuit** applies to a trade, profession, or avocation followed with zeal and steady interest, often as a source of livelihood <learn to adjust themselves to people whose tastes and *pursuits* are different from their own – Bertrand Russell> <set up a . . . program . . . to assist Negroes in the *pursuit* of scientific and technical careers – *Current Biog.*> **Business** may be used in the sense of *work* or *occupation* <I hated, and still hate, the awful *business* of research – Arnold Bennett> <students who must learn the difficult *business* of becoming effective adults – J. A. Perkins> <the *business* of keeping a lunatic asylum – Thomas Denman>

world – see EARTH

worldly – see EARTHLY

worry *vb* **worry, annoy, harass, harry, plague, pester, tease, tantalize** *shared meaning* : to torment to the point of destroying one's peace of mind or disturbing one acutely. **Worry** implies an incessant goading or attacking that tends to drive its victim to desperation or defeat <brother should not war with brother, and *worry* and devour each other – William Cowper>

<took on the mighty galleons like terriers *worrying* bulls – Nora Stirling & Ruth Knight> **Annoy** implies persistent interrupting, bedeviling, interfering with, or intruding on until the victim is angry or upset <clouds of flies . . . *annoyed* our horses – G. H. Borrow> <my movements are all along a regular beat, which enables me to avoid things that bore or *annoy* me – Edmund Wilson> **Harass** implies persecution with small attacks or exactions that wear down or distract or weaken <begins to *harass* her with questions – Donald Heiney> <the Indians *harassed* the settlements. They ambushed men working in the fields . . . , burned their houses, and laid waste their fields – Georgia C. Reed> **Harry** heightens the impression of maltreatment and oppression and commonly carries over from other senses a suggestion of driving in some way <*harrying* Southern sympathizers by arbitrary arrests – *Encyc. Americana*> <James I cordially disliked the Puritans; he boasted that he could make them conform, or *harry* them out of the land – S. E. Morison> **Plague** implies the tormenting affliction of painful disease or something felt as comparable in its persistent inflicting of distress <misfortune *plagued* the plotters at every turn – W. L. Shirer> <the gods are just, and of our pleasant vices make instruments to *plague* us – Shak.> **Pester** implies a continuous harassment with small persistent attacks (as of vermin or small children) <*pestered* with incredible swarms of flies – Tobias Smollett> <would *pester* people with irritating questions – Elsa Maxwell> **Tease** implies an attempt to break down resistance (as by repeated appeals and importunities) <children *teasing* to go to the circus> or a rousing to wrath or upsetting by persistent raillery or petty tormenting <an [excessively tall] . . . boy may be *teased* and taunted because of his height, and impelled either to withdrawal or aggression – M. F. A. Montagu> **Tantalize** implies teasing by repeatedly awakening then frustrating hopes or expectation <merciful love that *tantalizes* not, one-thoughted, never-wandering, guileless love – John Keats>

worry *n* – see CARE

worship – see REVERE

worth, value *shared meaning* : the quality of being excellent, useful, important, desirable, or meritorious or a measure or estimate of such quality. In much of their use these words are close synonyms whose choice depends more on the demands of idiom than on any inherent difference in meaning or connotation. Thus, when the reference is to an equivalence in money or other goods or services *worth* and *value* are frequently but by no means always interchangeable; the *value* (or *worth*) of these coins to collectors is greater than their monetary *worth* (not *value*); get full *value* (better than *worth*) for one's money. However, **worth** is likely to be chosen with reference to what is intrinsically excellent or enduringly meritorious <of ancient race by birth, but nobler yet in his own *worth* – John Dryden> <assumption . . . that the social whole has greater *worth* and significance than its individual parts – Aldous Huxley> <retaining their faith in the educative *worth* of history – R. G. Hanvey> while **value** tends to be applied with reference to qualities imputed to a person or thing or to the degree to which he or it is regarded as useful, important, or excellent, especially in relation to other things <he places high *value* on his wife's criticism of his work – *Current Biog.*> <one reason people flee to the suburbs is for a more natural environment . . . it shows the *value* people set on nature . . . In a city, nature has to have the correct, expansive dimensions in order to perpetuate itself, but what a *worth* it has then! – Anthony Bailey> Additionally, *value* can apply, as *worth* cannot, to something felt to have worth or value, either intrinsically or in relation to something else <citizens for

whom freedom is a fundamental *value* – Nat Hentoff> <preoccupation with products as physical objects rather than as *values* to the consumer – T. J. Murray>

wrangle – see QUARREL
wrath – see ANGER
wreck – see RUIN *vb*
wretched – see MISERABLE
wrong *n* – see INJUSTICE
wrong *adj* – see FALSE ***ant*** right

yank – see JERK
yardstick – see STANDARD
yarn – see STORY
yearn – see LONG
yield **1** see RELINQUISH
2 yield, submit, capitulate, succumb, relent, defer *shared meaning* : to give way to someone or something that one can no longer resist. **Yield** in reference to a person implies being overcome (as by force or entreaty) <after some further argument I *yielded* the point – W. H. Hudson †1922> <not a man to *yield* weakly – Havelock Ellis> but with reference to a thing it implies qualities (as elasticity or weakness) that facilitate giving way <a soft *yielding* mattress> <the door suddenly *yielded* to her hand – Jane Austen> **Submit** suggests surrendering after conflict or resistance to the will or control of another <not only has faith in divine Providence but *submits* to it humbly – Herbert Agar> <if the draft beckons . . . he might just go to jail rather than serve . . . [or] he might *submit* and work for changes from within the system – T. J. Bray> **Capitulate** stresses the fact of giving up in the face of a force or power beyond one's capacity to resist <the universities would *capitulate* to a young, vigorous and revolutionary creed – Walter Moberly> <his . . . refusal to *capitulate* to his emotions – Kenneth Rexroth> **Succumb** stresses weakness and helplessness in the one that gives way or overwhelming power in the one that causes the giving way <the best of constitutions will not prevent ambitious politicians from *succumbing* . . . to the temptations of power – Aldous Huxley> The word frequently implies a disastrous outcome (as death or destruction) <*succumb* to pneumonia> <true passion . . . must be crushed before it will *succumb* – George Meredith> **Relent** implies a yielding through mercy or pity by one who holds the upper hand <can you hear a good man groan, and not *relent?* – Shak.> <[had he been able] to see his sweetheart lying, crying and shivering . . . . He might have *relented* – Margaret Deland> **Defer** implies a voluntary yielding or submitting out of respect or reverence for or deference to another <everybody must *defer* . . . a nation must wait upon her decision, a dean and chapter truckle to her wishes – Victoria Sackville-West> <she *deferred* in all things to her uncle – Upton Sinclair> <even the bravest miners *defer* to the superstition – *Ford Times*>

zeal – see PASSION ***ant*** apathy
zest – see TASTE 2

MERRIAM-WEBSTER DICTIONARIES

WEBSTER'S THIRD NEW INTERNATIONAL DICTIONARY, *Unabridged*

The completely new authority of our language. Includes 100,000 new words and new meanings with 200,000 demonstrations of word usage. Every definition given in a single phrase of precise meaning. 3,000 illustrations; 20 plates in glorious color. 460,000 entries; 2,736 pages.

WEBSTER'S SEVENTH NEW COLLEGIATE DICTIONARY

This desk dictionary is the latest in the famous Merriam-Webster Collegiate series, the outstanding favorite in schools, homes, and offices. 130,000 entries include 20,000 new words and new meanings for more complete coverage than any other desk dictionary. Precise, clear definitions with 10,000 usage examples assure full understanding and accurate use of words. 1,244 pages.

WEBSTER'S NEW DICTIONARY OF SYNONYMS

This completely new word guide is the only thesaurus with words defined, discriminated, and illustrated with thousands of quotations that help you use the right word in the right place. Alphabetically arranged. Quicker to use and easier to understand. When you need a thesaurus, this is the book to ask for.

WEBSTER'S BIOGRAPHICAL DICTIONARY

Concise biographies of more than 40,000 noteworthy men and women of every historical period, every nationality, all walks of life.

WEBSTER'S GEOGRAPHICAL DICTIONARY

A quick-reference source of information about 40,000 of the world's important places. The greatest fund of current geographical information obtainable in a single volume to aid in a clear understanding of the vital news of the day.

WEBSTER'S ELEMENTARY DICTIONARY

An excellent dictionary written specifically for boys and girls in the fourth, fifth, sixth, and seventh grades. 18,000 vocabulary entries selected for school needs in the elementary grades.

G. & C. Merriam Co., Springfield, Mass. 01101, U.S.A.